From a Realist Point of View

OXFORD LEGAL PHILOSOPHY

Series Editors

Timothy Endicott, Irit Samet and Nicolaos Stavropoulos

Oxford Legal Philosophy publishes the best new work in philosophically oriented legal theory. It commissions and solicits monographs in all branches of the subject, including works on philosophical issues in all areas of public and private law, and in the national, transnational, and international realms; studies of the nature of law, legal institutions, and legal reasoning; treatments of problems in political morality as they bear on law; and explorations in the nature and development of legal philosophy itself. The series represents diverse traditions of thought but always with an emphasis on rigour and originality. It sets the standard in contemporary jurisprudence.

ALSO AVAILABLE IN THE SERIES

The Principle of Legality
A Moral Theory
Conor Crummey

Value and Circumstance
Justice, Consent, Equality, and Law
Timothy Macklem

Elucidating Law
Julie Dickson

The Right of Redress
Andrew S. Gold

Faces of Inequality
A Theory of Wrongful Discrimination
Sophia Moreau

Coercion and the Nature of Law
Kenneth Einar Himma

Property Rights
A Re-Examination
J. E Penner

A Theory of Legal Personhood
Visa AJ Kurki

Imposing Risk
A Normative Framework
John Oberdiek

Law and Morality at War
Adil Ahmad Haque

Ignorance of Law
A Philosophical Inquiry
Douglas Husak

Reason and Restitution
A Theory of Unjust Enrichment
Charlie Webb

Allowing for Exceptions
A Theory of Defences and Defeasibility in Law
Luís Duarte d'Almeida

Why Law Matters
Alon Harel

The Ends of Harm
The Moral Foundations of Criminal Law
Victor Tadros

From a Realist Point of View

BRIAN LEITER

Karl N. Llewellyn Professor of Jurisprudence and Director, Center for Law, Philosophy, and Human Values, University of Chicago, USA

OXFORD
UNIVERSITY PRESS

OXFORD
UNIVERSITY PRESS

Oxford University Press is a department of the University of Oxford.
It furthers the University's objective of excellence in research, scholarship,
and education by publishing worldwide. Oxford is a registered trade mark of
Oxford University Press in the UK and in certain other countries.

Published in the United States of America by Oxford University Press
198 Madison Avenue, New York, NY 10016, United States of America.

Library of Congress Cataloging-in-Publication Data
Names: Leiter, Brian author
Title: From a realist point of view / Brian Leiter.
Description: New York : Oxford University Press, 2026. | Series: Oxford legal philosophy series | Includes bibliographical references and index.
Identifiers: LCCN 2025048980 (print) | LCCN 2025048981 (ebook) |
ISBN 9780197749821 hardback | ISBN 9780197749838 epub |
ISBN 9780197749845 updf | ISBN 9780197749852 online
Subjects: LCSH: Jurisprudence | Law—Philosophy | Political science—Philosophy | Judicial process—Philosophy | LCGFT: Essays
Classification: LCC K230.L45 A37 2026 (print) | LCC K230.L45 (ebook)
LC record available at https://lccn.loc.gov/2025048980
LC ebook record available at https://lccn.loc.gov/2025048981

DOI: 10.1093/9780197749852.001.0001

Printed by Integrated Books International, United States of America

MIX
Paper
FSC FSC® C183721

The manufacturer's authorized representative in the EU for product safety is
Oxford University Press España S.A. of Parque Empresarial San Fernando de Henares,
Avenida de Castilla, 2 – 28830 Madrid (www.oup.es/en or product.safety@oup.com).
OUP España S.A. also acts as importer into Spain of products made by the manufacturer.

Note to Readers

This publication is designed to provide accurate and authoritative information in regard to the subject matter covered. It is based upon sources believed to be accurate and reliable and is intended to be current as of the time it was written. It is sold with the understanding that the publisher is not engaged in rendering legal, accounting, or other professional services. If legal advice or other expert assistance is required, the services of a competent professional person should be sought. Also, to confirm that the information has not been affected or changed by recent developments, traditional legal research techniques should be used, including checking primary sources where appropriate.

(Based on the Declaration of Principles jointly adopted by a Committee of the American Bar Association and a Committee of Publishers and Associations.)

for Sheila and our beautiful children,
Sam, William and Celia—once again

Series Editors' Preface

In films, in novels, in dreams, there are alternatives to realism. But in legal philosophy, we just have to face up to what is *really* going on.

In its historical reality as an *-ism* (i.e., a tendency or inclination that gets adhered to, more or less, by particular actors), legal realism has started from that uncontestable premise. And then it has gone very much further, through strands of work by many thinkers, to develop a theoretical account of what is real.

Brian Leiter has led the way in that pursuit. His previous works have developed a framework in the tradition of Nietzsche and Marx, Ayer and Quine, and, of course, the realist lawyers—especially Karl Llewellyn and Richard Posner. Leiter's disagreements with those other realists are themselves contributions to the tradition.

Now, in *From a Realist Point of View*, Leiter works out the implications across the wide terrain of legal, moral, and political philosophy and revisits the starting points. This book develops the realist impulse through many instances of Leiter's intense argumentative verve.

The impulse involves a denial that conclusions as to what is to be done can be objectively right or wrong. In fact, in Leiter's deep skepticism about normativity, there is no objective right or wrong even concerning *what is to be believed*. The impulse includes a heightened sensitivity to hidden ideologies and a vigorous distrust of the intuitions of bourgeois law professors (those intuitions are, at least, capable of being real, but they are incapable of providing a norm for action). And the impulse includes suspicion of the label "philosopher," and skepticism about the role in public affairs of public philosophy. And yet, readers who seek to use philosophical techniques as tools for effective political rhetoric should not give up: "in ways we cannot always anticipate, our labors in the service of discursive hygiene may matter" (see chapter 17).

The wide terrain encompasses disagreement about law, indeterminacy in law, the doctrine of precedent; the metaphysics of law, constitutional law, and democracy; and the role of judges, animal rights, naturalism, Marxism, and the human sciences. Through the pattern of this complex work, Brian Leiter's bracing leitmotif is skepticism about "moralizing"—by which he means, purporting to offer an objectively sound justification for a course of action or a public policy, or in fact for any conclusion as to what is right and wrong.

The book brings a new and arresting clarity to the legal realism that Leiter defends. And it offers a challenging criterion of success for moralizers: We had better find a way to explain what real reason there is for anyone else to agree with our views as to what is to be done.

We are very glad to present to you Brian Leiter's argument that, on that criterion, success is unattainable.

Timothy Endicott
Irit Samet
Nicolaos Stavropoulos

Preface and Acknowledgments

Over the last thirty-five years, I have written about and taught Nietzsche and Marx, as well as H. L. A. Hart, Michel Foucault, W. V. O. Quine, Sigmund Freud, and the American Legal Realists. I have also written and taught about topics in general jurisprudence, metaethics, free will, philosophical naturalism, and freedom of speech and religion. Most of that work does not appear here,[1] but some of it does, and all of it reflects the thinkers and topics that have occupied me since college and graduate school.

Philosophy is, as Nietzsche observed, "an unconscious memoir" that tells us something about the philosopher's "moral or immoral intentions," which themselves reveal, as he put it, the "rank-order of the inner drives of his nature" (*Beyond Good and Evil*, sec. 6). This volume is a partial memoir, whose title is suggestive about one of the animating "morals" of this philosopher: to eschew ideological illusions about the human situation and human society (including law), with which modern societies and the philosophies that emerge from them are awash, and to face up to our actual situation, without wishful thinking. My first loves in philosophy were Nietzsche and Marx, and then other thinkers like them, mostly lesser, but nonetheless notable for being concerned with what the world and human beings are really like—and not with the stifling, scolding moralizing of those philosophers (including almost all recent ones) who took their own moral wishes and prejudices seriously, either projecting them onto reality or offering reliably implausible rationalizations for them.

How did I arrive at this place? I do not really know, but as we learn from Nietzsche, there is no first-person privilege when it comes to knowing one's own motivations and character. So let me offer a data point that is probably highly relevant. I grew up in New York City (NYC), and the biggest influence on my life was my father, Maurice Leiter (1933–2020), who was born and raised in Brooklyn. Let me quote from portions of the memorial notice[2] I wrote upon

[1] Some of this work appears in the following books and articles: *Nietzsche on Morality* (Routledge, 2002; 2nd ed. 2015); *Naturalizing Jurisprudence* (Oxford University Press, 2007); *Why Tolerate Religion?* (Princeton University Press, 2013); "The Case against Free Speech," *Sydney Law Review* 38 (December 2016): 407–39; *Moral Psychology with Nietzsche* (Oxford University Press, 2019); "The Epistemology of the Internet and the Regulation of Speech in America," *Georgetown Journal of Law & Public Policy* 20 (2022): 913–45; and (with Jaime Edwards), *Marx* (Routledge, 2025).

[2] The full notice is here: https://www.dignitymemorial.com/obituaries/chicago-il/maurice-leiter-9215919.

his death in 2020 (due to the spectacular mishandling of COVID in the United States[3]):

> My father was born in Brooklyn, New York. . . . He was raised as a Jew—his mother's family had fled the Cossacks in Eastern Poland/Russia, who had the habit of forcibly conscripting teenage boys into the czar's army (one of many reasons it's hard to shed tears over the execution of Czar Nicholas)—but he became an atheist at the "age of 4" he told me. Perhaps that was an exaggeration, but probably not far off the truth. He was ill-suited to religion constitutionally: It was an offense against self-respect, among its many other problems. . . .
>
> His father, Harry Leiter, abandoned my father and his mother, Rose (nee Harris), when my father was still fairly young (I'm not sure the exact age, I think about 9). . . . My paternal grandmother was the youngest of six (as I recall), the others all boys (hence the need to flee the Cossacks). . . . My father graduated from Abraham Lincoln High School in Brooklyn and went on to Brooklyn College. His life revolved around baseball, radical politics, classical music, literature, and philosophy, which he studied at Brooklyn College.
>
> In the 1950s (after college) and into the early 1960s, my father bounced around between one thing and another, the details are not entirely clear to me. As I mentioned in an interview a number of years ago,[4] my birth in 1963 necessitated his earning a more regular income, and so his teaching in the public schools in NYC became his primary activity (he had started teaching in the schools earlier, I'm not sure exactly when). When my father (and mother) first started teaching in the public schools in the 1950s, schools were run by principals like personal fiefdoms, with hiring and promotion decisions made arbitrarily based on the whims of the local dictator. The United Federation of Teachers ("UFT"), the teacher union in NYC, changed all that during the 1960s. (This is obviously why capitalist apologists hate unions: "whims of the local dictator" is the essence of unregulated capitalism.[5])
>
> My father participated in the Brownsville teacher strikes of 1968,[6] eventually becoming "district representative" for the UFT in Bensonhurst (Brooklyn) during the 1970s. (Bensonhurst was then, and for many years after, a Mafia stronghold. One thing my father often did was help families with school

[3] In Singapore, a civilized and functional country, the death rate was roughly 30 out of 100,000; in the United States, it was roughly 350 out of every 100,000 people, one of the worst rates in the world.

[4] https://www.whatisitliketobeaphilosopher.com/brian-leiter.

[5] As my father's union colleague Marvin Reiskin said: "The principals and superintendents he worked with never wanted to lock horns. He was nicknamed 'The Slasher' because he could just tear you down with words." https://ufthonors.uft.org/leiter/. Another retired teacher wrote to me recently: "Your dad played a significant role in helping to rid us of a sociopathic/psychopathic principal. Fearless, outspoken, and relentless was he."

[6] The Wikipedia entry is informative: https://en.wikipedia.org/wiki/1968_New_York_City_teachers%27_strike

transfer issues within the district; one appreciative parent said to my father, "If you ever need someone's legs broken, let me know." He did not have occasion to take him up on the offer.) He continued to teach English at New Utrecht High School in Brooklyn (I can still recall attending one of his classes), the school featured in the opening clips of the 1970s American TV comedy *Welcome Back Kotter*. (My father also gave me the most important advice I ever got about teaching: "Never assume.")

My father was a courageous person with unshakeable confidence and self-respect, who never retreated from a fight or wrongdoing. I'll just give a few examples that stand out in my memory and will perhaps provide some flavor of the person.

When I was a small child in Manhattan, my father would have to look for street parking in Manhattan when he came home from work. One evening in the late 1960s, while parking his Volkswagen Beetle, he was accosted by two men, one with a handgun. They demanded that he take them to his apartment. He declined, since that was where my mother and I were. They then forced him into the car and made him drive around. As an empathetic working-class kid, my father started to talk to them, asking them about why they had resorted to robbery. It turned out they had both been laid off, and were desperate. They drove around for about an hour, as they unloaded their story of hardship. In the end, he offered them what money he had on him, but they declined, left and let my father go home.

In the late 1960s, the American labor union movement, under the influence of George Meany, lined up behind the then-ongoing US war of aggression, the Vietnam War. At the annual meeting of the American Federation of Teachers, members were instructed to vote in favor of a resolution supporting the Vietnam War. There were roughly five hundred members of the New York delegation; there was one "no" vote, by Maurice Leiter. Despite the defection from the union leadership on the Vietnam issue, my father continued working with the UFT, where he was again the lone dissenter among the leadership from the 1975 plan to avoid bankruptcy—fashioned by that representative of his economic class, Felix Rohaytn—to sacrifice teachers and other public workers.

My father was famously gregarious, quite generally, talking to everyone, everywhere, despite his self-professed preference for solitude. All the janitors and door-persons at his building: he knew them all, their life stories, their families, their difficulties. Give him thirty minutes with a new cleaning or repair person in the apartment, and he had quizzed them about their lives, and knew about their kids or parents, their travails or aspirations. Going to a restaurant with him could be challenging, because he would derail the plans by talking with the wait staff or the car valet. Although an elitist about some matters, he was the most deeply egalitarian person I have ever known, genuinely interested in people, especially the working-class people who often pass silently beneath our upper-middle-class radars.

I am pretty aggressive and forthright, but not as courageous as my father. I did learn from him respect for those who do the actual work that makes bourgeois life function. I also internalized the basic quasi-Hobbesian reality of New York City (which, as in so many matters, is a microcosm of a capitalist world defined by competition for resources): as my father often put it, there was the "Jewish Mafia," the "Irish Mafia," the "Catholic Mafia," and so on. Most were not literally composed of gangsters, but like the actual criminal Mafia, they were groups defined by tribal loyalties based on ethnicity or religion, who looked out for the interests of their co-tribalists (especially those in the same economic class), and pursued those interests against the interests of the other groups. The idea that one of these Mafias would "do the morally right thing" was laughable: they had to be forced, usually by understanding the costs that the other Mafias would impose upon them. (Students of Trump would do well to bear this point in mind.) Self-interest (including the interest of the group of which one is a member) defined politics and what actually happened. It was not the actual Hobbesian state of nature (except among the criminal Mafia, though even they took steps to mitigate the "war of all against all"), since it was governed by legal rules about interactions. Moral considerations, except to the extent they were encoded in the law, played no role in how disputes were resolved: This was the world of the Holmesian Bad Man, moved only by prudence. My father had definite normative views (he knew which side he was on), but he understood well that the capitalist class was not going to bend to demands of justice because that was the "morally right" thing to do. It was one reason he favored the default by New York City in 1975.

I am heir to this familial and cultural background, and I have now made a bit of the background to the "memoir" conscious here, although I am sure there is much more involved (and much that I am only dimly aware of). What, however, does any of this have to do with the "philosophy" in this volume? On some conceptions of philosophy, of course, none of the preceding should be relevant, after all. That is not my view, for epistemological reasons developed at greater length elsewhere,[7] and which I will explain more briefly here, however, since it does inform many of the essays in this volume. First, and most obviously, one's background explains what problems one finds important. Second, and more importantly, it also explains what reasons or considerations one deems

[7] See Brian Leiter, "On the Relevance of Etiology to Justification (with reference to Marx and Nietzsche)," *Midwest Studies in Philosophy* 47 (2023): 157–69. This paper explains why I often laugh when a philosopher tells me he only cares about the truth and the best arguments.

epistemically compelling. The late philosopher G. A. Cohen famously observed that, "people of my generation who studied philosophy at Harvard rather than Oxford for the most part *reject* the analytic/synthetic distinction."[8] The example is amusing for philosophers, and certainly has exemplars (e.g., Gilbert Harman was at Harvard around the time Cohen was at Oxford). Cohen then says something very important by way of explaining this phenomenon:

> I believe . . . that in each case [Harvard or Oxford] students were especially impressed by the reasons respectively for and against believing in the distinction, because in each case the reasons came with all the added persuasiveness of personal presentation, personal relationship, and so on.[9]

This is a rather key insight about graduate education and philosophical views. We can restate Cohen's point as follows: the causal influence of the "Personal Element" ("personal presentation, personal relationship") affects what philosophers take to be reasons justifying their views, often insulating them, as it were, from contrary epistemic considerations. The Personal Element plays a very large role in philosophy, as in other disciplines, and explains why scholars often have so many acolytes among their students. And it also makes clear that "philosophy" too needs social and personal context to be understood, and that is before one gets to the kinds of "unconscious" influences Nietzsche thought were crucial to explaining philosophical views.[10]

What, however, is "philosophy" (i.e., that which needs explaining)? Defining "philosophy" is surely a fool's errand, but there may be some lessons from history relevant here. Beginning with Plato's unhappy triumph over the Sophists in antiquity, "philosopher" has become an honorific, an honor most of its bearers do not deserve, but one many academics want to claim for themselves and their friends.[11] Almost no credentialed philosophers are courageous, independent, critical of received wisdom, truly in love with "truth" for the sake of truth, as Plato's Socrates was alleged to be (he wasn't either, but that is another story, well-told by Nietzsche[12]). The professionalization of the academy that began in

[8] G. A. Cohen, *If You're an Egalitarian, How Come You're So Rich?* (Harvard University Press, 2000), 18.

[9] Ibid.

[10] In my own case, the most formative part of my education were the three years of graduate coursework in philosophy at the University of Michigan, Ann Arbor, even though I now think the views of most of my teachers at that time are mistaken. I learned a kind of discursive hygiene (see Chapter 17) that is rare in the modern academy outside philosophy, but one that also equipped me to see how every argument fails, and thus the need to attend to the sociology of academic philosophy affects many of its conclusions.

[11] This is why charlatans so often want to self-present as "philosophers."

[12] See Brian Leiter, "The History of Philosophy Reveals that 'Great' Philosophy is Disguised Moral Advocacy: A Nietzschean Case Against the Socratic Canon in Philosophy," in M. van Ackern (ed.),

Germany in the early nineteenth century, and came to fruition in the advanced capitalist countries over the last 150 years, guarantees that anyone with the requisite credentials is a "philosopher," just like anyone with a different set of credentials is a "medical doctor" or a "chemist." Many credentialed philosophers are learned, or at least clever; relatively few are creative, original, free of conventional prejudices, or brave. "Philosopher" certainly does not designate any special insight or skill in understanding the world or what ought to be done. In the Anglophone world, it picks out a talent for logically precise dialectic within a particular Anglophone tradition (some of whose formative forebears, like Frege, wrote originally in German); outside the Anglophone world, especially in Europe, it picks out the learning (often philological and cultural) sufficient to locate oneself in the broader cultural tradition called "philosophical."

Anglophone "analytic" philosophers are notoriously ignorant of history and culture (often the history of their own supposed discipline), while their nonanalytic counterparts elsewhere sometimes give the impression of not knowing what an argument for a thesis would look like. Nietzsche wanted to preserve the honorific "philosopher" for those who "legislate values," but they are so few and far between that the label could rarely be used (something Nietzsche probably intended). Nietzsche was closer to the mark for our purposes when he observed that, "Those who know they are profound, strive for clarity. Those who would like to seem profound, strive for obscurity" (*The Gay* Science, sec. 173). Whatever philosophy is, and whatever role one's unconscious life or the "Personal Element" plays in it, I strive for clarity. Readers are welcome to apply to the views defended (clearly I hope!) in this volume Nietzschean lessons.

Within the Anglophone tradition, I don't think there is much more than precision and clarity of expression that philosophers can claim for themselves, to the extent they can still claim that.[13] The collapse of the idea that philosophers have a distinctive technique or method that other scholars lack—the primary conclusion, one might have thought, of philosophy of the last century (think of Wittgenstein or Quine)—should by now have shredded the honorific sense of the term. "Philosopher" today mostly denotes location in a professional or social network,[14] and thus it is fortuitous that one of my hobbies for many years was the sociology of the academic profession in the Anglophone world which

Proceedings of the British Academy 214: Philosophy and the Historical Perspective (Oxford University Press, 2018), 185–99.

[13] Standards of clarity have declined in Anglophone philosophy in the wake of Michael Dummett, whose influence on style was pernicious (e.g., John McDowell, Crispin Wright, Christopher Peacocke). The contrast would be with philosophers like Carl Hempel, Jaegwon Kim, and H. L. A. Hart.

[14] Perhaps it always did. Randall Collins, *The Sociology of Philosophies: A Global Theory of Intellectual Change* (Harvard University Press, 1998), is instructive.

sustains the label "philosopher."[15] I thus will have more to say about the sociology of philosophy than most academic philosophers because I think readers (especially those far removed from the Anglophone profession's sometimes unusual concerns) will not understand what has happened without some of that context. The current intellectual diversion of general jurisprudence ("legal philosophy") in the United States is a case study I will consider at greater length in the new material in chapter 9 in this volume. What has happened to general jurisprudence in the United States is hardly unique, especially given the condition of Anglophone "analytic" philosophy, which has adopted fully the research paradigm of the natural sciences (lots of researchers working on small pieces of [supposedly] big problems) but too often without any cognitive (especially, empirical) check on either the problems or the contributions (outside certain subfields, like philosophy of physics or cognitive science).[16] As a result, everything increasingly bottoms out in the "intuitions" or intellectual gimmicks of "important" professors of philosophy, so that much Anglophone philosophy is essentially ethnographic data about what prominent members of a certain social and economic class believe or "intuit."[17] (This is yet another reason why the socio-psychological background of philosophers is important.)

General jurisprudence is hardly one of the more notable cases on this score. For that, we would have to turn to the spectacle of Thomas Nagel, an eminent philosophy professor in the "analytic" tradition, who came to think Darwin's theory of evolution by natural selection could not be correct since if it were his moral views could not be true (see ch. 1 in this volume for further discussion). Nagel's very public intellectual collapse is a classic case of what the psychologists call "group polarization": too much time talking to a small group of likeminded philosophers, similarly parochial and similarly full of their own moral prejudices, led Nagel into the realm of the absurd.[18] It is difficult to take

[15] Starting in graduate school, and continuing for a quarter-century thereafter, I produced a report for students about what were regarded as the "best" philosophy programs in the Anglophone world. This enterprise was hugely useful to students seeking degrees and jobs, but it became so influential that it became controversial—partly among those in the grips of the delusion that "philosophy" was an honorific, but mostly from those teaching in programs that were not as highly ranked as they thought they deserved. My ambition, from the beginning, was to help young people who enjoy "philosophy" find a professional path into academia. In this regard, it was quite successful, but the self-serving hostility the project engendered raises questions about its future viability. Over the years, numerous scholars in other fields have sought my advice on similar initiatives in their disciplines, only to be deterred by the hostility and abuse my efforts have generated.

[16] See the scathing comments about much of analytic philosophy in Daniel Dennett, "Higher-Order Truths about Chmess," *Topoi* 25 (2006): 39–41.

[17] Again, there is an important epistemological point here. For the more technical discussion, see again Leiter, "On the Relevance of Etiology to Justification (with reference to Marx and Nietzsche)," above. The crucial idea is that "personal" influence of supervisors or *Doktorvaters* has a disproportionate influence on what views professional philosophers in training accept.

[18] As T. M. Scanlon recounted in an interview with the *Brown Political Review*, he participated in a small discussion group with Thomas Nagel, Ronald Dworkin, and other prominent philosophers in the 1960s and 1970s about moral and political philosophy, which had a substantial impact on him:

the long view when one is living in the present, but I am hopeful that this display will not age well, even if those lodged in positions of professional power sustain it for some time into the future within the narrow confines of professional Anglophone philosophy.[19]

Causal explanations of philosophical beliefs (in terms of social, psychological, or economic influences) are important for reasons Marx and Nietzsche understood: What to believe is always underdetermined by the reasons and evidence on offer.[20] Every argument in moral philosophy depends on a basic moral intuition that itself is unsupported; so too with every argument about what one ought to believe, which rests on an unsupported epistemic intuition.[21] In all normative matters, of action or belief, we bottom out in pure commitment, and the only question with some cognitive content is what the psychological or "sociological" explanation for the commitment is. (I use "sociological" broadly to include any explanation that goes beyond facts about individual psychology.) This is another facet of realism: to be realistic about the non-rational causal determinants of belief, whether in the juridical realm or outside it. This is also why I emphasize the ways in which a particular set of views and assumptions hang together--such as legal realism, legal positivism, moral skepticism, and a kind of "Marxism."[22] Someone who, because of their fundamental attitudes, opts out of some of the

> [I]t was something that provided me with confidence in two ways: One, there really was a subject matter there that you could learn more about because in the 1950s, moral philosophy had a kind of skeptical air to it. It was sort of conventionalist or emotivist, non-cognitivist, and so on, and so we were drawn together by the fact that most of us in the group tended to think that there were real facts about right and wrong, and that just by thinking really hard and clearly about them, you could make progress, and that wasn't what was going on in most of philosophy at the time. (https://brownpoliticalreview.org/a-realist-about-reasons/)

Alas, there are no "real facts about right and wrong," so this was all an illusion sustained by group polarization.

[19] The major centers of "philosophical importance" have always tracked the centers of economic and military power: Greece and Rome in antiquity, for example; or Prussia/Germany in the nineteenth century; or Britain in the nineteenth and- twentieth centuries, and America in the twentieth and twenty-first centuries. Because the Anglophone dominance in philosophy coincided with the real globalization of capitalist markets, it may survive the collapse of the American empire, which will surely be one of the main geopolitical events of the twenty-first century. On the other hand, the current Trump war on universities may shift the balance of "intellectual" power much more quickly, perhaps over the next generation.

[20] The American Legal Realists understood that something analogous was true in the case of judicial decision. See discussion in chs. 5, 6, 7, 10, and 16 in this volume, as well as in Leiter, *Naturalizing Jurisprudence.*

[21] See Brian Leiter, *Moral Psychology with Nietzsche* (Oxford University Press, 2019), 109–11. See also chs. 15 and 16 in this volume.

[22] Marx was wrong about the teleological structure of history, the labor theory of value (and the interpretation of the fetishism of commodities dependent on the former), the tendency of the rate of profit to fall, and the importance of "species-being," among other topics. He was right about many other topics, hence his continuing importance. See generally Edwards and Leiter, *Marx*, for an account and evaluation.

commitments and assumptions underlying these views—to naturalism, to skepticism about normative objectivity, to a realistic picture of human beings and their motivations—will find the whole package unacceptable. In philosophy, as in politics, there is value in knowing who your friends and who your enemies are,[23] and I hope this volume will help draw those lines.

One way I hope to show how a particular package of views hang together is by linking "realism" about law to realism about politics, in a way that has not yet occurred in these separate scholarly literatures. In fact, I think a "realist" outlook in both domains is distinctive, and for similar reasons. The goal of the (mostly) new material in chapter 1 of this volume[24] is to explain what it is to be a *realist*—not in the metaphysical sense of someone who takes the existence and character of the world to not depend (in some sense usually specified) on what human beings believe, but in the sense that links legal and political realists. Realists, in this latter sense, share a concern with correctly describing what human beings are really like and what really happens, without supposing that any of it is morally attractive or makes any kind of rational sense. The opponents of realists are "moralists," who may sometimes grudgingly acknowledge what is really happening, but are mostly concerned with what *ought* to happen given the prevailing moral conventions in the community of the philosophers and the economic class from which they come. Hegel, an extreme moralist in this regard, held that "the real is the rational" (and the rational is also the moral); by contrast, realists claim instead that "the real is irrational," and it is only the extreme moralism of mainstream philosophy that obscures that truth. Much recent philosophy has not simply been the "Owl of Minerva" (recording systematically the moral ideology of its own era as it ends), but also the "*scolding* Owl of Minerva," hooting disapprovingly at the actual world evolving before it while offering a falsification of it. As the United States gradually succumbs to an authoritarian political movement led by a strangely charismatic buffoon, the utter irrelevance of all philosophical output during this era is particularly striking. Moral philosophy, as Marx and Nietzsche both demonstrated in very different ways, is irrelevant noise in the history of the world, merely symptomatic.[25]

Part I of this volume is concerned primarily with general jurisprudence—realism about the nature of law and legal reasoning—with some of the chapters being fairly technical, some less so. Chapter 2, "Explaining Theoretical

[23] This is not an opaque reference to the Nazi sociopath Carl Schmitt: It is an acknowledgment that core fundamental commitments in philosophical matters are sometimes unbridgeable (because they depend on wholly nonrational factors).

[24] Some of the ideas about law in chapter 1 were first broached in Brian Leiter, "What Is a Realist Theory of Law?" *Journal of Institutional Studies* 6 (2020): 334–45.

[25] General jurisprudence may also be irrelevant noise, but at least it is part of theoretical, not practical, philosophy: It aims to give us knowledge about law and legal reasoning, not tell us what we ought to do. That knowledge can survive charismatic buffoons.

Disagreement," appeared originally in *University of Chicago Law Review* 76 (Summer 2009): 1215–50. This paper offered a positivist reply to Dworkin's theoretical disagreement challenge, one that combined a commitment to Hart's positivism with a legal realist-style explanation of what was actually going on in Dworkin's favorite example, *Riggs v. Palmer*. This essay has been widely translated and much discussed, and critiqued. In chapter 3, "Theoretical Disagreements in Law: Another Look" (which appeared originally in D. Plunkett, S. Shapiro, and K. Toh (eds.), *Dimensions of Normativity: New Essays in Metaethics and Jurisprudence* [Oxford: Oxford University Press, 2019)], I respond primarily to the most trenchant critic of the argument in chapter 2, Kevin Toh. I show that Toh misreads Hart and also misunderstands the talk of "presupposition" in Kelsen and Hart. I also defend my original error-theoretic interpretation of the semantics of theoretical disagreements against some other critics. In the new chapter 4, I revisit the theoretical disagreements debate, and consider some alternative proposals that have emerged in recent years, most distinctively, those that claim theoretical disagreements are not a problem for legal positivism, which is only a theory about "sources" of law. Here, I have the pleasure of responding to the stimulating arguments of three former students, among others.

Chapter 5, "Legal Positivism as a Realist Theory of Law," first appeared in *The Cambridge Companion to Legal Positivism*, edited by Torben Spaak and Patricia Mindus (2021), and I am grateful to Cambridge University Press for permission to reprint it here. The essay has been revised, especially the critique of Raz's unrealist jurisprudence at the end. In earlier work,[26] I had argued that American legal realism presupposed the positivist theory of legal validity. In this essay, I argue that Hart's legal positivism involves an essentially "realistic" outlook on law and adjudication, one congenial to legal realists. I revisit Hart's critique of realist "rule-skepticism," arguing that, given what little Hart says, it ultimately is not clear whether he and the American realists disagree once we clear up Hart's confusions about legal realism. I conclude by criticizing Raz's betrayal of Hart's realism, most clear in his moralized conception of the "authority" that law purportedly claims.

Chapter 6, "Realism about Precedent," appeared in T. Endicott, H. Kristjansson, and S. Lewis (eds.), *Philosophical Foundations of Precedent* (Oxford University Press, 2023). It offers a systematic defense of the legal realist view of precedent by identifying the key theoretical issue: judgments about "relevant similarity" between cases yield unavoidable indeterminacy in reasoning with precedent. Chapter 7, "How to Cabin the Realist Indeterminacy Thesis," was written in 2024 for T. Adams, K. Greasley, and D. Reaume (eds.), *The Morality*

26 Brian Leiter, "Legal Realism and Legal Positivism Reconsidered," *Ethics* 111 (2001): 278–301, repr. Leiter, *Naturalizing Jurisprudence*.

in Law: Themes from the Work of Leslie Green (Oxford University Press, forthcoming). It addresses the most important theoretical objection to my reconstruction of American Legal Realism, due to Leslie Green:[27] namely, why think indeterminacy in legal reasoning should be confined to the appellate courts, as most American Realists thought. The answer turns on their essentially "sociological" conception of "legitimate" legal arguments (i.e., arguments accepted by lawyers and judges in a legal community), which I defend on the merits.

Chapter 8, "The Demarcation Problem in Jurisprudence: A New Case for Skepticism," originally appeared in *Oxford Journal of Legal Studies* 31 (2011): 663–77 but has been revised substantially for inclusion here. In particular, the influential discussion of the idea that law is an artifact has, I think, been improved, and rejoinders to earlier critics have been added. The core idea remains intact, but I hope more clearly expressed: The metaphysical inflation of what is required to draw the line between law and morality makes a demand no one should reasonably expect to generate an answer applicable to all cases, let alone those cases that arise in the higher appellate courts. There we should be discussing what ought to be done, not what the "real" legal standards are.

Chapter 9, "Against the Metaphysical Turn in Recent American Jurisprudence," is new and continues the critique of "metaphysical inflation" in jurisprudence from chapter 8, focusing, in particular, on the work of Mark Greenberg, as well as its influence on Scott Shapiro, who is probably most responsible for popularizing Greenberg's mischaracterization of the questions of jurisprudence. (Shapiro, while nominally a legal positivist, adopts Greenberg's framework to ill effect.) I demonstrate that Greenberg has simply changed the topic in general jurisprudence, and for no good philosophical reasons. I also argue against Greenberg's own positive view. I hope this chapter will put a stop to the descent into irrelevant metaphysics in general jurisprudence, but given the sociology of the discipline in the United States, I am not hopeful.

Part II collects essays developing a realist perspective on courts, politics, and morality, although some issues from Part I occasionally recur. Chapter 10, "Legal Formalism and Legal Realism: What Is the Issue?" appeared originally in *Legal Theory* 16 (2010): 111–33 and I am grateful to Cambridge University Press for

[27] Leslie Green, "Realism and the Sources of Law," in Green, *The Germ of Justice* (Oxford University Press, 2024). Michael Steven Green raised interesting challenges to my interpretation of American Legal Realism in an earlier symposium on my *Naturalizing Jurisprudence* book in the journal *Law and Philosophy*. See Michael Steven Green, "Leiter on the Legal Realists," *Law and Philosophy* 30 (2011): 381–418; I replied to Green (and other critics) in "Naturalized Jurisprudence and American Legal Realism Revisited," *Law and Philosophy* 30 (2011): 499–516. I have mostly let pass in silence confused and sometimes incompetent critiques by others (chapter 10 is an exception). Alas, the secondary literature on the jurisprudence of American Legal Realism is still quite poor. The best piece of work in the last decade is Matthew Etchemendy, "Legal Realism and Legal Reality," *Tennessee Law Review* 88 (2021): 399–468. Scholars of American Legal Realism would do well to study this essay!

permission to reuse this essay here. The essay is a critical assessment of a book by Brian Tamanaha, a "law and society" scholar. My commentary explores the concepts of realism and formalism about judging, and clarifies them, while also exposing the serious confusions about both that mar Tamanaha's account. (I also raise some doubts about his historical evidence, which is not reliably presented.) Chapter 11, "In Praise of Realism (and Against 'Nonsense' Jurisprudence)" appeared in *Georgetown Law Journal* 100 (March 2012): 865–93. It represents my first attempt to draw the "realism" and "moralism" contrast drawn more thoroughly in chapter 1 of this volume, but this chapter covers additional ground. It juxtaposes the dispute between the realist Thucydides and moralist Plato in antiquity with the jurisprudential dispute between the realist Richard Posner and moralist Ronald Dworkin in recent legal theory. I also critically consider Raymond Geuss's treatment of Rawls and Dworkin's fanciful use of Cardozo, among other topics.

Chapter 12, "Constitutional Law, Moral Judgment and the Supreme Court as Super-Legislature" was first presented as the Twenty-fourth Mathew O. Tobriner Memorial Lecture in Constitutional Law at the University of California College of the Law, San Francisco (formerly "Hastings College of Law"), and appeared in *Hastings Law Journal* 66 (August 2015): 1601–16. This essay has already been translated into Spanish and Portuguese and anthologized in an Anglophone jurisprudence textbook. I defend a realist interpretation of the US Supreme Court, whose exercise of a quasi-legislative power is especially dramatic and consequential. It raises the question whether politicians should persist in trying to conceal from the public what the Supreme Court really does. Although US-specific, the essay identifies reasons why any high court will inevitably have a quasi-legislative power.[28]

Chapter 13, "The Role of Judges in Democracies: A Realistic View," first appeared in English in the Brazilian *Journal of Institutional Studies* 6 (2020): 346–75, and was reprinted unchanged in P. Chiassoni and B. Spaic (eds.), *Judges and Adjudication in Constitutional Democracies: A View from Legal Realism* (Springer, 2021). It was then revised in 2023 for publication in Italian as a "booklet" by Edizioni Scientifiche Italian, in a series edited by Massimo La Torre. It has been revised, and workshopped, further for inclusion here. Unlike some of the other essays, this one has attracted relatively little attention in the Anglophone world, although it has been translated already into Spanish and Portuguese (and Italian, as noted above), and was reprinted (in English) in a journal for judges in Romania. Here I pursue the question from chapter 12, namely, what judges ought to do (given the rational indeterminacy

[28] The point has been repeatedly confirmed to me by academic and practicing lawyers in Brazil, for example—a jurisdiction where Dworkin is "taken seriously" and thus provides "cover" for the quasi-legislative power the courts exercise.

that unavoidably infects the law) as a matter of their morals and politics, and as a matter of strategy. The standard jurisprudential advice about the "obligations" of judges is banal, so this essay takes a different approach. I endorse a realist view of democracy, arguing this undermines the so-called countermajoritarian difficulty; I identify the real problem with originalism (no one wants to be bound by the "dead hand" of the distant past), and I conclude that in thinking about what judges ought to do we must take account of their moral and political views, but also the latitude the courts have in any given polity.

The final chapters present a realistic view of morality—in which moral commitments are understood as historically and culturally variable, as manifestations of human attitudes, not reflections of a mind-independent reality—and of moral philosophy, which is irrelevant to actual political practice (using Marx and Foucault as case studies). The former view was fairly orthodox in the Anglophone world from the 1940s until the 1960s, but the creation of a cadre of employed faculty confident in their local moral prejudices changed all that. The view of morality evident in these final chapters still has more resonance in Europe, where the historicist traditions have had more influence (although as I note in chapter 18, the Frankfurt School tried to derail historicism in favor of Kantian delusions).

Chapter 14, "The Boundaries of the Moral (and Legal) Community," was presented as the Meador Lecture at the University of Alabama Law School in 2011 and subsequently appeared in *Alabama Law Review* 64 (2013): 511–31. Here I consider the question whether the best explanation for the increased recognition of the moral equality of human beings (independent of race, sex, nationality, etc.) and even nonhumans is best explained in "Whig" or "non-Whig" terms. Whigs think that the expanding boundaries of the moral community involve cognition of long-neglected moral facts; non-Whigs point to causal influences on our expanding moral sensibilities that have nothing to do with their epistemic reliability. As a realist, I side with the non-Whig explanations, including the "evolutionary" explanations that are all the rage in the social sciences these days (although they do not explain nearly enough). I suggest that the economic and psychological factors indicated by Marx and Nietzsche also offer important explanations for the change in sensibilities over the last two centuries. I conclude with some psychological and materialist speculation about why the moral community is unlikely to expand fully to include nonhuman animals, precisely, but not only, because of their lack of rational and discursive capacities.

Chapter 15, "Disagreement, Anti-realism about Reasons, and Inference to the Best Explanation," appeared in a special open-access, online issue on "disagreement" of *Ethical Theory & Moral Practice*. This is a more technical argument for skepticism about moral objectivity, which is central to the realist point of view defended in this volume. This essay will be of most interest to "analytic" philosophers. The same is true of chapter 16, "Normativity for Naturalists," which appeared originally in *Philosophical Issues: A Supplement to Nous* 25 (2015): 64–79 and I am grateful for permission from Wiley to reprint it here. This essay takes for granted the conclusion of chapter 15, that there are no objective facts about value (or normativity), and considers some of the arguments against that conclusion, in the process clarifying that for naturalists, there is no *real* normativity, just facts about human attitudes and practices.

Chapter 17, "The Paradoxes of Public Philosophy," was originally presented as a lecture in 2014 to the law faculty and student body at Jindahl University in India, outside Delhi, and appeared subsequently in the inaugural issue of *Indian Journal of Legal Theory* 1 (2016): 51–64. Here I pursue some of the implications of the conclusions from chapters 15 and 16 with respect to the neoliberal fad of "public philosophy," in which philosophers purport to address citizens and politicians about what they ought to do. This is primarily a comical spectacle,[29] in which moral philosophers, with no special epistemic authority for their claims, issue arguments and conclusions that no one in the public sphere takes seriously. Does that mean professional philosophers have no contribution to make to public life? Probably it does, but professional philosophers could try to offer "discursive hygiene," which, if combined with much more rhetorical skill, might make an impact on some political actors.

Chapter 18, "Why Marxism Still Does Not Need Normative Theory: A Polemic," appeared originally in *Analyse & Kritik* 37 (2015): 23–50, in an issue on "The Normative Turn from Marxism" edited by Anton Leist, and I am grateful for the permission of Lucius & Lucius to reprint the essay here—although this version is revised substantially, reflecting refinements of my view from my work with Jaime Edwards on our volume on *Marx* for *The Routledge Philosophers* series (which appeared in 2025). The basic themes, however, remain intact: Marx broke decisively with Hegel and Feuerbach after 1844–45,[30] and came to see that moral and political philosophy were wholly irrelevant to actually changing the world. To change society, what matters is to understand how socioeconomic relations really work, and how they have evolved historically; one can count on the self-interest of the vast majority, once enlightened about the real facts (the main task of a communist party, in Marx's view), to do the rest once global capitalism immiserates the vast majority in the service of producing profit for capitalists.[31] I also speculate about what led to the collapse of so-called Marxism after World

[29] It is not only comical but also dangerous, as the fiasco of "Effective [sic] Altruism" (EA) and its influence on Samuel Bankman-Fried demonstrated. EA grew out of Peter Singer's ideas, discussed in Chapters 14 and 17. It was never concerned with "effectiveness" as distinct from measurable short-term effects. But it provided a spectacular ideological whitewash of pursuit of money, hence its appeal in the "tech" and "finance" sectors of capitalism.

[30] For what will prove to be the seminal account, see Lawrence Dallman, "Marx's Naturalism: A Study in Philosophical Methodology," Ph.D. diss., University of Chicago, 2021.

[31] For the reasons that are built into the logic of capitalism, as even neoclassical labor economists have begun to notice, see Edwards and Leiter, *Marx*, 136–38.

War II into the kind of moral philosophy Marx always had contempt for, focusing in particular on G. A. Cohen's later work and on Habermas.

Chapter 19, "Foucault as a Kind of Realist: Genealogical Critique and the Debunking of the Human Sciences," appeared in *Inquiry* 67 (2024): 2129–146, and I am grateful to Taylor & Francis for permission to include that essay here. Foucault's corpus is undoubtedly animated by a normative impulse: to liberate humans from a kind of self-imposed oppression, one that depends on the unwarranted credibility of certain human sciences. His critique, however, is a realist critique, one that eschews moral argument in favor of exposing the moral and political influences on the human sciences that undermine their epistemic credibility. I argue that Foucault's critique, however, is not wholly successful, focusing in particular on a rather feeble excuse for pedophilia offered in his *History of Sexuality*.

Individual chapters acknowledge particular debts, and there are many. (That is a standard conceit, but the reality is that the existence of serious universities committed to teaching and research makes possible much better scholarly writing by everyone! So please read the footnotes to particular chapters!) Here I will note my more general debts. My temperament and tastes were, as already noted, decisively shaped by my father. I still think about him almost every day, and probably always will. Sheila Sokolowski is the kindest and most generous (and genuine) person I have ever known. I would not have been so productive except for her support and love. Together we also undertook the most interesting and important project of our lives, namely, Samuel, William, and Celia. On my deathbed, if I'm still thinking, I will think only of these splendid human beings.

I have learned the most about legal philosophy from Leslie Green, especially during the years he was a regular visiting professor at the University of Texas at Austin, when I taught there. Conversations, over many years, with other legal philosophers have been instructive and important, including Max Etchemendy, John Gardner, Mark Greenberg, Matthew Kramer, Stephen Perry, Joseph Raz, Scott Shapiro, and Kevin Toh. I disagree quite strongly with some of these jurisprudents, but I publish those disagreements here only because they are the most worthy opponents, and I have learned from all of them.

I have also benefited from the "globalization" of the community of legal philosophers over the last quarter-century, for which almost all the credit goes to the Europeans (although Leslie Green and I have made a point with *Oxford Studies in Philosophy of Law* to contribute to this trend). It has been particularly valuable for me to have learned from the community of European legal realists. So warm thanks are due to the following European legal philosophers (not all realists, however): Pierre Brunet, the late Bruno Celano, Pierluigi Chiassoni, Luis Duarte D'Almeida, Riccardo Guastini, Jakob Holtermann, Miodrag Jovanović, Jose Juan Moreso, Giorgio Pino, Giovanni Battista Ratti, Maria

Cristina Redondo, Bojan Spaić, Michel Troper, and Dmitrios Tsarapatsanis—with apologies to those I may have forgotten.

Since moving to the University of Chicago in 2008, I have learned a tremendous amount from the splendid students here, in both law and philosophy: I should mention, in particular, Nir Ben-Moshe, Andrew Biondo, Gabe Broughton, Sarah Cohen, Courtney Cox, Elena Di Rosa, Lawrence ("Dusty") Dallman, Jaime Edwards, Joshua Fox, Aaron Graham, Josh Kaufman, Claire Kirwin, Taylor Koles, Nethanel Lipshitz, Kate Petroff, Richard Stillman, Dan Telech, Bill Watson, and Helen Zhao. I am also indebted to the brilliant Ms. Zhao for excellent research assistance in completing this volume. I have learned a huge amount from Michael Forster, with whom I have been co-teaching for the last fifteen years. I have also benefited from several conversations with my political science colleague John Mearsheimer.

My colleagues in the law school at Chicago have been generous in reading and commenting on many of these chapters. The University of Chicago Law School is undoubtedly the most intellectually serious law school in the United States, in part because of the influence of neoclassical economics on the culture of the school: Argument and evidence are the coin of the realm, in a way that is very rare in American law schools, but is familiar to philosophers. The ideological limitations of neoclassical economics have also been instructive, and have certainly improved my work on Marx, for reasons John Stuart Mill understood. A very famous philosopher who left a Chair at Oxbridge a number of years ago in order to return to a US law school observed, correctly, that US law schools treat faculty as "gods" (which is not true in the UK). Only professors in US medical and business schools earn more, on average, but it is not just the salaries: the research support, teaching loads, and support for travel for American law professors, especially at the most elite schools, are remarkable. Those facts should make it less mysterious that the American legal academy is so far to the right on matters of economic policy among the industrialized democracies. My own background in a labor union family probably insulated me somewhat from the ideological impact of the material conditions of my intellectual production. At the same time, my personality, a product of my personal history described only partly, above, probably insulated me from some of the historically unaware moralistic tendencies of the contemporary academy, especially those in the increasingly insular world of Anglophone philosophy.

BL, Chicago, June 23, 2025

Contents

1
What Is Realism?

I. Realism and Moralism

There have been two main traditions of theorizing about society, politics, and law in Western thought, but they do not divide up along familiar lines of modern or ancient, Enlightenment or pre-Enlightenment, analytic or Continental, historical or systematic. On one side, we find, for example, Thucydides, Machiavelli, Marx, Nietzsche, Freud, and—to mention more recent thinkers who are generally on the realist side of the divide—H. L. A. Hart and Michel Foucault.[1] On the other side, we find Plato, Aristotle, Aquinas, Kant, Hegel, and—once again, to mention more recent theorists—John Rawls, Jürgen Habermas, and Ronald Dworkin. I will treat the former as representing "realism" in political and legal thought, the latter "moralism," terms whose meaning I explore in what follows.

It is important to emphasize, at the start, that I am using "realism" in a sense wholly different from the metaphysical sense used by many philosophers. In this latter sense, "realism" means, broadly speaking, the view that the existence and character of the world and its constituent parts do not depend on the mind; that is, they do not depend on our beliefs about the world or what we would be justified in believing about it under ideal conditions for inquiry; realism, in the metaphysical sense, contrasts with "idealism" (or "anti-realism"), the view that there is some dependence of reality on the "mind."

By contrast, "realists," for my purposes, are realistic (in the colloquial sense) about human beings and societies, about what they are "really" like, and that affects, in turn, their approach to theory. More precisely, realists are committed to most (if not necessarily all[2]) of the following ideas about human beings and theorizing about them:

(1) Human beings, throughout history and across cultures, are motivated primarily by their passions and interests (not by "reason"[3]) (call this "Humeanism" about motivation).

[1] On Thucydides and Nietzsche, see chapter 11; on Marx, see chapter 18; on Hart, see esp. chapter 5; and on Foucault, see chapter 19, all in this volume.
[2] I accept all of them, but many of the realists I mentioned at the start do not.
[3] Instrumental reason—choosing effective means to one's ends—is relevant, of course, but reason does not choose ends.

From a Realist Point of View. Brian Leiter, Oxford University Press. © Brian Leiter 2026.
DOI: 10.1093/9780197749852.003.0001

(2) Many (most?) important human passions and interests are antisocial or "immoral" (people are, for example, frequently selfish, cruel, self-aggrandizing, avaricious, self-deceived, lustful, envious, etc.) (call this "Nietzscheanism" about motivation).[4]

(3) Given what human beings are like (whether by nature or in virtue of the conditions existing in human societies to date[5]), theories devoted to articulating and discursively justifying people's supposed moral obligations and duties are irrelevant to changing people's behavior—rational arguments do not change passions and interests.

(4) Since there are no objective moral requirements (as most realists believe[6]), arguing about them is a scholastic exercise, more akin to codifying and quibbling about conventional etiquette norms at some place and time.

(5) People's beliefs about their actions and motivations are mostly self-serving and post hoc, designed to obscure or rationalize what they are really doing and what their real motivations are (philosophers are significant contributors to this obfuscation).

(6) Theories of society, politics, and law should try to explain *what is really going on* (e.g., the actual patterns and causes of human behavior, both individual and social).

(7) "Ordinary opinion," "common sense," and "folk intuitions" are data to be explained (causally), not resources for philosophical understanding or theory construction.

(8) Theories of society, politics, and law must *never* assume that their subject matter is morally defensible.

[4] Is there a gendered difference on this score? It is certainly fashionable to suppose so. As Nietzsche knew, the nineteenth-century stereotype of females—as irrational and moved by their passions—was true of all people, especially of the men who pretended otherwise. Whether the antisocial tendencies of women "by nature" are less extreme than those of men is a harder question, because of the effect of sexist social practices. Certainly, women with political power—Indira Ghandi, Golda Meir, Margaret Thatcher, Hillary Clinton—seem hard to distinguish from their male peers.

[5] The second disjunct is important for understanding Marx's views, since he recognizes that human beings are as realists describe them, but thinks this is mostly an artifact of the economic conditions under which people have existed so far. While it seems to me correct that certain familiar features of human beings in capitalist societies (e.g., calculating self-interest) are ones that the capitalist system incentivizes, at the end of the day I am more sympathetic to Nietzsche's and Freud's view that some of the antisocial characteristics of people would survive even the replacement of capitalism with a more humane economic system. (Marx's own confidence in the continual growth of productive power already seems to presuppose a powerful role for self-interest throughout human history, since the motivation for growing productive power before capitalism is exclusively that it creates wealth and leisure.)

[6] For good reasons, see chs. 15 and 16, in this volume, in particular.

Realists—from Thucydides to Machiavelli, Marx, and Nietzsche—are certainly animated by aspirations to change people's behavior,[7] but they eschew entirely the approach of moralists who think that moral arguments and discursive reasoning are an effective way to influence human affairs.[8] Realists are (per (1)) generally "Humeans" about motivation: One can move people to action by arousing their existing passions and desires, but one cannot reason anyone into action on the grounds that something is the right thing to do regardless of their preexisting desires and emotions. Some realists, like Machiavelli and Marx, provide explicitly instrumental advice: On the plausible assumption that princes want to remain in power, says Machiavelli, here is what you ought to do; on the plausible assumption that the vast majority want to escape their immiseration, says Marx, here is an explanation of the causes of their misery and how different ways of organizing the economy would eliminate it.[9] Other realists, like Thucydides and Nietzsche, employ a variety of rhetorical devices to arouse the emotions of their readers (or their "rightful" readers in Nietzsche's case). Thucydides puts before his audience in dramatic terms the catastrophic consequences of unbridled Athenian lust for power and glory; Nietzsche puts before his readers the destructive consequences of Christian morality on human excellence and flourishing. As Humeans, all hope that the emotions of their readers, once aroused through their writing, will lead them to act differently. Nowhere do realists offer normative arguments, logical or transcendental deductions, or geometric or other proofs about what is truly right, good, and valuable: The rationalizations of Plato, Spinoza, Kant, Hegel, and Rawls are all practically irrelevant exercises on this view. Realists, like all humans, have attitudes about what is "right, good, and valuable," but they reject the idea that what I will henceforth call *discursive theories* (those that proceed by argument or reasoning) about what is "right, good, and valuable" are informative or effective.

Moralists, by contrast, concern themselves first and foremost with such discursive theories about how individuals and institutions morally ought to act.[10]

[7] Thucydides, Machiavelli, and Nietzsche are all interested in influencing certain kinds of "elites": political elites in the case of Thucydides and Machiavelli, geniuses and nascent geniuses in the case of Nietzsche.

[8] Realists should also reject this approach because it delivers no actual knowledge, but that is a separate claim: Certainly Nietzsche accepts that, the others mentioned in the text may or may not.

[9] See generally Jaime Edwards and Brian Leiter, *Marx* (Routledge, 2025), esp. chs. 3 and 4.

[10] As David Runciman notes, it is tempting to see Bentham as "representative of a naïve form of moralism [in Runciman's slightly different sense], because he specified a single, pre-political value [utility] as the basis for assessing politics." David Runciman, "Political Theory and Real Politics in the Internet Age," *The Journal of Political Philosophy* 25 (2017): 5. But Runciman says that this is a "caricature" since "Bentham's writing exemplifies . . . the realist suspicion of the loose application of moralised language to politics, and in particular talk about rights, which for Bentham was meaningless in the absence of any underpinning in the terms of enforcement, or power." Ibid. More importantly, he thought this moralized nonsense was "dangerous because it serves as a smokescreen for those engaged in the practice of politics." Ibid., 6. That is right as far as it goes—it shows that Bentham is not a "moralist" in Runciman's limited sense of someone who thinks politics is just applied moral

Sometimes those in the moralist tradition scold people and institutions for their bad behavior, for their failure to honor their "real" obligations and duties, the "real" demands of justice, and so on, even though such scolding is irrelevant to what happens. Mostly, moralists proclaim what, morally, ought to be done, even in the most mundane aspects of life, without regard for any possible application or influence.[11] What is peculiar about the latter is that they almost all do so without any argument that the normative standards they invoke have any status, beyond that of conventional practices in their locale or among members of their class. To be sure, they almost all presuppose that the moral norms they invoke are more than just (geographically, temporally, socioeconomically) local conventions, but the parochiality of the norms should be obvious to anyone outside the "bubble" of bourgeois academic philosophers in the wealthy universities of the Anglosphere (and its appendages in, e.g., Germany). As an aside, one valuable contribution of the history of moral philosophy is that it reveals the figures of the past who continue to engage us, and these are more likely to represent more abiding concerns of more human beings (*vide* Hume on the question of taste). Even there, as Nietzsche showed in *On the Genealogy of Morality*, there is still a parochialism with much wider temporal horizons.[12]

philosophy. In other ways, Bentham is a moralist, though one, like Mill after him, with a finer talent for rhetoric than most contemporary moralists.

[11] I have been astonished when some contemporary academic philosophers deny this characterization. One need only look at a litany of recent titles from a major academic publisher of philosophy: *A Minimally Good Life: What We Owe to Others and What We Can Justifiably Demand*; *What to Save and Why: Identity, Authenticity, and the Ethics of Conservation*; *Stones and Lives: The Ethics of Protecting Heritage in War*; *Being Good in a World of Need*; *Spying Through a Glass Darkly: The Ethics of Espionage and Counter-Intelligence*; *The Virtue of Loyalty*; *A Relational Ethics of Immigration: Hospitality and Hostile Environments*; *The Ethics of Surveillance in Times of Emergency*; *What We Owe to Future People: A Contractualist Account of Intergenerational Ethics*; *What's Wrong with Lookism? Personal Appearance, Discrimination, and Disadvantage*; *Appealing to the Crowd: The Ethical, Political, and Practical Dimensions of Donation-Based Crowdfunding*; *Parenting and the Goods of Childhood*; *Food, Justice and Animals: Feeding the World Respectfully*; *On Taking Offense* ("defends taking offense as, under the right conditions, morally appropriate and politically significant"); *The Ethics of Animal Shelters*; *The Rationality of Love*; *The Rules of Rescue: Cost, Distance, and Effective Altruism*; *Green Light Ethics: A Theory of Permissive Consent and Its Moral Metaphysics*; *Perpetrator Disgust: The Moral Limits of Gut Feelings*; *Mobilizing Hope: Climate Change and Global Poverty* ("clarifies the moral dimensions of climate change by connecting the problem of climate change to the global priority to eradicate poverty"); *Responsible Citizens, Irresponsible States: Should Citizens Pay for Their States' Wrongdoings?*; *Just and Unjust Uses of Limited Force*; *No Refuge: Ethics and the Global Refugee Crisis*; *To Do, To Die, To Reason Why: Individual Ethics in War*; *The Morality of Defensive Force*; *Inheritance of Wealth: Justice, Equality, and the Right to Bequeath*; *The Duty to Vote*; *The Wrong of Rudeness*; *Climate Justice: Vulnerability and Protection*; *The Right to Be Loved*; *Permissible Progeny? The Morality of Procreation and Parenting*; *The Risk of a Lifetime: How, When, and Why Procreation May Be Permissible*. The list could be much longer: What is clear is that academic moral philosophers now take themselves to be in the business of telling people how they, morally, ought to act.

[12] See Michael N. Forster, "Nietzsche: Three Genealogies of Christianity," *Genealogy* 6 (2022): 38.

Not all philosophical moralists sit in judgment of leaders and citizens who fail to live up to the moralist's arguments about their obligations: Rather, as with Hegel (or, in a different tradition, Confucius), they engage in elaborate rationalizations on behalf of the status quo (or, more precisely, the interests of the dominant class in the status quo). Hegel's observation that philosophy is the "owl of Minerva" which only flies at dusk when an era is ending is an appropriate metaphor not only for Hegel's rationalizations of the Prussian state, but for much moralist philosophy since. Think of John Rawls's theoretical edifice in defense of the welfare state in the capitalist democracies, or Ronald Dworkin's jurisprudential defense of the idea that the progressive US Supreme Court led by Earl Warren in the 1960s was really just discovering existing law.[13] Both Rawls and Dworkin wrote shortly before the capitalist welfare state and the progressive judiciary were defeated by the forces of political reaction in the United States after 1980: Their work literally made no difference to what transpired in its wake.

Consider, more generally, the academic industry devoted to the "normative foundations" of tort law, contract law, punishment—the list is quite long. All these practices have functioned without any "normative foundations," and unsurprisingly so: They all arise in response to particular social and economic circumstances, often over extended periods of time, that render them both normatively incoherent (would anyone *really* expect a body of law developed over centuries to reflect a coherent set of moral principles?[14]) and yet practically robust without discursive normative foundations. Practices, after all, are sustained by habits of emotion and judgment, inbred from youth by parents, and under the ideological influence of economic necessity, church, culture, and schools. The best moralist "theory of the normative foundations" of tort or punishment is flotsam on the surface of social reality: an epiphenomenon. Yet this aspect of academic moralism, although irrelevant to practice, has proved a "full employment" act for academic moralists in the universities.[15]

Moralists sometimes profess an interest in human nature, but it has usually been a moralized forgery. The pattern was set by Plato's astonishing claim that it was better for a person to be a victim of injustice than a perpetrator of it. Plato, knowing the Homeric epics and the recent history of Greece (so memorably

[13] I applaud the Supreme Court under Chief Justice Earl Warren ("the Warren Court"), which made America slightly more civilized. But they were making good law, not "applying" or "discovering" existing law. See esp. chs. 12 and 13 in this volume.

[14] As Enzo Rossi rightly points out to me (in a Nietzschean spirit), the same is true of what gets called "morality."

[15] There are things to be learned from the "normative foundations" industry, but they are mostly in the vein of ethnographic data collection about the attitudes of particular classes at particular times. See esp. ch. 18 in this volume. And I do not want to deny the interest for those in the presence of such inquiries, however irrelevant they are to practice.

recorded by Thucydides), also knew that all of antiquity rejected that assessment; he could not know, but may well have suspected, that all subsequent history would reject it as well. Recognizing what humans are *really like*, Plato sees that his entire moralistic project must be shown to comport with real human motivations (i.e., their pursuit of self-interest). Later moralists abandon even Plato's one concession to reality, namely, about actual human motives. Adam Smith and David Hume, noticing the propensity of people in "polite" upper-class society to sympathize with others (at least of their class), posit a "sympathetic" disposition at the foundation of morality. This sympathetic disposition does not reach very far—and is quickly deadened by distance, physical and social—thus rendering it useless at the political level (as Marx well understood). As H. L. A. Hart, a thinker of a more realistic temperament, observed, "human altruism is limited in range and intermittent."[16]

In what follows I want to explore in more systematic detail realism about law and politics, and to identify some of the continuities between "legal realism"—an important tradition in twentieth-century jurisprudence that I have been expounding and defending for thirty years[17]—and "political realism," which has recently established an identity for itself in academic political philosophy, but whose history extends back to antiquity. Continuities between the two kinds of realism have not been noted, partly because in the Anglophone world too much attention has been devoted to the tepid form of "political realism" in the work of the late English philosopher Bernard Williams.[18] (It also has not helped that much writing on legal realism is quite philosophically feeble.[19]) In fact, as we will see, recent "political realism" is quite different from the historical tradition, which actually has deeper affinities with legal realism, or so I shall try to show.[20]

[16] H. L. A. Hart, *The Concept of Law*, 3rd ed. (Clarendon Press, 2012), 196.

[17] See especially Brian Leiter, *Naturalizing Jurisprudence: Essays on American Legal Realism and Naturalism in Legal Philosophy* (Oxford University Press, 2007), and chs. 5, 6, 7 10, 11, and 12 in this volume.

[18] Williams was something of the "bad boy" among boring and parochial analytic philosophers, since he was never as boring and parochial as they were. His views, however, were pedestrian and conservative by comparison to real skeptics about morality and moral philosophy (and, in the case of political realism, by comparison to the historical realists like Thucydides and Machiavelli). See, e.g., Brian Leiter, "Bernard Williams's Debt to Nietzsche: Real or Illusory?," in *Morality and Agency: Themes from Bernard Williams*, ed. A. Szigeti and M. Talbert (Oxford University Press, 2022), 17–35.

[19] See ch. 10 in this volume for a discussion of an example. I let the others pass in silence.

[20] A theme I also take up in ch. 11 in this volume.

II. Realism about Law

Moralism obviously has the upper hand in political philosophy in the contemporary academy[21]—a point to which I will return—but in legal theory, the situation is better: The most important figure in Anglophone legal philosophy of the last century, H. L. A. Hart, was mostly a realist, even as most of those influenced by him (like Joseph Raz and many of his students) sank into moralism. Realists about law have also been well-represented in France (e.g., Michel Troper), Italy (e.g., Giovanni Tarello and Riccardo Guastini), Scandinavia (e.g., Alf Ross), Australia (e.g., Julius Stone), and the United States (e.g., Karl Llewellyn, Richard Posner, and the present author).[22]

A realist theory of law, as I understand it, involves both a "realist" and a "naturalistic" component. In legal theory, realists aim to describe how law operates without romantic or moralizing illusions. We want to know what law and legal institutions are like, not what we might wish them to be. Realists also do not suppose that the way things are will make "moral sense" or will turn out to be morally defensible: It can (and often does) turn out that law and its operations are wrong, foolish, or worse. Realists can, of course, be animated by normative hopes, as we saw in section I, but they do not build them into the account of their subject matter (contrast, for example, Ronald Dworkin's jurisprudence, which builds a moral obligation to obey the law into his account of the nature of law). In the first instance, we need to understand *what is really going on*. For example, what are people's real motivations, what are they doing (independent of what they say they are doing)?

Because realism means understanding *reality*, realists are necessarily "naturalists" in the following precise sense: In describing and explaining what is really going on, they appeal only to mechanisms and entities that are explanatorily fruitful in the successful empirical sciences (those sciences being our only reliable guide to what is real). Naturalism is the second crucial commitment of realist jurisprudence. Of the historical legal realists, the Scandinavians were most explicit about commitment to naturalism, while the Italians and the Americans, in different ways, presuppose a naturalistic worldview (even though

[21] This is true even of the descendants of the Frankfurt School, who are now academic moralists indistinguishable from their colleagues in the Anglophone world in this regard. See ch. 18 in this volume for further discussion.

[22] Italian legal realism associated with the "Genoa School" is more radical in its claims about the indeterminacy of legal interpretation than the view I defend. See, e.g., Riccardo Guastini, "Rule-Scepticism Restated," in *Oxford Studies in Philosophy of Law*, ed. Leslie Green and Brian Leiter (Oxford University Press, 2011), 138–61. And for a more recent and important systematic treatment, see Pierluigi Chiassoni, *Interpretation without Truth: A Realistic Inquiry* (Springer, 2019). Chiassoni gives a useful summary of "Genoa" realism at ibid., 2–8. For reasons, my view is not as skeptical about interpretation as theirs, see esp. ch. 7 in this volume.

the American Realists of the 1920s and 1930s were philosophically unsophisticated, the *Zeitgeist* in which they grew up was a naturalistic one). My own legal realism is explicitly informed by philosophical naturalism.[23] Insofar as only what is naturalistically explicable can be real, naturalism must be central to the realist worldview.

It is important to understand what naturalism does and does not mean in this context. Quine, the most important philosophical naturalist of the twentieth century, was, ironically, often a very bad Quinean. The crucial commitment of naturalism, as even Quine professed, is a posteriori: Whatever works in the successful sciences is admissible into a naturalist ontology. Yet Quine remained committed for most of his career[24] to two failed scientific research programs: physicalism (the idea that everything real must be reducible to physics) and behaviorism in psychology. As another post-Quinean naturalist philosopher, Jerry Fodor, pointed out in the 1970s,[25] reduction to physics has not marked the last half-century of scientific research; instead, there has been a proliferation of special sciences—biological and cognitive sciences most notably—that proceed without even the pretense of being reducible to physics. As another important post-Quinean philosopher, Tyler Burge, has observed:

> Promoters of "naturalizing" [i.e., physicalist reductionist] projects are driven, I think, by misconceptions of science. These misconceptions breed misconceptions of mind. The notion of representation—of reference or attribution that can be correct or incorrect and that helps type-individuate kinds of psychological states—is entrenched not only in common-sense explanation but in scientific explanation in psychology. There is nothing unnatural or supernatural about such explanation. Some of the relevant psychology is well-supported, mathematically rigorous, mature science. There is no basis, even a prima facie one, to the worry that psychological notions are invitations to mystery or miracle. Even if there were such basis, the role that these notions play in powerful empirical science would undermine it. . . . I know of no good ground for thinking that [psychologists'] explanatory claims must be twisted into the mold of biological or information-theoretic explanation, or any other explanation in the natural sciences, in order to be explanatorily successful.[26]

[23] See esp. Leiter, *Naturalizing Jurisprudence*.

[24] In one of his late works, *Pursuit of Truth*, Quine professed commitment to Davidsonian anomalous monism, although for reasons that seem hard to square with his other commitments. See W. V. Quine, *Pursuit of Truth* (Harvard University Press, 1990), 70–73. Quine became slightly less austere near the end. See especially W. V. Quine, *From Stimulus to Science* (Harvard University Press, 1995). Whether this shift was a philosophically principled change is less clear.

[25] Jerry A. Fodor, *The Language of Thought* (Thomas Y. Crowell Co., 1975), 9–26.

[26] Tyler Burge, *Origins of Objectivity* (Oxford University Press, 2010), 296–97.

For naturalists, explanatory and predictive fruitfulness is the mark of the real and the knowable, not some a priori and empirically unmotivated assumption that everything must be reducible to physics. Quine himself was "officially" a resolutely methodological naturalist in this sense—even allowing that we would have to jettison "empiricism" (the view that all knowledge derives from sensory experience) if telepathy turned out to work[27]—yet in practice for most of his long life he remained wedded to the failed science of the middle of the last century. That also explains his behaviorism in psychology, long after the collapse of that research program, which began with Noam Chomsky's famous critique of B. F. Skinner[28] and was concluded by the flourishing of the cognitive sciences, which Fodor emphasized and to which he contributed.

In short, naturalism involves no commitment to physicalism, to the view that only physical events and properties are real. Naturalists take successful empirical sciences as a constraint on their ontology, and we now know that unreduced psychological facts are central to the scientific understanding of human phenomena, *contra* behaviorism. But it is an equally important upshot of naturalism, as I understand it, that it rules out appeal to all evaluative or normative facts, which play no role in any successful explanatory paradigms in any discipline.[29] Anti-realism about morals in particular—there are no attitude- or mind-independent facts about what is morally right and wrong—is central to naturalism: Psychological attitudes (e.g., beliefs or affective responses) about moral matters are often crucial to explaining human behavior, but we do not need to posit the existence of any mind-independent (objective) facts about moral values. This kind of anti-realism about morals is currently controversial among bourgeois philosophers in Anglophone universities, who spend too much time talking to moralistic members of their class and thus suffer from "group polarization," as the social psychologists call it.[30] It does, however, have the weight of intellectual history on its side: Since Nietzsche, most of modernity has rejected both God and an objectively true morality. The absence of objective facts about moral value is fatal to the views of Dworkin and to the Catholic natural lawyers,[31]

[27] Quine, *Pursuit of Truth*, 20–21.

[28] See Noam Chomsky, "A Review of B.F. Skinner's *Verbal Behavior*," *Language* 35 (1959): 26–58.

[29] See, e.g., Brian Leiter, "Moral Facts and Best Explanations," repr. *Naturalizing Jurisprudence*; Brian Leiter, *Moral Psychology with Nietzsche* (Oxford University Press, 2019), esp. chs. 1, 2, and 4; and ch. 15 and 16 of this volume.

[30] See, e.g., David G. Myers, "Discussion-Induced Attitude Polarization," *Human Relations* 28 (1975): 699–714; Charles G. Lord, Lee Ross, and Mark. R. Lepper, "Biased Assimilation and Attitude Polarization: The Effects of Prior Theories on Subsequently Considered Evidence," *Journal of Personality and Social Psychology* 37 (1979): 2098–2109; Johannes A. Zuber, Helmut W. Crott, and Joachim Werner, "Choice Shift and Group Polarization: An Analysis of the Status of Arguments and Social Decision Schemes," *Journal of Personality and Social Psychology* 62 (1992): 50–61; Cass R. Sunstein, "The Law of Group Polarization," *The Journal of Political Philosophy* 10 (2002): 175–95.

[31] See, e.g., Brian Leiter, "Politics by Other Means: The Jurisprudence of 'Common Good Constitutionalism,'" *University of Chicago Law Review* 90 (2023): 1685–1717.

among others, but I shall not dwell on that here. They are not part of modernity, and it would surely be best if we could pass over them in silence.[32]

Realism about law, then, is "realism" and "naturalism" about the social phenomenon known as "law." What do legal realists, so understood, reveal to us about law?

To start, realists about law acknowledge that in any functioning legal system, law operates primarily outside the courts. This was a central contention of H. L. A. Hart's jurisprudence: Legally valid norms guide how ordinary people buy homes, make wills, enter contracts, avoid taxes, and structure many other aspects of their lives. *Adjudication* is a fringe phenomenon in a functioning legal system: Most individuals consult lawyers to accomplish certain goals, not to end up in court. Jurisprudential theories—once again, Dworkin's most infamously—that organize their claims about the nature of law around what goes on in court are deeply unrealistic.[33] (As an aside, I should note that realists like Alf Ross focus on courts, but for nothing like Dworkin's reasons at all. Ross does so rather because of Kelsen's view that laws are primarily addressed to judges, together with Ross's ambition of locating law in a naturalistic picture of how the world works.[34])

Yet law outside the courts appears in two guises: what the "law books" say, and what legal and other actors do. "Law in the books" and "law in action" is how realists often mark the contrast, and the difference is important: Some norms for behavior can be legally valid, as Hart showed, but mostly ignored in practice. The posted speed limits on the roads are the most familiar example in many jurisdictions: It is *clearly* illegal to drive beyond a certain speed limit, and yet it is common for drivers to recognize that no one will be sanctioned unless they greatly exceed that limit. In any legal system that has existed, there is always a gap between the legally valid rules and the rules that are enforced: call this *realism about enforcement.*

Realism about enforcement is not just about the gap between enforcing the rule "in the books" and enforcing a different norm (as in the speed-limit case), but also between how the rules "in action" are enforced against different parties: Here facts about economic class, political power, and other salient demographic and social characteristics (e.g., race or ethnicity) figure in how the same legally enforced rules play out (this is perhaps most notorious in the arena of

[32] Given the current state of affairs in academic jurisprudence, it has not been possible to pass over all of them in silence!

[33] Most self-identified realists, including the Americans and the Italians, focus primarily on adjudication, but insofar as they do not generally equate what goes on in courts with a theory of the nature of law, they do not make Dworkin's mistake. Sometimes, however, they are not so careful.

[34] For doubts whether this was right, even from a naturalistic point of view, see Brian Leiter, "Alf Ross's Critique of American Legal Realism—and a Naturalistic Critique of Ross," available on SSRN at https://papers.ssrn.com/sol3/papers.cfm?abstract_id=4240991.

how police interact with citizens, but it extends well beyond that arena). A realist theory must also capture this second kind of gap between the "law in the books" and the "law in action." Realism about enforcement calls attention already to the way in which valid legal norms are and are not applied in real life. Still, a further realism about enforcement practices accepts that legally valid norms are applied in real life but notes how that application really works.

When we do get to those matters that arise in the courts, legal realists emphasize the inevitable indeterminacy of what we call "legal reasoning," at least in some range of cases (which will vary by jurisdiction, for reasons that will become apparent). Legal reasoning is supposed to be the "method" by which courts arrive at a judgment based on the facts of the case and the relevant valid law. In reality, in every modern jurisdiction, "legal reasoning" may circumscribe the outcome a court can legitimately reach, but it often affords the court latitude about the choice of outcome. More precisely, the most plausible version of the indeterminacy thesis about law[35] is that the *class of legal reasons*—that is, the reasons that may be invoked in public to justify a judicial decision—*underdetermines* the decision a judge must reach in many cases; legal reasons limit the justifiable outcomes to the case, but the judge often has available equally legitimate legal arguments for more than one decision even within the circumscribed field of possible decisions. The task of a realist theory of adjudication is to explain why legal reasoning is indeterminate and to identify what influences judges to choose the decision they do, within the realm of those that are legally available.

There are various possible grounds of legal indeterminacy: H. L. A. Hart emphasized the "open texture" of natural languages,[36] while the American and Italian realists have emphasized the interpretive latitude judges enjoy in how they construe statutory provisions and precedents.[37] It seems to me both considerations are correct, although their influence varies by jurisdiction. The idea that judges have interpretive latitude is a claim about the *legitimate* interpretive moves a judge can make when confronted with legal sources, whether legislative, constitutional, or judicial. The notion of "legitimacy" at issue here is a thoroughly naturalized one, to be understood in terms of psychosocial facts about legal actors: Differing interpretations are "legitimate" insofar as they are *accepted* in fact by other legal actors, especially other judges, as acceptable interpretations. This is often called a "sociological" conception of legitimacy—social acceptance by others is the mark of "legitimacy"—in contrast to the "philosophical" conception, which asks whether the interpretations are really justified by reference to some normative standard. That realists rely on a sociological

[35] Leiter, *Naturalizing Jurisprudence*, 9–12.
[36] Hart, *Concept of Law*, 124–36.
[37] See, e.g., Leiter, *Naturalizing Jurisprudence*, 73–78; Guastini, "Rule-Skepticism Restated."

conception of legitimacy means, of course, that the extent of indeterminacy will vary depending on the facts about the attitudes and practices of officials in different legal jurisdictions. This is as it should be: The scope of the indeterminacy of legal reasoning will vary by jurisdiction, even if every jurisdiction exhibits indeterminacy to some degree. That the conception is sociological also explains why, for example, the American realists can claim that indeterminacy is an issue primarily at the various stages of appellate review: This is an empirical claim about the interpretive latitude officials have in those kinds of cases, and is compatible, of course, with legal reasoning being determinate and judicial outcomes being predictable elsewhere in the legal system (see ch. 7 in this volume).

A realist theory of law is necessarily a positivist theory,[38] and a positivist theory is necessarily a realist one (see ch. 5 in this volume). This is not true, to be sure, of all theories that have claimed the "positivist" label, but it is true of the most important one, H. L. A. Hart's, despite his confusions about the American and Scandinavian realists that I have written about previously.[39] Hart, however, is a realist insofar as he recognizes that law operates mostly outside the courts; that inside the courts, some decisions are legally indeterminate; that the nature of law is naturalistically explicable in terms of psychosocial facts about human behaviors and attitudes, particularly those of officials; and that law is not necessarily a good thing, that it has costs, and that it is always an open question whether law generates moral obligations of compliance. Hart's mistake regarding legal realism was in taking both the Americans and the Scandinavians to be answering his questions, rather than their own. In both cases, he wrongly understood them to be proffering an analysis of the concept of law, understood as that concept implicit in ordinary language that captured features of law intelligible to an ordinary person familiar with a modern municipal legal system. The American realists had neither interest in nor even an understanding of a project of conceptual analysis, and in fact presupposed in their arguments for the indeterminacy of legal reasoning a positivist conception of legal validity.[40] The Scandinavian realist Alf Ross—the only one Hart really engaged with—was also quite clear that his project was not one of ordinary-language conceptual analysis but rather an effort to explain how central legal concepts like "obligation," "duty," and "right" could be located within a fairly austere naturalistic worldview; Ross explicitly acknowledged that this analysis could not do justice to the concept of law deployed by an insider to the legal system.[41] Hart's misguided, albeit

[38] See Leiter, *Naturalizing Jurisprudence*, 59–80.
[39] See ibid., 17–18, and chs. 5 and 7 in this volume
[40] See Leiter, *Naturalizing Jurisprudence*, 59–80.
[41] See Jakob H. Holtermann, "Naturalizing Alf Ross's Legal Realism: A Philosophical Reconstruction," *Revus* 24 (2014): 165–86. See also ch. 7 in this volume.

influential, dispute with legal realism has obscured the essential connection between positivist and realist views about law (see especially chs. 5 and 7 in this volume).

The connection is particularly clear in the case of the realist indeterminacy thesis. Any thesis to the effect that legal reasons fail to justify a unique decision in some range of cases presupposes that we know the difference between "legal" and "nonlegal" reasons, including "legal" and "nonlegal" norms (i.e., those that are and are not legally valid). Positivists and antipositivists will draw the line at different places, and how they draw the line bears on the indeterminacy thesis. If a realist says the judge's decision reflected his moral judgment about the merits of the case, and if the moral considerations the judge relied on would, in fact, only justify one decision (the one the judge reached), that only shows legal reasoning to be indeterminate if, in fact, those moral considerations were not "part of the law" or "legally binding." Hard positivism about law and legal validity can easily explain this[42]: The moral norms are not accepted as criteria of legal validity from an "internal point of view"—that is, they are neither invoked as justifying a decision nor are deviations from those norms criticized by reference to them—and so are not part of the rule of recognition.[43] That positivism is necessary for the realist arguments for indeterminacy to work does not show, of course, that positivism is correct. Positivism is vindicated, however, on naturalistic and explanatory grounds, precisely the same considerations that commend realism: That is, a positivist theory of law figures in the most explanatorily fruitful explanations of legal phenomena, such as judicial decisions.[44]

I mentioned already that a realist theory of law, because it is a naturalistic theory, eschews reference to objective moral values. Here again Hart is a model realist about law: It is not simply that the existence of law in some society is, on his view, a complicated empirical, not moral, fact (i.e., a psychosocial fact about the practices of officials in deciding questions of legal validity, their attitudes toward those practices, as well as about the obedience of citizens to legally valid norms[45]), it is that he correctly glosses normative concepts, like "obligation," entirely in behavioral terms, that is, what people are disposed to say and do, rather than in terms of any cognitive (i.e., referential) content those terms might have. So, for example, Hart says that "[r]ules are conceived and spoken of as imposing obligations when the general demand for conformity is insistent and the social pressure brought to bear upon those who deviate or threaten to deviate is

42 See Leiter, *Naturalizing Jurisprudence*, ch. 2. See also ch. 5 in this volume.

43 Even versions of "soft" positivism are compatible with this conclusion, given that realists most often point to nonlegal norms influencing decisions that are not norms judges do or would acknowledge as decisive.

44 See chs. 2 and 5 in this volume, and Leiter, *Naturalizing Jurisprudence*, 121–36.

45 Hart, *Concept of Law*, 116–17.

great. . . . [T]he insistence on importance or *seriousness* of social pressure behind the rules is the primary factor determining whether they are thought of as giving rise to obligations."[46] This is Hart's reasonable attempt at naturalizing normative talk in terms of things that do exist, namely, the observable behavior (including verbal behavior) of people. Alf Ross pursued a related but different strategy, namely, one of translation of normative talk into talk about predictions of behavior to preserve the apparently cognitive content of legal claims (admittedly, on a verificationist view of meaning). But both theorists share the same naturalistic impulse: to purge their theory of law of reference to moral (or moral-sounding) facts.[47] After Auschwitz (with apologies to Adorno), this seems a minimal commitment for a serious theory of law in modern societies.

One must acknowledge that far too many later positivists in the Anglophone tradition have abandoned the realism and naturalism of Hart's approach; Joseph Raz is the most striking case. Raz is a moral realist in the metaphysical sense: He takes there to be objective moral values,[48] although his reasons for thinking this are a bit obscure. Dogmatic confidence in the objectivity of morality became a feature of Oxford philosophy starting in the 1980s, finding its clearest theoretical articulation decades later in the work of Derek Parfit, as well as other defenders of explicitly nonnaturalist value realism or "realism about reasons."[49] At the same time, Raz remains committed to the positivist thesis that there can be no evaluative or content-based criteria of legal validity. Where Raz's moral realism (in the metaphysical sense) makes itself most apparent is in his view that law necessarily claims authority, even if it ultimately lacks a justification for that claim.

On Raz's view, law can only claim authority if it is possible to identify the content of a legal directive without reference to the underlying ("dependent") reasons for that directive. This is a "prerequisite" for claiming authority because what distinguishes a (practical) authority in the first place is that its directives preempt consideration of the underlying reasons (including, e.g., moral reasons) for what we ought to do, and in so doing actually makes it more likely that we will do what we really ought to do.[50] For my kind of realist, the problem with Raz's argument is that it presupposes a highly moralized and unrealistic conception

[46] Ibid., 86–87.

[47] Of the many dubious claims in Scott Shapiro's book *Legality* (Harvard University Press, 2011), the most startling is related to the issue noted in the text. See ch. 9 in this volume for further discussion.

[48] See, e.g., Joseph Raz, "Notes on Value and Objectivity," in *Objectivity in Law and Morals*, ed. Brian Leiter (Cambridge University Press, 2001).

[49] T. M. Scanlon, *Being Realistic About Reasons* (Oxford University Press, 2014), is the strongest representative of the genre in my view; for doubts even about this version, see Leiter, *Moral Psychology with Nietzsche*, ch. 4. See also chs. 15 and 16 in this volume.

[50] Raz offers this argument to show that no legal positivist can allow that there could be content-based criteria of legal validity; I mostly agree with his conclusion, but not at all for Raz's reasons. See ch. 5 in this volume.

of what it is for law to claim "authority." Raz understands authority in terms of what he calls "the Service Conception," in which a claim to authority is a claim to provide a subject of authority better "reasons" for acting in accordance with what Raz calls "right reason" than the subject would arrive at without the intermediation of the authority.[51] (We can gloss, for purposes here, "right reason" as *what one really ought to do.*) This view obviously presupposes Raz's moral realism (and realism about reasons quite generally), one that is incredible from a legal realist (i.e., naturalist) point of view: There are no *real* moral reasons for acting. More importantly, a legal realist can also rightly wonder: Why think that when law claims authority, it is claiming to perform a service (i.e., help its subjects do *what they really ought to do*)? I return to this issue in chapter 5, where I critique Raz's view in more detail.

Raz is explicit in rejecting Hart's realist approach to jurisprudence. Against Hart's realist aim of a "descriptive jurisprudence," Raz asserts "there is an interdependence between conceptual and normative argument" such that the account "does not necessarily conform to everyone's notion of authority in all detail. It does claim to be an explanatory account in singling out important features of people's conception of authority."[52] No theorist thinks their descriptive account conforms "to everyone's notion . . . in every detail," so this is just a strawman. Where is the evidence, however, that Raz's account even captures some "important features of people's [which people?] conception of authority"? There is none. Raz has simply smuggled in a moralized conception of authority[53]—as providing a service for its subjects—without even the pretense that it satisfies even lax evidential demands of a "descriptive sociology" as Hart, the realist, proposed.

Razian moralism is, plainly, not as pernicious as the massive ideological delusions about law that Dworkin's entire corpus represents. Yet it still represents a backsliding from the realism of Hart's jurisprudence, which legal realists should reject. One can grant that all law claims authority (i.e., the right to tell its subjects what to do) without supposing that the claim of right is to be analyzed in Razian terms. Legal systems claim the right to direct the conduct of their subjects, but whether that claim is ever justified, and on what grounds, is a question on which legal realists should be agnostic. Until we have evidence that legal systems have claimed this right to perform a "service" for their subjects, those committed to a

[51] See Joseph Raz, "Authority, Law and Morality," *The Monist* 68 (1985): 295–324.

[52] Joseph Raz, *The Morality of Freedom* (Oxford University Press, 1986), 63–65. The talk of "importance" obviously echoes John Finnis, *Natural Law and Natural Rights* (Oxford University Press, 1980), ch. 1, who had an alarmingly large impact on Raz.

[53] Moralized in the sense that its main aim is to explain why deference to authority by rational subjects can be justified.

realistic, naturalistic descriptive jurisprudence must treat the Razian analysis as a wrongheaded appendage to the realistic program in legal theory.

There are normative upshots of realism about law, although their precise content will depend on one's normative starting points, about which a realist theory itself is neutral.[54] Nonetheless, realism about law reveals the terms on which normative evaluation of law must proceed, if it is not to be evaluating make-believe. First, given *realism about law enforcement practices,* it is never sufficient to evaluate a legal system to know what the valid legal norms are; one must know both which valid norms are enforced and *how and against whom* they are enforced. Valid legal norms that are just can turn out to be unjust along either dimension, and unjust legal norms can turn out to be just along either dimension. The positivist account of legal validity, which is the only serious account we have, leaves these evaluative questions open (as it should, since it is only an account of validity), and no competing account of legal validity settles them. Those that purport to do so—like Dworkin's and those of some lesser antipositivists—serve only as ideological obfuscations. Second, given realism about adjudication, we need to rethink the role of judges, especially appellate judges, in a legal system. Since indeterminacy is an inescapable feature of a legal system, judges must be appointed with that fact in mind. Judges are never merely appliers of the law; they must always make new law, if only interstitially, although sometimes they do more than that.[55] The quality of their moral and political judgment thus matters as much as their distinctively legal competence. The lie that judges are simply the instruments of the lawmakers is an ideological illusion that all legal realists oppose, as it deceives the public about the essential role of courts in a polity. Political elites are rarely fooled on this score, of course, which is why they typically care a great deal about the composition of the judiciary. Since, however, there is no known political or economic system in which the preferences of elites are conducive to the well-being of the vast majority, legal realism here has an important role to play in promoting public, and perhaps even democratic, accountability.

III. Realism about Politics (and about Moral and Political Philosophy)

Realism in political philosophy, unlike in legal philosophy, has been less central to the Western academic canon of the last two centuries, which is infused with moralism, due to the influence of Kant and Hegel in Europe, Rawls in North

[54] See ch. 13 in this volume for one approach to these questions.
[55] See chs. 12 and 13 in this volume.

America, and, perhaps most importantly now, to the fact that political philosophy is written almost exclusively for other academics who earn their living by being favorably assessed by other moralist professors, who are almost all members of the economic classes that have the leisure to "reflect" on the morality of their actions according to local norms.[56] Chapter 18 discusses some of the political economy explanations for this state of affairs, but I will put those to one side for now.

The best characterization of political realism in the existing scholarly literature is due to Alison McQueen, who is sensitive to both the historical and contemporary traditions.[57] She characterizes political realism as involving four claims[58]:

1. "[R]ealists think that there is something distinctive about politics. It is a realm of activity with 'its own character, purposes, and means'" [quoting Matt Sleat].
2. "[R]ealists think that politics is agonistic or conflictual. They attribute this disagreement to a variety of causes, including human nature and the limits of rationality, competing identities and interests, and value pluralism. [Hans] Morgenthau, for example, locates the causes of conflict in human nature—our lust for power and will to dominate."
3. "[P]olitical realists tend to prioritize the requirements of order and stability over the demands of justice. They see order as a fragile accomplishment. Because disagreement and conflict are ineradicable, order and stability are always vulnerable."
4. "[R]ealists reject as utopian those approaches which seem to deny the distinctiveness of politics and the persistence of disagreement and conflict. Realists take aim at theories that fail to take seriously the psychological, sociological, and institutional constraints on political action."

McQueen's first thesis is a bit anachronistic. Thucydides, for example, was certainly not reacting against views that failed to treat politics as distinctive (e.g., by treating political philosophy as "applied moral philosophy"[59]), although

[56] This was not the case for Machiavelli, Hobbes, and Nietzsche, obviously, who had very different audiences, and generally wrote much better as a result!

[57] William Galston's account is also helpful, but less historically oriented, and not as succinct as McQueen's. See William Galston, "Realism in Political Theory," *European Journal of Political Theory* 9 (2010): 385–411. Galston's account is very much of a kind of "normative political realism" as I call it, below, in the text.

[58] Alison McQueen, *Political Realism in Apocalyptic Times* (Cambridge University Press, 2018), 10–11.

[59] The complaint common among contemporary political realists like Raymond Geuss and Bernard Williams.

Machiavelli arguably was (vis-à-vis Cicero).[60] Her first thesis clearly identifies, however, the main theme of "political realism" in recent Anglophone philosophy. As Enzo Rossi, a leading contributor to this literature, puts it: "[P]olitical realism is a view about the normative autonomy of the political," and, in particular, its rejection of the "ethics first" approach to political philosophy.[61] This leads naturally to the question about the "sources of realist normativity," as Rossi says.[62] McQueen's third and fourth theses, in turn, point to some of the "normative" concerns of "realist" political theory (most obvious in Hobbes, of course): a focus on order and stability, and rejection of utopianism and the priority of deontological moral concerns. I'll refer to the latter as Normative Political Realism.

Political realism, as I am concerned with it here, is somewhat different: It takes a lesson, as it were, from legal realism, whose fundamental ambition is to describe and explain how law and adjudication really work.[63] Similarly, political realism aims to *describe* and *explain* what is going on in politics and society, not to pass normative judgment, let alone to identify alternative "sources" of normativity.[64] The primary goal of realistic theories is to understand how things work. Theorists may have normative aspirations, but they have no interest in theoretical justifications of those aspirations since such justifications have no effect (and, at least for some realists, because they have no epistemic standing either). The only normativity this "Classical Political Realism" (as I will call it) recognizes (but does not try to justify) is the normativity of self-interest, because it is a psychological and sociological fact: It moves people to act. This is true even of realists like Marx, who appeal to the self-interest of a class, not their altruistic or other-regarding motives.[65] Let me say a bit more about Thucydides in

[60] See, e.g., Cicero, *De Officiis*, trans. Walter Miller (Harvard University Press, 1913). Machiavelli's subversion of the conventional political literature of his age has been extensively discussed. See, e.g., Quentin Skinner, *The Foundations of Modern Political Thought, Vol. 1: The Renaissance* (Cambridge University Press, 1978), 128–38.

[61] Enzo Rossi, "Being Realistic and Demanding the Impossible," *Constellations* 26 (2019): 639.

[62] Ibid., 641. Rossi frames his discussion around Bernard Williams's account in Bernard Williams, "Realism and Moralism in Political Theory," in *In the Beginning Was the Deed* (Princeton University Press, 2005), 1–17. Williams's tepid version of political realism is notable mainly for how moralistic it is: he thinks a "realist" [*sic*] political theory must still explain how "the state [can] offer a justification of its power *to each subject*" (ibid., 4), since this demand is constitutive of politics, thus not "prior" to it (ibid., 5). He then goes further and says that "a justification does not count if the acceptance itself is produced by the coercive power which is supposedly being justified" (ibid., 6). He aptly calls this the "critical theory principle" and notes that it has affinities with the arch-German moralist Habermas (ibid., 9). As often happens with Williams, what starts out looking like some "radical" break with the mainstream is, in the end, just a hedged and de minimis departure from the mainstream. See also note 18, above.

[63] See Leiter, *Naturalizing Jurisprudence*, especially ch. 1.

[64] Rossi's alternative "source" of normativity is purely epistemic, and thus also lays a considerable emphasis on correct description but in a different way than I emphasize here.

[65] See Edwards and Leiter, *Marx*, 134–35. Marx, of course, thinks the calculating form of self-interest familiar under capitalism is an artifact of the circumstances in which people find themselves. It is possible that under different conditions than have ever existed, all traces of self-interest will disappear, but that is irrelevant for Marxist advocacy of revolution under capitalist relations of

particular, as an example of the kind of classical political realism that is important for my purposes.

Thucydides lays considerable emphasis on *human nature* and the challenges it poses for maintaining order and stability, both within states and between them, as McQueen notes. There is not, however, anything like McQueen's contrast between "order and stability" and "justice," since for Thucydides, the latter has a meaning distinct from the modern connotation of, e.g., distributive justice (think of Rawls's *A Theory of Justice*). Here is how Paul Woodruff fairly summarizes the requirements of "justice" for Thucydides.

1. That traditional law be maintained.
2. That disputes be settled without violence by a duly constituted authority.
3. That an agreement be kept, even when it is in the interests of one party to abrogate it.
4. That punishment be meted out as retribution, proportional to the offense, and only to the guilty.
5. That overreaching and avarice be avoided.
6. That tyranny be avoided. (This follows from 1, as tyranny occurs when traditional law is abrogated.)[66]

For Thucydides—writing long before the triumph of moralism in the modern academy—"justice" is close to "order and stability."

Of course, as I remarked at the start of this chapter, Thucydides's *History* has a moral to it: namely, that unbridled lust for power and glory led Athens to ruin. As he says regarding the horrors of the civil war in Corcyra: "The cause of all this was the desire to rule out of avarice and ambition, and the zeal for winning that proceeds from those two" (Thucydides, 92). The same applies to Athens itself, although Thucydides never levels that charge directly: He never says, "Athens ought not to have acted as it did." His readers know that things ended badly for Athens (the empire collapsed). What Thucydides does is tell the story of the war by putting into the mouths of his speakers *their real motives and beliefs*; from these, readers can infer that it was these motives that produced the bad outcome. (This connects to McQueen's fourth thesis about political realism: Political actors need to be aware of the real motives of other actors.)

production. (Maybe under communism, moral theory would be practically effective?) At the same time, as noted earlier in note 5, the only explanation for why productive power should grow so relentlessly (if not consistently) throughout human history is that human beings are motivated by the benefits that accrue to them from its growth.

[66] See Thucydides, *Thucydides On Justice, Power and Human Nature*, trans. Paul Woodruff (Hackett, 1993), xxvii. All further citations to Thucydides will be to this edition and included in parentheses in the body of the text.

The most famous example of the latter is the Melian dialogue. It seems unlikely that the Athenians actually said the following to the Melians:

> [W]e will not make a long speech no one would believe, full of fine moral arguments—that our empire is justified because we defeated the Persians, or that we are coming against you for an injustice you have done to us . . . Instead, let's work out what we can do on the basis of what both sides truly accept: we both know that decisions about justice are made in human discussions only when both side are under equal compulsion [e.g., before the law]; but when one side is stronger, it gets as much as it can, and the weak must accept that. (Thucydides, 103)

In fact, the Athenians probably did justify their actions as a response to the injustice the Melians had done them. Thucydides, however, cuts beneath their actual rhetoric and makes them say out loud what they are really thinking, namely, that "justice" only applies to those who are equals in power. More generally, he portrays with unflinching candor a world in which actors are driven by lust for power and glory, and in which any talk about justice or fairness in relations between states is simply window-dressing.[67]

Nietzsche's own commentary on the Melian dialogue highlights the realism he so admires in Thucydides (and Machiavelli):

> Do you suppose perchance that these little Greek free cities, which from rage and envy would have liked to devour each other, were guided by philanthropic and righteous principles? Does one reproach Thucydides for the words he puts into the mouths of the Athenian ambassadors when they negotiated with the Melians on the question of destruction or submission?
>
> Only complete Tartuffes [i.e. Socrates and Plato] could possibly have talked of virtue in the midst of this terrible tension—or men living apart, hermits, refugees, and emigrants from reality—people who negated in order to be able to live themselves.[68]

Two characteristics, then, distinguish Thucydides from contemporary "political realists." First, he relies explicitly on claims about human nature on the

[67] In an unpublished manuscript, Andrew Biondo points out that "there is not a single 'diagnostic' passage [cites omitted], where Thucydides claims a [political actor] is driven by any moral motivation whatsoever." Andrew Biondo, "Is Thucydides an Amoral Realist?" (unpublished manuscript, University of Chicago, 2023).

[68] Friedrich Nietzsche, *The Will to Power*, trans. Walter Kaufmann and R. J. Hollingdale (Vintage Books, 1967), 233–34.

real motives of human beings. Second, there is an absence of explicit normative judgments (he lets the history "speak for itself" as it were). On the first point, two aspects of human nature are a recurring concern in the *History*: first, the desire for glory, power, and honor, and second, the powerful role of self-interest. (In a sense, Thucydides's main implicit normative standard of judgment is *long-term* self-interest: The pursuit of short-term self-interest, and the lust for glory and power, if unchecked, lead to ruin, as it did for Athens.) Pericles's "funeral oration," in particular, is an exercise in unbridled self-congratulation for Athens—for the exemplary way fellow Athenians supposedly deal with each other (see especially Thucydides, 40–41) ("justice" among equals, as it were), but most importantly for its glorious empire:

> For Athens is the only power now that is greater than her fame when it comes to the test. Only in the case of Athens can enemies never be upset over the quality of those who defeat them when they invade; only in our empire can subject states never complain that their rulers are unworthy. We are proving our power with strong evidence, and we are not without witnesses: we shall be the admiration of people now and in the future.... For we have compelled all seas and all lands to be open to us by our daring; and we have set up eternal monuments on all sides, of the evil we have done to our enemies, and of the good we have done to our friends....
>
> [T]o famous men, all the earth is a monument, and their virtues are attested not only by inscriptions on stone at home; but an unwritten record of the mind lives on for each of them, even in foreign lands, better than any gravestone ... [T]he love of honor is the one thing that never grows old, and useless old age takes delight not in gathering wealth (as some say) but in being honored. (Thucydides, 43, 45)

The "natural" ambition for glory and power is also expressed starkly in the Melian dialogue:

> Nature always compels gods (we believe) and men (we are certain) to rule over anyone they can control. We did not make this law, and were not the first to follow it; but we will take it as we found it and leave it to posterity forever, because we know that you would do the same if you had our power, and so would anyone else. (Thucydides, 106)

The central role of self-interest for Thucydides is perhaps most apparent in his rendering of the Athenian debate about how to treat Mytilene, after the rebellion: Both sides appeal only to the self-interest of Athens. Cleon, who favors killing everyone in Mytilene, remarks that:

> [Athenian] softness [i.e., in possibly sparing the Mytileneans] puts you in danger and does not win you the affection of your allies; and you do not see that your empire is a tyranny, and that you have unwilling subjects who are continually plotting against you. They obey you not because of any good turns you might do them to your own detriment, and not because of any good will they might have, but only because you exceed them in strength. . . .
>
> Long ago we should have given the Mytileneans no more privileges than our other allies, and then they would not have come to this degree of insolence, for generally it is human nature to look with contempt on those who serve your interests, and to admire those who never give in to you. . . .
>
> [Y]ou ought not to make the mistake of giving in to the three things that are most damaging to an empire: pity, delight in speeches, and a sense of fairness. (Thucydides, 67, 69, 70)

Diodotus's contrasting case *against* killing the Mytileneans is also framed exclusively in terms of self-interest:

> Our dispute, if we are sensible, will concern not their injustice to us, but our judgment as to what is best for us. Even if I proved them guilty of terrible injustice, I still would not advise the death penalty for this, unless that was to our advantage . . . [W]e are not at law with them, and so have no need to speak of justice. We are in council instead, and must decide how the Mytileneans can be put to the best use for us. (Thucydides, 72)

After making the case that it is in their interest to spare many of the Mytileneans, he concludes: "I want you to accept my proposal because you see that it is the best course and not because you are swayed more by pity or a sense of fairness" (Thucydides, 74).

For Thucydides, moralism about politics is wholly irrelevant to the practice of politics[69]: Political actors do what they do in pursuit of glory and power, and entirely with an eye to the interest of their states. You can appeal to that latter interest, but that is all. This is different than the primary objection to moralism in contemporary political theory. Enzo Rossi's influential account of "radical realism" has emphasized (quoting Raymond Geuss) that " 'ethics is usually dead politics; the hand of a victor in a past conflict reaching out to extend its grip

[69] It is a bit like the legal realist Jerome Frank's attitude toward normative theories of adjudication: There is no point in theories of how judges ought to decide cases, because judges just decide as they do, given the nature of the human mind. See Jerome Frank, "Are Judges Human? Part 1: The Effect on Legal Thinking of the Assumption That Judges Behave Like Human Beings," *University of Pennsylvania Law Review* 80 (1931): 17–53; Jerome Frank, *Law and the Modern Mind* (Steven & Sons Limited, 1949), 100–17. Thucydides is on stronger empirical footing than Frank!

to the present and the future'. . . . Insofar as morality is influenced by political power, moral advocacy for political actions and institutions should be the object of critical suspicion—more so than most mainstream, ethics-first political theory allows."[70] Rossi and political realists who follow him propose, instead, developing critiques based on purely epistemic considerations. One can hardly disagree with their kind of skepticism about moralistic critiques of politics; certainly, the class position of the leading academic moralists tends to support this worry.[71] One can agree, as well, that epistemic norms are more robust, in terms of cross-temporal and cross-cultural acceptance, than moral norms.[72] This is still, however, a different kind of critique than that characteristic of classical political realism: Moralism is practically ineffective, a mere academic exercise, irrelevant.[73]

As Nietzsche observes regarding Kant and Hegel, moralists simply "press[] into formulas . . . some large class of given values."[74] Yet these philosophical formulas have no effect on practice, even though their subject is practice. Sometimes the "given values" are efficacious in the world (precisely because they are dominant), but they do not require philosophical formulation to be so; other times, they are merely ideological obfuscations for what is really going on, and so rendering them philosophically precise just obscures reality. The latter has been true from Hegel's rationalization of the Prussian State[75] to Nozick's rationalization of the marketplace,[76] but the worry can be generalized on both counts. Charles Lindblom, a leading American scholar of politics, observed a generation ago that:

[70] See again, Rossi, "Being Realistic and Demanding the Impossible," 641.

[71] The leading contemporary academic moralists in political philosophy in the United States, especially those appointed in law schools, earn salaries that put them in the top 1 percent in America. The idea that their class position would have no influence on their moral and political views is astonishing, and, predictably, none of them are radical critics of capitalism.

[72] See ch. 16 in this volume.

[73] Rossi and Matt Sleat, in their useful overview of recent political realism, note that it has been disengaged from the "classical realism" of international relations (IR) scholars from earlier in the twentieth century, thinkers like Hans Morgenthau. See Enzo Rossi and Matt Sleat, "Realism in Normative Political Theory," *Philosophy Compass* 9 (2014): 689–701. Rossi and Sleat describe those earlier IR writers as showing "an appreciation of the political as a sphere of human activity that provides a context of disagreement which cannot be reduced to morality, a skepticism towards the power of reason and morality in political life and the difficulties in judging political action." Ibid., 697. I am not sure this is an entirely apt characterization. Some IR theorists think the behavior of states is due entirely to human nature, for example, the instinct for self-preservation or for power (Morgenthau was himself influenced by Nietzsche). The dominant strand of IR theory links the motive for self-preservation to the anarchic character of the international system: the international arena is the Hobbesian state of nature, so only the most powerful will survive. Human nature and self-interest are the dominant themes, which is like what I call in the text "classical political realism."

[74] Friedrich Nietzsche, *Beyond Good and Evil*, trans. Judith Norman, ed. Rolf-Peter Horstmann and Judith Norman (Cambridge University Press, 2002), 211.

[75] See G. W. F. Hegel, "Preface," *Elements of the Philosophy of Right*, trans. H. B. Nisbet (Cambridge University Press, 1991).

[76] Robert Nozick, *Anarchy, State and Utopia* (Basic Books, 1974).

> [T]here is no clear, unmistakable, demonstrated connection between . . . the distinguished contributions of a whole history of political philosophy and any of society's major ventures.... We have to face, at one extreme, the *possibility* that the world of the 1940s and 1950s—and today's world, too—would look pretty much as it does had there never been a Plato or Aristotle or their equivalents; never a Hobbes, a Locke, a Weber, or their equivalents.[77]

Lindblom is arguably wrong to mention realists like Hobbes and Weber, but he is certainly right that we have no evidence at all that the work of moralist philosophers has influenced political action: Decades, and sometimes centuries, later, politicians may invoke some now-recognized moralist as authority, but this is a sociological fact that requires diagnosis, not evidence of causation.[78] The enormous academic energy devoted to systematic articulation of our (alleged) moral obligations and duties is an exercise in philosophical onanism: It is serious and intense, but its primary benefit accrues to the producer.

Sometimes, alas, it is much worse than that. Theorists during the Nazi era in Germany, for example, assimilated Hegel to the Nazi cause. The legal theorist Karl Laurenz found in Hegel justification for the supremacy of public over private law, and for the supremacy of the "community's way of life" over that of the individual.[79] Laurenz was hardly alone. Ernest Rudolf Huber, a student of Carl Schmitt, explained that "[t]he [Nazi] state is the actuality of the *völkisch* idea—this is how we might today modify the spirit of Hegel's famous words ['the state is the actuality of the ethical Idea']."[80] Other Nazi theorists marshalled quotes and ideas from Rousseau and Kant to justify the Nazi's racist ideology.[81] These famous figures of European political philosophy served as a menu of "authorities" for intellectual apologists for Nazism, a phenomenon that harbors a general warning for moralizing political philosophy.

[77] Charles Lindblom, "Political Science in the 1940s and 1950s," *Daedalus* 126 (1997): 241–42.

[78] Locke's ideas were mimicked in the US Declaration of Independence a century on, no doubt because they were so advantageous for the ruling elite who wanted to break ties with England. On this, see Charles Beard, *The Economic Basis of Politics* (Alfred A. Knopf, 1928), and, more recently, Michael Klarman, *The Framers' Coup: The Making of the United States Constitution* (Oxford University Press, 2016). Marx had enormous influence, but not by virtue of having a moral theory, but by virtue of having an explanatory/descriptive theory. Nietzsche was so influential in Europe by the 1910s that everyone claimed his mantle: socialists, anarchists, romantics, and, of course, proto-Nazis—but he was no moralist, trying to persuade with discursive arguments. The political victory of the latter extinguished the other readers in Germany. See, e.g., Brian Leiter, "Nietzsche's Hatred of 'Jew Hatred,'" review of *Nietzsche's Jewish Problem: Between Anti-Semitism and Anti-Judaism* by Robert C. Holub, *The New Rambler Review*, December 21, 2015, https://newramblerreview.com/book-reviews/philosophy/nietzsche-s-hatred-of-jew-hatred.

[79] See the discussion of Laurenz's *Deutsche Rechtserneurung und Rechtsphilosophie* (J. C. B. Mohr, 1934) in Herlinde Pauer-Studer, *Justifying Legal Injustice: Legal Theory in Nazi Germany* (University Press, 2020), 10.

[80] Pauer-Studer, *Justifying Legal Injustice*, 65.

[81] Ibid., 10–12.

We need not confine our attention, however, to the horrible Nazi past to see the practical irrelevance of moral philosophy to making the world morally better. Let us consider the United States, whose university system has given rise to a massive industry of moralistic rationalizing and scolding.[82] During the imperial hegemony of the United States since World War II, the United States has intervened militarily in or invaded outright at least a dozen different countries,[83] killed tens of millions of people through military aggression or predictable collateral consequences of military intervention, and harmed tens of millions more. During this same time, the modest American welfare state—stingy by the standard of affluent capitalist countries[84]—has been rolled back, starting with the reactionary Reagan administration in the 1980s and accelerated by the Clinton Administration in the 1990s, reflecting the reality of one-party rule in America during that time. Now there is a two-party rule, one committed to a modest form of social democracy, the other to authoritarianism in the service of rapacious capital and a malignant narcissist. The wages and income of most Americans have stagnated (the losses have been obscured to some extent by the entry of women into the workforce and the rise of "two-career" families[85]), the rich have gotten obscenely wealthier, while death rates among middle-aged working-class Americans have risen in the wake of the world crisis of capitalism in 2008,[86] confirming the long-standing phenomenon that economic distress and lower economic status increase health problems and mortality.[87]

[82] Here it shares something with ancient Greece and Rome at their high points. The Greek Empire produced Plato's moralizing nonsense (e.g., it is better to be a victim of injustice than perpetrate it), and the Roman Empire produced the equally absurd advice of the Stoics, who, in one of the great reaction formations in human history, decided that the only way to deal with normal human responses to inevitable suffering and loss was to renounce all emotional responses. The Stoics embody Nietzsche's diagnosis of parts of post-Socratic antiquity as the reaction formation of the sick.

[83] I am thinking of Greece, Dominican Republic, Nicaragua, Iran, Vietnam, Guatemala, Indonesia, Iraq, Afghanistan, Panama, Brazil, Chile, Cambodia, Laos, and Cuba. The body count goes up if one adds the tyrants and murderous regimes heavily dependent at different times on American support, from the Philippines to Iran to Brazil in the 1950s and 1960s, to Egypt and Saudi Arabia in the twenty-first century—and, most recently, Israel in its murderous rampage in Gaza and Lebanon.

[84] See, for example, the comparative data presented in Francis G. Castles, *Comparative Public Policy: Patterns of Post-War Transformation* (Edgar Elgar, 1998).

[85] For this point, see Fatih Guvenen et al., "Lifetime Incomes in the United States over Six Decades," Working Paper No. 23371 (National Bureau of Economic Research, April 2017), http://www.nber.org/papers/w23371, which suggests that decreasing income inequality between men and women has masked increasing income inequality within both groups.

[86] On these points, see Anne Case and Angus Deaton, "Rising Morbidity and Mortality in Midlife among White Non-Hispanic Americans in the 21st Century," *Proceedings of the National Academy of Sciences* 112 (2015): 15078–83; Anne Case and Angus Deaton, "Mortality and Morbidity in the 21st Century," *Brookings Papers on Economic Activity*, Spring 2017: 397–476.

[87] On this, see Richard G. Wilkinson, *Unhealthy Societies: The Afflictions of Inequality* (London: Routledge, 1996), as well as the helpful discussion in Helen Epstein, "Life and Death on the Social Ladder," *The New York Review of Books* 45 (1998): 26–30.

Contemporaneous with all these events, academic philosophers in the United States explained, however, that everyone is entitled to equal regard and that a legal system that did so would create a moral obligation to obey the law (Ronald Dworkin);[88] that altruism is rationally obligatory, a lesson apparently missed by every American president ever since (Thomas Nagel);[89] that democracy and law discharge our moral duty of equal respect to one another, and that law can only work in a democratic context (Seana Shiffrin).[90] Perhaps most remarkably, the premier moralist of the last half-century, John Rawls, explained that "liberal" and "decent" peoples can "defend" themselves against "outlaw" nations that violate human rights and engage in foreign aggression.[91] Rawls never made clear, though, who would undertake defense against the United States, one of the two most significant "outlaw" aggressors in the post-World War II world, along with Russia (a distant second).

Moral and political philosophers are not to blame for the horrors of Nazism or the depravities of American politics. They have been, however, wholly irrelevant to preventing, ameliorating, or even diagnosing them. Their activity has been the proverbial flotsam on the surface of the ocean.

Many ideas, to be sure, have been "misused" in history, and not just those from normative philosophy. No one in Russia, Eastern Europe, or China needs to be reminded, for example, about the misuse of Marx on behalf of tyrannical regimes that Marx—who recognized the progress represented by liberal freedom of expression and similar rights[92]—would have condemned. The crucial difference is that theorists like Marx (and other realists) provide actual knowledge of how human beings and societies work: Empirical knowledge can be misused, but it is still knowledge. Almost all that moralist philosophers do—as Nietzsche remarked in the passage I quoted earlier—is "press into formulas" popular moral opinions. Much moralist philosophy no doubt gets its appeal from its valorization of normative ideals appealing to its propounders, much like religious preaching and even some artistic achievements do: think of Picasso's *Guernica* or Conrad's *Heart of Darkness*.[93] Yet moralist philosophers usually arrive on the scene *after* the ideals have emerged, as Nietzsche observed, and they are rarely, if ever, as effective in arousing people's passions as the artists or the preachers.[94] Academic moralists do get to feel good about themselves, however, and it would

[88] See Ronald Dworkin, *Law's Empire* (Harvard University Press, 1986).

[89] See Thomas Nagel, *The Possibility of Altruism* (Princeton University Press, 1970).

[90] See Seana Shiffrin, *Democratic Law* (Oxford University Press, 2021).

[91] See John Rawls, *The Law of Peoples* (Harvard University Press, 1999).

[92] See Edwards and Leiter, *Marx*, 197.

[93] Moralist philosophers usually emphasize normative ideals popular among members of their class (e.g., concern for animals or "diversity").

[94] See Richard Posner's idea of "moral entrepreneurs." Richard Posner, "The Problematics of Moral and Legal Theory," *Harvard Law Review* 111 (1997): 1638, 1642, 1664–67.

be wrong, as a sociological matter, to underestimate how important that fact is in explaining the academic moralist industry.

Anyone who doubts the irrelevance of academic moralizing should recall Thomas Nagel's response to the argument of the former Marxist-turned-academic-moralist G. A. Cohen that justice, in fact, applies not just to institutions but to "the personal choices of [individuals in] their daily lives."[95] Cohen, an excellent scholar and analytic philosopher, led Anglophone Marxism into Christian moralizing in his late work, as I argue in chapter 17. He did correctly diagnose the moral hypocrisy of Ronald Dworkin (and his friends and colleagues like Thomas Nagel) in his book *If You're an Egalitarian, How Come You're So Rich?*[96] The title was a jab at Dworkin, who owned real estate fit for plutocrats in both London and New York while pontificating about equality. (Nagel was not as rich, but owned an apartment in Paris, and earned a salary putting him in or close to the top 1 percent in United States.)

A turn to Protestant moralizing was the distinguishing feature of Cohen's late work, when he became obsessed with the bad motives of individuals. Cohen objected that the Rawlsian Difference Principle takes for granted that some people—those who can command more income for their work—are "acquisitive maximizers in daily life"[97]; that is, they want to get as much as possible for themselves, and thus the difference principle is necessary to insure that some "of the extra which they will then produce can be recruited on behalf of the worst off."[98] Rawls here is closer to Marx than Cohen, ironically enough, for Cohen's objection is that the "talented" high earners have unjust motivations, though as Marx (and presumably Rawls) recognize, those motivations can hardly be extinguished under capitalist relations of production: Anyone without those motivations will be destroyed in the market. Yet Cohen declares that "we must care equally about the [informal social] ethic that sustains . . . inegalitarian incentives."[99] That moralizing arguments might affect the informal social ethos is ludicrous, as evidenced most clearly by the fact that it cannot even affect the ethos of those who purport to be egalitarian philosophers like Thomas Nagel.

Let us recall, now, Nagel's response to Cohen's argument:

> I must admit that, although I am an adherent of the liberal conception of [justice and equality], I don't have an answer to Cohen's charge of moral incoherence. It is hard to render consistent the exemption of private choice from the

[95] G. A. Cohen, *If You're an Egalitarian, How Come You're So Rich?* (Harvard University Press, 2000), 122.

[96] See ibid.

[97] Ibid., 140.

[98] Ibid., 124.

[99] Ibid., 140.

> motives that support redistributive public policies. I could sign a standing banker's order giving away everything I earn above the national average, for example, and it wouldn't kill me. I could even try to increase my income at the same time, knowing the excess would go to people who needed it more than I did. I'm not about to do anything of the kind, but the equality-friendly justifications I can think of for not doing so all strike me as rationalizations.[100]

Nagel, one of the preeminent moralizing philosophers of the day, understood the force of Cohen's arguments, had no response to them, yet admitted it would have no effect whatsoever on his behavior.

This is admirably candid, but it also stands as an indictment of a whole generation of moral and political philosophy in the Anglophone world.[101]

More importantly for our purposes, it confirms the ideological character of so much normative philosophical work[102]: Its normative commitments do not affect the practice of those who produce it, and yet its production allows them to advertise an appealing-looking moral seriousness against the backdrop of economic relations that systematically harm the well-being of the vast majority. These moralist philosophers devote their time to parsing the intuitions and feelings about nice (or "just" or "moral") behavior shared by members of their social and economic class (bourgeois professors at universities in capitalist countries), while the actual systemic issues that affect human well-being—for example, global capitalism and the accelerating displacement of wage slavery by technology or the rise of authoritarianism in Russia, America, Hungary, Poland, and India and the accompanying massive ideological delusions that render most people incapable of assessing their interests or even what is true—receive little analysis, comment, or illumination. The irony, of course, is that the moralizing etiquette or "scold" manuals produced by Western academics have no discernible impact on what political actors do. No one who exercises real power cares at all that professors deem their behavior "unjust," "unfair," or "wrong."

Nietzsche famously said that "my *cure* from all Platonism has always been *Thucydides*. Thucydides and, perhaps, Machiavelli's *Principe* are most closely related to myself by the unconditional will not to gull oneself and to see reason in *reality*."[103] The Cohen-Nagel exchange might encourage more philosophers

[100] Thomas Nagel, "Getting Personal: Why Don't Egalitarians Give Away Their Own Money?," *Times Literary Supplement*, June 23, 2000, 6.

[101] As Enzo Rossi points out to me, Peter Singer is sometimes cited as a counterexample, but he is not; his work has influenced charitable donations (and trivia like eating habits), but has quite explicitly excluded consideration of aggregate human well-being. See the discussions of Singer in chs. 14, 17, and 18 in this volume.

[102] It is, in Marxian terms, a "distraction ideology." See Edwards and Leiter, *Marx*, 162–64.

[103] Friedrich Nietzsche, "Twilight of the Idols," in *The Portable Nietzsche*, ed. and trans. Walter Kaufmann (Viking, 1954), 558 (ch. X, sec. 2).

not to "gull themselves," as it were. Machiavelli, of course, followed Thucydides in seeing humans (and especially political leaders) as essentially motivated by selfish concerns, for whom moral considerations are at best rhetorical window dressing. Machiavelli says, "[I]t seems to me better to concentrate on what really happens rather than on theories or speculations" and thus we should "set aside fantasies about rulers . . . and consider what happens in fact."[104] He proceeds with a point-by-point refutation of the utterly unrealistic "wisdom" of antiquity, especially in the person of Cicero.[105] Machiavelli denies that generosity is a virtue;[106] he says that "because men are excessively self-interested," it is better to be feared than loved, since fear appeals more directly to the self-interest of the subjects;[107] he argues that a ruler should only feel bound by his promises "if all men were upright; but because they are treacherous and would not keep their promises to you, you should not consider yourself bound to keep your promises to them."[108] Much of Machiavelli's advice is predicated on the supposition that "men are so naive, and so much dominated by immediate needs" that deception is both quite possible and profitable.[109] "The common people," he says, "are impressed by appearances and results."[110]

In the present, one thinks immediately of the comically inept Donald Trump or, several years earlier, Silvio Berlusconi, but let us remember that Trump's predecessor Barack Obama also rode to victory on "appearances": His primary promise when running for president of the United States was "change we can believe in," as vacuous a slogan as Trump's "make America great again." While Obama was a more civilized human being than the undeveloped shell of a human, Trump, he, too, was still symptomatic of the appeal of "appearances" to the masses.

IV. What Is to Be Done?

If one is a realist and an intellectual—someone whose medium is ideas, analysis, and argument—then what should one do? This volume offers an example, I hope, but only one example. I try to explain what law is and how it really operates; I critique and debunk moralizing theories of law; I describe and explain how politics, including the politics of law, really operate; and I try to *curate*

104 Niccolo Machiavelli, *The Prince*, ed. R. Price and Q. Skinner (Cambridge University Press, 1988), XV.
105 See Quentin Skinner, "Introduction," in ibid., XVII–XX.
106 Machiavelli, *The Prince*, XVI.
107 Ibid., XVII.
108 Ibid., XVIII.
109 Ibid.
110 Ibid.

our best insights on these questions from the past (one of the main goals of many chapters in this volume). I also try to do all this while being clear and analytically precise. Those more gifted can also try to do what the classical political realists—Machiavelli, Marx, Nietzsche—did, although this would require a much deeper engagement with topics and figures the current university tends to assign to the "human sciences" rather than philosophy as currently conceived.[111] How to pursue realistic inquiry will depend on methodological competence, unavoidably, but one should not forget the crucial role of speculative hypotheses in all the human sciences.[112]

One thing realist philosophers can do is offer "discursive hygiene," as I call it in chapter 17, that is, making clear what we are talking about and what its inferential implications are.[113] Almost all public life, and much academic discourse in many fields, trades on "dirty" discourse: conceptual confusions, invalid inferences, factual mistakes, and so on. (This is Quinean philosophy as the handmaiden of the sciences, as it were.) It is no part of realism that "ideas" never matter: It is only the arguments of scolding moral philosophers that do not matter. John Maynard Keynes famously quipped that "[t]he ideas of economists and political philosophers, both when they are right and when they are wrong, are more powerful than is commonly understood. Indeed, the world is ruled by little else. Practical men, who believe themselves to be quite exempt from any intellectual influences, are usually slaves of some defunct economist."[114] It is a mistake, however, to run together the claims of economists (whether Keynesian or Marxian) about how the economic realm works with the "ought" claims of moralizing political philosophers. The former (economic theories) are sometimes influential, but they are not moralistic theories; they are theories that appeal to those looking for the means to realize their preexisting ends. Over centuries, the moralizing ideas of earlier philosophers do sometimes appear in the mouths of those who wield political power, but I can think of no case where this was due to the philosophical justification or defense of the ideas rather than circumstances that eventually made the normative ideas salient or advantageous for ruling elites.[115]

Nietzsche's Zarathustra remarks that "the world revolves" around those who create values, though it does so "invisibly," that is, without most of those influenced by those values realizing their origin.[116] Nietzsche's point is related

[111] Many chapters in this volume draw on the human sciences, which a realist must do.
[112] See especially the discussion in Leiter, *Moral Psychology with Nietzsche*, 4–9.
[113] Enzo Rossi's conception of political realism has a similar aspiration.
[114] John Maynard Keynes, *The General Theory of Employment Interest and Money* (Harcourt, 1936), 383.
[115] See notes 78–81 and the accompanying text.
[116] Friedrich Nietzsche, "Thus Spoke Zarathustra," *The Portable Nietzsche*, ed. and trans. Walter Kaufmann (Viking, 1954), 164.

to, but subtler than, Keynes's. Nietzsche's paradigmatic example of a creator of values around whom the world has revolved for two millennia is, of course, Plato, but crucially this was only because "Christianity" became "Platonism for the people" (as he put it in the preface to *Beyond Good and Evil*).[117] That the rise of Christianity popularized Platonism is to be explained not by the potency of Plato's arguments—which I assume we all know are almost never successful—but by what Nietzsche famously called "the slave revolt in morals"; that is, the way in which the Platonic revaluation of earlier Homeric values was in the interest of a large class of oppressed people, which was, in turn, advantageous for the early "ascetic priests" in their battles with the warrior classes of antiquity (this is the argument, in very condensed form, of the first essay of the *Genealogy*, though the explanation of the triumph of Christianity is complicated considerably in the other two essays of the *Genealogy*[118]). Plato's creativity is, in any case, anomalous; most moral philosophy is, as noted earlier, what Nietzsche aptly said about Kant and Hegel, namely, just "press[ing] into formulas" values that were "once *posited* and created, but which have for a time become dominant."[119] It is probably not accidental, in that regard, that the most successful creator of values in the Western tradition adopted a literary, rather than discursive, form. Platonic/Christian ideas have mattered, but not because masses of humanity were swayed by the power of the arguments of scolding moral philosophers.[120]

From a realist point of view, what we should *not* do is obvious. Eschew the "scholarly" etiquette and scold manuals that have been a feature of the ideological obfuscation of reality by philosophers from Confucius to Joseph Butler to G. W. F. Hegel to W. D. Ross to the present; what is needed is understanding how the world and its institutional structures work, not how some moralistic Tartuffe thinks individuals ought to behave—or why some ideological moralist thinks how things are is exactly how they ought to be. Moral etiquette manuals can, of course, be written, but institutions of scientific research should not be enlisted in such ethnographic trivia, unless in the anthropology department.[121]

[117] See Nietzsche, *Beyond Good and Evil*, 4. Briefly, Plato, like Christianity, devalued this world as apparent and transitory, made knowledge of the truth a condition of a good life or "salvation," and elevated reason over the passions and desires.

[118] For a more serious treatment, see Brian Leiter, *Nietzsche on Morality*, 2nd ed. (Routledge, 2015), esp. chs. V–VIII.

[119] Nietzsche, *Beyond Good and Evil*, 211.

[120] It is particularly ironic that academic moralism is also morally bankrupt: its primary accomplishment is ideological obfuscation, distracting increasingly large portions of the intellectual class and thus rendering them impotent and irrelevant with respect to the central practical problems affecting human well-being in our current time and place (see the discussion of Peter Singer in ch. 18 in this volume).

[121] Anthony Appiah, a Ghanian aristocrat and prominent contemporary philosopher, literally writes a column for *The New York Times* answering "ethical" questions (an "advice" column, as it were). That is exactly where most moralistic philosophy should appear, and at least Appiah writes well.

Insofar as realists do want to write about *what ought to be done*, they are probably well-advised to write in a way that is intelligible to literate citizens who are not academics, with attention to the value of good rhetoric, and with regard for what people actually want in the circumstances in which they find themselves.[122] Moralistic scolding influences no one (unless they are five years old or under your doctoral supervision).

It will no doubt be recorded by history—assuming history is still written by scholars interested in what really happened—that the moral and political philosophy of the era in which authoritarianism triumphed over democracy, reliable epistemic authority collapsed,[123] and the regime of wage slavery began giving way to mass immiseration[124] was wholly irrelevant to these events: to diagnosing it, to preventing it, even to influencing what anyone did. The official moral and political philosophy of this era should, of course, be commended for having provided an often exquisitely detailed etiquette manual about what one should feel as the *Ancien Regime* collapses—for example, how one should feel about the treatment of chickens on farms or, even more remarkably, how Thomas Nagel felt about Darwin's theory of evolution by natural selection (the best-confirmed theory in the biological sciences), since it undermined his "confidence in the objective truth of [his] moral beliefs."[125] On that basis, recall, Nagel concluded Darwin's theory could not be correct. Perhaps I am a hopeless romantic optimist, but I do believe there will come a time when it is obvious to philosophers that Nagel's rejection of the theory of natural selection based on his taking his own moral opinions seriously deserves as much regard as Lysenko's rejection of

[122] "Public philosophy" is now the label for this in the capitalist countries, and has now branded itself and become a self-promoting industry of its own, distinguished primarily by the legions of credentialed, but trite, mediocrities it attracts. It is irrelevant to serious realist theory: see the University of North Texas philosophy program or the "Public Philosophy Network." I wrote one book of "normative" political/legal philosophy, on the justification for religious exemptions to generally applicable laws. See Brian Leiter, *Why Tolerate Religion?* (Princeton University Press, 2013). The book generated responses from *First Things*, the leading journal of Catholic intellectual thought, and from an Elder of the Mormon Church; it was also condemned by an evangelical Christian organization. I suppose this means I succeeded!

[123] See Brian Leiter, "Free Speech on the Internet: The Crisis of Epistemic Authority," *Daedalus* 153 (2024): 91–104.

[124] See Edwards and Leiter, *Marx*, 136–37.

[125] Thomas Nagel, *Mind and Cosmos* (Oxford University Press, 2012), 28. See also the review by Michael Weisberg and me: Brian Leiter and Michael Weisberg, "Do You Only Have a Brain? On Thomas Nagel," *The Nation*, October 3, 2012, https://www.thenation.com/article/archive/do-you-only-have-brain-thomas-nagel/.

Mendelian genetics for its anti-Marxist implications. Lysenko's name now stands for politically motivated charlatanism in the sciences; how will Nagel's name fare (even allowing for the moral luck that no one with power has yet taken his feelings seriously)? The answer to that question may tell us something about the respective fates of realism and moralism in political thought.[126]

[126] I am grateful to Otto Pfersmann for the opportunity to present an overview of legal realism at seminars at the Ecole des Hautes Etudes en Sciences Sociales in Paris and for the feedback from him and his students; to Enzo Rossi for very helpful comments on an earlier draft of some of this material; to Brian O'Connor for sharp comments on a later draft; to John Mearsheimer for very good advice on an early draft; and, once again, to Enzo Rossi for comments on the penultimate draft and very helpful correspondence. James Pearson also offered helpful feedback on the penultimate draft. I also want to thank the audience at a conference in Turin in 2017 for helpful questions and challenges regarding a very early version, especially Günter Figal. A later version was presented as the opening plenary address at the 30th World Congress of the International Association for the Philosophy of Law and Social Philosophy at the Christian Dimitrie Cantemir University, in Bucharest, and I am grateful to the organizers for the invitation and the audience for questions. My understanding of political realism benefited greatly from teaching and discussion with Carlo Burelli. Finally, I thank Joshua Fox, when he was a PhD student at the University of Chicago, for his typically excellent research assistance, and Helen Zhao, University of Chicago Law School Class of 2025, for her excellent research assistance on the final version.

PART I

REALISM ABOUT LAW AND LEGAL REASONING

2

Explaining Theoretical Disagreement

I. Theoretical Disagreement

Scott Shapiro agrees, "to some extent,"[1] with my verdict that the "winner" of the so-called Hart-Dworkin debate about the nature of law was Hart's legal positivism.[2] Where he disagrees is that he thinks Dworkin posed a new kind of objection to positivism in *Law's Empire*,[3] to which positivists have not adequately responded. According to this new objection, positivists have no satisfactory account of what Dworkin calls "theoretical disagreement" about law. "Positivism," says Shapiro, "is particularly vulnerable to Dworkin's critique in *Law's Empire*."[4] If that were true, this would, indeed, be significant. I shall agree with Shapiro that Dworkin's critique in *Law's Empire* is different from the earlier ones that have long ago been deflected or discredited.[5] I shall disagree that the "new" critique is compelling or that positivists have failed to respond to it. Notwithstanding Shapiro's heroic effort at resuscitation, my verdict on the "Hart-Dworkin debate" stands.

When lawyers or judges have a theoretical disagreement about law in Dworkin's sense they are disagreeing about what most legal philosophers call the criteria of legal validity (and what Dworkin calls the "grounds of law"): That is, they are disagreeing about the criteria some norm must satisfy to count as *legally valid* (or, as I shall sometimes say, *legally binding* or *a norm of that legal system*). So, for example, judges might "disagree about whether statute books and judicial decisions exhaust the pertinent grounds of law,"[6] that is, they might disagree about whether a legally binding norm must *necessarily* be found in a statute book or judicial decision. Perhaps the Koran or the New Testament of the Bible is also

[1] Scott J. Shapiro, "The 'Hart-Dworkin' Debate: A Short Guide for the Perplexed," in *Ronald Dworkin*, ed. A. Ripstein (Cambridge University Press, 2007), 49.

[2] See Brian Leiter, "Beyond the Hart/Dworkin Debate: The Methodology Problem in Jurisprudence," *American Journal of Jurisprudence* 48 (2003): 17–51, reprinted in Brian Leiter, *Naturalizing Jurisprudence: Essays on American Legal Realism and Naturalism in Legal Philosophy* (Oxford University Press, 2007) (subsequent page references are to the reprinted version). For a shorter, punchier, and more polemical version of these doubts, see Brian Leiter, "The End of Empire: Dworkin and Jurisprudence in the 21st Century," *Rutgers Law Journal* 36 (2006): 165–81.

[3] Ronald Dworkin, *Law's Empire* (Harvard University Press, 1986).

[4] Shapiro, "Short Guide," 50.

[5] See generally Leiter, "Beyond the Hart/Dworkin Debate," 155–64.

[6] Dworkin, *Law's Empire*, 5.

From a Realist Point of View. Brian Leiter, Oxford University Press. © Brian Leiter 2026.
DOI: 10.1093/9780197749852.003.0003

a pertinent ground of law? Perhaps what is morally obligatory is a ground of law? Perhaps economic efficiency is a ground of law? Insofar as jurists disagree about these questions, they are engaged in a theoretical disagreement.[7]

In fact, though, the theoretical disagreements to which Dworkin calls attention neither deny that statutes and judicial decisions are grounds of law nor claim that judges must turn to sacred texts or economics journals to figure out what the law is. The theoretical disagreements that interest Dworkin presuppose that statutes and judicial decisions are, indeed, grounds of law, but deny that this settles the question of what the criteria of legal validity *really* are: The key theoretical disagreements for Dworkin concern the *meaning* of the acknowledged sources of law, such as statutes and constitutional texts.[8]

Consider two of Dworkin's central examples of theoretical disagreement. In *Riggs v. Palmer*,[9] the question was whether Elmer was entitled to inherit under the will of his grandfather, whom he had murdered, to claim the inheritance.[10] The majority of the New York court held that he was not entitled to inherit, the dissent thought otherwise. But the two sides disagreed not simply about the result: "[T]heir disagreement—or so it seems from reading the opinions they wrote—was about what the law actually was, about what the statute required when properly read."[11]

The dissent, says Dworkin, opted for "a theory of 'literal' interpretation," according to which the words have "the meaning we would assign them if we had no special information about the context of their use or the intentions of their author."[12] Since the plain meaning of the statutes governing wills made clear that

[7] I shall follow Shapiro in treating the argument from theoretical disagreement as independent of what Dworkin calls "the semantic sting" argument. Shapiro, "Short Guide," 54. As Shapiro puts it: "The semantic sting argument is used to explain why positivists require the grounds of law to be determined by consensus [i.e., by the social rule constituting the Rule of Recognition]. Dworkin hypothesizes that positivists insist on consensus because they tacitly subscribe to a criterial semantics, according to which concepts may be shared only if the criteria for the proper application of the concepts are shared." Ibid. There is, as various writers have pointed out, no reason to think that the positivist theory of the concept of law is committed to a criterial semantics. A *locus classicus* for this point is Joseph Raz, "Two Views of the Nature of the Theory of Law: A Partial Comparison," *Legal Theory* 4 (1998): 249–82, esp. 258–65. The argument from theoretical disagreement survives the refutation of the "semantic sting" argument because it calls our attention to cases in which people disagree about the "grounds of law" even in the absence of *any* criteria (even criteria unknown to the speakers) that settle what the grounds of law are.

[8] There are two levels at which judges might disagree about the "meaning" of an authoritative legal source: they might, most obviously, disagree about the meaning of the text, or they might agree about the meaning but *disagree* about the correct theory of meaning or interpretation that explains why the text means what it means. This distinction shall prove important in sections II and III.

[9] 22 N.E. 188 (1889).

[10] Dworkin discussed the case in his famous 1967 paper, "Model of Rules I," reprinted in *Taking Rights Seriously* (Harvard University Press, 1977), but in *Law's Empire*, he refers to it as "Elmer's Case." The change in name is probably not accidental, since the features of the case that are important for Dworkin's argument twenty years later in *Law's Empire* are rather different than those he emphasized in 1967. I shall return to that point in section III.

[11] Dworkin, *Law's Empire*, 16.

[12] Ibid., 17.

the grandfather's will was valid, Elmer was entitled to inherit. The majority, by contrast, had a "a very different theory of legislation"[13] according to Dworkin. Since "it would be absurd . . . to suppose that the New York legislators who originally enacted the statute of wills intended murderers to inherit" and since "a statute does not have any consequence the legislators would have rejected if they had contemplated it,"[14] the majority concluded that Elmer could not inherit, since the legislature never would have intended a murderer to benefit from his misdeed in this way. So in *Riggs v. Palmer*, the judges were having a theoretical disagreement because they disagreed about the relevant criterion of legal validity: Is it the *plain meaning* of the statute the legislature enacted, or is it *the counterfactual intention* of the legislators had they considered the application of the statute to the facts at hand?

Dworkin offers the US Supreme Court's decision in *Tennessee Valley Authority v. Hill*[15] as another central example of theoretical disagreement. The Endangered Species Act of 1973 included within the scope of its protection an obscure fish called the "snail darter." The Tennessee Valley Authority (TVA) had already spent $100 million building a dam, which, as fate would have it, threatened the snail darter's habitat. The question before the Court was whether construction must stop because of the danger to the protected fish. The majority said yes, the dissent no, but, as with *Riggs*, the crux of their purported theoretical disagreement concerned the meaning of the Endangered Species Act. The majority, though giving a nod to the relevance of legislative intention, took the view, according to Dworkin, "that when the text is clear the Court has no right to refuse to apply it just because it believes the results silly."[16] The dissent, by contrast, thought that the statute must be read to "'accord[] with some modicum of common sense and the public weal,'"[17] which Dworkin glosses as meaning "that the courts should accept an absurd result only if they find compelling evidence that *it* was intended."[18] The *TVA* dissent, then, shares with the *Riggs* majority the view that *legislative intention*—including hypothetical or counterfactual legislative intention—controls the meaning of a statute, hence controls what the law is.

Now, theoretical disagreements are not the only disagreements lawyers and judges have about the law. Some disagreements are, in Dworkin's terms, merely "empirical."[19] That is, the parties agree about the criteria of legal validity (e.g., being approved by a majority of the legislature and not vetoed by the executive suffices to make a norm legally binding) but disagree about whether those

13 Ibid., 18.
14 Ibid., 19.
15 437 U.S. 153 (1978) (hereinafter *TVA*).
16 Dworkin, *Law's Empire*, 21.
17 Ibid., 23.
18 Ibid.
19 Ibid., 5.

criteria are satisfied in a particular case. (Did a *majority* really approve the legislation? Didn't the executive veto the legislation in a timely way?) Certain kinds of empirical disagreements are relatively few and far between in court decisions: It is rare to find the courts debating, for example, whether a statute was or was not vetoed, or whether it received enough votes to pass. More common, of course, are empirical disagreements about the *intentions* of the legislature: Even when judges agree that intention is controlling, they may disagree about what the intention *really* is or would have been given legislative history, the reasonable meaning of statutory language, contemporaneous events and legislation, and the like. These "empirical" disagreements are, in any case, not at issue in Dworkin's new objection to legal positivism.

Dworkin describes *Law's Empire* as a book "about theoretical disagreement in law" which "construct[s] and defend[s] a particular theory" of law that explains such disagreement and how it is possible.[20] He declares that "[i]ncredibly, our jurisprudence"—by which he means legal positivism—"has no plausible theory of theoretical disagreement in law,"[21] and that, in consequence, this jurisprudence "distorts legal practice,"[22] and is therefore "an evasion rather than a theory."[23]

II. The Positivist Account of Theoretical Disagreement

Before turning to the positivist account (and why Dworkin deems it inadequate), it is worth pausing a moment to notice the curious dialectical structure of Dworkin's argument. Why should a theory of law be organized around the phenomenon of theoretical disagreement about law, absent some showing—nowhere to be found in Dworkin's corpus—that it is somehow *the* central (or even *a* central) feature of law and legal systems? And why think a competitor theory, positivism, should be abandoned because it fails to have an account of theoretical disagreement? No physicists, after all, have abandoned the theory of gravity, even though no one knows how to square it with the fact that the rate of expansion of the universe is increasing.[24] The reason, of course, is that the rate of expansion of the universe is one of only a multitude of empirical phenomena

[20] Ibid., 11. To explain "theoretical disagreement," Dworkin argues, we must treat law as an "interpretive concept," and his theory, Law as Integrity, provides the best interpretation of that concept. But notice that the central rationale for treating law as an "interpretive concept" is that doing so is necessary to make sense of theoretical disagreement.

[21] Ibid., 6.

[22] Ibid., 15.

[23] Ibid., 11.

[24] There are, to be sure, competing theories, see, for example, Brian Greene, *The Fabric of the Cosmos: Space, Time, and the Texture of Reality* (Knopf, 2004), 230. But none of them is well-established. See Margaret Warner, *Expanding Universe*, PBS Online NewsHour (Feb. 27, 1998), accessed Feb. 5, 2025, https://www.pbs.org/newshour/show/expanding-universe

to which a theory of gravity must answer, and the theory answers quite well to almost all the others. So, even if we agreed with Dworkin that legal positivism had an unsatisfactory account of theoretical disagreement in law, this would be of no significance unless we thought that this phenomenon was somehow central to an understanding of the nature of law and legal systems. We shall return to this issue below.

But what do legal positivists say about theoretical disagreement, and why is their account inadequate according to Dworkin's view? Recall the basic contours of the positivist theory as developed by Hart. Law, according to Hart, is the "union of primary and secondary rules," that is, of (primary) rules that tell people what they can and cannot do, and of (secondary) rules that instruct us how to create, change, identify, and resolve disputes about rules, both primary and—with one exception—secondary.[25] The exception is that secondary rule Hart calls the "Rule of Recognition," the rule that specifies the criteria of legal validity (the "grounds of law" in Dworkin's terminology) all *other* rules must satisfy if they are to count as rules of that legal system.[26] That a rule of recognition is the rule for any particular legal community cannot, itself, be established by reference to other criteria, on pain of infinite regress.[27] Rather, Hart says, the rule of recognition is constituted by a certain kind of social practice which gives rise to what Hart calls a "social rule."[28] Social rules exist when there is a practice of convergent behavior by people who evince a certain attitude toward that behavior: They do not simply converge mindlessly, as it were, but instead take themselves to have obligations to engage in that behavior.[29] The content of the rule of recognition, in turn, is constituted by the actual criteria of legal validity officials use, insofar as they evince an attitude of having an obligation to decide questions of legal validity by reference to these criteria.[30] Judges in the United States, for example, engage in a convergent practice of invalidating statutes forbidden by the US Constitution. But it is not just an accident that they engage in such behavior; rather, they take themselves to have an obligation to do so. Ask Chief Justice John Roberts of the US Supreme Court, "Why do you invalidate statutes inconsistent with the Constitution?" and after he is done being puzzled, he will reply roughly as follows: "Because that is what I have an obligation to do as a federal judge."[31] In offering that kind of answer, he would be evincing what

[25] H. L. A. Hart, *The Concept of Law*, 2nd ed. (Oxford University Press, 1994), 80–81.
[26] Ibid., 106.
[27] Ibid., 107–10.
[28] Ibid., 109.
[29] Hart, *Concept of Law*, 91.
[30] This is the "positive" aspect of the positivist theory of law: what the rule of recognition is in some community, hence what the law is, is just a complicated psychosocial fact about the practices of officials and their attitudes toward that practice. See Hart, *Concept of Law*, 97.
[31] Perhaps, as Mark Greenberg suggested to me, Chief Justice Roberts's first response would be, "Because the Constitution is the highest law." But then, if we replied, "Yes, we agree it is the highest

Hart calls acceptance of the rule of recognition of the American legal system—which includes "constitutionality" as one of its criteria of legal validity—from an "internal point of view"—that is, acceptance of it as an obligation-imposing rule.[32]

In what sense, then, does the Hartian positivist have difficulty explaining theoretical disagreement about law? Recall that a theoretical disagreement is a disagreement about the *criteria of legal validity*, that is, about the *content* of what Hart calls the rule of recognition. But the rule of recognition, on Hart's view, is a social rule, meaning its content (i.e., the criteria of legal validity) is fixed by a complex empirical fact, namely, the *actual practice* of officials (and the attitude they evince toward the practice). So it looks like the only dispute about the criteria of legal validity that is possible, on Hart's view, is an empirical or "head count" dispute: namely, a dispute about what judges are doing, and how many of them are doing it, since it is *the actual practice of officials in employing certain criteria of legal validity and their attitudes toward that practice* that determines the content of the rule of recognition according to the positivist.

Yet, this latter kind of disagreement is manifestly not at issue in Dworkin's examples of "theoretical disagreement." The claim of the dissent in *Riggs*, after all, is not that the majority is mistaken because, *in fact*, most judges do not apply the counterfactual intention test favored by the *Riggs* majority. It is, rather, that the *plain meaning* of the statute controls the disposition of the case, and it is not the court's business to override the will of the legislature.[33] Judges engaged in Dworkinian theoretical disagreements are disagreeing about the *meaning* of the authoritative sources of law, and thus about what the law requires them to do in particular cases; they are not engaged in an empirical dispute about how their colleagues on the bench *typically* or *generally* resolve disputes.

So the positivist theory fails to explain theoretical disagreement in the following precise sense: It fails to explain what I will call the "Face Value" character of the disagreement, that is, what it appears the judges are disputing when we take at "face value" what they actually say in the opinions they write and

law, but so what? Why invalidate lower laws just because they are contradicted by the highest law?" At some point, we would elicit a version of the (perplexed) reply I described in the text.

[32] A more striking, recent example from the US context involves former Alabama Chief Justice Roy Moore, who refused to comply with a federal court order requiring the Alabama Supreme Court to remove a display of the Ten Commandments on the grounds that it violated the Establishment Clause of the First Amendment. See Glassroth v. Moore, 279 F. Supp. 2d 1290 (M.D. Ala. 2002). His refusal to recognize the legal validity of that higher court's decision resulted in his being removed from office by a state judicial ethics commission. Other legal officials, in short, manifested their acceptance from an internal point of view that part of the rule of recognition in the United States which requires lower courts to abide by the decisions of higher courts, and they did so by (severely) sanctioning Moore for his divergence from the normal practice embodied in the rule.

[33] I will return to the details of what the judges *actually* said in *Riggs* shortly.

publish.[34] They write *as if* there is a fact of the matter about what the law is, even though they disagree about the criteria that fix what the law is. The positivist explanation for this "disagreement" cannot vindicate what it *appears* they are disagreeing about.

The particular character of the explanatory failing bears emphasizing precisely because there are multiple contexts in which the face value character of a phenomenon is not what cries out for explanation. Sigmund Freud's Rat Man, to take an extreme case,[35] can give elaborate explanations for why he must purge all the fat from his body. However, Freud's account *explains away* the face value of what he says: It shows that he is obsessed with getting rid of his fat (*Dick* in German) not because the Rat Man has any interest in being slim, but because of a repressed wish to get rid of (i.e., kill) his cousin Dick, his competitor for the affections of the woman he loves.[36] If there is a failing of Freud's account, it surely is *not* that it fails to take the Rat Man's statements at face value: It would be, rather, that it has identified the wrong causal and psychological mechanism by which the Rat Man became consciously obsessed with losing weight.

The Rat Man case is extreme, however, in the sense that the consciously articulated reasons he gives for wanting to purge the fat from his body cannot figure in any remotely plausible reconstruction of his motives: The reasons are bad, they do not rationally support his obsession, and they cannot be intelligibly integrated into a general account of his actions and motivations. The face value reasons of the Rat Man are, in short, not plausibly taken as his *real* reasons. Matters are not so stark, by contrast, in the case of Dworkin's examples of theoretical disagreement. We might think that taking those disagreements at face value is warranted precisely because it seems possible to reconstruct them as rational disagreements on their own terms. Or so, in any case, someone sympathetic to Dworkin's complaint must argue.

So how do positivists explain theoretical disagreement? There are two candidate explanations, neither of which attempts to vindicate the face value disagreement.[37] According to positivists, either theoretical disagreements are

[34] As Jane Stapleton correctly reminds me, Dworkin is silent on the many cases where common-law judges explicitly (i.e., at face value) acknowledge making law and weighing considerations of policy. That fact already considerably reduces the universe of cases for which the Dworkinian theory purportedly has the better explanation.

[35] Sigmund Freud, *Notes upon a Case of Obsessional Neurosis*, in *The Standard Edition of the Complete Psychological Works of Sigmund Freud*, ed. James Strachey, trans. James Strachey (Hogarth, [1909] 1955), 151, 188–89.

[36] Ibid., 189.

[37] More precisely, the positivist accounts do not try to vindicate the face value of the disagreement in the sense that the positivist explanation for theoretical disagreement does not rely on the assumption that there is a fact of the matter about what the law is about which the disputants disagree. Yet this latter assumption is either explicit or can be reasonably imputed to the parties based on the face value of their disagreement.

disingenuous, in the sense that the parties, consciously or unconsciously, are really trying to *change* the law, that is, they are trying to say, as Dworkin puts it, "what it should be" not "what the law is,"[38] or they are simply in *error*, that is, they honestly think there is a fact of the matter about what the grounds of law are, and thus what the law is, in the context of their disagreement, but they are mistaken, because, in truth, there is no fact of the matter about the grounds of law in this instance precisely because there is no convergent practice of behavior among officials constituting a rule of recognition on this point.[39] Call the first possibility the Disingenuity Account and the second the Error Theory Account. Notice that the disingenuity account presupposes the *truth* of the error theory: A judge cannot be disingenuous in arguing *as if* there were a clear criterion of legal validity operative in a dispute without knowing that, in fact, there is no such criterion. The error theory account, by contrast, attributes a pure mistake to the parties: They *genuinely* think there is a right legal answer about the applicable criteria of legal validity, even though there is no convergent practice (no social rule) supporting such an answer. On the disingenuity account, by contrast, the parties to the dispute know, at some level, that it would be a mistake to genuinely believe there is a right answer as a matter of law.

The disingenuity account can be put in terms that are more or less accusatory. In the harsher version, the disingenuity account claims that judges engaging in theoretical disagreements know full well (i.e., consciously) that there is no "law" to be found, that the issue is very much up for grabs, and that their purported theoretical disagreement about what the law requires is nothing more than rhetorical posturing designed to facilitate acquiescence to their preferred quasi-legislative outcome. In the more mild version, the Disingenuity Account claims only that judges have an unconscious or preconscious awareness that there is no "law" to be found—that is, under optimal conditions for rational reflection they would be able to acknowledge that there is no binding criterion of legal validity in the case at hand—but, because of the various familiar psychological and emotional influences on human decision-making in the heat of a legal dispute,[40] they come to believe, at least in the moment, that there is a right answer as a matter of law, and it is an answer that favors their view of the case.

[38] Dworkin, *Law's Empire*, 11.

[39] Dworkin puts this second possibility somewhat misleadingly: he says that positivists "say that theoretical disagreement is an illusion, that lawyers and judges all actually agree about the grounds of law." Ibid., 7. It is true that on this second account, theoretical disagreement is a kind of illusion, but nothing requires the positivist to claim *in addition* that "lawyers and judges all actually agree about the grounds of law." If they did, then they would not think they were disagreeing!

[40] Judge Richard Posner's account is illuminating in this regard. See Richard Posner, *How Judges Think* (Harvard University Press, 2008), 105–7.

Error theories are familiar in many areas of philosophical inquiry, from ethics[41] to the philosophy of mathematics.[42] In all cases, they are motivated by the need to reconcile some part of our thinking and discourse with what we take to be well-established theories about what there is.[43] So, for example, in the case of ethics, J. L. Mackie argues that if there were ethical properties, they would have the extraordinary feature of being categorical imperatives for action for those who acquired knowledge of them.[44] Since nowhere else in our picture of the world and its component parts do we find any evidence of properties with such remarkable action-guiding powers, it seems incredible that they should exist in the ethical case. Mackie's conclusion is that ethical judgments—judgments which systematically ascribe such action-guiding properties to states of affairs—are all in error.[45]

A standing puzzle about error-theoretic accounts is why a particular discourse persists when all its judgments are false. Religious discourse is our paradigm case of an ongoing discourse that nonetheless invites error-theoretic treatment, since its persistence (notwithstanding its systematic falsity) seems explicable by the powerful psychological satisfactions it affords sincere participants.[46] The case of moral discourse is more complicated, as it also obviously serves to coordinate and regulate social interactions, which has led many philosophers sympathetic to Mackie's picture of what there is to conclude that ethical talk should be construed noncognitively, that is, as expressing attitudes that help shape social interaction.[47]

Theoretical disagreements about law present a special case, precisely because the range of claims to which the error theory applies is rather limited within the total scope of disputes one might have about law. It is one thing to say that *all* mathematical judgments or *all* ethical judgments are false; it is quite another to say that *all judgments about what the criteria of legal validity really are in the absence of a social rule constituting a rule of recognition* are false. After all, the latter class of judgments represents only a fraction of the disagreements lawyers and judges

41 See, for example, J. L. Mackie, *Ethics: Inventing Right and Wrong* (Penguin, 1977), 35.

42 See, for example, Hartry H. Field, *Science without Numbers: A Defence of Nominalism* (Princeton University Press, 1980), 1–2.

43 Error theories are, strictly speaking, semantic theories, theories to the effect that certain expressions or judgments (e.g., about ethical or mathematical properties) are genuinely referential, and thus truth-evaluable, yet systematically fail to refer because the properties in question do not exist. In the text, I am going to prescind from the particulars of the *semantic* account, since I do not see them as at issue in Dworkin's critique of positivism.

44 Mackie, *Ethics*, 33.

45 Ibid., 35.

46 Nietzsche has a more complex account of the motivations for religious belief. See Friedrich Nietzsche, *On the Genealogy of Morality* (Cambridge University Press, 1994), 66–71. See also Brian Leiter, *Nietzsche on Morality* (Routledge, 2002), 235–44. But Nietzsche's account is also quite compatible with the error-theoretical treatment of religious discourse.

47 The classic contemporary treatment is Allan Gibbard, *Wise Choices, Apt Feelings: A Theory of Normative Judgment* (Harvard University Press, 1990).

have. More importantly, theoretical disagreements about law represent only a minuscule fraction of all *judgments* rendered about law, since most judgments about law involve *agreement*, not disagreement. This bears emphasizing, given the mysterious centrality assigned to theoretical disagreements by Dworkin in his later theory of law.

One may think of the universe of legal questions requiring judgment as a pyramid, with the very pinnacle of the structure captured by the judgments of the highest court of appeal (where, one may suppose, theoretical disagreements in Dworkin's sense are rampant), and the base represented by all those possible legal disputes that enter a lawyer's office. This is, admittedly, a very strange-looking pyramid, as the ratio of the base to the pinnacle is something like a million to one.[48] It is, of course, familiar that the main reason the legal system of a modern society does not collapse under the weight of disputes is precisely that *most* cases that are presented to lawyers never go any further than the lawyer's office; that *most* cases that lawyers take do not result in formal litigation; that *most* cases that result in litigation settle by the end of discovery; that most cases that go to trial and verdict, do not get appealed; and that most cases that get appealed do not get appealed to the highest court, that is, to the court where theoretical disagreements are quite likely rampant.

Why the preceding is true is familiar to anyone knowledgeable about law and litigation: There is *massive* and *pervasive* agreement about the law throughout the system.[49] It is precisely because just about everyone agrees about the law that lawyers can tell most prospective clients who wander through the doors that they have no claim, and should go home; it is precisely because just about everyone agrees about the law that most cases settle after discovery, since by then the facts are clear and both sides know what the legally required result will be (and so the only question is putting a price tag on the resolution); it is precisely because just about everyone agrees about the law that most cases are not appealed; and so

[48] Consider: Administrative Office of the U.S. Courts, *Statistical Tables for the Federal Judiciary*, Table C-4 (Dec. 2007), online, accessed Feb. 5, 2025, https://www.uscourts.gov/data-news/reports/statistical-reports/statistical-tables-federal-judiciary/statistical-tables-federal-judiciary-december-2007 (reporting that out of 236,256 cases in 2007, 53,581 were resolved without court action, and only 9,858 were resolved by the court at trial); Administrative Office of the U.S. Courts, *Judicial Case Load Indicators: 12-month Periods Ending March 31, 1998, 2003, 2006, and 2007* (Mar. 2007), online, accessed Feb. 5, 2025, https://www.uscourts.gov/sites/default/files/statistics_import_dir/IndicatorsMar07.pdf (reporting that in 2007, 254,850 cases were terminated in the US district court system and that only 60,668 appeals were filed in the US court of appeals system).

[49] The point was made in the jurisprudential literature against reckless claims about legal indeterminacy by the Critical Legal Studies writers a generation ago. See, for example, Frederick Schauer, "Easy Cases," *Southern California Law Review* 58 (1985): 399–440; Ken Kress, "Legal Indeterminacy," *California Law Review* 77 (1989): 283–337; Brian Leiter, "Legal Indeterminacy," *Legal Theory* 1 (1995): 481–92. There is a certain irony in now needing to reemphasize a similar point against Dworkin, the true believer in global legal determinacy! The difficulty, of course, is that Dworkin's belief in the determinacy of legal reasoning is only a *metaphysical* thesis, not an *epistemological* one—were it epistemological, then there would be no room, of course, for theoretical disagreement.

on. To be sure, there are a variety of strategic and other considerations that may explain why some parties litigate and appeal verdicts quite independent of agreement about the law, but if there were not massive convergence about *what the law is*, we should expect the universe of legal cases to look less like a pyramid and more like a lopsided square (e.g., a trapezoid), whose base was somewhat bigger than its top.[50]

One of the great theoretical virtues of legal positivism as a theory of law is that it explains why the universe of legal cases looks like a pyramid precisely because it explains the pervasive phenomenon of *legal agreement*. Legal professionals agree about what the law requires so often because, in a functioning legal system, *what the law is* is fixed by a discernible practice of officials who decide questions of legal validity by reference to criteria of legal validity on which they recognizably converge. Only as we approach the pinnacle of the pyramid do we approach those cases where the practice of officials breaks down, and the "law" is up for grabs. Indeed, there is an obvious "selection effect"[51] in favor of appealing the cases where the law is not clear and so judges have room for theoretical disagreement, and thus room for siding with the appellant's version of the case.

When we put the phenomenon of theoretical disagreement in this kind of realistic perspective, the oddity of Dworkin's dialectical tact in *Law's Empire* becomes apparent. Dworkin would have us focus on the pinnacle of the pyramid, and construct a theory that explains *it*—explains it, moreover, in the sense of taking discourse at the pinnacle at face value! That legal positivism makes happy sense of *the overwhelming majority of legal phenomena* appears to count for naught.[52] It would be as if the adequacy of a theory of gravity were measured by its comportment with the rate of expansion of the universe rather than with

[50] I simplify, unavoidably, the complexity of considerations that influence parties in a modern legal system. My colleague Adam Muchmore has emphasized to me three other important scenarios, though ones consistent with the basic hypothesis about massive agreement about the law. First, large law firms are less likely to tell their corporate clients to "go home," as opposed to give them odds on their chances of success—and corporate clients, even with low odds, may for all kinds of reasons proceed with litigation. Second, even where the law is not clear, pretrial rulings may "clarify" it—at least for purposes of the dispute at hand—such that parties can calculate what they are willing to pay given what juries are likely to believe about the facts. Third, and finally, criminal defendants have more compelling reasons for appeal, even in the face of relative clarity about the law and the facts, than others, and so their rate of appeal would not count against the hypothesis that there is massive agreement about the law.

[51] Leiter, "Legal Indeterminacy," 490–91.

[52] A defender of Dworkin's view might say that even if theoretical disagreements are not *frequent*, they are *qualitatively* important to a legal system since, for example, they arise in cases where the courts must license the exercise of the coercive power of the state, as well as in cases that attract considerable attention because of their overlap with ethical matters that are the subject of public controversy. Of course, no legal positivist accepts the idea that a general jurisprudence must explain how the exercise of coercive power by the courts is generally justified or the idea that cases that attract attention in the newspaper are a central datum to which a theory of law must answer. To be sure, the positivist explanations for theoretical disagreement explain such cases, though not in terms congenial to Dworkin's theory.

its ability to predict the observable behavior of midsize physical objects as they fall to earth, or the movement of the planets, and so on.

Perhaps, however, this way of framing the dispute is too facile.[53] To be sure, we must concede the obvious: Massive agreement about the law—not disagreement—is the norm in modern legal systems. However, this apparent agreement, a Dworkinian might assert, belies a deeper disagreement: namely, about the law itself. Perhaps "plain meaning" theorists and "counterfactual intentionalists" end up agreeing about the resolution of most cases. But that is just because the plain meaning and the counterfactual intention converge most of the time, and so lawyers and jurists who would *otherwise* have a theoretical disagreement about the *real* grounds of law avoid such disagreements simply because their competing theories of statutory or constitutional meaning yield the same result in so many cases.[54]

This is, I suppose, a possibility, but the first question to raise about it is *evidential*: namely, what reason is there to suppose that this is the actual state of affairs? Certainly from the standpoint of Dworkinian earnestness about the face value of legal discourse there is no support for this supposition: Agreement is agreement, and surely, one might think, only someone presupposing the truth of Dworkin's view would *impute* to these agreements abstract, and hidden, theoretical disagreements lurking in the background.

On the other hand, one might argue that since apparent theoretical disagreements (e.g., between plain meaning theorists and counterfactual-intention theorists) do emerge explicitly in other contexts (e.g., toward the pinnacle of the pyramid), it is reasonable to suppose that these same views about the *meaning* of authoritative legal sources inform lower-level agreements about the law, even if not explicitly articulated. Let us call this the Consistency Supposition, namely, the supposition that those jurists who will mount an explicit theoretical disagreement about the law (based on some theory of legal meaning) in some cases (like *Riggs* or *TVA*) may be supposed to operate with the same theory of legal meaning even in those cases that elicit agreement among all parties.

Unfortunately, the Consistency Supposition seems unwarranted by any evidence of what courts do, at least in America.[55] Judges and especially lawyers

[53] Here I benefited from discussion with Mark Greenberg.

[54] To be clear, *mere* silence does not show there is no theoretical disagreement: the parties have a theoretical disagreement if they have conflicting beliefs about the "grounds of law," whether or not those are clearly expressed. But, of course, what the parties say will be our evidence for imputing such conflicting beliefs to them, so the absence of explicit disagreement creates a serious evidential problem for the claim that there is a genuine theoretical disagreement. I take up that issue in the text.

[55] Since Dworkin's central examples of theoretical disagreement are drawn from the US context, I am going to focus on the American legal system, which, arguably, will present the strongest case for Dworkin's view. It is worth noting, of course, that in many legal systems, among the authoritative rules binding on officials are rules of interpretation, which eliminate much of the theoretical disagreement familiar in the American context. One possibility that needs to be considered is that as we move up the pyramid of cases in the US legal system, there is simply less and less law and more and

tend to be *opportunistic* when it comes to their approach to the meaning of authoritative sources in contested cases, a point famously made by Karl Llewellyn in his paper on the canons of statutory interpretation,[56] and confirmed in a different way by Philip Bobbitt in his well-known study of the six "modalities" of constitutional argument and interpretation, where Bobbitt found none of the six approaches dominated the others.[57] Moreover, when eminent jurists—even those on appellate courts—profess what Dworkin would call "theoretical disagreements," these turn out to have little impact on the actual outcomes of the cases.[58] The theoretical disagreements appear, as it were, to be epiphenomenal to the decision-making process, though the face value approach would have us treat them as nonetheless central.

Someone familiar with mundane legal practice—the ordinary problems and issues that arise, most of which do not lead to litigation—might reasonably conclude that if there is a governing rule of interpretation at work in law, it is something like "ordinary meaning controls, except when its import is absurd or repugnant, at which point interpretive opportunism takes hold."[59]

more lawmaking, more so, perhaps, than in those legal systems with judiciaries more disciplined by binding rules of interpretation.

[56] Karl N. Llewellyn, "Remarks on the Theory of Appellate Decision and the Rules or Canons about How Statutes are to be Construed," *Vanderbilt Law Review* 3 (1950): 395–406.

[57] Philip C. Bobbitt, *Constitutional Fate: Theory of the Constitution* (Oxford University Press, 1982).

[58] See Daniel A. Farber, "Do Theories of Statutory Interpretation Matter? A Case Study," *Northwestern University Law Review* 94 (2000): 1409–44. Farber examined statutory interpretation decisions by Judges Richard Posner and Frank Easterbrook of the US Court of Appeals for the Seventh Circuit, noting that "in terms of their theoretical writings about interpretation, Posner (a leading pragmatist) and Easterbrook (a leading textualist) are as far apart as two judges could be." Ibid., 1409. Yet Farber found that

> [T]he cases in which Posner and Easterbrook disagree also provide a test of how closely theories of interpretation are linked to outcomes. Somewhat to my surprise, I have concluded that the effect is quite limited. Posner and Easterbrook are as serious about legal theory (and certainly as capable of theoretical analysis) as any two judges we are ever likely to see. Their theories of interpretation are sharply opposed. In the four opinions that I examine in detail, however, these theoretical differences seem to have had only a marginal relationship with outcomes. Moreover, it turns out that Posner and Easterbrook are somewhat less likely to dissent from each other's opinions than is typical for judges on their court, the Seventh Circuit.
>
> There is, in short, a resounding absence of evidence that these judges' sharp theoretical difference has any substantial effects on their judicial votes. This means either that their theoretical difference does not matter or that it is precisely offset by their similarities in other respects. Like other federal appellate judges, they agree on the outcome in the vast majority of the cases on which they sit. At the very least, it seems fair to say, the differences in their work as judges are dramatically smaller than the differences in their jurisprudential writings.

Ibid., 1410–11. See also Posner, *How Judges Think*, 346.

[59] For the classic example of statutory construction to avoid absurdity, see *Holy Trinity v United States*, 143 U.S. 457, 460–61 (1892) ("If a literal construction of the words of a statute be absurd, the act must be so construed as to avoid the absurdity . . . [T]he Bolognian law which enacted 'that whoever drew blood in the streets should be punished with the utmost severity,' did not extend to the surgeon who opened the vein of a person that fell down in the street in a fit."). Peter Cane suggests to me

Bearing in mind that the universe of legal cases is a pyramid, this should hardly be surprising. At the base of the pyramid, ordinary language and ordinary meaning hold sway, which, together with the convergence of officials on criteria of legal validity, render most cases clear and produce massive agreement in legal judgments. Only as we move up the pyramid—either because parties are motivated by strategic considerations or because the clear legal doctrine as applied to the facts leads to absurd or repugnant results—does what Dworkin calls theoretical disagreement become more and more common. In opposition to Dworkin's consistency supposition—supposed to show that theoretical disagreement, though rarely apparent, is in fact (latently) omnipresent—we might propose what I will call the Plain Meaning Default Supposition, according to which ordinary meaning (or stipulated technical meaning by reference, for example, to statutory preambles or contractual terms), together with the criteria of legal validity, gives us the content of law, *except in a select range of cases.*[60] If it were otherwise, we should expect almost every legal question that arises to look like the disputes in *Riggs* and *TVA*, when, of course, they do not.

that in common-law jurisdictions, there is a related rule for cases of ambiguity: if the plain meaning is ambiguous, then consult the purpose. See William Blackstone, 1 *Commentaries on the Laws of England* (University of Chicago Press, 1979), 58–62.

[60] Theoretical disagreement is also possible, of course, about case law: what it means, which case is controlling, and so on. If there is an analogue to the plain meaning default supposition in this context, it would be something like what Hart said about precedent:

> *First,* there is no single method of determining the rule for which a given authoritative precedent is an authority. Notwithstanding this, in the vast majority of decided cases there is very little doubt. The head-note is usually correct enough. *Secondly,* there is no authoritative or uniquely correct formulation of any rule to be extracted from cases. On the other hand, there is often very general agreement, when the bearing of a precedent on a later case is in issue, that a given formulation is adequate. *Thirdly,* whatever authoritative status a rule extracted from precedent may have, it is compatible with the exercise by courts that are bound by it of ... two types of creative or legislative activity. On the one hand, courts deciding a later case may reach an opposite decision to that in a precedent by narrowing the rule extracted from the precedent, and admitting some exception to it not before considered, or, if considered, left open. . . . On the other hand, in following an earlier precedent the courts may discard a restriction found in the rule as formulated from the earlier case, on the ground that it is not required by any rule established by statute or earlier precedent. . . . Notwithstanding these two forms of legislative activity, left open by the binding force of precedent, the result of the English system of precedent has been to produce, by its use, a body of rules of which a vast number, of both major and minor importance, are as determinate as any statutory rule.
>
> Hart, *Concept of Law*, 134–35.

Even though, as I have argued, this is not an adequate response to the Realist arguments for indeterminacy in appellate cases (toward the pinnacle of the pyramid, as it were) (see Brian Leiter, "Legal Realism and Legal Positivism Reconsidered," in Leiter, *Naturalizing Jurisprudence*, 74–79), this seems wholly apt for describing, even in the American system, how case law functions on the vast majority of occasions when legal judgments are required—hence the massive agreement about the law, to which we have already alluded. For further discussion of this issue, see chapter 9, especially the discussion of "the Real Standard Picture" in section I(B).

Suppose the plain meaning default supposition is correct as a characterization of one part of the US rule of recognition. In that case, error-theoretic treatments of theoretical disagreements will not raise the kinds of puzzles that afflict error-theoretic treatments of, for example, moral discourse. The latter, recall, faced the burden of explaining why a discourse that is systematically mistaken nonetheless persists. The error theory of theoretical disagreements, however, does not claim that legal discourse is *systematically* mistaken, only that it falls into error at the pinnacle of the pyramid. That should hardly be surprising, given that the mistake involved is fairly abstract and theoretical—misunderstanding the conditions of possibility of legal validity itself—and the opportunities for the mistake arise only in a minuscule range of cases. Systematic mistakes at the margins of any social practice are hardly surprising, especially when avoiding them would require a degree of reflective theoretical awareness that practitioners have no reason to acquire.

So, the positivist has two straightforward explanations of theoretical disagreement: the disingenuity account and the error theory. *Why are these explanations not wholly adequate to the phenomenon in question?* That is the key question, and the answer to it will determine the success of Dworkin's new argumentative strategy in *Law's Empire*. But, before we can adequately address that question, we need to revisit his central examples themselves.

III. The "Face Value" of *Riggs* and *TVA* Revisited

If Dworkin's account has anything to commend it, it is supposed to be that it does justice to the Face Value of theoretical disagreements. But does it? Attention to what the judges were really saying in *Riggs* and *TVA* casts some doubt on this claim.

On Dworkin's view, the judges in *Riggs* are disagreeing, as Shapiro puts it, about "the proper method for interpreting the law,"[61] that is, about whether the literal reading of the statute or the "counterfactual intention" theory is controlling. There is a sense in which such a disagreement might be *imputed* to the judges, but there is no sense in which that disagreement is central to the face value of the majority and dissenting opinions. Neither opinion engages the "method of interpretation" employed by the other opinion, let alone assesses its validity or merits, let alone argues for its own preferred method of interpretation. The *Riggs* opinions are far more mundane, in ways that are familiar to lawyers, if not to those motivated by antecedent jurisprudential axes to grind.

[61] Shapiro, "Short Guide," 35.

The majority opinion in *Riggs* is written in the classic "shotgun" fashion of many opinions and lawyers' briefs: Canvass all possible arguments in support of your position, repeat them for emphasis, and present them all without any regard for how they actually hang together as a coherent, principled position. The majority concedes that the statute "literally construed"[62] favors Elmer (it even concedes—nowhere noted by Dworkin—that precedent supports Elmer's position, but simply proclaims that the majority is "unwilling to assent to the doctrine of that [earlier] case"[63]). But then it makes two *different* arguments: first, that "a thing which is within the [counterfactual] intention of the makers of a statute is as much within the statute as if it were within the letter,"[64] and second,

> *Besides*, all laws, as well as all contracts, may be controlled in their operation and effect by general, fundamental maxims of the common law . . . [such as] "No one shall be permitted to profit by his own fraud, or to take advantage of his own wrong. . . . These maxims are dictated by public policy, have their foundation in universal law administered in all civilized countries, and have nowhere been superseded by statutes."[65]

The first argument is an argument about statutory interpretation, which invokes what we have been calling the "counterfactual intention" theory of the meaning of a statute. The second simply abandons the first argument—hence the "besides" (which, in the lawyer's brief, would have been "in the alternative")—for a natural law-style argument to the effect that there is a binding legal principle which trumps the statute and precludes inheritance by Elmer.[66]

It is worth noting that the second argument was the *only* one emphasized by Dworkin thirty years ago in his first systematic critique of Hart in "The Model of Rules I,"[67] whereas in *Law's Empire*, he calls attention only to the second, "counterfactual intention" argument. (So much for taking the opinion at face value!) But there is an obvious reason for Dworkin's selective attention to the actual opinion, namely, that the earlier objection to positivism that it could not accommodate "principles" like "no one shall be permitted to . . . take advantage of his own wrong"[68] was decisively met,[69] requiring Dworkin to shift grounds to the argument from theoretical disagreement, which is our focus here.

62 *Riggs*, 22 N.E. 188 at 189.
63 Ibid., 190–91.
64 Ibid., 189.
65 Ibid., 190 (emphasis added).
66 What I am calling the "natural law" argument could ground a different kind of theoretical disagreement, to be sure; my point here is only that in *Law's Empire*, Dworkin does not so utilize it.
67 Dworkin, "Model of Rules I," 23.
68 *Riggs*, 22 N.E. at 190.
69 See, for example, Leiter, "Beyond the Hart/Dworkin Debate," 155–62.

In its first "shotgun blast," the *Riggs* majority hammers home the idea that the legislature never could have intended someone like Elmer to inherit. The court says, variously,

> [I]t never could have been [the legislature's] intention that a donee who murdered the testator to make the will operative should have any benefit under it.[70]
>
> If the lawmakers could, as to this case, be consulted, would they say that they intended by their general language that the property of a testator or of an ancestor should pass to one who taken his life for the express purpose of getting his property?[71]
>
> What could be more unreasonable than to suppose that it was the legislative intention in the general laws passed for the orderly, peaceable, and just devolution of property that they should have operation in favor of one who murdered his ancestor that he might speedily come into the possession of his estate? Such an intention is inconceivable.[72]

This legislative intention, though, is easily conceivable, if we frame it at the right level of generality: not as the intention to let Elmer benefit from his wrongdoing, but as the intention to make it a matter of clear "public policy" (as the dissent puts it[73]) to enforce wills in accord with the intent of their makers—even those testators who, foolishly, leave property to their nascently felonious descendants! The majority's repetitious, rhetorical overkill on behalf of the counterfactual intention theory is, perhaps, indicative of awareness that the argument has problems.[74] That impression is confirmed by the way in which the majority abruptly abandons the counterfactual intention argument—with the remarkable "besides" passage quoted above—in favor of the natural law argument.

Even more striking is the dissenting opinion, which does not even deign to consider the counterfactual intention theory, let alone respond to it! "We are bound by the rigid rules of law, which have been established by the legislature, and within the limits of which the determination of this question is confined," the dissent announces.[75] Furthermore, since the legislature has clearly "prescribed exactly when and how wills may be made, altered, and revoked," there is "left no room for the exercise of an equitable jurisdiction by courts over such matters."[76] Since the law is clear, there is no call for a judgment of equity; in any case, the

70 *Riggs*, 22 N.E. at 189.
71 Ibid.
72 Ibid., 190.
73 Ibid., 192 (Gray dissenting).
74 The historical context of the decision, discussed below, confirms this worry.
75 *Riggs*, 22 N.E. at 191 (Gray dissenting).
76 Ibid.

equities are not entirely clear—or so the dissent seems to suggest in the following three representative observations:

> [T[he demands of public policy are satisfied by the proper execution of the laws and the punishment of the crime.[77]
>
> Practically the court is asked [by the plaintiffs] to make another will for the testator [which is in tension with the public policy of enforcing the intentions of testators as written].[78]
>
> The law has punished him [Elmer] for his crime, and we may not say that it was an insufficient punishment.[79]

From the standpoint of an equitable remedy, permitting the inheritance has as strong a claim as the alternative. The legislature does not want courts rewriting wills, and Elmer is already in jail for his crime: How could it be equitable for the court to substitute its own version of the will for the testator's or to deem Elmer's punishment insufficient?

The merits of the dissent's arguments do not really concern us. What is striking is that the dissent is not, at Face Value, having a disagreement about "what the statute required when properly read."[80] To disagree about *that* would be to disagree about competing readings of the statute: But there is none of that in the dissent's opinion. Its posture is far closer to what I earlier called the plain meaning default supposition: The statute is clear and the result is not absurd, all things considered. Since the statute's meaning is plain, the *only* question is one of the equities, not of the merits of competing theories of statutory meaning.

TVA, on examination, is even more clearly mischaracterized by Dworkin.[81] Recall that on Dworkin's rendering, the *TVA* majority (in an opinion by Chief Justice Burger), though giving a nod to the relevance of legislative intention, took the view "that when the text is clear the Court has no right to refuse to apply it just because it believes the results silly."[82] The dissent (in an opinion by Justice Powell), by contrast, thought that the statute must be read so as to "accord[] with some modicum of common sense and the public weal,"[83] which Dworkin glosses as meaning "that the courts should accept an absurd result only if they

[77] Ibid., 192.
[78] Ibid.
[79] Ibid., 193.
[80] Dworkin, *Law's Empire*, 16.
[81] Dworkin's account is also usefully contrasted with the more realistic account of *TVA* by Richard Lazarus, based on a study of Justice Blackmun's papers. See Richard Lazarus, "Human Nature, the Laws of Nature, and the Nature of Environmental Law," *Virginia Environmental Law Journal* 24 (2005): 231–61.
[82] Dworkin, *Law's Empire*, 21.
[83] *TVA*, 437 U.S. at 196 (Powell, J., dissenting).

find compelling evidence that *it* was intended."[84] In fact, it seems far more plausible to construe Burger and Powell as having an empirical disagreement about a criterion of legal validity they *both* accept, namely, that the intention of Congress controls the interpretation of the statute. Their dispute concerns the intention of Congress, and *not* the criterion of legal validity.

The majority opinion by Chief Justice Burger spends some time rehearsing in detail the various versions of the Endangered Species Act and the objections registered against each one, before concluding:

> The plain intent of Congress in enacting this statute was to halt and reverse the trend towards species extinction, *whatever the cost*. This is reflected not only in the stated policies of the Act, but in literally every section of the statute . . . In addition, the legislative history undergirding [the pertinent section of the Act] reveals an explicit congressional decision to require agencies to afford first priority to the declared national policy of saving endangered species. The pointed omission of the type of qualifying language previously included in endangered species legislation reveals a conscious decision by Congress to give endangered species priority over the "primary missions" of federal agencies.[85]

Although Dworkin then quotes Burger's assertion "that when the text is clear the Court has no right to refuse to apply it just because it believes the results silly,"[86] he fails to note that both before and after this declaration, the majority opinion engages in an extensive consideration of the possible intention of Congress, and does not rest its opinion solely on "plain meaning." Moreover, Burger explicitly deems the congressional intent to be to protect endangered species "whatever the cost,"[87] which plainly encompasses counterfactual possibilities as well.

One would not know from reading Dworkin's account that the dissenting opinion agrees with the majority's understanding of the relevant criterion of legal validity! Justice Powell, writing for the dissent, says that he cannot

> believe that Congress could have intended this Act to produce the "absurd result"—in the words of the District Court—of this case. If it were clear from the language of the Act and its legislative history that Congress intended to authorize this result, this Court would be compelled to enforce it. It is not our province to rectify policy or political judgments by the Legislative Branch, however egregiously they may disserve the public interest.[88]

[84] Dworkin, *Law's Empire*, 23.
[85] *TVA*, 437 U.S. at 184–85 (emphasis added).
[86] Dworkin, *Law's Empire*, 21.
[87] *TVA*, 437 U.S. at 194.
[88] Ibid., 196 (Powell, J., dissenting).

So the majority and dissent, in fact, accept the same criterion of legal validity: The statute, and the intent of Congress, are controlling, and if Congress intended an absurd result, it is not for the Court to undo it. Their disagreement is, in Dworkin's terms, purely empirical, namely, about the evidence bearing on congressional intent, actual and possible. When Dworkin says that "if we take the opinions of these two justices at face value, they did not disagree about any historical matter of fact,"[89] he exactly misstates what a fair reading of the opinions shows them to be disagreeing about, namely, the *actual* and *possible* intentions of Congress as evidenced by the legislative history and the facts about the words they chose to enact.

IV. Theoretical Virtues and the Best Explanation of Theoretical Disagreement

Let us recall Dworkin's charges against legal positivism with respect to the phenomenon he dubbed "theoretical disagreement." "Incredibly," he says, legal positivism "has no plausible theory of theoretical disagreement in law,"[90] and that, in consequence, positivism "distorts legal practice,"[91] and is "an evasion rather than a theory."[92] One might expect that such dramatic pronouncements might be accompanied by at least a gesture toward articulating what constitutes a *good explanation* or what theoretical virtues are at stake. Such expectations will, alas, be disappointed. Even though positivism has two rather obvious explanations for the phenomenon Dworkin dubs "theoretical disagreement"—the disingenuity and error theory accounts that Dworkin himself acknowledges in passing—Dworkin spends little time explaining why they are not, in fact, quite "plausible" accounts of the phenomenon in question.[93]

Even his defender, Shapiro, finds Dworkin's objections to these accounts rather feeble. As Shapiro writes:

> Dworkin objected to the repair argument [what we have been calling the Disingenuity Argument] by wondering why, if the positivist is correct, the public has yet to pick up on the judicial ruse. But the explanation for such a fact—if it is a fact—is simple: The law is a professional practice and lay persons

[89] Dworkin, *Law's Empire*, 23.
[90] Ibid., 6.
[91] Ibid., 15.
[92] Ibid., 11.
[93] Ibid., 37–43.

> are either ignorant of its ground rules or too intimidated by legal officials to challenge them.[94]

Even if one thought Dworkin's kind of argument had some merit, it would still not suffice for the issue at hand: for what we need to know is what makes one explanation of the phenomenon better than another, not simply that one account (arguably) has some deficiencies.

Borrowing a bit loosely from the philosophical literature that examines the rationality of belief and theory choice in the sciences,[95] we may try to articulate some of the theoretical virtues or desiderata that should lead us to prefer one explanation of a phenomenon—like theoretical disagreement in law—to another. To avoid being hopelessly derailed into the question of what an "explanation" is, I am going to assume—unhelpfully, but hopefully with enough intuitive resonance so as to be adequate here—that a basic theoretical desideratum for an explanation is that it helps us "understand" or "make sense" of some data, however it is "understanding" or "making sense" is ultimately to be cashed out. But what happens when we have more than one explanation that "makes sense" of a phenomenon: say, by hypothesis, Dworkin's explanation of theoretical disagreement[96] versus the positivist account articulated above? Why prefer one

[94] Shapiro, "A Short Guide," 42. Shapiro, however, thinks there is a stronger argument available to Dworkin. He writes:

> One need notice only that judges are not the only ones who engage in theoretical disagreements—legal scholars do so as well. The law reviews, after all, are filled with articles arguing for the legal propriety of one interpretive methodology over another. Indeed, the great disputations of legal theory—those between originalism and dynamism, textualism and purposivism, documentarianism and doctrinalism—have been precisely about theoretical disagreements in the law. Judges may have a great political interest in hiding the true nature of their activities, but scholars generally do not.
>
> Ibid., 42–43.

Put to one side that academic debate about law must count as an even more marginal phenomenon for a theory of law than even debates at the pinnacle of the pyramid by courts, the crucial (but unsupported) claim here is that these academic debates are about the "*legal* propriety" of these interpretive methods, as opposed to their *moral* and *political* virtues. So, to take but one current and much-noted example, Randy Barnett argues for *originalism* not on the grounds that "the law" requires it, but on the grounds that it is morally required given a certain conception of individual rights and the constraints they impose upon morally legitimate government. See Randy Barnett, "Scalia's Infidelity: A Critique of Faint-Hearted Originalism," *University of Cincinnati Law Review* 75 (2006): 7–24. The merits of the argument do not matter here; the point is that Barnett is typical of how legal scholars more generally often debate these questions, namely, not in terms of their "legal propriety" but in terms of the moral and political considerations that favor or disfavor competing approaches.

[95] See, e.g., W. V. O. Quine and J. S. Ullian, *The Web of Belief*, 2nd ed. (McGraw-Hill, 1978), especially ch. VI; Paul Thagard, "The Best Explanation: Criteria for Theory Choice," *Journal of Philosophy* 75 (1978): 76–92; Lawrence Sklar, "Methodological Conservatism," repr. in Lawrence Sklar, *Philosophy and Spacetime Physics* (University of California Press, 1985).

[96] As set out, for example, in *Law's Empire*.

account to the other? Here are three familiar theoretical desiderata often thought relevant:

(1) *Simplicity*. We prefer simpler explanations to more complex ones, *all else being equal* (i.e., without cost to *other* theoretical desiderata).
(2) *Consilience*. We prefer more *comprehensive* explanations—explanations that make sense of more different kinds of things—to explanations that seem too narrowly tailored to one kind of datum.
(3) *Conservatism*. We prefer explanations that leave more of our other well-confirmed beliefs and theories intact to those that do not, *all else being equal* (i.e., without cost to *other* theoretical desiderata).

Our earlier objections to the face value explanation of the Rat Man illustrate the intuitive role of these considerations. The Rat Man's reasons for his obsession, we said, did "not rationally support his obsession, and they cannot be intelligibly integrated into a general account of his actions and motivations." At the most basic level, the face value explanation failed to "make sense" of the Rat Man's extreme obsession, but it also failed along the dimension of *consilience*, that is, it did not allow us to understand how the Rat Man's obsession could be squared with all the other evidence about the Rat Man's values, goals, actions, and motivations. To be sure, the psychoanalytic account of the Rat Man's obsession was not, at least when proffered, especially conservative, since it required us to revise standing folk-psychological views about conscious motivational structures and their role in action. By the same token, it also *complicated* the necessary picture of the mind and its psychic economy—but this illustrates the trade-offs that are possible between the desiderata when we evaluate competing theories and try to decide what we ought to believe. There will be no simple metric showing us how to make the trade-offs and comparisons.

As we saw in section III, Dworkin's theory has the immediate difficulty that it does not even make sense of the *actual* face value of the decisions that are offered as central examples of the phenomenon in question. We may put *TVA* to one side, since if I am correct, it is not even a case of theoretical disagreement. *Riggs* is the stronger candidate for the face value explanation, though even here, as we saw, Dworkin cannot point to any *actual* disagreement about the merits of competing interpretive approaches, and he also now brackets that aspect of the majority opinion (the "natural law" argument as I called it) that he had made central to his account of *Riggs* in 1967.[97] Yet, Dworkin can fairly claim that the judges in *Riggs* do appear to have conflicting beliefs about the correct way to read statutes, even if they fail to engage that conflict directly in their opinions.

[97] Compare Dworkin, *Law's Empire*, 15–20, with Dworkin, "Model of Rules I," 14.

In any case, let us suppose the deficiencies of Dworkin's purportedly "face value" account of *Riggs* are in equipoise with the deficiencies of the disingenuity or error theory accounts. We would still be handicapped by looking at the majority and dissenting opinions in *Riggs* in a vacuum, for the *best* explanation of these opinions would have to show how they fare along dimensions of *consilience* and *conservatism*: for example, how they fit with our other theoretical beliefs about law, about the behavior of these jurists in other cases, and so on.

That the best explanation of *Riggs* is not, in fact, the face value explanation becomes quite apparent when we turn to an illuminating account by Kim Lane Scheppele of the historical background to *Riggs*.[98] Cases like *Riggs* had not arisen previously because they had been dispensed with by the courts using the legal fiction of "civil death," according to which, "If a person were convicted of a serious crime, the law would consider the person to be civilly dead, incapable of existing at law. And if a person were dead to the law, then this would surely affect the ability to inherit."[99] In 1870, however, England passed a statute that addressed, among other things, the civil consequences for conviction of a serious crime.[100] As Professor Scheppele explains:

> [A convict's] property was not to be forfeited any longer—and this was an important alteration in the English law—but it would instead be put under the control of an administrator . . . Under this new statute, convicts were allowed to retain ownership of their property, even though it fell under the control of someone else. But the statute was silent about an important matter: it did not say explicitly whether a convict could inherit or not. It even implied that the convict *could* now inherit, by referring to real and personal property that might come into the convict's possession after his conviction, which, since the convict could no longer contract, was most likely to occur through inheritance. For American courts that still looked to English law as a source of inspiration for American practices and standards, these new views about convicts' property represented a major change.[101]

As Professor Scheppele goes on to note, a year before *Riggs*, the New York Court of Appeals had occasion to consider "the English statute and the issue of civil death" in *Avery v. Everett*.[102] The case raised "the question of the status of a convict's property,"[103] in particular, whether a convict could designate an

98 Kim Lane Scheppele, "Facing Facts in Legal Interpretation," *Representations* 30 (1990): 42–77.
99 Ibid., 50.
100 Ibid., 51–52.
101 Ibid., 52.
102 110 N.Y. 317 (1888).
103 Scheppele, "Facing Facts," 52.

heir of his choosing. The majority, citing the English statute of 1870 (among other sources), answered the question in the affirmative, finding, as Professor Scheppele puts it, that a convict "was allowed to keep his property, even though he was civilly dead."[104]

Far more notable for our purposes, however, is that the dissenter in *Avery*—the one, recall, who wished to maintain the rule that civil death meant a convict lost his property rights—was the same judge (Judge Earl) who wrote the majority opinion in *Riggs*![105] If Judge Earl's view had prevailed in *Avery*, then there would have been no need for recourse to the counterfactual intention of the legislature or to natural law in *Riggs*.[106] But having lost in *Avery*, Judge Earl needed a new way to reach the preferred result.

Knowing now what we do about Judge Earl's views about inheritance by convicts, how should we view his interpretive moves in *Riggs*? Should we accept them at face value, as reflecting his deep theoretical commitments about interpretation, or as interpretive opportunism, designed to change the law to undo the effects of *Avery* at least in certain kinds of egregious cases, like those involving convicts whose crimes facilitate an inheritance? One might think there is a certain unreality—a kind of naivety about legal practice—involved in selecting the former option. Yet charity toward the innocent is no doubt a virtue in scholarship as in life, so we should, at least, entertain the face value interpretation a bit further.

We need look no farther, however, than the very same volume of the case reporter in which *Riggs* appears to find pertinent evidence bearing on the extent to which Judge Earl (of the *Riggs* majority) and Judge Gray (of the *Riggs* dissent) were *really* having a theoretical disagreement about the merits of intentionalist versus "plain meaning" interpretations. Handed down on the very same day as *Riggs*, we have the case of *Bockes v. Wemple*,[107] regarding statutory compensation for retired trial court judges, in which Judge Gray, writing for the majority, seems to have wholly forgotten the literalism of his *Riggs* dissent:

[104] Ibid., 53.
[105] Ibid.
[106] Professor Scheppele suggests that a case like *Riggs* could have been distinguished from *Avery* on the grounds that "[d]epriving people of property they already have in their possession [at issue in *Avery*] is a very different matter from restricting the ways in which they can come by property in the first place [at issue in *Riggs*]." Scheppele, "Facing Facts," 53–54. In that event, Judge Earl could have simply appealed in *Riggs* to "a quite straightforward view of legislative intent" (ibid., 60) since the "statute of wills was undoubtedly drafted against a background where the civil death fiction was assumed to be part of the existing law," and so there was no need to *explicitly* address the question of inheritance by convicted murderers. Ibid., 59. The distinction suggested by Professor Scheppele might well have been drawn, but it is far from obvious that it marks a relevant difference between the cases against the background of a repudiation of the principle that convicts forfeit their property rights. One suspects that is why Judge Earl in *Riggs* opted for a different approach.
[107] 22 N.E. 272 (N.Y. 1889).

> It is an elementary rule that statutes are to be interpreted according to their intent. The intention of the legislature is undoubtedly the great principle which controls the office of interpretation; but, as Chancellor Kent says . . . "The words of a statute, if of common use, are to be taken in their natural, plain, obvious, and ordinary significance." It is only where the literal acceptation [sic] of the words used will work a mischief, or some absurd result, or where some obscurity in the sense compels it, that we need resort to extrinsic aids of interpretation.[108]

It was, to be sure, a contention of the *Riggs* majority that a great "mischief" and "absurd result" would follow from permitting a murdering grandson to profit from his crime, which is why the majority opinion by Judge Earl demanded consideration of legislative intention. But the reader will recall that Judge Gray did not even deign to respond to the majority's argument, let alone acknowledge the relevance of legislative intention, in that context—and notwithstanding his resounding endorsement of intentionalism in *Wemple*!

So, notwithstanding the literalism of his *Riggs* dissent, Judge Gray was obviously not above deeming statutory provisions "too literally construed."[109] Indeed, in *Post* et al. *v. Weil* et al.,[110] involving the interpretation of the terms of a deed that was part of a trust, Judge Gray declared:

> Mere words should not be, and have not usually been, deemed sufficient . . . to entail the consequences of forfeiture of an estate [the fate that would befall Riggs], unless, from the proof, such appears to have been the distinct intention of the grantor, and a necessary understanding of the parties to the instrument. Nor should the formal arrangement of the words influence us wholly in determining what the clause was inserted to accomplish; but in this, as in every other case, our judgment should be guided by what was the probable intention, viewing the matter in the light of reason.[111]

To be sure, this case did not involve a matter of statutory interpretation, though it is not obvious why the intentionalism—indeed counterfactual intentionalism ("the probable intention . . . in the light of reason")—endorsed here should not also be applied in a context like *Riggs*.

Judge Earl, who regularly authored decisions involving probate issues for the New York Court of Appeals, generally took the familiar view of probate courts that the intention of the testator must be upheld. Thus, for example, in *Haynes*

[108] Ibid., 273.
[109] See Warner v. Fourth Nat'l Bank, 22 N.E. 172, 173 (N.Y. 1889).
[110] 22 N.E. 145 (N.Y. 1889).
[111] Ibid., 145.

v. Sherman,[112] decided not quite two months after *Riggs*, Judge Earl wrote, regarding the creation of trusts, some of which arguably violated the rule against perpetuities: "The courts will strive to uphold so much of a will as they can, without frustrating the main intention of the testator, or violating any rule of law."[113] That sentiment, alas, was nowhere in evidence in *Riggs*, where the intentions of the grandfather counted for naught in the majority opinion (the argument, recall, was that the *legislature* would not have intended the grandson to inherit). Furthermore, while Judge Earl did argue in *Riggs* that the inheritance would violate a natural law prohibition on benefiting from criminal wrongdoing, the core argument (the crux of the "theoretical disagreement" as Dworkin would have it) pertained to the correct theory of statutory interpretation, a topic which figures rather little in Judge Earl's many other opinions for the Court.[114]

This kind of interpretive opportunism of appellate courts was documented decades ago by the American Legal Realists and is familiar to every lawyer. But it still leaves the explanatory question unanswered: *Why* the opportunism, and why in the pattern that we find it? Short of a comprehensive biographical and historical study, we may not know the answer. However, even within the confines of Volume 22 of the *Northeastern Reporter* some possibilities leap out. In a quite lengthy decision in *People v. Budd*,[115] the New York Court of Appeals upheld the constitutionality of the power of the legislature to regulate private grain elevators, since the commerce in which they figured affected, so the legislature thought, the public interest.[116] To the modern ear, the decision, of course, resonates with the issues central to the *Lochner* era at the turn of the twentieth century (when the US Supreme Court held unconstitutional, for example, New York's attempt to regulate the hours worked by bakers[117]) and to its undoing thirty years later during Roosevelt's New Deal.[118] A vigorous dissent in *Budd* was written by none other than Judge Gray, who was joined by Judge Rufus Peckham, who went on to write, as an Associate Justice of the US Supreme Court, the majority opinion in *Lochner* sixteen years later! Judge Gray wrote (in terms echoed by his colleague Peckham in *Lochner*[119]):

[112] 22 N.E. 938 (N.Y. 1889).

[113] Ibid., 939.

[114] See, for example, O'Brien v. Home Benefit Soc'y of New York, 22 N.E. 954, 955 (N.Y. 1889) (setting aside the language of a contract without discussion based on common-law doctrine and thus rejecting the defendant's defense of breach by the plaintiff); People v. Charbineau, 22 N.E. 271, 272 (N.Y. 1889) (resolving the case on a literal reading of the relevant statute without attempting to justify his interpretive method). On the other hand, in one opinion, *Wood v. Mitchell*, 22 N.E. 1125 (1889), Judge Earl, in a rather brief opinion, did appeal to the idea that "it may also be supposed that it was the purpose of the legislature . . ." in interpreting a statute. Ibid., 1126 (relying on a literal reading of the text as well as hypothetical legislative intent to find the case to be an easy one).

[115] 22 N.E. 670 (N.Y. 1889)

[116] Ibid., 674–75.

[117] See Lochner v. New York, 198 U.S. 45, 53 (1905).

[118] See, for example, West Coast Hotel Co. v. Parrish, 300 U.S. 379, 396–97 (1937).

[119] See *Lochner*, 198 U.S. at 53–55.

> This legislation . . . is said to fall within the scope of the police power of the state. If this is true of this measure, then I fail to see where are the limits within which the exercise of that power can be confined. This act undertakes to regulate the prices which can be charged by an individual in the prosecution of his private business . . . This plea for the extension of the police power to the extent named, of interfering with the conduct of a legitimate private business enterprise, seems to me to find no support and reason, and it certainly tends to nullify that provision of the constitution which is supposed to guaranty to each individual that he shall not be deprived of his life or liberty or property without due process of law . . . I understand it to be the general rule that the individual has absolute liberty to pursue his advocations, and to contract with respect to his property, subject only to the restriction that he may not interfere therein with his neighbor's rights or use of his property . . . That liberty I take to be guarantied by the constitution to him, and to be a most valuable right.[120]

Since Judge Gray clearly subscribed to the view that so-called economic liberty—the "absolute liberty" to do what one wants with one's property, subject only to the constraints of John Stuart Mill's Harm Principle[121]—is constitutionally inviolable, it should hardly be surprising that he objected to the effort of the majority in *Riggs* to undue a testator's liberty to dispose of his property as he had intended. Judge Gray's opportunistic literalism in *Riggs* likely has more to do with his ideological opposition to state interference with property rights than with a considered view of statutory interpretation.

Judge Earl, based on his published opinions, is somewhat harder to pin down. We may at least note that in one of his longest authored opinions in Volume 22 of the *Northeastern Reporter*, namely, his majority opinion in *Moller v. Moller*,[122] he agrees with the lower court's "low estimate of the value in divorce cases of the evidence of prostitutes and private detectives" but then goes to great lengths to repudiate its application in this case.[123] Indeed, Judge Earl provides extraordinary detail documenting the evidence of Mr. Moller's dalliance with a prostitute. Although "the illicit amours of faithless husbands" were "clandestine" and "hidden from public observation," Judge Earl concludes that "corroboration gives such strength and weight to the evidence of the prostitute and detective as to induce belief in its truth."[124] In *Moller*, one senses the powerful indignation of a jurist who is repulsed by immorality, so much so that he would overturn

[120] *Budd*, 22 N.E. at 680–81 (Gray dissenting).
[121] See John Stuart Mill, *On Liberty* (Bobbs-Merrill, 1956), 13.
[122] 22 N.E. 169 (N.Y. 1889).
[123] Ibid., 169 (finding the defendant guilty of engaging in adultery with a prostitute based on the testimony of the prostitute).
[124] Ibid., 169–70.

the verdict of a trial court, notwithstanding the ordinary norms of appellate deference. If this diagnosis is correct, should we be surprised that Judge Earl was equally eager to "punish" the felonious and self-serving grandson, beyond the punishments already prescribed by the criminal law?[125]

These "Realist" explanations for the disagreement in *Riggs*, dispensing as they do with the face value of the dispute, are the flip side of the disingenuity accounts noted earlier. They do not necessarily suppose that the jurists are aware that there is no settled law in support of their view; rather, the jurists may simply be motivated subconsciously by their moral view of the merits, such that they convince themselves of the legal propriety of their preferred outcome. Or perhaps they lack even a subconscious awareness of the absence of settled law? In that case, the error theory account explains why they talk *as if* there were a fact of the matter about the applicable criteria of legal validity. Of course, given their moral views of the merits, it should hardly be surprising that they make a systematic mistake about the nature of law at a certain rarefied level of abstraction. In any case, what the preceding shows, rather clearly, is that when Dworkin declares "there is no positive evidence of any kind that when . . . judges seem to be disagreeing about the law they are really keeping their fingers crossed"[126] (as the disingenuity account would have it), what he really ought to have said is, "There may be lots of evidence, but I have made no effort to consider any of it."

That the debunking explanation—the disingenuity or error theory account—squares with other behavior by the jurists in question is only one of its virtues: the virtue of consilience noted earlier. That it also does not require us to do violence to a theoretical account of law, which explains the pervasive agreement about what the law is, may be its primary virtue. If theoretical disagreement were

[125] Perhaps there is a final way for Dworkin to redeem his preferred account against the Realist explanation of the decision. For could not Dworkin argue that the moral and political visions that animate Judges Gray and Earl are really just the touchstones for their conflicting constructive interpretations of the law in *Riggs*? In other words, the correct reconstruction of their differing approaches to statutory interpretation in *Riggs* is that each judge is relying on a principle that he judges to be the morally best of those that have some dimension of fit with prior decisions—where the determination of which is morally best grows out of the moral and political visions that the purportedly Realist interpretation of their behavior makes explicit. This is an intriguing, though I fear ultimately fanciful proposal. Most obviously, there is not even the pretense in *Riggs* that the argument is explicitly motivated by competing moral principles, a significant problem for a theorist emphasizing the "face value" of the disagreement. More importantly, though, it is unclear how Judge Earl's moralistic prudery translates into a principled argument against inheritance by felons. Equally important, we would need some evidence that the moral and political visions evidenced in the cases noted in the text are actually operating across a range of cases in a way that could be described as "constructive interpretation" in the Dworkinian sense. Finally, even if we could reconstruct the evidence adduced by the Realist in support of a Dworkinian account of the behavior of the judges in *Riggs* and other cases, we would still have to show that the explanatory power of that account is such that it warrants including within the class of valid legal norms moral and political principles that lack any recognizable pedigree in authoritative sources. In any case, let this footnote stand as a challenge to Dworkin's remaining defenders to offer an account that meets the explanatory burden.

[126] Dworkin, *Law's Empire*, 39.

something other than a marginal phenomenon—if it were not primarily the provenance of the pyramid of the universe of legal phenomena—then the claims of a theory, like Dworkin's, that give it pride of place[127] might be theoretically significant. But, when the most striking feature about legal systems is the existence of massive *agreement* about what the law is, then any satisfactory theory has to do a good job making sense of that to be credible. Not only does positivism have such an explanation, noted earlier,[128] but Dworkin's theory makes the massive agreement about law, at best, surprising, since for Dworkin, the positive history of institutional actions and decisions (e.g., by courts and legislatures) does not exhaust a community's law. Rather, on Dworkin's view, the law includes the moral principles that figure in the best explanation and justification of that history, as well as whatever concrete decisions follow from those principles. Thus, the law, on Dworkin's view, is in principle esoteric, since much, indeed all, of the "law" in a community might be unknown, indeed never known, by members of that community insofar as they fail to appreciate the justificatory moral principles and their consequences. If this were the true nature of law, the existence of massive agreement might seem puzzling indeed.[129]

We need not stop with appeal to the phenomenon of massive agreement about what the law is, for the positivist theory explains more than that: It purports to explain how the ordinary person familiar with a modern municipal legal system understands law; it purports to explain how the distinction between legal and moral norms is drawn; it purports to explain the *general* concept of law, not just the idea of law in any *particular* legal system; and so on. Dworkin's theory, by contrast is far less consilient. It can only make sense, for example, of legal systems whose institutional history falls above the threshold required for *moral* justification of that legal system to be possible, since Dworkin's theory aims to "explain how what it takes to be law provides a general justification for the exercise of coercive power by the state."[130] Dworkin's theory is also less simple than its positivist competitor, since it demands that we assume the existence of *legally right answers* no one knows about, as well as the existence of *moral facts*

[127] Recall that Dworkin describes *Law's Empire* as being "about theoretical disagreement in law. It aims to understand what kind of disagreement this is and then to construct and defend a particular theory about the proper grounds of law." Ibid., 11.

[128] On the positivist account, legal professionals agree about what the law requires so often because, in a functioning legal system, *what the law is* is fixed by a discernible practice of officials who decide questions of legal validity by reference to criteria of legal validity on which they recognizably converge. See text accompanying notes 59–60.

[129] Dworkin would be forced to appeal to *epistemic* considerations to explain why there is this massive agreement, notwithstanding the strange metaphysics of the situation (i.e., that what the law is might be unknown by all existing jurists and lawyers). Dworkin's theory has, of course, long depended on this distinction. Nevertheless, Dworkin has never explained why the epistemic constraints under which jurists and lawyers operate should lead to massive convergence.

[130] Dworkin, *Law's Empire*, 190.

that determine what these answers are.[131] Its apparent primary virtue—at least as presented in *Law's Empire*—is that it explains something of the face value of theoretical disagreements, treating them as interpretive disputes about the point or purpose of our legal practices.[132] Why this explanatory achievement (if that is what it is) should trump positivism's greater ones is nowhere explained by Dworkin.

V. Conclusion

There is, to repeat, no simple formula for deciding how to tally up the theoretical and explanatory virtues of competing accounts. We may, at least, sum up the conclusions about the debate defended here:

(1) Dworkin explains some of the face value of some theoretical disagreements, for example, in *Riggs*. Even Dworkin's account goes beyond, or ignores parts of, the face value disagreement.
(2) The positivist has an explanation of theoretical disagreement in cases like *Riggs*, which "explains away" the face value of the disagreement, but is more consilient with an account of other behavior by the jurists in question.
(3) That Dworkin's explanation of the theoretical disagreement in *Riggs* is less plausible than the positivist account does not, of course, establish that the positivist explanations are generally superior. Perhaps Dworkin's example was ill-chosen, even though he has made it central to his attack on positivism.
(4) Theoretical disagreements are relatively marginal phenomena within the scope of a general theory of law, emerging primarily at the pinnacle of the pyramid of legal questions that arise. Massive agreement about the law is a far more common phenomenon that a theory must address.
(5) Positivism fares better at preserving the face value of massive agreement about law than Dworkin's theory does.
(6) There are other legal phenomena for which positivism has a prima facie plausible account, which are untouched by Dworkin's objections to the positivist account of theoretical disagreement.

[131] For doubts about the latter, see ch. 15, in this volume.

[132] Notice that even Dworkin's "interpretivist" reading of theoretical disagreement goes far beyond the face value of the opinions, even in *Riggs*.

(7) Dworkin's own account of theoretical disagreement is embedded in a theory of law and adjudication which is both less consilient and more complex than the positivist account.

It is true, as Shapiro argued, that the objection to legal positivism in *Law's Empire* is different from the objections on which Dworkin built his reputation as a critic of Hart. Yet, as I have argued, the objection does not appear to amount to much, either when it is considered on its own terms (as an account, for example, of *Riggs* or *TVA* in competition with the positivist account) or when considered in light of the plethora of theoretical desiderata that should inform a plausible theory of law. To the extent readers disagree with that conclusion, I hope this chapter will at least have succeeded in framing the theoretical issues at stake for a critic of positivism who is impressed by the phenomenon of theoretical disagreement.[133]

[133] Thanks to John Gardner, Leslie Green, Mark Greenberg, and Scott Shapiro for useful discussion of these issues on various occasions, and to Greenberg for quite helpful discussion of an early draft of this essay. I also benefited from questions and comments by students in my Spring 2007 Jurisprudence class at the University of Texas at Austin when we discussed this topic. Workshop audiences at a variety of venues provided valuable feedback and discussion: the Faculty of Law and Program in Social and Political Theory, Research School of Social Sciences, Australian National University; the Law School, University of California, Los Angeles; the Institute for Philosophical Investigation, National Autonomous University of Mexico; the jurisprudence departments of the Faculties of Law at the Universities of Genoa in Italy and Girona in Spain, and the Law School at the University of Chicago. Of the many who helped me on these occasions, I should mention especially Peter Cane, Riccardo Guastini, Larry Laudan, Adam Muchmore, Martha Nussbaum, Giovanni Ratti, Jane Stapleton, and Ed Stein.

3

Theoretical Disagreements in Law

Another Look

I. The Problem Stated

Just when Dworkin's decades-long campaign against legal positivism seemed moribund,[1] a new Dworkin-inspired challenge, with new champions, arrived on the scene. Scott Shapiro argued[2] that positivists had not responded adequately to the argument from theoretical disagreement (TD) from Dworkin's *Law's Empire*.[3] I agreed with Shapiro that the argument from TD demanded a systematic positivist reply, and offered one (see ch. 2 in this volume). Since then, a number of other writers have expressed doubts about this reply, some from a position sympathetic to positivism, some less so.[4] I begin by reviewing Dworkin's criticism of the positivist account of TD and my original response to it, and then turn to the doubts raised by the critics. I hope, once again, to lay the problem of TD to rest.

Judges sometimes agree on the applicable criteria of legal validity (e.g., they agree the intention of the legislature controls), but disagree on its application (e.g., what did the legislature *really* intend?). In *Law's Empire*, Dworkin noted judges sometimes appear to disagree about what the applicable criteria of legal validity are (the "grounds of law" in Dworkin-speak) (Dworkin, 5). Dworkin claimed that positivists could not explain such disagreements—though his *real* objection was that they could not explain such disagreements *without explaining them away*—that is, without offering an interpretation of those disagreements that did not see them as involving a mistake. In many contexts, the best explanation of a phenomenon does involve attributing a mistake to the parties,[5] so

[1] See Brian Leiter, "The End of Empire: Dworkin and Jurisprudence in the 21st-Century," *Rutgers Law Journal* 35 (2005): 165–81.

[2] Scott Shapiro, "The Hart/Dworkin Debate: A Short Guide for the Perplexed," in *Ronald Dworkin*, ed. A. Ripstein (Cambridge University Press, 2007).

[3] Ronald Dworkin, *Law's Empire* (Harvard University Press, 1986).

[4] See, e.g., Luis Duarte d'Almeida, "The Grounds of Law," in W. Waluchow and S. Sciaraffa (eds.), *The Legacy of Ronald Dworkin* (Oxford University Press, 2016); Barbara Baum Levenbook, "Dworkin's Theoretical Disagreement Argument," *Philosophy Compass* 10, no. 1 (2015): 1–9; Kevin Toh, "Jurisprudential Theories and First-Order Legal Judgments," *Philosophy Compass* 8, no. 5 (2013): 457–71; Kevin Toh, "Four Neglected Prescriptions of Hartian Legal Philosophy," *Law and Philosophy* 34 (2015): 333–68.

[5] See ch. 2, esp. pp. 56–59, in this volume.

From a Realist Point of View. Brian Leiter, Oxford University Press. © Brian Leiter 2026.
DOI: 10.1093/9780197749852.003.0004

the fact that positivists *explain away* TDs settles nothing. The question is always what is the *best* explanation of the phenomenon.

Take *Riggs v. Palmer* (a late nineteenth-century case from the highest court in the state of New York, and Dworkin's favorite example for decades), which considers the question whether the grandson (Elmer) who murdered his grandfather to inherit under the latter's will should be permitted to do so. According to Dworkin, the majority and dissent are having a dispute about the *criteria of legal validity* ("the grounds of law"). The majority and dissent, according to Dworkin, agree that the statutes governing wills control this case, but the majority opinion by Judge Earl (denying the inheritance) argues as though the *meaning* of the statute is given by the *counterfactual intention* of the legislature (i.e., what the legislators would have intended had they thought of this sordid case, in which case Elmer loses), while the dissenting opinion by Judge Gray (permitting the inheritance) argues as though the *meaning* of the statute is given by the *plain meaning* of its provisions, in which case Elmer inherits.

On the positivist view, where a legal system exists, there exists a rule of recognition (RR) that specifies the criteria of legal validity for that system. The RR is, itself, merely a "social rule": its content is fixed by (1) a convergent pattern of behavior, and (2) acceptance of a rule describing that behavior from an "internal point of view" (i.e., treating the behavior described by the rule as more-or-less obligatory). In the case of the RR, this means its content will consist of (1) the criteria of legal validity on which judges actually converge, and (2) which they also treat as obligatory. So the existence of an RR is just a complex psychosocial fact about officials of the system.

Let us now suppose that officials in the New York legal system at the time of *Riggs* did not converge upon either the *counterfactual intention* theory of statutory meaning or the *plain meaning* theory. It follows, then, on the positivist view, that there is no fact of the matter about which criterion of legal validity is correct. Insofar as Judge Earl, writing for the majority, and Judge Gray, writing for the dissent, think there is a fact of the matter, they are both mistaken: perhaps an innocent error, perhaps not so innocent (i.e., perhaps they know there is no fact of the matter, and are really trying to change the content of the RR or are simply trying to get their preferred outcome in the case).

According to Dworkin, what the law is follows from the best "constructive interpretation" of the institutional history of the legal system (the latter being, roughly, the authoritative sources a positivist theory might identify: legislative enactments, prior court decisions, a constitution, executive orders, etc.). A constructive interpretation identifies moral principles that explain a sufficient amount of that institutional history and then decides the present case in a way consistent with the explanatory moral principle that provides the best moral justification for that history (i.e., shows that history in its best "moral" light). A TD for Dworkin, then, is just a case of conflicting constructive interpretations. Is that really the best explanation of the phenomenon Dworkin identifies?

II. The Problem Resolved from a Positivist Point of View

In a 2009 article (reprinted as ch. 2 in this volume), I argued that the positivist had a better explanation of TD in cases like *Riggs*. The fact that the positivist explanation of *Riggs* treats the judges as mistaken in thinking there was a fact of the matter about the meaning of the statute is no objection to it as an explanation: the better explanation of a phenomenon, as we have already noted, often treats the surface phenomena as misleading or illusory. (Even Dworkin's reading of the dispute in *Riggs* does violence to the actual dispute between the majority and the dissent: neither side, for example, even acknowledges the opposing reading, so neither side writes *as if* this is a dispute about the best constructive interpretation of the statutory materials, *contra* Dworkin's reading.) A good explanation should not only make sense of what the judges said and did in *Riggs*, but what they said and did in other cases: this is the explanatory virtue of *consilience*. But as soon as we look beyond *Riggs*, we find that Judge Gray is often an intentionalist about interpretation, and Judge Earl is usually a severe textualist, with little enthusiasm for speculations about counterfactual intentions.[6] Their rhetorical posturing in *Riggs* turns out to be wholly opportunistic, driven by underlying legal and political differences that far transcend the particulars of *Riggs* (Judge Earl was really trying to salvage some remnants of the "civil death" doctrine recently repudiated by the New York Court of Appeals, while Judge Gray was simply vindicating his absolutist view of property rights against government meddling [it is not for the courts to correct the murdered grandfather's foolish decision to leave his wealth to his felonious grandson].) The positivist, with some legal realist instincts, offers a much more plausible account of what is really going on precisely by *not taking seriously* the TD on which the Dworkinian focuses.[7]

[6] See ch. 2, 59–64, in this volume.

[7] Tim Macklem presses on me a different kind of positivist response: namely, that a RR identifies the sources of law but does not adjudicate among all the ways of interpreting them. Here I agree, I take it, with Dworkin (as well as Shapiro): namely, that this austere conception of the RR would be inadequate to discharge the functions of an RR as Hart originally conceived them, namely, eliminating some (if not all) uncertainty about what the valid legal norms are in a particular system. I thus agree (infrequently as that may be) with Dworkin that saying the duly enacted statute is a source of law is not enough for an RR that resolves uncertainty: It is necessary that the RR provide guidance as to what norms the statute enacts as legally valid. This, of course, can be done by content-neutral criteria (the intent of the legislature, the plain meaning of the text, etc.). And, indeed, these content-neutral criteria can come in hierarchical orderings, such that some sources trump others. But an RR that did not resolve some number of TDs would not, in fact, be adequate to support a functioning legal system. (I return to this topic in ch. 4 in this volume.)

How a particular jurisprudential theory explains a particular TD is not, despite Dworkin's framing, sufficient for deciding its theoretical merits. Even though the positivist has a more consilient explanation than Dworkin of the judicial behavior in *Riggs*, that does not show that positivism is a more plausible theory of law precisely because theoretical disagreements are only one kind of phenomenon a theory of law should explain, and a relatively marginal one at that (being confined largely to the upper reaches of appellate litigation). *Massive agreement* about what the law is remains the most striking feature of functioning legal systems, and positivism has always had the most straightforward explanation of that phenomenon. Legal professionals agree about what the law requires so often because, in a functioning legal system, *what the law is* is fixed by a discernible practice of officials who decide questions of legal validity by reference to criteria of legal validity on which they recognizably converge and which they treat as obligatory. If what the law is were really what follows from the best constructive interpretation of the institutional history of the legal system, then one would expect controversy about what the law is to break out all the time and everywhere, given how contestable constructive interpretations are. But beyond the fact of massive agreement, positivism also fares better at explaining other familiar features of modern legal systems, such as the distinctions everyone recognizes between what is *legally* binding and what is *morally* required, between legal expertise and general "good judgment," and so on. Moreover, legal positivism offers explanations that do not depend, unlike Dworkin's, on tendentious (perhaps incredible?) metaphysical commitments, such as the existence of objective moral truths.[8]

A number of recent writers—Kevin Toh, Barbara Levenbook, and Luis Duarte D'Almeida[9]—think this kind of reply to the argument from TD is the wrong response. Crucial to my account (and also to the restatement of Dworkin's challenge by Shapiro) was the supposition that Dworkin is correct that on a positivist view, a dispute about the criteria of legal validity is a dispute about the *content of the rule of recognition*, and that since the content of the RR is fixed by the criteria of legal validity on which officials converge and which they accept from an internal point of view, a *genuine* dispute about the criteria would be nothing more than a "head count" dispute (see ch. 2, 42, in this volume), that is, a dispute about what the actual "internal point of view" practice of the officials was. Kevin Toh has posed the most direct challenge to that latter assumption, so I begin by considering his view (especially since D'Almeida depends crucially on it).

[8] See, e.g., chs. 15 and 16 in this volume.
[9] See *supra* note 4.

III. Toh's Basic Objection

I should note at the start that debating with Toh on this issue is complicated by his hermeneutic posture. He denies offering a "correct understanding" of Hart, only "an alternative to the standard understanding," one supposedly vindicated by "the new possibilities in legal philosophy that it opens up, rather than on its fidelity to what Hart actually said or thought" (Toh 2015, 335).[10] Toh is happy to ascribe "commitments" to Hart on the basis of remarks in essays prior to *The Concept of Law*, even when Toh admits that "Hart himself was not always consistent in" honoring the alleged commitments subsequently and, indeed, that some of the alleged commitments "are only implicit in Hart's writings" (2015, 334). And when Hart's explicit statements in *The Concept of Law* are in tension with Toh's "alternative" understanding, Hart is sometimes deemed to be guilty of an "unforced error" (2015, 344) or we are simply advised to "dispense with Hart's view" on a particular question (2015, 344). Indeed, when what Hart actually says is flatly incompatible with one of the alleged commitments Toh deems central to Hart, Toh warns us against being "easily blind[ed]" to the commitment by what Hart actually writes (2015, 360).[11] My interpretive posture is different: I think we should take seriously what Hart actually says, especially in *The Concept of Law* (unless recanted later) and especially as it bears on the question of TDs. We should be loath to attribute error to him based on alleged "commitments" that Hart himself does not honor or sometimes even explicitly embrace. Until the clear theoretical advantages of an alternative approach are demonstrated, discounting Hart's actual views seems to me unwarranted.[12]

Toh (2013) thinks the assumption that a dispute about the content of the RR must be resolved by appeal to the actual practice of officials wrongly ignores Hart's distinction between "internal" and "external" statements about law. That a RR exists is an "external" fact about the behavior and attitudes of officials in some society. However, it is not true, says Toh, that these external facts about behavior and attitudes set the correctness conditions for "internal" judgments of legal validity made by officials in the system. (An "*internal statement*" manifests "the internal point of view"—the view of someone who accepts the rules as standards of conduct—and "is naturally used by one who, accepting the RR and without

[10] What those possibilities actually are is, in the end, not entirely clear. Of particular concern here is what the alternative account of TD would look like. Toh (2013, 2015) does not address this directly, though one can infer the general structure of the account. TDs would be disagreements in "attitudes," namely, attitudes about RR acceptance. But from a Dworkinian perspective, that would be as bad as the error-theoretical interpretation, since the disagreement is not factual but attitudinal, and, more seriously, it obscures the fact that the TD disputants in Dworkin's examples are arguing *about the content of the RR purportedly accepted*, not the subsidiary rules validated by that RR.

[11] I return to this last case below, pp. 79–81.

[12] As I argue in ch. 4 in this volume, Toh's supposed alternative has no advantages.

stating the fact that it is accepted, applies the rule" in deciding a question of legal validity.[13])

Thus Toh claims that Hart accepts the following proposition: "(L1) A community's being governed by (a system of) laws consists only of certain social facts existing in that community." But Hart purportedly rejects (or at least does not endorse) "(L3) Any first-order legal judgment is correct ultimately in virtue only of certain social facts existing in the relevant community" (2013, 461).[14] Toh claims that "there is no explanatory payoff from accepting (L3) that Hart ever discusses—that is, there is no explanandum that would require (L3) as a part of the explanans" (2013, 461). This, I will argue, is mistaken as a matter of Hart exegesis, a point to which we return shortly.

Toh proposes an analogy to meta-ethical noncognitivism like that defended in Allan Gibbard's work.[15] While it might be true, says Toh, that a community has a "morality" only in virtue of certain complex psychosocial facts obtaining—for example, "when its members regulate their emotions of guilt and impartial anger by a set of norms, and those emotions of guilt and impartial anger in turn regulate the members' behavior and practical thought" (Toh 2013, 462)—it would be a non sequitur on the preceding to say (as a matter of first order and internal moral judgment) that "any first-order moral judgment is correct ultimately in virtue only of certain social facts existing in the relevant community" (Toh 2013, 462). Toh's worry, then, is that Dworkin's challenge to Hart, as well as my response on behalf of Hartian positivism, involves precisely that non sequitur.

IV. Toh's Basic Objection: Moral vs. Legal Conventionalism

Toh's analogy to metaethical noncognitivism of the Gibbard variety is misconceived. Let us call "moral conventionalism" the view that what is morally right and wrong depends ultimately on the behavior and attitudes of most members of a community. So, for example, action X is morally right if most members of the community act as if X is right and, when pressed, will affirm that X is indeed something that ought to be done. Gibbard's metaethical view is *not* committed to this kind of moral conventionalism, and perhaps moral

[13] H. L. A. Hart, *The Concept of Law*, 3rd ed. (Oxford University Press, 2012), 103–12. Cf. ibid. at 101: "In the day-to-day life of a legal system its RR is very seldom expressly formulated as a rule . . . but its existence is *shown* in the way in which particular rules are identified." As Hart will say elsewhere, it is "presupposed." I will have more to say about presupposition in the text below, pp. 78–83.

[14] I take it "correct" in (L3) means that the judgment is a true statement of the law in the jurisdiction, and nothing more. So (L3) can be both an "external" judgment in Toh's sense and a first-order judgment about which propositions of law are true. Presuppositions can perform this semantic function, as discussed later.

[15] Allan Gibbard, *Wise Choices, Apt Feelings: A Theory of Normative Judgment* (Harvard University Press, 1990).

conventionalism is false. The key question is whether the legal analogue to moral conventionalism is also false, that is, that law is not conventional in precisely the sense that morality would be on the moral conventionalist view? I take it to be central to the positivist theory as defended by Hart and others that law is conventional in precisely the way the moral conventionalist thinks morality is conventional. In other words, the positivist view is that which norms are legally valid in any society, and thus which judgments of legal validity are correct, depends ultimately on the conventional practice of officials, that is, on the criteria of legal validity on which they converge and accept from an internal point of view (i.e., it depends on their behaviors and attitudes): roughly, Toh's (L3).

Crucial to Toh's position is the claim that (L3) ("Any first-order legal judgment is correct ultimately in virtue only of certain social facts existing in the relevant community") has "no explanatory payoff" in Hart's theory. His argument for this claim, however, again exposes his odd hermeneutic posture vis-à-vis Hart's texts. According to Toh (2013, 2015), (L3) does not help explain the kinds of phenomena that Hart thought Bentham's and Austin's theories could not adequately explain, and which Hart focused on in chapters 2 through 4 of *The Concept of Law*: for example, the transfer of sovereign power, the continuity of laws across sovereigns, the existence of power-conferring rules, and so on. Hart's theory, of course, aims to explain these phenomena, and does so more successfully, by almost universal consensus, than his positivist predecessors. From the preceding, however, it simply does not follow that (L3) has no explanatory power in Hart's theory: the idea that what needs explaining are only the phenomena that Bentham and Austin failed to explain is incorrect. For it is precisely Hart's more complicated theoretical apparatus of a union of primary and secondary rules—and secondary rules understood as social rules—that leads Hart to be committed to Toh's (L3) or what I have been calling legal conventionalism. Let me explain.

Although Hart is offering an analysis of the concept of law, one supposedly adequate to what an ordinary person familiar with a modern municipal legal system understands, we also know the analysis has a revisionary dimension, aiming to purge the folk concept of incompatible elements in favor of a more satisfactory and coherent theoretical account.[16] For example, the folk—not to mention theorists from Austin to Kelsen—think there is some kind of necessary connection between law and coercion, but that aspect of the folk concept cannot be reconciled with the idea of *obligations* to act as the law requires, as Hart famously argues. Legal conventionalism, in particular, is necessary to explain an

[16] For discussion of this aspect of Hart's methodology, see Alex Langlinais and Brian Leiter, "The Methodology of Legal Philosophy," in *The Oxford Handbook of Philosophical Methodology*, ed. H. Cappelen, T. Gendler, and J. Hawthorne (Oxford University Press, 2019), esp. 678–79.

even more prosaic set of observations. Where legal systems exist, we can distinguish between those norms that are legally valid and those that are not. A theory of law should explain this. Hart's theory does so by noting that for a legal system to exist there must be a special kind of secondary rule, a rule of recognition specifying the criteria of legal validity, which is itself simply an instance of the phenomenon that Hart calls a "social rule": a convergent practice of behavior (e.g., judges applying particular criteria of legal validity) and acceptance of the rule describing that practice from an internal point of view (e.g., judges treat applying such criteria as obligatory, or something like that). The introduction of the idea of a rule of recognition naturally raises Dworkin's worry: Sometimes judges in modern legal systems engage in TDs (i.e., disputes about the content of the rule of recognition or the criteria of legal validity). How are we to explain what's going on in such disputes? Hart answers this question as well: He is explicit that internal judgments of legal validity *presuppose* the RR that validates them, and we already know that an RR exists only if the relevant internal-point-of-view practice exists.[17] If there is a dispute about the presuppositions of a legal judgment—a TD in Dworkin's sense—then there is only one way to resolve it on Hart's view. Consider the following three claims made by Hart:

(1) Hart says that an internal judgment of legal validity which "makes use of a RR which [the legal official] accepts as appropriate for identifying the law" (*The Concept of Law*, 108) also presupposes that this RR is "actually accepted and employed in the general operation of the system. *If the truth of this presupposition were doubted, it could be established by reference to actual practice: to the way in which courts identify what is to count as law, and to the general acceptance of or acquiescence in these identifications*" (*The Concept of Law*, 108 [emphasis added]). In other words, internal judgments of legal validity presuppose that the RR has a particular content, and if that were "doubted" (as it would be in a TD), the content would be established by empirical facts about "actual practice." This, I take it, is a direct endorsement of what Toh calls (L3), and what I, Dworkin, and Shapiro were all assuming is a feature of Hart's view.

(2) In addressing uncertainty about the content of the RR—about the "ultimate criteria of legal validity" in a legal system (*The Concept of Law*, 149), using the English rule about the sovereignty of Parliament as his example—Hart says that its content "is an empirical question concerning

[17] I agree with Toh (2013, 2015) that the existence of an RR is a matter of external fact, and that there is no sense to the question whether an RR is legally valid, but as far as I can see, that is wholly irrelevant to the TD problem, which is not about the "legal validity" of the RR, but about its content. I should add that I also agree with Toh (2015, 349-353) that the supposed problem of the "normativity of law" is a pseudo-problem (though not quite for all of Toh's reasons).

the form of rule which is accepted as the ultimate criterion in identifying the law. Though it is a question about a rule lying at the base of a legal system, it is still a question of fact to which at any given moment of time, on some points at least, there may be a quite determinate answer." He concludes, based on the practice of the English courts, "that the presently accepted rule is one of continuing sovereignty, so that Parliament cannot protect its statutes from repeal" (*The Concept of Law*, 150). In this case, then, the *content* of the RR is explicitly established by Hart by appeal to statements of fact about official practice—once again, demonstrating an explanatory role for Toh's (L3), since the first-order judgment that Parliament cannot protect its statutes from repeal is established by answering this "empirical question."

(3) Hart goes on to say that "the fact that the rule of parliamentary sovereignty is determinate at this point [in time] does not mean that it is so at all points. Questions can be raised about it [i.e., about the content of the RR with respect to parliamentary sovereignty] to which at present there is no answer which is clearly right or wrong. These can be settled only by a choice, made by someone to whose choices in this matter authority is eventually accorded" (*The Concept of Law*, 150). (Hart's example concerns legislation that imposes special voting rules for its own repeal.) So here "we are in the area of open texture of the system's most fundamental rule . . . a question may arise to which there is no answer—only answers" (*The Concept of Law*, 151), and some court may subsequently make "determinate . . . the ultimate rule by which valid law is identified" (*The Concept of Law*, 152). In these cases—cases of TD in Dworkin's sense—"when courts settle previously unenvisaged questions concerning the most fundamental . . . rules, they *get* their authority to decide them accepted after the questions have arisen and the decision has been given. Here all that succeeds is success" (*The Concept of Law*, 153). In other words, a new official practice (converging on particular criteria of legal validity) settles the questions about the content of the RR, and thus settles disputes about presuppositions like the kind we saw in (2), above—which is exactly the supposition of my positivist account of TD (see ch. 2 in this volume).

As the two preceding passages ((2) and (3)) indicate, for Hart, judgments about the content of the RR can be first-order judgments about the content of the law.[18] That is because they are not judgments that *presuppose* the RR, they are

[18] "Ultimate" rules like the RR are neither valid nor invalid, but "[w]e can ask whether it is the practice of courts, legislatures, officials, or private citizens . . . actually to use this rule as an ultimate RR" (*The Concept of Law*, 107). But when we ask such questions we are "no longer attempting to

judgments about the RR itself, and those are, as Hart says, factual or empirical, but the truth of these factual judgments, according to Hart, are "presupposed" by the internal judgment that the law is X. And, as the first quote makes clear, a dispute about that presupposition is resolved by "reference to actual practice," or what I glossed as a "head count."

V. Presuppositions

Since Toh's claim that legal conventionalism (i.e., his L3) plays no explanatory role in Hart's theory is flatly contradicted by what Hart says, perhaps we should consider a different tact: namely, what is the best way to understand Hart's talk of "presupposition"? Perhaps there is a reading of Hart's talk about presupposing the RR that can be explained in a way that supports Toh's position.

Toh addresses this question, but makes two mistakes in his treatment of it. First, after noting correctly that Hart criticized "Kelsenian talk of presuppositions [as] misleading" and that Hart argued instead that the " 'existence' of rules of recognition [is] a complex empirical fact" (2015, 359), Toh goes on to claim that "[w]hatever the real or full nature of Kelsen's notion of presupposition, it seems to bear sufficient resemblance to the one that Hart himself deploys for [Hart's] simple dismissal of Kelsen's talk of presupposition of the basic norm to be quite misleading" (2015, 359–60). Here Toh betrays his excessive enthusiasm for dismissing what Hart actually says.

Kelsen's and Hart's talk of presuppositions is, to start, completely different. Kelsen is a neo-Kantian: his talk of "presupposition" is talk of a transcendental condition on the possibility of the intelligibility of some judgment (in the legal case, the possibility of ultimate judgments about legal normativity). That is not surprising when one remembers that Kelsen's was supposed to be a "pure" theory of law, one untainted by empirical claims: Whatever exactly transcendental conditions on the possibility of judgment are, they are not empirical facts. Hart, by contrast, is no neo-Kantian, and he has no use for talk of transcendental conditions on the possibility of judgment. Hart's is plainly not a "pure" theory of law: Unlike Kelsen, it grounds a legal system in complex psychosocial facts about the behavior and attitudes of officials, not in talk of transcendental conditions. More precisely, Hart was influenced by ordinary language philosophy—appeal to how people actually speak—so his references to "presuppositions" have an empirical dimension, one grounded in the pragmatics of ordinary language.

answer the same kind of question about it as those which we answered about other rules with its aid" (ibid.), precisely because "we have moved from an internal statement of law asserting the validity of a rule of the system to an external statement of fact" (ibid., 108). But that external statement answers the first-order question.

That is utterly absent from Kelsen. We will return to that crucial aspect of Hart's ideas about "presupposition" shortly.

Toh's second mistake in his treatment of presupposition follows not from the misunderstanding of Kelsen but from his willingness to disregard what Hart says. According to Toh's rendering of Hart's "oblique" analysis of "internal" legal judgments, a judgment by an official of the system that "This rule is the law" can be analyzed as follows:

> [He] expresses his acceptance of some rule that he deems validated by the rule of recognition of his community's legal system, and furthermore *presupposes* (i) the content of that rule of recognition, and also (ii) the efficacy of that rule of recognition . . . [He thus] presupposes not only the content of the rule of recognition of his community, but also that the relevant rule of recognition is accepted and followed by the officials of his community. *The content of this second, factual presupposition—as opposed to the first, normative presupposition—is the same as the content of the external legal statement about the existence of the relevant rule of recognition.* (Toh 2015, 360 [emphasis added])

In other words, it seems that, even on Toh's view, an official of the system who judges that, "This rule is the law" presupposes that "any first-order legal judgment is correct ultimately in virtue only of certain social facts existing" (Toh 2013, 461, stating his [L3]), and thus presupposes what Toh calls the "external legal statement about the existence of the relevant rule of recognition." This might suggest, of course, that someone engaged in a TD is disputing precisely the factual statement about the practice constituting the RR, and the truth of that statement is an empirical question as Hart put it in the passage from p. 108 of *The Concept of Law*, which I quoted earlier. Toh, no doubt realizing that this analysis defeats his claims, cautions us not to be "easily blind[ed]" (2015, 360) to Hart's real view. The other possibility, of course, is that Hart has expressed his real view accurately, and we should be blinded to that!

Toh's attempt to have us disregard what Hart actually says depends on two claims. First, Toh (2015, 362) quotes a lengthy passage from Hart's 1959 essay on "Scandinavian Realism" in which, on Toh's gloss, "Hart . . . warns explicitly against conflating internal and external statements," which is correct, but the conflation Hart is reacting to is Alf Ross's (supposed) claim that statements of law are just predictions of official behavior,[19] not the problem of TDs, which are cases in which the presuppositions are explicitly in dispute. Second, Toh goes on

[19] Ross, as we now know, did not proffer this as a claim about the ordinary concept of law, but as a kind of reforming definition meant to reconcile the intelligibility of law in a world naturalistically conceived. See the discussion of Ross in ch. 7 in this volume.

to note that "presuppositions are defeasible and could be cancelled" in ordinary language (2015, 362–63). In TDs, however, they are not cancelled, they are directly disputed, so the phenomenon of cancellation is not relevant.

If Toh's argument that what Hart actually says "blinds" us to his real meaning is not compelling, then let us see whether we can take seriously what Hart actually says. We should begin with the fact that Hart, unlike Kelsen, seems to be thinking of presupposition in the empirical manner of ordinary language philosophers, who were always sensitive to the pragmatics of language use, a theme that has come to the fore in subsequent philosophy of language and linguistics. One familiar view about presuppositions in this tradition, the "semantic" view, requires that presuppositions hold even when the statement that presupposes them is negated: so "a proposition that *P* presupposes that *Q* if and only if *Q* must be true in order that *P* have a truth value at all."[20] The proposition ("P") that, "It is unconstitutional to execute juveniles in the United States" clearly presupposes that the United States has a constitution, and that presupposition does survive negation of (P): it cannot be true that it is really constitutional to execute juveniles in the United States unless the United States also has a constitution! In Hart's view, however, (P) also presupposes something else, namely, ("Q"): "A Supreme Court decision about the constitutionality of such executions under the Eighth Amendment decides the question of its constitutionality," which is one small part of the general RR of the American legal system. That presupposition cannot be a semantic presupposition of (P) since some negations of P do not require it: for example, Some speakers might simply deny (Q) and endorse "Z": "Such executions are constitutional unless they are really cruel." So it looks like a judgment about the unconstitutionality of executing juveniles in the United States, in which Q is presupposed, cannot be a presupposition *in the semantic sense.*

There is a different view of presuppositions that is, I will suggest, more adequate to Hart's usage, but before setting that out explicitly, it will be useful to imagine how a dispute about the preceding propositions *P*, *Q*, and *Z* might actually go between two lawyers, call them Leslie and Jeremy. Leslie asserts, "It is unconstitutional to execute juveniles in the United States." Jeremy retorts, "No, it isn't." They continue:

Leslie: "Of course it is, the Supreme Court settled the issue with its decision in *Roper v. Simmons* in 2005."

Jeremy: "I know the Court made that decision, of course, but that doesn't mean it is really unconstitutional, it depends on whether it is *really* cruel."

[20] Robert Stalnaker, *Context and Content: Essays on Intentionality in Speech and Thought* (Oxford University Press, 1999), 48.

Leslie: "No, its constitutionality in the United States right now has been settled by the Supreme Court. Your opinion, or anyone else's, about its cruelty isn't relevant to the state of the law, unless you can persuade the High Court to reverse itself."

Jeremy: "Why do you talk as if the Supreme Court's decision in *Roper* settles anything about the constitutionality of executing juveniles?"

Leslie: "Are you being serious? That issue has been settled since *Marbury* and *Cooper v. Aaron*!"

Jeremy: "Just more court decisions, who cares?"

Leslie: "Did you pass a bar exam? Supreme Court decisions about constitutionality are binding on the lower courts and the other branches of government."

Jeremy: "Says you!"

Leslie: "No, says all the courts and other lawyers in this jurisdiction."

Jeremy: "But they could all be wrong!"

Leslie: "I'm not even sure what that would mean."

Jeremy: "It means they're all wrong about what the law really is."

Leslie: "I understand you would like the law to be different, and so maybe you want the High Court to overrule itself, but the law right now is settled."

Jeremy: "No it's not, it only *appears* to be settled because of the consensus among the lower courts following the High Court."

Leslie: "But that's just what the law is today!"

To be sure, someone might really press Jeremy's line against Leslie's, and if it were false that the content of the RR is settled by actual practice, then Jeremy's pressing this line of criticism would not be ridiculous. The latter, however, is not our immediate question here; our question is whether it could be Hart's view that the *actual practice of officials* settles questions about the content of the RR—that is, Leslie's position in this debate (which I do take to be both the positivist's posture and the ordinary lawyer's posture). And in assuming that the actual practice does settle that, as Leslie does, it seems wholly in line with what Hart actually says in the passages quoted earlier. Hart holds the view that actual practice settles the question of the content of the RR in contested cases, and such a view is compatible with how a putative disagreement between a positivist and Dworkinian lawyer would go, as the case of Leslie and Jeremy illustrates. Moreover, if I am right that Leslie's position is the ordinary lawyer's position in this debate, and that Jeremy's position is as puzzling as Leslie finds it, then that would also count in favor of Hart's view as against Dworkin's.[21]

[21] Of course, Jeremy might reasonably be understood to be arguing that the Supreme Court *got the law wrong*, a point to which I return below, p. 83, in the text.

Now, there is a view of presupposition in ordinary language, the pragmatic view, that comports much better with how Hart is thinking about presupposition when he treats the empirical fact that the RR has such-and-such a content as the presupposition of first-order legal judgments. According to the pragmatic view, "Presuppositions . . . are something like the background beliefs of the speaker—propositions whose truth he takes for granted, or seems to take for granted, in making his statement."[22] Leslie starts the debate with Jeremy assuming that it is "common ground" between them that a Supreme Court decision about constitutionality settles the legality of executing juveniles. Their dispute breaks down, and descends into Leslie's incredulity, precisely because Jeremy seems to reject the idea that any competent American lawyer accepts, namely, that since *Marbury*, the Supreme Court has the final word on constitutional validity. Leslie, like Hart in *The Concept of Law*, takes it for granted that *official practice* is decisive, which in the American context, with regard to constitutionality of legislation, means decisions of the US Supreme Court. From this point of view, as already noted, Jeremy's dissent from what Leslie (speaking for Hart) took to be the "common ground" appears mysterious.

Although on the pragmatic view, "[p]resupposing is . . . not a mental attitude like believing, but is rather a linguistic disposition—a disposition to behave in one's use of language as if one had certain beliefs, or were making certain assumptions," this "does not rule out a semantic *explanation* for the fact that a certain presupposition is required when a certain statement is made,"[23] though the pragmatic view does not require it. On the pragmatic view, presuppositions can vary by context of utterance and, more importantly, presupposition and logical entailment can go together or come apart. On the semantic view, *A* presupposes *B* iff *both A* and its denial require *B*. But the pragmatic account allows for the fact that "sometimes when a presupposition is required by the making of a statement, what is presupposed is also entailed, and sometimes it is not,"[24] and this is helpful when it comes to the dispute between Leslie and Jeremy. For Jeremy denies that executing juveniles is unconstitutional, but does *not* presuppose, as Leslie does, that a Supreme Court decision settles the matter. Their disagreement results precisely from presupposition and entailment coming apart. Leslie believes that (A) it is unconstitutional to execute juveniles, presupposes (B) constitutionality is settled by decisions of the US Supreme Court, such that someone who denies (A) must still presuppose (B). But Jeremy denies (A) while also rejecting (B), meaning that he denies Leslie's presupposition and thus has a TD. Yet, as we have seen, on Hart's view, that kind of dispute is settled by reference to

[22] Stalnaker, *Context and Content*, 48.
[23] Ibid., 52, 53.
[24] Ibid., 54.

the empirical facts about official practice. So we can say that on Hart's view, any first-order judgment presupposes pragmatically an official practice constituting the relevant rule of recognition, while Dworkin denies that.

Perhaps that is too quick, though. Cannot a lawyer *intelligibly* argue that a question of American constitutional law settled by the US Supreme Court was wrongly resolved and should be overruled in a subsequent decision? The simple answer is, of course, yes, any lawyer can so argue, and they may well be right: Perhaps the law would be morally improved by being overruled, or perhaps the High Court misunderstood the law. Only the latter claim is at issue (anyone can argue that the law would be morally better if construed differently, of course). But the latter claim involves a TD, which, according to Hart, is resolved by reference to actual practice, which is what the Dworkinian denies, of course. This just shows, however, that arguments for overruling based on "what the law *really* requires" are not neutral data points for adjudicating between competing accounts of the content of the RR. Legal arguments for overruling earlier decisions in a common-law system are even less frequent data points requiring explanation than TDs themselves, which occur against the background of massive agreement about the law, as noted earlier.

VI. Some Other Objections and Concluding Remarks

Once we see that Hart assumes that the RR, as fixed by official practice, functions as a pragmatic presupposition of first-order legal judgments, we can dispense with D'Almeida's objections fairly easily. D'Almeida follows Toh in thinking the internal/external judgment distinction is crucial, and notes that when officials make what he calls "general internal statements" (2016, 176)—statements of the form, "This decision is legally required because of this criterion of legal validity" (e.g., in the example I have been using, "A state can not execute a juvenile because the U.S. Supreme Court has deemed such executions unconstitutional")—they do not *justify* them by appeal to the fact that officials accept such a criterion (D'Almeida 2016, 193). In ordinary discourse, however, one does not *justify* one's statements by reference to their pragmatic presuppositions: one takes the *common ground* to actually be the common ground of the discourse! Of course judges do not claim the correctness of their "statements of law depends on everyone else or even a majority agreeing with them" (D'Almeida 2016, 193); the correctness of their statements of law depends on their correctly applying the criteria of legal validity, which in cases of constitutionality, presupposes that the criteria are fixed by Supreme Court decisions (where the Supreme Court has ruled on the matter). Even D'Almeida concedes that judges do "presuppose the truth of the external statement that that rule [that criterion of legal validity] is actually generally accepted as appropriate for that purpose" (2016, 194), which is to concede the point: The external fact that the RR is what it is based on official practice is pragmatically presupposed as the common ground of the debate. That issue, of course, does not arise when speakers agree about the law; it only arises when they *disagree* about the common ground, which is why, *contra* Duarte D'Almeida, one would not expect the character of theoretical agreement and disagreement to be symmetrical.

By contrast, Levenbook (2015, 5) echoes Shapiro's attempt to motivate Dworkin's critique by claiming that since "criticism for engaging" in TDs "is notably absent," it is not plausible that those engaged in them are being disingenuous. The idea would be that if a dispute about the common ground were a mere pretense—an attempt to change the law, rather than dispute its fundamental grounds—then we would expect criticism of judges for engaging in what look like Dworkinian TDs, but she thinks there is none. In fact, some scholars do criticize judges on this ground,[25] but put that to one side since there is a more basic point. To argue against the error-theoretical interpretation of TD, it is never enough to appeal to the ordinary practice of those committing the error, including those acceding to it. Many objections have been made against Mackie's error theory of ethical discourse, but no one, to my knowledge, has argued that Mackie *must* be wrong because those engaged in ethical discourse think their claims are true. Error-theoretic treatments of religious and theological discourse are an even better case: such discourse generally does not admit of noncognitive analysis (as ethical discourse does), and yet no one would seriously argue that because many participants in the discourse think, for example, that there is a real question about how one being, God, could be realized in three distinct "divine" beings, the Father, the Son, and the Holy Spirit, that the error-theoretic interpretation of the discourse is misguided. Legal positivism stands to theoretical disagreements about law, as error-theoretic naturalism stands to theological debates about the Trinity. One can forgive, and even explain, how participants in these discourses come to make the mistakes they do, and in the legal case, it is quite a bit easier, given that neither the judiciary nor practitioners have a reason to have well-developed views on the foundational questions about their practice (why would judges need to recognize the truth of legal conventionalism?), so their error in these unusual cases may well be innocent. Moreover, judges and lawyers have obvious practical motivations for misconceiving their disputes,

[25] See, e.g., Richard Fallon, "Constitutional Precedent Viewed through the Lens of Hartian Positivist Jurisprudence," *North Carolina Law Review* 86 (2008): 1107–64.

something that is also true of other discourses that warrant error-theoretic treatment. In the end, as I argued originally (see ch. 2 in this volume), the *only* relevant question is whether the *best explanation* of law and legal systems is one that involves an error-theoretic interpretation of TDs, when they actually occur. That is also the question we are left with by what Hart actually says.[26]

[26] A very early version of this paper benefited from discussion at the conference on "Deep Disagreements" at Humboldt University in Berlin in June 2015. I can recall particularly useful questions and comments on that occasion from Don Loeb, Ralf Poscher, and Ernie Sosa. A later version benefited from detailed comments by Kevin Toh. The current version was improved by discussion at a legal and political philosophy workshop with faculty from Chicago, King's College, London, and the National University of Singapore at the University of Chicago in May 2016—especially Ryan Doerfler, Ben Laurence, Tim Macklem, and John Tasioulas—and by written comments from Max Etchemendy. Finally, I am grateful to Tim Grinsell for guidance on linguistic presuppositions; to Taylor Coles, University of Chicago Law School Class of 2018, for research assistance; and to the Alumni Faculty Fund of the Law School for research support.

4

Postscript on Theoretical Disagreements

In chapter 3 (in this volume), I considered several responses to my original argument from 2009 (reprinted as ch. 2 in this volume) that legal positivists can explain theoretical disagreements (TDs) about law, by, in short, explaining them away within a more plausible general explanatory framework that does a better job explaining all the relevant data points about law, including the fact of massive agreement about the law. In chapter 3, I also demonstrated that the most interesting rejoinder to my original argument, due to Kevin Toh, involved a serious misunderstanding of Hart. Here, I want to consider some different responses from Toh's to the problem of TD that have won support from several legal philosophers.[1]

In chapter 2, I agreed with Dworkin that, on a positivist view, a dispute about the criteria of legal validity is a dispute about the *content of the rule of recognition* (RR), and that since the content of the RR is fixed by the criteria of legal validity on which officials converge and which they accept from an internal point of view, a *genuine* dispute about the criteria would be nothing more than a "head count" dispute, that is, a dispute about what the actual "internal point of view" practice of the officials was. In the 2019 essay—reprinted as chapter 3 in this volume—I noted in a footnote a possible response to Dworkin's challenge that I did not consider in that chapter:

> Tim Macklem presses on me a different kind of positivist response: namely, that a RR [rule of recognition] identifies the sources of law, but does not adjudicate among all the ways of interpreting them. Here I agree, I take it, with Dworkin (as well as [Scott] Shapiro): namely, that this austere conception of the RR would be inadequate to discharge the functions of an RR as Hart

[1] See, e.g., Luka Burazin and Giovanni Battista Ratti, "Rule(s) of Recognition and Canons of Interpretation," in *Judges and Adjudication in Constitutional Democracies: A View from Legal Realism*, ed. P. Chiassoni and B. Spaic (Springer, 2021); Torben Spaak, "The Scope of Legal Positivism: Validity or Interpretation?" in *The Cambridge Companion to Legal Positivism*, ed. T. Spaak and P. Mindus (Cambridge University Press, 2021). Bill Watson defends a similar view, with some modest differences (discussed below in the notes), in "How to Answer Dworkin's Argument from Theoretical Disagreement without Attributing Confusion or Disingenuity to Legal Officials," *Canadian Journal of Law & Jurisprudence* 36 (2023): 215–40. See also Richard Stillman, "Statutory Interpretation and Denotational Disagreement," *Canadian Journal of Law & Jurisprudence* (forthcoming), also discussed below, 90 n8.

From a Realist Point of View. Brian Leiter, Oxford University Press. © Brian Leiter 2026.
DOI: 10.1093/9780197749852.003.0005

> originally conceived them, namely, eliminating some (if not all) uncertainty about the valid legal norms are in a particular system. I thus agree (infrequent as that may be) with Dworkin that saying the duly enacted statute is a source of law is not enough for a RR that resolves uncertainty: it is necessary that the RR provide guidance as to what norms the statute enacts as legally valid. This, of course, can be done by content-neutral criteria: e.g., the intent of the legislature, the plain meaning of the text, and so on. And, indeed, these content-neutral criteria can come in hierarchical orderings, such that some sources trump others. But a RR that did not resolve some number of TDs would not, in fact, be adequate to support a functioning legal system.[2]

Macklem's proposed response is developed systematically (and independently of Macklem) by Luka Burazin and Giovanni Battista Ratti, and I will concentrate on their version.[3] Burazin and Ratti give a succinct statement of the assumption I share with Dworkin:

> [T]he reasoning behind this [assumption] might be the following: (a) the rule of recognition sets the criteria for identifying valid legal norms (i.e., the criteria of validity); (b) the "what is the law" question cannot be answered only on the basis of the formal criteria of validity (i.e., whether the norm was enacted by a competent authority in a duly prescribed procedure); (c) in order to determine what is the norm in force, one needs to determine its content; (d) in order to determine the content of the norm, one needs to interpret its linguistic formulation (i.e., the sentence expressing it or the norm-formulation); (e) hence, the rule of recognition includes among its criteria of validity canons of interpretation. (Burazin & Ratti, 123–24)

This is not quite right, since a "norm" necessarily has content, so the "formal criteria" do not identify a "norm" "enacted by a competent authority" but rather a source of legal norms.[4] Their subsequent formulation of their own position

[2] See ch. 3, n. 7 (in this volume).

[3] Torben Spaak has a similar view, but mischaracterizes what theoretical disagreements are: he treats them as all disputes about the "interpretation and application of law" (Spaak, "The Scope of Legal Positivism," 455). But theoretical disagreements are not disagreements about the "interpretation and application of law," they are disputes about the criteria of legal validity. For example, everyone can agree that the intention of the legislature controls the meaning of a statutory provision (the relevant criterion of legal validity), but a dispute about what the intention of the legislature was is not a theoretical disagreement: that is, in Dworkinian terms, an "empirical disagreement." And even when there is theoretical and empirical agreement, there can still be uncertainty *in application* of a norm in a particular case: for example, everyone can agree the legislature intended to prohibit the "vehicles in the park," and then disagree about whether that applies to Segues. That latter disagreement is also *not* a theoretical disagreement. As we will see, below, when Spaak discusses *actual* theoretical disagreements about the criteria of legal validity, he smuggles in an interpretive criterion.

[4] Burazin & Ratti (127) distinguish between "norm-formulations" and "norms," but by the former they appear to mean only the words used in a legal source to express a norm, which does not yet tell

is better in this regard: they endorse the view that "the rule of recognition sets the criteria only for sources of law and not legal norms themselves" so that we need to distinguish "between normative texts (sources of law) and legal norms (as meanings of legal texts)" (Burazin & Ratti, 124).

Burazin and Ratti point out that "Hart does not say much about how the content of law is identified," but that he does seem to "equate[] legal rules with their linguistic formulations" (Burazin & Ratti, 128). This seems to me right, and I agree it is plausible that Hart "at least implicitly . . . endorsed the view that at least one canon of interpretation (i.e., the literal or plain-meaning canon) is a necessary part of the rule of recognition and is thus covered by a consensus of convention among officials" (Burazin & Ratti, 137). Yet Burazin and Ratti admit that it is "extremely rare in practice" for the linguistic articulation of a norm to express "only one norm" (Burazin & Ratti, 133): that is the standard legal realist point about legal indeterminacy.

Although Burazin and Ratti reject my view of theoretical disagreements (ch. 2 in this volume)—for reasons that we can confine to a footnote[5]—they acknowledge, following Andrei Marmor, that "since the rule of recognition identifies norms (and not simply texts), it is necessary to include canons [of interpretation], which allow one to pass from the relevant sources to norms" (Burazin & Ratti, 131). They suggest that we distinguish between two kinds of rules of recognition: one about sources, another about how to interpret sources and thus identify the actual norms enacted (Burazin & Ratti, 134–35). Their thought, I take it, is that there is convergence on sources (thus constituting one rule of recognition), but not with respect to the "rule of recognition of norms [which] has a disjunctive content, consisting in different norms that depend on use of different canons" (Burazin & Ratti, 136–37).

us what the norm is. See, e.g., ibid., 132: "Norms are the meaning-contents of norm-formulations." They also acknowledge that a "norm-formulation" can "express more than one norm." Ibid., 133.

[5] Burazin and Ratti mischaracterize my view as consisting in "a sociological-empirical thesis that aims at denying the pervasive character of disagreements within contemporary legal systems" (131). But that is not my argument at all: my argument (ch. 2 in this volume) is that theoretical disagreements are best explained by a positivist theory that involves a realistic explanation of the dispute in Dworkin's favorite case, *Riggs v. Palmer*. This explanation imputes error to appellate judges in some cases, at least when they think there is a fact about the criteria of legal validity when there is not. The attribution of error is not serious since it turns on an abstract jurisprudential proposition and is not very common. Burazin and Ratti complain that the last point (they think, wrongly, it is the main part of the argument) involves "the fallacy of improper generalization, in so far as it derives from the (supposed) absence of interpretive disagreement in the lower levels of the US judiciary system a general thesis according to which legal systems in general are not characterized by the presence of widespread . . . disagreements" (131). What I claim is that in all functioning legal systems, massive agreement about the law is the norm, and Burazin and Ratti offer no evidence to the contrary (unsurprisingly). If, in fact, theoretical disagreements (what they call "interpretive disagreement") are more widespread, let them adduce the evidence. They do not.

Multiplying rules of recognition does not, however, respond to Dworkin's objection, it simply concedes the force of his point: if there is no convergence on the canons of interpretation (as they put it), then there is no fact of the matter about which norm a source enacts. Yet judges, as Dworkin argued, write in cases of "theoretical disagreements" as if there is a fact: hence we are forced back into attributing an error theory to judges engaged in such disagreements (as I argued originally).[6] More important, how is agreement on sources enough for a rule of *recognition*? Knowing sources does not tell us which norms are legally valid, unless one assumes—as Burazin and Ratti argue Hart seems to—that the literal meaning of the words is equivalent to the norm.[7] Yet as Burazin and Ratti themselves rightly argue, this is implausible. So a rule of recognition that identifies *only* sources is not a rule that allows us to recognize legally valid norms, and so fails in its central epistemic function.[8]

I want to conclude by considering a somewhat different proposal, although one related to the preceding. Perhaps we need to distinguish between the validity of legal norms and their application in particular cases, as Aaron Graham has

[6] See ch. 2. in this volume.

[7] Spaak makes a similar assumption: he says, "a legal norm is more or less identical with its formulation" ("The Scope of Legal Positivism," 459). The problem with this assumption has nothing to do with Stanley Fish's implausible meaning skepticism (discussed in Spaak, "The Scope of Legal Positivism," 459–60), but with the point that Burazin and Ratti make about the many other canons of interpretation that go far beyond the literal meaning of the linguistic formulation.

[8] Bill Watson's view confronts a similar problem. Watson ("How to Answer Dworkin's Argument," 240) suggests that officials do converge on "imprecise grounds of law" (what he calls "coarse-grained agreement" [224]), such as that a statute's "meaning" or a court's "holding" (217) is a source of law. A bit like Hart (and Spaak), Watson is tempted by the thought that "much of the time, anyone familiar with the usages of American legal English can read an enacted text and immediately and unreflectively see what the text directs in the case at hand" (229), but of course that is not going to be true in most cases that reach the stage of appellate review. In such cases, Watson suggests that "judges recognize that legal content is unsettled," but he claims, "[W]e do not expect them to expressly acknowledge as much in their official capacities; we expect them instead to speak as any lawyer would, i.e., to *advocate* for an answer to a legal question" (240). This, of course, just gets us back to a variation on my error-theoretic account. From the standpoint of Dworkin's objection, it is no improvement since Watson explains away the face value of what judges say they are doing in such cases (which is "discovering" the legal answer, not "advocating" for one).

Richard Stillman ("Statutory Interpretation and Denotational Disagreement") develops an interesting variation (and, I think, improvement) on Watson's view (which Stillman discusses helpfully in section 2 of his paper). Stillman argues that some (not all!) supposed theoretical disagreements are merely "denotational" disagreements—that is, disagreements about what the criterion of legal validity refers to. For example, officials may converge on the idea that courts should be the agent of the legislature, but then disagree about what this requires. He makes a prima facie plausible case that this is what is happening in the federal courts in the United States, but this account may not work for other jurisdictions or other interpretive disputes (Stillman does not claim otherwise). Even in the United States, moreover, the upshot would still be that the "denotational disagreement" undermines the epistemic function of the RR: it may no longer be a TD in Dworkin's sense, but it still means that judges and lawyers may not know which norms are legally valid. These disputes may be sufficiently rare, however, that they are compatible with the RR's basic function.

argued.[9] According to this view, in *Riggs v. Palmer,* there was, in fact, convergence on the valid legal norm (and not just the source):

> [T]he governing valid legal norm was simply that contained in the statutory text. It specified the conditions a will had to meet in order to be legally enforceable. Then an unforeseen and difficult question arose: may an heir who murdered his testator to prevent modification of the will inherit?[10]

What looks like a TD is really a disagreement about the "reasons supporting diverging applications of the norm that the respective judges favored."[11] It is the trademark Dworkinian mistake throughout his career to conflate the question, "What is the law?" with the question, "How ought a court to decide this case?," and one might think of Graham's line of response as extending this general criticism of Dworkin to the case of TDs. I certainly think Graham is correct that there are cases where this might work, but I do not see that *Riggs v. Palmer* is such a case. The majority and dissent in that case disagree precisely about what the valid legal norm is, as Dworkin originally argued: they do not agree on it.[12] In the dispute about statutory interpretation that Dworkin emphasized in *Law's Empire*, the majority and dissent disagree about the statutory norm—that is, whether it is to be understood literally or in terms of the majority's preferred "counterfactual intention" theory.[13] Rather than preserving the "face value" of their disagreement or explaining it away, Graham's account proposes a description of the disagreement (quoted above) that does not fit the evidence. That means there are still TDs in Dworkin's sense, even if some putative TDs admit of Graham's interpretation.

What one can say, correctly I believe, is that outside the appellate courts, there is massive convergence on not only the valid sources of law but the valid legal norms themselves: This is why, as Hart recognized, law exists and functions primarily outside the courts. While it is certainly true that, as Bill Watson puts it, "legal agreement does not entail theoretical agreement,"[14] it is a plausible explanatory hypothesis that it usually does, given what we find in functioning legal

[9] See, e.g., Aaron Graham, "Theoretical Disagreements, Hard Cases, and the Positivist Theory of Legal Validity" (Ph.D. diss., University of Chicago, 2023); Aaron Graham, "Hard Cases and Theoretical Disagreements," *Journal of Legal Philosophy* (forthcoming).

[10] Graham, "Hard Cases and Theoretical Disagreements," 28 (of the manuscript version).

[11] Ibid., 29

[12] The majority's argument that the statutory norm is trumped by the maxim of the common law that no one should profit from their own wrongdoing fits better with Graham's characterization, but that is not the crucial argument for Dworkin in framing the objection to legal positivism from TDs.

[13] See the discussion in ch. 2 in this volume.

[14] Watson, "How to Answer Dworkin's Argument," 223 (citing Barbara Baum Levenbook and Dale Smith as legal philosophers pressing this point). Watson recognizes that I have a response to this argument at 224 n. 40, which I discuss in the text.

systems, where most legal questions do not end up in court. (If TDs were pervasive, it would be surprising to find so much convergence not just on sources but on valid legal norms.) To repeat a theme from chapter 2, the crucial question is which theory provides the *best explanation* for all the relevant phenomena, not just TDs, but massive agreement about the law, as well as the distinctions familiar to the layperson that Hart identified in 1961. Theories of law, like theories of any subject, stand or fall as corporate bodies, not as isolated hypotheses. The debate about TDs still needs to come to terms with that. It also needs to overcome its aversion to the idea that sometimes judges are confused about abstract jurisprudential questions. Think of it this way: Throughout the world, intelligent theologians are earnestly engaged in debates about beings that do not exist, and the only naturalistically plausible interpretation of their debates must attribute to them significant error. The error involved in TDs is very modest, by comparison, but equally understandable: of course, the clergy of the law sometimes believe there are facts about matters central to their practice even when there are not. This is no objection at all to a theory of law that succeeds in explaining both the error and so much else about the practice.

5

Legal Positivism as a Realist Theory of Law

I. Introduction

By "legal positivism," I mean the view about the nature of law that H. L. A. Hart articulated most powerfully in 1961 (while learning from and modifying the work of Hans Kelsen), and that Joseph Raz developed further (although not always in a realist direction) in the 1970s and 1980s, according to which (1) where a legal system exists, there exists a "rule of recognition" specifying the criteria in virtue of which norms are valid law; and (2) a rule of recognition is nothing more than a complex psychosocial artifact constituted by the practice of officials, in particular, the criteria of legal validity they converge upon and which they treat as obligatory (in Hartian lingo: that they accept from "an internal point of view").[1] That means laws and legal systems rest at bottom on the conventional practices of officials.

By realist theories of law, I mean theories that (1) describe without sentimental or moralizing illusions what law is and how it actually operates in human societies (descriptive adequacy takes priority over moralizing sermons); (2) recognize that law is never adequate to explain how courts adjudicate all cases that come before them; and (3) account for law and adjudication within the constraints of a naturalistic theory of the world; that is, one that eschews appeal to any entities or properties that do not find a place in successful empirical scientific accounts of natural and social phenomena.[2] Both the American and Scandinavian (self-identified) "legal realists" were proponents of realist theories of law in this sense, albeit in very different ways, a point to which I return. Hart was a critic of both American and Scandinavian legal realisms, though in both cases, he missed his mark. The irony is that Hart's legal positivism is also a realist theory of law (more in the American than Scandinavian sense), and once we sort out the misunderstandings and confusions, it will be clear that legal positivists

[1] I take Hart's view to be an improvement on Kelsen's kind of positivism in several crucial respects, most importantly, in naturalizing the notion of validity via appeal to certain kinds of social practices (Hart, in this regard, has more in common with the Scandinavian Realist Alf Ross than he acknowledges, a point to which I return, below). There are other self-proclaimed positivists, some of whom are and some of whom are not. I put to one side the plethora of views that sometimes travel under the "positivist" label.

[2] See ch. 1 in this volume for the more detailed account of "legal realism."

From a Realist Point of View. Brian Leiter, Oxford University Press.
DOI: 10.1093/9780197749852.003.0006

and realists form a unified theoretical front against the moralizing and ideological obfuscators about law, from Lon Fuller to Ronald Dworkin. It will also turn out that one of Raz's additions to Hart's theory, namely, the idea that law necessarily claims authority in Raz's "Service Conception" sense, betrays the realist ambitions of Hart's theory.

II. The Realism of Hart's Legal Positivism

Hart's theory of law, as developed in *The Concept of Law*, is a realist theory in four important respects.

First, Hart recognizes that law in modern societies operates primarily outside the courts, namely, as a way of guiding ordinary people (sometimes with the help of lawyers) as to what they can and cannot do and, in particular, how they can acquire various legally created powers, such as the power to get married (and accrue the associated legal benefits) or the power to dispose of their property after their death. Any general *theory of law* that focuses primarily on courts is not realistic. It is not simply that courts decide only a minuscule fraction of all legal disputes (massive agreement about what the law requires, after all, is the norm in functioning legal systems [see ch. 2 in this volume]), it is that the primary function of law in modern societies is to help people organize their affairs to avoid disputes, either with other citizens or with the state: in other words, *to avoid* adjudication. Law tells people what they need to do to buy a house, to get divorced, to avoid tax penalties, and to enter into business relationships; it also sets conditions under which their freedom can be restricted or their property seized.

Second, adjudication of some legal disputes inevitably involves judgments that are not constrained by law but instead require the exercise of discretionary judgment, informed by non-legal considerations: the law is sometimes *rationally indeterminate* (i.e., the class of legitimate legal reasons underdetermines the decision the adjudicator must reach[3]). Any theory that presents adjudication as a matter of discovering preexisting answers in a legal heaven is not realistic. Rules determinate in their application in most instances can never be without uncertainty, unless they adopt patently absurd approaches, such as "When the rule is unclear, the plaintiff wins."[4] Hart saw, correctly, that indeterminacy in law was inevitable—though he was wrong in thinking the "open texture" of language was its primary cause (a point to which I return)—and he also saw correctly that this was not a feature of law anyone should try to remedy[5]: We are far better off

[3] See Brian Leiter, *Naturalizing Jurisprudence* (Oxford University Press, 2007), 9–12.
[4] Even such rules might be indeterminate, insofar as there can be penumbral cases of "unclear."
[5] H. L. A. Hart, *The Concept of Law*, 3rd ed. (Oxford: Clarendon Press, 2012), 128–30.

with officials who can produce an authoritative resolution of disputes that no one anticipated than we would be with a system that tried to settle every matter well in advance.

Third, the social phenomenon of law is explicable in wholly naturalistic terms, without recourse to objective moral values, or Kantian transcendental conditions on judgment: Law and legal systems exist entirely because of psychological and sociological facts about persons. On one reading, the claim that law is part of the natural order is bound to seem trivial (theists and others in the grips of religious illusions to one side): Is not everything part of the "natural order" of the world? But positivists and realists understand this claim in a more demanding way: Everything real is part of the causal account of nature developed by successful empirical sciences, whether physics, biology, or cognitive science. There are no facts outside the causal order of nature as described by the various sciences. Legal systems have important "normative" dimensions—officials and sometimes subjects take the system's demands to be obligation-imposing, for example—but this is really a complicated psychological and sociological fact about persons and their attitudes, not a fact about the world apart from those psychosocial facts about persons. Any theory that posits transcendental conditions on legal judgment (e.g., Kelsen) or mind-independent moral values (e.g., Dworkin) is not realistic.

Fourth, Hart recognizes that law is not necessarily a good thing, that governance by law has costs, and as a result, we should never presuppose that law is morally good or obligatory. This has been the central idea of the positivist tradition in legal theory: We can say what the normative system called "law" requires while recognizing that what the law demands may not be what we should do. Talk of law not being "morally binding" must, of course, be given a noncognitivist gloss, consistent with Hart's actual way of marking normative practices.[6] Any theory, like Dworkin's, that builds the justification of coercive power into the nature of law is not realistic.

III. Legal Realisms, American and Scandinavian

Hart contributed to the perception that legal positivism was not a realist theory of law by his famous, but ultimately misguided, criticisms of the American and Scandinavian legal realists. The fault is not entirely his, to be sure: the American legal realists were rhetorically exuberant, rather than analytically precise, and an

[6] Recall that for Hart, the ascription of the "internal point of view" to agents is based entirely on behavioral criteria (i.e., what actors do and say). This no doubt betrays the influence of Gilbert Ryle's behaviorism in philosophy of mind. See my discussion in "Back to Hart," *Belgrade Law Review* 69 (2021): 749–60.

unfortunate translation of Alf Ross's *Of Law and Justice* probably exacerbated the misunderstandings of the Scandinavian position.[7]

Hart also solidified the unfortunate assimilation of the two realisms, American and Scandinavian, when, in reality, they have almost nothing in common: Calling them both instances of "realism" is mainly an accident of intellectual history and a confusion about words. While the Scandinavians adopted the label "realism" to signal their opposition to metaphysical idealists, who thought the nature of reality was dependent on the human mind and its categories,[8] the Americans invoked a different sense of "realism"—partly colloquial and partly corresponding to an intellectual tradition stretching from Thucydides to Machiavelli and beyond—as being candid about *what really happens* (especially when courts decide cases), without sentimental or moralistic illusions.[9] The latter is the sense of realism I am mainly concerned with here.

The difference should hardly be surprising given the very different professional and intellectual backgrounds of the two groups. The major American Realists—Karl Llewellyn, Jerome Frank, Herman Oliphant, Max Radin, Underhill Moore, and William O. Douglas, among others—were law professors, lawyers, and jurists, with no philosophical training and, rather obviously, no aptitude for or interest in philosophical questions.[10] What they were all interested in was how courts actually decide cases, and what lawyers and law students needed to know if they were to reliably advise their clients about how they would fare in the courts. They advanced no theses about the nature of law apart from these practical litigation-oriented concerns, though it is striking that their tacit assumptions about the nature of law were all positivist ones, a point to which we will return.[11]

The Scandinavians were different: They were either primarily philosophers or had some formal training in philosophy, and all were primarily academics and scholars who conceived of their jurisprudential questions in philosophical terms. In contemporary terminology,[12] they were occupied with variations on what philosophers call the "location problem," that is, the problem of how to

[7] See the discussion in Brian Leiter and Max Etchemendy, "Naturalism in Legal Philosophy," in *The Stanford Encyclopedia of Philosophy*, ed. E. Zalta, § 5.1, *https://plato.stanford.edu/entries/lawphil-naturalism/* (drawing on and discussing work by Jakob Holtermann).

[8] Hägerstrom is a case in point. See Patricia Mindus, *A Real Mind: The Life and Work of Axel Hägerström* (Springer, 2009), 48. Mindus also notes other writers skeptical about the lumping together of Scandinavian and American Realism (ibid., 137 n. 2).

[9] See ch. 11 in this volume.

[10] Felix Cohen was the exception—although his philosophy PhD served him badly. *See, e.g.*, "Transcendental Nonsense and the Functional Approach". *Columbia Law Review* 35 (1935): 809-849, which arguably adopts an indefensible version of rule-skepticism. For discussion, *see* Leiter, *Naturalizing Jurisprudence*, 68-73.

[11] See Brian Leiter, "Legal Realism and Legal Positivism Reconsidered," reprinted in Leiter, *Naturalizing Jurisprudence*.

[12] Frank Jackson, *From Metaphysics to Ethics* (Oxford University Press, 1998).

locate some phenomenon (e.g., consciousness or moral value) in a world naturalistically conceived—that is, conceived in the causal terms described by the empirical sciences. So, for example, philosophers interested in the location problem might ask how we make sense of subjective conscious experience, or of the idea that something is morally wrong, in a world that is exhaustively explained by physics, chemistry and biology? Or how can we locate the experience of Beethoven's 9th Symphony as beautiful, or the sense that genocide is a moral abomination, in a world thought to be composed of nothing other than physical, chemical, biological, and/or psychological facts?

For the Scandinavian realists, the precise issue was how to locate a system of legal norms in a world so conceived. The Scandinavians were philosophically diverse on some issues, so generalizing about them will no doubt run roughshod over some individual differences. Yet there are two basic issues at stake: metaphysical (do these norms really exist?) and semantic (what is the *meaning* of legal statements mentioning such norms?). On the metaphysical question, there are elements of eliminativism in the views of Olivecrona and Ross. Just as the eliminativist about religious discourse thinks that the entities that religious discourse refers to (gods, souls, spirits) do not exist, and so should be eliminated from any realistic picture of what the world is like, the legal eliminativist thinks that legal obligations, legal rights, and legal duties do not really exist either, since such concepts play no role in a scientific explanation of the world. Because the Scandinavians sometimes seem to be eliminativists at the metaphysical level, they (generally) opt for "noncognitivist" views about the semantics, that is, views according to which *statements* about legal obligations, rights, and duties do not really try to refer to anything, but are simply the expression of the "attitudes" of legal actors.[13] So, for example, judgments about legal obligations and duties are interpreted as expressing certain noncognitive attitudes or feelings: A court's judgment of the form, "Mr. Smith has a contractual obligation to pay Mr. Jones $5,000 for those widgets" really means something like, "I, the judge, feel the force of the legal demand that Mr. Smith pay under these circumstances, and if he doesn't, I will sanction him!" The psychologism of some of the Scandinavians held that legal norms, both their existence and their effects on behavior, were to be explained in terms of the psychological states of persons who accepted these norms, rather than the reality of the norms: that X *believes* or *feels* he has a duty or obligation is what is explanatory of behavior, not the existence of the duty.[14]

[13] See the more detailed discussion in Leiter and Etchemendy, "Naturalism in Legal Philosophy," § 5.1. See also Torben Spaak, "Karl Olivecrona on Judicial Lawmaking," *Ratio Juris* 22 (2009): 483–98; Torben Spaak, "Karl Olivecrona's Legal Philosophy: A Critical Appraisal *Ratio Juris* 24 (2011): 163–65. As Patricia Mindus reminds me, Hägerstrom is an unusual case, opting for an error theory about "rights," but a kind of emotivism about judgments of moral value.

[14] See Mindus, *A Real Mind*, 142 n. 31.

A similar kind of psychologism is, I think, implicit in Hart, though he sometimes cannot quite acknowledge it, perhaps because of the influence of J. L. Austin's ordinary language philosophy on his thinking. This requires further explication.

Hart was a metaphysical antirealist about moral norms: Such norms do not really exist, since the best explanation of the world would not include facts about what is morally right and wrong. This might suggest that the *normativity* of morals—the ability of what is morally right and wrong to give people efficacious reasons to act—should be understood in exclusively psychological terms—i.e., as a psychological fact about what particular people believe and feel when they are told that "[i]t is morally wrong to do X" or "[i]t is morally right to Y." The most charitable reading of Hart should understand him as accepting something like this view, since, unlike Hans Kelsen, his was an "impure" theory of law, in which anti-realism about norms was conjoined with noncognitivism about the semantics of normative judgment: to judge that doing X is morally (or legally) wrong is just to express a certain kind of attitude or feeling, presumably one tied—psychologically—to motivation and action.[15] Hart did, of course, reject the view he attributed to Alf Ross, namely, that legal *validity* consists in "a verifiable hypothesis about future judicial behavior and its special motivational feeling."[16] (Hart failed to realize that this was a stipulative account in Ross, not an ordinary language account: Ross wanted to show how we could "locate" doctrinal or "external" statements about what the law is in a world naturalistically conceived,[17] a point to which I return.) For Hart, to say that a legal rule is *valid* is just to say that it satisfies the criteria of legal validity in the rule of recognition. But neither I nor Ross is denying Hart's conceptual point about judgments by legal actors about legal validity, namely, that its meaning is not reducible to predictions about behavior: Even Ross's treatment of such judgments was noncognitive, like Hart's.[18] Rather, the point at issue here concerns what an anti-realism about *norms*, which Hart accepts, entails about motivation and action. On the realist/naturalist view, to the extent an agent's judgment that X is *morally right* (or *legally obligatory*) has normative force for the agent, that normative force is explicable in terms of certain psychological facts about the agent. Hart sometimes seems to deny this, for example, when he says that "the internal character of [normative legal judgments, like, 'You must stop at the red light'] is not a mere matter

[15] Cf. Kevin Toh, "Hart's Expressivism and His Benthamite Project, *Legal Theory* 11 (2005): 75–123.

[16] See H. L. A. Hart, "Scandinavian Realism," in *Essays in Jurisprudence and Philosophy* (Oxford University Press, 1983), 165.

[17] Ross took naturalism to require verificationism about meaning. I discuss Ross's view in more detail in "Alf Ross's Critique of American Legal Realism—and a Naturalistic Critique of Ross," available at https://papers.ssrn.com/sol3/papers.cfm?abstract_id=4240991.

[18] See Alf Ross, *On Law and Justice*, ed. J. Holtermann, trans. U. Bindreiter (Oxford University Press, 2019), 20–26.

of the speaker having certain 'feelings of compulsion"; for though these may indeed often accompany the making of such statements they are neither necessary nor sufficient conditions of their normative use in criticizing conduct, making claims and justifying hostile reactions by reference to the accepted standard."[19] But Hart is best understood here as simply revealing his commitment to a kind of Rylean behaviorism about attitude ascriptions: agents manifest the "internal point of view" simply by virtue of using the right kind of normative language and making the right kinds of justificatory or critical comments about, respectively, conforming or deviant behavior vis-à-vis some rule.[20] Contemporary naturalists have no reason to accept the behaviorism, given the explanatory fruitfulness of psychological explanations in so many domains.

In sum, the Scandinavians have deeper affinities with the great Austrian legal positivist Hans Kelsen and the great English legal positivist H. L. A. Hart than they do with the American realists: the latter want to figure out why courts decide as they do, and then let lawyers in on the *real* causes accordingly; while all the former (i.e., Kelsen, Hart, and the Scandinavians) are interested in traditional philosophical questions about the nature of law and (in the case of Hart and the Scandinavians) how it can be located within a naturalistic worldview, that is, one that takes for granted that the world is, more or less, as the sciences describe it. Hart and the Scandinavians differ from Kelsen in their willingness to think the answer can involve "naturalizing" certain normative concepts in law, that is, understanding them as complicated psychological and sociological artifacts, and thus as part of what Kelsen would have understood to be an "impure" theory of law.[21]

IV. Hart's Mistaken Critique of Legal Realism

Hart attributes to legal realism a view he calls "rule-skepticism," a view he deems correct in certain instances (consistent with his own realism about adjudication). Hart considers two different kinds of rule-skepticism. One, which I will call "Conceptual Rule-Skepticism," holds that "talk of rules is a myth, cloaking the truth that law consists simply of the decisions of courts and the predictions of them."[22] The second is the only important kind for his putative dispute with legal realism, which I will call "Empirical Rule-Skepticism." According to this view, "rule-skepticism has a serious claim on our attention, but only as a theory

[19] Hart, *The Concept of Law*, 167

[20] See again, Leiter, "Back to Hart."

[21] I've explored that possibility as well: see the essays in Part II of Leiter, *Naturalizing Jurisprudence*.

[22] Hart, *Concept of Law*, 133.

of the function of rules in judicial decision"[23]; more precisely, this realist/skeptic claims "that it is false, if not senseless, to regard judges as themselves subject to rules or 'bound' to decide cases as they do."[24]

Conceptual rule-skepticism grows out of Hart's conflation of the American and Scandinavian realists. Conceptual rule-skepticism is a claim about the nature of law—that is, that it consists only in what courts say or in predictions of what courts will do. Hart's critique of this as an account of the nature of law as reflected in ordinary language is wholly persuasive, in my view[25]: such a theory of the ordinary concept of law cannot account for how judges think about what the law "obligates" them to do, or about the way in which lawyers and citizens criticize judicial conduct by reference to the law. But did either the Scandinavians or the Americans endorse conceptual rule-skepticism?

Alf Ross, as we have seen, did proffer something like this, but not because he thought it was adequate to the "ordinary" usage of the concept of law, or because he was insensitive to the points Hart raised. He proffered such an analysis as part of a philosophical reconstruction of statements about what the law is by scholars, one that would make sense of its normative concepts in a world naturalistically conceived: by reinterpreting normative claims about "duties" and "obligations" as empirical predictive claims, Ross aimed to show that law was not polluted with metaphysical nonsense but rather was empirically verifiable. Ross was not doing ordinary language philosophy about how things looked to legal insiders; Hart was. Hart criticized Ross as offering an implausible analysis of the "ordinary" concept; Ross would have agreed. Hart offered no direct response to the actual "location problem" Ross was concerned with.

In the case of the American realists, Hart was also guilty of misreading, although in fairness to him, at least one realist, Felix Cohen, was, arguably, a conceptual rule-skeptic, although Cohen is nowhere cited by Hart: Hart's American legal realism relies on an amalgamation mainly of Frank, Holmes, and Llewellyn. Plainly these writers do talk about the importance of "predicting" what courts will do. The question is whether, in so talking, they are fairly read as offering an analysis of the concept of law. Only Hart's grossly anachronistic reading suggests an affirmative answer.

The idea that philosophy involves "conceptual analysis" via the analysis of language (or appeals to intuitions about how concepts or terms apply) is an artifact of Anglo-American analytic philosophy of the twentieth century; indeed, as practiced by Hart, it really reflects the influence of fashionable views in philosophy of language current at Oxford in the 1940s and 1950s. The American

[23] Ibid., 135.
[24] Ibid.
[25] Cf. Leiter, *Naturalizing Jurisprudence*, 69–73.

realists were not philosophers, let alone analytic philosophers, let alone students of G. E. Moore, Russell, and Wittgenstein, let alone colleagues of J. L. Austin. The idea that what demands understanding about law is the "concept" of law as manifest in ordinary language and ordinary intuitions would have struck them as bizarre. While the realists had much to say about adjudication and how legal rules work in practice, they had nothing explicit to say about the "ordinary" concept of law or our intuitions about it.[26]

So what did the American realists mean in talking about "prediction"? In *Law and the Modern Mind*, Jerome Frank cautions the reader early on that he "is primarily concerned with 'law' as it affects the work of the practicing lawyer and the needs of the clients who retain him."[27] Holmes begins "The Path of the Law" by emphasizing that he is talking about the meaning of law to lawyers who will "appear before judges, or . . . advise people in such a way as to keep them out of court."[28] Against this background, infamous statements like Llewellyn's—"What these officials do about disputes is, to my mind, the law itself"[29]—make perfect sense. Theirs is not a claim about the "concept" of law, but rather a claim about a practical heuristic, how it is helpful to think about law for attorneys who must advise clients what to do. For your client the franchisee in Connecticut doesn't simply want to know what the rule on the books in Connecticut says; he wants to know what will happen when he takes the franchisor to court. So from the practical perspective of the franchisee, what one wants to know about the "law" is what, in fact, the courts will do when confronted with the franchisee's grievance. That is all the law that matters to the client, all the law that matters to the lawyer advising that client. And that is all the American realists wanted to emphasize.

Ironically, it turns out the American realists could not have been conceptual rule-skeptics, because their arguments for the indeterminacy of law actually presuppose the positivist's concept of law. The central claim of legal indeterminacy is the claim of rational indeterminacy: the claim that the "class of legal reasons" fails to justify a unique outcome in some or all cases. The "class of legal reasons" is the class of reasons that are taken to properly justify a legal conclusion (and thus "compel" it insofar as legal actors are responsive to valid legal reasons). So,

[26] Raz and his followers often obscure this point. Raz, for example, claims that the argument for his "hard" or "exclusive" positivism "is not an argument from the ordinary sense of 'law' or any other term. It relies on fundamental features of our understanding of a certain social institution, the primary examples of which are contemporary municipal legal systems. . . ." Joseph Raz, *The Authority of Law* (Oxford University Press, 1979), 50. But all his examples are examples of ordinary or familiar distinctions people draw between law and other normative systems, between legal and other kinds of normative competence. The giveaway is the appeal to "our understanding of a certain social institution": What could that possibly be other than an armchair report of what Raz takes people to say and believe about law?

[27] Jerome Frank, *Law and the Modern Mind* (Brentano's, 1930), 47 note.

[28] O. W. Holmes, "The Path of the Law," *Harvard Law Review* 10 (1897): 457.

[29] Karl Llewellyn, *The Bramble Bush* (Oceana, 1930), 3.

for example, appeal to a statutory provision or a valid precedent are parts of the class of legal reasons in the United States, while appeal to the authority of Plato's *Republic* is not: A judge is not obliged to decide one way rather than another because Plato says so. Any argument for indeterminacy, then, presupposes some view about the boundaries of the class of legal reasons. When Herman Oliphant[30] argues, for example, that the promise-not-to-compete cases are decided not by reference to law but by reference to uncodified norms prevalent in the commercial culture in which the disputes arose, this only shows that the law is indeterminate on the assumption that the normative reasons the courts are actually relying upon are not themselves legal reasons.[31] So, too, when Holmes chalks up judicial decisions not to legal reasoning but to "a concealed, half-conscious battle on the [background] question of legislative policy"[32] he is plainly presupposing that these policy concerns are not themselves legal reasons. The famous American realist arguments for indeterminacy which focus on the conflicting, but equally legitimate, ways lawyers have of interpreting statutes and precedents[33] only show that the law is indeterminate on the assumption either that statutes and precedents largely exhaust the authoritative sources of law or that any additional authoritative norms not derived from these sources conflict. It is the former assumption that seems to motivate the realist arguments. Thus, Llewellyn says that judges take rules "in the main from authoritative sources (which in the case of law are largely statutes and the decisions of the courts)."[34] In short, the American realists presuppose something like the positivist idea of a rule of recognition whose criteria of legality are exclusively ones of pedigree: A rule (or canon of construction) is part of the law by virtue of having a source in a legislative enactment or a prior court decision.[35]

Matters are more interesting with respect to what I am calling empirical rule-skepticism. Here is Hart's characterization of the view in question:

[30] Herman Oliphant, "A Return to Stare Decisis," *American Bar Association Journal* 14 (1928): 71–76.

[31] According to Oliphant, the courts found ways to enforce promises by sellers of business not to compete with purchasers, because this made good economic sense: there would be no point to the transaction otherwise. By contrast, courts found ways to invalidate promises not to compete by employees by employers, since such arrangements were disfavored by trade guilds and took unfair advantage of the bargaining position of employees.

[32] Holmes, "The Path of the Law," 467.

[33] The classic discussions are Llewellyn, *The Bramble Bush,* 72–76; Max Radin, "Statutory Interpretation," *Harvard Law Review* 43 (1930); Karl Llewellyn, "Remarks on the Theory of Appellate Decision and the Rules or Canons about How Statutes Are to Be Construed," *Vanderbilt Law Review* 3 (1950): 395–406.

[34] Karl Llewellyn, "Some Realism about Realism—Responding to Dean Pound," *Harvard Law Review* 44 (1931): 13.

[35] One difference is that most positivists recognize customary practices as sources of valid law, whereas it is not clear what the realists think about this.

> [I]t amounts to the contention that, so far as the courts are concerned, there is nothing to circumscribe the open texture [of language in which rules are framed]: so that it is false, if not senseless, to regard judges as themselves subject to rules or "bound" to decide cases as they do. They may act with sufficient predictable regularity and uniformity to enable others, over long periods, to live by courts' decisions as rules. Judges may even experience feelings of compulsion when they decide as they do, and these feelings may be predictable too; but beyond this there is nothing which can be characterized as a rule which they observe.[36]

Empirical rule-skepticism on this rendering, then, involves two claims: (1) legal rules are indeterminate; and, as a result, (2) legal rules do not determine or constrain decisions.

Obviously (1) is not an empirical claim, but a philosophical or jurisprudential one. But (2) could be true even if (1) were false (that would be pure empirical rule-skepticism, we might say). Yet Hart is surely correct that most American realists endorse both (1) and (2). Unfortunately, Hart is mistaken about the realist argument for (1), and thus underestimates the amount of indeterminacy in law. And the real dispute, if there is one, between the American realists and Hart turns in the end on (2).

Remember that Hart acknowledges that legal rules are indeterminate but claims that is a phenomenon at "the margin of rules"[37]; the realist skeptic, on Hart's rendering, is simply "a disappointed absolutist,"[38] someone who set the bar for legal determinacy too high. But the American realists, with some exceptions (notably Jerome Frank), recognized that law was mostly rationally determinate; they pointed out that it tended to be indeterminate, however, in those cases that reached the stage of appellate review. And they argued for that proposition based on the empirical evidence of lines of appellate cases that could not be rationalized in terms of the official doctrine. Their argument for indeterminacy was different from Hart's, which may help explain the *apparent* disagreement.

According to Hart, legal rules are indeterminate because "there is a limit, inherent in the nature of language, to the guidance which general language can provide."[39] Language is, in Hart's famous phrase, "open-textured":

> There will indeed be plain cases constantly recurring in similar contexts to which general expressions are clearly applicable ("If anything is a vehicle a

[36] Hart, *Concept of Law*, 135.
[37] Ibid.
[38] Ibid.
[39] Ibid., 123.

> motor-car is one") but there will also be cases where it is not clear whether they apply or not. ("Does 'vehicle' used here include bicycles, airplanes, roller skates?"). The latter are fact-situations, continually thrown up by nature or human invention, which possess only some of the features of the plain cases but others which they lack.[40]

Language is "open-textured" in that while words have "core" instances—aspects of the world that clearly fall within the extension of the word's meaning—they also have "penumbras," cases where it is unclear whether the extension includes the aspect of the world at issue. In cases in which the facts fall within the penumbra of the key words in the applicable legal rule, a court "must exercise a discretion, [since] there is no possibility of treating the question raised . . . as if there were one uniquely correct answer to be found, as distinct from an answer which is a reasonable compromise between many conflicting interests."[41]

While some writers have challenged the implicit semantics that informs this argument for the indeterminacy of language (a fortiori of law),[42] I think we should agree with Hart that legal rules must necessarily be indeterminate in some measure given the indeterminacy of language itself, and that this type of indeterminacy resides "at the margin of rules."[43] What bears noting here is that the American realist arguments for indeterminacy did not rely on these claims about language.

The American realists located the indeterminacy of law not in general features of language itself, but in the existence of equally legitimate, but conflicting, canons of interpretation that courts could employ to extract differing rules from the same statutory text or the same precedent.[44] Indeterminacy resides not in the rules themselves, but in the ways we have of characterizing what rules statutes and precedents contain. Llewellyn, for example, argues that any precedent can be read "strictly" or "loosely," and that either reading is "recognized, legitimate, honorable."[45] The strict interpretation characterizes the rule of the case as specific to the facts of the case; the loose interpretation abstracts (in varying degrees) from the specific facts to treat the case as standing for some general norm. But if "each precedent has not one value [that is, stands for not just one rule], but two, and . . . the two are wide apart, and . . . whichever value a later court assigns to it, such assignment will be respectable, traditionally sound, dogmatically correct,"[46]

40 Ibid., 128.
41 Ibid.
42 For criticism of such approaches, see Leiter and Etchemendy, "Naturalism in Legal Philosophy," § 5.3.
43 Hart, *Concept of Law*, 132.
44 I take it something similar is true of the Italian legal realists of the Genoa School.
45 Llewellyn, *Bramble Bush*, 74.
46 Ibid., 76.

then precedent, as a source of law, cannot provide reasons for a unique outcome, because more than one rule can be extracted from the same precedent.

Llewellyn thinks the same is true of statutory interpretation, where one can find "'correct,' unchallengeable rules of 'how to read' which lead in happily variant directions."[47] By mining the cases, Llewellyn shows that courts have endorsed contradictory canons of construction, like "A statute cannot go beyond its text," but also "To effect its purpose a statute must be implemented beyond its text."[48] But if a statute can properly be construed in contradictory ways to stand for different rules, then reasoning from the statute will not justify a unique outcome in the case at hand.

One difficulty with these realist arguments is that they rely on a tacit conception of legitimate legal argument. The assumption is that if lawyers and courts employ some form of argument—a "strict" construal of precedent, a particular canon of statutory construction—then that form of argument is legitimate in any and all cases. Put in this strong form, the assumption cannot be right: not every strict construal of precedent will be legally proper in every case. Even Llewellyn must recognize this, as suggested by his famous—but clearly facetious—example of the strict reading that yields, "This rule holds only of redheaded Walpoles in pale magenta Buick cars."[49] But that would never be a legitimate construal of a precedent (barring some bizarre scenario in which all these facts turned out to be legally relevant), and Llewellyn surely knows as much. The claim cannot be, then, that any strict or loose construal of precedent is always valid. It must only be that lawyers and judges have this interpretive latitude often enough to inject a considerable degree of indeterminacy in to law.[50]

Notice that the realist argument for empirical rule-skepticism is conceptually severable from the claim that the law is indeterminate. Centrally, it is based on the observation that the decisions courts reach do not fall into patterns that correlate with the rules they invoke; rather, the decisions reflect judges' responses to the underlying facts of the cases. This was the point of Oliphant's example of the promise-not-to-compete cases mentioned earlier; it is Llewellyn's point too in his discussion of the New York sales cases.[51] What causes judges to decide as they

[47] Llewellyn, "Remarks on the Theory of Appellate Decision," 399.
[48] Llewellyn, *Bramble Bush*, 90.
[49] Ibid., 72.
[50] Leslie Green has objected that there appears no principled explanation why the indeterminacy should not go "all the way down," as it were. See Leslie Green, "Realism and the Sources of Law," in *The Germ of Justice* (Oxford University Press, 2023). The key to an answer, however, is precisely that the argument depends on a "sociological" notion of which interpretations of sources are "legitimate," meaning accepted by most lawyers and judges. Lawyers and judges may, of course, treat interpretive moves as acceptable even without a principled basis for doing so. For a more extended discussion of this issue, see ch. 7 in this volume.
[51] Karl Llewellyn, *The Common Law Tradition* (Little, Brown, 1960), 22–124. According to Llewellyn, a series of New York cases applied the rule that a buyer who rejects the seller's shipment by formally stating his objections thereby waives all other objections. Llewellyn observed that the rule

do, according to the realist, is not legal rules[52] but a sense of what would be fair or appropriate on the facts of the case at hand. All American realists agreed on this point. Judge Hutcheson claimed that "the vital, motivating impulse for the decision is an intuitive sense of what is right or wrong for that cause."[53] Frank invoked the example of "a great American judge," Chancellor Kent, who had confessed that "[h]e first made himself 'master of the facts.' Then (he wrote) 'I saw where justice lay, and the moral sense decided the court half the time; I then sat down to search the authorities . . . but I almost always found principles suited to my view of the case."[54] Llewellyn noted that to understand what appellate courts are really doing, one must appreciate "how far the proposition which seems so abstract has roots in what seems to be the due thing on the facts [before the court]."[55] As a result, Llewellyn's advice for the lawyer was "on the facts . . . [to] persuade the court your case is sound," even if the lawyer must also provide a "technical ladder" to the "sound" result.[56] Frank pointed out that a former president of the American Bar Association had given the very same advice.[57] In short, the core of the realist defense of empirical rule-skepticism is, in fact, empirical: They looked at what the courts (primarily the appellate courts) really did, and found that legal rules were clearly not the determining factors in a large number of cases.

At the same time, the realists—unlike many of the later Critical Legal Studies writers—did not overstate the irrelevance of rules. For one thing, the American realists were (generally) clear that their focus was indeterminacy at the stage of appellate review, where one ought to expect a higher degree of uncertainty in the law. Cases that have determinate legal answers are, after all, less likely to be litigated to the stage of appellate review. Most of the time, the realists seemed to understand this point. Thus, Llewellyn explicitly qualified his indeterminacy

seemed to have been harshly applied in some cases where the buyers simply may not have known at the time of rejection of other defects, or where the seller could not have cured in any case. Upon looking at the underlying facts of the cases, however, Llewellyn discovered that in each case where the rule seemed to have been harshly applied, what had really happened was that the market had gone sour, and the buyer was looking to escape the contract. The court, being "sensitive to commerce or to decency" (ibid., 124) applied the unrelated rule about rejection to frustrate the buyer's attempted violation of a basic norm of commercial conduct: namely, parties should honor their commitments even under changed market conditions. It is, in short, the "background facts, those of mercantile practice, those of the situation-type" (ibid., 126) that determine the court's decision.

[52] Some legal rules, of course, structure the presentation of facts to the court, and thus "the facts of the case at hand" are unintelligible without legal rules. Conceding this point does not change the fact, however, that there still may be a disjunction (as the realists claim) between the substantive rules of law that judges invoke in their decisions and the real bases for their decisions.

[53] Joseph C. Hutcheson, "The Judgment Intuitive: The Function of the 'Hunch' in Judicial Decisions," *Cornell Law Quarterly* 14 (1929): 285.

[54] Frank, *Law and the Modern Mind*, 104 note.

[55] Llewellyn, *Bramble Bush*, 29.

[56] Ibid., 76.

[57] Frank, *Law and the Modern Mind*, 102 note.

claim by saying that "in any case doubtful enough to make litigation respectable the available authoritative premises . . . are at least two, and . . . the two are mutually contradictory as applied to the case at hand."[58] And Max Radin noted that judicial "decisions will consequently be called for chiefly in what may be called marginal cases, in which prognosis is difficult and uncertain. It is this fact that makes the entire body of legal judgments seem less stable than it really is."[59] Empirical rule-skepticism is surely more plausible when it is not advanced as a global claim about adjudication and the law.

Notice now that even if we agreed with Hart that the open texture of language affects rules only "at the margins" (whatever that means, a point to which we return), the realists have now given us an additional reason (beyond Hart's) to expect indeterminacy in law. If the realists are right, then not only do legal rules suffer from the open texture that Hart describes, but statutes and precedents will frequently admit of "manipulation"—legally legitimate manipulation, of course—and thus be indeterminate in this additional respect as well. The combination of sources of interdeterminacy (the open texture of language and the conflicting canons of interpretation) seems sufficient to move indeterminacy from the margins to the center of cases actually litigated through the stage of appellate review.

Hart is not wholly insensitive to the realist arguments, though he treats them cursorily. In response to Llewellyn's point, for example, that a court can interpret a precedent both "loosely" and "strictly" and thus extract two different rules from the same prior decision, Hart says simply this: "[I]n the vast majority of decided cases there is very little doubt [as to the rule of the case]. The head-note is usually correct enough."[60] Alas, a first-year litigation associate knows that this approach to precedent would be a recipe for disaster. To extract "holdings" without regard to the facts of the case—which is all a head-note typically provides—is mediocre lawyering. Skillful lawyers know exactly what Llewellyn describes: that the "rule" of a prior case can be stated at differing degrees of specificity, and so made to do very different rhetorical work depending on the needs of the case at hand.

So both Hart and the American realists acknowledge indeterminacy in law, and both acknowledge, accordingly, that rules do not determine decisions in some range of cases. Hart seems to think they disagree over the range of cases about which these claims hold true, but that is not entirely clear. Consider Hart's ultimate rejoinder to Realist skepticism about the influence of legal rules on court decisions:

[58] Llewellyn, "Some Realism about Realism," 1239.
[59] Max Radin, "In Defense of Unsystematic Science of Law," *Yale Law Journal* 51 (1942): 1271.
[60] Hart, *Concept of Law*, 131.

> [I]t is surely evident that for the most part decisions . . . are reached either by genuine effort to conform to rules consciously taken as guiding standards of decision or, if intuitively reached, are justified by rules which the judge was antecedently disposed to observe and whose relevance to the case in hand would generally be acknowledged.[61]

There is, alas, no argument here: "[I]t is surely evident" is simply a denial of what the realist affirms, yet offers no evidence for the denial other than Hart's armchair confidence in the correctness of his own view.

But perhaps Hart and the American realists are not really disagreeing? That may seem surprising, but I now think it is the most plausible interpretation, given the clear realist elements in Hart's own views, and the clear positivist elements in the views of the American realists. After all, when Hart limits indeterminacy to the "margin of rules," this is against the backdrop of one of his central insights, namely, that law exists mainly *outside* the courts as a way for individuals to plan their affairs and guide their conduct. The American realists sometimes make the "American mistake" (think of Dworkin) of focusing far too much on courts, but if we put that parochial prejudice aside, they have no theoretical reason to deny Hart's insight. And that insight is compatible with recognition that cases that reach the stage of appellate review are especially likely to be ones where the law is indeterminate, precisely for "selection effect" reasons: [P]arties have more incentive to pursue further litigation when the law is unclear and the result could go either way. Hart has no theoretical reason to deny this latter point.

Remember also that the American realists explicitly did not discount the role of rules in adjudication. Llewellyn is representative when he asks, "Do I suggest that . . . the 'accepted rules,' the rules the judges say that they apply, are without influence upon their actual behavior?" and answers, "I do not."[62] The realist approach, says Llewellyn, "admits . . . some relation between any accepted rule and judicial behavior" but then demands that what that relation is requires empirical investigation, since it is not always the relation suggested by the "logic" (or content) of the rule.[63] As he puts the point elsewhere: Realists deny that "traditional . . . rule-formulations are the heavily operative factor in producing court decisions."[64] But to deny only this claim is to admit that rules play some causal role in decisions.

We thus arrive at a possible *rapprochement* between two schools of Anglophone realist jurisprudence, that of Hart's positivism and the legal realists. Both Hart and the American realists agree that valid legal rules (i.e., those with

[61] Ibid., 137.
[62] Llewellyn, "A Realistic Jurisprudence—The Next Step," *Columbia Law Review* 30 (1930): 444.
[63] Ibid.
[64] Llewellyn, "Some Realism about Realism," 1237.

the relevant pedigree) matter, that they are often determinate in their application, and that at the higher levels of adjudication, indeterminacy obtains and judges must exercise discretion. In addition, the Scandinavian realists can agree that Hart has a satisfactory account of the "ordinary" concept of law, while disagreeing whether the best attempt to solve the location problem for law in a world conceived naturalistically requires the theoretical artifice of recasting normative talk in law in predictive terms or whether a noncognitivist approach, that arguably Hart favors, will suffice for statements about the law by both legal actors and observers. And all the realists and the positivists agree that law does not always suffice to explain what happens in adjudication, and all reject the objectivity of moral values. Even if there can be reasonable doubts about whether the muddle-headed American realists understood all these points, or whether the Scandinavian realists, in the grips (generally) of logical positivism, did, we can affirm that sensible realist jurisprudence can and must affirm them.

V. Realism, Positivism, and Raz's Authority Argument

In the recent positivist tradition, the most influential contribution to the theory comes from Hart's student Raz, who argued, against Hart, that no rule of recognition at the foundation of a legal system could incorporate moral, or content-based, criteria of legal validity.[65] Although the practice of officials determines the content of a rule of recognition—those criteria of legal validity that they converge upon and treat as obligatory—it cannot, on Raz's view, rely on criteria of legal validity that require judges to assess the content of the norms to determine their legal validity. According to Raz, law necessarily claims authority, even if it ultimately lacks a justification for that claim, and only source-based criteria of legal validity are compatible with the possibility of law claiming authority. A legal system can only claim authority if it is possible to identify its directives without reference to the underlying ("dependent") reasons for that directive. This is a "prerequisite" for claiming authority because what distinguishes a (practical) authority in the first place is that its directives preempt consideration of the underlying reasons (including, e.g., moral reasons) for what we ought to do, and in so doing actually makes it more likely that we will do what we really ought to do. Hart's "soft positivism," as well as Dworkin's view, however, make the identification of law depend on the very reasons that authoritative directives are supposed to preempt, and thus makes it impossible for law to fulfill its function of providing authoritative guidance. Thus, to the extent judges purport to treat norms as legally binding based on their appealing moral or other normative

[65] Joseph Raz, "Authority, Law and Morality," *The Monist* 68 (1985): 295–324.

content, they are simply exercising discretion under the mask of doing what the law requires.

Soft positivists, defenders of Hart's own official view in his "Postscript," have lodged various objections to Raz's argument. From a realist point of view, however, the worry about Raz's argument is that it presupposes a highly moralized and unrealistic conception of what it is for law to claim "authority." Raz understands authority in terms of what he calls "the Service Conception," in which a claim to authority is a claim to provide a subject of authority better "reasons" for acting in accordance with what Raz calls "right reason" than the subject would arrive at without the intermediation of the authority.[66] (We can gloss, for purposes here, "right reason" as *what one really ought to do.*) We can bracket for a moment the extravagant metaphysics of reasons such a view requires—though it is hard to see how to make sense of the objective existence of such reasons from a naturalistic point of view[67]—and make a more modest objection: Why think that when law claims authority, it is claiming to help its subjects do *what they really ought to do*? Of course, law always *claims authority* in the sense of claiming the right to tell those subject to its jurisdiction what they must do, but the idea that this claim to authority is a claim to Raz's service conception looks like ideological obfuscation. On the one hand, the ruling class that controls any legal system will always claim the right to command, and will often offer moralized rationalizations for that right, but why take that seriously? On the other hand, legal systems claim authority to direct their subjects' behavior for all kinds of reasons that have nothing to do with performing a "service" for their subjects (the greater glory of Rome, pleasing the King or God, defending the honor of the King or God, etc.). One can imagine a Razian redescribing these justifications as reasons for acting that purport to perform the service of bringing the subjects closer to "right reason," but this mischaracterizes what most legal systems in history, and even in the present, are doing when they claim the right to command: whether their subjects have reasons to obey these commands (beyond prudential ones, i.e., fear of sanction) is irrelevant to most legal authorities.

Raz's account of authority exposes his repudiation of realism in legal theory: Against Hart's realist aim of a "descriptive jurisprudence," Raz asserts, "there is an interdependence between conceptual and normative argument"[68] such that the account "does not necessarily conform to everyone's notion of authority in every detail. It does claim to be an explanatory account in singling out important features of people's conception of authority."[69] Of course, no theorist thinks their descriptive account conforms "to everyone's notion . . . in

[66] Ibid.

[67] See chs. 15 and 16 in this volume.

[68] Raz, *The Morality of Freedom* (Oxford Clarendon Press, 1986), 63.

[69] Ibid., 65.

every detail," so this is just a distraction. But where is the evidence that Raz's account even captures some "important features of people's [which people?] conception of authority"? Raz, I fear, has simply smuggled in a moralized (and ideologically loaded) conception of authority[70]—as providing a service for its subjects—without even the pretense that it satisfies even lax evidential demands of a "descriptive sociology" as Hart, the realist, proposed.

Does that mean Hart was correct in the "Postscript" that rules of recognition can incorporate content-based criteria of legal validity?[71] Not quite, though perhaps not for the reasons I have given previously. Hart himself, recall, agrees that a satisfactory account of law must explain how the law fulfills an *epistemic* function, i.e., enabling *at least* officials to recognize what the law is in many if not all cases. (Hart himself in "The Postscript" thought soft positivism was compatible with such an epistemic function.) I am, however, now skeptical about the argument I defended in 2007,[72] about what I called the "Extreme Scenario." In this scenario, it would be part of the conventional practice of officials to treat "Natural Law" as the obligatory criterion of legal validity. Of course, the whole history of the world shows the requirements of the putative "natural law" are a subject of massive controversy (because there is no such thing),[73] which might appear to mean that if a rule of recognition treated "natural law" as the sole criterion of legal validity, it could not discharge any epistemic function. The problem with this kind of objection—apart from its trading on conceptual possibilities not nomic actualities—is that under concrete historical and social circumstances, agents often do converge on parts of what they take to be "natural law," and thus appeals to natural law can serve an epistemic function.

[70] Moralized in the sense that its main aim is to explain why deference to authority by rational subjects can be justified.

[71] Scott Shapiro offers a slightly different argument against soft positivism, one that relies not on a claim about authority but on a claim about what it is to be "guided" by a rule. "On Hart's Way Out," *Legal Theory* 4 (1998): 469–507. (As Shapiro rightly notes, "Hart . . . has always claimed that the essence of law is the guidance of conduct" [ibid., 487]). According to Shapiro, one is "motivationally" guided by a legal rule when one's "conformity is motivated by the fact that the rule regulates the conduct in question" (ibid., 490). Shapiro argues that on Hart's view, the rule of recognition must provide motivational guidance to officials (ibid., 492) but that a rule of recognition incorporating content-based criteria cannot make a "practical difference" to the judges: "The rule makes a practical difference to one's practical reasoning [reasoning about what one ought to do] only if, in this counterfactual circumstance, the agent might not conform to the rule" (ibid., 495). But, argues Shapiro, a rule of recognition incorporating moral criteria could provide no motivational guidance, since judges are already motivated to do what morality requires. It should be obvious why this argument fails, even if its conceptual claim about "providing guidance" is correct: first, it is unrealistic to think that judges are already motivated to do what morality requires (sometimes they may be, sometimes they may not be); and second, even if individual judges were motivated to act morally, there is no evidence that their understanding of morality coincides with what the rule of recognition demands of them.

[72] Leiter, *Naturalizing Jurisprudence*, 126–27.

[73] See Brian Leiter, "Politics by Other Means: The Jurisprudence of 'Common Good' Constitutionalism," *University of Chicago Law Review* 90 (2023): 1699–1704. See also ch. 15 in this volume.

Hart's own view of meaning—in terms of what competent speakers of a language would take to be extensions of particular terms—should have led him to realize as much: "due process" and "equal protection" may have bigger penumbras than "vehicle," but they still also have a core set of applications which speakers of the same language—and thus adherents to the same moral ideology manifest in that language—will agree upon. And that means that content-based tests of legal validity are not all the same: Some are really ideological covers for exercises of discretion (as hard positivists have always correctly emphasized), but others may simply involve *exactly the same* kind of interpretive approach as with respect to any rule with the right pedigree—that is, appeal to a competent speaker's understanding of the term (except, of course, where pedigreed rules of interpretation dictate otherwise). We may still, from a positivist/realist point of view, reject the idea of *genuine* content-based criteria of legal validity, but that would be on the grounds of the explanatory fruitfulness of that way of demarcating the legal from the nonlegal[74] and not from claims about the concept of authority. Law claims authority, but not in Raz's sense; judges sometimes treat moral considerations as criteria of legal validity, but in the same way they treat the ordinary understanding of "vehicle" as a criterion of applied legal validity in a particular case, and the best explanation of law does not need to countenance as "law" those cases where judges treat moral considerations as criteria of legal validity where that judgment depends entirely on substantive moral judgment and argument.[75]

[74] Leiter, *Naturalizing Jurisprudence*, 175–80.

[75] Thanks to participants in the conference in Stockholm in November 2018 for useful discussion and comments—especially Patricia Mindus, Torben Spaak, and Kevin Toh. Thanks also to Michael Sevel for helpful discussion of Raz's views and Joshua Fox for research assistance.

6

Realism about Precedent

I. Precedent and Judgments of "Relevant Similarity"

In jurisdictions with a doctrine of precedent (or *stare decisis*), later courts are supposed to be bound by the decisions (the *ratio* or holding) of earlier courts, either those above them in a chain of authority (vertical precedent) or their own earlier decisions (horizontal precedent, where the later incarnation of the same court usually retains the option of overruling its earlier decision). The later court, in either the vertical or horizontal cases, is bound *only* by those decisions which are "on point" or "the same in relevant respects" to the case currently before the court. Since cases are never identical in all particulars, this always requires figuring out which general categories that subsume the particulars of different cases are the *relevant* ones: I will call this "relevant similarity" in what follows. Relevant similarity is typically assessed in light of either the reasons the earlier court actually gave for the decision or the reasons that can be imputed to the earlier court based on the legal decision that court reached.[1] Analogical reasoning figures crucially in determining whether an earlier case that might be precedent is, in fact, "relevantly similar." Indeed, there is no doctrine of precedent without analogical reasoning,[2] since in any jurisdiction with a doctrine of *stare decisis,* any earlier decision by a court is a possible precedent for a later

[1] Joseph Raz suggests—*contra* skeptics about identifying the holding (*ratio*) of the case—that "the *ratio* is the reason(s) by which the court justifies its decision" and this is "partly a matter of the interpretation" of the written decision. Joseph Raz, *The Authority of Law: Essays on Law and Morality* (Clarendon Press, 1979) 184. That Raz thinks this is a response to skepticism is surprising. Indeed, Raz echoes Hart's mistaken confidence on this score: "[T]he identification of the *ratio* of a case is reasonably straightforward." Ibid. Raz does recognize the great "freedom" courts have when it comes to precedent, and that it is "unreasonable to attribute great weight to the actual formulation of the rule in the hands of the" earlier court. Ibid., 188. Raz suggests that sometimes the later court may try to formulate a "modified rule that was really the rule the original court had in mind." Ibid.

[2] Grant Lamond understates this point in "Precedent and Analogy in Legal Reasoning," *Stanford Encyclopedia of Philosophy*, June 20, 2006, https://plato.stanford.edu/entries/legal-reas-prec/. He writes: "Arguments by analogy complement arguments from precedent in two ways: (i) they are used when the facts of a case do not fall within the *ratio* of any precedent, in order to assimilate the result to that that in the analogical case; and (ii) they are used when the facts of a case *do* fall within the *ratio* of a precedent, as a basis for distinguishing the case at hand from the precedent." Ibid., § 4. But whether the facts of a case actually fall within a *ratio* itself depends on at least *sotto voce* analogical reasoning, since no two cases are identical, and whether the particulars in a new case really do fall under the general categories of the prior case is often arguable—a point the realist approach to precedent calls attention to. We shall examine an instance of this in the text below, 117–20.

From a Realist Point of View. Brian Leiter, Oxford University Press. © Brian Leiter 2026.
DOI: 10.1093/9780197749852.003.0007

court considering the same legal question, and any earlier decision considering the same legal question is potentially distinguishable as involving facts that are not "relevantly similar." Uncontroversial judgments of relevant similarity deal with most of the former cases.

Realists about precedent—from Karl Llewellyn[3] to Julius Stone[4] to this author[5]—are skeptical that precedent really binds courts[6] (especially, as we will see, appellate courts). Realists are skeptical about the constraint of precedent not because they believe judges improperly disregard binding precedents (they may sometimes do so, but that would not be an interesting theoretical point); the worry, rather, is that judges can often quite properly and justifiably distinguish precedents that might impede the decision they want to reach on moral or political grounds. They can do so precisely because judgments of "relevant similarity" that are central to distinguishing precedents are largely unconstrained by law. First, such judgments depend on inchoate and sometimes unconscious norms that govern general classifications of particulars, about which reasonable people can and do differ, and about which the law is mostly silent. Second, given the range of permissible characterizations of the earlier court's reasons in many instances, the requirement that the judgment of relevant similarity or difference be consistent with those reasons imposes only a limited constraint on the general classification employed.[7] This is particularly important in the cases that reach the stage of appellate review precisely because of selection effects: advocates

[3] Karl N. Llewellyn, *The Bramble Bush: Some Lectures on Law and Its Study* (Oceana, 1951), 56–69. I return to Llewellyn, below, 118–19 in the text.

[4] Julius Stone, *Precedent and Law: Dynamics of Common Law Growth* (Butterworths, 1985), 2. Stone notes that most studies "tend to take for granted that the ambit of a precedent, that is, the range of circumstances for which it is binding, is normally clear and known. When this is taken for granted, all the sources of appellate leeways of choice to which this work is devoted are . . . often . . . ignored." Ibid. Stone references Rupert Cross as an example of those who take it for granted, but the same is true of H. L. A. Hart, Joseph Raz, and many others. Stone identifies various sources of "appellate leeways," including "equally licit and competing methods of finding the purported *ratio decidendi* of a case, and of distinguishing *ober dicta* from it. They include more than one—often many—alternative ratios which even a single method can reveal. They also include an array of levels of generality at which any 'material' fact can usually be described, delimiting the purported *ratio* more widely as the level of generality of each such fact is raised."

[5] See, e.g., Brian Leiter, *Naturalizing Jurisprudence: Essays on American Legal Realism and Naturalism in Legal Philosophy* (Oxford University Press, 2007); Brian Leiter, "Constitutional Law, Moral Judgment, and the Supreme Court as Super-Legislature," *Hastings Law Journal* 66 (2015): 1601.

[6] More precisely, realists are skeptical about how often precedent really permits the court to justify one and only one decision on legal grounds. More often, precedent may *restrict* the range of possible decisions, but that is consistent with the realist point that legal reasoning is *under*determinate, not, strictly speaking, *in*determinate.

[7] Prior cases and legal experience can *influence* the unconscious norms governing classifications and the imputation of reasons, but that is a weak constraint. Still, when precedent is relevant for a court, it is more of a constraint than in a case of "first impression."

often pursue cases through the stage of appellate review when the "precedents" could go either way.[8]

A caveat at the start: Legal systems with doctrines of precedent differ in important respects. Even Joseph Raz (decidedly not a legal realist) concedes, regarding his treatment of precedent in the English system, that it may not be representative: "[T]he English judiciary is small and highly centralized. It is recruited exclusively from the Bar (itself small), comes from a more or less homogeneous social background, and is unified by strong professional and social ties into a relatively cohesive social group."[9] That is surely part of the explanation for why no legal realism movement developed in England.[10] Raz adds that his account is "meant to be faithful to the accepted theory of the practice [of precedent] rather than to the practice."[11] The realist account of precedent concerns itself with the practice, not the theory, and its primary evidence is *the actual decisions of the courts.*[12] According to the realists, judgments about relevant similarity are sufficiently flexible that precedent is less a constraint on decision than a tool that judges can either use to avoid decisions they would rather not reach on other normative grounds or to justify decisions they want to reach on other normative grounds, but for which they need a legal precedent. How flexible judgments of relevant similarity are will depend, however, on the inchoate norms governing such judgments in a particular legal culture, as well as the norms governing the imputation of reasons to a prior court. The realistic view of precedent may have wider or narrower scope in different legal systems, depending on these factors.

[8] This is why realists emphasize indeterminacy in appellate adjudication. See, for instance, Stone, *Precedent and Law*, ch. 1; Leiter, *Naturalizing Jurisprudence*, 11–12, 20, 79–80. My view now is that it is not clear that this states any dispute with Hart's account of legal indeterminacy; see generally chs. 5 and 7 in this volume.

[9] Raz, *Authority of Law*, 181.

[10] Other factors include (1) the civil service system of the judiciary in England, where appointment and advancement depend on evaluation by other judges, who are likely to enforce adherence to norms of interpretation; and (2) the fact that English law students start studying law at age 17 or 18, without exposure to other disciplines, so are presented with law as though it is actually a discipline unto itself. Theology students, for example, tend not to attend to non-theological explanations for the beliefs of theologians, and perhaps something similar happens with law students in England.

[11] Raz, *Authority of Law*, 181.

[12] Raz puts to one side the question of what happens in practice by saying "[o]nly an empirical study" could settle the matter. Ibid. Only a very sophisticated empirical study could settle the matter decisively, but familiarity with what courts do, emerging from practice or reading cases (or both, in the case of most realists), can surely suffice to suggest that the "theory" may be bogus. The latter constituted the *actual,* and generally compelling, methods of the American legal realists. See Brian Leiter, "Legal Realisms, Old and New," *Valparaiso Law Review* 47 (2013): 67.

II. A Nonlegal Example of the Problem Afflicting Judgments of "Relevant Similarity"

Let us start with a nonlegal example. Children often take parental decisions about siblings to have precedential force, mostly on the grounds of "equal treatment": for instance, claims of the form, "why did my brother get to do X, but I can't?" (The general justification for a doctrine of precedent is not my concern here, but "equal treatment" looms large on many accounts.) Suppose the father tells his fourteen-year-old son that he can stay up late in the evening on a school night to watch a movie but forbids his eleven-year-old daughter from doing the same. The daughter objects: "You are letting my brother stay up for the movie!" She here makes an appeal to precedent, one that assumes that the relevant general category covering the particulars of the case is "child of the father." The father, unlike a court, probably has said less than would illuminate his *reasons* for the prior decision about the brother. Here are some reasons that are compatible with—and thus perhaps imputable to (depending on what precisely was said)—the father's earlier decision about the brother:

(1) Older children need less sleep, so they can stay up later than younger children and still perform adequately at school the next day.
(2) Younger children are more likely to wet their beds if they stay up late.
(3) Boys deserve more privileges than girls, since a boy's life is harder.
(4) The boy has fewer responsibilities than the girl, so if he is tired the next day it hardly matters.
(5) The boy has gone above and beyond the call of duty with regard to family responsibilities lately, and deserves the privilege.
(6) Past experience shows that the son needs less sleep than his sister.

Appeals to "equal treatment" are vitiated when the principle governing the treatment is of dubious moral merit (for instance, sexist assumptions about boys and girls, as in (3)), but that is most relevant in cases of (horizontal) precedent where overruling is an option.[13] Even putting (3) aside, the reasons established by the father's precedent include subsuming the particulars of the precedent case under general categories like "ability to perform the next day's duties" ((1) and also (4)), "avoiding wetting the bed" ((2)), "desert based on merit" ((5)), and "physical and psychological need" ((6), although there is possible overlap with (1)). The choice of any one of these ways of characterizing the particulars of the precedent case will affect the application of the precedent to the present case (i.e., the daughter's

[13] It is not wholly irrelevant in cases of vertical precedent, since courts, sometimes, should not do what the law requires, but that is a separate issue.

demand to stay up to watch the movie given the precedent). The daughter wins her "appeal" if the only relevant category is "child of the father," but she may lose her appeal on all the other ways of stating the relevant similarity, *unless* she can argue that the general category does not, in fact, apply to her: For example, she doesn't need more sleep than her brother, she never wets the bed, and so on.

Perhaps the father gave reasons that rule out some of these possible descriptions of the categorization of the relevant facts, justifying his decision. But it is a feature of precedent in ordinary life and in the law that parties can later raise distinctions that the precedent decision did not explicitly contemplate, subject to the constraint that these distinctions can be made consistent with the earlier outcome. Sometimes it is proper to identify the rule of the precedent by appeal to a pattern of decisions: For instance, how has the father treated the fourteen-year-old vis-à-vis his older brother? But courts do this too when they locate a particular precedent case in the context of related decisions, to elucidate the *real* or *more general* rationale at work in an area of law.

Much of the latitude in identifying the reasons and the "relevant similarity" between cases arises from the fact that, as H. L. A. Hart pointed out in chapter VII of *The Concept of Law*, precedent is a form of instruction by "example," rather than explicit linguistic guidance formulated in a rule,[14] and as a result, it "may leave open ranges of possibilities, and hence of doubt, as to what is intended."[15] Sometimes, an appeal to the reasons given in connection with the "example" may help, but not always. Let us consider an American case from the US Supreme Court that illustrates the case for realism about precedent.[16]

III. A Legal Example of Realism about Precedent

New York v. United States from 1992[17] was one of the early cases[18] that signaled the intent of some members of the US Supreme Court to redraw the boundaries of federal power after an earlier incarnation of that Court—appointed in large part by President Franklin Roosevelt—redrew them in the late 1930s and early 1940s to make Roosevelt's New Deal possible. *New York* concerned the

[14] Of course, linguistic formulations admit of many kinds of interpretation, another aspect of realism I am not considering here.

[15] H. L. A. Hart, *The Concept of Law*, 3rd ed. (Oxford University Press, 2012), 125. There are exceptions, of course, to the "example" model of precedent in which the earlier court offers a precise linguistic formulation of its rule that it expects later courts to follow.

[16] The classic American realist example of skepticism about precedent is Edward Levi's discussion of *MacPherson v. Buick Motor Co.*, 217 N.Y. 382 (1916), and the privity doctrine in Edward Levi, *An Introduction to Legal Reasoning* (University of Chicago Press, 1949), 8–10. For discussion, including contrast of Levi's and Cardozo's treatment with Dworkin's, see ch. 11 in this volume.

[17] 505 U.S. 144 (1992).

[18] Earlier, see Gregory v. Ashcroft, 501 U.S. 452, 461 (1991).

Low-Level Radioactive Waste Policy Amendments Act of 1985, ("Radiocative Waste Act") which the State of New York now challenged as betraying "federalism" values—the value of preserving certain regulatory questions for the states, and thus as beyond the reach of the federal government—by infringing upon state autonomy. Under what one might have thought the controlling precedent, *Garcia v. San Antonio Metropolitan Transportation Authority*[19] just seven years earlier, this might have seemed an "easy" case in which the law clearly dictated that New York should lose. *Garcia*, which concerned federal regulation of wages and working hours, held that the only protection for federalism values, like state autonomy, came from the political process itself, that is, from the fact that the states were all represented in the US Congress; only if there were a breakdown in the political process, so the *Garcia* court suggested, would the Supreme Court intervene. *New York v. United States* seemed a clear case from the standpoint of *Garcia*: the Radioactive Waste Act had been enacted by Congress *after being drafted by the various states*; the states, in effect, wanted Congress to bind them to the agreement they had reached among themselves. This would seem to be a paradigmatic case of federalism values in action: autonomous states strike a bargain about how to dispose of their radioactive waste, and then ask Congress to enforce the bargain.

Because the "doctrine of precedent" is malleable, once the Supreme Court agreed to review the case, everyone was on notice that what might have seemed clear as a matter of *stare decisis* was not. In the majority opinion, Justice Sandra Day O'Connor effectively took a page from the American legal realist Karl Llewellyn's explanation of the malleability of precedent from his 1930 book *The Bramble Bush*.[20] In Llewellyn's famous rendering, appellate courts approach precedents in one of two ways: They read "unwelcome" precedents strictly, that is, they characterize their holding in a way that is highly specific to the facts of the earlier case in order to distinguish it from the case currently before the court. In Llewellyn's obviously facetious example, a strict reading of an earlier court's holding might be, "This rule holds only of redheaded Walpoles in pale magenta Buick cars."[21] By contrast, a "loose" reading of a precedent abstracts away from the particular facts of the case in favor of a generic rule of law that the court would like to treat as binding in the present instance. Not every "strict" or "loose" reading is going to be plausible, but Llewellyn, as the smart and experienced lawyer he was, is plainly correct that in the American legal system the doctrine of precedent affords courts enough latitude in construing the holdings of earlier

[19] 469 U.S. 528 (1985).

[20] Llewellyn, *The Bramble Bush*, 56–69.

[21] Ibid., 66–67. Llewellyn was an experienced lawyer, and obviously knew that limiting the *ratio* of a prior case by the names of the parties or the color of their cars was not going to be effective. But rhetorical excess, rather than analytical precision, was Llewellyn's trademark.

cases—in identifying the "relevant similarity" between the earlier case and the present one—to make precedent a weak constraint on present decision in many cases. And that is precisely what happened in *New York v. United States.*

Justice O'Connor, in the majority opinion, faced a prima facie problem as mentioned already: under *Garcia*, the Radioactive Waste Act looked like a clear case of the political process operating to protect the interests of the states—after all, the states had drafted the Act in negotiations with each other, and then asked Congress to enact it. Presumably O'Connor lacked the votes to overrule *Garcia*—a move that would have been unseemly, in any case, given that *Garcia* had overruled another case, *National League of Cities*,[22] from less than a decade before!—and so, taking a page from Llewellyn, she set out to *distinguish Garcia* by reading it strictly. According to Justice O'Connor's majority opinion,[23] the rule in *Garcia*—that the only protection for federalism values comes from the political process itself—applies *only* in cases where the federal regulation applies to *both* public and private entities, as was true of the wage and hour regulations at issue in *Garcia*. *Garcia* itself did not make an issue out of this factual difference, but Justice O'Connor did: for the federal Radioactive Waste Management Act applied only to public entities, namely, states, and so, according to Justice O'Connor, presented a different issue than in *Garcia*. In other words, the relevant similarity/difference is whether the challenged legislation regulated *only* state actors or both public and private actors. With *Garcia* distinguished and left intact, Justice O'Connor proceeded to a historical analysis and ultimately invalidated a portion of the Act being challenged in *New York*. Those details do not matter for our purposes.

The dissenting opinion by Justice Byron White[24] can also be read as taking a page from Llewellyn: he effectively accused the majority of distinguishing *Garcia* on the basis of factual differences that did not make a difference. Justice White, we might say, complained that the majority opinion said the rule in *Garcia* applies only to "redheaded Walpoles in pale magenta Buick cars"[25] (i.e., an irrelevant factual dissimilarity). From Justice White's perspective, the difference between a federal regulation that reached public and private entities as opposed to only public ones was irrelevant, *New York v. United States* was an easy case, and *Garcia* should have controlled the result.

Crucial to the interest of this example for my purposes is that I believe neither the majority nor the dissent was right "as a matter of law" in this case (i.e., neither side had stronger legal reasons for their decision than the other). That the federal law at issue in *Garcia* applied to both public and private employers was not

22 426 U.S. 833 (1976).
23 New York v. United States, 505 U.S. at 149–88.
24 Ibid., 188–211.
25 Llewellyn, *The Bramble Bush*, 66–67.

emphasized in *Garcia*, but the reasoning of the *Garcia* majority opinion is not inconsistent with that distinction. To be sure, Justice O'Connor did a poor job of explaining why the factual difference between *Garcia* and *New York* actually mattered, but an explanation is not hard to come by: Surely it is reasonable to worry that state autonomy might be more at risk when a federal regulation *only applies to the states*, as opposed to regulating activity, regardless of whether public or private actors perform it. Justice O'Connor's opinion says, in effect: When federal law controls only the operations of state governments, a different kind of judicial scrutiny is warranted to ensure protection for federalism values. At the same time, Justice White's view was equally plausible as a matter of law: the *Garcia* rule emphasized the importance of the political process as a safeguard for state autonomy, and the underlying facts in *New York* seemed to indicate a political process functioning well, indeed, driven by the states themselves, until the State of New York had some buyer's remorse. Justice O'Connor and Justice White made different judgments about the "relevant similarities" between *Garcia* and *New York*, and the law was compatible with both judgments. In that sense, precedent did not constrain the decision.[26]

IV. A Rejoinder to Realism about Precedent

A rejoinder to the realist account of precedent in *New York* must argue that, in fact, either Justice O'Connor or Justice White was *correct as a matter of law*. In other words, either Justice O'Connor found a "legally relevant" difference between *Garcia* and *New York* or she did not (as Justice White argued). To make that case, one must show that the inchoate norms governing judgments of relevant similarity and difference are, in fact, governed (or constrained) by more demanding legally obligatory norms than the realist argument has so far allowed. The clearest (perhaps only) example of such an alternative account would be Ronald Dworkin's theory of law as "constructive interpretation."[27] According

[26] On the realist account, it is natural to ask what really explains the decision in *New York v. United States*. *New York*, as students of American federalism know, was near the beginning of a series of Supreme Court cases in which, for the first time since the triumph of the New Deal, the Court began placing some limits on the exercise of federal power. President Reagan, who appointed Justice O'Connor a decade earlier, ran partly on the issue of state autonomy from federal overreach. And so for Justice O'Connor, a newfangled conservative in the Reagan mold, *New York* presented an opportunity to state loud and clear that there really are limits on federal power. By contrast, for Justice White, an oldfangled conservative appointed by President Kennedy in the early 1960s, the New Deal revolution had settled all the questions about the scope of federal power. Justice White was a law-and-order conservative, skeptical of the expanding rights of criminal defendants, as well as of abortion rights, but he was fully accepting of the transformation of the constitutional system effected by the New Deal.

[27] See Ronald Dworkin, *Law's Empire* (Belknap Press, 1986). Scott Brewer suggests there is more constraint in reasoning by analogy than realist skeptics allow, but even he admits his preferred methodology is "admittedly far from determinate" and that there is "inevitably an uncodifiable imaginative

to Dworkin, judgments about the relevant similarity of a precedent are part of a broader "constructive interpretation" of the prior case and (in principle) all other aspects of the prior institutional history of the legal system (although only a Hercules could do that): that is, an interpretation that both fits or explains some portion of the prior institutional history and shows it in the best moral light. A non-Herculean Dworkinian judge considering *New York* must ask whether distinguishing the facts in *Garcia* from the facts in *New York* (as Justice O'Connor did) is really part of the best constructive interpretation of (at least) the federalism line of cases: that is, whether a principled explanation of the distinction (between federal laws that apply only to public entities, as opposed to those that apply to all economic actors, regardless of public/private status) would provide the best moral justification for the law. Put more simply, the Dworkinian judge asks whether ours is a morally better legal system if it applies the *Garcia* rule in all federalism cases or adopts a different approach (as Justice O'Connor would have it) when federal regulations target only state actors (on the assumption that both approaches fit well enough with some of the prior cases). On this approach, intuitive judgments about "relevant" similarity and difference are now "disciplined" by moral arguments about the merits and demerits of different approaches to federalism. The "discipline" involved is, to be sure, only as compelling as the objective force of the moral arguments in question. If equally good moral arguments can be marshalled in favor of both Justice O'Connor's and Justice White's views, without any further way to adjudicate between them, then Dworkinian constructive interpretation imposes no additional constraint at all.

Legal realists like me are inclined to think that the idea that judgments of "relevant similarity" are constrained by "moral argument" is comical: It is not only that there are arguments against Dworkinian optimism about moral argument,[28] but also that it seems implausible that morality takes sides in the O'Connor–White dispute. One need not agree wholeheartedly with the legal realist's metaethical views to nonetheless concede that the proposed Dworkinian rejoinder to the realist argument about precedent requires several highly

moment in . . . analogical reasoning." See Scott Brewer, "Exemplary Reasoning: Semantic, Pragmatics and the Rational Force of Legal Argument by Analogy," *Harvard Law Review* 109 (1996): 954–55. This is not surprising given the central role of abductive inference in his account (ibid., 962), since inferences to the best explanation (in this case, of similarities and differences between cases) are hostage to a variety of values about what makes one explanation better than another. The evidence that Brewer thinks constrains (confirms or disconfirms) the abductive hypothesis is also quite flexible, as his extended discussion of "pragmatics" makes clear (ibid, 989–1003). Brewer's aim is, in any case, to show that analogical arguments can have "rational force," not that they uniquely determine outcomes in a way that would defeat realist skepticism.

[28] See, e.g., J. L. Mackie, "The Third Theory of Law," in *Ronald Dworkin and Contemporary Jurisprudence*, ed. Marshall Cohen (Rowman & Allanheld, 1984); Leiter, *Naturalizing Jurisprudence*, ch. 8; and chs. 15 and 16 in this volume.

contentious assumptions: that the law depends on constructive interpretation; that there is an objective answer to the moral question about the different approaches to federalism in the O'Connor–White dispute; and that this answer, if it exists, constrains judgments of relevant similarity. Even though few legal philosophers now accept these latter assumptions, the possible Dworkinian rejoinder to the realist view underlines the point that realism about precedent, like any argument about the indeterminacy of legal reasoning, depends on a view (tacit if not explicit) about which norms are legally valid and thus prima facie binding on the courts.[29]

When the realist about precedent claims that judgments of relevant similarity and difference between cases are often indeterminate, that presupposes that valid legal norms are silent on the choice between, for instance, Justice O'Connor's or Justice White's interpretation of *Garcia.* If valid legal norms were not silent on that point, then the choice would not be (what I call) "rationally indeterminate," or indeterminate with respect to the reasons the court may properly invoke. Obviously, many norms for decisions are not silent on the choice confronting the Supreme Court in *New York*. For example, the norm "one ought to promote federal over state power whenever possible" would decide the case in favor of Justice White. The latter norm, however, is not legally valid in the United States, even on Dworkin's view I suspect.[30]

Even if judgments about relevant similarity are at some point legally unconstrained, they are not wholly unconstrained: The demand for "relevant" difference (or similarity) with regard to the reasons for the precedent operates in all legal systems, as in ordinary lives. The latitude a decision maker has about "relevance" will always be constrained by the inchoate norms governing those judgments, as our initial example of the father setting bedtimes suggests. The father could not justify (by his lights or the children's) his decision to the eleven-year-old daughter by appealing to her hair color compared to her brother's, for example. Although this is a difference between the daughter's case and her older brother's case, it is not "relevant" in the sense that there is no general principle that anyone accepts that would explain its relevance, unlike the examples given earlier.

[29] See Leiter, *Naturalizing Jurisprudence*, ch. 2.

[30] Hart's "soft positivism" in the "Postscript" to *The Concept of Law* does not help either, absent a showing that the moral considerations American judges treat as legally binding would have rendered *New York* an improper decision. But since *New York* was not met with a chorus of disapproval by American judges, it does not seem that Hart's one concession to Dworkin's early critique helps here. (Recall that American legal realists, at least, accept a positivist criterion of legal validity: see Leiter, *Naturalizing Jurisprudence*, ch. 2; and ch. 5 in this volume.

That law depends in this way on nonlegal norms of judgment should hardly be surprising. The normative force of grammar, math, and deductive inference also constrains legal judgments, although none of the latter are legally valid norms. Unlike the norms governing judgments of "relevant similarity," however, the norms of grammar, math, and deductive inference impose more constraints, although grammar has a more dynamic element (dependent as it obviously is on practice) than the others. However, even grammatical norms are more demanding than norms about "relevant similarity." Grammatical norms may evolve over time given the linguistic practices of large groups of people, but "relevance" norms are subject to extensive contestation in the present moment, as the nonlegal example we began with illustrates. Analogical reasoning is central to legal reasoning and (as noted at the start) central to precedent, but it is also hostage to the norms governing judgments of relevant similarity. Since those norms are contested and fluid—meaning that the constraint imposed by them is quite limited—it should be unsurprising how often the valid legal norms in the jurisdiction underdetermine judicial decisions. That is the foundation of realism about precedent, although its scope may vary in different legal systems and different cultures as noted at the start.[31]

[31] My thanks to Hafsteinn Dan Kristjánsson and Claudio Michelon for their helpful comments on an earlier version, and Sarah Cohen, University of Chicago Law School Class of 2022, for research assistance, and the Alumni Faculty Fund of the Law School for financial support.

7

How to Cabin the Realist Indeterminacy Thesis

On Green, Positivism, and the Sources of Law

I. Green's Challenge, the Realist Indeterminacy Thesis, and "Legitimate" Interpretations

The American Legal Realists (hereafter "Realists"), as I have reconstructed their views,[1] are tacit legal positivists in that they assume that the content of the law is exhausted by certain sources, such as court decisions and legislative enactments. Their distinctive claim is that law is indeterminate primarily in cases that reach the stage of appellate review. More precisely, they argue that the valid law and legal reasons justify more than one, but not simply any, outcome (what I call "rational indeterminacy"). I have argued, primarily on expository grounds, that the realists (with the notable exception of Jerome Frank[2]) primarily made claims about the indeterminacy of law in the appellate courts, without explicitly answering the important question Leslie Green raises,[3] namely, why think their "rule-skepticism" (as Hart calls it) is confined to the appellate courts? Green observes, for example, that:

> Any realist who is any kind of rule skeptic faces a challenge in keeping his skepticism under control. A dose is needed in respect of the reasoning of appellate courts; but not so much that it will dissolve those institutions, and not so much that it makes ordinary law—law-in-action, law-in-the-solicitor's office—unintelligible. Legal institutions, courts, officers, and decisions are rule-constituted things. (Green 116)

How can the Realist "keep[] his skepticism under control" so that it doesn't undermine all the "rule-constituted things" required for a legal system to exist at

[1] See Brian Leiter, *Naturalizing Jurisprudence* (Oxford University Press, 2007), esp. chs. 1 and 2.
[2] Ibid., 17.
[3] Leslie Green, "Realism and the Sources of Law," in *The Germ of Justice: Essays in General Jurisprudence* (Oxford University Press, 2023), 105–25. All further citations to this essay will be included in the body of the text by author name and page number.

From a Realist Point of View. Brian Leiter, Oxford University Press. © Brian Leiter 2026.
DOI: 10.1093/9780197749852.003.0008

all? How can the Realist cabin skepticism about the determinacy of rules to cases that reach the stage of appellate review? The answer turns, unsurprisingly, on what the argument for that skepticism is. When understood correctly, the claim that it is largely confined to the appellate courts is, I shall argue, plausible.

Green says indeterminacy (or "empirical rule-skepticism" as he calls it, following my characterization of the kind of rule-skepticism at issue between Hart and the realists) follows from the core positivist thesis that "[a]ll law is positive law" (105),[4] given that:

(1) "The sources of law are finite" (Green 108).
(2) "All legal sources are somewhat indeterminate, owing to the related phenomena of ambiguity, vagueness, and the fact that there is always more than one permissible way of applying a legal norm, even a mandatory norm" (Green 108–9).
(3) "There are unresolved conflicts among laws" (Green 109).

Strictly speaking, positivism need not make indeterminacy inevitable: A system of positive, sourced law could have sourced metarules that resolve all these cases (e.g., gaps or indeterminacy in the law should be resolved in favor of the defendant; conflicts in the law should be resolved in favor of the older law). This point is minor, since no actual legal system adopts such blanket, arbitrary metarules. The more important point is that Green's discussion of the sources of indeterminacy for the positivist either omits or misunderstands the crucial argument for the Realists.

So what is the realist argument for the rational indeterminacy of law? The distinctive realist argument appeals to the existence of conflicting, but *equally legitimate*, ways of interpreting precedents and statutes. (I return to the crucial notion of "legitimacy" below.) Llewellyn demonstrated, for example, that American courts had endorsed *both* the principle of statutory construction that "[a] statute cannot go beyond its text," but also the principle that "[t]o effect its purpose a statute must be implemented beyond its text."[5] But if a court could, in some cases, legitimately appeal to either canon when faced with a question of statutory interpretation, then the "methods" of legal reasoning (including canons of

[4] More precisely, that "all law has sources, where a source can be identified in a content-independent way, apart from its merits" (Green 106). See also Green's correct observation that on a positivist view, "Law can even be made unintentionally: a custom may emerge by invisible hand mechanisms yet satisfy the prevailing criteria for legal validity in that legal system; a ruling can be made solely to settle a particular dispute but have the upshot of changing the law governing many future cases; a piece of judicial reasoning can silently introduce, en route to its conclusion, a presupposition that is later treated as legally binding" (Green 106).

[5] Karl Llewellyn, "Remarks on the Theory of Appellate Decision and the Rules and Canons about How Statutes Are to Be Construed," *Vanderbilt Law Review* 3 (1950): 395, 401.

statutory construction) would justify at least two different interpretations of the statute (i.e., two different readings of what norm the statute enacted).[6] In that case, the question for the Realists was: Why did the judge reach that particular result, given that law and legal reasons did not require him to do so?

Llewellyn offered a similar argument about the conflicting, but (again) equally legitimate, ways of interpreting precedent in his 1930 book *The Bramble Bush*. According to Llewellyn's (incautiously) strong statement of the argument, *any* precedent can be read "strictly" or "loosely," and either reading would be "recognized, legitimate, honorable."[7] The strict interpretation characterizes the rule of the case as specific to the facts of the case; the loose interpretation abstracts (in varying degrees) from the specific facts to treat the case as standing for some general norm. But if "each precedent has not one value [that is, stands for not just one rule], but two, and . . . the two are wide apart, and . . . whichever value a later court assigns to it, such assignment will be respectable, traditionally sound, dogmatically correct,"[8] then precedent, as a source of law, cannot provide reasons for a unique outcome, because more than one rule can be extracted from the same precedent.[9]

The crucial claim in this argument for indeterminacy is that the conflicting ways of reading statutes or precedents are both "legitimate." The Realist assumption is that if lawyers and courts employ some form of argument—a "strict" construal of precedent, a particular canon of statutory construction—then that form of argument is *legitimate* in any and all cases. Put this incautiously, the assumption cannot be right: Not *every* strict construal of precedent will be legally proper (or "legitimate") in every case. Llewellyn himself (a very experienced lawyer[10]) recognized this, as suggested by his famous—but clearly facetious—example of a "strict" reading of precedent that yields, "This rule holds only of redheaded Walpoles in pale magenta Buick cars."[11] That, however, is unlikely ever to be a legitimate construal of a precedent, barring some bizarre scenario in which all these facts turned out to be legally relevant, and Llewellyn surely knows as much. The claim cannot be, then, that *any* strict or loose construal of precedent

[6] Green says, correctly, that the mere existence of conflicting canons of construction "does not show them to be in equipoise" in any particular case (Green 11), which is certainly right and which Llewellyn, a very accomplished lawyer, surely knew. It suffices for Llewellyn's purposes that *sometimes* they are in equipoise in the sense of "equally legitimate."

[7] Karl Llewellyn, *The Bramble Bush* (Oceana, 1930), 74.

[8] Ibid., 76.

[9] For a striking example of conflicting readings of precedent in action in American constitutional law, see Brian Leiter, "Constitutional Law, Moral Judgment, and the Supreme Court as Super-Legislature," *Hastings Law Journal* 66 (2015): 1601–16, esp. 1608–11.

[10] Llewellyn not only practiced law with the leading New York law firm of Shearman & Sterling, he also drafted the Uniform Commercial Code, adopted by all states in America. He maintained a deep involvement with commercial law practice throughout his career.

[11] Llewellyn, *Bramble Bush*, 72.

is *always* legitimate. It must only be that lawyers and judges have this interpretive latitude often enough to inject a considerable degree of indeterminacy into law.

If the preceding is the realist argument, then the relevant sense of "legitimate" here is different than what we might call the philosopher's conception. For philosophers, a law, a government, or a bit of coercion is "legitimate" if it is *justified*. The realist arguments, by contrast, depend entirely on what is often called the "sociological" conception of legitimacy: A law or a government or coercion is "legitimate" in the sociological sense if people *actually accept it* as legitimate (i.e., they deem it appropriate, acceptable, correct). Hitler enjoyed massive legitimacy, in the sociological sense, through most of the 1930s in Germany; Stalin enjoyed massive legitimacy in the Soviet Union, in the same sense, until his death.[12] But no one can argue their rule was *justified*. Nothing is more common than the gap between perceptions of "legitimacy" and what the best philosophical account would deem a morally *justified* claim to legitimacy. When the Realists claim that conflicting interpretations of sources of law are "equally legitimate," they mean only that both interpretations would be recognized by lawyers and judges as colorable, defensible, and appropriate (i.e., that they are sociologically legitimate). If that is true, then legal reasoning is indeterminate because the same sources of law can yield two (or more) different valid rules, and lawyers and judges would accept those arguments.[13]

Green acknowledges, recall, that, "[a]ll legal sources are somewhat indeterminate, owing to the related phenomena of ambiguity, vagueness, and the fact that there is always more than one permissible way of applying a legal norm, even a mandatory norm" (Green 108–9). The distinctive realist argument, as we saw, is *not* about ambiguity or vagueness (although Realists have no reason to deny that those could be sources of indeterminacy): The central issue is that a recognized valid source of law, admits of interpretation. Green acknowledges there may be "more than one permissible way of applying a legal norm, even a mandatory norm," but what the Realist argument above claims is different: The claim is that a valid *source* of legal norms can be interpreted as creating different "legal norms," even different "mandatory norms." The sources of law may be determinate—and they may be social, as the positivist claims—but it may be indeterminate what norms they enact if how to interpret the sources is indeterminate.

How does this help cabin Realist rule-skepticism, in response to Green's initial objection? Since the notion of "legitimate" but conflicting interpretations

[12] The examples could be extended well beyond Hitler and Stalin, but philosophers tend to have a more difficult time realizing that their own states and rulers may not be legitimate in the philosophical sense.

[13] Someone, like Dworkin, who thought there were criteria for identifying which readings of precedents or statutes were legitimate in the philosophical sense will not be impressed by these considerations. For the Realists, the touchstone of theorizing was, however, the *actual practice*, not what some philosopher might like the practice to be.

of sources of law is entirely a sociological one, indeterminacy will be cabined to appellate cases if, as a matter of empirical fact, it is primarily in appellate cases that lawyers and judges recognize the possibility of equally legitimate, but conflicting, interpretations of the sources of law. Why might that be true? Cases that are appealed are subject to a "selection effect": They are often (not always) selected for appeal precisely because lawyers can see that there are equally legitimate (in the sociological sense) but conflicting ways of interpreting the authoritative sources. A fresh set of appellate eyes may yield a different decision, on this view, since a different decision could be "legitimately" justified. Where the "legitimate" interpretations are all perceived to yield the same mandatory legal norm, by contrast, there is less incentive to appeal an adverse decision.[14]

Green suggests that limiting Realist rule-skepticism to appellate cases "would drain a lot of blood from their theory" (Green 121), but that is a strange objection if the reasons for so limiting it are empirically justified. Certainly, the limitation would drain the "contaminated blood" of several decades of sophomoric misrepresentations of the Realists by the Critical Legal Studies professors in American law schools. But the thesis that American appellate courts, given indeterminacy, are *really* making decisions based on their nonlegal judgment about what would be "fair" or "sensible" on the underlying facts of the case is not trivial: It contradicts the self-presentation of these courts, in both practice and in theory (e.g., Ronald Dworkin and his remaining acolytes).

Green's complaint is ironic since he commends Hart's "plea to look" (Green 120), yet looking at court opinions, in exacting detail, is exactly what the Realists did. Hart's problem was precisely that he did not look, at least not beyond the English law of his day.[15] That would be fine if Hart were doing merely "specific" jurisprudence, but he was not: He presented his theory as a general one about law in modern municipal legal systems. Hart's is, in fact, such a theory of law, and a quite successful one, but that is not true of his brief foray into the theory of adjudication. Hart certainly did not look at the voluminous and detailed studies of American decisions that were the primary work of the American Legal Realists.[16] From his English armchair, Hart declared that,

[14] Some of these considerations *might* apply at the trial level, but they will surely apply much more often at the appellate level. Civil cases are selected for litigation at the trial level primarily when, given the law, it is possible to persuade the trier of fact in one's favor.

[15] It is, for Realists, certainly "an open question to what extent the trial courts follow the high courts" (Green 120), and the Realist arguments were based on the empirical evidence in their jurisdiction. It could turn out to be different elsewhere, of course. Whether it was different in the UK in 1961, as Hart apparently believed, is something a scholar might investigate.

[16] For just a small sampling, see, e.g., Milton Handler and Charles Pickett, "Trade-Marks and Trade Names—An Analysis and Synthesis I," *Columbia Law Review* 30 (1930): 168; Karl Llewellyn, "On Warranty of Quality, and Society I," *Columbia Law Review* 36 (1936): 699; Karl Llewellyn, "On Warranty of Quality, and Society: II," *Columbia Law Review* 37 (1937): 341; Karl Llewellyn, "On Our Case-Law of Contract: Offer and Acceptance, I," *Yale Law Journal* 48 (1938): 1; Karl Llewellyn, "Our Case-Law of Contract: Offer and Acceptance, II," *Yale Law Journal* 48 (1939): 779; Karl Llewellyn,

> [I]t is surely evident that for the most part decisions . . . are reached either by genuine effort to conform to rules consciously taken as guiding standards of decision, or, if intuitively reached, are justified by rules which the judge was antecedently disposed to observe and whose relevance to the case at hand would generally be acknowledged.[17]

But this was precisely what Realists denied, *with evidence based on looking*.[18]

II. Permissive Sources and Reasons for Decision

Now Green agrees with me that Realists accept the positivist view that all law is source-based. He suggests that the real dispute between positivists and Realists is that the latter "consider *many* sources to be permissive—not only Llewellyn's canons of interpretation but also case law and even statutes, judicially construed" (Green 120). "Permissive" sources get their "merit-independent force from the fact that they are recognized and applied as reasons for decision in the practice of the courts, even though they fall short of binding authority" (Green 120).

Green seems to be using the idea of a "source" of law in the capacious sense introduced by Joseph Raz:

> The sources of law are those facts by virtue of which it is valid and which identify its content. This sense of "source" is wider than that of "formal sources" which are those establishing the validity of a law (one or more Acts of Parliament together with one or more precedents may be the formal sources of one rule of a law). "Source" as used here includes also "interpretive sources", namely all the relevant interpretive materials. The sources of a law thus understood are never a single act (of legislation, etc.) alone, but a whole range of facts of a variety of kinds.[19]

"Across Sales on Horseback," *Harvard Law Review* 52 (1939): 725; among many others by Llewellyn; Underhill Moore and Theodore S. Hope, Jr., "An Institutional Approach to the Law of Commercial Banking," *Yale Law Journal* 38 (1929): 703; Herman Oliphant, "A Return to Stare Decisis," *American Bar Association Journal* 14 (1928): 71.

[17] H. L. A. Hart, *The Concept of Law*, 3rd ed. (Clarendon Press, 2012), 141.

[18] See *supra* note 16 for examples. To describe just one case: When Herman Oliphant in "A Return to *Stare Decisis*" argued that there was no general contracts doctrine about the validity of a promise not to compete, he did so by looking at cases, showing that the pattern of the results could not be reconciled with the contractual arguments given. The *actual* pattern only becomes clear when one looks at the underlying situation types: Courts enforce those promises when made by sellers of businesses to buyers, for (loosely speaking) economic efficiency reasons; courts invalidate the promises when made by employees to their employers, for (loosely speaking) fairness reasons.

[19] Joseph Raz, *The Authority of Law* (Oxford University Press, 1979), 47–48.

What are "all the relevant interpretive materials"? I assume this includes canons of statutory interpretation, general theories of statutory interpretation (e.g., textualism and intentionalism), and analogical reasoning about precedents—but I confess, I'm not entirely sure what is meant, or why Raz calls them *materials*. Hart himself does not utilize the idea of "interpretive sources," although I take it Hart recognizes that the rule of recognition could specify how the norm enacted by a social source should be determined (e.g., intention).

Terminological quibbles aside, the real problem facing Green's suggestion that the dispute between Realists and legal positivists is about what Green calls "permissive sources" seems to me this: Green's "permissive sources" are, for Realists, mostly just rhetorical devices for justifying a decision that is reached based on considerations nowhere stated. "Interpretive canons" (or "strict" or "loose" readings of precedent) are not "permissive sources" for the judge, they are instead "window dressing" (at least in cases where the law is indeterminate) that allows the judge to justify in print a decision based on reasons nowhere explicitly acknowledged (i.e., they are accepted as "legitimate" reasons by other lawyers and judges). That is the whole point of the Realist critique. As part of his elaboration of the notion of a permissive source, Green endorses (Green 119) Hart's comments in the notes to *The Concept of Law,* but they are worth quoting in full to make clear how Hart conceives of them:

> In systems where a statute is a formal or legal source of law, a court in deciding a case is bound to attend to a relevant statute though no doubt it is left considerable freedom in interpretation the meaning of the statutory language . . . But sometimes much more than freedom of interpretation is left to the judge. Where he considers that no statute or other formal source of law determines the case before him, he may base his decision on, e.g., a text of the Digest, or the writings of a French jurist . . . The legal system does not *require* him to use these sources, but it is accepted as perfectly proper that he should do so. They are therefore more than merely historical or causal influences since such writings are recognized as "good reasons" for decision. Perhaps we might speak of such sources as "permissive" legal sources to distinguish them both from "mandatory" legal or formal sources such as statute and from [merely causal influences on the decision].[20]

Hart plainly contemplates persuasive sources as supplying a basis for decision when the formal sources run out, but that is not the role of conflicting but equally legitimate ways of interpreting sources for the Realists: Their availability to the judge is precisely what makes the formal sources amenable to being enlisted on

[20] Hart, *Concept of Law*, 294.

behalf of differing legal conclusions. The actual reasons for decision—for example, moral and political intuitions about how to respond to "situation types"—are nowhere given as reasons by the court, although the Realist efforts at law reform aimed to bring these hidden reasons into the canon of authoritative legal sources.[21]

The primary reason Realists engaged in law reform efforts was because they realized that the *actual reasons* for decisions were often unstated, and they wanted to make those reasons explicit in the formal sources of law. That is what Llewellyn accomplished with the Uniform Commercial Code, and what Oliphant accomplished when his reading of the promise-not-to-compete cases was reflected in the *Second Restatement of Contracts* in the United States. They hoped to turn *sotto voce* reasons that were in fact the causes of the decision into "formal sources" of law so that everyone would know what to expect should their affairs end up in court.

I would suggest that we assimilate something like Green's idea of "permissive sources" to what I have called for many years "the class of legal reasons,"[22] that is, the reasons judges can legitimately give *in their opinions* for their decisions, in the sociological sense of legitimacy. But being a member of the class of legal reasons in this sense does not make a consideration (or "source") an actual reason for the decision. The class of legal reasons includes "formal" sources but also includes ways of interpreting sources that allow them to be enlisted on behalf of a decision reached for ulterior, and often silent, reasons. These kinds of reasons, according to the Realists, are not "sources" of law but "tools" for (legitimately, in the sociological sense) justifying in public decisions reached on other grounds.

III. Some Disagreements with Green on Realism

Green's work, including the essay under discussion here, is a welcome exception to the dogmatism of Oxford jurisprudence, which has remained attached to Hart's misunderstandings of Realism many years after its debunking. As I have argued elsewhere, the "Personal Element"[23] of influence by authoritative teachers exercises a much more profound influence on what scholars believe than one might hope for in a *Wissenschaft*. Disagreeing with Hart is not easy

[21] See Brian Leiter, "Legal Realism and Legal Doctrine," *University of Pennsylvania Law Review* 163 (2015): 1975.

[22] Brian Leiter, "Legal Indeterminacy," *Legal Theory* 1 (1995): 481. The basic ideas are also presented, in slightly different form, in Leiter, *Naturalizing Jurisprudence*, 9–12.

[23] Brian Leiter, "On the Relevance of Etiology to Justification (with reference to Marx and Nietzsche)," *Midwest Studies in Philosophy* 47 (2023): 157. See also the discussion in the Preface in this volume.

for those trained at Oxford,[24] and in some ways, even less easy for those trained by Raz,[25] even though Raz betrayed, without announcing it, important realistic aspects of Hart's approach to jurisprudence.[26] Even though Green is the exception who proves the truth of the preceding generalization, I hope it will not be too churlish to conclude by noting two disagreements with Green's criticisms of Realism, while also acknowledging that most of what he says seems to me both right and salutary for a long overdue *rapprochement* between realism and positivism.

A. Green says, rightly, that I believe "we have been misled by" Hart," since "the most important realists hold views that are either compatible with Hart's positivism or, to the extent of any compatibility, superior" (Green 112) (they are superior on the question of what American appellate courts are actually doing, per the discussion above). He continues with a very fair description of my view:

[24] Those who fell under Dworkin's malign influence "disagree" with Hart mostly by misrepresenting him. The work of David Dyzenhaus in general jurisprudence is a striking and somewhat embarrassing example. For an amusing evisceration, see Matthew H. Kramer, "Dogmas and Distortions: Legal Positivism Defended," *Oxford Journal of Legal Studies* 21 (2001): 673.

[25] Many years ago, Green and I went up to Raz's rooms at Balliol, and as we entered the room, Green joked about experiencing feelings of "posttraumatic stress disorder," which also made Raz laugh! On my philosophy blog, Alon Harel shared the following about Raz's teaching style on a post noting Raz's death (https://leiterreports.typepad.com/blog/2022/05/in-memoriam-joseph-raz-1939-2022.html):

> Joseph did not waste time on giving compliments. On the first meeting in his office he started with what he called "terminological remarks." These remarks lasted about an hour in which he thoroughly scrutinized each and every term I used and exposed why these terms should never be used. At this point when I was half conscious and without warning he said as following: "And now on page 13 a disaster is happening." The disaster was my failed attempt to develop an argument whose assumptions were too reckless. Then began another monologue that lasted about two hours in which Joseph made it clear to me that not only was my argument invalid and that its assumptions were false but the assumptions I made would inevitably lead to the opposite conclusion from the one I was trying to defend.
>
> Readers will surely understand that it was not easy to work with Joseph. I knew at least two people who started working with Joseph and abandoned the doctoral project and there were others as well. At the same time, there were very many who worked with Joseph and who set up what could be called a "support group of Raz's doctoral students," sharing the difficulties of working with him. Oxford had at the time many superstars in the field of moral and political philosophy: Derek Parfit, Ronald Dworkin, Amartya Sen, Jerry Cohen, and of course Joseph Raz. Jerry Cohen and Joseph were extremely popular supervisors as both of them were highly committed to their students. Unlike many others in the academy of then and today (including some followers of Joseph) there was no trace of arrogance in Joseph, but a genuine belief in the power of reason to discover the truth. He had a real curiosity and lust to find the truth alongside an uncompromising willingness to seek it through the use of reason.

Raz was, as this recollection reveals, an important mentor during his decades at Oxford, but he was also a dominating presence. Important legal philosophers outside his immediate sphere of influence (i.e., those not affected by "the Personal Element") have been more critical of his work. See, e.g., Kevin Toh, "Some Moving Parts of Jurisprudence," *Texas Law Review* 88 (2010): 1283.

[26] Esp. ch. 5 in this volume.

> Realists do not deny the possibility of legal rules and they do not offer a predictive analysis of the concept of a rule—those are forms of conceptual rule-skepticism, and the realists eschew conceptual analysis altogether. They are committed only to empirical rule skepticism, the view that, owing to indeterminacy, the decisions of appellate courts cannot be predicted on the basis of (positive) law but they can be predicted by extra-legal considerations. (Green 113)

Green suggests, however, that some Realists were, *contra* Leiter, conceptual rule-skeptics. He points, first, to Holmes's "The Path of the Law,"[27] noting that Holmes claims that "there are 'really' no primary obligations in tort or in contract; there are only remedial obligations to pay damages if so ordered by a court" (Green 114). The context for Holmes's claim about obligations was a broader thesis, namely, that a "Bad Man"—someone who either did not care what was morally right or wrong, or did not know what was morally right or wrong—could nonetheless make sense, for his purposes, of talk about legal obligations. A claim about how a "Bad Man" understands the law is obviously not the same as a claim about the ordinary understanding of the concept of law. Recall how Holmes begins his lecture:

> [In studying law] [w]e are studying what we shall want in order to appear before judges, or to advise people in such a way as to keep them out of court. The reason why it is a profession, why people will pay lawyers to argue for them or to advise them, is that in societies like ours the command of the public force is intrusted to the judges in certain cases, and the whole power of the state will be put forth, if necessary, to carry out their judgments and decrees. People want to know under what circumstances and how far they will run the risk of coming against what is so much stronger than themselves, and hence it becomes a business to find out when this danger is to be feared. The object of our study, then, is prediction, the prediction of the incidence of the public force through the instrumentality of the courts.[28]

Holmes could hardly be more explicit that his topic is how it is useful to think about "law" if one is advising clients about what will happen if their dispute ends up in court. Holmes—like every other Realist (except Felix Cohen, about whom more in a moment)—*never* made any explicit claim about the "concept of law," because that topic (namely, the "concept") was not a topic Holmes recognized. (It was not even a central topic in philosophy until the middle of the twentieth century!) There is law, there are questions about what the law is on particular

[27] Oliver Wendell Holmes, Jr., "The Path of the Law," *Harvard Law Review* 10 (1897): 457.
[28] Ibid.

topics, there are the decisions of courts, but the "concept of law" as an abstract object to be elicited from all these practices simply did not exist as a topic of intellectual inquiry for Holmes or almost all of the later Realists. Holmes, like every other Realist, made the now banal, and obviously correct, observation that when your client, who is paying money for your services, asks "what is the law," what she really wants to know is "what will judges do if we go to court?" or "what will legal officials do if we pursue this matter?" The client does not want to know what is morally right or wrong, or what the esteemed legal authorities have to say on the question, or what the "paper rule" says will happen: the client wants to know what will *really* happen (e.g., will she be able to reclaim her property or get monetary damages for her losses? Or will she be told to go home?).

Green's second example of Realists offering a predictive analysis of the concept of law (what I call conceptual rule-skepticism) is Felix Cohen (Green 114). Here the charge is fair, but as I noted many years ago,[29] Felix Cohen was nowhere cited by Hart, and no other Realists endorsed his view. Cohen, who did have a doctorate in philosophy and was influenced by Percy Bridgman's "operationalism" in philosophy of science, did, alas, defend something like conceptual rule-skepticism. This is a case study in "a little knowledge of philosophy is a dangerous thing." Cohen's mistake has no bearing on what the Realists were actually doing in the vast majority of their work.

B. Green's second mistake about legal realism concerns the Scandinavian tradition, which continues to be misunderstood due to Hart (and even though it has almost nothing to do with American legal realism[30]). Green writes:

> [E]ven if judges do not experience any special psychological states like "feelings of compulsion" they may nonetheless have an obligation to decide in a certain way [citing Hart, *The Concept of Law*, 136]. This point is addressed to the crude behaviorism of Alf Ross or Axel Hägerstrom's reductionism, or maybe eliminativism about legal entities. (Green 121)

I bracket Hägerstrom, whose work I do not know as well, and focus only on Ross, who was the opposite of a "crude behaviorist," and whose dispute with Hart on the issue of "obligation" is greatly complicated by Hart's *sotto voce* views in philosophy of mind. Let me explain.

In his major work, *On Law and Justice*,[31] Ross is explicitly committed to verificationism, to the view that meaningful (cognitive) statements are ones that

[29] Leiter, *Naturalizing Jurisprudence*, 70.

[30] Brian Leiter, "Legal Realisms, Old and New," *Valparaiso Law Review* 47 (2013): 949.

[31] Alf Ross, *On Law and Justice*, ed. Jakob Holtermann, trans. Uta Bindreiter (Oxford University Press, 2019). All citations are included by author name and page number in parentheses either in the body of the text or the footnotes.

admit of verification by experience (Ross 14) (so, e.g., the claim from physics that "pressure and volume of a given mass of confined gas are inversely proportional" [Ross 13] is meaningful because "we are aware of what experiences these sentences are referring to, that is, how we should proceed in order to verify their truth" [Ross 14]).[32] As he puts it later, "[s]cientific sentences must possess representative meaning" (Ross 18).[33]

Ross then takes up the question of how we are to understand a legal proposition like the one he made famous from the Danish Bill of Exchange Act (DBEA): "The acceptor is obligated to pay the bill of exchange on the due day for payment" (Ross 14). From the verificationist point of view, the problem is the word "obligation": "what is an 'obligation' and how can one empirically determine if it has arisen?" (Ross 14). Since we cannot empirically verify the existence of an obligation, Ross concludes that the "Danish Bill of Exchange Act does not seek to disclose information about reality, it does not have what is called logical meaning" (Ross 15) (i.e., verifiable, cognitive meaning).

In Ross's terms, the DBEA provision is a kind of "expressive" utterance, namely, a "directive": It is expressive insofar as it arises from "emotional-volitional circumstances" (Ross 15) and does "not symbolize anything" (Ross 16), and it is a "directive" insofar as it aims "to exert influence" on action (Ross 16). Since "directives," like all statements with *only* expressive meaning, are not verifiable, and since "science" deals only with assertions (i.e., statements that can be true or false), Ross says, "*the problem of 'the nature of law' is the problem of how to interpret the concept 'scientifically valid law' as an integral element of every juridico-scientific sentence*" (Ross 19)—that is, how to understand every statement of legal doctrine that involves a normative concept like "obligation" as an empirically verifiable statement. The new edition of *On Law and Justice* usefully introduces the technical term "scientifically valid law" to capture Ross's Danish, which distinguishes the latter from what Hart and so many others would call "valid" law, that is, norms that *are treated as part of the law* by officials of the relevant legal community. "Scientifically valid law," by contrast, consists of norms that are empirically verifiable. But how precisely?

Ross distinguishes two kinds of norms in a legal system: what he calls "norms of conduct" (those which "prescribe a certain course of conduct" [Ross 43]); and

[32] As Ross writes later, the "logical meaning" of a "statement about reality" "is identical with the immediate experience through which the truth of the statement is tested" (Ross 51–52). "[A] statement about reality... implies, directly or indirectly, that when following a certain procedure one will, under certain conditions, have certain direct experiences. This procedure is called verification: it is concerned with the method of testing the truth of a statement and, at the same time, defines its meaning content" (Ross 52).

[33] Cognitivism and verificationism are not equivalent; one could think a class of statements is cognitive even if one could not specify how it would be verified. We can ignore this for purposes of discussion here.

"norms of competence (or procedure)" which "create a competence (power, authority) . . . to the effect that norms created in conformity with a given mode of procedure shall be considered norms of conduct" (Ross 43–44). Consistent with Kelsenian dogma, Ross views both kinds of norms as directives to judges. Thus, norms of conduct operate as a "directive to the judge, telling him how, should the occasion arise, he should exercise his judicial authority" (Ross 44) (i.e., whether he should impose sanctions). So too norms of competence: they constitute "an instruction to the judge (and other law-applying authorities), namely, to make a decision in accordance with the detailed instructions issued by [the competent authority]" (Ross 45). (One consequence of this view, as Ross recognizes [Ross 64-65], is that competence norms cannot be "scientifically valid" unless reviewable and voidable by judges.) Thus, all law, on Ross's view (and following Kelsen), "consists of directives for *organizing the exercise of specific coercion through the courts*" (Ross 45).

"Scientifically valid" law, then, consists of the norms (of conduct and competence) that are "felt by [the judge] to be socially binding" and with which the judge thus "complie[s] efficaciously" (Ross 47). (Efficacious compliance with laws by citizens is irrelevant on Ross's view, which he recognizes is a "paradox," since when "courts do not have the opportunity to display their reaction" in response to law, its scientific validity is uncertain [Ross 64–65].[34]) In sum, any statement about "scientifically valid law" is really a

> prediction that *if an action in which the conditional facts, given in [the law in question], are considered to exist, is brought before a court; and if in the meanwhile there have been no alterations in the circumstances which motivate A, the direction to the judge contained in [the law] will form an integral part of the reasons for the court's decision.* (Ross 54)[35]

This is the source of the attribution of a "prediction theory" to Ross, although it bears noting (as the new translation of his work makes clear) that this applies

[34] One possibility is that Ross could account for the scientific validity of such norms by appeal to counterfactual predictions about what courts would do if, in fact, they had to display their reaction. As Dimitrios Tsarapatsanis calls to my attention, Eugenio Bulygin, correctly, pointed out that for such a counterfactual prediction to be true, we would have to attribute something like a *disposition* to judges to abide by the law were the question to arise. See Eugenio Bulygin, *Essays in Legal Philosophy* (Oxford University Press, 2015), 50. Bulygin reports that, in correspondence, Ross accepted this suggestion. Ibid., 289. I am not sure how, within Ross's original naturalistic framework, this is an admissible response: The only proof of a disposition, after all, is in the behavior of the court. If there is no behavior evincing the disposition, then the posit looks like pernicious and metaphysical wishful thinking. Either judicial behavior is a criterion of scientific validity or it is not: *Possible* judicial behavior seems neither here nor there.

[35] One consequence of this view is that "scientific validity" of a legal norm is a matter of degree, "depending on the degree of probability with which it can be predicted that the rule will be applied" (Ross 57).

only to the concept of *scientifically valid law*, that is, law as understood within the constraints of Ross's verificationism, and not to the concept of valid law as used by the judge or lawyer. (Hart, by contrast, is interested in explaining the latter.) We also see here Ross's antibehaviorism about psychology, since the idea of scientifically valid law supposes that the ideology of the law is "felt . . . to be socially binding," that is, it rests, as he admits, "upon hypotheses concerning the inner life, or thought processes, of the judge" (Ross 48). Although he later associates the view with what he calls "behavioristic realism" (Ross 87), that would be misleading if one confuses it with behaviorism in psychology (Ross counsels against that mistake at p. 88). What he means is that the behavior of judges entitles us to infer abductively the presence of an "ideology which animates the judge and motivates his actions," since that posit facilitates "the meaningful understanding and effective prediction of the course of events" (i.e., it is verifiable) (Ross 49).[36]

Hart did, to be sure, take issue with Ross's talk of judges "feeling bound," preferring to analyze essentially the same phenomenon Ross identified in terms of *behavior* (officials actually converging on a criterion of legal validity, officials applying that criterion regularly, officials criticizing in strongly normative terms deviation from the criterion, etc.). Ross glosses the same phenomenon as "feeling bound," and I cannot see a strong theoretical reason to prefer Hart's approach to Ross's (except, ironically, that Hart's is easier to "verify").[37] Indeed, I have argued elsewhere[38] that Hart's approach reflects his uncritical acceptance of Gilbert Ryle's behaviorism about mental states, another view that was part of the philosophical air Hart was breathing at Oxford. Ryle claimed that to be in a mental state is just to manifest certain behaviors, or to have the disposition to engage in certain kinds of behavior.[39] My hypothesis is that this Rylean view is what motivates Hart's behavioral gloss on what it is to adopt the internal point of view; Ross, who was less taken with behaviorism, felt no such compulsion and so spoke more simply of the psychological state of "feeling bound" as the mark of the internal point of view. Ross thought positing this psychological state could only be justified if it was verified by judicial behavior, but we can just as well

[36] The reference to "meaningful understanding" is puzzling, since prediction can be possible without that. Is this a nod to Weberian *Verstehen*? I'm not sure.

[37] Hart's view also has the vice that it suggests that judges could just "talk the talk, and walk the walk," but not actually have the internal point of view as a matter of internal phenomenology. Yet if we ask *why* the existence of a legal system requires officials to take the "internal point of view" (rather than the merely prudential view of the Holmesian Bad Man), the answer must surely be that it contributes to the stability and functionality of the system. And the latter is only true *if* judges really do "feel bound" as Ross puts it.

[38] Brian Leiter, "Back to Hart," *Annals of the Faculty of Law-Belgrade Law Review* 69 (2021): 749.

[39] More precisely, Ryle spoke about sentences about mental states being equivalent in meaning to sentences about behavioral dispositions. I give this a metaphysical, rather than semantic, gloss in the text.

say that we are justified in positing it because it is part of the best explanation of judicial behavior: if judges did not "feel bound," they would not so reliably converge.[40]

In sum, Ross's mistake is not behaviorism (he is not a behaviorist, in the way, say, Quine was throughout most of his career), it is verificationism which leads him to endorse something like a prediction theory of law to explain how legal propositions employing normative concepts (like "obligation," "duty," right," etc.) can be "scientifically valid."[41] Ross explicitly recognizes that this notion of "scientific validity" is unrelated to the way in which lawyers and judges discuss "validity."[42]

IV. Conclusion

Everyone who knows Green, whether from his writing or from conversation, knows that he is very good at turning a pithy phrase to make a deep jurisprudential point. The essay under discussion here is replete with examples, some of which I have already quoted. One of the gems I have not had occasion to mention so far comes in the context of his response to mistaken objections to legal positivism. The objection in question claims that "[i]f law were positive, legal systems could not be identified by their contribution to human goods" (Green 108), as natural law theorists believe. Green's retort:

[40] On this point, the difference between Hart and Ross is subtle, but important. On Hart's view, the theory that best explains the legal phenomena recognizes that "[t]he acceptor has an obligation to pay the bill of exchange" (Ross's main example) as a complex descriptive and normatively inert fact about the verbal and physical behavior of officials and other legal actors in a particular system as seen from the outside, but also as a statement with normative force when uttered by some actors within the system. Judicial behavior is relevant to the former only insofar as it is relevant to specifying the rule of recognition of that system. However, judicial behavior in *applying that particular norm* is irrelevant to the question of whether a particular norm is valid. It is on this latter point—because of his conception of "scientific validity" as dependent on empirical verifiability—that Ross differs, but here I think Hart has the more explanatorily fruitful view. This also explains why Hart's view is not, *contra* Ross, a case of jurisprudential idealism: validity for Hart is not an "a priori concept" (Ross 78), and it is not merely "formal" as it is for Keslen, since for Kelsen the "validity of a norm . . . can never derive from a natural fact (Ross 79). "Validity" is the status of norms (as made manifest in the behavior of officials and legal actors) that, from an external point of view, satisfy the criteria in the rule of recognition. Which those are is an empirical question. And there is no *derivation* of validity from a natural fact, but rather the reduction of talk about validity to psychosocial facts about behavior.

[41] I critique Ross's view, from a naturalistic perspective, in "Alf Ross's Critique of American Legal Realism—and a Naturalistic Critique of Ross," available on SSRN at https://papers.ssrn.com/sol3/papers.cfm?abstract_id=4240991.

[42] See Ross's discussion regarding an attempt to analyze the rules of chess while ignoring the point of view of the players (Ross 22–24), which basically mirrors Hart's later point about the "internal point of view."

> *But*: Institutions and artefacts may have constitutive aims to promote well-being. Nothing is a sewage system that is not oriented to promoting public health, yet the existence (and content) of a sewage system is a matter of plain empirical fact. (Green 108)

Antipositivism about sewage systems has not gotten as much traction as antipositivism about law, but perhaps if this succinct rejoinder were more widely appreciated, that would change.

Another important cautionary note about legal philosophy that we owe to Green comes from a 2019 interview, where he aptly remarked that "many people [in jurisprudence] care more about saying something new than about saying something true."[43] The incentives of the academy encourage producing new but preposterous theories, alas, but perhaps one way to change the incentives is by recognizing that a really crucial task for professors of jurisprudence or philosophy more generally is what Green calls "curating." On his blog, also in 2019, he writes:

> I am now wondering whether we might think of some of our work in jurisprudence, or in philosophy more generally, as more like *curating*... Like research, curating can find out things; like scholarship it can communicate things in a way unique to, or bearing the indelible imprint of, the creator. But curating also does something else.
>
> A curator attempts to *care for* knowledge and culture we already have. Not by freezing it or ensuring no others can touch it, but by conserving it while placing it in a new context, or displaying it from a new angle, or in the company of new ideas, so as to make it intelligible and perhaps useful to those who follow us. A curator protects what we already know (and value), not only against forgetting, but also against the disintegrating forces of self-importance (including national self-importance) and against the blaring noise of the news cycle.[44]

Green has not given us a new but untrue "theory of law," but his corpus represents jurisprudential curation at its best, saying new and (almost always) true things

[43] "Leslie Green," University of Oxford Faculty of Law, accessed March 21, 2025, https://www.law.ox.ac.uk/content/leslie-green. He did not name names, but I would guess he is thinking of, among others, Scott Shapiro's "Planning Theory of Law" and Mark Greenberg's "Moral Impact Theory of Law," both undoubtedly new, both undoubtedly not true. See generally ch. 9 in this volume.

[44] Leslie Green, "Research, Scholarship, and Curating," *Semper Viridis*, published September 8, 2019, https://ljmgreen.com/2019/09/08/research-scholarship-and-curating/.

about every major topics in general jurisprudence, and every major figure on whom he has written, from Kelsen to Hart to Dworkin to the Realists—and without purporting to reinvent the subject from the ground up. Green has indeed "conserve[ed] [jurisprudential knowledge] while placing it in a new context . . . displaying it from a new angle . . . [and] in the company of new ideas, so as to make it intelligible and perhaps useful to those who follow us." We need more work on the exemplary model of his.

8

The Demarcation Problem in Jurisprudence

A New Case for Skepticism

I. The Demarcation Problem

For more than two hundred years, legal philosophers have been preoccupied with specifying the differences between two systems of normative guidance that are omnipresent in all modern human societies: law and morality. In the last hundred years, what I will call the "Demarcation Problem"—the problem of how to distinguish these two normative systems—has been *the* dominant problem in jurisprudence and the theory usually denominated 'legal positivism' has offered the most important solution.[1] Legal positivists such as Kelsen, Hart and Raz claim that the *legal validity* of a norm cannot depend on its being *morally valid*, either in all or at least some possible legal systems (the range of the scope operator here marks the distinction between "Hard" and "Soft" versions of positivism).

Kelsen tells us on the first page of the *Pure Theory* that the theory "attempts to answer the question what and how the law *is*, not how it ought to be"[2] and the second chapter on "Law and Morals" sets out to establish that the "science of law"—the science of the legal validity of norms—is not to be confused with "ethics," the science of the social norms denominated "moral" (Kelsen 59). "[L]aw and morals" must be "recognized as different kinds of normative systems" (Kelsen 62), Kelsen says, a difference he locates in the fact that law involves "a socially organized coercive" sanction, while morals lacks such sanctions, substituting "merely the approval of the norm-conforming and the disapproval of the norm-opposing behavior" (Kelsen 62).

The first sentence of *The Concept of Law* states Hart's aim "to further the understanding of law, coercion, and morality as different but related phenomena."[3]

[1] See Leslie Green, "Legal Positivism," *Stanford Encyclopedia of Philosophy*, accessed January 3, 2003, http://plato.stanford.edu/entries/legal-positivism/, for a recent clean statement of the view.

[2] Hans Kelsen, *Pure Theory of Law*, trans. Max Knight (University of California Press, 1967), 1. Further citations are included by page number in the body of the text.

[3] H. L. A. Hart, *The Concept of Law*, 3rd ed. (Clarendon Press, 2012), vi. All further references will be included by page number in the body of the text.

From a Realist Point of View. Brian Leiter, Oxford University Press.
DOI: 10.1093/9780197749852.003.0009

He famously identifies as one of the three main issues driving jurisprudential inquiry the question, "How does legal obligation differ from, and how is it related to, moral obligation?" (Hart 13). That issue looms so large because "law and morals share a vocabulary so that there are both legal and moral obligations, duties, and rights" and "all legal municipal legal systems reproduce the substance of certain fundamental moral requirements" (Hart 7). This, of course, leads positivism's most important competitor, natural law theory, to claim "that law is best understood as a 'branch' of morality or justice" (Hart 7).[4] Positivists, of course, deny this. Finally, and as is well-known, Hart devotes an entire chapter of *The Concept of Law* to the relationship between "Law and Morals," noting that positivists deny that "the criteria of legal validity of particular laws used in a legal system must include, tacitly if not explicitly, a reference to morality or justice" and that, in consequence, "it is in no sense a necessary truth that laws reproduce or satisfy certain demands of morality, though in fact they have often done so" (Hart 185–86).

Raz, similarly, devotes fully half of his classic collection of essays, *The Authority of Law*, to "criticiz[ing] various attempts to establish a conceptual connection between law and morality"[5] and the seminal chapter on "Legal Positivism and the Sources of Law" makes clear that the identification of law "is a matter of social fact" thus independent of its "moral merit" (Raz 37).[6]

If it is familiar and uncontroversial that the demarcation problem has been central to legal philosophy, it perhaps requires more emphasis on what kind of answer to the demarcation problem jurisprudents have demanded. Hart himself says we want to understand "the nature (or the essence) of law," though he views that framing as "obscure[]" (Hart 6). But what is it to understand the *nature* or the *essence* of law? Julie Dickson, following Raz (but not Hart), says that:

> A successful theory of law . . . is a theory which consists of propositions about the law which (1) are necessarily true, and (2) adequately explain the nature of law. . . . I am using "the nature of law" to refer to those essential properties which a given set of phenomena must exhibit in order to be law.[7]

[4] Ronald Dworkin's last book, *Justice for Hedgehogs* (Harvard University Press, 2011), endorsed this absurd view explicitly, although he was hardly the first. The notorious Nazi judge Roland Freisler, for example, also believed that "[t]here can be no divide between a requirement of law and a requirement of morality. For requirements of law are requirements of [moral] decency." Herlinde Pauer-Studer, *Justifying Injustice: Legal Theory in Nazi German* (Cambridge University Press, 2020), 205. See ch. 11 in this volume for further discussion.

[5] Joseph Raz, *The Authority of Law: Essays on Law and Morality*, 2nd ed. (Oxford University Press, 2009), x. All further references will be included by page number in the body of the text.

[6] Raz's role in this story is complicated for reasons discussed in ch. 11 in this volume.

[7] Julie Dickson, *Evaluation and Legal Theory* (Hart Publishing, 2001), 17. Dickson faithfully follows Raz's lead here, though he has not always been so immodest. Thus, in the earlier essay "Legal Positivism and the Sources of Law," reprinted in his *The Authority of Law*, 2nd ed. (Oxford University Press, 2009), Raz notes that it is no part of the argument for the Sources Thesis "that a similar

She is echoed by Scott Shapiro, who says that in inquiring into "the fundamental nature of law" we want to "supply the set of properties that make (possible or actual) instances of [law] the things that they are"[8] and offers the example of water being H2O:[9] "Being H2O is what makes water *water*. With respect to law, accordingly, to answer the question 'What is law?' on this interpretation is to discover what makes all and only instances of law instances of *law* and not something else."[10] In addition, says Shapiro (here again echoing Dickson who is following Raz), "to discover the law's nature" is also "to discover its necessary properties, i.e., those properties that law could not fail to have."[11]

Legal philosophy has, unsurprisingly, always been hostage to its philosophical climate—jurisprudents are rarely, if ever, innovators in philosophy. They, instead, are the jurisprudential Owls of Minerva, bringing considered philosophical opinion in its maturity (sometimes, alas, on its death bed) to bear on theoretical questions that arise distinctively in the legal realm. Thus, Kelsen's jurisprudence bears the stamp of neo-Kantianism and the moral anti-realism common among logical positivists; Ross's jurisprudence presumes the correctness of logical positivist semantics and epistemology; and Hart's jurisprudence reflects the methodological influence of ordinary language philosophy and the substantive influence of post-World War II Oxford-style noncognitivism. The early Kelsen and Hart had (or at least often appeared to presuppose) what seems to me to be the correct metaethical position (broadly antirealist[12]), but did not, perhaps, fully appreciate its import with respect to some of their central jurisprudential concerns. What is particularly striking is that, even at the start of the twenty-first century, legal philosophers set conditions for a successful analysis of the demarcation problem—to identify the "necessary" and "essential" properties of law that distinguish it from morality in all cases—that would strike most

conception of legal systems is to be found in all cultures and in all periods." Ibid., 50. That is only one kind of theoretical modesty, for one might still think that it is possible to state necessary truths that explain the essential nature of a culturally and temporally bounded human practice; as noted in the text, our experience in the philosophy of science in the twentieth century invites skepticism.

[8] Scott J. Shapiro, *Legality* (Harvard University Press, 2011), 8–9.

[9] In fact, as the philosopher of science, Michael Weisberg has written, "Water Is *Not* H_2O," in *Philosophy of Chemistry: Synthesis of a New Discipline*, ed. David Baird et al. (Springer, 2006), 337–45. Briefly, hydrogen and oxygen both have multiple isotopes (atoms with the same number of protons and electrons, but different neutrons), and the natural language category of "water" doesn't distinguish between them; in addition, chemical kinds are individuated by their "structural" properties (at the macro, molecular, and atomic level) and "reactive" properties (how the substance transforms, either over time or when interacting with other substances); isotopic differences matter here.

[10] Shapiro, *Legality*, 9.

[11] Ibid. Certainly, Hart would not have found this "essentialist" characterization of the demarcation problem satisfactory.

[12] Noncognitivist semantics of moral discourse have some appeal, but so does error theory. In any case, it is a mistake to let the semantic tail wag the metaphysical dog, and with respect to the latter, moral anti-realism is the most plausible view. See generally, ch. 15 in this volume.

philosophers in other fields, even forty years ago, as wholly incredible. The persistence of the demarcation problem means that the most recent jurisprudential Owl of Minerva has not yet taken flight. I hope here to set this venerable philosophical bird on her path and to lay this most recent version of the demarcation problem to rest.

II. Law Is an Artifact

The concept of law is the concept of an *artifact*, that is, something that necessarily owes its existence to human activities, often (but not always) intended to create that artifact (I refine the definition below). Even John Finnis, the leading natural law theorist of recent decades, does not deny this point.[13] I certainly do not understand Kelsen, Bobbio, Hart, Raz, or other self-identified positivists to deny this claim. Those who might want to deny that law is an artifact concept are not my concern here; the extravagance of their metaphysical commitments would, I suspect, be a subject for psychological, not philosophical, investigation.

Artifact concepts, even simple ones like "chair," are notoriously resistant to analyses in terms of their essential attributes, both because they are hostage to changing human ends and purposes and because they cannot be individuated by their natural properties (chairs, after all, can be made of stone, wood, metal, etc.). Artifacts can be made of almost anything; natural kinds, by contrast, are often thought in recent Anglophone metaphysics to have distinctive microconstitutions, whether characterized in chemical, molecular, or genetic terms.[14] To be clear, I am a Quinean about natural kinds: "natural kinds" just pick out those ways of grouping things over which the sciences can produce lawful generalizations, groupings we would be especially loath to abandon given the disruption to the rest of our theoretical picture of how the world works. That is the only sense of "natural kind" that can make sense for empiricists and fallibilists, and it's the sense I endorse here. That means, of course, that at bottom, "natural kinds" also answer to human interests—the various pragmatic interests that inform theory-choice given the underdetermination of theory by evidence and

[13] Finnis, after all, admits that positivism gives the correct account of "what any competent lawyer . . . would say are (or are not) intra-systematically valid laws, imposing 'legal requirements.'" John Finnis, "On the Incoherence of Legal Positivism," *Notre Dame Law Review* 75 (2000): 1611. Finnis complains instead that positivism does not have an adequate answer to questions it was not asking, such as when there is a moral obligation to obey the law. See the critical discussion in Brian Leiter, *Naturalizing Jurisprudence: Essays on American Legal Realism and Naturalism in Legal Philosophy* (Oxford University Press, 2007), 163–64, 193–94.

[14] That is the more recent "metaphysical" view of natural kinds, rather different than the Whewell/Mill/Quine empiricist view, well-defended in Muhammad Ali Khalidi, *Natural Categories and Human Kinds* (Cambridge University Press, 2013).

logic[15]—and so the difference between them and artifacts will be one of degree. But differences of degree can still be vast and theoretically and practically significant, and that is true about the way we demarcate stuff with a distinctive microconstitution from stuff that is notable mainly for how human beings use it.

Things on the artifact side of the divide do not have distinctive microconstitutions, but perhaps they can have essential or necessary properties of some other kind? Perhaps, for example, the essential property of an artifact is its function? Even in the case of "chairs," however, this seems a difficult analysis to provide. Their apparent function—providing support for those who sit—can be discharged by boxes, tortoises, car seats, and steps. Moreover, some chairs have as their actual function ornamental decoration, not sitting; some serve primarily as shelves for stacking papers or books. Some chairs have arm rests, some do not; some have back rests, some do not. Because human ends and purposes shift, the concept of a "chair" has no essential attributes that transcend a particular time and place.

Hart, who is more metaphysically cautious than, for example, Dickson or Shapiro, only claims to be analyzing the concept of law used by someone familiar with the "modern municipal legal system" (Hart 7). If the *essentialist* project can be salvaged with these boundaries, that is a question that can only be resolved a posteriori. The inductive case for skepticism developed below does not, in any case, depend on assuming that the account on offer is atemporal. Notice, of course, that this kind of move—deflating the ambitions of the analysis by bounding it temporally, perhaps culturally and geographically as well—represents a major deflation of the rhetoric of those committed to the demarcation problem in recent jurisprudence.

Most philosophers who think artifacts can have essential functions appeal to a different consideration to determine that function: the intention of the maker of the artifact. Let us consider a recent paper by the legal philosopher Luka Burazin, who has given the most systematic account of law's artifactual nature in the jurisprudential literature and its relationship to claims about function.[16] Burazin begins with a well-known philosophical account of artifacts due to Risto Hilpinen, according to which an artifact is "an object that has been intentionally made for a certain purpose" (Burazin 388).[17] This way of thinking about

[15] On this see generally, W. V. O. Quine and Joseph Ullian, *The Web of Belief* (Random House, 1978).

[16] Luka Burazin, "Can There Be an Artifact Theory of Law?," *Ratio Juris* 29 (2016): 385–401. All further citations to Burazin are by page number in the body of the text. For a somewhat similar account, see Jonathan Crowe, "Law as an Artifact Kind," *Monash University Law Review* 40 (2014): 737–57. Crowe's account has the virtue of acknowledging the problem that law does not necessarily involve an author, but his positive account is similar to Burazin's, and faces similar difficulties. (Crowe also aims to vindicate a natural law theory, which is no part of Burazin's ambition.)

[17] Risto Hilpinen, "Artifact," *Stanford Encyclopedia of Philosophy*, accessed November 11, 2016, http://plato.stanford.edu/entries/artifact/. A different account of artifacts as functional kinds holds only that the function is the one the artifact has "historically reproduced to serve." Beth Preston,

artifacts poses an immediate difficulty in the case of law, due to the ambiguity of what "law" refers to. *Particular laws*—say, a particular statute or a particular court decision—may be created intentionally "for a certain purpose," though in the case of legislation, *what* purpose is often a particularly vexed question.[18] (It can also be vexed in the case of a judicial decision, since the law created by the decision may be different from what the judges explicitly intended, and it may be unclear whether the purpose was, e.g., a fair resolution of the dispute before the court or to create a rule that will influence subsequent behavior.) The positivist theory of law, however, is not a theory about *particular laws*; it is rather a theory about why "particular laws" are tokens of a type "law." And the type law is a social phenomenon that is only implicit and inchoate in the actual practice of judges, lawyers, and ordinary citizens familiar with "modern municipal legal systems," as Hart put it (Hart 7). This is a crucial problem for the traditional way of thinking of artifacts due to Hilpinen, and which Burazin follows. For it is not the case that the *type law*—the phenomenon of law captured by our concept of it—was "intentionally made for a certain purpose."[19] The difficulty becomes apparent when Burazin says that "the intention of legal officials to create an instantiation of the legal system is based on their substantive concept of the legal system" (Burazin 398). But there is no evidence that legal officials have any such intentions let alone a substantive concept "of the legal system"—even if some philosophers do!

Law is not alone in being an artifact without an intentional creator. Think of etiquette: Even the particular norms of etiquette are rarely intentionally created, and the institution of regulating the boundaries of informal social interaction by, for example, norms of politeness, respect, and courtesy[20]—"etiquette"—is a kind of human social practice that was not created by anyone or any group for any particular purpose, though it has served several different ones in societies (e.g., reducing social friction, preserving hierarchy, marking degrees of intimacy

"Philosophical Theories of Artifact Function," in *Philosophy of Technology and Engineering Sciences*, ed. Anthonie Meijers (Reidel, 2009), 226. Such a proposal runs into the difficulties discussed below in the text regarding the idea that law's distinctive function is to "guide conduct."

[18] See generally Max Radin, "Statutory Interpretation," *Harvard Law Review* 43 (1930): 863–85; Frank H. Easterbrook, "Judicial Discretion in Statutory Interpretation," *Oklahoma Law Review* 57 (2004); Richard Ekins, *The Nature of Legislative Intent* (Oxford University Press, 2016).

[19] Burazin, following other authors, allows that "an artifact can have properties . . . acquired through its use in practice," but this is secondary to the primary properties, which are due to the author's intentions (Burazin 391). Burazin also denies that "patterns of behavior or behavioural regularities alone can constitute institutional artifacts" (law being an institutional artifact), again insisting that "a substantive concept" of that artifact must be intentionally applied and recognized by the community (ibid., 395). But an inchoate concept, like the concept of law (or etiquette) cannot satisfy that demand, since agents have the concept only partially and inchoately.

[20] Note that the instantiation of such norms varies wildly by culture: crossing legs, showing one's feet, sitting down at a particular moment, can all violate etiquette norms or be compatible with them.

in relationships, among others). Yet etiquette, like law, does not exist without humans producing it, and what comes into existence is not reducible to or even supervenient upon any cluster of natural properties about which the sciences can identify nomic regularities. Yet the practice "etiquette" is still a human artifact, not only because humans produce it, but because *humans care about it.* So I suggest we think of the category of "artifacts" more broadly, as the category of phenomena that *result from human action*, which are *responsive to human interests*, and which are not otherwise natural kinds.[21] That captures both law and etiquette. Burazin's error is to define artifactuality in terms of intentionality, and then to suppose that the distinctive function is traceable to intention.

Notice that law and etiquette are also no different than "science" in this regard. No one set out to create the domain of human inquiry we now call "science" to serve a particular function; what happened, of course, in the scientific revolution is that individuals set out to try to discover different kinds of regularities in nature, and found out that they could do so through certain methods, with the resulting amalgamation of theories being deemed "science." Science is a human artifact too, but like law and etiquette, it has no intentional maker of the type of social phenomenon it is, though people and whole political cultures care about science immensely. Is there a distinctive *function* of science nonetheless? Certainly, initially, it seemed to be the *prediction and control* of nature, but that will hardly help explain the sense in which geology and evolutionary biology are part of science. Indeed, as Larry Laudan has shown,[22] there is no criterion at all, let alone a functional one, that essentially demarcates science from nonscience. We shall return to this point shortly, but first I want to consider one other rejoinder on behalf of artifacts having essential functions.

Leslie Green has recently expressed skepticism about what lesson we should draw from the preceding about the prospects for individuating artifact types by their functions. He gives the amusing purported counterexample of a "printer-driver": "[N]o string of code is a printer-driver," he observes, "unless it is written in order to, or has or could have some capacity, to drive a printer."[23] As a matter of metaphysics, we can agree with Green that artifacts, like other entities, are self-identical, which is all his purported analysis of the function shows. The real question is whether there is any account of the *functional kind* of an artifact that does not trade on self-identity and does not avert to the intentions of

[21] Some words pick out phenomena that lead dual existences. A "wolverine" can be a biological kind of animal, but it is also an artifact: the mascot for the University of Michigan sports teams.

[22] Larry Laudan, "The Demise of the Demarcation Problem," in *Physics, Philosophy and Psychoanalysis: Essays in Honor of Adolf Grünbaum*, ed. R. S. Cohen and Larry Laudan (Springer, 1983). All further citations will be included by page number in the body of the text.

[23] Leslie Green, "The Morality in Law," in *Reading HLA Hart's* The Concept of Law, ed. Luis Duarte d'Ameida, James Edwards, and Andrea Dolcetti (Bloomsbury, 2013), 200. Additional references are included by page number in the body of the text.

the creator—which for the reasons already noted, is not available in the case of law. In short, could phenomena that are produced by humans and responsive to human interests still have distinctive functions, where distinctive means "type-individuating" functions?

One possibility, it might seem, is that facts about the etiology of the artifact *apart from the intentions of a creator* could individuate a function characteristic of the type. We are, of course, familiar with this idea from selectionist accounts not of artifactual but biological kinds. Yet even in the latter context, the claim is controversial. As the philosopher of biology David Hull asked, in an influential paper a quarter-century ago:

> [W]hat is the normal function of the [human] hand? We can do many things with our hands. We can drive cars, play the violin, type on electronic computers, scratch itches, masturbate, and strangle one another. Some of these actions may seem normal; others not, but there is no correlation between commonsense notions of normal functions and the functions which hands were able to fulfill throughout our existence. About all a biologist can say about the function of the human hand is that anything that we can do with it is "normal."[24]

Hull's view is by no means uncontroversial,[25] but I mention it only to underline that even in the biological domain, function talk is complicated. What then of artifacts, which have no biological etiology (and no intentional creator), how are their functions to be determined?

Law, like etiquette, serves many functions, and no evolutionary story—certainly none with the explanatory power of natural selection—picks out any distinctive one. When we untether artifacts from creators, I fear, functions are always hostage to rather variable interests, since that is all that is left to us to individuate the artifacts. Sometimes it is said that the "essential" function of law is to guide conduct,[26] but perhaps we should pause for a moment to make clear why this will not work. Many valid laws do not, of course, guide conduct (think of many laws against jay-walking, or many speed limits on highways). But even

[24] David Hull, "On Human Nature," in *Arguing about Human Nature*, ed. S. Downes and E. Machery (Routledge, 2013), 31.

[25] See Edouard Machery, "A Plea for Human Nature," in *Arguing about Human Nature*, ed. S. Downes and E. Machery (Routledge, 2013), 65–68, explaining the relevance of etiology to function talk.

[26] Those influenced by speculative evolutionary psychology and anthropology sometimes think that law's function is a certain kind of "social coordination," which is an even more demanding standard than the fairly thin idea of "guiding conduct." I do not consider such proposals here, given how thin the scientific evidence is that this picks out a distinctive function of law. Consider: If law's function were really "social coordination," then why does the actual content of the law in societies at similar levels of economic development differ so dramatically? Evolutionary functionalists need to answer that question.

if we say the essential function of law is to *try* to guide conduct, there is the obvious problem that morality, for example, also tries to guide conduct, but moral guidance is not necessarily legal guidance. Law and morality also share this aim with the differing sets of rules that govern the Catholic Mass, dining in a fancy restaurant, and playing cricket. So if law were "essentially" about guiding conduct, that by itself would not pick it out from other normative systems. More problematically, however, law serves other functions besides attempted guidance of conduct: For example, some laws are meant to signal the values or aspirations of a community (or a class), and some are simply ceremonial (think of commemorations of national heroes). Law sometimes guides conduct, often attempts to guide conduct, but it cannot claim that as its distinguishing essential function, since it shares guidance and attempted guidance with too many other normative systems, and, itself, discharges other functions as well. The only thing that would demarcate law's guidance of function, when it does, would be an answer to the demarcation problem!

Green also accuses me of a *tu quoque* fallacy: "Leiter even holds," he says, "that it is a necessary feature of something being an artifact that it has no (other) necessary features," and then claims that this shows, *contra* my skepticism, that there is, in fact, a necessary difference between law and morality since, as Green asserts, "morality does *not* owe its existence to human activities intended to create morality" (Green 200). Green takes as his target here an earlier formulation in which I mistakenly claimed that artifacts had to be *intentional* human creations, a view I now repudiate for the reasons given above. My worry then was about human babies, which are not, it seems, artifacts, but are human creations, although not always intentional. But human babies are biological kinds, just like calves and lion cubs, and so are not artifacts in the sense proposed earlier: they result from human actions, human beings care about them, but they are biological kinds, so not artifacts.[27]

[27] I want to mention one other interesting objection to an earlier version of this paper, presented in Mark Murphy, "Two Unhappy Dilemmas for Natural Law Jurisprudence," *American Journal of Jurisprudence* 60 (2015): 121–42. Murphy wrote:

> Consider a kind that clearly counts as artifactual by the proposed standard [at 125: "in part to be something that owes its existence to the activity of persons who are its makers, and that *somehow* the intentions of those who are its makers enter constitutively into the explanation of its existence conditions"] but which does not at all seem to be subject to the claim [by Leiter] that artifactual kinds are matters of shifting, contingent interest. Consider kinds of illocutionary acts, acts of doing things with words. Take *assertion*, for example. Assertions are made by people. Their existence and identity-conditions may not be well-understood, but it is pretty plain that assertion is connected to agents' intentions in a way that is characteristic of artifacts . . . [T]here is a thriving philosophical enterprise of working through the question of what the necessary features are of different sorts of illocutionary act, and assertion especially . . . *Id.* at 125–26.

Murphy is right that speech acts (or particular kinds of speech acts, like "assertions") are artifacts on a definition I had utilized earlier. It was in part because of objections like this, and objections by

Green's objection, however, does not depend on the specific claim about intentionality: It depends on my thinking there is a way to mark the artifact/natural kind distinction, which seems to commit me to artifacts having some necessary features after all. Of course, "artifacts" could have necessary features, even if particular artifacts do not. Everything turns here, in any case, on the sense of "necessity": If the artifact/natural kind distinction is theoretically fruitful, as I think it is, then we need to say what that distinction is. As with natural kinds themselves, on the Quinean view, the boundaries could shift: In that sense, they are not necessary. But as theorizing stands today, if artifacts have essential features or functions, unrelated to intentions, then someone should name them! Green does not, and no one has.[28]

III. Science and the Demarcation Problem

Those working in general jurisprudence attracted to the recent "essentialist" version of the demarcation problem should be given special pause by the failure of twentieth-century philosophy of science to identify the essential features of science, one of the most important human artifacts of modernity. Karl Popper, Rudolf Carnap, and Carl Hempel, to name three luminaries of twentieth-century philosophy, were interested in a version of this demarcation problem—not how to demarcate law from morality, to be sure, but how to demarcate epistemically reliable forms of inquiry from epistemically unreliable ones, that is, how to demarcate science from pseudo-science or nonsense. Like the recent legal philosophers, they sought to identify the essential properties of a human artifact (namely, science). They failed, and spectacularly so. Perhaps there is a lesson for legal philosophers in this story?

In philosophy of science, the demarcation problem was the problem of figuring out which kinds of human inquiry were *epistemically special*, that is, which had epistemic properties or characteristics that warranted the inference that the conclusions of such an inquiry were likely to be true. Those epistemically special forms of inquiry were to be deemed *scientific*, and so deserving of

Green, that it seemed important to characterize artifacts as "the category of phenomena that *result from human action*, which are *responsive to human interests*, and which are not otherwise natural kinds." Speech acts are features of *natural languages* that admit of empirical investigation and description; particular kinds of speech acts are just *natural kinds*, i.e., recurring types of speech acts in natural languages, whose characteristics, inferential properties, etc., can be studied and analyzed.

[28] This is more minor, but it is not my view that morality "does not owe its existence to human activities"—like law and etiquette, it does not owe its existence to *intentional* human activities, but it is a wholly conventional normative system, as Nietzsche, among many others, knew. I do not think this is a point of disagreement between me and Green.

credence, while all others were not. Permit me to quote from Larry Laudan's seminal treatment of the rise and fall of the demarcation problem, which he characterizes as follows:

> [W]e expect a demarcation criterion to identify the *epistemic* or *methodological* features which mark off scientific beliefs from unscientific ones. We want to know what, if anything, is special about the knowledge claims and the modes of inquiry of the sciences... [A]ny philosophically interesting demarcative device must distinguish scientific and non-scientific matters in a way which exhibits a surer epistemic warrant or evidential ground for science than non-science. If it should happen that there is no such warrant, then the demarcation between science and non-science would turn out to be of little or no philosophic significance. (Laudan 118)

Attempts to solve the scientific demarcation problem were, in turn, precisely efforts to specify the "conditions which are both necessary and sufficient" for some form of inquiry to be scientific (Laudan 119).

The history of the search for such a criterion is quite a long one, going back to antiquity (though the artifact Aristotle wanted to understand is different than ours, not surprisingly) (Laudan 112–13). In the nineteenth century, there were attempts to specify the distinctive "method" of scientific inquiry (Laudan 115–17), but the solutions to the scientific demarcation problem most familiar to us now were those associated with the Logical Positivists and Karl Popper. "Verificationist" theories held that scientific propositions were genuinely meaningful (i.e., empirically verifiable). These theories, however, ran into trouble because, on the one hand, as Laudan observes, "many statements in the sciences [are] not open to exhaustive verification (e.g., all universal laws)" (Laudan 120), while many false statements—like "the Earth is flat"—are verifiable (though false!) since "we can specify a class of possible observations which would verify" the statement (Laudan 121). Popper's alternative, eschewing verification in favor of falsifiability, ran into different problems: it could not explain the scientific status of most "singular existential statement[s]" (e.g., "there exists a Black Hole"), and it deems "scientific" "every crank claim which makes ascertainably false assertions" (Laudan 121).[29]

[29] Other objections were raised to Popper's falsificationism. Paul Feyerabend called attention to the commitment of natural scientists to theories some of whose predictions had actually been falsified. The so-called Duhem-Quine thesis about the underdetermination of theory by evidence suggests that no theoretical claim can ever be falsified, since there is always a choice, when confronted with recalcitrant evidence, to reject *either* the claim being tested *or* the background assumptions underlying the test. (Laudan, however, is a critic of the Duhem-Quine thesis: see, e.g., Larry Laudan, *Science and Relativism* (University of Chicago Press, 1990).)

As Laudan observes, we cannot "prove that there is no conceivable philosophical reconstruction of our intuitive distinction between the scientific and the non-scientific" (or we might add, between the "legal" and the "moral") (Laudan 124). But we can conclude, as Laudan does, that "none of the criteria which have been offered thus far promises to explicate the distinction" (Laudan 124). We should, therefore, ask *why solving the demarcation problem* matters? For what philosophical or practical purposes do we need a solution to the demarcation problem?

In the case of science, the solution mattered for explicitly *practical* reasons. As Laudan remarks, "demarcation criteria are typically used as *machines du guerre* in a polemical battle between rival camps" (Laudan 119). So, for example, "Popper was out to 'get' Marx and Freud" (Laudan 119) by showing that their theories were not falsifiable. Popper, alas, had no real understanding of either Marx's or Freud's views,[30] but that is tangential to our concerns here. What matters, as Laudan notes, is that:

> the labeling of a certain activity as "scientific" or "unscientific" has social and political ramifications which go well beyond the taxonomic task of sorting beliefs into two piles. . . . Precisely because a demarcation criterion will serve as a rationale for taking a number of *practical* actions which may well have far-reaching moral, social and economic consequences, it would be wise to insist that the arguments in favor of any demarcation criterion we intend to take seriously should be especially compelling. (Laudan 120)

In other words, the demarcation problem was thought to matter because *knowledge* matters, because what we *know* affects what we think ought to be done. As Laudan remarks, "It remains as important as it ever was to ask questions like: When is a claim well confirmed? When can we regard a theory as well tested? What characterizes cognitive progress?" (Laudan, 124). What the failure in philosophy of science to solve the demarcation problem shows is that we cannot take a shortcut to answer these questions by simply dividing forms of inquiry into the "scientific" and "nonscientific" based on some necessary and essential properties distinguishing the two forms of inquiry.

30 See generally Brian Leiter, "The Hermeneutics of Suspicion: Recovering Marx, Nietzsche, and Freud," in *The Future for Philosophy*, ed. Brian Leiter (Oxford University Press, 2004).

IV. Implications for Jurisprudence

So what then about the demarcation problem in jurisprudence? I do not need to rehearse for this audience the doubts about the positivist analysis of law, the most powerful and successful analysis of law we have. Many of these doubts may be, as I am inclined to think, misguided, yet who can deny that there are genuinely hard cases for the positivist to explain. Can the idea of a rule of recognition really account for the reasoning of common-law courts interpreting precedents? And what of the rule of recognition itself? Hart says the "rule of recognition" is merely a social rule, so its content is fixed by whatever the practice of officials in a particular legal system happens to be.[31] Raz says the practice cannot include an appeal to moral criteria of legal validity consistent with the law's claim to authority.[32] Scott Shapiro says it cannot include such appeals consistent with the law's claim to guide conduct.[33] Wil Waluchow argues the law's claim to authority is compatible with an official practice of employing moral criteria of legal validity if authoritative directives are merely weighty, rather than exclusionary, reasons for action.[34] And so on.

If, in the history of philosophy, there is not a single successful analysis of the "necessary" or "essential" properties of a human artifact, why should we think law will be different? If hundreds, perhaps thousands, of philosophers in the last century—both the innovators like Carnap and Popper and the legions of less well-known philosophical laborers—could not specify the essential and necessary features of *science*, perhaps the most important and transformative human artifact of recorded history, should we really hold out hope that an analysis of *law* will yield "necessary" and "essential" criteria (i.e., criteria that will classify every norm in either the "legal" or the "nonlegal" camp)?

A skeptical induction over past failure is not a conclusive refutation, just as the failure to solve the demarcation problem in philosophy of science does not prove that there is no account of the *essential* and *necessary* properties of a scientific inquiry. Rather than belabor the no doubt familiar disputes about the demarcation problem in jurisprudence, let us follow Laudan's lead and ask a different question: namely, Why does solving this problem matter?

In surveying the writings of the great writers on the demarcation problem in jurisprudence—I here mean Kelsen, Hart, and Raz—it seems that two practical concerns (sometimes implicit, sometimes explicit) explain the importance

[31] See H. L. A. Hart, "Postscript," in *The Concept of Law*, ed. Penelope Bulloch and Joseph Raz (Clarendon Press, 2012), esp. 250–54.

[32] Joseph Raz, "Authority, Law, and Morality," reprinted in *Ethics in the Public Domain* (Oxford University Press, 1994).

[33] Scott J. Shapiro, "On Hart's Way Out," *Legal Theory* 4 (1998): 469–507.

[34] W. J. Waluchow, *Inclusive Legal Positivism* (Clarendon Press, 1994).

for these writers, and those who follow them, of demarcating *legal* from *moral* norms[35]:

(1) The fact that a norm is *legally valid* does not mean it is *morally obligatory* (or even *morally attractive*).
(2) The fact that a decision by a legal official would be *morally attractive* does not mean it is *legally obligatory.*

In other words, legal positivists—those who have insisted that the demarcation problem can be solved—are keen to emphasize that *legality does not entail morality* and, conversely, that *morality does not entail legality.* You will notice, of course, that the need to draw this distinction, to solve the demarcation problem, turns on the assumption that the *moral validity* of a norm entails a practical consequence (i.e., it entails acting in accordance with the norm). If we grant that assumption, then confusing law and morality has serious practical consequences indeed: It means that if the *legal validity* of a norm is equivalent to its moral validity, then every law *ought to be obeyed* (something no legal positivists believe, of course). And, conversely, it means that if a norm is morally valid, then a legal actor *ought to apply it.*

The demarcation problem in philosophy of science was meant to solve a normative problem about theoretical rationality, about what we ought to believe. As Laudan correctly observed, its solution had consequences for practical reasons, for what *ought* to be done, and it was these that motivated the ultimately futile search for a theoretical shortcut. The demarcation problem in jurisprudence also purports to resolve a theoretical dilemma: what to believe about the nature of law. The connection of an answer to this question to matters of practical import may seem even more apparent.[36] Perhaps we can defuse interest in the demarcation problem in jurisprudence if we tackle its underlying assumption—namely, that the *moral validity* of a norm is overriding in practical reasoning? (Legal positivists, of course, recognize that the legal validity of a norm does not entail anything about a moral obligation to follow it.)

Suppose it were agreed that the *moral validity* of a norm was *not* overriding in practical reasoning. Suppose morally valid norms merely give defeasible (even easily defeasible) reasons for acting, just like legally valid norms and norms of

[35] I do not mean to deny that these writers also have a purely theoretical concern (i.e., figuring out what they take to be necessarily true about law). But since I am arguing that there is no reason to think this is a viable theoretical project—unless ethnographically and temporally bounded in ways that are not obviously congenial to the essentialist ambitions of Raz and progeny—it seems useful, following Laudan's lead, to think about its import for practical reasoning.

[36] Some writers draw the connection explicitly: For example, Shapiro says that "analytical jurisprudence [meaning a solution to the Demarcation Problem] has profound practical implications for the practice of law." Shapiro, *Legality*, 25.

instrumental rationality. That a norm was legally valid might, in some cases, also mean it is morally valid, but what if that did not change reasoning about what ought to be done? That a norm was morally valid might be an interesting fact for a judge to note, but it would not require the judge to make one decision rather than another. In such a world, would solving the demarcation problem in jurisprudence matter? It is hard to see why.

Kelsen and Hart were both metaphysical antirealists about moral norms; that is, they denied that such norms had any objective existence, and they denied that the best metaphysical account of what the world contains would include facts about what is morally right and wrong. This might suggest that the *normativity* of morals—its ability to give people reasons to act—should be understood in exclusively psychological terms—that is, as a psychological fact about what particular people believe and feel when they learn that "It is morally wrong to do X" or "It is morally right to Y." I believe the most charitable reading of Hart should understand him as accepting something like this view, since, unlike Kelsen, his was an "impure" theory of law, in which anti-realism about norms was conjoined with noncognitivism about the semantics of normative judgment: To judge that doing X is morally (or legally) wrong is just to express a certain kind of attitude or feeling, presumably one tied—psychologically—to motivation and action.[37] Hart did, of course, reject the view he associated with Alf Ross, namely, that legal *validity* consisted in "a verifiable hypothesis about future judicial behavior and its special motivational feeling."[38] This dispute traded on Hart's misunderstanding of what Ross meant by "validity" (for Ross, it was a term of art, not applicable to the ordinary concept of law) and by the tacit philosophical behaviorism Hart had inherited from Ryle, and which made him think that a mental state (like acceptance from an internal point of view) could be adequately captured in terms of behavior (e.g., convergence on a norm in practice, criticism of those who deviate from the norm, etc.).[39] We can, happily, put those confusions aside here. The point at issue here concerns what an anti-realism about *norms*, which Hart accepts, entails about motivation and action. On the view I am proposing, to the extent an agent's judgment that X is *morally right* has normative force for the agent, that normative force is explicable in terms of certain psychological facts about the agent. It is possible Hart did not always understand this, as when he says:

[37] For the legal case, see Kevin Toh, "Hart's Expressivism and His Benthamite Project," *Legal Theory* 11 (2005): 115.

[38] H. L. A. Hart, "Scandinavian Realism," repr. *Essays in Jurisprudence and Philosophy* (Oxford University Press, 1983), 65.

[39] On Hart's misunderstanding of Ross, see Brian Leiter, "Alf Ross's Critique of American Legal Realism—and a Naturalistic Critique of Ross," available on SSRN at https://papers.ssrn.com/sol3/papers.cfm?abstract_id=4240991; and on the Ryle influence specifically, see Brian Leiter, "Back to Hart," *Annals of the Faculty of Law-Belgrade Law Review* 69 (2021): 749–60.

> [T]he internal character of [normative legal judgments, like, "You must stop at the red light"] is not a mere matter of the speaker having certain "feelings of compulsion"; for though these may indeed often accompany the making of such statements they are neither necessary nor sufficient conditions of their normative use in criticizing conduct, making claims and justifying hostile reactions by reference to the accepted standard.[40]

On one reading, all Hart might mean is that agents manifest the "internal point of view" simply by virtue of using the right kind of normative language and making the right kinds of justificatory or critical comments about, respectively, conforming or deviant behavior vis-à-vis some rule. But to the extent the "internal point of view" of the actor making the legal judgment is *normative* for that agent (i.e., motivates him to act), then that is a psychological fact about the agent, about his "feelings" as it were. If Hart really meant to deny that, then he was, alas, just mistaken.

Insofar as one believes that people feel moral rightness demands action, then one has good reason to worry about the demarcation problem. The "purity" of Kelsen's theory—his reluctance to assimilate the normativity of law to psychosocial facts about behavior and attitudes—might seem to block the naturalization of the problem suggested by the approach sketched above. So as not to be taken far afield, I shall simply declare, somewhat dogmatically, my allegiance to Hume, Nietzsche, and (I would hope) Hart in being skeptical that any sense can be given to the neo-Kantian idea of the grounds of intelligibility of the application of norms apart from a psychological one.[41] We need, accordingly, to approach the demarcation problem in that spirit.

If we understand the idea of the *morally obligatory* or *morally attractive* in purely psychologistic terms, then the practical import of solving the demarcation problem changes. What is legally valid is not necessarily morally obligatory, and what is morally attractive is not necessarily legally obligatory: Those are the two key (often implicit) contentions of recent proponents of the positivist answer to the demarcation problem. But this only seems important to emphasize because *people actually think the moral is overriding in practical reasoning.* In a world in which people, for example, viewed *moral obligation* as on a par in practical reasoning with "would feel pleasant," it is hard to see why the demarcation problem would matter. Perhaps legal norms are *morally obligatory*, but that does

[40] Hart, "Scandinavian Realism," 167.

[41] I am also fairly confident (*contra* Quine's naturalism, with its unprincipled commitment to psychological behaviorism even in the face of the a posteriori failure of that research program) that our best explanatory theory of the world will need to presuppose the reality of the mental states of persons, though it will not need to make explanatory appeal to moral norms. See Brian Leiter, "Moral Facts and Best Explanations," repr. Leiter, *Naturalizing Jurisprudence.*

not answer the question of what should be done. And perhaps certain norms are morally attractive: That does not decide, at all, the question whether a judge should apply them. And that, I will suggest, is really what we are interested in.

Admittedly, the world as the moral philosophers imagine it is one in which morality is overriding in practical reason. We may bracket, for the moment, Nietzschean and Thucydidean skepticism about whether this is the real world.[42] The point that bears emphasizing is that if the solution to the demarcation problem is supposed to answer a practical question about *what ought to be done*, one that is reducible to a psychosocial question about the attitudes people have about morality and legality, then we should ask: Is there any reason to think a *theoretical* solution to the demarcation problem will affect the actual psychological attitudes of persons?

Defenders of legal positivism, the dominant answer to the demarcation problem (in both its essentialist and nonessentialist forms) in the last two hundred years, are surely familiar with the contention that a solution to the demarcation problem has far-reaching consequences for practice. This was, after all, the central thought behind Lon Fuller's famous 1957 attack on H. L. A. Hart,[43] which has been a target of philosophical derision ever since for its odd mischaracterizations of the claims of legal positivists, including Hart. Fuller thought, simply put, that the blame for the moral depravity of Nazi judges could be laid at the door of their "positivism"—that is, their view that they were bound to apply the legally valid norms of their immoral system (Fuller 649). According to Fuller, positivism's "definitions of 'what law really is' are not mere images of some datum of experience, but direction posts for the application of human energies" (Fuller 632), and he reminds us that "words have a powerful effect on human attitudes" (Fuller 649). Thus, Fuller deems it worth asking "whether legal positivism, as practiced and preached in Germany, had, or could have had, any causal connection with Hitler's ascent to power" (Fuller 658) and concludes that, due to the ideas of legal positivism, the "German lawyer was therefore peculiarly prepared to accept as 'law' anything that called itself by that name" (Fuller 659), even, of course, when the law was morally abhorrent.

Fuller's attack has been criticized for its many misstatements of Hart's views, for example, when he claims that Hart believes there is an "amoral datum called law, which has the peculiar quality of creating a moral duty to obey it" (Fuller 656). That Hart's version of the positivist theory of law had none of the implications that Fuller described is not the issue.[44] What requires notice here, however, is that the main practical rationale for solving the demarcation problem we have identified appears

[42] See ch. 11 in this volume.

[43] Lon Fuller, "Positivism and Fidelity to Law—A Reply to Professor Hart," *Harvard Law Review* 71 (1957): 630–72. Further citations will be by page number in the body of the text.

[44] See, e.g., Brian Leiter, "The Radicalism of Legal Positivism," *National Lawyers Guild Review* 66 (2009): 165–72.

to be the mirror image of Fuller's attack on positivism: that the correct or incorrect view about legality will affect action, namely, judicial decision! To be sure, many legal philosophers might object that their only concern is a theoretical one, namely, figuring out what is *true* about law. Since we have never found any essential truths about any artifact concepts that would satisfy the desiderata legal philosophers like Raz and Dickson and Shapiro announce, it is hard to see why we should take seriously the idea that there is a purely theoretical reason for solving the demarcation problem the way they want. That would leave us, then, only with the practical reasons, and they are real enough, assuming one thinks that confusions about *morality* and *legality* have consequences in political practice.

Let us suppose that they do, much as Fuller did. *Why, then, think that a jurisprudential solution to the demarcation problem would resolve them*? That is the key question. If I am right about the perceived practical importance of solving the demarcation problem in jurisprudence, then positivism confronts a psychosocial phenomenon: People think that *morally obligatory* means *overriding* in practical reasoning, and they think *legally valid* means *morally obligatory*. Does anyone seriously believe Kelsen's *Pure Theory of Law* or Hart's *The Concept of Law* are the manifestos to counteract these psychosocial phenomena? To think so would be to commit Fuller's mistake, but in reverse.[45]

Fuller sought to lay at the door of positivism the reprehensible behavior of Nazi legal officials.[46] A positivist solution to the demarcation problem would, by contrast, teach the Nazis that legal obligations are defeasible, since they are not moral obligations—or so the anti-Fullerian positivist must suppose. But if Fuller was mistaken, not only in his characterization of positivism but in his claim that it had some "causal connection with Hitler's ascent to power" (Fuller's words), then why should there be any practical reason to try to solve the demarcation problem in jurisprudence? (To be sure, there might be theoretical reasons to solve the demarcation problem, but that is not the claim at issue.)

Law and morality, as we noted at the start, are pervasive normative phenomena in modern societies. We generally believe that judges have a defeasible obligation to apply the law; we also generally believe that judges, like other persons, ought to do what is morally right. These two normative demands can conflict, raising hard practical questions to answer. The idea that a putative solution to the demarcation problem gives us the answer—which seems to be what Fullerians and anti-Fullerians think—is an illusion.

[45] Not the mistake of misunderstanding legal positivism, but the mistake of thinking a certain legal theory (denominated "positivist") constitutes the actual explanation for why Nazi judges did abhorrent things. (Thanks to Matt Kramer for clarification on this issue.)

[46] I am assuming, of course, that Fuller's speculation is preposterous. That he adduced no actual evidence on its behalf is only one of many reasons for thinking it silly. And the actual evidence now available points in the opposite direction. See Herlinde Pauer-Studer, *Justifying Injustice: Legal Theory in Nazi Germany* (Cambridge University Press, 2020).

Even though we cannot demarcate science and nonscience, we still need to assign degrees of epistemic credence to differing claims about what the world is like. And even if we cannot precisely demarcate law and morals, we still need to decide what it is we ought to do, and what it is we have an obligation to do. Solutions to demarcation problems, if they worked, would give us shortcuts in some cases. But if they do not work, then we have to tackle the practical questions directly. In philosophy of science, this has meant concentrated attention on the epistemology of the various sciences, from physics to biology to psychology, and whether their distinctive claims are well-supported by the available evidence. In philosophy of law, that would mean focusing on *particular* legal systems and the practical demands they make upon officials. To take a very American example, the question is *not* whether the original public meaning of the Constitution is the criterion of legal validity in the US legal system—as, for example, the far right Supreme Court Justice Antonin Scalia believes—the question is whether applying the original public meaning in resolving concrete controversies could be justified: How, one might ask, should we be bound by the dead hand of the past, especially a dead hand that had terrible judgment on a multitude of issues? Even if Justice Scalia were right about the legal meaning of the Constitution, the right conclusion might be that the legal meaning should be discounted.

V. Objections

Two objections to the preceding now demand explicit attention. Am I not already supposing a distinction between law and morality? After all, I have conceded that judges have a defeasible obligation to apply the law and that judges, like other persons, ought to do what is morally right. This statement already supposes that the two source of norms, law and morality, are different. But of course they are *obviously* different in many cases, and many contexts! It is a mistake to assume that a distinction, to be useful for *many* purposes, has to be made in terms of *essential* properties that will demarcate *all* cases for all purposes, the way the molecular constitution of water definitely settles the status of all clear potable liquids. It has been precisely the claim of recent jurisprudents who offer solutions to the demarcation problem that they have identified the criterion that cuts the normative world at the legal and nonlegal joints.[47] Even after the almost-universal admission that philosophers failed to solve the demarcation problem in philosophy of science, philosophers, and the "folk," can still happily recognize that chemistry is a fairly good bet for telling us what the world is like, and

[47] This is explicit in Raz, Dickson, and Shapiro. Perhaps their ambitions, suitably deflated, survive the criticisms developed here.

astrology is not, even though there is no criterion that will tell us the scientific status of any and all propositions about the world. For most purposes, we operate quite well with the method of paradigm cases, and analogies to those cases; for those purposes, Hart's legal positivism does better than any competitors, or so it seems to me (and others, of course). The real practical problems the demarcation problem might solve rarely arise in the ordinary cases, but in the extraordinary ones, where the demands of what seems paradigmatically to be law pull in one direction and the demands of what seem paradigmatically to be moral considerations pull in the other. Does the Eighth Amendment of the US Constitution, prohibiting "cruel and unusual punishments," prohibit, in particular, the imposition of the death penalty? Some traditional jurisprudents think a solution to the demarcation problem would help.[48] But given what is at stake, how could it? Why would we think the state is justified in terminating the life of a citizen just because it turns out to be *constitutional* on one reading of the constitutional provision? Perhaps the death penalty is a *legally valid* punishment in the United States; it is hard to see why that would change the fact (if it is a fact) that it is morally abhorrent to empower the state to deprive citizens of their life. A legal positivist might agree that the death penalty in the United States is *legally valid*, but deem it so morally abhorrent a penalty that equitable considerations require judges to override their valid legal obligations. An antipositivist who thinks the immorality of the death penalty means it is not legally obligatory will reach the same conclusion. In each case, the *key* question is: *What is the moral status of the death penalty*?[49] The rest is just jurisprudential window dressing.

A second worry about the argument of this chapter also naturally arises at this point. Has not my posture here brought me surprisingly close to the position of Ronald Dworkin in his recent work?[50] Has not Dworkin chastised legal positivists for attempting to divorce legal philosophy from political philosophy, to divorce questions about what the law is from questions about what it ought to be, and what judges ought to do? Indeed, he has, but for reasons wholly unrelated to the considerations adduced here. Dworkin thinks that solving the demarcation problem leads to answers to the practical questions, and that the two kinds of questions stand and fall together. Thus, Dworkin claims that the positivist solution to the demarcation problem entails claims about how judges should decide

[48] Shapiro, *Legality*, 28–30.

[49] The hypothetical positivist here will get one extra question, to be sure: namely, does the law require the immoral decision? And that question *could* affect the practical reasoning of the positivist judge, depending on her view of the moral weight of legal validity. But notice, then, that the extra question for the hypothetical positivist judge is also a *moral* one. In the end, it is hard to see how the overriding consideration could not be the seriousness of the moral inequity of the death penalty. (Thanks to an anonymous referee for pressing this issue.)

[50] See, e.g., Ronald Dworkin, "Hart's Postscript and the Point of Political Philosophy" and "Thirty Years On," in *Justice in Robes* (Harvard University Press, 2008).

particular cases—though as I and others have noted, this reading involves such a wild fabrication of the positivist position that Fuller looks like a paragon of interpretive charity by comparison.[51] For positivists, the fact that a norm is legally valid certainly creates a prima facie legal reason to decide in accordance with the legal norm, but one that is defeasible by other equitable considerations. And, conversely, Dworkin thinks his own theory of law as integrity both solves (or should we say, "dissolves") the demarcation problem *and* tells judges how to decide concrete cases.

The skeptical argument developed here is different. It suggests we abandon the demarcation problem in its essentialist form in favor of arguing about *what ought to be done*, whether by judges confronted with novel cases, or citizens confronted with morally objectionable laws. This is the practical consideration that animates interest in the demarcation problem, but since human artifacts never admit of successful analysis in terms of their essential characteristics—the inductive lesson to be learned from twentieth-century philosophy, especially philosophy of science—why not address the practical considerations directly? The lesson, frankly, seems well-confirmed by the increasingly baroque attempts by legal positivists to solve the demarcation problem after the valiant and seminal efforts of Kelsen, Hart, and Raz. And it seems equally well-confirmed by the efforts of natural law theorists like John Finnis and Mark Murphy, who *really* want theorists to focus on *morally good* law or *practically reasonable* legal systems, but who insist on claiming that their transparent change of the subject is *really* an answer to the demarcation problem, *really* a case of saying what "nondefective" law is or what the "focal" cases of law are.[52] The professionalization of philosophy, including legal philosophy, guarantees, I fear, continued attention to the demarcation problem, since specialization always runs the risk of generating both an audience and performers for ultimately pointless disputes. In the spirit of Marx's second *Thesis on Feuerbach*, let me suggest that a "dispute . . . that is isolated from practice is a purely *scholastic* question."[53]

[51] See Brian Leiter, "The End of Empire: Dworkin and Jurisprudence in the 21st Century," *Rutgers Law Journal* 36 (2004): 165–81, esp. 175–77.

[52] See, e.g., the useful survey piece by Mark Murphy, "Natural Law Theory," in *The Blackwell Guide to Philosophy of Law and Legal Theory*, ed. M. Golding & W. Edmundson (Blackwell, 2005), 15–28. See generally ch. 9 in this volume.

[53] This article owes its existence to a conversation with Larry Laudan many years ago. An earlier version benefited from the discussion at the international conference on "Neutrality and the Theory of Law" at the University of Girona, May 20–22, 2010. I can recall particularly helpful questions or comments on that occasion from Eugenio Bulygin, Pierluigi Chiassoni, Luis Duarte D'Almeida, Dan Priel, Veronica Rodriguez-Blanco, Stefan Sciaraffa, and Scott Shapiro. I am also grateful to Frederick Schauer for his written comments on that draft. A later version was improved by astute criticisms of an anonymous referee for *Oxford Journal of Legal Studies* and by questions from an audience at the international conference on "The Nature of Law," sponsored by McMaster University in Hamilton, Ontario on 12–15 May 2011; I can recall particularly helpful questions or comments on that occasion from Matthew Kramer, Mark Murphy, Giovanni Ratti, and Kevin Toh. I was helped to see the need to clarify my view by comments from Charles Barzun on the penultimate draft of the essay in this volume.

9

Against the Metaphysical Turn in Recent American Jurisprudence

In this chapter, I want to address the most influential—but utterly unrealistic and antinaturalistic—development in recent jurisprudence in the United States.

I. Greenberg and the Metaphysical Turn

General jurisprudence has been concerned for at least two centuries with a "metaphysical" or "ontological" question in a fairly modest sense of those terms: namely, what is required for a norm *to exist* as a norm of a legal system? (Many legal philosophers have also tried to explain what it is for a legal system to exist in a particular society, but that inevitably requires an answer to the first question as well.) The "metaphysical turn" I am concerned with here goes much further, involving what I shall refer to as a "layer cake" model of reality, in which the philosophical project is to explain how different layers of reality map on to other layers: so, for example, in jurisprudence, the question is how are "legal facts" determined by "social facts" and so-called moral facts (and, perhaps also, how are all the latter facts determined by physical facts). What I mean by this metaphor will become clearer in the discussion that follows.

The paper in general jurisprudence in the United States that initiated this new metaphysical turn is Mark Greenberg's "How Facts Make Law" from 2004[1] (although, as we will see, Scott Shapiro's book *Legality* from 2011 is perhaps most responsible for popularizing Greenberg's misguided conceptualization). Very few scholars endorse Greenberg's own unusual view (about which more below), but many have adopted his new and idiosyncratic formulations of the problems of general jurisprudence,[2] often without recognizing that they are both

[1] Mark Greenberg, "How Facts Make Law," *Legal Theory* 10 (2004): 157–98. (All further citations will be included by page number in the text.) This article was published when I was an editor of *Legal Theory*, and rightly so, though as will be clear, I think it is quite misconceived.

[2] To pick one recent general jurisprudence paper, chosen almost at random (it popped up in my Twitter feed [before I quit that right-wing cesspool]): "Anglo-American jurisprudence is usually [sic] presented as a debate about the grounds of law—about what constitutively explains

From a Realist Point of View. Brian Leiter, Oxford University Press. © Brian Leiter 2026.
DOI: 10.1093/9780197749852.003.0010

new and idiosyncratic. This appears to have been more true in the United States than the United Kingdom (and so far, it has had almost no impact in Europe or Latin America[3]), where more scholars have traditionally had serious training in the history of jurisprudence.[4] In America, an influx into the academy of very smart PhD philosophers (some with law degrees, some not) attuned to the latest fads in analytic philosophy but with an "interest" in law found Greenberg's formulations seductive, without realizing how little they had to do with the traditional problems of general jurisprudence or how little reason there was for legal philosophers to think these were real questions.

Here is how Greenberg opens his influential discussion:

> Nearly all philosophers of law agree that nonnormative, nonevaluative, contingent facts—*descriptive facts*, for short—are among the determinants of the content of the law. In particular, ordinary empirical facts about the behavior and mental states of people such as legislators, judges, other government officials, and voters play a part in determining the content. It is highly controversial, however, whether the relevant descriptive facts, which we can call *law-determining practices*, or *law practices* . . . are the only determinants of legal content, or whether legal content also depends on normative or evaluative facts—*value facts*, for short. In fact, a central—perhaps *the* central—debate in philosophy of law is a debate over whether value facts are among the determinants of the content of law (though the debate is not usually characterized in that way) (Greenberg, "How Facts Make Law," 157).

legal facts, such as the fact that murder is a crime in a certain jurisdiction." Felipe Jimenez, "Legal Positivism for Legal Officials," *Canadian Journal of Law & Jurisprudence* 36 (2023): 359. The citation for this mischaracterization of the debate is not Hart or Kelsen or Raz, but rather David Plunkett, "Robust Normativity, Morality, and Legal Positivism," in *Dimensions of Normativity: New Essays on Metaethics and Jurisprudence*, eds. David Plunkett, Scott Shapiro, and Kevin Toh (Oxford University Press, 2019), a paper by a very smart philosopher without a law background. Jimenez acknowledges that this "picture is distortive in several ways, and many have expressed their dissatisfactions with it," but then goes on to employ it on the grounds that it has "become a standard framing." Jimenez, "Legal Positivism for Legal Officials," 359. The recent frequency of a mischaracterization in one parochial jurisprudential community should not redeem it. One finds similar mischaracterizations, often presented as obvious and without any citations, in recent work by—among other serious contributors to the recent jurisprudential literature—Emad Atiq, Mitchell Berman, Daniel Wodak, and, of course, David Plunkett.

[3] Much of Europe and Latin America is insulated from the latest fads in American jurisprudence by other factors: the influence of Kelsen, in particular, but also Bulygin, Ross, Guastini, and the legal realist traditions indebted to antimetaphysical philosophical views. The fact that English is the *lingua franca* of scholarship poses a risk, however, to these other jurisprudential traditions.

[4] The decline in importance of general jurisprudence at Oxford, since the death of John Gardner and the retirement of Leslie Green, may change that, given Oxford's outsized presence, at least historically, in the field.

The last parenthetical is apt and also revealing: the debate was *never* before characterized as being about the "determinants of content,"[5] and, as I will argue, it should not be so understood. I will take up both points in the following sections. Before doing so, let me also quote at the start Greenberg's formulation of his preferred metaphysical question (which gives expression to the "layer cake" metaphor), namely:

> whether law practices are the sole determinants of legal content . . . [T]he determination relation with which we are concerned is primarily a metaphysical, or constitutive, one. . . . [N]o legal-content facts are plausibly metaphysically basic or ultimate facts about the universe, facts for which there is nothing to say about what make them the case. Legal-content facts, like facts about the meaning of words or facts about international exchange rates . . . hold in virtue of more basic facts. The important implication for present purposes is that the *full story* [emphasis added] of how the determinants of legal content make the law what it is cannot take any legal content as given . . . (Greenberg, "How Facts Make Law," 158–59).

The particular determination relation that Greenberg is interested in, he calls "rational" determination, in which the account "explains why the legal facts should depend on the legal practice in some specific way rather than another one."[6] I shall argue against both Greenberg's "rational determination" formula and against the whole idea of thinking "grounding" language illuminates any issues in general jurisprudence in the rest of this chapter. But I want to start with a

[5] Here, for example, is Kelsen, writing in 1941 in the *Harvard Law Review*, explaining his "pure theory of law":

> The pure theory of law is a theory of positive law; a general theory of law, not a presentation or interpretation of a special legal order. From a comparison of all the phenomena which go under the name of law, it seeks to discover the nature of law itself, to determine its structure and its typical forms, independent of the changing content which it exhibits at different times and among different peoples. In this manner it derives the fundamental principles by means of which any legal order can be comprehended. As a theory, its sole purpose is to know its subject. It answers the question of what the law is, not what it ought to be. The latter question is one of politics, while the pure theory of law is science.

Hans Kelsen, "The Pure Theory of Law and Analytical Jurisprudence," *Harvard Law Review* 55 (1941): 44. Hart describes the disagreement between legal positivism and natural law as follows: "Legal Positivism [is] the simple contention that it is in no sense a necessary truth that laws reproduce or satisfy certain demands of morality, though they have often done so" while natural law views all aim to show "the ways in which legal validity is connected with moral value." H. L. A. Hart, *The Concept of Law*, 3rd ed. (Oxford University Press, 2012), 185–86.

[6] This is David Enoch's apt formulation in an unpublished manuscript, "That's Just What It Is to Be Legally Valid: A Quick Refutation of Greenberg's 'How Facts Make Law'" (2009). Enoch, alas, accepts Greenberg's framing that the determination question has been central to general jurisprudence, but rejects, as his title suggests, Greenberg's challenge to legal positivism.

more modest historical point: namely, that Greenberg's formulation of the "central debate in philosophy of law" is not, in fact, the central debate.

A. The Historical Debate Was about "Validity," Not "Content"

None of the canonical figures in the history of twentieth-century jurisprudence—not Kelsen, not Hart, not Bobbio—thought the central question of legal philosophy was about the metaphysical "determinants" of "legal content."[7] The central question was about the legal validity of sources (especially on the European Continent)[8] or of norms (typically valid in virtue of their sources),[9] whose content was necessarily assumed (norms just are propositions [e.g., "Do not talk with your mouth full"], and thus necessarily have content). There were certainly questions about how valid norms were to be *applied* in particular cases, but even then there were no questions about "determinants of content," and it was not the topic of general jurisprudence. One can think of the *actual* topic of general jurisprudence as follows. Everyone knows that there are many norms governing human conduct in any society: do not talk with your mouth full at the table; do not drive faster than a certain speed limit on the highway; do consider how your actions affect the interests of others; do say "please" and "thank you"; do not cheat on exams; do not assault other people; and so on. Some of these norms are legal norms ("legally valid," i.e., they exist as norms of the legal system), and some are not. Ordinary people familiar with a modern municipal legal system, as Hart observed, know that there are differences: they know (this is my example, not

[7] The closest one gets comes much later in Dworkin's talk in *Law's Empire* (Harvard University Press, 1986) about the "grounds of law," but even he did not mean the *metaphysical grounds*, just the considerations (or "propositions") that would justify identifying some norms (some "legal propositions") as legally valid (or "true"). (Dworkin, who liked to invent new vocabularies, eschewed the Kelsenian talk of "validity" that Hart and others used.) Another recent writer, considering Dworkin's theoretical disagreement argument, frames the issue this way: "What is the metaphysical relationship between legal texts and legal content? Or as I will sometimes put it: How do legal texts contribute to legal content? Positivists have not always focused on this question, and even today, it is not clear that they have fully answered it," citing to Greenberg. Bill Watson, "How to Answer Dworkin's Argument from Theoretical Disagreement without Attributing Confusion or Disingenuity to Legal Officials," *Canadian Journal of Law & Jurisprudence* 36 (2023): 225. Watson correctly notices that this is not what legal positivists were talking about, although he treats the question as a serious one.

[8] See, e.g., Giorgio Pino, "Sources of Law," in *Oxford Studies in Philosophy of Law, Volume 4*, ed. J. Gardner, L. Green, and B. Leiter (Oxford University Press), esp. pp. 67–68; Torben Spaak, "The Scope of Legal Positivism: Validity or Interpretation," in *The Cambridge Companion to Legal Positivism*, ed. T. Spaak and P. Mindus (Cambridge University Press, 2021), 448. See also the discussion in ch. 4 in this volume. On the European Continent, it is more common to frame the question in terms of what the valid sources of legal norms are, and to treat then the question of how to interpret sources to identify norms as a separate issue.

[9] Following Kelsen, a norm is "legally valid" if it exists as a norm of the legal system. I use "norm" loosely to encompass all the prescriptions, prohibitions, permissions, rights, powers, etc. that the law promulgates.

Hart's) that norms of etiquette are not legally required, and that assaulting another person is legally prohibited. What explains the differences? Why are some norms legally valid, and some are not (and some are both)? What is it for norms to exist as norms of a legal system (i.e., to be valid)? In this much more conventional formulation of the topic there is no question about the metaphysical determinants of "legal content." The content (the norms) are taken for granted.

In support of his different formulation, Greenberg cites only Raz, who did indeed say things like "the existence and content of every law is fully determined by social sources."[10] However, when Raz first introduced the idea that "the positivist social thesis is that what is law and what is not is a matter of social fact," he himself called it a "crude formulation" (Raz, *Authority of Law*, 37).[11] Although the initial "crude" formulation does not mention "content," Greenberg construes it as involving an ambitious metaphysical claim about the "social facts" that determine legal content. (Raz's focus, by contrast, is mostly on the existence question, which is a matter of the law's social source [hence Raz's "sources thesis"]). One occasion when Raz does explicitly address the question of content is this curious passage:

> The sources of law are those facts by virtue of which it is valid and which identify its content. This sense of "source" is wider than that of "formal sources" which are those establishing the validity of a law (one or more Acts of Parliament together with one or more precedents may be the formal sources of one rule of a law). "Source" as used here includes also "interpretive sources," namely all the relevant interpretive materials. The sources of a law thus understood are never a single act (of legislation, etc.) alone, but a whole range of facts of a variety of kinds (Raz, *Authority of Law*, 47–48).

This is an odd formulation: What are "interpretive materials"? In what sense are they social sources?[12] A way of interpreting sources is not obviously itself a

[10] Joseph Raz, *The Authority of Law* (Oxford University Press, 1979), 46. All further citations will be included by page number in the text. Hart very rarely used a similar formulation. But as Luka Burazin and Giovanni Battista Ratti correctly note, "Hart does not say much about how the content of law is identified." Luka Burazin and Giovanni Battista Ratti, "Rule(s) of Recognition and Canons of Interpretation," in *Judges and Adjudication in Constitutional Democracies: A Realistic View*, ed. P. Chiassoni and B. Spaic (Springer, 2021), 128. See the further discussion of Burazin and Ratti's view about theoretical disagreements in ch. 4 in this volume.

[11] Raz, alas, was too often impressionistic and "crude" in his formulations. For a useful discussion in this regard, see Kevin Toh, "Some Moving Parts of Jurisprudence," *Texas Law Review* 88 (2010): 1283–1321, and the example discussed below in the text. So many Anglophone legal philosophers are students or friends of Raz that this point is not acknowledged as often as it should be.

[12] Here, the Continental European practice of distinguishing the valid sources of law from the correct *interpretation* of the sources to determine what legal norm they enact seems a clearer demarcation. See again Pino, "Sources of Law," 68. But for doubts about how this works in the case of theoretical disagreements, see ch. 4 in this volume.

"source," as opposed to a way of reading a source (a hermeneutic technique or method). I assume what Raz has in mind is something like the source-based hermeneutic principle in the Canadian system that the original intent of the framers of the Canadian Charter is irrelevant to the meaning of the Charter's provisions. Surely, however, it would be clearer to distinguish between sources of law and ways of interpreting those sources, many of which are not obviously "source-based" except in the sense that they are part of established legal practice.[13]

In any case, the mention of "interpretive materials" as "social sources" for determining the *content* (or norm) enacted by a "formal source" may seem to open the door to Greenberg's idea that explaining content is one of the questions the positivist theory is trying to answer—although it bears emphasizing that, even in Raz's elliptical remarks, there is no suggestion that this explanation involves determination relations, or what Greenberg calls a "constitutive explanation" about how different layers of reality map on to each other. That is the crucial point. No one prior to Greenberg thought the central question of general jurisprudence was "how facts make law," that is, how it is social facts constitutively explain the content of the law. No one should think that is an important question, as I will argue.

B. Law Exists outside the Courts: Against Greenberg's Theory of Legal Content

It should not be surprising that Hart mostly ignored the issue of content, given one of his central insights about law as a social phenomenon: Law exists primarily outside of courts and serves primarily to guide people's conduct. Almost all the mistakes of Anglophone jurisprudence after Hart are traceable to failure to recognize this fact, about which Hart was obviously right. Hart took for granted that the interpretive disputes about content that occupy the appellate courts did not play a large role in the life of the law. No one consulting a lawyer about taxes, a will, or a contract, after all, is aiming to end up in court. They want to know what the law is to structure their affairs in order to accomplish their goals and avoid litigation. Lawyers advise people about the content of the law in part by reference to court decisions on point, but also by reference to statutory definitions of terms, administrative rulings, and, most fundamentally, by knowing the authoritative sources for rules framed in the public, natural language of the community.[14]

[13] See, again, Burazin and Ratti, "Rule(s) of Recognition and Canons of Interpretation."

[14] Of course, on Hart's view, official, including judicial, behavior matters, since the content of the rule of recognition in a legal system is just the criteria of validity the officials converge upon and accept from an "internal point of view." This fact is precisely part of the explanation for why most lawyers can give reliable answers about the content of the law, and keep their clients out of the

The hard questions about the *content* of the law (about the norms the "formal sources" enact) arise in the courts, and especially the appellate courts. Dworkin, who wrote as though law exists only as the output of "constructive interpretation" of the formal sources of law by the appellate courts, pushed the discussion much further toward questions of "content," but it is not news to anyone in jurisprudence that Dworkin often changed the topic. Ironically, even he did not think determining the content of law was a matter of metaphysical or, more precisely, rational determination relations, as Greenberg does.

Greenberg makes the question of legal content even more opaque than Dworkin does. Greenberg argues that what he calls "the Standard Picture"[15] of "legal content" (in which, most generally, "the content of law is the meaning of certain legal texts (or utterances)" [Greenberg, "Standard Picture," 42][16]) is, in fact, controversial, a point of jurisprudential contention. This raises three questions: Is this picture really "standard"? Can it really be a point of jurisprudential contention? And what is the alternative?

In favor of what Greenberg dubs the Standard Picture is a simple thought: If the meaning of words in legal texts in the public language of the community were not the starting point for all questions about what the law is, it would be hard to see how law could guide conduct outside the courts (or even outside the seminar room). The meaning of legal texts in the public language of the community is central to law. Yet everyone also acknowledges that the law can use the public meaning of words to radically alter the meanings of legal texts (through statutory definitions of terms, judicial holdings about the interpretation of legal texts, administrative agency interpretations of texts, etc.). This already suggests the standard picture is not as central as Greenberg suggests.

Indeed, Greenberg himself acknowledges that legal positivists recognize custom as a source of law, and custom does not depend on the standard picture (Greenberg, "Standard Picture," 52). He also notes that the way lawyers and later courts interpret cases does not conform to the standard picture (ibid., 73–75). The question is why these latter facts are an objection to the standard picture

court: The existence of a rule of recognition facilitates the massive agreement about law that is the hallmark of a functioning legal system. See ch. 2 in this volume, esp. pp. 46–50.

[15] See Mark Greenberg, "The 'Standard Picture' and Its Discontents," in *Oxford Studies in Philosophy of Law, Volume 1*, ed. L. Green and B. Leiter (Oxford University Press, 2011).

[16] In his more precise and complex formulation: "the primary way in which law is determined is that the linguistic content of a legally authoritative pronouncement becomes a legal norm simply because it was authoritatively pronounced. . . . [T]he content of the law consists of these legal norms, perhaps along with some other legal norms that are constituted in peripheral ways." Greenberg, "Standard Picture," 54. Greenberg needs the last qualification because all legal positivists acknowledge custom as a source of law, and custom does not partake of the standard picture—which, as I argue below in the text, raises the question whether this picture is in any meaningful sense "standard."

(as Greenberg seems to think they are), rather than evidence that it is a fabrication to say, as Greenberg does, that the standard picture is common ground among legal theorists—except in the limited sense just noted? Although unmentioned by Greenberg, his example of case law evokes Hart's starting point in Chapter VII of *The Concept of Law*, namely, that one of the two ways of communicating what ought to be done does not involve language at all—namely, when we communicate by example, as precedent does on Hart's rendering.[17] This already shows that Hart should not be saddled with allegiance to the standard picture, such that the interpretation of case law counts against him, since he explicitly recognizes a nonlinguistic way in which the law guides conduct. Something similar might be said about Greenberg's examples of special rules of interpretation that apply to criminal statutes (Greenberg, "Standard Picture," 76); indeed, Greenberg admits that "[s]tatutes are regularly interpreted in ways that diverge from their ordinary content" (ibid., 77), but that just seems evidence that the standard picture is not so standard.

So it is right that the public, natural language in a community is the starting point for law, since law can only fulfill its guidance function if, in fact, it can rely on that shared language as the benchmark for guidance: Law simply cannot do without the "meaning of certain legal texts" (as Greenberg puts it), even if that meaning can vary quite dramatically from the meaning of the same words in the natural language. Let us call the following the "Real Standard Picture," to distinguish it from Greenberg's invention: *the meaning of words in the public language of the community is the starting point for the content of law, with all kinds of modifications of those meanings possible in accordance with the rule of recognition of that legal system, which itself often utilizes the public language.*[18] Since the content of the rule of recognition is equivalent to the content (the criteria of legal validity) officials actually converge upon and accept from an internal point of view, it is generally available to lawyers advising citizens about what the content of the law is (part of learning the law is learning the rule of recognition in a particular legal system).

[17] Hart, *Concept of Law*, 124–25.

[18] This is somewhat different than Jeffrey Goldsworthy's version of what he also calls "the Real Standard Picture" in Jeffrey Goldsworthy, "The Real Standard Picture and How Facts Make It Law: A Response to Mark Greenberg," *American Journal of Jurisprudence* 64 (2019): 163–213. Although Goldsworthy also believes that the "standard picture" does not describe common-law interpretations of precedent or statutory interpretation in all jurisdictions, he does think it fits rather well "the limited domain of statute law in Anglo-American legal systems" (ibid., 167–68). He thinks this in part because he focuses on the aspect of the standard picture that emphasizes authoritative pronouncements as the basis of legal norms, and its relation to constitutional doctrines about legislative supremacy (ibid., 169). My focus has been, by contrast, on Greenberg's "Linguistic Content Thesis," according to which the content of a legal norm is equated with the ordinary linguistic (or mental) content of the words in the pronouncement. This, it seems to me, is not, in fact, standard for the reasons discussed in the text.

Is the *Real* Standard Picture objectionable? It would be if one thought the *real* content of the law depends on Hercules's best "constructive interpretation" of the sources of law that the positivist recognizes,[19] or if one thought it depends on how God reads the relevant sources. These kinds of views, however, are hard to square with the reality that law actually guides conduct, and does so mostly outside the context of adjudication in every functioning legal system. Greenberg's own view faces similar problems. According to Greenberg, the real content of the law consists of "the moral impact of [the moral obligations created by] the relevant actions of legal institutions."[20] To be clear, Greenberg means the *real* moral obligations created by the "relevant"[21] actions of legal institutions.[22] How can law guide conduct if what the law is consists not in the meaning of legal texts produced by authoritative legal actors but rather in the *actual moral obligations* created by ("relevant") actions of legal institutions?[23] Lawyers are not trained in moral philosophy (or the detection of "real" moral obligations), and, in any case, moral philosophers themselves often disagree profoundly about morality.[24] (If I asked my lawyer to make an estate plan for my family, I would fire him if he thought thinking about the "moral" impact of the actions by the Illinois legislature or courts were relevant to the question!) If what the law really requires depends on figuring out the *true* moral impact of what legal actors have done,

[19] Greenberg recognizes that Dworkin's view also rejects the standard picture, although he has a somewhat unusual reading of Dworkin's theory. But the details do not matter here. See Greenberg, "Standard Picture," 56–59.

[20] Mark Greenberg, "The Moral Impact Theory of Law," *Yale Law Journal* 123 (2014): 1290.In his later formulation, "The content of law is that part of the moral profile created by the actions of legal institutions" (ibid., 1309), where the "moral profile" consists of all the moral obligations, powers, privileges, and permissions that are created (ibid., 1308), or which are "*altered* or *reinforced* by the actions of legal institutions" (e.g., outlawing murder and specifying sanctions for it) (ibid., 1320).

[21] This qualification creates its own problems. Greenberg admits that only changes to our moral obligations that are brought about in the "legally proper way" count (Greenberg, "Moral Impact Theory," 1321) (i.e., only those that aim to improve the moral profile). Sometimes a legal system can pass wicked laws, which create moral obligations of resistance on the part of citizens, but this way of changing the moral profile is "paradoxical" (ibid., 1322). Why paradoxical? "[A] legal system, by its nature, is supposed to change the moral situation for the better" (ibid., 1322). No direct argument is given for this astonishing claim about the "nature" of legal systems, a point to which we return in the text. (On the serious problems with Greenberg's idea of the "legally proper way" of generating moral obligations, see the penetrating critique in Hasan Dindjer, "The New Legal Anti-Positivism," *Legal Theory* 26 (2020): 181–213, esp. at 202–4.)

[22] I was astonished to see Greenberg say "that much of our concern with law presupposes that . . . [moral] skepticism [or anti-realism] is false" on the grounds that the anti-realist believes that "people have interests and desires and wield raw power, but there is no reason to be concerned with unfairness, inequality, cruelty, or injustice" (Greenberg, "Moral Impact Theory," 1308 n.43). As fraudulent libels of moral antirealists go, this one is extraordinary coming, as it does, from a professional philosopher. Moral antirealists can have all kinds of attitudes about unfairness, inequality, cruelty, and injustice, and those supply all the reasons that are needed to care about those matters.

[23] As Hasan Dindjer shows, Greenberg's view fails to pick out familiar examples of "legal obligations." Dindjer, "New Legal Anti-Positivism," 188–91, and thus fails as a recognizable account of the content of law.

[24] See ch. 15 in this volume.

then the epistemic barrier to figuring out what the law requires seems daunting indeed.

The difficulty Greenberg's view confronts in explaining how law guides conduct outside courts is only the tip of an iceberg of problems. His "moral impact theory" seems on its face more a stipulation than an explication of any recognizable concept of law. Of course, Greenberg explicitly denies that considerations of "English usage or even lawyers' intuitions" about law are relevant; he has to, since he also claims that on his view "the law can never include truly evil norms," among other bizarrely counterintuitive claims (Greenberg, "Moral Impact Theory," 1337–38).[25] Greenberg adduces a few considerations that are supposed to count in favor of his counterintuitive "moral impact" view as a theory of *law* (rather than a stipulation), but none seem to me compelling.

First, Greenberg asserts, "it is plausible[26] that moral reasoning has a place in legal interpretation" (ibid., 1304). Everyone, however, agrees that moral reasoning has "a place in legal interpretation." What is in dispute is whether that place is essential to establishing what the law is, or rather comes into play only when the law runs out or when the requirements of law are sufficiently unjust that a judge ought to think twice about enforcing them. Greenberg presumably believes the place of moral reasoning is essential to saying what the law is, but that is not a data point to be explained by a theory but a conclusion of a particular theory.

Second, Greenberg says, "legal systems treat legal obligations as genuinely binding obligations that are generated by the legal institutions" and claims his view "vindicates this treatment," whereas the positivist theory allows that "it can

[25] Greenberg remarks that a "true" theory can have "counterintuitive consequences," and justifies that by noting that "a great deal of what we now think about the world and about human beings would once have been thought to be absurd" (Greenberg, "Moral Impact Theory," 1338). That is true, but we know roughly what the criteria of success are for counterintuitive physical, biological, and psychological theories (e.g., their explanatory and predictive power). Greenberg's view has little explanatory power, a point to which I will return (it obviously does not aspire to predictive power). Even serious theories highly revisionary of ordinary understandings of social practices and institutions (e.g., Marx's) motivate their counterintuitive claims based on explanatory and predictive power. See Jaime Edwards and Brian Leiter, *Marx* (Routledge, 2025), ch. 2.

[26] Claims about what seems "natural" or "plausible" or "intuitive" do far too much work in Greenberg's "Moral Impact Theory," and most of the claims said to be "natural" or "plausible" or "intuitive" do not seem to me to be anything of the kind: they range from the idiosyncratic to the debatable to the bizarre. A partial catalogue of some of the astonishing, and mostly undefended, *ex cathedra* pronouncements of this kind: "it is part of the nature of law that a legal system is supposed to change our moral obligations to improve our moral situation" (Greenberg, "Moral Impact Theory," 1294); "a legal system, by its nature, is supposed to change the moral situation for the better" (ibid., 1322); while allowing that, in fact, "it is controversial what the functions of law are, or even whether law has functions" (ibid., 1339) he then claims "for purposes of argument" that "settling disagreements is an important function of law" (ibid.) and that it is "at least as plausible" that law's other functions include "that government coercion is used only in accordance with past political decisions," that law is "acting for the public good," and (of course) "improving our moral situation" (ibid.). I return to several of these in the text.

be true that one has a legal obligation despite the fact that one has no [genuine moral] obligation" (Greenberg, "Moral Impact Theory," 1304).[27] Here we see the characteristic conservatism of much Anglophone analytic philosophy: even if we grant that "legal systems treat legal obligations as genuinely binding obligations,"[28] why should we expect that pretense to be vindicated? Even Raz, who believes that all law claims legitimate authority, does not try to vindicate law's claim: On his view, most law probably lacks legitimate authority, despite claiming it. A rather different assumption than Greenberg's seems far more "plausible" (to use Greenberg's favorite word), not by virtue of my armchair intuitions, but in light of the actual history of the world: namely, that legal systems adopt lots of moral pretenses (including claiming that their legal requirements are also "moral" requirements) because their real role is to protect and legitimize the position of the dominant class in society. By feigning to impose moral obligations, they can more effectively discharge their real function.[29] Call this the "Realistic Assumption." From the perspective of the realistic assumption, it is a virtue of a theory of law that it does not entail that every legal institution's claim to have generated a genuine (moral) obligation is vindicated. (Indeed, one might think [as everyone in the legal positivist tradition arguably did] that disabusing people of the false notion that the law's commands are morally obligatory is both a practical and theoretical virtue of the positivist theory, as Hart argued long ago.[30])

Greenberg, unsurprisingly, rejects the realistic assumption about legal institutions. He declares, for example, that "it is part of the nature of law that a legal system is supposed to change our moral obligations to improve our moral situation" (Greenberg, "Moral Impact Theory," 1294); or similarly, "a legal system, by its nature, is supposed to change the moral situation for the better" (ibid., 1322); and so too "a necessary condition on a legal institution . . . that it be an organization that, by its nature, is supposed to improve the moral situation" (ibid., 1324). The only argument given for these astonishing assertions about the "nature" of law, legal systems, and legal institutions—assertions rejected by every major figure in the history of general jurisprudence in the last century (who

[27] See also Greenberg's discussion of the "bindingness hypothesis" in Greenberg, "Standard Picture," 84–100. As Greenberg formulates it: "[A] legal system is supposed to operate by arranging matters in such a way as to reliably ensure that, for every legal obligation, there is an all-things-considered moral obligation with the same content—but *not* necessarily so that for every moral obligation, there is a corresponding legal obligation" (ibid., 84). The objections in the text apply equally to the later discussion.

[28] I doubt they do this in most cases: Mostly they treat legal obligations as things that must be done, *or else* (i.e., they are strong prudential reasons for acting, not moral obligations).

[29] Greenberg denies that he is defending a claim about the "function" of law (Greenberg, "Standard Picture," 88), and I agree that he is not. But I am defending such a claim, in the context of showing that law's actual function provides a better context for explaining the superficial features of legal talk that Greenberg notices.

[30] See Hart, *Concept of Law*, 207–12.

were, presumably, also interested in the truth about the nature of law)—is that they "explain . . . the fact that an organization of powerful thugs that controls a community is not a legal system or a legal institution" (ibid.).[31] This, however, is a feeble consideration, since a positivist theory of law has an easy way to explain why a Mafia regime need not be a legal system.[32] First, Mafia-controlled areas almost never (if ever) satisfy what Hart identified as the Minimum Content of Natural Law,[33] that is, they rarely address the full range (or even a partial range) of the distributive and harm-related issues that arise from the human situation of equal vulnerability to harm, limited altruism, and limited resources which legal systems address through rules of tort, criminal law, and property, among others. (Indeed, the Mafia contributes to the problems the minimum content of natural law is there to address!) Second, whether the rules of the Mafia system are accepted by "officials" from an "internal point of view" is often doubtful (witness the massive defections of Mafia members as informers). Third, and perhaps most strikingly, the rules of the "Mafia system" often presuppose the existence of the actual legal system, even in areas where the Mafia is dominant: For example, they include rules forbidding cooperation with law enforcement, requiring secrecy about Mafia operations, and the like. Thus, even the "Mafia system" presupposes a concept of law and a legal system different from its own regime.

Given that there is overwhelming evidence from both Marxist and public choice perspectives that legal systems serve purposes other than improving the moral situation (e.g., promoting the interests of the ruling class or the most powerful interest groups), why exactly are we to believe that law "by its nature" improves the moral situation? Greenberg's *ex cathedra* pronouncements about the "nature" of law and legal institutions seem a particularly preposterous instance of armchair philosophy.

[31] Greenberg makes a similar argument in Greenberg, "Standard Picture," 91–92. Scott Shapiro, in *Legality*, follows Greenberg on this score, and claims that law must necessarily have a "moral aim," namely, "the aim of remedying the moral deficiencies of the circumstances of legality . . . to compensate for the infirmities of custom, tradition, persuasion, consensus, and promise." Scott Shapiro, *Legality* (Harvard University Press, 2011), 213. It is easy to see how Greenberg, as an avowed antipositivist, could accept such a view; that Shapiro thinks it is compatible with legal positivism is puzzling.

[32] John Gardner and Timothy Macklem, in their critical review of *Legality*, offer some additional considerations: "Contrary to the impression given by Shapiro, traditional Mafias, such as the *'Ndrangheta,'* tend to have a strongly moralistic self-image, and often regard themselves as better placed than the law of the land to provide security against social disorder by use of a tough code, firmly enforced. In particular, it is far from clear, *pace* Shapiro, that a Mafia don could not properly be criticized for corruption in his role as an official of his clan, just as a legal official might be. He could certainly be criticized (and possibly end up sleeping with the fishes) for failing in his duties of honour towards the rest of the clan, e.g., by passing business to the clan's competitors or tipping off the *Carabinieri*." John Gardner and Timothy Macklem, "Review, *Legality*," *Notre Dame Philosophical Reviews* (2011), https://ndpr.nd.edu/news/legality/.

[33] See Hart, *The Concept of Law*, 193–200.

Greenberg offers one final consideration on behalf of his idea that the content of the law consists of the real moral obligations that "relevant" actions of legal institutions produce. He says his view "makes it easy to explain our dominating concern with law" since, "If the legal institutions change what we are obligated to do, it is vital to work out that change" (Greenberg, "Moral Impact Theory," 1304–5). This, again, is a rather weak consideration. In an early critique of Greenberg's view,[34] Brian Bix correctly observed that it is not controversial to note that the law can affect our moral obligations (even on an antirealist construal). It suffices, however, for us to care about the law for moral reasons as long as it affects our "moral obligations," regardless of whether that is the actual content of the law. Of course, the real reason in modern societies that people care about the law on a regular basis have little to do with moral considerations and everything to do with self-interested considerations. A bit of realism about law—there is none in Greenberg's view—would acknowledge that.

One could agree that Greenberg's own positive view about the content of law is implausible and also agree that the historical debate in general jurisprudence was about validity, not content. Yet this would not show that we should not want a theory of law that explains the *content* of law (that explains, in Greenberg's terms, "how facts make law"), not just the validity of norms. Why should we reject that aspiration? It is to that final question I now turn.

C. Against Greenberg's Metaphysical Question

Greenberg's preferred metaphysical question, recall, is . . .

> whether law practices are the sole determinants of legal content[?] . . . [T]he determination relation with which we are concerned is primarily a metaphysical, or constitutive, one. . . . [N]o legal-content facts are plausibly metaphysically basic or ultimate facts about the universe, facts for which there is nothing to say about what make them the case. Legal-content facts, like facts about the meaning of words or facts about international exchange rates . . . hold in virtue of more basic facts. The important implication for present purposes is that the *full story* [emphasis added] of how the determinants of legal content make the law what it is cannot take any legal content as given (Greenberg, "How Facts Make Law," 158–59).

[34] Brian Bix, "When Law Becomes Morality: Comments on Mark Greenberg's Moral Impact Theory of Law" (2014), available at https://papers.ssrn.com/sol3/papers.cfm?abstract_id=2434075.

Notice that Greenberg's "full" story is not one anyone in the history of jurisprudence has tried to offer (and for good reasons, as we will see[35]). More precisely, Greenberg says, we are looking to understand not "bare metaphysical determination" but what he calls "rational determination" (ibid., 160), according to which: "The A facts rationally determine the B facts just in case the A facts metaphysically determine the B facts *and* the obtaining of the A facts makes intelligible or rationally explains the B facts' obtaining" (ibid., 163).

Why, however, should we want or even expect an account that gives us the "rational determination" relationship between some lower-level facts and "legal facts"? It cannot be because Joseph Raz said the "existence and content of law" is a matter of social fact, since what he meant by that clearly had nothing to do with rational determination relations between lower- and higher-order facts. Moreover, it is easy to understand what Raz meant without any reference to determination relations: Norms are legally valid in virtue of their sources (the relevant social facts), including the "sources" (as he called them) about how to interpret the formal sources. Greenberg has smuggled into jurisprudence a question that no one was asking, without explaining why anyone else should ask it (it does open the door to his own view, discussed in the prior section). I shall argue that there are good reasons why the question is historically anomalous, and why it is still not worth asking.

From a naturalistic point of view, Greenberg's kind of metaphysics is epistemically suspect. Theorizing about metaphysical determination relations invites armchair speculation based on ordinary language untethered from any epistemically reliable process. Anglophone philosophy has been in the grips of metaphysical speculation since the 1990s, of a kind foreign to the philosophical *Geist* that prevailed from the 1940s until the 1970s. The philosophical pendulum will swing again, no doubt, and hopefully back to a more naturalistic point of view, in which successful empirical science imposes a real constraint on theorizing, and questions about how different categories of "facts" relate to each other are a question for empirical science to answer (if it even has an answer). That anyone speculates now about how "moral facts" (which do not exist) might "determine" legal facts is an indication of how far we are from serious naturalistic scruples.[36] Kelsen, Ross, Bobbio, and Hart would have all been astonished and perplexed.

[35] The closest case, ironically (since Greenberg appears unaware of it), would be Alf Ross, but as a logical positivist, he was not looking to establish metaphysical relations between "legal facts" and "moral facts" (there are none of the latter). But Ross did try to offer an account of the meaning of legal propositions consistent with an ontological view derived from the empirical sciences: In that sense only, his ambition was a metaphysical one, but driven by epistemological considerations (in particular, verificationism). See generally, Brian Leiter, "Alf Ross's Critique of American Legal Realism—and a Naturalistic Critique of Ross," available at https://papers.ssrn.com/sol3/papers.cfm?abstract_id=4240991.

[36] See Brian Leiter, "Moral Facts and Best Explanations," in *Naturalizing Jurisprudence: Essays on American Legal Realism and Naturalism in Legal Philosophy* (Oxford University Press, 2007), 203–24, as well as chs. 15 and 16 in this volume.

One might object, of course, that the ordinary "intuition pump" methods of Anglophone legal philosophy are also epistemically suspect for somewhat different reasons,[37] even when they eschew ambitious metaphysics of Greenberg's sort.[38] And that is why a second objection to Greenberg's preferred question is important: Greenberg's question imposes upon legal philosophy a metaphysical burden that has not been met successfully elsewhere in philosophy.[39] Greenberg acknowledges,[40] for example, that the demand for "rational determination" has affinities with the question famously posed by Saul Kripke about meaning in the context of his reading of Wittgenstein[41]: namely, in virtue of what facts does any rule have the meaning it does? Kripkenstein's answer is that there are no more "basic" facts that ground (let alone "rationally determine") "meaning facts." Meaning facts arise from a kind of ineffable (and rationally inexplicable) communal consensus. That conclusion parallels the conclusion of Nelson Goodman's much earlier "new riddle of induction"[42]: There are no facts that determine (even in Greenberg's metaphysically "brute" way) how scientific predicates should be projected into the future. Once again, purely "pragmatic" (not rational) considerations fix (or "entrench") certain predicates for projection into the future.

One might say that this just shows that evaluative (e.g., pragmatic) considerations influence the determination of legal content, just as they do, say, in the cases of projectible predicates. That is probably right,[43] but no one in legal philosophy has ever denied that (or claimed otherwise): In contemporary lingo, one might say that legal philosophy has sometimes been interested in a semantic question (what is the meaning of this statutory provision?), but not in the meta-semantic question of what makes it the case that a particular meaning is the meaning.[44] Strikingly, Greenberg also concedes that, "*even if* morality were the relevant value [needed for rational determination] . . . it would not follow

[37] See, e.g., Leiter, *Naturalizing Jurisprudence*, 178–81.

[38] For a partial defense of Hart's methodology, however, see Alex Langlinais and Brian Leiter, "The Methodology of Legal Philosophy," in *The Oxford Handbook of Philosophical Methodology*, ed. Herman Cappelen, Tamar Szabo Gendler, and John Hawthorne (Oxford University Press, 2016), 671–89.

[39] More weakly, one might say it has not been met convincingly elsewhere in philosophy; obviously some metaphysicians will disagree. For some pertinent discussion, see Alexander Miller and Olivia Sultanescu, "Rule-Following and Intentionality," *Stanford Encyclopedia of Philosophy*, https://plato.stanford.edu/entries/rule-following/, esp. sections 3.3 and 4.

[40] Greenberg, "How Facts Make Law," 164 n.18.

[41] Saul Kripke, *Wittgenstein on Rules and Private Language* (Harvard University Press, 1982), 24, 29.

[42] See Nelson Goodman, *Fact, Fiction, and Forecast*, 4th ed. (Harvard University Press, 1983), 59–83.

[43] For a related thought about the role of "pragmatics" in fixing legal content, see Bill Watson's critique of Greenberg's view in Bill Watson, "In Defense of the Standard Picture," *Legal Theory* 28 (2022): 59–88, esp. pp. 77–78.

[44] Thanks to Jed Lewinsohn for pressing this point on me.

that the content of the law would necessarily be morally good or even that the moral goodness of a norm would "count in favor" of its being legally valid.[45] That makes it more puzzling why general jurisprudence should care. Legal positivists, for example, deny that legally valid norms are necessarily morally defensible, yet there is no reason to think that evaluative judgments about "rational" determination will implicate morality: So why does this matter for any actual jurisprudential debate?

In short, if legal content is in the same metaphysical (determination) boat as semantic content and the content of projectible predicates in scientific theories, then why expect legal philosophers to solve the problem?[46] Even other philosophical domains concerned with the understanding of artifacts have also eschewed framing their problems in Greenberg's metaphysical terms. In philosophy of art, for example, the question arises: What makes something "art"? Why is Marcel Duchamp's urinal on its back (the "Fountain") a work of "art"? The question is much discussed by philosophers, but no one has thought it was a question about what metaphysically basic facts determine "art facts." Arthur Danto famously argued that if the institutions of the "art world" treat something as art, it is art (I oversimplify).[47] In philosophy of science in the mid-twentieth century, philosophers considered the question: What distinguishes science from pseudo-science? Karl Popper famously proposed the answer that scientific hypotheses are "falsifiable." In neither case did anyone ask about the metaphysical determinants of "art facts" or "science facts." One can imagine how the answers actually given might be translated into Greenberg's metaphysical determination question, but the question is why one should want to do that? It might create publication opportunities for recent PhDs trained in metaphysics, but what would we learn that we have not learned from the existing debates?[48]

What were the existing debates about? Think of it this way. Not every act people think is "morally required" is legally required; not everything that

[45] Greenberg, "How Facts Make Law," 193.

[46] Gideon Rosen has argued that another metaphysical relation, supervenience, is not adequate to account for the positivism/antipositivism dispute. See Gideon Rosen, "Metaphysical Dependence: Grounding and Reduction," in *Modality: Metaphysics, Logic and Epistemology*, ed. Bob Hale and Aviv Hoffmann (Oxford University Press, 2010), 113–14. His argument for "grounding" as the preferred metaphysical relation faces some of the problems noted in the text here, but also those articulated by Bosko Tripkovic and Dennis Patterson, "The Promise and Limits of Grounding in Law," *Legal Theory* 29 (2023): 202–28, esp. 217. The demonstration that supervenience is an inadequate metaphysical account is, in any case, just grist for my mill that we should not try to reframe the debate in terms of metaphysical relations between "layers" of reality. The debates have been clear enough for decades, without translating them, even if analytic philosophers outside philosophy of law were confused. (A smart Princeton graduate once explained to me that the "grounding" formulation made the debates in general jurisprudence easier to understand for metaphysicians at Princeton. That hardly seems like a good reason to talk that way, given how much is lost, as we will see in the section of this chapter on Shapiro.)

[47] See Arthur Danto, *The Transfiguration of the Commonplace* (Harvard University Press, 1981).

[48] We have learned nothing in jurisprudence either, although we have obscured plenty of issues, as I discuss in the section of this chapter on Shapiro.

people think is "morally prohibited" is legally prohibited; not everything legally required coincides with what people think is "morally required," and so too with legal prohibitions. Law and morality both address human behavior in multivarious ways, which is why the standing question of their relation has been so important.[49] What we want to know, as a theoretical matter, is not "how facts" determine legal content; what we want to know is whether the moral value of a norm does or should make it legally valid, and whether the immorality of a norm does or should make it legally invalid. That is what general jurisprudence has been about for at least a century (if not two). The old question was not an irrelevant one, and it is also perfectly clear without any additional metaphysical apparatus.[50]

To sum up: Since we do not know how "facts" make a predicate projectible into the future, and we do not know how facts make it the case that a rule has a particular meaning, why would anyone think we should know "how facts make law"? No one in the history of jurisprudence before 2004 thought that was the question. No one after 2004 should think it is a serious question either. Anyone interested in a theory of legal content already has the resources for answering that question, and, more importantly, that answer will vary by legal jurisdiction, as it should. The content of the law is determined by a mix of authoritative (and hierarchically organized) sources, their meanings based on the meaning of the words in the public language of the community, but with substantial modifications to those meanings involving authoritative stipulation, precedent, custom, and rules of interpretation specified by the rule of recognition in a particular legal system.

II. Shapiro's Metaphysical Turn

> "Although [the earlier chapters] do give a keen sense of what is at stake and a decent introduction to key concepts in philosophy of law, they will mislead students in respect of the menu of problems, the solutions that have been proposed, and the order in which these should be investigated. If treated as the state of the art, these chapters may well set the art back."
>
> —Review of Shapiro's *Legality* by John Gardner (late Professor of Jurisprudence, Oxford University) and Timothy Macklem (Professor of Jurisprudence, King's College, London) (*Notre Dame Philosophical Reviews*, 2011)

[49] That remains true even if the boundaries are sometimes fuzzy (see ch. 8 in this volume).

[50] This question is also closely tied, at least for Dworkin, with the question of how judges should decide cases, although actual positivists have generally thought the questions about which norms are valid and how judges should decide cases were separate questions.

Greenberg's idiosyncratic conception of the questions of general jurisprudence has been most consequential, I suspect, through its huge influence on Scott Shapiro's 2011 book *Legality*,[51] which, while ostensibly a defense of a legal positivist view, adopts wholesale Greenberg's conceptualization of the issues (as well as adopting various antipositivist theses[52]). It is to Shapiro's version of Greenberg's view, and its problems, that I now turn.

Shapiro explicitly frames his inquiry in the metaphysical terms popularized by Greenberg: "[A]nalytical jurisprudence examines [the] *metaphysical* foundations" of law he says (Shapiro, *Legality*, 2), meaning the supposed metaphysical determination (or grounding relation) between "legal facts," "social facts," and "moral facts" (ibid., 27). As discussed in section I, "analytical jurisprudence" has never understood its questions this way. Indeed, as we will see, it is not clear whether any legal positivists actually accept Shapiro's "metaphysical foundations" formulation of positivism, namely, that "social facts determine legal facts" (certainly H. L. A. Hart does not). The metaphysical framing is, however, one of the two reasons his book has been favorably received in some quarters,[53] despite serious mistakes and confusions, some of which we will soon discuss (although not all the mistakes depend on the metaphysical framing Shapiro favors).[54] It captures the *Zeitgeist* of very recent Anglophone jurisprudence to try to fit Hart-style questions into the language of metaphysical determination or "grounding" relations, the stage set by Greenberg.[55] Yet Shapiro's metaphysical reframing of the debates in general jurisprudence, rather than adding depth or illumination to the main questions, manages either to render obscure or simply erase the existing positions in the field. Legal positivists and Dworkin disagree about whether a norm can be legally valid (i.e., exist as a norm of the legal system) without also being morally justified in some measure: Dworkin

[51] Scott Shapiro, *Legality* (Harvard University Press, 2011). All further citations will be by page number in the body of the text.

[52] See the discussion, *supra* note 32, regarding the Mafia and the idea that law must have a "moral aim."

[53] The second factor affecting the book's reception is that those sympathetic to Dworkinian, natural law, and antipositivist views more generally have welcomed it, because Shapiro's framing of questions, and his mistakes, are all favorable to those views, even as he purports to offer a positivist view. The only notable legal positivists to review the book reached a very different verdict: see John Gardner and Timothy Macklem's detailed review (2011) in *Notre Dame Philosophical Reviews*, with which I mostly agree.

[54] Mistakes and confusions in Shapiro's account have also been discussed in Kevin Toh, "Plan-Attitudes, Plan-Contents, and Bootstrapping," in *Oxford Studies in Philosophy of Law, Volume 3*, ed. Leslie Green and Brian Leiter (Oxford University Press, 2018), 1-48; and Matthew Kramer, "In Defense of Hart," *Legal Theory*, 19 (2013): 370–402.

[55] Greenberg's 2004 paper precedes the "grounding" fad in Anglophone philosophy, but is naturally assimilated to that development. See, e.g., Samuele Chilove and George Pavlakos, "Law-Determination as Grounding: A Common Grounding Framework for Jurisprudence," *Legal Theory* 25 (2019): 53–76. This is hardly surprising, given the sociology of the academy: ideas percolate, inchoate, in elite graduate programs before crystallizing in a research program, even a pointless one.

thinks legally valid norms must satisfy some kind of moral test;[56] positivists either deny that it is necessary that they do so (e.g., Hart) or deny that it is possible for a moral test to be a criterion of legal validity (e.g., Raz). Positivists and John Finnis disagree about whether the "central cases" of law for purposes of jurisprudential theorizing must be identified by first figuring out what kinds of laws and legal systems would generate genuine moral obligations: Finnis affirms this; positivists deny it. Positivists and Mark Murphy disagree about whether it is part of the law's nature to have success conditions that can only be specified by moral argument: Murphy affirms this, and positivists deny it. None of these debates is illuminated by the misleading framing in terms of metaphysical determination relations, and the latter two are not even captured by it. One could, of course, modify the preceding characterizations to nominally capture these views in metaphysical determination terms: For example, Finnis holds that in the "central cases" of law, moral facts determine legal facts. But this adds nothing: the whole question is what is meant by the "central cases," why are they central, and how is morality relevant to specifying them? None of these actual questions is illuminated by saying Finnis believes that "moral facts determine legal facts" in "central" cases of law.

I begin by examining Shapiro's curious discussion of his "methodology"—which, when the metaphysical clutter is cleared away, is just a familiar mix of intuition-pumping examples and reflective equilibrium—but readers mainly interested in the substantive problems with Shapiro's view can safely skip ahead to subsection (B).

A. Shapiro On Jurisprudential Methodology

Shapiro claims one of the two main questions for jurisprudence is "the Identity Question." He defines it thus: "[T]o ask about the identity of X is to ask what it is about X that makes it X and not Y or Z or any other such thing. . . . A correct answer to the Identity Question must supply the set of properties that make (possible or actual) instances of X the things that they are" (Shapiro, *Legality*, 8).

This is an instance of the "demarcation problem" in jurisprudence, namely, how to demarcate legal norms from other kinds of norms (see ch. 8 in this volume). Hart, however, avoided this metaphysical framing in terms of the "set of properties that make (possible or actual) instances of X the things that they are"; among other things, Hart had no interest in the "possible" cases, as opposed

[56] This does not mean legally valid norms must be morally good ones, just that they must satisfy the moral justification component of what Dworkin calls "constructive interpretation." See Ronald Dworkin, *Law's Empire* (Harvard University Press, 1986).

to the actual ones. And even with respect to the latter, he eschewed any essentialist interpretation of his project. In *The Concept of Law,* Hart begins by noting the surprising diversity of answers to the "What is law?" question since about 1800, explicitly "neglect[ing] classical and medieval speculation about the 'nature' of law" (Hart, *Concept of Law*, 1; note Hart's quote marks!). (He later refers to "What is the nature (or the essence) of law?" as a "more obscurely framed" variant on "What is law?" [ibid., 6].)[57] Hart's allergy to talk of "nature" and "essence" reflects a philosophical commitment Hart does not state but has clearly absorbed from the later Wittgensteinian *Zeitgeist* in England at the time (all his mentions of the word "essence" are in quotes[58]): This is the view that concepts like "law" or "game" (or "knowledge" or any other concept of interest) do not have necessary and sufficient conditions that one can explicate via analysis, but rather are "family resemblance" concepts, ones with invariably fuzzy borderline cases.[59] This way of thinking is obviously anathema to the metaphysical turn in jurisprudence. (Hart slips a bit when he states the two "necessary and sufficient conditions" for the existence of a legal system.[60])

The strength of the metaphysical commitments Shapiro has signed on to becomes apparent in the analogy he suggests for answering the identity question, namely, the metaphysical interpretation of what makes water what it is: "Being H_2O is what makes water *water.* With respect to law, accordingly, [we need] to discover what makes all and only instance of law instances of *law* and not something else" (Shapiro, *Legality,* 9). In fact, it is false according to chemistry that "[b]eing H_2O is what makes water *water*,"[61] but I will put that to one

[57] Hart suggests the real concerns of jurisprudence are three: "How does law differ from and how is it related to orders backed by threats? How does legal obligation differ from, and how is it related to, moral obligation? What are rules, and to what extent is law an affair of rules?" (Hart, *Concept of Law*, 7–13). I am not sure this is a very apt characterization, even of what Hart achieves in *The Concept of Law.* The first question is certainly important, and well states the dispute with views like John Austin's, and Hart offers a clear answer to it. The second question is never really answered in the 1961 book as far as I can see, although suggestions are made. The status of the third question is curious: Hart tells us precisely the way in which law is an affair of rules, but he never offers an analysis of what a rule is, only of what it is to accept a rule.

[58] See, e.g. Hart, *Concept of Law*, 8.

[59] Ludwig Wittgenstein, *Philosophical Investigations*, trans. G. E. M. Anscombe (Oxford: Blackwell, 1953).

[60] Hart, *Concept of Law*, 116. Later in *The Concept of Law*, Hart also accepts that law *necessarily* satisfies what he calls the "minimum content of natural law" (ibid., 193–200). But this is not a conceptual necessity, but something like a "nomic" one: given what our world is like and what people are like, any society with a legal system will necessarily try to satisfy some recognizable moral aims, even if it does so poorly. Matt Kramer offers somewhat different objections to this language in his book on Hart. See Matt Kramer, *H.L.A. Hart* (Polity Press, 2018), 107–9.

[61] See Michael Weisberg, "Water Is *Not* H_2O," in *Philosophy of Chemistry: Synthesis of a New Discipline*, ed. Davis Baird, Eric Scerri, and Lee McIntyre (Springer, 2006), 337–45. Briefly, hydrogen and oxygen both have multiple isotopes (atoms with the same number of protons and electrons, but different neutrons), and the natural language category of "water" doesn't distinguish between them; in addition, chemical kinds are individuated by their "structural" properties (at the macro,

side (except as a cautionary note about armchair metaphysics) since the example has gained so much traction in the era of Kripke-Putnam semantics for natural kind terms.[62]

What is surprising about Shapiro's framing of the question is that—even granting the Kripke-Putnam background—law is *not* something that could be individuated the way water is, that is, by its "essential" micro-constitution at the chemical level. "Law" is like "science," "chess," "art," and "chair" in not having a distinctive micro-constitution: These are all human artifacts, some created intentionally (e.g., most chairs), some not (e.g., science[63]). If the objects picked out by these categories have identity conditions in Shapiro's sense, they would have to be wholly different.[64] But Shapiro lets this disanalogy pass in silence.

Shapiro calls his method "conceptual analysis," and says it is equivalent to "descriptive metaphysics," "reflective equilibrium," and "rational reconstruction" (Shapiro, *Legality*, 13). The disjunction is surprising, since most understandings of "conceptual analysis" would not make it equivalent to these other methods. Shapiro is, however, clear about his stipulated understanding: He purports to endorse a version of what is known as "the Canberra plan."[65] Here is one gloss:

> [The Canberra Plan] argues that philosophy starts with an initial analysis of concepts employed by everyday thought, such as *free will*, say, or *knowledge*, or *moral value*, or *conscious experience*. Once this stage has been completed, philosophy can then turn to "serious metaphysics" to demonstrate how a limited number of ingredients (for example, physical ingredients) might satisfy these everyday concepts. This second stage is likely to appeal to synthetic *a posteriori* scientific knowledge about the fundamental nature of reality. But the purely analytic first stage, according to the Canberra Plan, also plays an essential part

molecular, and atomic level) and "reactive" properties (how the substance transforms, either over time or when interacting with other substances); isotopic differences matter here.

[62] Even if water is not H_2O, it suffices for Kripke-Putnam semantics that it have some *essence* according to our best natural science. There are, however, different, nonmetaphysical ways of thinking about "natural kinds," for example, in terms of their explanatory fruitfulness. See, e.g., Muhammad Ali Khalidi, *Natural Categories and Human Kind* (Cambridge University Press, 2013).

[63] Particular scientific hypotheses and instruments are intentional human creations, but the social practice we pick out with "science" is not.

[64] Most writers—not Shapiro—suggest that the essential nature of artifacts can be identified by appeal to the intentions of their makers. This will not work in the case of law, however, since while some particular legally valid norms may have intentional creators, *law* as a social phenomenon does not. See ch. 8 in this volume

[65] See, e.g., Frank Jackson, *From Metaphysics to Ethics: A Defence of Conceptual Analysis* (Oxford University Press, 1998); but David Lewis—who was very close to the Australians in matters metaphysical—also used something like this method. See David Lewis, "How to Define Theoretical Terms," *Journal of Philosophy* 67 (1970): 427–46.

> in setting the agenda for the subsequent metaphysical investigation. [internal citations omitted]
>
> An initial question about this programme relates to its scope. It is by no means clear that all, or indeed any, philosophically interesting concepts can be subject to the relevant kind of analysis. Jackson himself assumes that pretty much all everyday concepts can be analysed as equivalent to "the kind which satisfies such-and-such folk assumptions." But it is arguable that many everyday concepts are not so constituted, but rather have their semantic contents fixed by observational, causal or historical relations to their referents.[66]

Here is how Shapiro explains it:

> Conceptual analysis can easily be thought of as a kind of detective work.... In conceptual analysis, the philosopher ... collects clues and uses the process of elimination for a specific purpose, namely, to elucidate the identity of the entity that falls under the concept in question ... The philosophical clues ... are not merely true, but *self-evidently* so. The key to conceptual analysis ... is the gathering of truisms about a given entity (Shapiro, *Legality*, 13).

Shapiro's approach to "truisms about law," however, departs not only from Hart but arguably also from Frank Jackson,[67] who, like Hart, took *folk understandings* of the concepts at issue *as the starting point*.[68] (Hart, influenced by Austin's ordinary language philosophy, treated as a starting point what an ordinary person familiar with a modern municipal legal system knows about law.) By contrast, Shapiro writes:

> [T]he legal philosopher must assemble a preliminary list of truisms about law. Doing this does not however mean identifying what the layperson [i.e., Hart's ordinary person] would recognize as obvious truths about the law. It means identifying those truths that those who have a good understanding of how legal institutions operate (lawyers, judges, legislators, legal scholars, and so on) take to be self-evident, or at least would take to be so on reflection (Shapiro, *Legality*, 15).

66 David Papineau, "Naturalism," *Stanford Encyclopedia of Philosophy*, https://plato.stanford.edu/archives/sum2020/entries/naturalism/.

67 And not simply because Shapiro has no use for scientific knowledge, as Jackson's approach does.

68 It was only a starting point, of course: the goal was to make coherent the inchoate folk concept. Thus, one familiar feature of the folk understanding—that law involves coercion—is discarded by Hart, precisely because it doesn't fit other familiar features of law (e.g., rules that confer powers).

Why this approach, rather than Hart's, is the preferred one for "conceptual analysis" is never explained. The evidence that the adduced truisms are those actually shared by "lawyers, judges, legislators, legal scholars and so on" is also absent. And one might have hoped for some clarification about the oxymoronic idea of "self-evident . . . on reflection," but Shapiro is again silent. There may be a reason for these omissions. Shapiro's suggested "truisms" (ibid., 15) are not obviously true, let alone self-evidently true: they range from the "sometimes true" (Shapiro exploits that) to the "philosophically contentious" to the "false." For example:

(1) "Legal authority is conferred by legal rules." This depends on what one means by rules, and one's view of the relation between positive and natural law (i.e., either divine or otherwise supra-human law). Insofar as legal authority arises from customary practices, as Hart believes, this "truism," on one way of understanding it, may be false.
(2) "Legal authorities have the power to obligate even when their judgments are wrong." This just trades on an ambiguity about "obligate" (moral or legal?). It is either false (in the case of morally obligate) or tautological and irrelevant (in the case of legally obligate).
(3) "Simply knowing that the law requires one to act in a certain way does not motivate one to act in that way." It seems a plausible *empirical* generalization that it does not *necessarily* motivate one to act that way, but as stated by Shapiro it is obviously false.[69]
(4) "One can be a legal official even though one is alienated from one's job." This is perhaps true if alienation is interpreted in its colloquial sense, but it is then irrelevant to every theory of law; but the claim is false if it implies that there could be a legal system in which officials did not accept the secondary rules from an internal point of view: that is a contested jurisprudential thesis, and could not be treated as a truism.[70]

Now, even nonessentialist, nonmetaphysical accounts of law, like Hart's, have need of something like "truisms," but they are more like those in Hart's list in *The Concept of Law*[71] (although he could take on board *some* of Shapiro's): In short, the contestable nature of Shapiro's purported "truisms" is not ultimately that important. The real question is: what if we disagree about Shapiro's truisms (as I do)? In the end, *Shapiro's real method is one of reflective equilibrium*, as he eventually makes clear: "We must consider the totality of our responses and be willing to give up some of our views when they don't cohere with other judgments

[69] There are, sadly, people for whom "It's the law" always answers the question of what must be done. Lon Fuller, rather notoriously, tried to defame all legal positivists as holding this view.
[70] On this point, see Brian Leiter, "Back to Hart," *Belgrade Law Review* 69 (2021): 749–60.
[71] Hart, *Concept of Law*, 3.

to which we assign a higher priority and are therefore less willing to abandon" (Shapiro, *Legality*, 17). It would seem, then, that the references to the Canberra plan, truisms, and conceptual analysis are beside the point: the "method" is just the familiar one of appeals to intuitions about particular cases that fall within the extension of a proposed analysis, and some mutual adjustment between theory and those intuitions.[72] One could adopt this "method" without any of the talk about metaphysical determination relations. Shapiro is in the unhappy position of trying to do legal philosophy the way everyone has since Hart, while offering a metaphysical framing orthogonal to his project.

B. Why Jurisprudence Is (Supposed) to Matter and the Metaphysics of Positivism vs. Natural Law

"Why care?" asks Shapiro. He quotes Judge Richard Posner's demand for "payoff," that "*something* ought to turn on the answer to the question 'What is law?'" (Shapiro, *Legality*, 22). The standard philosophical answer to "what turns on the answer" is knowledge of the truth, and thus understanding of an important social phenomenon. Shapiro, unlike all legal positivists, treats the Posner challenge seriously and tries to offer an answer:

> [A] great deal *does* turn on the question of "What is Law?" . . . One of the main goals of this book will thus be to show that analytical jurisprudence has profound practical implications for the practice of law—or, in other words, that the answer to what the law is *in any particular case* depends crucially on the answer to what law is *in general*. . . .
>
> In order to prove conclusively that the law is thus-and-so in a particular jurisdiction, it is not enough to know who has authority within the jurisdiction, which texts they have approved, and how to interpret them. One must also know a general philosophical truth, namely, how legal authority and proper interpretive methodology are established in general. In other words one must know which facts *ultimately* determine the existence and content of legal systems (ibid., 25).

Here Shapiro sounds like Dworkin, who said, "Jurisprudence is the general part of adjudication, silent prologue to any decision at law"[73]—something legal

[72] This was Rawls's method, and he did not think it one of conceptual analysis. See John Rawls, *A Theory of Justice* (Harvard University Press, 1971). The method has, of course, its own problems: see, e.g., Robert Cummins, "Reflections on Reflective Equilibrium," in *Rethinking Intuition*, ed. Michael DePaul and William Ramsey (Rowman & Littlefield, 1998).

[73] Dworkin, *Law's Empire*, 90.

positivists have always denied. "What is the law?" constitutes one question; "how should the court decide a particular case?" another. With respect to Shapiro's formulation, it is especially surprising to be told that to know what the law is, "it is not enough to know who has authority within the jurisdiction, which texts they have approved, and how to interpret them": *How could that not be enough for knowing what the law is*? Isn't that all most (very good) lawyers know? Why should knowing the *origins* of legal authority and interpretive methodology matter at all? On its face, this is a non sequitur.

Shapiro's attempt to deflect the apparent non sequitur takes him back into Greenbergian metaphysics. He says, plausibly, that "[l]egal facts are never *ultimate* facts," where the latter (his example is quarks) admit of no further explanation. By contrast, "if it is against the law to jaywalk in New York City, then this legal fact obtains in virtue of the fact that, say, the city council voted to approve a bill that set out in writing that jaywalking is prohibited within the city and the fact that the mayor signed the bill" (Shapiro, *Legality*, 26). But he goes from this banal point (which is all a lawyer or citizen would need to know) to asking, "What facts might we appeal to in order to establish the authoritative status of fundamental laws such as the Constitution?" (ibid., 27). Why, however, do we need to know the answer to that question, if we already know that the Constitution "has authority within the jurisdiction . . . and how to interpret" it? That is, after all, exactly what Shapiro earlier said we were entitled to assume (ibid., 25).

Shapiro is correct that positivists and "natural lawyers" (ibid., 27) have different answers to the question what grounds authority in a legal system, although his description of the competing answers leaves much to be desired. He describes them as follows. For positivists, "all legal facts are ultimately determined by social facts alone. . . .[C]laims about the existence or content of a legal system must ultimately be established by referring to what people think, intend, claim, say, or do" (ibid., 27). A bit later, Shapiro admits one way in which this is, in fact, clearly false: the positivist "does not seriously mean that the law is *ultimately* determined by social facts alone" since social facts are not among the "ultimate constituents of the universe" (ibid., 44). Social facts might, after all, be reducible (or token-identical) to other kinds of facts. He notes that "some even maintain that moral facts are reducible to other, more basic, nonmoral facts" (ibid.). This latter possibility would, of course vitiate the way the positivist/natural law distinction is being drawn. Surprisingly, Shapiro declares that "these deep metaphysical questions will largely be ignored. We will draw a methodological line at the social and the moral and treat social and moral facts as though they were ultimate. Our taxonomy of legal philosophers, therefore, will only consider those 'above the line' positions" (ibid.). From the standpoint of metaphysics, this seems a rather thin answer, and might be thought a reason to try to avoid metaphysical grounding claims in stating the issues! After all, almost no legal positivists have ever had developed views on the "ultimate constituents of the universe," and never needed to, as we saw in section I.

Which positivist, however, actually accepts the view that "all legal facts are ultimately determined by social facts alone"? Take Shapiro's own example: "if it is against the law to jaywalk in New York City, then this legal fact obtains in virtue of the fact that, say, the city council voted to approve a bill that set out in writing that jaywalking is prohibited within the city and the fact that they mayor signed the bill" (ibid., 26). Yet this legal fact about jaywalking also "obtains" in virtue of a whole set of semantic facts that are not "social" facts, although this may depend on one's views about semantic content (but most positivists have been agnostic on this, Alf Ross being an exception, and his view was certainly not that meaning depends on social facts). This legal fact also obtains in virtue of various geographical facts (e.g., "in New York City") that are not simply social facts ("being *New York City*" might be a social fact, but being particular landmasses, partly separated by water, denominated "New York City" is not a social fact). It also obtains in virtue of biological and psychological facts about those who comprise the city council and their actions and mental states, which are presumably not all social facts. The slogan "legal facts" depends on "social facts," when given the metaphysical gloss, does not describe anyone's position.

The problem is worse than this. Even Hart acknowledges in Chapter IX of *The Concept of Law* the truth of the "minimum content of natural law" (Hart, *Concept of Law*, 193–200): Any society with a legal system will (as a matter of "nomic" necessity,[74] as it were) use law to deal with limited resources, limited altruism, our shared vulnerability to harm, and so on. Is this minimal moral content of any legal system a matter of social facts? Only on a disputed conventionalist conception of morality would the latter be true. No legal philosopher, as far as I can tell, accepts the metaphysical thesis that "all legal facts are ultimately determined by social facts alone." Some legal philosophers do believe that legally valid norms must have a social source, and some others believe that whether a norm is legally valid depends on the conventional practice of officials. The talk of metaphysical determination relations just obscures the actual positivist theses at issue, and commits the positivist to a thesis that is obviously false. Conceding effectively that it is false, as Shapiro does, by dropping a footnote that social facts are not "ultimate facts" does not help.[75]

[74] That is, in virtue of the facts and laws about our world, including the facts and laws about human psychology.

[75] Jed Lewinsohn points out, correctly, that the "orthodox" view of grounding among its proponents allows that "X facts can fully determine/ground Y facts" even if the X facts have further determinants/grounds, so Shapiro has made various concessions he should not have. There is a cautionary tale here: legal philosophers should not adopt metaphysical framing if they do not

According to Shapiro, for natural lawyers, "legal facts are ultimately determined by moral *and* social facts. . . . [C]laims of legal authority and proper interpretation must in the end be justified through morally sound reasoning" (Shapiro, *Legality*, 27). In a footnote, Shapiro admits this does not fit Mark Murphy's Weak Natural Law thesis,[76] but he claims Murphy's view is compatible with positivism anyway, but that is not correct. If it is internal to the nature of law that it has moral success/defectiveness conditions, as Murphy argues, then law is not just a matter of social facts, to use Shapiro's idiom. On Murphy's view, one must do normative moral and political philosophy to say what law's success-and-defectiveness conditions are, contrary to Hart's claim that we can do descriptive jurisprudence while prescinding from normative theory. Since Murphy's is the only philosophically interesting version of natural law theory currently on offer, Shapiro's framing, by excluding it, is even less useful.[77]

Back, however, to Shapiro's official formulation of the natural law view: "legal facts are ultimately determined by moral *and* social facts. . . . [C]laims of legal authority and proper interpretation must in the end be justified through morally sound reasoning" (Shapiro, *Legality*, 27). Note the (Dworkinian) slippage in this formulation from talk about what the law is to talk about justifying "legal authority and proper interpretation." Again, it is surely enough for a lawyer to "know who has authority within the jurisdiction, which texts they have approved, and how to interpret them" (ibid., 25)? Answers to the further questions are irrelevant.

Shapiro tries to defend his ongoing non sequitur by pointing to a disagreement about how to interpret the Eighth Amendment prohibition (in the US Constitution) on "cruel" (and unusual) punishment. His framing, which I have quoted repeatedly, claimed that even the lawyer who knew "how to interpret" the authoritative sources would still need to answer the jurisprudential question

understand it! None of this has any bearing, of course, on the other reasons offered for rejecting the metaphysical question.

[76] Mark Murphy, "Natural Law Theory," in *The Blackwell Guide to the Philosophy of Law and Legal Theory*, ed. Martin P. Golding and William A. Edmundson (Blackwell, 2005), 21–23.

[77] The fact that Murphy's view gets so little attention in recent American jurisprudence—in comparison, say, to Greenberg's eccentric views—itself raises an interesting sociological question about the profession. Murphy, a long-time professor at Georgetown University, has not taught in an elite "analytic" department, and he works very much in the Thomist Catholic tradition (to which I should add, lest it not be obvious, I am wholly unsympathetic). His engagement with the jurisprudential tradition, however, is quite a bit more serious than most antipositivist work in Anglophone jurisprudence, and his level of argument is much higher than Finnis, who spent his career at Oxford, where he produced many acolytes, but none at Murphy's philosophical level. That Murphy's work is not the central case of antipositivism for recent writers in jurisprudence is yet another indication of how the sociology of the academic profession warps research. (After I pointed out the relevance of Murphy's work to his own work, Emad Atiq, much to his credit, included a serious discussion of Murphy's views in his recent book, Emad Atiq, *Legal Anti-Positivism* (Cambridge University Press, 2025), which may help change the situation.)

(ibid., 25), and now he has subtracted even that bit of legal knowledge (about correct interpretation). Shapiro asks: "How are we to resolve this disagreement" between the positivist and natural lawyer (ibid., 29)?

Let us distinguish some different ways of understanding what is at issue here. First, we might be looking for the *legally correct* interpretation, the one the law requires. A particular view about the nature of law *could* affect that question, but might not: Presumably, Shapiro would allow that not every particular legal question ("Is this punishment forbidden by the 8th Amendment?") necessarily has an answer, and that might be true on either the positivist or natural law view about the nature of law. Second, and more importantly, even the *legally correct* interpretation would not answer the question of what a judge *ought* to do. On the positivist view, of course, it never does. The punishment might not be "cruel" as a matter of law, but should still be forbidden as an equitable matter, or it might be "cruel" as a matter of morality but should still be permitted (because of settled expectations generated by the law, separation of powers concerns, deference to a strong social consensus, etc.). Why not just resolve the disagreement by appeal to whatever normative considerations are relevant to deciding whether a particular punishment should or should not be forbidden?[78] The only thing Shapiro's preferred approach gets us—perhaps sometimes—are merely "labels," precisely what Shapiro claimed to avoid (Shapiro, *Legality*, 30): We get to say that what we are doing is *legally correct*.

C. Shapiro's "Possibility Puzzle"

According to Shapiro, to have the power to make laws, one must already have law investing one with that power: "the Possibility Puzzle arises because it appears that anybody with power to create legal norms must derive its power from some norm, while any norm that could confer such a power must itself by created by someone with the power to do so" (ibid., 42). As he rightly notes, this is a kind of chicken-egg problem: "all chickens must hatch from chicken eggs" but "all chicken eggs must be laid by chickens" (ibid., 39). There is, in fact, an evolutionary solution to the original chicken-egg problem—Shapiro does not mention it—which is to deny that "all chicken eggs must be laid by chickens." It suffices that some evolutionary ancestor, a proto-chicken, through some random genetic mutation, lays a chicken egg from which emerges a chicken. This is not that far off the legal positivist answer: Legal power arises, often enough accidentally, from a nonlegal customary practice, which is one of the reasons that the

[78] See ch. 8 in this volume for that kind of answer.

idea of "planning" (the centerpiece of Shapiro's alleged alternative to Hart) is irrelevant to the phenomenon we are trying to understand.

Shapiro frames the natural law and positivist responses to the Possibility Puzzle as follows. Natural lawyers say "legal authority must ultimately derive from some moral norm"—for example, "certain political communities' moral right to determine the terms and direction of social cooperation. . . . This sovereign right . . . derives from the rules or principles of political morality" (ibid., 43). Positivists, by contrast, "ground legal authority not in moral but in social facts" (ibid., 43; see also his characterization of Hart at ibid., 44). Note the crucial ambiguity in Shapiro's phrase "the fundamental rules of the legal system are ultimate norms that rest purely on social facts" (ibid., 44) that is involved in the "rest" metaphor. "Rest" for the positivist does not mean *justifies*, unlike in the natural law case. Unfortunately, Shapiro's argument trades precisely on this ambiguity and leads to some of the more seriously misleading claims in the book.

From Hume, we are supposed to know, according to Shapiro, that you cannot get a normative conclusion (an "ought") from merely descriptive premises (an "is") (ibid., 45–46). What does this have to do with the possibility puzzle? The positivist says that legal authority arises from a psychosocial fact (i.e., from *being taken to have such authority by officials*). Having legal authority is not a normative fact; it is a descriptive fact about those who satisfy the relevant power-conferring rules in a particular jurisdiction. Recall Shapiro's own gloss on Hart: Those who wield legal authority or legal power can do so "because courts and other legal officials follow rules mandating deference to their choices" (ibid., 44). Shapiro mistakenly thinks that to say X has "a legal right is to draw a normative conclusion" (ibid., 47), but it need not be: it can simply be a statement of a descriptive fact about the rights X has in a particular jurisdiction (see ibid., 47 for the same claim: "knowledge of the law is normative"). This is a serious mistake. When Shapiro offers the example of the father telling the child what to do, he has to change the topic into how the father "can justify [his] claim to authority" (ibid., 48). It is a good question how legal systems can justify their claim to authority, but that answer is very different from the answer to the question, "Is there a legal system here?"[79]

[79] The confusions noted in the text vitiate most of Shapiro's foray into "expressivism" (Shapiro, *Legality*, 98–99). (For one critical discussion of Shapiro's treatment of those issues, see Toh, "Plan-Attitudes, Plan-Contents, and Bootstrapping.") I do want to say something about one aspect of Shapiro's discussion. Shapiro objects that expressivism cannot explain how the Holmesian Bad Man can make legal judgments, despite not accepting the rule of recognition from an internal point of view (Shapiro, *Legality*, 111), and second, that the legal/moral distinction (e.g., regarding obligation) is "unstable and unsupportable. . . . The claims of law are far too serious to accept the possibility that they are amoral in nature" (ibid.). Let us look at these in turn.

Shapiro says that law's "redescribability" is a problem for Hart's (alleged) assumption that "legal reasoners always engage practically with the social facts of legal practice when deriving legal conclusions" (Shapiro, *Legality*, 112) (i.e., by adopting the internal point of view). Shapiro objects,

D. The Rule of Recognition and Shapiro's Main Objection to Hart

Here is Shapiro's first gloss on the rule of recognition (RR):

> The most salient property of the rule of recognition is that it is a *secondary* rule. It is a rule about other rules, that is, the primary rules. The rule of recognition is also a *social* rule. . . . First, the rule of recognition exists and has the content it does because, and only because, of certain *social facts*. In particular, its existence and content is determined by the fact that members of a group take the internal point of view toward a certain behavioral regularity and use it to evaluate the validity of norms that fall within their purview. . . (Shapiro, *Legality*, 84).
>
> [T]he rule of recognition is a *duty-imposing* rule. It imposes a duty on legal officials to apply rules that bear certain characteristics. For example, the British rule of recognition requires British officials to apply the rules enacted by the Queen-in-Parliament. . . . might be wondered, then, why Hart presents the rule

"[t]he bad man does not accept these norms [i.e., the RR], but can nonetheless truthfully redescribe the law in terms of obligations, rights, and legal validity" (ibid., 112). Just as a threshold matter, anyone who knows anything about law must be puzzled by this claim. What could be more common in legal practice than a lawyer saying something like this: "You have an obligation to do X, even though it's stupid/the court decision is wrong/the statute is absurd" etc. Surely Hart also knew this! The standard positivist account of such judgments is that they are, per Raz, "detached" rather than "committed" (see, e.g., Joseph Raz, *The Authority of Law: Essays on Law and Morality* (Oxford University Press, 1979), 153–57), but Shapiro rejects that view in a long footnote that appears to trade on a misunderstanding of Raz (Shapiro, *Legality*, 415 n.44).

Shapiro's attack on the legal/moral "obligation" distinction raises some more complex issues. He says that "concepts such as AUTHORITY and OBLIGATION are characteristically employed in contexts where moral notions are uniquely apt, namely, where the conduct being guided and evaluated is contrary to our self-interest, requires considerable sacrifice, significantly affects the lives of others, and subjects the actor to punishment and censure for failure to comply. . . . In legal contexts, we require people to pay their taxes, join the army, pass difficult licensing exams before practicing a profession, and testify in a criminal trial, under the threat of jail or heavy fines. Only moral concepts have the heft to make such serious claims" (ibid., 114). Put aside that this paragraph turns a lot on fuzzy metaphors (e.g., the "heft" of moral concepts—how does one weigh them?), and recall instead Hart's own discussion of duties and obligations (Hart, *Concept of Law*, 86–87). Hart says that "the insistence on importance or *seriousness* of social pressure behind the rules is the primary factor determining whether they are thought of as giving rise to obligations" (ibid., 87), and says later, "[O]bligations and duties are [also] thought of as characteristically involving sacrifice or renunciation, and the standing possibility of conflict between obligation or duty and interest is, in all societies, among the truisms of both the lawyer and the moralist" (ibid.). Hart is, in some sense, a non-cognitivist. He does not think that normative concepts have a distinctive representational content; rather, they are picked out by the practical or expressive role they play: how much pressure is brought to bear for conformity, how the concepts interact with self-interest, and so on. One possibility, then, is that the difference between "legal" and "moral" obligation might be one of degree: "legal obligation" will involve not as much "social pressure" to conform as "moral obligation," for example. However, Hart says the crux of the distinction is in terms of the kind of rule (moral or legal) on behalf of which the social pressure is exercise. See H. L. A. Hart, *Essays on Bentham* (Oxford University Press, 1982), 127–61. This way of thinking about it comports with the linguistic data points identified by Daniel Wodak, "What Does 'Legal Obligation' Mean?," *Pacific Philosophical Quarterly* 99 (2018): 790–816. (Thanks to Alma Diamond for helpful discussion of these issues.)

> of recognition as a test of legal validity, when in reality it is a duty-imposing norm (ibid., 85).

Let me begin with a few observations about these formulations, which anticipate some of the issues to come.

First, the RR *is also* a rule about the other *secondary* rules (not just the primary rules); that is, the rules of adjudication and legislation are legally valid by virtue of meeting RR criteria, but this is a minor mistake. Second, Shapiro's formulation *in the quoted passage* is correct: The *content* of the RR is determined by (the content of) the social practice (i.e., what criteria officials converge upon and accept from an internal point of view). Shapiro, alas, forgets his own formulation soon enough. Third, Hart presents the RR as a "test of legal validity" because that is all it is: if an RR exists, then officials *take (believe) themselves* to have a duty to apply those criteria,[80] but that does not mean the rule "imposes" a duty.[81] This confusion, however, is important to Shapiro. Later he says: "In the legal [as distinct from moral] sense . . . the rule of recognition *is* self-justifying. By law, officials ought to follow the rule of recognition for the trivial reason that the rule of recognition ultimately defines what the law is" (ibid., 91). This makes no sense: the RR is not self-justifying legally, since it is not part of the law, so it is not necessarily the case that "by law" officials ought to follow the RR.[82] If they *believe they ought to follow it*, then there is a legal system (*ceteris paribus*); otherwise not.[83] That is the crux of Hart's view.

The central argumentative move in the book is Shapiro's criticism of Hart's account of the RR:

[80] That they so take themselves is manifest in what they say and do, since Hart's ascriptions of mental states are generally based on behavioral criteria, reflecting Gilbert Ryle's influence (see Gilbert Ryle, *The Concept of Mind* (University of Chicago Press, 1949). See again Brian Leiter, "Back to Hart."

[81] Shapiro here follows a mistake propagated by Raz and others; a useful discussion is Giorgio Pino, "Farewell to the Rule of Recognition?," *Problema* 5 (2011): 265–99, esp. at 277 ff. Pino rejects my characterization of the rule of recognition, claiming that the latter is simply "redundant" on the rules of change and adjudication. His argument, however, depends on never specifying the content of the latter rules. To start, the rule of recognition picks out *those parts* of the rules of change and adjudication that are actually relevant to legal validity. But beyond that, it also picks out criteria of validity that are no part of the rules of changes or adjudication (e.g., in the United States, the Supreme Court has the final word on what the Constitution means).

[82] Officials might have a legal obligation to "follow the law" depending on their oath of office, but that has nothing to do with the RR or its existence conditions: the existence of a legally required "oath of office" presupposes the RR.

[83] Of course, the evidence for what officials "believe" is simply what they say and do (apply the criteria in the rule of recognition, criticize those who fail to do so, justify their own conduct by reference to the rule, etc.).

> Hart tries to demystify the creation of social rules by reducing them to social practices. In other words, social practices generate rules because these rules *are nothing but* social practices (Shapiro, *Legality*, 95).

and, a bit later,

> Social rules cannot be reduced to social practices because rules and practices belong to different metaphysical categories. Rules are *abstract objects*.... Practices, on the other hand, are *concrete events*. They take place within the natural world and causally interact with other physical events.... Because rules and practices are different kinds of things, one cannot be reduced to the other... (ibid., 103).

Gardner and Macklem reply as follows:

> Hart thought that this particular social practice, the practice of the proto-officials, was in two ways normative. It was a practice of purportedly following a rule which also supplied the content of a rule. This is a point about a particular social practice, not about social practices generally. Hart never says, and indeed goes to some trouble to deny, that 'social practices ... necessarily generate social rules', which is the view that Shapiro attributes to him (103). Nor does Hart identify the practice exactly with the rule. He identifies the content of the practice, or part of it, with the content of the rule. Shapiro says nothing to suggest that this is a category mistake (just as well, because it isn't one).[84]

Gardner and Macklem's point is consistent with Shapiro's original formulation of Hart's account of the RR, which was in terms of its *content* being determined by the *content* of a social practice: semantic contents are in the same metaphysical category, for those keeping track.

I think, however, that there is a much stronger reply to Shapiro's criticism, which is that Hart simply has no reductive analysis of rules at all.[85] Hart has a reductive, behavioral analysis only about what it is to "*accept a rule* from an internal point of view"; Hart's analysis concerns *accepting a rule*, not *rule*.[86] This

[84] Gardner and Macklem, "Review of *Legality*."

[85] I owe the general point to Kevin Toh. But I would go further: Hart has no "practice theory of rules," a myth started by Warnock and Hacker in the 1960s and perpetuated by Raz (Michael Sevel suggests to me the genealogy may be more complicated, and I urge readers to consult his forthcoming monograph on Raz for the further details). For an important critique of the idea that Hart has a "practice theory" of rules, see Thomas Adams, "Practice and Theory in *The Concept of Law*," in *Oxford Studies in Philosophy of Law, Volume 4*, ed. John Gardner, Leslie Green, and Brian Leiter (Oxford University Press, 2021). Adams's demonstration of the lack of a textual pedigree for a so-called practice theory of rules is plausible independent of his less plausible Wittgensteinian commitments, which I am skeptical Hart shared in the same form.

[86] Adams also makes this point in Adams, "Practice and Theory," 22–23.

is explicit in *The Concept of Law*, where he says he is answering the question, "What is the acceptance of a rule?" (Hart, *Concept of Law*, 55):

> What is necessary is that there should be a critical reflective attitude to certain patterns of behavior as a common standard, and that this should display itself in criticism (including self-criticism), demands for conformity, and in acknowledgments that such criticism and demands are justified, all of which find their characteristic expressions in the normative terminology of 'ought', 'must', and 'should', 'right' and 'wrong' (ibid., 57).

Hart here describes the behavioral evidence that people accept a rule from an internal point of view; he does not offer any analysis of what a "rule" is here, or elsewhere ("rule" functions as a kind of theoretical primitive in his account of law). Shapiro's "category mistake" objection to Hart is wrong.[87] Yet this is the fundamental basis on which we are supposed to think it worthwhile to think that law has anything to do with planning.

Hart identified a key weakness in John Austin's and Jeremy Bentham's views about law: They omitted the idea of a "rule," relying instead on the ideas of sovereignty, sanctions, and command. Hart, himself, has no further, reductive analysis of "rule"[88]: It functions effectively as a theoretically primitive notion in his jurisprudential theory. Hart, by common consensus now, was correct that you cannot understand the phenomenon of law without reference to the idea of "rule" and its surrogates ("principle," "standard," etc.). The idea that law consists of "rules" (of varying types) certainly has ordinary language and legal common sense on its side; the idea that law consists of "plans" does not. The basic reason Shapiro alleges the idea of "planning" is even relevant to jurisprudence is because Hart made a "category mistake." But Hart did not, and given that, there is no reason to proceed down Shapiro's rabbit hole. Leslie Green's joke about Shapiro's "planning theory" is worth recounting:

A: We have a problem with murder around here; we need to do something about it.
B: Yes, let's make a plan!
A: Great idea, what's the plan?
B: Don't murder!

[87] There is an interesting question about the social epistemology of academia here. Every expert in legal philosophy knows that the "category mistake" objection to Hart is wildly mistaken ("categorically mistaken" as Les Green put it to me), but the *jejune* do not, even the *jejune* with jobs teaching law. Fortunately, mistakes by legal philosophers are not as important as mistakes by doctors: On the "why does it matter?" scorecard, mistakes by those doing general jurisprudence do not kill anyone (contrary to Lon Fuller).

[88] Perhaps such an analysis can be given, but Hart proceeds as though none is required for his purposes.

III. Conclusion

The real mischief of Shapiro's approach has had less to do with the mistakes catalogued above than with his wholesale adoption of Greenberg's new metaphysical framing of the supposed questions of general jurisprudence in terms of determination relations. No one, however, prior to 2004 thought the central question in jurisprudence concerned the metaphysical determinants or "grounding" of the content of law, of "how facts make law." Those prior to 2004 were not missing something, but many people after 2004 are. Certainly, for legal realists, who are also philosophical naturalists, this unfortunate metaphysical turn in general jurisprudence needs to be purged if one wants to understand what law is and how law and especially courts *really* operate.[89]

[89] Earlier versions of the material on Shapiro were presented to and discussed with an excellent group of JD and PhD students in my Autumn 2019 graduate seminar at the University of Chicago on recent work in general jurisprudence. Tom Adams from Oxford was also a regular participant in the seminar, and I am grateful as well for his insights. I have been helped, as always, by many discussions with Leslie Green over the years, as well as by his comments on a later draft. Thanks to Adams, Gabe Broughton, and Michael Sevel for comments on an earlier draft of the material on Shapiro, and Mitch Berman and Jed Lewinsohn for comments on a later draft of the same. A later version of the Shapiro material also benefited from discussion with an audience at Cambridge University. Jed Lewinsohn (again) and Alma Diamond both gave me excellent comments on an early draft of the Greenberg material. An early draft of that material also benefited from discussion at the Harvard Law & Philosophy Workshop in Fall 2023. David Enoch offered comments on a later version of the Greenberg material, as did audiences at Cambridge and Oxford Universities in March 2025: Comments by Thomas Bullemore, Hasan Dindjer and Nicos Stavropoulos were particularly useful. I thank Sarah Cohen, University of Chicago Law School Class of 2022, and Helen Zhao, University of Chicago Law School Class of 2025, for research assistance and the Alumni Faculty Fund of the Law School for support.

PART II

REALISM ABOUT COURTS, POLITICS, AND MORALITY

10

Legal Formalism and Legal Realism

What Is the Issue?

In teaching jurisprudence, I typically distinguish between two different families of theories of adjudication, theories of how judges do or should decide cases.[1] "Formalist" theories claim that (1) the law is "rationally" determinate—that is, the class of legitimate legal reasons available for a judge to offer in support of his decision justifies one and only one outcome either in all cases or in some significant and contested range of cases (e.g., cases that reach the stage of appellate review); and (2) adjudication is thus "autonomous" from other kinds of reasoning; that is, the judge can reach the required decision without recourse to nonlegal normative considerations of morality or political philosophy. I also note that "formalism" is sometimes associated with the idea that judicial decision-making involves nothing more than mechanical deduction on the model of the syllogism—Beccaria, for example, expresses such a view.[2] I call the latter "Vulgar Formalism" to emphasize that it is not a view to which anyone today cares to subscribe. It is true enough that deductive reasoning on the model of syllogism is a characteristic feature of most well-done judicial opinions—that is, the conclusion can be reconstructed as following deductively from a statement of the applicable rule of law and the statement of the facts. But most of legal reasoning in common-law jurisdictions[3] is given over to explaining why the *applicable rule of law* is, in fact, the applicable rule of law, and what the legally significant facts are. And such reasoning is rarely "mechanical" in the sense of "obvious" or machine-like, as the pejorative label implies. Such reasoning is often contestable and contested, which is why "mechanical" does not illuminate much about the nature of legal reasoning. But there are plenty of jurists and scholars committed to (1) and (2) above—we might call them "Sophisticated Formalists." They are "sophisticated" precisely because they recognize that legal reasoning is not mechanical, that it demands the identification of valid sources of law, the

[1] Such theories can be cast in descriptive or normative terms, but I will mostly focus on the descriptive version here. I will turn, later, to what we might call formalist views of rule-application, associated in particular with Frederick Schauer.

[2] Cesare Beccaria, "Interpretation of the Law," in *Of Crimes and Punishments* (1764).

[3] In some civil-law jurisdictions, the opinions are often written precisely in the form of Vulgar Formalism!

From a Realist Point of View. Brian Leiter, Oxford University Press. © Brian Leiter 2026.
DOI: 10.1093/9780197749852.003.0012

interpretation of those sources, the distinguishing of sources that are relevant and irrelevant, and so on, and they offer a theoretical account of how these various bits of reasoning are done "rightly." Their leading theoretical spokesman is Ronald Dworkin,[4] but in different ways, Robert Bork and Justice Scalia are committed to such a picture of adjudication (at least as a normative ideal),[5] as is the popular culture more generally, as any observer of a Supreme Court confirmation hearing can attest (indeed, one might think the popular culture is the last preserve of Vulgar Formalism!). Judges, of course, continue to write their opinions in sophisticated formalist manner, presenting the binding rules of law as given by the materials correctly interpreted and as then requiring, as a matter of logic, a particular decision.

Against the Sophisticated Formalist theory stands the views of the "realists," theorists who purport to give us an unsentimental and honest account of what judges *really* do—the theorists who, most famously, came to be known as American Legal Realists, scholars and lawyers and jurists like Karl Llewellyn, Jerome Frank, Underhill Moore, Herman Oliphant, Leon Green, Max Radin, and others. (I shall henceforth use Realists, with a capital "R," to name this group of thinkers whose views I endorse.)[6] As I have argued at some length, the majority of Realists advanced a descriptive theory of adjudication according to which (1) legal reasoning is indeterminate (i.e., fails to justify a unique outcome) in those cases that reach the stage of appellate review; (2) appellate judges, in deciding cases, are responsive to the "situation-types"—recurring factual patterns (e.g., "seller of a business promises not to compete with the buyer, and then tries to break the promise")[7]—that elicit predictable normative responses ("this is unfair" or "this is economically foolish") from most jurists, responses that are not, however, predictable based on existing "paper" rules and doctrine; and (3) in the commercial law context (a primary focus of the Realists), judges look to the "normal" practices in the existing business culture in deciding what is the right outcome (i.e., the judges treat normal economic practice as the normative benchmark for decision).[8] My former colleague, the late Charles Alan Wright,

[4] See, e.g., Ronald Dworkin, "Hard Cases," in *Taking Rights Seriously* (Harvard University Press, 1977); and Dworkin, ch. 6 in *Law's Empire* (Belknap Press, 1986).

[5] They do not think, to be sure, that every legal question has a unique answer, but where the law, especially the constitutional law, is unclear, they opt for deferring to legislative majorities.

[6] Richard Posner is a contemporary representative: see Richard Posner, *How Judges Think* (Harvard University Press, 2008).

[7] The example is from Herman Oliphant, "A Return to *Stare Decisis*," *American Bar Association Journal* 14 (1928): 75. In this situation-type, courts found a way to enforce the promise. By contrast, in cases involving the "situation-type" "employees promise not to compete with an employer after leaving his employ," courts found a way to invalidate the promise.

[8] For detailed discussion and evidence, see Brian Leiter, *Naturalizing Jurisprudence: Essays on American Legal Realism and Naturalism in Legal Philosophy* (Oxford University Press, 2007). See esp. chs. 1–3. For a more concise account, see Brian Leiter, "American Legal Realism," in *The*

senior author of the preeminent treatise on *Federal Practice and Procedure* in the United States, told me that he thought of himself as a Realist in this sense; my first "boss" in practice, Milton Handler, late professor of law at Columbia for forty-five years and name partner of a leading New York law firm, understood his scholarly work as Realist in the same way.[9] In their scholarly work, Wright and Handler tried to recast the norms of legal decision in ways that reflected the specific situation-types to which they found the judges to be sensitive—that is, they tried to articulate explicitly the norms of decision (some of them previously inchoate or unstated in the decisions) at a greater level of factual specificity than might be found as boilerplate doctrine in a treatise or court decision.

Brian Tamanaha's provocative book *Beyond the Formalist-Realist Divide: The Role of Politics in Judging*[10] might seem, on casual perusal, to upset this distinction, though in fact (and notwithstanding its title) it ultimately does nothing of the kind. Tamanaha's primary target is an historical, not philosophical, thesis,[11] namely, that, contrary to the presentation by many legal historians and theorists (including Jerome Frank, Grant Gilmore, Thomas Grey, Morton Horwitz, Duncan Kennedy, William LaPiana, and G. Edward White, among others), there was not a "formalist" age in American legal thought that only ended with the arrival of the American Legal Realists in the 1920s and 1930s. In fact, judges and scholars expressed "realist" ideas during what is alleged to be the heyday of "legal formalism." Tamanaha adduces evidence which will, as Sanford Levinson puts it on the book's dustjacket, "generate very wide interest, controversy, and ... changes in the way American legal history is presented." Although it seems to me that the evidence is problematic in a variety of ways (especially regarding realism), and that Tamanaha consistently overstates his conclusions, I concur with Levinson that Tamanaha has articulated a prima facie challenge to the standard historical narrative about a certain kind of formalism, identifying, in particular, several instances where Frank and Gilmore grossly mischaracterized earlier writers.

Blackwell Guide to Philosophy of Law and Legal Theory, ed. M. Golding and W. Edmundson (Wiley-Blackwell, 2005). The description in the text pertains to what I call the "Sociological Wing" of Realism, which was the dominant strand. The views of Jerome Frank were a bit different on the second and third points.

[9] See, e.g., Milton Handler & Charles Pickett, "Trade Marks and Trade Names: An Analysis and Synthesis," in two parts: *Columbia Law Review* 30 (1930): 160, 759.

[10] Brian Tamanaha, *Beyond the Formalist-Realist Divide: The Role of Politics in Judging* (Princeton University Press, 2010).

[11] He also wants to take on contemporary political scientists in chapters 7 and 8, who have often taken a strawman view of adjudication as their target. I have no brief here on behalf of their accounts, and if Tamanaha's book has the salutary effect of improving the quality of their work, that will be to his lasting credit. (I do agree with Fred Schauer, though, who points out to me that the political science work on courts is a useful corrective to much doctrinal scholarship in constitutional law, which talks as though the doctrine is *really* explanatory of Supreme Court decisions.)

Tamanaha, however, also purports to have a substantive jurisprudential thesis—suggested by the volume's title and the explicit ambition of the final two chapters—namely, that he is moving us "beyond" the distinction between formalism and realism about judging: "legal theory discussions of legal formalism are irrelevant, misleading, or empty. Debates about judging are routinely framed in terms of antithetical formalist-realist poles that jurists do not actually hold" (Tamanaha 3).[12] Unfortunately, the thesis that jurists do (or do not) "hold" formalist or realist views turn on sloppy characterizations of these views by Tamanaha (sometimes simply echoing sloppy characterizations by others). And even if jurists did not hold the views when precisely characterized, that would do nothing to show there was not an important jurisprudential distinction between formalist and realist conceptions of adjudication: the question is whether these conceptions count as plausible reconstructions of judicial practice (regardless of what judges say), ones that illuminate important conceptual and normative issues about adjudication. The argument of Tamanaha's book is, in the end, irrelevant to philosophy of law. Perhaps more seriously from the standpoint of Tamanaha's primary ambition—namely, to revise the standard historical narrative about American legal thought—some of the sloppiness in stating the competing positions, formalism and realism, creates problems for the historical evidence Tamanaha adduces and raises questions about the reliability of his presentation of it.

I. Formalism and Realism: The Historical Narrative

Let us begin with the historical thesis, which is a coin with two sides, one about formalism and one about realism. Regarding legal formalism, Tamanaha's target is legal historians and theorists like Gilmore, Horwitz, and Kennedy[13] who claim that the 1870s to the 1920s in the United States were "the heyday of legal formalism" according to which "lawyers and judges saw law as autonomous comprehensive, logically ordered, and determinate and believed that judges engaged in pure mechanical deduction from this body of law to produce single correct outcomes" (1). On this account, legal formalism was brought to an end by the Realists, who "building upon the insights of Oliver Wendell Holmes, Roscoe Pound, and Benjamin Cardozo" showed "that the law is filled with gaps and contradictions, that the law is indeterminate, that there are exceptions for almost

[12] This non sequitur is not simply an artifact of the introduction to the book. Tamanaha repeats it again much later: "Any approach that defines 'formalism' in these terms has doubtful validity, as earlier chapters demonstrated. These ideas were *not* widely held in the U.S. legal tradition, if they were held by any jurists at all" (Tamanaha 160).

[13] See esp. Tamanaha 60–61.

every legal rule or principle, and that legal principles and precedents can support different results" (Tamanaha 1). Judges, according to these realists, "decide according to their personal preferences" and come up with *post-hoc* legal rationales for the decisions so reached.[14]

Tamanaha distinguishes between two aspects of the "formalism" assigned by legal historians to thinkers of the nineteenth century (see ch. 2). First, there was a "formalist" "theory of the nature of law (the common law, in particular)" according to which "in new situations judges *did not make law* (even when declaring new rules) but merely discovered and applied preexisting law" (Tamanaha 13). Second, there was a "formalist" theory about judicial decision, about "how judge mechanically apply law (precedents and statutes) to the facts in particular cases" (Tamanaha 13). Tamanaha claims the connection between the two stories "is tight" (13),[15] though I do not see that he makes the case, and as a conceptual matter, the two theses are obviously distinct. The first "formalist" view—call it "Natural Law Formalism" — is an instance of a standard "natural law" canard according to which there is always a pre-existing answer to every legal question, usually one that requires moral reflection (or, in earlier forms, insight into the divine will) to discover. One could, quite obviously, reject Natural Law Formalism and still think that *where there are binding legal sources*, judicial decision is a matter of mechanical application of the rules derived from those sources to the facts of the case.[16]

Tamanaha spends an entire chapter (ch. 2) showing that lots of jurists and scholars in the nineteenth century thought that judges do make law in new circumstances, but that is perhaps not surprising, since one would expect this to be common wisdom among common lawyers in the modern era in the wake of Bentham's attack on the natural law canard in the early nineteenth century (an attack Tamanaha notes in passing at 15). Every beginning law student is taught, for example, that one of the key differences between common-law and (at least a caricature of) civil-law systems is that in the former *judges make law*.[17] An attack

[14] It's not clear the Realists held the views so described, as I discussed many years ago in Brian Leiter, "Rethinking Legal Realism: Toward a Naturalized Jurisprudence," *Texas Law Review* 76 (1997): 267, reprinted as ch. 1 in my *Naturalizing Jurisprudence*. But we can bracket that issue for the moment.

[15] Later remarks suggest that Tamanaha may only mean that those he is criticizing think the connection is tight: see esp. Tamanaha 54.

[16] This appears to be very roughly what H. L. A. Hart thinks, for example, about "easy" cases. See H. L. A. Hart, *The Concept of Law*, 2nd ed. (Oxford University Press, 1994): 126–30, and the discussion below, pp. 219–20.

[17] I was surprised to see Tamanaha acknowledge the point toward the end of the book: "*All lawyers know that judges make the common law*. This has been acknowledged for at least two centuries, as earlier chapters documents" (175). The surprise is that this recognition did not lead Tamanaha to suspect the triviality of the issue, and the fact that it is orthogonal to any interesting formalist theory of adjudication. To be sure, this contrast, though indeed drawn in common-law classrooms, is a caricature of what really goes on in civil-law courtrooms, as the legions of Legal Realists in civil-law

on Natural Law Formalism was no significant part of the attack on "formalism" by the American Legal Realists, and, in any case, is of little jurisprudential interest, given how few proponents the alternative view has.[18]

Against the second formalist thesis, about "mechanical" adjudication, Tamanaha argues *contra* Roscoe Pound that "judges at the time [i.e., the purported 'formalist' age] did not widely believe that judging was an exercise in mechanical deduction" (28). Of course, "mechanical deduction," while central to Vulgar Formalism, also has little to do with any philosophically interesting jurisprudential thesis about formalism, and it is not wholly surprising that skeptics about mechanical deduction are to be found in the nineteenth century too. Still, Tamanaha's approach to Pound is representative of the general argumentative strategy of the book, and so warrants notice: Tamanaha adduces quotes from nineteenth-century jurists and scholars—whom Tamanaha generally describes as important or leading figures (some of them are, while some, one worries, have been rescued from obscurity by the needs of Tamanaha's argument) or who published their views in prominent journals—that are inconsistent with the historical thesis in question.[19] Is this method adequate to establish the claims at issue in this chapter and elsewhere in the book?

Tamanaha gives insufficient attention to two key evidential questions. First, are the antiformalist quotations he adduces representative of views in the putatively "formalist" age? Second, even if the quotations are representative, are they as common as such sentiments became in the 1920s and 1930s? We are trying to assess, remember, whether there was something that deserves to be called a "formalist" age. Presumably, no one committed to the existence of such a period thinks that everyone thought monolithically at that time. It is often said, for example, that "free market" thinking triumphed in the West in the 1980s, giving rise to a so-called neoliberal era. That obviously doesn't mean that Marxists, socialists, and free-market skeptics stopped writing or thinking. Indeed, it would be easy to adduce prominent examples of market skeptics publishing their views in prominent journals during the last thirty years. But this would hardly show

countries—from François Gény in France a century ago to Riccardo Guastini in Italy and Michel Troper in France today—have demonstrated.

[18] While historically, Natural Law Formalism was associated with Blackstone, it does still have one well-known defender, who is almost entirely absent from Tamanaha's book: Ronald Dworkin. For Dworkin does believe that the duty of the judge is always to discover the law that already exists in every case, though Dworkin does not subscribe to Tamanaha's second "formalist" thesis, about which more momentarily. The absence of Dworkin, the "ideal type" of the interesting legal formalist, from Tamanaha's analysis betrays the superficiality of the jurisprudential argument of the book.

[19] See Tamanaha 34: "All of the preceding statements were made in the heart of the so-called formalist age. They were made by leading lawyers and judges in high-profile settings. What they say is manifestly at odds with the conventional story about purportedly dominant legal formalist beliefs at the time."

that the past thirty years were not properly characterized as a "neoliberal era" in the West.

The evidential questions here are, admittedly, hard, but Tamanaha does not even attempt to tackle them. It is not enough to quote this-or-that judge or scholar saying antiformalist, proto-realist things in 1880. We need to know: How were these remarks received by their professional peers? Were they widely echoed and repeated? Or were they criticized and rejected by others at the same time—or simply ignored? Tamanaha demonstrates in several different cases that thinkers alleged to be "formalists" by later historians and theorists in fact held some antiformalist views, and that is a welcome and important corrective. But it simply does not establish his central historical theses.

The evidential issue, however, is even more complicated than this.[20] Even if we suppose, in the best-case scenario for Tamanaha, that a significant minority or even a bare majority of scholars and jurists in the late nineteenth century were saying "realist-sounding" or "antiformalist" things, we will still need to know how this *compares* to the received professional wisdom of the 1920s and 1930s. After all, it would still make perfectly good sense to call the late nineteenth century the "formalist age" if it turns out that a larger proportion of leading scholars and jurists said "realist-sounding" things in the 1920s and 1930s than in the 1870s and 1880s. Tamanaha, alas, sheds no light on this issue.

These worries are compounded by the fact that Tamanaha's historical evidence is only probative to the extent his account of the competing positions is illuminating.[21] We have already noted that showing that nineteenth-century jurists and scholars recognized that common-law judges "make law" in new circumstances and that they do not decide cases "mechanically" does not illuminate much about formalism as a philosophically interesting theory of adjudication. But let us turn to the flipside of Tamanaha's historical thesis about formalism: "Realism about judging was commonplace decades before the legal realists came on the scene" (68). This historical claim turns out to trade on a sloppy and loose characterization of realism, that does no justice to the distinctive theses of Realists like Karl Llewellyn, Herman Oliphant, Max Radin, Underhill Moore, and others.

Tamanaha offers a motley assortment of "evidence" that there was realism about judging before the Realists.[22] It runs the gamut from Teddy Roosevelt's

[20] Here I am indebted to Stefan Vogenauer.

[21] There is also the question whether Tamanaha represents his quoted sources fairly. I discuss some cases where he has not, below. I leave it to intellectual historians to carry out a more systematic examination of the sources on which Tamanaha's argument depends.

[22] Some of the "evidence" from scholars and jurists in the early 1900s is hardly apposite: no one thinks Realism arose *ex nihilo*; it, of course, had a pre-history in earlier thinker, like Holmes and Cardozo. And Jerome Frank famously cited Chancellor Kent, writing a century earlier in support of the thesis that judges *first* get a "hunch" about the fair outcome, and then search for legal reasons to support that conclusion. See footnote 3 in Chapter XII of Jerome Frank, *Law and the Modern Mind*

claim in 1908 that "[t]he decisions of the courts on economic and social questions depend upon their economic and social philosophy" (71–72); to an 1893 law review article observing that "[t]o say that no political prejudices have swayed the court . . . is to maintain that is members have been exempt from the known weaknesses of human nature" (75); to an unsigned essay in *Albany Law Review* in 1870 claiming that "the excision of politics from the judicial mind is impossible" (77). From all this, Tamanaha concludes that "[b]y the time the legal realists arrived on the scene [in the 1920s], realism about judging had circulated inside and outside of legal circles loudly and often for at least two generations" (78).

But does Tamanaha's evidence show anything of the kind? Critical Legal Studies (CLS) writers may have believed that "law is politics," but this was barely a footnote in Realism, which was largely silent on the political influences on decision.[23] Yet Tamanaha's mistaken reduction of Realism to the view that judges are influenced by politics runs throughout his discussion, and is even reflected in the title of the book and the extensive attention he accords the recent political science literature on courts. Thus, it is unsurprising that at the conclusion of his purported exposition of Realism in chapter 6, Tamanaha announces that, "Rantoul in 1836, Hammond in 1881, the legal realists in the 1920s and 1930s, and Critical Legal Studies in the 1970s and 1980s (and others along the way) all argued in interchangeable terms that judges have the freedom to decide cases in accordance with their political views . . ." (107). *But it was not the thesis of the Realists that judges decided in accordance "with their political views"*![24] Tamanaha himself adduces no textual evidence otherwise. If one looks at classic Realist studies like Llewellyn on sales law[25] or Moore on check-cashing

(Brentano's Publishers, 1930). Even Tamanaha notices that Frank cites jurists from the nineteenth century (see 93). I concentrate on Tamanaha's evidence that is further removed from the 1920s.

[23] The closest one comes in a central Realist text is the following comment in Oliver Wendell Holmes, "The Path of the Law," *Harvard Law Review* 10 (1897): 457, about the three possible explanations for why a judge might make a particular legal argument (e.g., implying a condition in a contract in a particular case): "It is because of some belief as to the practice of the community or a class, or because of some opinion as to policy, or, in short, because of some attitude of yours upon a matter not capable of exact quantitative measurement, and therefore not capable of founding exact logical conclusions." Ibid., 466. The Realists of the 1920s and 1930s focused almost wholly on the first and third possibilities, not the second.

It should be noted that the CLS version of "law is politics" is generally not the same as the political science version, which Tamanaha mostly emphasizes. For the CLS writers, law was often "political" in the sense that the indeterminacies in the law were filled in based on underlying but inchoate philosophical views of a moral and political kind. The *locus classicus* for that kind of CLS view is Duncan Kennedy, "Form and Substance in Private Law Adjudication," *Harvard Law Review* 89 (1976): 1685–1778. But this theme was also not one of interest to the Realists.

[24] I discuss this, and the evidence, in chs. 1 and 3 of my *Naturalizing Jurisprudence*.

[25] See, e.g., Karl Llewellyn, *The Common Law Tradition: Deciding Appeals* (Little, Brown and Co., 1960): 122.

practices,[26] there was no interest, at all, in the political party of the judge, the judge's political ideology, or the political objectives of the appointing president. Rather, in each case, the Realists tried to show that nonlegal norms of fairness or efficiency, often deriving from normal practice in the relevant business context, explained the decisions. Rather than judges imposing an "economic and social philosophy" (as Teddy Roosevelt put it, in the quote above), the emphasis in most Realist writings was on the sensitivity of judges to nonlegal norms prevalent (e.g., in the regular practices of merchants or banks).

Even when Tamanaha tries to produce evidence that *more precise and distinctive* Realist theses about adjudication were common well before the Realists came on the scene, he mostly either produces inapposite evidence or, more seriously, mischaracterizes his sources. Noting, for example, that Realists believed that to predict judicial decisions, one needed to attend to "the reactions of the judges to the facts and to the life around them" (quoting Llewellyn at 80), Tamanaha claims "this too was said much earlier" and then cites Frederick Pollock noting that "legal science" aims to predict "the decisions of courts of justice" (80). *But Pollock endorses nothing like Llewellyn's claim about the need to attend to the factual "situation-types" to which the judges were sensitive in order to predict the decision.* So the Pollock quote is irrelevant: what was distinctive of Realism was its view about the factors relevant to predicting a decision, not some vague and general interest in prediction, which was, of course, a common concern of all lawyers faced with the prospect of going to court.

Tamanaha also quotes Judge Thomas Cooley observing in 1886 that "when a case is such that just and well-instructed minds differ as to its coming within the intent of the statute, the rule laid down by the [presiding judge] or the prevailing majority of its members becomes a rule of law" (81). But this banal observation—that if there is a dispute about the intent or purpose of the statute, the court's decision will settle the matter and create a binding precedent—has nothing to do with the distinctive Realist theses about statutory interpretation,[27] which suggest that across a wide range of statutory interpretation cases, the judge has available equally proper, but utterly conflicting, methods of statutory interpretation to invoke so that the actual "rule" of the statute is "up for grabs."

On the key issue of the influence of situation-types on judicial decision (which Tamanaha says "has been identified by a theorist [citing me] as *the* distinctive innovation the legal realists brought to American jurisprudence" [Tamanaha 83]),

[26] See, e.g., Underhill Moore and Theodore S. Hope, Jr., "An Institutional Approach to the Law of Commercial Banking," *Yale Law Journal* 38 (1929): 703–19.

[27] See Max Radin, "Statutory Interpretation," *Harvard Law Review* 43 (1930): 863–85; Karl Llewellyn, "Remarks on the Theory of Appellate Decision and the Rules and Canons about How Statutes Are to Be Construed," *Vanderbilt Law Review* 3 (1950): 395–406.

he cites *only one* earlier author, James C. Carter, who, in fact, says *nothing of the kind.* Here is what Tamanaha quotes from Carter (83–84):

> It is in *new* cases that nearly all the difficulty in ascertaining and applying the law arises. The great mass of transactions of life are indeed repetitions of what has before happened—not exact repetitions, for such never occur—but repetitions of all substantial features. They have once or oftener been subjected to judicial scrutiny and the rules which govern them are known. They arise and pass away without engaging the attention of lawyers or the courts. The great bulk of controversy and litigation springs out of transactions which present material features never before exhibited, or new combinations and groupings of facts. It is here that doubt and difficulty make their appearance.... Several different rules—all just in their proper sphere—are competing with each other for supremacy.[28]

What does this have to do with the distinctive Realist thesis according to which appellate judges are largely applying nonlegal norms to recurring situation-types, while reciting general legal doctrines that are mere window dressing and which obscure the normative considerations influencing their decisions? Literally nothing, as far as I can see, which is quite apparent when one attends to the context of Carter's argument.

Carter wants to defend the common-law tradition of judges making new law for new situations against proponents of complete codification of the law, such as Jeremy Bentham, the target of the preceding pages in Carter's article. Against the proponents of codification, Carter argues that codification is impracticable, but also that it is undesirable because it will entail arbitrary and unjust decisions in "new" or "future" transactions:

> Our power to subject objects to a scientific classification being necessarily limited to those which are submitted to observation, the jurist, or the codifier, can no more classify future human transactions, and, consequently can no more frame the law concerning them, than the naturalist can classify the *fauna* and *flora* of an unknown world.[29]

To be sure "unwritten" common law,

[28] James C. Carter, "The Provinces of the Written and the Unwritten Law," *American Law Review* 24 (1890): 1, 15.
[29] Ibid., 10.

> takes the transactions of the past, and, by classifying them, makes its rules; but it makes them *provisionally* only. It declares that they are binding upon courts only so far as respects transactions substantially like those from the examination of which the rules have been framed. In respect to future cases which may wear different aspects, it suspends judgment.[30]

So the "future cases" at issue for Carter are those which are sufficiently different from the past cases, on the basis of which common-law doctrines were crafted, that the unwritten rules of the common law should not be binding. Codification, for a radical reformer like Bentham, was meant to do away with the "unwritten" judge-made rules, but at the cost, says Carter, of laying down rules for unknown situations. What leads to the passage Tamanaha quotes is Carter's consideration of the rejoinder of the "Benthamite" that, even if codification might produce unjust and arbitrary results for genuinely new cases, such cases are "so small in number" that the "miscarriages" of justice resulting would be trivial.[31] The quoted passage is then Carter's response, and thus part of his continued defense of the need for "unwritten" rules crafted by judges in response to new circumstances. We can now see that what Carter *really* says in this passage has nothing at all to do with the Realist theory of appellate decision based on responsiveness to situation-types. Rather, Carter makes the sensible point that where the problems are familiar ones, settled common-law doctrines are so clear that the matters do not end up in court at all, which means it is precisely the *new* or "future" cases—ones for which no legal rule governs—that will command the attention most often of judges. The genuine Realist, by contrast, would be skeptical that even the settled common-law doctrines, at least at the level of abstraction at which they are typically articulated, will really explain the decisions of the courts in later cases. On this distinctive Realist thesis, Carter is completely silent.

Tamanaha's overreaching of the evidence in this and other instances leads me to think that legal historians would do well to consider his other examples with care and some skepticism. Even when Tamanaha seems to do better—for example, finding examples of earlier writers (in particular William Hammond, whom he cites quite a bit) making something like Llewellyn's point about the "strict" and "loose" view of precedent (81) and Frank's point about the latitude judges have in characterizing the facts of a case in terms of their legal significance (82)—one has the sense that he is too quick to be satisfied with quotes and snippets considered in isolation. Tamanaha does not mention, for example, that Hammond concedes that his Realist-sounding claims constitute "a bold and harsh statement," but one that can be backed up "on much higher authority than

[30] Ibid.
[31] Ibid., 15.

my own"[32]—that is, Hammond appears to recognize that his claims go against the common wisdom (perhaps because his was a "formalist" age?) and thus demand some support. Also unnoted by Tamanaha is that Hammond's article is quite clearly a brief for *university education of lawyers by full-time academics*, in the place of "schools . . . in the hands of busy lawyers and judges" who devote "their scanty leisure to this (commonly ill-paid and too often underrated) work."[33] This is hardly surprising, given that Hammond was dean of the law schools at the University of Iowa and then Washington University, St. Louis. Hammond's realist-sounding description of the state of the law[34]—his "bold and harsh statement"—is quite clearly, in context, something he *deplores*, but that he offers as a reason for entrusting legal education to full-time academics, who might, it is implied, set things right (making the law more formalistic, perhaps?). Given his rhetorical objectives, one might at least wonder how representative Hammond's realist-sounding claims are of the prevailing understanding. Tamanaha does not.

Let me conclude by recapping the main lines of argument regarding Tamanaha's historical thesis. Tamanaha adduces enough evidence, in my view, to state at least a prima facie case against any historian who wants to claim that in the nineteenth century, jurists and scholars generally believed that common-law judges did not make law in new circumstances and that judging was simply a mechanical exercise in deductive reasoning. We still need to know how representative Tamanaha's evidence is, and its relation to the received wisdom of the time. It would certainly not be at all surprising to find that most common-law jurists and scholars did not accept Natural Law Formalism, and it would also not be wholly surprising if most jurists and scholars then were not really Vulgar Formalists. Whether nineteenth-century jurists and scholars held or rejected more sophisticated forms of formalism is simply not addressed at all by Tamanaha's evidence. With regard to realism, Tamanaha's evidence is much less probative: he shows that many people recognized the influence of politics on the courts in the nineteenth century, but it was no significant part of Realism to establish this thesis. With respect to more distinctive Realist theses, Tamanaha's evidence fares worse: in several important cases, it is either inapposite or its content is misunderstood. In the end, Tamanaha does not make even a prima facie case that the distinctive theses of the Realists had widespread traction in the nineteenth century.

[32] William G. Hammond, "American Law Schools, Past and Future," *Southern Law Review* 7 (1881): 400, 413.

[33] Ibid., 417.

[34] Ibid., 412.

II. Formalism and Realism: The Jurisprudential Issues

Tamanaha says he wants to rebut a "common misapprehension about the realists . . . [namely] that they were radical skeptics about judging" (68).[35] Rather, the Realists embraced what Tamanaha calls "balanced realism" (6), an awareness that,

> judges sometimes make choices, that they can manipulate legal rules and precedents, and that they sometimes are influenced by their political and moral views and their personal biases (the skeptical aspect [of balanced realism]. Yet [balanced realism] conditions this skeptical awareness with the understanding that legal rules nonetheless work; that judges abide by and apply the law; that there are practice-related, social, and institutional factor that constrain judges; and that judges render generally predictable decisions consistent with the law (the rule-bound aspect). (Tamanaha 6; cf. 95–96)[36]

Since Frederick Schauer and I developed more refined versions of these same points about American Legal Realism in widely cited scholarship going back twenty years now,[37] it is puzzling, indeed, to see Tamanaha announce this as though it were a discovery. Of course, the bulk of our work was devoted to rendering precise issues such as (1) the actual influences on judicial decision, (2) how often judge "make choices," (3) when legal rules *really* constrain decisions and when they don't, and (4) the difference between *legal* factors constraining decisions (and rendering it predictable) versus nonlegal factors that have the

[35] He also denies that "the legal realists formed a group or movement" (68). His evidence is that "the main characterizations of legal realism put forth by theorists and historians"—he cites only Laura Kalman, Robert Summers, John Henry Schlegel, and Morton Horwitz—are "the promotion of an instrumental view of law as a means to serve social ends, the pursuit of social scientific approaches to law, the efforts of reformers to transform legal education in order to improve legal practice and judging, and attempts by reformers to advance a progressive political agenda in and through the law—or some amalgamation of all four" (70). He then fairly notes that those often listed as Realists "did not agree among themselves on these positions." Ibid. Since he, inexplicably, omits attempts by jurisprudential writers to explicitly state distinctive jurisprudential theses characteristic of Realism—namely, mine and Fred Schauer's (though he otherwise cites our work)—this is hardly surprising. But we will return to this issue below, in the text.

[36] Note that Balanced Realism is not simply an empirical observation about judicial behavior; it is predicated on a jurisprudential view about the indeterminacy of legal reasoning, such that judges do have choices to make and can *quite properly* construe rules and precedents in different ways, etc.

[37] See, e.g., Brian Leiter, "Legal Realism," in *A Companion to the Philosophy of Law and Legal Theory*, ed. D. Patterson (Oxford: Blackwell, 1995); and Leiter, "Rethinking Legal Realism," which Tamanaha does cite *but not for its precise characterization of realism.* And for Schauer's work on Realism, see Frederick Schauer, "Judging in a Corner of the Law," *Southern California Law Review* 61 (1988): 1717–34 and Frederick Schauer, *Playing by the Rules* (Oxford: Clarendon Press, 1991), esp. pp. 191–96; Schauer gives a concise summary of his views on Realism in chapter 7 of his recent *Thinking Like a Lawyer* (Harvard University Press, 2009) (although he mischaracterizes my views there).

same effects (Tamanaha runs them together under the heading of "rule-bound aspect").[38] In this respect, Tamanaha's treatment of Realism in chapter 6 marks a somewhat unhappy step backward in the jurisprudential discussion of Realism.[39]

To make matters worse, though, Tamanaha also argues that Schauer and I have gotten the Realists wrong on the basis of either mischaracterizations of our views or misuse of evidence. For example, Tamanaha quotes (93–94) Schauer as follows:

> The Realists believed that decision-makers, especially judges deciding hard cases, initially make an "all things considered" judgment about who ought to win. That preliminary judgment, taking into account moral, political, economic, and psychological factors, is not arbitrary, but is particularistic in focusing on the optimal results *for this case*. . . .To the Legal Realist, rules serve not as sources of *ex ante* guidance, but as vehicles of *ex post* legitimation of decisions reached without regard for the rules."[40]

According to Tamanaha, Schauer "misconstrues their position" (94). His argument against Schauer bears quoting:

> The realists believed in the law and fervently labored to improve it. Llewellyn unabashedly proclaimed his "faith about the Good in this institution of our law"; and he waxed poetically on "the aesthetics of certain legal arts I deeply love." In defense of the realists, Eugene Rostow, the dean of Yale Law School who knew many of the key players, remarked that "the legal realists were among our most devoted and effective reformers, both of law and of society." Jerome Frank confessed, "I am—I make no secret of it—a reformer."
>
> The various goals of the realists were to increase the certainty and predictability of law, to train better lawyers, to advance legal justice, and to reform the law to better serve social needs. (Tamanaha 94)

It is unclear, however, how these points are relevant to the adequacy of Schauer's gloss on the Realist position, unless one assumes that his use of "especially" means that Schauer is claiming that Realists believe judges *always* decide in the

[38] In my own case, an important part of the aim was to show that the Realist theory can be reconstructed in a way that reflects recognizable philosophical motivations, of a naturalistic kind, and insulates it from well-known criticisms in the philosophical literature. But these points are not at issue here.

[39] A contrast is usefully drawn here with the work by Michael Steven Green on Realism. See, e.g., his "Legal Realism as Theory of Law," *William & Mary Law Review* 46 (2005): 1915–2000. While I think Green wrong, partly on textual and partly on philosophical grounds, Green's work is jurisprudentially interesting because it articulates precise and distinctive Realist theses about law and adjudication.

[40] Schauer, *Playing by the Rules*, 192.

way described, as opposed to so deciding in that small number of "selected"-for cases that reach the stage of appellate review, which has always been Schauer's expressed view.[41] That judges in those kinds of cases make result-oriented decisions based either on particularistic grounds or by reference to nonlegal norms prevalent in the context where the dispute arose, and then cite legal doctrines as a post-hoc rationalization for the decision, is compatible with, inter alia, loving the law, thinking the law delimits the range of permissible outcomes, thinking most legal cases (e.g., those that do not reach the stage of appellate review) are determinate as a matter of law, thinking that decisions can be made more predictable by attending to the situation-types to which the judges were actually responsive, restating the law to capture the pertinent level of fact-specificity to which judges were sensitive, and so on.[42]

If Tamanaha's positive claims about realism are (mostly) old news—albeit somewhat loosely repackaged and with the "law is politics" thesis much overplayed—his thesis in the final two chapters is more ambitious and radical: namely, that the distinction between formalism and realism, once each view is rightly understood, should be abandoned. It is not always clear why exactly it should be abandoned, but I take it Tamanaha's argument boils down to two kinds of considerations. First, Tamanaha does not think the distinction illuminates what judges do, or what they say they are doing, because everyone is alleged to be a "balanced realist" (I will refer to this claim as "the Banality of Balanced Realism"). Second, it is impossible to state an interesting or relevant version of "formalism" (I will refer to this claim, following Tamanaha's chapter title, as "the Emptiness of Formalism").

The Banality of Balanced Realism is a recurring theme in Tamanaha's argument. "Judges . . . have consistently and candidly expressed a balanced realism

[41] See Schauer, "Judging in a Corner of the Law," and, even earlier, Frederick Schauer, "Easy Cases," *Southern California Law Review* 58 (1985): 399–440.

[42] I confine my comments on Tamanaha's mistaken criticisms of me to a footnote. I have already commented, above, on Tamanaha's misrepresentation of James Carter's views in the context of his criticism of my claim that the distinctive Realist thesis is about responsiveness to situation-types as the best explanation of appellate decisions. Tamanaha also purports at one point to be disputing my claim that "American Legal Realism was, quite justifiably, the major intellectual event in 20th-century American legal practice and scholarship" (*Naturalizing Jurisprudence*, 1), but since he does not, as we have seen, actually discuss the distinctive views of the Realists, on which my claim was predicated, there is no dispute. Everyone can agree with Tamanaha that before Realism, there were at least some jurists and scholars who recognized the influence of politics on judicial decision and were skeptical that mechanical deduction did any justice to the nature of legal reasoning, but this would do nothing to show that "Realism about judging was commonplace decades before the legal realists came on the scene" (Tamanaha 68). A more egregious case—because I had pointed out the error to Tamanaha in an earlier version of this material—is the purported criticism (on p. 2 of his book) of my account of formalism in Brian Leiter, "Positivism, Formalism, Realism," *Columbia Law Review* 99 (1999): 1138–64, without noting that I was articulating competing substantive views of adjudication, not making an historical claim of the kind he is criticizing. Even if most late nineteenth-century writers were "realists" instead of "formalists," this would have no bearing on the jurisprudential question about how we ought to understand adjudication.

about judging," he says (7).[43] "The formalist-realist antithesis obscures . . . balanced realism, a view that the legal realists shared with their entire generation as with their historical jurisprudence forebears" (69). "[R]ealist insights about judging" are, in fact, "*plainly evident aspects of judging*" (91). Is it really evident that in appellate cases, judges are primarily responding to factual situation-types and then finding post-hoc legal rationales for what they think would be "fair" or "sensible" given the situation-type? (The critics of my interpretation of Realism certainly have not thought so![44]) But as we have already seen, by "realism" Tamanaha often does not mean the views distinctive of the Realists. What is "plainly evident," he says, is that "the law has inconsistencies, runs out, and routinely comes up against unanticipated situations and that judges possess a substantial degree of flexibility when working with legal materials. It was obvious to observers that the law can be interpreted differently by judge with different views" (91).[45] A *That* view, stated at this level of generality, may be banal (except for Natural Law Formalists), but it is not clear it is what is really at issue. The key questions are what is meant by "a substantial degree of flexibility when working with legal materials" and that "law can be interpreted differently by judges with different views." The American Realists, as I have argued, thought that appellate judges routinely confronted cases in which there are equally legitimate (i.e.,

[43] Alas, most of Tamanaha's examples are of Realist judges like Cardozo or post-Realist judges like Walter Schaefer.

[44] See, e.g., Green, "Legal Realism as Theory of Law"; see also Michael S. Moore, *Educating Oneself in Public: Critical Essays in Jurisprudence* (Oxford University Press, 2000): 32–35. H. L. A. Hart, who seems to embrace what Tamanaha is calling "balanced realism" (again, it is hard to say for sure, because the characterization is vague and shifting), thought he had a dispute with the Realists.

[45] In chapter 10 (esp. 186–96), Tamanaha expands on his earlier description of "balanced realism," attributing to realism about adjudication nine claims (his rambling discussion is somewhat repetitive, so I have trimmed the list a bit here): (1) "When judges perceive facts, interpret the law, and render judgments, they are influenced by cognitive framing in the same ways that all cognition is influenced" (187), but the inevitability of cognitive framing is not the same as "willful judging," which, unlike the former, "is not ubiquitous and is not inevitable" (188); (2) "when judges render legal decisions, except in the most routine cases, the purposes behind the applicable rules and the consequences of the decision will have a bearing" (189); (3) "uncertainties will inevitably arise in interpretation and application of legal rules and principles" (190); (4) "the region of legal uncertainty is where judges render decisions with the least legal guidance, and where judges' mix of legal and social views has the most leeway and impact—though still in a context thick with legal norms" (190); (5) "judges are sometimes confronted with what they consider 'bad rules' or 'bad results,'" though they "do not take a uniform position or follow the same course in such situations" (191) though sometimes in cases of this kind there "is an enhanced potential for the influence of the personal values of" the judge to affect the decision (192); (6) "the common law and statutes contain a variety of standards like fairness and reasonableness, or provisions that require balancing, or that requires judges . . . to make judgments. The judgments called for cannot be made in a rule-like fashion and are not determined by legal factors alone," though judges may often agree due to their sharing "similar training in the legal tradition and its values" as well as "social views" (192); (7) "judges are not machines or computers" (194); (8) "judicial decisions frequently are consistent with and determined by the law" (194); (9) "law is continuously being worked out by judges" (195). Some of these claims are, at this level of generality, quite banal or merely the flipside of the denial of Vulgar Formalism (e.g., 3, 7, and 9); some are of dubious Realist pedigree (e.g., 1, 2, and 6); and some are contested by other accounts of adjudication, as discussed in the text.

legally proper) ways of interpreting authoritative sources of law, and so there is generally more than one decision that could be justified with the available legal materials and the tools of legal reasoning and interpretation. If there is evidence that that view is or was widely accepted, Tamanaha does not produce it.

But perhaps the dispute is about how *often* the preceding is true—that is, about what "routinely" in this context means? Tamanaha appeals to comments by Cardozo, Patricia Wald, and Harry Edwards to the effect that 5–15 percent of appellate cases are "very hard" or indeterminate as a matter of law, and so judges in those cases have great latitude in deciding (e.g., 144). So perhaps it is *this* claim that is the hallmark of Balanced Realism and is supposedly banal? Here is Judge Edwards, presumably a "balanced realist" in Tamanaha's sense:

> Appellate judges sometimes make law. Both participants in and observers of the judicial process have recognized this fact for many years [citing Frank, Dewey, and Roger Traynor]. One might expect that today, more than a half-century after the Legal Realist movement, the phenomenon of the exercise of "judicial discretion" would have been so exhaustively studied as to merit no more than a passing reference in preparation for the examination of more controversial matters. That turns out not to be true. Not only does the activity of judicial lawmaking remain mysterious, but a surprisingly large number of people, both within and without the legal community, question its legitimacy in any form.[46]

Judge Edwards recognizes that his "balanced realism" is a controversial position, contrary to Tamanaha's supposition of banality. His evidence, in a footnote to the passage I have just quoted, includes the jurisprudential views of Ronald Dworkin and the representative comments of a U.S. Senator during Judge Wald's confirmation hearings. Both data points are surprisingly absent from Tamanaha's book. At one point, in the course of a generally dismissive discussion of Judge Posner's Realism, Tamanaha quotes Posner's comment that, "most judges are cagey, even coy, in discussing what they do. They tend to parrot an official line about the judicial process (how rule-bound it is), and often to believe it, though it does not describe their actual practices."[47] In reply, Tamanaha allows that,

> Judges no doubt bear some responsibility for perpetuating the belief that they are deluded or deceptive. They *occasionally* say things that ring false, like

[46] Harry T. Edwards, "The Role of a Judge in Modern Society: Some Reflections on Current Practice in Federal Appellate Adjudication," *Cleveland State Law Review* 32 (1983): 385, 388. Notwithstanding the admission of "Balanced Realism" by Judge Edwards, it is perhaps worth noting that he, himself, may be understating the role of nonlegal influences on the decisions of his own court, as the discussion in Richard L. Revesz, "Ideology, Collegiality, and the D.C. Circuit: A Reply to Chief Judge Harry T. Edwards," *Virginia Law Review* 85 (1999): 805–51 suggests.

[47] Posner, *How Judges Think*, 2.

Justice Roberts's claim in his Senate confirmation hearing that judging on the Supreme Court is akin to calling balls and strikes (124).

"Occasionally" seems an understatement. Judge Sotomayor of the Second Circuit spoke like a true "balanced realist" before her nomination to the US Supreme Court,[48] but toed the official formalist line at her confirmation hearings about the role of the judge to apply the law, not "make" law, leading Georgetown law professor Louis Michael Seidman to denounce her as a liar.[49] Formalism (both Natural Law and Vulgar versions!) is, quite obviously, the official story about adjudication in the public culture in the United States, as confirmation hearings, including the most recent one,[50] regularly confirm. Thus, already, there appears to be a useful role for the formalist-realist distinction, namely, as a way of framing political discourse about adjudication.

If such affirmations of formalism were merely an artifact of the pathologies of American political life, then perhaps we should simply concede that "all insiders" are Balanced Realists, even if the hoi-polloi and the grandstanding politicians are not? Yet surely it also matters that Tamanaha's "Balanced Realism" is not the norm in the other major common-law jurisdiction, England. I have recounted the story elsewhere[51] of the quip from Peter Birks, late Regius Professor of Civil Law at Oxford University, that legal realism is "immoral"—not simply wrong, but reprehensible, precisely because it encouraged what he took to be the false view that legal categories and concepts do not in fact and should not constrain and explain the decisions of the courts. Birks was not Vulgar Formalist, nor was he a Natural Law Formalist, but he was certainly a Sophisticated Formalist, who

[48] See the video of her remarks in 2005 regarding policymaking by courts at: morgenr, "Judge Sonia Sotomayor: Court Is Where Policy Is Made," YouTube Video, 0:34, May 3, 2009, http://www.youtube.com/watch?v=OfC99LrrM2Q (visited July 19, 2010).

[49] The Federalist Society Online Debate Series, "The Sotomayor Nomination, Part II," July 13, 2009, http://www.fed-soc.org/debates/dbtid.30/default.asp (visited July 10, 2010). Seidman says: "I was completely disgusted by Judge Sotomayor's testimony today. If she was not perjuring herself, she is intellectually unqualified to be on the Supreme Court. If she was perjuring herself, she is morally unqualified. How could someone who has been on the bench for seventeen years possibly believe that judging in hard cases involves no more than applying the law to the facts? First-year law students understand within a month that many areas of the law are open-textured and indeterminate—that the legal material frequently (actually, I would say always) must be supplemented by contestable presuppositions, empirical assumptions, and moral judgments. To claim otherwise—to claim that fidelity to uncontested legal principles dictates results—is to claim that whenever Justices disagree among themselves, someone is either a fool or acting in bad faith. What does it say about our legal system that to get confirmed, Judge Sotomayor must tell the lies that she told today? That judges and justices must live these lies throughout their professional careers? Perhaps Justice Sotomayor should be excused because our official ideology about judging is so degraded that she would sacrifice a position on the Supreme Court if she told the truth. Legal academics who defend what she did today have no such excuse. They should be ashamed of themselves."

[50] Consider Elena Kagan's repeated claim, reported in multiple news outlets, that it is "law all the way down" in appellate adjudication.

[51] Brian Leiter, "Rule and Reason," *Times Literary Supplement* (Feb. 26, 2010): 24.

thought the duty of the scholar was to take seriously the way courts reason with legal concepts, and then help them do it even more successfully. In the land where the law is still standardly taught from black-letter treatises written by the leading scholars, it should hardly be surprising that Balanced Realism is manifestly not the received wisdom of scholars and jurists.

Perhaps, though, we should interpret Tamanaha's thesis about the Banality of Balanced Realism as confined to the United States—though such a restriction would require him to abandon his broad claims about the uselessness of the distinction between formalism and realism. (If the distinction helps make sense of major jurisdictions, it has some utility!) But here the failure to even discuss Dworkin's jurisprudential views is especially surprising, since Dworkin is *manifestly* not a Balanced Realist, and his Sophisticated Formalism (in the terms I introduced at the start) is offered as a way of making theoretical sense of American judicial practice, among other jurisdictions. Perhaps Tamanaha does not see the relevance of Dworkin because of his own excessive emphasis on "mechanical deduction" and his repeated tendency to run together the autonomy of legal reasoning with the claim about mechanism, For example, "No one thinks that law is autonomous and judging is mechanical deduction" (Tamanaha 197). Or perhaps since not many other scholars accept the full package of Dworkin's views,[52] and since most legal philosophers find Dworkin's actual jurisprudential theory implausible,[53] Tamanaha deems it not worth noting. If so, he should have at least said so clearly. If the slogan "we are all Balanced Realists now" means we should not take Dworkin seriously, I am happy to sign on,[54] though I fear I am not typical. Still, if a distinction between realism and formalism is useful for thinking about the dispute between a well-known contemporary theoretical edifice and its critics, must we really just give it up? It is hard to see why.

If Balanced Realism is not, then, wholly banal, perhaps the problem is really with the Emptiness of Formalism? Tamanaha begins his explicit discussion of jurisprudential issues in chapter 9—tellingly titled "The Emptiness of 'Formalism' in Legal Theory"—by invoking H. L. A. Hart, who devoted a whole chapter of *The Concept of Law* to "Formalism and Rule-Scepticism" (159). Tamanaha emphasizes Hart's puzzlement about the meaning of formalism, yet fails to mention that *the whole point of chapter VII* was to render the issue more precise.

[52] The "Dworkin Lite" that is popular among constitutional theorists does not appear to commit them to Dworkin's views about the rational determinacy of law and the autonomy of legal reasoning. Most constitutional theorists are simply attracted to the idea that moral considerations are relevant to adjudicating weighty constitutional issues—a view, of course, that does nothing to distinguish Dworkin's jurisprudence from that of the legal positivists. See Brian Leiter, "The Radicalism of Legal Positivism," *National Lawyers Guild Review* 66 (Fall 2009): 165–72.

[53] See, e.g., Brian Leiter, "The End of Empire: Dworkin and Jurisprudence in the 21st Century," 36 *Rutgers Law Journal* 36 (2004): 165, and the references therein.

[54] See esp. ch. 11 in this volume.

"Easy" cases, for Hart, are cases in which the facts of the case fall squarely within the core meaning of the words in the applicable legal rule; these cases can be decided largely "mechanically" by deducing the required result from the rule and the facts. "Hard" cases, by contrast, are ones for Hart in which the facts fall within the "penumbra" of the meaning of the words in the applicable rule; these cases require the judge to exercise discretion. Hart is, in Tamanaha's terms, probably a "balanced realist," but his discussion certainly does *not* show that we can move "beyond the formalist-realist divide." Rather, it shows that there is an important question about where and how often the formalist model of decision in "easy" cases applies, and where and how often the "realist" model of decision in "hard" cases applies—which is precisely Hart's dispute with Realism.[55] Again, that looks like a useful conceptual role for the formalism/realism divide in thinking about adjudication.

The relevance of the formalist-realist divide is also suggested by Tamanaha's subsequent discussion of formalism, though that was not his intent. Considering the views of Duncan Kennedy and Frederick Schauer on formalism, Tamanaha concludes that "formalism entails rule-bound judging that prohibits consideration of purposes or consequences" (166). So here is a clear formalist thesis, if not about legal reasoning as a whole, then about one important piece of it, namely, rule-application: judges should, on this view, apply the rule without regard for its ultimate purposes. Tamanaha, in response, tries to argue that it is impossible to distinguish applying a rule as written from consideration of its purposes. To do so, he revisits one part of the old Hart-Fuller debate, arguing that Fuller was correct that there is an "artificial separation of purposes from rule interpretation" (167). Tamanaha points, fairly enough, to Hart's famous example of the rule: "No vehicles in the park." Tamanaha asks why Hart is entitled to think that automobiles are "obviously" prohibited while "bicycles and roller skates" fall in the penumbra of the rule (168). Tamanaha thinks this is only obvious if one assumes something about the "purpose" of the statute. To show that the distinction is not obvious (and to establish that there is no "meaning of the rule"/"purpose of the rule" distinction), he quotes an internet dictionary[56] as follows, but omitting the part I have put in bold:

> (1) any means in or by which someone travels or something is carried or conveyed; **a means of conveyance or transport: *a motor vehicle; space vehicles;*** (2) a conveyance moving on wheels, runners, tracks, or the like, as a cart, sled, automobile, or tractor.

[55] See Brian Leiter, "Legal Realism and Legal Positivism Reconsidered," *Ethics* 111 (2001): 278, reprinted in Leiter, *Naturalizing Jurisprudence*. See also ch. 5 in this volume.

[56] Dictionary.com, "Vehicle," http://dictionary.reference.com/browse/vehicle (viewed July 2, 2010).

Put to one side the fact that Hart's method of ordinary-language philosophy was not meant to track lexicographic results, Tamanaha's omission is telling: the fact that *even an internet dictionary* uses as its core example "motor vehicle" does jibe nicely with Hart's intuition that automobiles are indeed core instances of "vehicles" (without any regard for the "purpose" of the rule) while bicycles and roller skates are not. Remember, too, that Hart was not claiming that it was a clear mistake of language to deem a bicycle a "vehicle," but rather that competent speakers of English will have different intuitions about that usage (with some adopting it, some eschewing it), such that it is indeterminate whether or not a rule covering "vehicles" covers bicycles. By contrast, competent speakers will all agree that an automobile is a "vehicle," as the very dictionary Tamanaha cites, but selectively quotes, demonstrates. To be sure, there can be contexts of interpretation where the pragmatics, as distinct from the semantics of meaning, come to the fore, and "meaning and considerations of purposes are intertwined" (170), as Tamanaha puts it, but his discussion does not show that the distinction between meaning and purposive interpretation is not a real one.

Tamanaha is aware, of course, that there are self-described formalists in America today.[57] Yet in discussing contemporary self-identified formalists, like Justice Scalia and Harvard law professor John Manning, the best Tamanaha can do is to note that they are not, in my terms, Vulgar Formalists (i.e., they don't think judicial decision is just mechanical deduction) (178). Ironically, Tamanaha himself gives a perfectly apt characterization of their Sophisticated Formalism (footnotes omitted):

> [T]hey want clear contractual terms to be enforced as written rather than be modified by courts; they prefer the constraint and predictability of legal rules over the openness of legal standards; they emphasize the text of legislation; they objective to giving weight to legislative history in the interpretation of statutes; they would not permit purpose to trump the plain meaning of statutory terms; they advocate adherence to precedent; they argue that courts ought to defer to other institution bodies (legislatures, administrative agencies, etc.) when the applicable legal provisions are vague or uncertain, or not rule-like; most argue that courts should decide in accordance with clear rules even if the legally indicated outcome in a particular case would be unjust (179).

These views give expression to "formalism" as a kind of normative ideal of completeness for the legal system:[58] There may well be indeterminacies and gaps in the law now, but the ambition of the formalist is to eliminate them, to produce

[57] In the year 2024, there are even more!
[58] I owe this way of putting the point to Scott Shapiro.

a system of law and legal reasoning that is determinate throughout. Tamanaha admits that these views mark a distinction between "contemporary jurists" who self-identify as "formalists and their opponents" (179), and it certainly does: Many theorists, Hart perhaps most famously, rejected formalism as a normative ideal.[59] Given this concession, one wonders why Tamanaha thinks his argument moves one "beyond the formalist-realist divide"? Perhaps the correct title of Tamanaha's book should have been: *refining the formalist-realist dispute about adjudication.* I suppose such an ambition, though intellectually legitimate, would have been less exciting and would overlap too obviously with well-traversed terrain.

Let me conclude by recapping the main lines of argument regarding Tamanaha's jurisprudential thesis that we can (or should) move "beyond" formalism and realism. Tamanaha attributes to the Realists a view he calls "balanced realism," a somewhat looser version of the account of Realism developed by Schauer and me in the 1990s, though Tamanaha's version tends to overemphasize the role of politics in judicial decision-making. He claims, falsely, that everyone is a "balanced Realist" largely on the basis of remarks by post-Realist judges, and, at the same time, accords little or no attention to the evidence that "balanced realism" is not accepted, such as public political debate about adjudication in the United States (which is quite formalistic in its assumptions), theoretical accounts of adjudication like Ronald Dworkin's, and the self-understanding of other common-law legal cultures, like England's. Tamanaha also argues, unsuccessfully, that "formalism" is "empty," but, in the process, actually reveals its substantive meaning as a normative theory or ideal of adjudication and rule-application.

III. Conclusion

Tamanaha's book reflects some striking research into the views of (largely forgotten or neglected) nineteenth-century law professors and jurists, and the material he has brought to our attention will demand attention from legal historians. One often has the sense, though, that having unearthed this material, Tamanaha was determined (no matter what!) to show that it really matters, that it really *must* change our views about realism and formalism, and about the originality of the Realists. Tamanaha's lack of conceptual clarity about the different kinds of formalist and realist theses about adjudication, together with his penchant to sometimes poach quotes out of context, warrants some skepticism about this ambition of the book. At the same time, one must acknowledge that many of

[59] Hart, *The Concept of Law*, 130–31.

Tamanaha's targets are as conceptually confused as he is, and that by disabusing those readers of the idea that most jurists thought legal decision-making was mechanical (Vulgar Formalism) or that common-law judges never make law (Natural Law Formalism), the book will have a salutary effect. Although mostly irrelevant to serious jurisprudential discussion of realism and formalism, Tamanaha has given future legal historians reason to exercise more caution and modesty before engaging in casual talk about a "formalist" age in American legal thought.[60]

[60] I am grateful to Mark Tushnet for helpful feedback and Frederick Schauer and Scott Shapiro for detailed comments.

11

In Praise of Realism (and Against "Nonsense" Jurisprudence)

I. Jurisprudence: Nonsense and No-Nonsense

Ronald Dworkin describes an approach to how courts should decide cases that he associates with Judge Richard Posner and Professor Cass Sunstein as "a Chicago School of antitheoretical, no-nonsense jurisprudence."[1] Since Professor Dworkin takes his own view of adjudication to be diametrically opposed to that of the Chicago School, it might seem fair, then, to describe Dworkin's own theory as an instance of "protheoretical, nonsense jurisprudence."

That characterization is not one that Professor Dworkin would welcome. To be sure, he describes his preferred approach to jurisprudential questions as "theoretical," in opposition to what he calls the "practical" orientation of the Chicago School. He writes, as he says, "in praise of theory," while the Chicago School he opposes views court decisions as "a political occasion" in which there is an "immediate practical problem" which demands of us an answer to the question: "How can we make things better?"[2]

It is familiar to students of jurisprudence that Dworkin is an unreliable guide to the views of his opponents,[3] and matters are no different in this instance. Judge Posner has a "theory" in any recognizable sense of that term.[4] He argues that the cases confronting appellate courts are frequently indeterminate as a matter of law and that, in fact, judges are often influenced by their nonlegal views about questions of morals and politics. Judge Posner suggests resolving those cases with a rough-and-ready cost-benefit analysis, in which costs and benefits are understood (again loosely) in terms of utility, which is, in turn, understood as the economists understand it, namely, in terms of revealed preferences (e.g., willingness to pay). The claims that the law is indeterminate, that judges are influenced

[1] Ronald Dworkin, *Justice in Robes* (Harvard University Press, 2006), 51.

[2] Ibid., 49–50.

[3] See, e.g., Brian Leiter "Beyond the Hart/Dworkin Debate: The Methodology Problem in Jurisprudence," in *Naturalizing Jurisprudence: Essays on American Legal Realism and Naturalism in Legal Philosophy* (Oxford University Press, 2007), esp. 155–160 & n. 32)

[4] See, e.g., Richard Posner, *The Problematics of Moral and Legal Theory* (Harvard University Press, 1999); Richard Posner, *How Judges Think* (Harvard University Press, 2008).

From a Realist Point of View. Brian Leiter, Oxford University Press. © Brian Leiter 2026.
DOI: 10.1093/9780197749852.003.0013

by nonlegal factors, that judges ought to employ cost-benefit analysis, and that utility should be understood in terms of revealed preferences certainly sound like theoretical claims to my ear. What else could they be? There is, to be sure, a real dispute between Dworkin and Posner (I shall bracket Sunstein's views, since they are, as Dworkin himself ultimately acknowledges,[5] quite different from Posner's), but it is not a dispute illuminated by the contrast between theory and practice. It is, rather, a dispute about the kind of theory that is relevant and illuminating when it comes to law and adjudication. And the fault line marked by this dispute is profound indeed, one that extends far beyond Dworkin and Posner and has a venerable and ancient history that runs through Plato and Thucydides, Kant and Nietzsche, Hegel and Marx, as well as Rawls and Geuss in the present. I shall describe it, instead, as a dispute between Moralists and Realists, between those whose starting point is a theory of how things (morally) ought to be versus those who begin with a theory of how things really are.[6] That is only a crude first approximation of what is at stake, but it will be the burden of this essay to fill it out. In the end, I will argue that the Realist approach to questions of legal and political theory is the superior one.

II. Plato vs. Thucydides

We shall return shortly to Dworkin and Posner, but let us go back in time to the first emblematic instance of this dispute: between the Moralist Plato and the Realist Thucydides in antiquity. There will prove to be a sense in which our contemporaries, Ronald Dworkin and Richard Posner, are merely reenacting a version of the dispute between the paradigmatic philosophical moralist Plato and the paradigmatic realist Thucydides.

Plato is both a moralist—a philosopher with a robust conception of the good life and the just society which he advocates—and a moralizing philosopher, whose metaphysical and epistemological views are in the service of his moral aims, a philosopher who illustrates Nietzsche's dictum that "the moral . . . intentions in every philosophy constitute the real root from which the whole plant has always grown."[7] For Plato, immoral behavior is irrational behavior,[8] and it is in the interest of rational beings to forego the selfish satisfaction of their desires in favor of acting justly. The true nature of reality, justice, and what is in

[5] Dworkin, *Justice in Robes*, 24–25.

[6] See ch. 1 in this volume for my more recent development of this contrast.

[7] Friedrich Nietzsche, *Beyond Good and Evil: Prelude to a Philosophy of the Future*, trans. Walter Kaufmann (Vintage Books, 1989): 13.

[8] The later Plato arguably has a different view, so consider this a point about the earlier, and better-known, Platonic view.

our interests, are all possible objects of rational cognition for Plato, though the objects of such cognition are a realm of facts that transcend the merely empirical world. The world around us, the one visible to our senses, is merely apparent, a pale imitation of the true world in which the rational is the moral, self-interest coincides with justice, and a harmony obtains between objective knowledge, objective reality, and the good. The Cambridge political philosopher Raymond Geuss aptly characterizes this Platonic "optimism" (as he calls it) in terms of a number of propositions, of which the most important for our purposes is the Platonic assumption "that when the world was correctly understood, it would make moral sense to us."[9] Dworkin, the jurisprudential Moralist, wants the correct understanding of what courts do to make a certain kind of "moral sense" as well, namely, that court decisions are morally justified in licensing the exercise of the state's coercive power in virtue of their conforming to a kind of Dworkinian ideal of judicial decision. We shall return to that ideal shortly.

Platonic optimism and moralism, as Nietzsche most famously argued, is the dominant theme in Western philosophy from Plato onward, and it is for this reason that Nietzsche so much prefers the pre-Socratic philosophers, especially the fifth-century Sophists, whom Nietzsche takes (somewhat, though not wholly, idiosyncratically) to be best exemplified by the historian Thucydides. In Thucydides, Nietzsche says

> that culture of the most impartial knowledge of the world finds its last glorious flower: that culture which had in Sophocles its poet, in Pericles its statesman, in Hippocrates its physician, in Democritus its natural philosopher; which deserves to be baptised with the name of its teachers, the Sophists.[10]

In Thucydides, in other words, "the culture of the Sophists, by which I mean the culture of the realists [*die Realisten-Cultur*], reaches its perfect expression."[11] "Realism," here, means not Plato's metaphysical doctrine about the reality of a supra-empirical world, but rather "the courage of all strong spirits to know their own immorality,"[12] that is, to face up to the role that (for example) avarice, malice, and selfishness play in what is otherwise instrumentally rational

[9] Raymond Geuss, *Outside Ethics* (Princeton University Press, 2005), 223.

[10] Friedrich Nietzsche, *Daybreak: Thoughts on the Prejudices of Morality*, trans. R. J. Hollingdale, ed. Maudemarie Clark and Brian Leiter (Cambridge University Press, 1997), 103. Cf. Friedrich Nietzsche, *The Will to Power*, trans. R. J. Hollingdale and Walter Kaufmann, ed. Walter Kaufmann (Vintage Books, 1968), 233: "The Greek culture of the Sophists had developed out of all the Greek instincts; it belongs to the culture of the Periclean age as necessarily as Plato does not; it has its predecessors in Heraclitus, Democritus, in the scientific types of the old philosophy; it finds its expression in, e.g., the high culture of Thucydides."

[11] Friedrich Nietzsche, "Twilight of the Idols," in *The Portable Nietzsche*, ed. & trans. Walter Kaufmann (Penguin Books, 1988), 463, 558.

[12] Nietzsche, *The Will to Power*, 234.

behavior by people. Thus, Thucydides, the quintessential realist, is described by Nietzsche as

> the last revelation of that strong, severe, hard factuality which was instinctive with the older Hellenes. In the end, it is courage in the face of reality that distinguishes a man like Thucydides from Plato: Plato is a coward before reality, consequently he flees into the ideal; Thucydides has control of himself, consequently he also maintains control of things.[13]

Plato "flees into the ideal" by pretending, for example, that it is always in the rational self-interest of agents to act justly and that no rational person ever knowingly acts wrongly. Thucydides's "courage in the face of reality," by contrast, is on display in his portrayal of the dialogue between the Athenians and the vanquished Melians—a dialogue that one distinguished scholar, W. K. C. Guthrie, has called "the most famous example of amoral realism."[14] Negotiating over the terms of surrender, the Athenians address the Melians, in relevant part, as follows:

> For our part, we will not make a long speech no one would believe, full of fine moral arguments—that our empire is justified because we defeated the Persians, or that we are coming against you for an injustice you have done to us. . . . Instead, let's work out what we can do on the basis of what both sides truly accept: we both know that decisions about justice are made in human discussions only when both sides are under equal compulsion [i.e., only among equals does right prevail over might]; but when one side is stronger, it gets as much as it can, and the weak must accept that.
>
> Nature always compels gods (we believe) and men (we are certain) to rule over anyone they can control. We did not make this law, and we were not the first to follow it; but we will take it as we found it and leave it to posterity forever, because we know that you would do the same if you had our power, and so would anyone else.[15]

Nietzsche's own commentary on this particular dialogue highlights some of the key themes of Sophistic Realism:

> Do you suppose perchance that these little Greek free cities, which from rage and envy would have liked to devour each other, were guided by philanthropic and righteous principles? Does one reproach Thucydides for the words he puts

[13] Nietzsche, *Twilight of the Idols*, 558–59.

[14] W. K. C. Guthrie, *The Sophists* (Cambridge University Press, 1971), 85.

[15] Thucydides, *On Justice, Power and Human Nature*, ed. & trans. Paul Woodruff (Hackett, 1993), 103, 106 (¶¶ 89, 105).

into the mouths of the Athenian ambassadors when they negotiated with the Melians on the question of destruction or submission?

Only complete Tartuffes [i.e., Socrates and Plato] could possibly have talked of virtue in the midst of this terrible tension—or men living apart, hermits, refugees, and emigrants from reality—people who negated in order to be able to live themselves....

[The English scholar] Grote's tactics in defense of the Sophists are false: he wants to raise them to the rank of men of honor and ensigns of morality—but it was precisely their honor not to indulge in any swindle with big words and virtues.[16]

Contempt for any "swindle with big words and virtues" may be one of the hallmarks of Realism, but what exactly does it mean? In the case under discussion, Realist impatience with the "swindle with big words and virtues" signifies the candid recognition that the Athenians in their dealings with the Melians are not moved at all by "philanthropic and righteous principles," but are driven, instead, by selfish and self-aggrandizing concerns, restrained only by the limits of their own power. (We should notice here the resonance with contemporary "realist" theories of international relations, which frequently acknowledge Thucydides as their inspiration.[17]) Socrates and Plato, by contrast, engage in a "swindle with big words and virtues" when, as Thucydides makes plain, virtue and justice play little role in human affairs.

Of course, the speeches Thucydides presents are his own creations; in many cases (as with the Melian dialogue), he could not even have been present to hear them. Yet this is precisely why Thucydides is a Realist in Nietzsche's view: How he chooses to reconstruct events reflects his Realism about human affairs. As the classical philosophy scholar Paul Woodruff aptly observes, "Thucydides' speakers are made to say what Thucydides thinks they actually believe, whether they would have said those things in public or not.... He shows us their speeches refracted through a lens of honesty."[18] Thucydides, in other words, puts into the speakers' mouths their true, amoral motives, reflecting Thucydides's realistic view of human nature and human affairs, in contrast with the idealistic fantasies of a Socrates or Plato.[19] Thus, Nietzsche declares:

[16] Nietzsche, *The Will to Power*, 234.

[17] See, e.g., David Boucher, *Political Theories of International Relations: From Thucydides to the Present* (Oxford University Press, 1998).

[18] Woodruff, *Thucydides on Justice, Power, and Human Nature*, ix, xxiii. As Geuss puts it: Thucydides's "project is to exhibit what really moves people to act, and what then happens to them and to others as a consequence of how they act, not to write an edifying treatise or a partisan tract." Geuss, *Outside Ethics*, 226.

[19] Of course, on one prevalent understanding of Plato, he too accepts that humans are self-interested, and tries to show them simply that "justice" and "virtue" are in their self-interest. The Realist may reasonably object that this identification of morality with self-interest is so implausible as to be no different from preaching "justice" and "virtue" quite apart from any appeal to self-interest.

> my cure from all Platonism has always been Thucydides. Thucydides and, perhaps Machiavelli's *Principe* are most closely related to myself by the unconditional will not to gull oneself and to see reason in reality—not in "reason," still less in "morality."[20]

Thucydides views political leaders as essentially motivated by selfish concerns—power, fear, wealth—and as creatures for whom moral considerations are rhetorical window dressing, rather than a reason for action.[21] The *History of the Peloponnesian War* is a microcosm for what happens when these perennial facts about motivation encounter the recurring circumstances of human social existence. Rather than delude his readers with a "swindle of big words and virtues," Thucydides puts into the mouths of his actors their actual self-serving motives: for glory and for power.[22]

III. Posner, Llewellyn, and Realism about Adjudication

We have traveled far from Dworkin and the "Chicago school of no-nonsense jurisprudence,"[23] but some points of contact between the ancient quarrel between Moralism and Realism and the contemporary jurisprudential dispute may have already suggested themselves.

Dworkin, as is no doubt familiar, believes that there exists a right answer as a matter of law in every (or almost every) dispute, and that judges discover that answer by the process of what he calls "constructive interpretation," that is, by figuring out which result would cohere with the moral principles that best explain and justify the prior official acts—the court decisions, legislation, and so on—constituting the institutional history of the legal system.[24] Dworkin's "nonsense jurisprudence," then, takes what judges say they are doing at face value: if they say they are reaching the result the law requires (and they usually do say that), then that is what they are doing and so we must interpret them. If judges invoke moral and political principles in deciding hard cases, then we must view those principles as legally binding on them, and construct a theory of law that

20 Nietzsche, *Twilight of the Idols*, ch. X, sec. 2.

21 Cf. Guthrie, *The Sophists*, 85: "It is remarkable how seldom even [Thucydides'] orators, aiming at persuasion, see any point in appealing to considerations of right, justice or other normally accepted moral standards: it is taken for granted that only an appeal to self-interest is likely to succeed."

22 In the case of Thucydides, none of the preceding is incompatible with his having a "moral" to convey to his readers about the consequences of naked lust for power and glory. But his method for conveying this is to illustrate the consequences of the conduct of the Athenians, rather than to construct a moral theory about why such conduct is not justified. In this respect, Thucydides is something like one of Judge Posner's "moral entrepreneurs," discussed below, 244–252.

23 Dworkin, *Justice in Robes*.

24 See generally Ronald Dworkin, *Law's Empire* (Belknap Press, 1986).

shows it to be so. Nonsense jurisprudence treats the judicial "swindle of big words and virtues" (to borrow Nietzsche's provocative phrase) as not a swindle, but a faithful report of the essence of legal reasoning, and thus the central data point to which any theory of law and adjudication must answer. Moreover, it treats the results of adjudication—the recognition of apparently new rights and remedies and causes of action—as making a kind of "moral sense," that is, as being morally justified exercises of coercive power when they arise from "constructive interpretation" and the integrity that method imparts to the legal system.

No-nonsense jurisprudence, from Karl Llewellyn to Richard Posner, sees matters otherwise. What judges say they are doing is one thing; what they are really doing is another. Official legal reasoning often fails to justify a single outcome as a matter of law—that, of course, is a theoretical claim in jurisprudence—so the idea that one could really understand what courts (especially appellate courts) are doing by attending only to the legal arguments they present in their opinions is an illusion. Just as Thucydides shows us the Athenian "speeches refracted through a lens of honesty," so too Realists from Llewellyn to Posner strip away the obfuscating doctrinal rationales judges offer to identify the real nonlegal considerations influencing the decisions.

To be sure, our jurisprudential Realists need not ascribe to judges self-aggrandizing motives! Judges are not necessarily like our ancient Athenians in pursuing "power and glory," though, as it happens, Posner himself has explored the possibility that judges are rationally self-interested maximizers of leisure, reputation, and prestige, among other desiderata.[25] From the Legal Realism of the 1920s and 1930s[26] to the contemporary political science literature,[27] though, the primary emphasis has been on the role that nonlegal value judgments—for example, judgments about the fairness of a particular business practice, or simply value judgments reflecting a particular political ideology—play in explaining why judges decide as they do, even when those nonlegal values are absent from the opinions.

Now Judge Posner has sometimes expressed unhappiness with the "Realist" label, notwithstanding the obvious affinities between the law and economics revolution he brought to fruition in the 1970s and the Legal Realist movement of the 1920s and 1930s. He has written that "[w]e economic types have no desire

[25] Richard A. Posner, "What Do Judges Maximize?" in *Overcoming Law* (Harvard University Press, 1995), 135–36. And see more recently Posner, *How Judges Think*, 35–36, which also notes limitations of this approach.

[26] See esp. Brian Leiter, "Rethinking Legal Realism: Toward a Naturalized Jurisprudence," in *Naturalizing Jurisprudence*, 15.

[27] See Frank B. Cross, *Decision Making in the U.S. Courts of Appeals* (Stanford University Press, 2007): 3–4; Thomas J. Miles and Cass R. Sunstein, "The New Legal Realism," *University of Chicago Law Review* 75 (2008): 831, 835–41. See generally Jeffrey A. Segal and Harold J. Spaeth, *The Supreme Court and the Attitudinal Model* (Cambridge University Press, 1993) (examining the way Supreme Court Justices' attitudes and values affect their decisions).

to be pronounced the intellectual heirs of Fred Rodell, or for that matter William Douglas, Jerome Frank, or Karl Llewellyn. The law and economics movement owes little to legal realism."[28] Whatever the chain of influence, it seems clear that economic analysis of law, like American Legal Realism, is predicated on a thorough-going skepticism about the adequacy of existing legal categories, and the need for an alternative explanation of the actual course of decisions.[29] The legal historian Neil Duxbury aptly summarizes Posner's approach to economic analysis of law as follows: "Owing to the fact that judicial opinions are frequently suffused with rhetoric, it is invariably very difficult to figure out what types of concerns lead judges to reach the decisions that they do."[30] Yet the resonance with familiar Realist refrains is obvious here—to take but one example, here is Karl Llewellyn:

> [I]f I am right, finding out what the judges say is but the beginning of your task. You will have to take what they say and compare it with what they do. You will have to see whether what they say matches with what they do. You will have to be distrustful of whether they themselves know (any better than other men) the ways of their own doing, and of whether they describe it accurately, even if they know it.[31]

The task Llewellyn identifies is, of course, precisely the task the Posnerian lawyer-economist would discharge. Indeed, Alan Schwartz has argued[32] that Llewellyn was a proto-economic efficiency theorist when it came to the optimal rules for contract law, a thesis which, if correct, would suggest an even deeper affinity between Posnerian law and economics and Legal Realism.[33]

[28] Posner, *Overcoming Law*, 3.

[29] Judge Posner tells me that he arrived at his views about adjudication quite independently of the Legal Realists and that he is mainly concerned not to be associated with some of the more extreme and sillier aspects of Legal Realism in writers like Fred Rodell or Jerome Frank's armchair psychoanalytic speculations about judicial motivations.

[30] Neil Duxbury, *Patterns of American Jurisprudence* (Oxford University Press, 1995): 410.

[31] Karl Llewellyn, *The Bramble Bush* (Oceana, 1930): 5.

[32] Alan Schwartz, "Karl Llewellyn and the Origins of Contract Theory," in *The Jurisprudential Foundations of Corporate and Commercial Law*, ed. Jody S. Kraus and Steven D. Walt (Cambridge University Press, 2000), 12, 15–16.

[33] Llewellyn, as Schwartz argues persuasively, "used commercial practice as the best evidence of the efficient transaction" (id. at 16), and thus by treating normal commercial practice as the benchmark for decision-making, he effectively privileged economic efficiency as the goal of the rules of commercial law, on the assumption that the norms of ordinary commercial practice will tend towards efficiency. (I should note that Schwartz does, however, misunderstand the meaning and nature of Llewellyn's rule- skepticism, as I discuss in Leiter, *Naturalizing Jurisprudence*, 108-112. But that disagreement does not affect the point at issue here.) It is also striking that Llewellyn and Judge Posner have strikingly similar views on precedent: compare Posner, *How Judges Think*, 45 with Llewellyn, *The Bramble Bush*, 51-66.

These historical details, however, do not matter for our purposes. What matters are the broad thematic affinities that set "Realists" like Holmes, Llewellyn, and Posner against Moralists like Dworkin when it comes to thinking about adjudication. Realists want to tell us what really goes on when courts decide cases; moralists want to understand adjudication in terms that they adjudge morally defensible, which means, for Dworkin, taking what judges say at "face value." The dispute between Realists and Moralists would be clear-cut if it were only a descriptive question about what is actually happening. After all, in recent years, much evidence has been adduced that strongly supports the conclusion that the political ideology of the judge has a strong influence on their decisions.[34] In a widely noted article on "The New Legal Realism," for example, Thomas Miles and Cass Sunstein identify what they call a "Standard Pattern of Judicial Voting" in "ideologically contested cases"—such as those involving "environmental protection, labor law, sex discrimination, abortion, and campaign finance law"—in which "the political affiliation of the appointing president greatly matters to judicial votes."[35] Moreover, while "in many areas of law, Democratic appointees cast liberal votes more often than Republican appointees do," in some areas, the composition of the panel matters: "the liberal voting rate typically increases with the number of co-panelists who are Democratic appointees—and correspondingly falls with the number of Republican appointees."[36]

The Standard Pattern is not, as Miles and Sunstein readily concede, universal, even with respect to subjects that might seem to be fraught with ideological discord. As they remark: "Republican appointees and Democratic appointees do not differ in their voting patterns in some areas in which significant differences might well be expected; examples include criminal appeals, property rights, congressional power under the Commerce Clause, and standing to sue."[37] As to what explains this convergence, Miles and Sunstein offer two possibilities: "Perhaps the law imposes a great deal of discipline in these domains, so that ideological differences cannot emerge; perhaps Republican and Democratic appointees do not much disagree in such areas."[38]

Beyond political ideology, studies have also found that "in sex discrimination cases a judge's sex matters" to the outcome,[39] and the race of the judge appears

[34] See, e.g., Cass R. Sunstein, David Schkade, Lisa M. Ellman, & Andres Sawicki, *Are Judges Political? An Empirical Analysis of the Federal Judiciary* (Brookings Institution Press, 2006); Frank B. Cross, *Decision Making in the U.S. Courts of Appeals* (Stanford University Press, 2007).

[35] Miles and Sunstein, "The New Legal Realism," 837–39.

[36] Ibid., 838. Cases where panel composition does not seem to matter include those dealing with abortion and capital punishment. As Miles and Sunstein write: "In those domains, judges apparently vote their convictions and are not influenced, at least in their conclusions, by the other judges on the panel." Ibid., 839.

[37] Ibid., 839.

[38] Ibid.

[39] Ibid.

to affect outcomes in voting rights cases.[40] Judge Posner, in his book *How Judges Think*, notes that "the outcome of Supreme Court cases can be predicted more accurately by means of a handful of variables, none of which involves legal doctrine, than by a team of constitutional law experts."[41] That most people, including many legal professionals, are surprised by this indicates what an "unrealistic" view they have, Posner says, of what judges do. The explanation for this state of affairs is partly attributable to the judges themselves. Judge Posner writes: "[M]ost judges are cagey, even coy, in discussing what they do. They tend to parrot an official line about the judicial process (how rule-bound it is), and often to believe it, though it does not describe their actual practices."[42]

Their "actual practices," according to Judge Posner, are better described by a variety of theories that emphasize their political attitudes, their strategic behavior (as in the "panel effects" noted by Miles and Sunstein[43]), their behavior as "rational, self-interested utility maximizer[s]," and, most importantly for Posner, their "preconceptions" which shape, often subconsciously, their "responses to uncertainty" in the face of new cases.[44] To be sure, Judge Posner, like the Legal Realists of the 1920s and 1930s, acknowledges that law matters,[45] that it constrains, often determines, decisions at the lower court level, but that as we move up through the levels of appellate review, nonlegal factors matter more and more to the outcomes—until we get, of course, to the US Supreme Court which is, as Judge Posner candidly acknowledges, "a largely political court."[46]

[40] Ibid., 840.

[41] Posner, *How Judges Think*, 24.

[42] Ibid., 2. Judge David F. Levi, former Dean of Duke Law School, takes issue with Judge Posner in "Autocrat of the Armchair," *Duke Law Journal* 58 (2009): 1792, claiming that Posner's "generalizations about the ways of the judge and the world are ex cathedra pronouncements that generally lack any identified objective support outside of his own experience and belief." Ibid., 1792–93. This is an odd charge to make against a book which synthesizes a massive amount of empirical literature from the social sciences about courts, judges, and human decision-making. See Posner, *How Judges Think*, 19–56. Judge Levi identifies a dozen *very specific* observations and claims (Levi, "Autocrat of the Armchair," 1796–97) that are offered by Judge Posner without empirical citation, but many of them are, as Judge Levi concedes, "not . . . clearly untrue" (most are, in fact, prima facie plausible), and they are in any case fairly minor points, rather than central themes. Levi, "Autocrat of the Armchair," 1797. (Those that are more central—like Judge Posner's claim about the central role of "intuition" in decision-making by judges—are, indeed, fair inferences from the empirical literature cited and discussed.) But the key difficulty with Judge Levi's critique is that he appears to misunderstand the central argumentative structure of the book, which is to claim that the *best explanation* for the massive empirical evidence about judicial decision-making is that "legalism" is false as a descriptive theory of adjudication.

[43] Miles and Sunstein, "The New Legal Realism," 837–40.

[44] Posner, *How Judges Think*, 35.

[45] For pertinent citation and discussion, see Leiter, *Naturalizing Jurisprudence*, 77–78.

[46] Posner, *How Judges Think*, 8. See also ch. 12 in this volume.

IV. A Dworkinian Rejoinder

What is the Moralist Dworkin to say in the face of such overwhelming evidence that judges, especially appellate judges, are often—though to be sure not always—political actors? They do not, to be sure, write opinions saying, "Since I was appointed by the Republican Reagan, I cannot possibly find in favor of the appellee," nor do they say, "As an African-American man, I cannot countenance the electoral practices of Georgia in this instance."[47] Yet if the Realists, now armed with their empirical studies, are right, then this may actually be the correct explanation for the decisions. Dworkin has, throughout his career, called attention to the fact that judges write their opinions as if they are discovering the right answer as a matter of law. But none of the empirical studies just noted deny that fact about the opinions they write: they simply confirm—again and again and again—that nonlegal considerations and influences actually explain the decisions, and there is no way for Dworkin's interpretive theory of law to accommodate what at times appears to be naked political partisanship.[48]

So how is a Dworkinian Moralist to respond? Although Dworkin claims to be describing what judges actually do—"the hidden structure of their judgments" as he says[49]—his theory is quite explicitly driven by a normative vision. Like Plato, Dworkin wants his subject matter to make "moral sense," which, for Dworkin, means that unless judges are deciding cases through the Dworkinian method of "constructive interpretation," their decisions could not supply a moral justification for coercing the losing party before the court.[50] It does not matter for our purposes that Dworkin's own unusual theory of the conditions under which

[47] Since on Dworkin's view of adjudication, moral/political judgments are, of course, central to fixing the content of the law, perhaps he should simply claim that the empirical literature confirms his theory of adjudication! To be sure, so the argument would go, judges differ in their moral judgments, but it has never been part of Dworkin's theory to claim that we always *know* what the right answer is, only that one exists, and that it follows from a process of constructive interpretation that requires moral/political judgment. The difficulty, however, for this rejoinder is twofold: first, to show that the patterns of decision identified in the empirical literature can be reconstructed in terms that look anything like a constructive interpretation, and second, to explain why the "face value" of the opinions fails to correspond to the social scientific explanation for the pattern of decisions. I am hard-pressed to see how either difficulty can be overcome, but invite a reader sympathetic to Dworkin's view to undertake the theoretical challenge the empirical literature poses.

[48] Note that Posner's view is that "naked political partisanship" is relatively rare, but only because he thinks the ideologies of the political parties are not themselves coherent. See Posner, *How Judges Think*, 94. That just means, however, that the category of the "political" needs to be individuated in a more fine-grained way.

[49] Dworkin, *Law's Empire*, 265. He means, of course, the hidden "logical" or "rational" structure that underlies the opinions they write, not the "hidden" psychological motivations.

[50] It is important to recognize that Judge Posner, like most theorists, is silent on this question. To be sure, he think utility-maximizing decisions are good ones, but that is because he thinks maximizing utility is good, not because he thinks it is necessary for the moral justification of court coercing the losing party. Indeed, like a good realist, he thinks that question is largely idle. See esp. Richard A. Posner, *Law, Pragmatism, and Democracy* (Harvard University Press, 2003).

coercion is justified is so implausible[51] that it has only one adherent. What is more significant is that we have no reason (and Dworkin supplies none) for assuming that it will or should turn out that the exercise of coercive power by courts *is* morally justified. We may certainly hope it is justifiable (at least in otherwise morally commendable legal systems) for courts to decide even "hard" cases where the law seems up for grabs, and there are reasons to think it is quite apart from the law supplying a "right answer" in every case—most obviously, by appeal to the Hobbesian idea that the alternative to authoritative and final resolution of societal disputes by courts would be an intolerable war of all against all, given how unrealistic it is that legislature could address all these problems.[52] But we need not derail our discussion into the justification of political authority, since the key point is that Dworkin is not entitled to his assumption that a theory of adjudication must show the exercise of coercive power by courts to be morally justified.

Now this response to Dworkinian moralism no doubt seems too quick, as well it should. For there is, in fact, another way of framing the Moralist's challenge to Realism about adjudication. Perhaps we have good realist reasons to be skeptical about the surface of judicial opinions, with their feigned supine posture before the force of the law and legal reasoning, and certainly we have no reason to assume in advance that courts are actually justified in bringing the coercive power of the state to bear against individuals in matters where the law seems to be uncertain. But a realistic Dworkinian—I assume, for sake of argument, that this is not an oxymoron—might concede both points, and still note that, in principle, all legal arguments have the property of being susceptible to what Dworkin has recently called "justificatory ascent." By "justificatory ascent," Dworkin means that in any legal argument it is always possible that a particular principle on which we are relying "is inconsistent with . . . some other principle that we must rely on to justify some other and larger part of the law."[53] And what that means is that even if, in reality, judges are not really deciding based on the legal principles they invoke, it is still the case that we, as observers, might demand that their decisions answer to the demand of a principled justificatory ascent suggested by the arguments they offer. (Here Dworkin signals his profound debt to the Legal Process school of thought.) Moreover, the Dworkinian Moralist might say, when such an ascent is carried out properly—namely, as Dworkinian "constructive

[51] See, e.g., the critique of Dworkin's theory of associative obligations in Leslie Green, "Law and Obligations," in *The Oxford Handbook of Jurisprudence and Legal Philosophy*, ed. J. Coleman and S. Shapiro (Oxford University Press, 2002), 521–22.

[52] Hart, himself, endorses a variation on this response. See H. L. A. Hart, *The Concept of Law* (Oxford University Press, 1994), 275.

[53] Dworkin, *Justice in Robes*, 53.

interpretation"—it even yields results that would justify the court's exercise of its coercive powers.

Dworkin must surely be right that there is "no a priori limit to the justificatory ascent into which a problem will draw" lawyers and judges, but everything turns on what legal constraints actually govern this ascent. The Realist worry is that, at some point, there are no meaningful legal constraints on justificatory ascent, and that all Dworkin has noticed is what the Realistic Sophists noticed 2,500 years ago, namely, that a skilled rhetorician can give arguments for conflicting propositions. The Realist worry, in short, is that this new Dworkinian mantra about "justificatory ascent" is just another "swindle with big words and virtues."

V. Dworkin, Cardozo, and "Justificatory Ascent"

Let us consider Dworkin's own central example in his recent work[54] on justificatory ascent—namely, Judge Benjamin Cardozo's seminal 1916 decision in *MacPherson v. Buick Motor Co.*[55] *MacPherson* established that manufacturers of potentially dangerous products could no longer escape liability to the consumers injured by their products based on lack of contractual privity, which was usually absent since consumers typically purchased the product from some intermediary. As the former Attorney General and late University of Chicago Law School Dean Edward Levi—exemplar of an earlier and also Realistically minded "Chicago School"—noted in his famous book *An Introduction to Legal Reasoning*,[56] *MacPherson* is a powerful illustration of the basic pattern of evolution of legal concepts, which moves from creation of the concept (in this case, that of the "inherently dangerous" product for which contractual privity is not required for liability), to "the period when the concept is more or less fixed," to the final "breakdown of the concept, as reasoning by example has moved so far ahead as to make it clear that the suggestive influences of the word is no longer desired."

Thus, we move from *Langridge v. Levy* in 1837, in which the son, injured by a gun sold to his father, was able to recover against the seller since the seller "knew it was defective and . . . was to be used by the" son,[57] to *Winterbottom v. Wright* in 1842, where recovery against the supplier of a carriage was denied to the coachman injured when it broke down due to a latent defect, on the grounds that carriages were not a "weapon of a dangerous nature" and, in any case, there was

[54] Ibid., 55.
[55] 111 N.E. 1050 (N.Y. 1916).
[56] Edward H. Levi, *An Introduction to Legal Reasoning* (University of Chicago Press, 1949), 2–3.
[57] Ibid., 11.

no evidence the supplier was aware of the latent defect.[58] By 1851, in *Longmeid v. Holliday*, "the concept of things dangerous in themselves . . . finally won out," as Levi puts it, even though the wife injured by an exploding lamp was denied recovery against the storekeeper who sold it to her husband.[59] The key to the decision, however, was the finding that "the lamp was not in its nature dangerous," which meant the absence of privity decided the matter.[60]

The next stage in the movement of the concept, according to Levi, was *Thomas v. Winchester* in 1852, in which recovery against the packager was permitted for mislabeled poison purchased from an intermediary, since "defendant's negligence had 'put human life in imminent danger.' "[61] Soon enough, privity was waived when we were dealing with a defective hair wash, but not "a defective balance wheel for a circular saw."[62] Yet by 1883, in *Heaven v. Pender*, a defective scaffold was found inherently dangerous (and so recovery permitted), though emphasis was laid upon the fact that "the necessary workmen were in effect invited by the dock owner to use the dock and appliances."[63] By the turn of the century—from the nineteenth to the twentieth that is—Levi notes that, "The dangerous concept had in it a loaded gun, possibly a defective gun, mislabeled poison, defective hair wash, scaffolds, a defective coffee urn, and a defective aerated bottle. The not-dangerous category, once referred to as only latently dangerous, had in it a defective carriage, a bursting lamp, a defective balance wheel for a circular saw, and a defective boiler."[64] If this is Dworkinian "justificatory ascent," its principled basis is, shall we say, a bit obscure.

Just one year before *MacPherson*, our story of "justificatory ascent" seems to culminate with the opinion of the US Court of Appeals for the Second Circuit (the Circuit encompassing New York, of course) in *Cadillac Motor Car Co. v. Johnson*, in which we learn that there is no requirement of privity when it comes to manufacturers of "articles inherently dangerous," but "one who manufactures articles dangerous only if defectively made, or installed"—including automobiles—"is not liable to third parties for injuries caused by them, except in cases of willful injury or fraud."[65]

A year later, that rule simply vanished in the hands of Judge Cardozo in *MacPherson*.[66] Cardozo rehearses the narrative of the concept of "inherently dangerous" products, much as Levi does, but starting with *Thomas v. Winchester*,

[58] Ibid.,12.
[59] Ibid.,13.
[60] Ibid.
[61] Ibid., 14–15, quoting Thomas v. Winchester, 6 N.Y. 397 (1852).
[62] Ibid., 15.
[63] Ibid., 16.
[64] Ibid., 18.
[65] Ibid., 19–20, quoting 221 F. 801, 802–3 (2d Cir. 1915).
[66] Of course, the New York Court of Appeals would not have been bound by the Second Circuit decision, but Judge Cardozo did feel the need to mention it, as discussed below in the text.

and admitting, at the start, that in the application of the so-called principle of that case, "there may at times have been uncertainty or even error."[67] Soon enough, Cardozo tells us that even if the rule in *Thomas v. Winchester* was restricted to "things imminently dangerous to life" like "poisons, explosives, deadly weapons," that no longer governs: the rule, he says, "no longer has that restricted meaning."[68] What matters, Cardozo says, is "the trend of judicial thought."[69] And that trend quickly leads Cardozo to the conclusion that if a thing is "reasonably certain" to be dangerous if negligently made, "it is then a thing of danger."[70] At that point, privity does not matter as to the right of the injured plaintiff to recover.

But what then of the prior year's contrary decision in the US Court of Appeals for the Second Circuit on essentially the same set of facts as at issue in *MacPherson*? It merits only passing notice by Cardozo that its holding was "contrary," and that there was "a vigorous dissent," yet Cardozo offers barely any discussion of the reasoning.[71] He does observe that the "contrary" view holds "that the contractor who builds a bridge, or the manufacturer who builds a car, cannot ordinarily foresee injury to other persons than the owner as the probable result," to which Cardozo retorts—in probably the crucial line of the whole opinion: "We think that injury to others is to be foreseen not merely as a possible, but as an almost inevitable result."[72]

That the majority opinion by Cardozo had, quite obviously, changed the law[73]— not via any justificatory ascent, but by a bit of quasi-legislative fiat—was not lost on the now-forgotten dissenter, Judge Bartlett, who remarked:

> It has heretofore been held in this state that the liability of the vendor of a manufactured article for negligence arising out of the existence of defects therein does not extend to strangers injured in consequence of such defects but is confined to the immediate vendee. The exceptions to this general rule which have thus far been recognized in New York are cases in which the article sold was of such a character that danger to life or limb was involved in the ordinary use thereof; in other words, where the article was inherently dangerous.[74]

After reviewing the long history of cases, Judge Bartlett concludes that the majority's decision is tantamount to "overruling what has been so often said by

[67] *MacPherson*, 111 N.E. at 1051.
[68] Ibid., 1052.
[69] Ibid.
[70] Ibid., 1053.
[71] Ibid., 1053–54.
[72] Ibid., 1054.
[73] Cardozo's opinion was also a bit loose with the facts of the case, as discussed in James A. Henderson, Jr., "*MacPherson v. Buick Motor Company*: Simplifying the Facts While Reshaping the Law," in *Torts Stories*, ed. R. Rabin and S. Sugarman (Foundation Press, 2003), 41.
[74] *MacPherson*, 111 N.E. at 1055 (Bartlett, C.J., dissenting).

this court and other courts of like authority in reference to the absence of any liability for negligence on the part of the original vendor of an ordinary carriage to any one except his immediate vendee."[75]

You will notice that neither the Dworkinian Moralist nor the Posnerian Realist has reason to disagree with Cardozo's result: Both can agree about the soundness of the outcome, which is why Cardozo is a celebrated figure and Bartlett a footnote. The question is whether we describe Cardozo's decision as an exercise in "justificatory ascent," or whether we describe it, more realistically, as an exercise in sensible legislation by the courts?

As Levi noted in his original discussion of the transformation of a legal concept, "matters of kind vanish into matters of degree and then entirely new meanings turn up," and judges will, of course, pretend that "some overall rule" governs.[76] Yet, as Levi remarks, "the rule will be useless," adding "The statement of the rule . . . is window dressing."[77] One doubts Judge Cardozo would have disagreed. The new rule of *MacPherson*, after all, made good economic sense in an age of retailers who distributed mass-produced goods to thousands (sometimes millions) of consumers. Here, the potential for injury was enormous, but producers (not retailers) were obviously in the best position to minimize the dangers. Cardozo's decision is thus justly celebrated as skillfully eliding clear precedents (including, of course, the Second Circuit Court case directly on point one year earlier!), establishing the necessity of contractual privity for liability, to create the best new rule for new social circumstances[78]—precisely the kind of outcome-oriented decision Judge Posner often commends. As Dean Prosser noted, in his seminal 1960 article on "The Assault on the Citadel"—the citadel being the immunity from liability afford by the requirement of contractual privity—Cardozo "wielding a mighty axe, burst over the ramparts, and buried the general rule under the exception."[79]

Dworkin, by contrast, wants to celebrate the opinion as an exercise in "justificatory ascent." Yet if we are to distinguish legally principled justificatory ascent in Dworkin's sense from Levi's or Posner's enlightened, albeit incremental, policymaking by courts, we need some compelling explanation of how the result in *MacPherson* was required by the existing legal materials and the principles they embodied.[80] Dworkin does not even try to provide one, and Cardozo

[75] Ibid., 1056.
[76] Levi, *An Introduction to Legal Reasoning*, 9.
[77] Ibid.
[78] Ibid., 24.
[79] William L. Prosser, "The Assault Upon the Citadel (Strict Liability to the Consumer)," *Yale Law Journal* 69 (1960): 1100.
[80] Two students of Dworkin who are leading tort theorists, John Goldberg and Benjamin Zipursky, have tried to defend a "moral concept of duty" against the prevailing "duty-skepticism" of William Prosser and contemporary law & economics, the latter of whom sees *MacPherson* as embodying it. See John C. P. Goldberg and Benjamin Zipurksy, "The Moral of *MacPherson*," *University of Pennsylvania Law Review* 146 (1998): 1733–1847. They note, rightly, that Cardozo's opinion does

himself, in reflecting on the decision, does not pretend that there is such an account:

> What . . . was the posture of affairs before the Buick case had been determined? Was there any law on the subject? A mass of judgments, more or less relevant, had been rendered by the same and other courts. A body of particulars existed on which a hypothesis might be reared. None the less, their implications were equivocal.[81]

Indeed, Cardozo explicitly repudiates the "extreme" notion that "[l]aw is fixed and immutable, that the conclusion which the judge declares . . . has a genuine preexistence, that judgment is a process of discovery, and not in any degree a process of creation,"[82] which is to say that he rejects precisely Dworkin's view of the case.

None of this will be surprising to those who recall Cardozo's 1923 book *The Nature of the Judicial Process*,[83] where he declares early on: "I take judge-made law as one of the existing realities of life."[84] To be sure, says Cardozo, "in countless litigations, the law is so clear that judges have no discretion,"[85] but "within the confines of [the] open spaces [of language] and those of precedent and tradition, choice moves with a freedom which stamps its action as creative. The law which is the resulting product is not found, but made."[86] When Cardozo titles one of his chapters "The Judge as Legislator," there can be little doubt that the author of *MacPherson* is a Realist and not a Moralist when it comes to understanding what judges really do, at least some of the time. Dworkin often takes Judge Posner to task for purporting to renounce moral theory, while at the same

talk about "duty" (but no one denies that), but, more ambitiously, they also argue that the decision identified the manufacturer's duty as growing out of "the line of cases dealing with 'inherently dangerous' products" (ibid., 1814), that these "'thing of danger' cases were not a haphazard collection" (ibid., 1815) but rather give rise to a principle about the duty of care manufacturers owe to non-privy parties that arises under three specific conditions which Goldberg and Zipursky characterize in detail (without quoting Cardozo) (ibid.). Goldberg and Zipursky's reconstruction of Cardozo is more amenable to Dworkin's justificatory ascent story, but it seems to this reader a "just so" story in tension with Cardozo's own understanding of the cases and his decision (see below, in the text), and with the "haphazard" line of cases that Levi describes.

[81] Benjamin N. Cardozo, *The Growth of the Law* (Yale University Press, 1924), 41.

[82] Ibid., 54. See, too, Cardozo's discussion of one of the seminal cases in the history of English contract law, *Strangborough v. Warner* from 1588, about which he observes: "Before the rendition of that judgment, we cannot say with justice that there was a preexisting principle or rule which the judges were extending or applying. They formulated the rule or principle for themselves, and gave it potency thereafter by a process of creation." Ibid., 39.

[83] Benjamin N. Cardozo, *The Nature of the Judicial Process* (Yale University Press, 1923).

[84] Ibid., 10.

[85] Ibid., 129.

[86] Ibid., 115.

time asking judges to reach the "best" decisions, on crudely utilitarian grounds, without excessive regard for past practice, except to the extent that practice had affected reasonable expectations. As Dworkin has quite plausibly argued, Posner "is himself ruled by an inarticulate, subterranean . . . but relentless moral faith,"[87] namely, in the utilitarian perspective that informs his analyses of concrete legal problems. Perhaps Cardozo was, himself, so too ruled? He does say, after all, in *The Nature of the Judicial Process* that, "when [judges] are called upon to say how far existing rules are to be extended or restricted, they must let the welfare of society fix the path, its direction, and its distance."[88] And it is, of course, now familiar to read Cardozo as a proto-economic analyst of the law, designing rules that would minimize the costs of accidents.

Perhaps these facts might explain a subject on which Dworkin has always remained oddly silent, namely, the extraordinary influence of Judge Posner's opinions (just like Judge Cardozo's) with other courts,[89] which might suggest that, even without theoretical foundations, Posner is the proverbial Hegelian "Owl of Minerva," who has captured the moral ethos of his time and place. That Dworkin's own writings about concrete legal problems, by contrast, have had almost no influence at all on the American courts[90] might also be thought confirmation of Judge Posner's infamous skepticism about moral theory,[91] at least

[87] Dworkin, *Justice in Robes*, 94.

[88] Cardozo, *The Nature of the Judicial Process*, 67.

[89] See William M. Landes, Lawrence Lessig, and Michael E. Solimine, "Judicial Influence: A Citation Analysis of Federal Courts of Appeals Judges," *Journal of Legal Studies* 27 (1998): 291–318, ranking Richard Posner at or near the top of various statistical analyses of the influence of federal courts of appeals judges, while noting that this outsize influence may be due in part to the fact that judges on the Seventh Circuit "publish more signed opinions per year than do judges in other circuits"; see also Jeffrey S. Sutton, "A Review of Richard A. Posner, *How Judges Think* (2008)," *Michigan Law Review* 108 (2010): 859, 859–60, noting that Richard Posner "is a judge who has left a deep imprint on American law, frequently including decisions of the United States Supreme Court." Sutton, a judge on the US Court of Appeals for the Sixth Circuit, ibid., at 859 n.*, also writes that "I often look to him for insights in resolving difficult cases of my own, telling my clerks, 'See if Posner has written anything on the topic.' Other judges, I suspect, do the same thing." Ibid., 860.

[90] For example, Ronald Dworkin's writings have only been cited in seven Supreme Court decisions, most in dissents or concurring opinions. See Washington v. Glucksberg, 521 U.S. 702, 747 (1997) (Stevens, J., concurring in the judgments) (quoting Ronald Dworkin, *Life's Dominion: An Argument About Abortion, Euthanasia, and Individual Freedom* (Alfred A. Knopf, 1993), 213); Planned Parenthood of Se. Pa. v. Casey, 505 U.S. 833, 914 n.2 (1992) (Stevens, J., concurring in part and dissenting in part) (quoting Ronald Dworkin, "Unenumerated Rights: Whether and How Roe Should Be Overruled," *University of Chicago Law Review* 59 (1992): 381, 400–1); Webster v. Reprod. Health Servs., 492 U.S. 490, 539 n.1 (1989) (Blackmun, J., concurring in part and dissenting in part) (citing Ronald Dworkin, "The Great Abortion Case," *New York Review of Books*, June 29, 1989, at 49); Bd. of Pardons v. Allen, 482 U.S. 369, 375-76 (1987) (quoting Ronald Dworkin, *Taking Rights Seriously* (Harvard University Press, 1977), 31–32, 69); Young v. Cmty. Nutrition Inst., 476 U.S. 974, 988 (1986) (Stevens, J., dissenting) (quoting Dworkin, *Law's Empire*, 352); Delaware v. Van Arsdall, 475 U.S. 673, 697 n.9 (1986) (Stevens, J., dissenting) (quoting Dworkin, *Taking*, 198–99); Hewitt v. Helms, 459 U.S. 460, 484–85 (1983) (Stevens, J., dissenting) (quoting Dworkin, *Taking*, 263).

[91] Richard Posner, *The Problematics of Moral and Legal Theory* (Harvard University Press, 1999). I am in the somewhat odd position of being a philosopher by training who is basically in agreement

if we agree that Dworkin is the more skillful moral theorist. In any case, when Dworkin castigates Posner as purportedly "avoiding moral theory but keeping its use dark, cloaked under all the familiar phlogistons like the mysterious craft of lawyerlike analogical reasoning," one thinks that Posner might as easily have castigated him for not acknowledging the role of lawmaking by courts "but keeping its use dark, cloaked under all the familiar phlogistons like the mysterious justificatory ascent."

How are we to adjudicate this dispute between Moralists like Dworkin and Realists like Posner about adjudication? At bottom, as Nietzsche noticed long ago, such fundamental philosophical disputes often seem to reflect differences of temperament and disposition.[92] In this instance, the Moralist finds solace in a vision of how the world works that is morally upright and defensible, while the Realist expresses his impatience with what he deems childish illusion and empty rhetorical posturing. Is there any more to be said, or must we simply declare our allegiance (predetermined or otherwise) to one temperament or the other? Notice that the Moralist Dworkin and the Realist Posner need have no dispute about the epistemology of judicial decision, only about its metaphysics. Dworkin can agree that Cardozo in *MacPherson* takes himself to be crafting a new utility-maximizing rule for changed economic circumstances, and still insist that, in reality, his decision can be understood as an exercise in "justificatory ascent"—that is, that the outcome in *MacPherson* was, in fact, required by the "logic" of legal reasoning over all the prior cases surveyed by Levi and cited by Cardozo.[93] To be sure, that was not Cardozo's view or Levi's, but they, so Dworkin must contend, are confusing their Realism about the process by which the result was reached, with the metaphysical question whether there exists a right answer as a matter of law.[94] The hope that there is a "justificatory ascent" story to be told about the

with Posner's skepticism. See, e.g., Brian Leiter, "Marxism and the Continuing Irrelevance of Normative Theory," *Stanford Law Review* 54 (2002): 1127–49, as well as ch. 17 in this volume. My Nietzschean and Marxian sympathies in philosophy no doubt explain my heresy.

92 See generally Brian Leiter, "The History of Philosophy Reveals that 'Great' Philosophy is Disguised Moral Advocacy: A Nietzschean Case Against the Socratic Canon in Philosophy," in *Proceedings of the British Academy 214: Philosophy and the Historical Perspective*, ed. M. van Ackern (Oxford University Press, 2018), 185–99.

93 This, in effect, is what Goldberg and Zipursky do. See Goldberg and Zipursky, "The Moral of *MacPherson*."

94 This has been Dworkin's familiar rhetorical trope throughout his career: to be sure, he allows, reasonable judges and lawyers disagree about the right answer as a matter of law, but that fact about our epistemic situation settles nothing about whether such an answer really exists. But the skeptic about right answers need not, as Dworkin falsely claims, be committed to "verificationism"—roughly, the view that there are no nonverifiable truths or right answers—he need only ask what the best explanation for intractable disagreement about the truth really is. Dworkin, *Taking*, 279–90. If there were right answers, one would expect, absent a non-question-begging specification of cognitive defects, that jurists would converge on them. If they do not converge, one natural explanation is that there is nothing there to converge upon; that is, there is no fact of the matter, no right answer

decision in *MacPherson* is just the Moralist's hope that the decision conforms to what Dworkin takes to be a morally attractive picture of adjudication, in which courts always aspire to find rather than make the law, and in which all possibly relevant moral considerations are, themselves, always part of the fabric of the law that is binding on the judge. It is an uplifting picture and aspiration, but is it, says the Realist, complete obscurantist nonsense, denying the cogency of the settled law prior to *MacPherson*, as well as Cardozo's genius in his quasi-legislative role as law reformer transforming antiquated rules of liability in response to the demands of a new economy?

VI. From Dworkin and Rawls to Posner and Geuss: Moral Theory vs. Moral Entrepreneurs

Raymond Geuss, in defending Thucydides's Realism against Plato's Moralism, remarks, "What Plato takes to be morally reprehensible behavior must, he thinks, finally be a form of irrationality that is self-defeating, and this puts such narrow limits to his ability to understand humans that it renders him unfit to be a serious guide to the world in which we live."[95] Thucydides, by contrast, fully appreciates that historical actors can be both quite rational and morally abhorrent, which is one of several reasons why his *History* is a source of insight into historical events more than two thousand years after its composition.

But might we not have a similar worry about the Dworkinian Moralist, namely, that he is "unfit to be a serious guide to the world in which we live"? After all, if we were all Dworkinian Moralists, then we would take every judicial opinion at face value, and never inquire into the politics or the individual or group psychology of the decisions, as Realists like Posner and Llewellyn and the contemporary political scientists do. We would only ask about the theory of "justificatory ascent" that supports the decision, and never entertain the hypothesis that the best way to make sense of what judges like Cardozo or tribunals like the US Supreme Court[96] are really doing is that they are making decisions on nonlegal grounds and then offering legalistic window dressing for those quasi-legislative decisions. As Geuss notes, when "the most reflective members [of society] are committed to the search for abstract definitions, general principles, [and] dialectically sustainable hypotheses . . . Thucydidean political thinking informed by a study of the reality of what actually happens will be likely to wither away."[97] Dworkin's

to discover. See generally Brian Leiter, "Objectivity, Morality, and Adjudication," in *Naturalizing Jurisprudence*, and especially ch. 15 of this volume.

[95] Geuss, *Outside Ethics*, 220.
[96] See ch. 12 in this volume.
[97] Geuss, *Outside Ethics*, 230.

"nonsense jurisprudence" has almost nothing to do with "what actually happens" in the courts: it is a just-so story, about "justificatory ascent," constructed after-the-fact— constructed, moreover, even in cases like *MacPherson* where the central actor, namely Cardozo, renounces the Moralist's story!

Yet is it any worse for that? Why should we *not* articulate ideal standards of conduct, even if they currently have no purchase in actual practice? It cannot simply be because of Geuss's curious worry about deflecting "reflective members" of society from Thucydidean political thinking! After all, most academic disciplines that might be interested in empirical study of political and social life—political science, economics, sociology, anthropology, social psychology—are notoriously unaffected by academic philosophy, with its emphasis on "abstract definitions, general principles, [and] dialectically sustainable hypotheses."[98] Why not let "a thousand flowers bloom"? Let the academic moralists in philosophy articulate ideal standards of conduct, and let the empiricists tell us what is *really* happening now? The latter do not seem to be dissuaded by the activities of the former.

This is the dilemma over which Geuss's recent Realist broadside[99] against Anglophone political philosophy, as exemplified by Rawls, founders. On the one hand, Geuss suggests that we should "reject" a Moralistic approach to politics according to which we do ideal ethical theory first (a theory that abstracts from empirical particulars) and in which politics is then just a kind of applied ethics.[100] Yet he admits that he thereby fails to "distinguish sharply between a descriptive theory and a 'pure normative theory' (the former purportedly giving just the facts; the latter moral principles, imperatives, or ideal norms)."[101] But why shouldn't he distinguish between those two kinds of theoretical inquiries, one "Realistic" and one "Moralistic" in the terminology I have been using here? His reasons for repudiating this "is/ought distinction" as he calls it are, alas, utterly obscure.[102]

And yet the particulars of Geuss's indictment of Rawlsian Moralism in political philosophy are in many ways damning.[103] As he observes,

[98] Ibid.

[99] Raymond Geuss, *Philosophy and Real Politics* (Princeton University Press, 2008). See also *Outside Ethics*, chs. 1 and 2, which in many ways constitute a more effective polemic; its criticisms of Rawls, in particular, are more cogent than those in *Philosophy and Real Politics*.

[100] Ibid., at 7–9.

[101] Ibid., at 16.

[102] See ibid., 16–17. I have no idea what the argument is here, or if there even is one.

[103] The attack in *Philosophy and Real Politics* is, it seems to me, less successful, involving often sophomoric mischaracterization of the Rawlsian view—for example, in complaining that "the 'original position' is obviously not at all a very good model for political deliberation or action" (ibid., 72), when Rawls, of course, never presented it as any such thing!

> [I]t is extremely striking, not to say astounding, to the lay reader that the complex theoretical apparatus of *Theory of Justice*, operating through over 500 pages of densely argued text, eventuates in a constitutional structure that is a virtual replica (with some extremely minor deviations) of the arrangements that exist in the United States.[104]

A version of that charge has long been familiar with respect to Dworkin's jurisprudence as a theoretical rationalization of the decisions of the Warren Court.[105] And just "as Rawls's purportedly egalitarian theory became more entrenched and more highly elaborated, social inequalities in fact increased drastically in virtually all industrialized countries,"[106] so too the elaboration of Dworkin's jurisprudential theory (though without the same army of acolytes) over the past fifty years has coincided with the demise of his preferred picture of constitutional adjudication.

Again, though, we may ask what conclusions to draw from this. The time frame in which a highly articulated moral theory makes its impact (if it makes any) may be longer than a generation or two, so the fact that the theory has had little or no impact on practice so far is hardly an objection.[107] As Nietzsche says in *Thus*

[104] Geuss, *Outside Ethics*, 23. Cf. Geuss, *Philosophy and Real Politics*, 90.

[105] See, e.g., Daniel A. Farber and Suzanna Sherry, *Desperately Seeking Certainty: The Misguided Quest for Constitutional Foundations* (University of Chicago Press, 2004), 122–23 (noting that, while the authors themselves found Dworkin's views "unexpectedly nuanced and illuminating," nonetheless "Dworkin's conclusions track the agenda of liberal judges like William Brennan, opening Dworkin to the charge of being merely a clever rationalizer"); Lino A. Graglia, "'Interpreting' the Constitution: Posner on Bork," *Stanford Law Review* 44 (1992): 1019, 1022 ("Because leftward is the direction generally favored by Dworkin, Ackerman, and nearly all of their fellow constitutional theorists, they have taken it as their professional responsibility to seek justification for what the courts have done"); cf. Raoul Berger, "The Founders' Views-According to Jefferson Powell," *Texas Law Review* 67 (1989): 1033, 1076 (citing Ronald Dworkin's writing as an example of "[a]ctivist apologetics for [the Warren Court's] judicial revision of the Constitution [that] often exhibit a cavalier attitude toward historical evidence").

[106] Geuss, *Outside Ethics*, 34. Geuss offers a number of interesting, and prima facie plausible, explanations for the success of Rawlsian Moralism in political philosophy, even in the face of growing inequality and un-Rawlsian outcomes in society at large. He suggests, for example, that "Rawls's theory gained in attractiveness as a compensatory fantasy," that is, as compensating for "inability to understand or exercise any control over" the actual world. Ibid., 35. Alternatively, Geuss notes that, "Rawls's system . . . is intricately elaborated and self-contained, and it also claims to embody a particularly well-grounded moral view of the world. Perhaps the pleasure in discussing such an aesthetically attractive and purportedly morally serious construction, and the associated sense of being part of an elite group of people who are both very clever and highly righteous, is a sufficient explanation of the omnipresence of the theory." Ibid., 36–37. He omits an equally important consideration, namely, the emergence of normative moral and political philosophy as an area of professional specialization precisely during the massive expansion of higher education in the 1960s. The Rawls industry is surely, in part, a consequence of the creation of a professional infrastructure supporting academic careers in its service.

[107] In her spirited response to Judge Posner's polemic against academic moral theory, Martha Nussbaum calls attention to purported examples in which philosophical "arguments have mattered in public life," including "the influence of Locke and Montesquieu on the American founding" and "the influence of Marx on many modern governments" and "the influence of John Dewey on American education." Martha Nussbaum, "Still Worthy of Praise," *Harvard Law Review* 111

Spoke Zarathustra, the world "revolves" around the creators of new values.[108] The crucial question is whether systematic, discursive moral philosophers are those creators. Nietzsche certainly did not think so,[109] nor, I take it, does Posner—a point to which we return, below.

There is another objection to the method of Rawlsian Moralism about politics worth noting, namely, its inherent conservatism given its methodology.[110] As Geuss puts it:

(1998): 1776, 1779–80. The examples are striking, however, for how well they actually confirm Judge Posner's thesis. No one, including Professor Nussbaum, thinks that the American Revolution was brought about by arguments from Locke; to the contrary, the Revolution is most plausibly explained by a variety of more familiar economic and power-seeking motivations by elites in the American colonies. (The classic source is Charles A. Beard, *An Economic Interpretation of the Constitution of the United States* (Macmillan, 1913). And see, more recently, *The U.S. Constitution: 200 Years of Anti-Federalist, Abolitionist, Feminist, Muckraking, Progressive, and Especially Socialist Criticism*, ed. B. Ollman and J. Birnbaum (New York University Press, 1990); Michael J. Klarman, *The Framer's Coup: The Making of the United States Constitution* (Oxford University Press, 2016).) Locke's conclusions, not his arguments, proved useful fodder for those instigating the revolt. The Marx example is even worse: He developed no moral or political theory, no arguments about the injustice of capitalism, no Marxian counterpart to the Rawlsian theory of justice. Instead, Marx, in both his popular polemics (of which there were many) and his scholarly investigations, exposed the mechanisms by which capitalism operated and its effects on the vast majority. Marx took for granted, quite reasonably, that the victims of capitalism (whom he thought were multiplying) were motivated to do something *once they understand, realistically, what was really happening to them*. Dewey shared with Marx a skill at popular prose and polemics; his poor reputation among academic philosophers, to the present, is some evidence that his influence on pedagogy, to the extent it is real (even at the University of Chicago Lab School, which he founded, his "influence" is nowhere felt much beyond the second or third grade), was due more to his skills as a moral entrepreneur than his philosophical acumen. What Professor Nussbaum misses is that the case against the efficacy of "academic moralism" is a case against the ability of systematic, discursive reasoning to change people's views and motivate action.

It is often suggested to me that a stronger case for the practical import of moral philosophy is Peter Singer's influence on the animal rights movement. Yet even Singer has admitted that the most influential part of his book *Animal Liberation* was chapter 3, which was an evocative *description* of factory farming, one designed to elicit a strong emotional reaction from those with a pre-existing empathy for animals and sensitivity to apparent suffering. See Singer's reply to Judge Richard Posner, in Peter Singer vs Richard Posner, "Animal Rights," *Slate*, June 13, 2001: http://www.slate.com/articles/news_and_politics/dialogues/features/2001/animal_rights/_4.html

> That the quality of the discursive reasoning has little or nothing to do with Singer's purported influence on "animal rights" should be evident from the fact that the line of reasoning—based on the moral importance of sentience and the utilitarian imperative to maximize pleasure over pain—that leads Singer to vegetarianism also leads him, quite naturally, to positions that are widely rejected and denounced, such as his willingness to countenance infanticide and the killing of the handicapped. Singer draws the correct conclusions from his premises; if people were *actually* influenced by his arguments, then there would be as many advocates for infanticide of the mentally defective as there are for not eating meat.

[108] Friedrich Nietzsche, "The Flies in the Marketplace," *Thus Spoke Zarathustra: A Book for All and None, in The Portable Nietzsche*, 103, 164.

[109] As Nietzsche says about Kant and Hegel in *Beyond Good and Evil*, they merely "press into formulas" existing valuations. *Beyond Good and Evil*, section 211.

[110] Obviously this sense of "conservatism" has little to do with the use of the term current in the United States, where it mostly picks out views that involve a retreat from the status quo, not an attempt to conserve it.

> Despite the conscientious angst of Rawls the man, and his openness to well-focused criticism of individual sections of his work, the structure and ethos of this theory as a whole is deeply complacent, not to say smug. We who have the great good fortune to live in countries that are sufficiently like the United States in structure have got our politics basically right; all we really need to do is fine-tune our economies in various ways, particularly so as to maximize equality (while respecting the principle of difference). . . . [A] major danger in using highly abstractive methods in political philosophy is that one will succeed merely in generalizing one's own local prejudices and repackaging them as demands of reason. . . . Rawls [on this view] is not a major moral and political theorist, whose work self-evidently deserves and repays the most careful scrutiny. Rather he was a parochial figure who not only failed to advance the subject but also pointed political philosophy firmly in the wrong direction.[111]

R. M. Hare, the late White's Professor of Moral Philosophy at Oxford (who, unlike Geuss, is certainly no critical theorist), identified more than a generation ago the source of the conservatism, namely, in the method of "reflective equilibrium" (RE) central to Rawls's theory of justice.[112] In this method for doing normative philosophy, we test our general theory—of justice, or of what is morally right, or of what is good—against our intuitive judgments about particular moral cases, and we either adjust our theory to do justice to the intuitions or give up some of our intuitions about the particular cases, until we achieve a theoretical equilibrium between the two. But as Hare scathingly, and correctly, observed:

> It is certainly possible, as some thinkers even of our times have done, to collect all the moral opinions of which they and their contemporaries feel most sure, find some relatively simple method or apparatus which can be represented, with a bit of give and take, and making plausible assumptions about the circumstances of life, as generating all these opinions; and then pronounce that that is the moral system which, having reflected, we must acknowledge to be the correct one. But they have absolutely no authority for this claim beyond the original convictions, for which no ground or argument was given. The "equilibrium" they have reached is one between forces which might have been generated by prejudice, and no amount of reflection can make that a solid basis for morality.[113]

[111] Geuss, *Outside Ethics*, 38–39.

[112] See generally R. M. Hare, "Rawls' Theory of Justice—1," *The Philosophical Quarterly* 23 (1973): 144 (reviewing John Rawls, *A Theory of Justice* (Belknap Press, 1971)).

[113] R. M. Hare, *Moral Thinking: Its Levels, Method and Point* (Clarendon Press, 1981), 12. Hare does not, however, draw the skeptical (and, in my view, correct) conclusion that morality lacks a solid basis, but instead thinks its content follows from claims about the logic of moral language.

The now notorious parochialism of the method of RE afflicts subjects far afield of ethics,[114] but it is the case of Rawlsian Moralism that concerns us here.[115] Is Moralism in political or legal theory *necessarily* conservative in the way Rawls is?[116] Why should it be once severed from the method of RE?

Yet we may also fairly ask if anything other than moral exhortation, polemics and rhetoric is left once RE is off the table.[117] RE had the advantage of all methods of "internal" critique, of appealing to what it is the audience already believed, however inchoately. But if we are not going to systematize and make theoretically explicit inchoate moral commitments we already share (as the later Rawls claims he is doing), what *can* we do except become what Judge Posner has aptly dubbed "moral entrepreneurs"—rhetoricians who aim to change fundamental moral commitments? His prime example is feminist theorist and advocate Catharine

Hare's positive program has, it is fair to say, been a failure, inspiring nothing comparable to the Rawls industry.

[114] See, e.g., Robert Cummins, "Reflections on Reflective Equilibrium," in *Rethinking Intuition: The Psychology of Intuition and Its Role in Philosophical Inquiry*, ed. Michael DePaul and William Ramsey (Oxford, 1998) (discussing kindred problem in philosophy of mind); Jaakko Hintikka, "The Emperor's New Intuitions," *Journal of Philosophy* 96 (1999): 127 (same, for philosophy of language); Jonathan Weinberg, Shaun Nichols, and Stephen Stich, "Normativity and Epistemic Intuitions," *Philosophical Topics* 29 (2001): 429 (same, for epistemology).

[115] In an otherwise judicious critical review of *Philosophy and Real Politics*, Samuel Freeman's response to this kind of worry is telling. He writes: "[G]iven that we have to begin somewhere in moral theorizing, it seems more reasonable to begin with our considered moral and evaluative intuitions rather than with anyone else's or anywhere else." Samuel Freeman, Book Review, *Ethics* 120 (2009): 175, 181. No argument is given for this assumption, or the assumption—surely the main one that Geuss, Posner, Marx, et al. deny—namely, that we need to "begin" moral *theorizing* at all.

[116] The conservativism of the Rawlsian approach is most clear in one of his last, and least successful works, *The Law of Peoples*, which, as Geuss notes, "even on the most superficial inspection" articulates "a specifically American political position—more enlightened, perhaps, than that of George W. Bush or Condoleezza Rice, but generically the same kind of thing. Of course, no one can object *in principle* to citizens helping to elaborate the national ideology (provided it is not actively vicious), but philosophy has in the past aspired to something more than that." Geuss, *Outside Ethics*, 34.

[117] I am assuming that the goal of moral and political philosophy is to have some influence upon practice or at least on what others believe, but that is a controversial assumption and not one shared by all (or maybe even most) moral and political philosophers. As the Harvard moral philosopher T. M. Scanlon observed, responding to Posner's critique of "academic moralism":

> "Posner gets off on the wrong foot . . . by assuming that the only point of moral philosophy is to convince people to change their moral views. This is one of the reasons that I do not find his book very enlightening or challenging. My aims in engaging in moral philosophy are (1) to get a clearer understanding of what kind of question I am thinking about in thinking about right and wrong and (2) to make up my mind what to think about it (both how to understand certain crucial terms such as rights, blame, responsibility, and so on, and which moral claims to accept.). . . . Insofar as I find my thoughts about morality to be unclear and conflicted, I imagine that some others may share these difficulties. So if I come up with what seems to me a satisfactory way of resolving one of them, I imagine that others might take these thoughts into account in deciding what to think. But persuading them to do so is not my main aim."

Tim Scanlon, Comment to Posner's Pragmatic Moral Skepticism (Nadelhoffer), *Leiter Reports* (June 21, 2006, 4:45 PM), http://leiterreports.typepad.comIblog/2006/06/posners-pragmat.html.

MacKinnon: "Her influential version of radical feminism is not offered without supporting arguments. But her influence is not due to the quality of those arguments. It is due to her polemical skills, her single-mindedness, her passion."[118] MacKinnon's work, even her most theoretically ambitious work,[119] is notorious for its analytical and argumentative weaknesses: It is no one's idea of sound moral or political philosophy. And yet her ideas have changed the law and the discourse about women and feminism well beyond the walls of the academy. It has done so through the rhetorical power by which MacKinnon forces readers to see inequities in the treatment of women heretofore rendered invisible, but which, when illuminated with MacKinnon's polemical prose, arouse her readers' preexisting distaste and antipathy for such injustice.

Judge Posner has a straightforward explanation for MacKinnon's success (and Dworkin's and Rawls's failure), based on the assumption (shared by Hume and Nietzsche, among others) that there is no necessary or intrinsic connection between knowing what is morally right[120] and being motivated to act accordingly. On the Humean/Nietzschean view, only if some idea engages our preexisting desires or emotions can it give rise to motivation and action. Thus, Judge Posner claims that academic moral theory, of the Rawlsian or Dworkinian kind,

> has no prospect of improving human behavior. Knowing the moral thing to do furnishes no motive, and creates no motivation. Motive and motivation have to come from outside morality. Even if this is wrong, the analytical tools employed in academic moralism—whether moral casuistry, or reasoning from the canonical texts of moral philosophy, or careful analysis, or reflective equilibrium, or some combination of these tools—are too feeble to override either narrow self-interest or [pre-existing] moral intuitions. And academic moralists have neither the rhetorical skills nor the factual knowledge that might enable them to persuade without having good methods of inquiry and analysis. As a result of its analytical, rhetorical, and factual deficiencies, academic moralism is helpless when intuitions clash or self-interest opposes, and otiose when they line up.[121]

We could hardly invent a more stunning confirmation of Judge Posner's Realist skepticism about Moralism than the reaction to an important book of moral and political philosophy by the late Chichele Professor of Social and Political Theory

[118] Posner, *Problematics*, 42–44. Judge Posner also suggests that her difficulties getting tenure constituted a kind of academic martyrdom that helped her cause, but that strikes me as implausible speculation for which he adduces no evidence.

[119] See, e.g., Catharine MacKinnon, *Towards a Feminist Theory of the State* (Harvard University Press, 1989).

[120] Or: believing one knows what is morally right.

[121] Posner, *Problematics*, 7.

at Oxford, G. A. Cohen, *If You're an Egalitarian, How Come You're So Rich?*,[122] a book whose title was a jab at Dworkin, the egalitarian political philosopher who jets between luxurious homes in London and New York. Cohen argues that genuine egalitarians (at least those who are not welfarists) are moral hypocrites if they do not give away significant portions of their money consistent with their egalitarian principles.[123] The argument is careful and often ingenious.

Now consider the response of a committed liberal, and nonwelfarist, egalitarian like Thomas Nagel:

> I have to admit that, although I am an adherent of the liberal conception of [justice and equality], I don't have an answer to Cohen's charge of moral incoherence. It is hard to render consistent the exemption of private choice from the motives that support redistributive public policies. I could sign a standing banker's order giving away everything I earn above the national average, for example, and it wouldn't kill me. I could even try to increase my income at the same time, knowing the excess would go to people who needed it more than I did. I'm not about to do anything of the kind, but the equality-friendly justifications I can think of for not doing so all strike me as rationalizations.[124]

If high-quality moral theory cannot even influence high-quality moral philosophers to change their behavior, then why in the world should we resist Judge Posner's Realist conclusion that Moralism "has no prospect of improving human behavior"?[125]

Here, then, is a Realist conclusion on which thinkers as different as Hume, Marx, Nietzsche, and Posner converge: Unless a normative position engages the antecedently existing desires, passions, and emotions of persons, it will get no purchase in practice. No discursively articulated system of moral norms will yield action unless the actors are already affectively disposed to the force of those norms. But if that is correct, then normative theorizing can serve only two *practical* purposes, namely, (1) to make vivid to the agent what he or she is already disposed to care about, or (2) to change the affective predispositions of its audience, such that they will care about, or value, other things. Since affective dispositions are nonrational, the medium of traditional philosophy—discursive reasoning—will be causally inert with respect to (2). And *vivid* and *emotionally moving* representation of what the agent is already disposed to care about

[122] G. A. Cohen, *If You're An Egalitarian, How Come You're So Rich?* (Harvard University Press, 2000).

[123] Ibid., 148–79.

[124] Thomas Nagel, "Getting Personal: Why Don't Egalitarians Give away Their Own Money?" *Times Literary Supplement*, June 23, 2000, 6.

[125] Posner, *Problematics*, 7.

has never been the strong suit of traditional philosophy, per (1).[126] So for both purposes, it seems moral entrepreneurs like MacKinnon, Nietzsche, or Marx will be far more effective than Moralistic philosophers like Rawls or Dworkin. Judge Posner's impact on his fellow judges and academic contemporaries, on this account, is not attributable to his superior skills of rational discursiveness but to his being the more effective moral entrepreneur, one who exploits the antecedent intuitions of jurists in a thoroughly capitalist and commercialized society, for whom "efficiency" and welfare-maximization require no argument.[127]

There is a further consideration that supports skepticism about the efficacy of Moralism, and that is an obvious complement to what I have been calling the Humean/Nietzschean view embraced by Realists like Posner (and also, arguably, Llewellyn). If one thinks—as Hume, Nietzsche, and Posner do—that there are no moral truths, then there is nothing to *know* about what's morally right and wrong that could be the upshot of discursive reasoning. More precisely, on this view, there's nothing to *know* that's *distinctively moral*, since, of course, rational inquiry might illuminate nonmoral facts that causally affect one's moral judgments (if I think efficiency is good, and discover through rational inquiry that the nonmoral fact that a certain rule maximizes efficiency, then I will change my moral judgment).[128] To the extent moral theory is committed to systematic discursive reasoning about the *moral*, its target is an illusion: there is no subject matter there about which one could make a cognitive mistake.[129] Arouse the passions, or make vivid the nonmoral facts, and one might well cause a change in moral view. Discursive reasoning of the kind practiced by systematic moral philosophers can do neither.

[126] Even Nussbaum, in her rejoinder to Judge Posner, admits as much: "the jargon-laden nonwriting of the philosophical journals is a good style for persuading no human being . . ." Nussbaum, *Still Worthy of Praise*, 1795.

[127] As Judge Posner writes: "I do not argue that economic analysis should convince opponents of [a particular position recommended by economic analysis] to give up their opposition. I do not believe that economics (or any other body of thought, for that matter) can compel a moral judgment." Richard A. Posner, *Frontiers of Legal Theory* (Harvard University Press, 2001), 47.

[128] See generally Brian Leiter, "Objectivity, Morality, and Adjudication," in *Naturalizing Jurisprudence*, 251–55. And for classic discussions, see Alfred Jules Ayer, *Language, Truth and Logic* (Oxford University Press, 1936); Charles L. Stevenson, *Ethics and Language* (Yale University Press, 1944).

[129] To be sure, there may be a sociological datum, like the "intuitions" of bourgeois academics who have been appropriately socialized, but it is hard to see why armchair sociology masquerading as moral philosophy will be compelling to those who don't share the relevant socialization experiences.

VII. Conclusion

Praise for Realism is praise for clarity about *what really happens*, since what really happens is the very stuff on which instrumental reasoning—reasoning about how to achieve what we already want or prefer or value—operates. By the same token, opposition to Moralism is not opposition to entrepreneurial advocacy for a normative vision, to moral polemics, and skillful rhetoric: People change their moral views, to be sure, but they do so, as Humeans and Nietzscheans claim, because their passions and emotions are suitably engaged and aroused, not because they follow through the conclusions of discursive reasoning—since such reasoning can establish the *truth* of no moral position. If there is a case for Realism and against Moralism—whether in the form of "nonsense jurisprudence" or Rawlsian political philosophy—it is captured by a paraphrase of Marx's second *Thesis on Feuerbach*: a philosophical dispute "which is isolated from practice is a purely *scholastic* question." If one subscribes, as I do, to Judge Posner's Humean/Nietzschean assumptions about how moral views change (as well as their moral skepticism), then the case against Moralism, whether Rawlsian or Dworkinian, is complete.[130]

[130] An early version of this essay was presented as the Dunbar Lecture in Law and Philosophy at the University of Mississippi in 2008 and as the 1st Annual Distinguished Lecture in Jurisprudence at Northwestern University School of Law in 2009; I am grateful to the audiences on both occasions for their questions. That version also benefited from workshops at the law schools at Arizona State University, University of Miami, University of Tulsa, and the University of Wisconsin at Madison. A later version was subjected to constructive criticism at a work-in-progress session with colleagues at the University of Chicago Law School; I should mention especially comments or questions from Aziz Huq, Jonathan Masur, Richard McAdams, Martha Nussbaum, David Strauss, and David Weisbach. I am grateful to Mark Gergen for helpful advice on privity; to Adam Hosein for useful discussion of Geuss's realism in political theory; and to Thomas Miles and Richard Posner for comments on a very early draft.

12

Constitutional Law, Moral Judgment, and the Supreme Court as Super-Legislature

I. Introduction

I propose to defend and explore three claims in this essay. First, there is very little actual "law" in federal constitutional law in the United States, especially with respect to cases that end up at the US Supreme Court: There, the Court operates as a kind of super-legislature, albeit one with a limited jurisdiction. The jurisdiction is limited in two important ways: First, the Court can only pass on issues that are brought before it; and second, the Court is "constrained," to some extent, by past decisions of the Court and by constitutional and legislative texts. The problem, however, is that the constraints *underdetermine* the Court's decisions in most cases, so the Court essentially makes its final choice among the legally viable options based on the moral and political values of the Justices, and not simply on the basis of legally binding standards.[1] The latter claim is, in part, a jurisprudential thesis about what counts as "legally binding standards," one that I shall defend by reference to the most plausible account of the nature of law, the legal positivist theory developed by H. L. A. Hart. Second, the absence of law in so many parts of federal constitutional law means that the quality of moral and political judgment exercised by judges is of decisive importance in how they fulfill their role and thus should be the overriding factor in the appointment of federal appellate judges, especially Supreme Court Justices. That brings me to my third claim, namely, that all political actors know that the US Supreme Court often operates as a super-legislature, and thus that the moral and political views of the Justices are decisive criteria for their appointment. This almost banal truth is, however, rarely discussed in the public confirmation process, but is common knowledge among political and legal insiders. To be sure, there is media speculation about the political predilections of the nominees, but their actual moral and political views are treated as off limits in the real confirmation process. This

[1] Even when the precedential "constraint" is clear, the Supreme Court always has the option of overruling itself. The only limit on doing so is political backlash. See Michel Troper's discussion of the idea that in the highest court "anything goes," and the only limits are political, not legal in his "Legal Realism in France," in L. Green & B. Leiter (eds.), *Oxford Studies in Philosophy of Law, volume 5* (Oxford University Press, 2025), 153-155.

From a Realist Point of View. Brian Leiter, Oxford University Press. © Brian Leiter 2026.
DOI: 10.1093/9780197749852.003.0014

antidemocratic secrecy is, in my view, deeply wrong and must be replaced with a realistic acknowledgment of the role of the Supreme Court as a political actor of limited jurisdiction. I will illustrate these claims by discussing a number of important public law cases, recent and not so recent.

II. There Is Very Little "Law" in American Constitutional Law: Hart and the Rule of Recognition

What does it mean to say there is very little "law" in American constitutional law? That requires us to have some view about what it means to say law exists, and so I must begin with some discussion of basic jurisprudential questions. I will here follow the most promising theory about the nature of law, the legal positivism of H. L. A. Hart and his student Joseph Raz.[2] Let us start with some terminology. Human societies are awash in norms, by which I mean demands of the form, "You ought to do X" or "You ought not do Y."[3] Some norms are merely norms of etiquette: for example, "You ought not talk on your cell phone during the lecture" or "You ought not talk with your mouth full at the table." Others are norms of prudence or self-interest: "You ought to attend class, lest you fail the exam!" Some are moral norms: "You ought to consider how your actions will affect the well-being of others." And some are *norms of the legal system*, for example, "You ought not go faster than 55 mph on the highway." The categories are not mutually exclusive: Sometimes moral norms (e.g., "You ought not murder innocents") are also legal norms, and sometimes norms of prudence are too (e.g., "You must wear a seatbelt while driving"). Norms of etiquette are rarely legal norms in modern legal systems; many moral norms are not legal ones, and many legal norms are not ones we think of as representing moral or ethical obligations (we do not think the English are immoral for driving on the left rather than the right, but we recognize they have a legal obligation to do so). The jurisprudential question is: How do we mark the difference? And the legal positivist answer is: Norms are *legally valid* (i.e., norms of the legal system) by virtue of satisfying criteria in that system's "rule of recognition," as Hart called it. A rule of recognition specifies the criteria by virtue of which particular norms are taken to be norms of the legal system. Such criteria can include legislative enactment, executive orders, judicial decisions, and so on.

[2] On legal positivism generally, *see* Brian Leiter, "Legal Positivism about the Artifact Law: A Retrospective Assessment," in *Law as an Artifact*, ed. L. Burazin et al. (Oxford University Press, 2018).

[3] There are many kinds of norms (prescriptions, proscriptions, permissions, rights, powers, etc.) I use deontic norms as the central case only for purposes of exposition, but I mean the term "norm" broadly.

Rules of recognition in modern legal systems are, admittedly, complex. Consider: A norm is a valid norm of the California legal system if it has been enacted by the California legislature and signed by the governor, and has not been deemed unconstitutional as a matter of state or federal law by a state or federal court and has not been preempted by a federal law (that has not itself been constitutionally invalidated by a federal court); a norm can also be a valid norm in the California system if it has been enacted by the US Congress and signed by the president, and has not been deemed unconstitutional by the US Court of Appeals for the Ninth Circuit or by the US Supreme Court; a norm can also be a legally valid norm in the California legal system if it figures in the holding of a California court that a higher California or federal court has not reversed; and so on. This omits executive orders and administrative rulings, also subject to various kinds of judicial review.

A good part of legal education is education in the rule of recognition of one's legal system (and, of course, the norms valid under it), although it is rarely denominated as such in the law school classroom. But what makes it the case that California's rule of recognition is what it is? H.L.A. Hart's great insight was that, at bottom, legal systems rest upon nothing more than a conventional practice of officials, most importantly judges. The California Constitution is a binding norm of the California legal system *only because* judges in California treat it as binding on their decisions; so too with the federal Constitution, and so too with legislative enactments, administrative decisions, and the like. That a rule of recognition exists, and that it has the particular content it does, depends entirely on officials converging on certain criteria of legal validity and on their treating such criteria as obligatory or binding—accepting them from an "internal point of view" as Hart famously said. That they converge on certain criteria is an empirical question, manifest in their decisions and sometimes the reasons given for them; that they treat such criteria as obligatory is manifest in their language and their behavior (e.g., in their willingness to criticize other judges who depart from those criteria, and in the language they use to justify their own conduct).

A wonderful example of Hart's point comes from the case of Chief Judge Roy Moore of the Alabama Supreme Court, who in 2003 refused to abide by a decision of the US Court of Appeals for the Eleventh Circuit that the presence of a statue of the Biblical Ten Commandments in the Alabama Supreme Court building violated the Establishment Clause of the US Constitution.[4] There was no doubt that under the applicable rule of recognition, the Eleventh Circuit had authority over Judge Moore with regard to the constitutionality of the placement of that statue. And when Judge Moore defied the Eleventh Circuit's decision, the officials of the Alabama legal system made manifest their acceptance of this

[4] Glassroth v. Moore, 335 F.3d 1282 (11th Cir. 2003).

aspect of the rule of recognition from an internal point of view: They not only criticized Judge Moore's refusal to comply with the order, but they also convened the necessary procedures to remove him from office. (Moore was subsequently reelected, which, alas, says more about the Alabama electorate than about the officials of the legal system, who acted appropriately.)

We may imagine a more fanciful example to illustrate Hart's view that where a rule of recognition exists, officials of the system accept that rule from an internal point of view, that is, they treat it as obligatory (or something like "obligatory"). Suppose Chief Justice Roberts comes to the University of California law school in San Francisco, and a student asks, "Justice Roberts, why are you and the other Justices always worried about whether laws are constitutional? I mean, who cares? Why not just make a sensible decision?" Once he gets past being surprised, the Chief Justice, we can be sure, would *not* give the following answer: "I'll tell you why we're always talking about the Constitution: being Chief Justice is a great job, it's got prestige, lifetime tenure, a great pension too. If I didn't treat the Constitution as a constraint on what we do, I'm worried I'd get impeached and have to give up this wonderful sinecure I have." Instead of averting to crass self-interested reasons like these for taking the Constitution seriously, the Chief Justice is far more likely to appeal to the professional oath of office he took as a Justice to uphold the Constitution, as well as to the moral and political virtues of our constitutional system as he understands them. I want to be clear: I am quite sure those are the *actual* reasons the Chief Justice, like other justices and judges, take the constitutionality of statutes seriously. Where legal systems exist, officials of the system, including the judges, really do accept the criteria of legal validity, such as constitutionality, from an internal point of view.

This now brings us back to the problem with which we started. Constitutionality is only a criterion of legal validity in the rule of recognition of the American legal system if judges generally treat it as such and accept it from an internal point of view. The difficulty is that while all judges treat the constitutional document as legally binding, they differ wildly on how to ascertain the meaning of its provisions. Justice Scalia thought the original public meaning of the provisions of the Constitution determines its requirements; Justice Thomas sometimes agreed with him, but no one else did until recently.[5] As a matter of the rule of recognition of American constitutional law, it is obviously false that the original public meaning of the Constitution is what is legally binding on the courts[6]: Some judges treat the plain meaning as binding, some appeal to the

[5] Recent appointments to the Supreme Court, such as Justices Barrett and Gorsuch, do profess allegiance to originalism. Other judges will avert to originalist considerations but do not regard them as decisive the way Justice Scalia purports to do.

[6] Cf. Richard H. Fallon, Jr., "Constitutional Precedent Viewed Through the Lens of Hartian Positivist Jurisprudence," *North Carolina Law Review* 86 (2008): 1107–63. Of course, this may change!

structure of the Constitution, and almost all defer to past judicial interpretations of constitutional provisions (whether based on original meaning or not) as binding, an example of what David Strauss calls our "constitutional common law."[7] Since federal judges do not converge on a single way of fixing constitutional meaning, it follows, on the positivist view, that in large parts of so-called "constitutional law" there really is no law because there are no criteria of legal validity generally accepted and applied by judges.[8]

III. Some Examples

Not all areas of what we call constitutional law are so unsettled—unanimous decisions by the Supreme Court on many constitutional issues are rather good evidence in support of that point. But even divided decisions can turn out to be. Let us recall the 1989 case *Texas v. Johnson*,[9] in which the US Supreme Court decided that a law prohibiting desecration of the flag violated the First Amendment, a decision in which Justices Scalia and Kennedy joined the majority opinion by Justice Brennan. More than thirty years later, the case stands as good law: The government cannot, constitutionally, punish burning the American flag. Lower court judges understand that a Supreme Court decision like *Texas v. Johnson* binds them to invalidate any blanket ban on flag-burning, and thus the issue has hardly arisen since.

Then, however, we have an issue like whether the Second Amendment protects an individual right to own guns. For most of the twentieth century, it was settled law that it does not; after all, the Amendment reads, "A well-regulated militia being necessary to the security of a free State, the right of the People to keep and bear arms shall not be infringed." One natural reading, one that dominated for most of our constitutional history, was that this protected the right of states to arm their militias. That the Amendment really protects an individual right to bear arms was famously deemed a "fraud on the American public" by the late Chief Justice Warren Burger, a Republican appointee (albeit before the Republican Party went off the rails in America).[10] The "fraud" is now the law of the land, thanks to the decision in 2008 by the super-legislature in *District of Columbia v. Heller*, which bypassed precedent and received wisdom in favor

[7] See David A. Strauss, "Common Law Constitutional Interpretation," *University of Chicago Law Review* 63 (1996): 877–935. In the lower federal courts, something like the "common law constitutionalism" approach dominates, due to convergence among officials on the binding force of Supreme Court decisions. But even there, plenty of room remains for the exercise of quasi-legislative powers.

[8] This extends beyond constitutional law in some measure in the United States. See ch. 2 in this volume

[9] Texas v. Johnson, 491 U.S. 397 (1989).

[10] *The MacNeil/Lehrer NewsHour: First Freedoms* (PBS television broadcast Dec. 16, 1991).

of the original public meaning as declared by Justice Scalia in the majority and disputed at length by Justice Stevens in the dissent.[11] The historical evidence is obviously mixed, and Judge Richard Posner's verdict on the decision, in a well-known *New Republic* article at the time,[12] still seems apt:

> Lawyers are advocates for their clients, and judges are advocates for whichever side of the case they have decided to vote for. The judge sends his law clerks scurrying to the library and to the Web for bits and pieces of historical documentation. When the clerks are the numerous and able clerks of Supreme Court justices, enjoying the assistance of the capable staffs of the Supreme Court library and the Library of Congress, and when dozens and sometimes hundreds of amicus curiae briefs have been filed, many bulked out with the fruits of their authors' own law-office historiography, it is a simple matter, especially for a skillful rhetorician such as Scalia, to write a plausible historical defense of his position.
>
> But it was not *so* simple in *Heller*, and Scalia and his staff labored mightily to produce a long opinion (the majority opinion is almost 25,000 words long) that would convince, or perhaps just overwhelm, the doubters. The range of historical references in the majority opinion is breathtaking, but it is not evidence of disinterested historical inquiry. It is evidence of the ability of well-staffed courts to produce snow jobs.
>
> ....
>
> .... For more than two centuries, the "right" to private possession of guns, supposedly created by the Second Amendment, had lain dormant. Constitutional rights often lie dormant, spectral subjects of theoretical speculation, until some change in the social environment creates a demand for their vivification and enforcement. But nothing has changed in the social environment to justify giving the Second Amendment a new life discontinuous with its old one: a new wine in a decidedly old wineskin. There is no greater urgency about allowing people to possess guns for self-defense or defense of property today than there was thirty years ago, when the prevalence of violent crime was greater, or for that matter one hundred years ago. Only the membership of the Supreme Court has changed.
>
> If constitutional decisions are to be determined by the balance between liberals and conservatives on the Supreme Court, the fig-leafing that we find in *Heller*—the historicizing glaze on personal values and policy preferences—will continue to be irresistibly tempting to the justices, with their large and tireless

[11] District of Columbia v. Heller, 554 U.S. 570 (2008).

[12] Richard A. Posner, "In Defense of Looseness," *The New Republic* (Aug. 27, 2008), http://www.newrepublic.com/ article/ books/ defense-looseness.

> staffs and their commitment to a mystique of "objective" interpretation. There is no way to purge political principles from constitutional decision-making, but they do not have to be liberal or conservative principles. A preference for judicial modesty—for less interference by the Supreme Court with the other branches of government—cannot be derived by some logical process from constitutional text or history. It would have to be imposed. It would be a discretionary choice by the justices. But judging from *Heller*, it would be a wise choice. It would go some distance toward de-politicizing the Supreme Court. It would lower the temperature of judicial confirmation hearings, widen the field of selection of justices, and enable the Supreme Court to attend to the many important non-constitutional issues that it is inclined to neglect.

A preference for judicial modesty is, however, also a political choice,[13] as Judge Posner recognizes, one that will serve to immunize from judicial review whatever the prevailing ideology of the other branches of the government is at that time. So the real question is, why, when we confirm Justices to the super-legislature, do we not have a public discussion of their political principles? That is the question Judge Posner's apt critique raises.

The Supreme Court's role as super-legislature emerges again in the important voting rights case, *Shelby County v. Holder* (2013).[14] Here, a bare majority of the super-legislature invalidated section 4 of the Voting Rights Act, which the actual legislature (i.e., the US Congress), had evaluated and extended in 2006.[15] The *Shelby* decision did so based on the finding of five members of the super-legislature that section 4—which specified the formula for determining which states with a history of voting discrimination required federal preapproval for election law changes—is no longer necessary, contrary to the view, apparently, of the actual legislature seven years earlier. In an opinion by Chief Justice Roberts, the five super-legislators explained that while "Congress compiled thousands of pages of evidence before reauthorizing the Voting Rights Act," these did not justify the original 1965 formula for preclearance.[16] Why not? According to Chief Justice Roberts, there was "no logical relation" to the section 4 requirements, that these requirements are "irrational" given the record, indeed, "played no role" in

[13] There is ambiguity in the notion of a "political" choice, though the basic idea is that it is a choice motivated by adherence to a norm that has no legal status but instead reflects commitments for how the polity as a whole should be organized—such norms may run the gamut from partisanship for the narrow agenda of a particular party to a vision of the just society.

[14] Shelby Cnty., Ala. v. Holder, 133 S. Ct. 2612 (2013).

[15] Note that the fundamental question in *Shelby County* was a constitutional, not statutory one: namely, was Section 4 a constitutional (i.e., rational) exercise of congressional power to enforce the Reconstruction Amendments (i.e., the Fourteenth and Fifteenth Amendments) to the US Constitution?

[16] *Shelby County*, 133 S. Ct. at 2629.

the preclearance formulas.[17] This is all just rhetorical flourish, of course, for a different legislative judgment: It is obviously not irrational to rectify a wrong with a possibly overinclusive measure when the wrong is sufficiently serious that one wants to secure its elimination. As Justice Ginsburg, for the dissenters, observed:

> Congress determined, based on a voluminous record, that the scourge of discrimination was not yet extirpated. The question this case presents is who decides whether, as currently operative, [pre-clearance in accordance with the Section 4 formula] remains justifiable, this Court, or a Congress charged with the obligation to enforce the post-Civil War Amendments "by appropriate legislation." With overwhelming support in both Houses, Congress concluded that, for two prime reasons, [the preclearance formula] should continue in force, unabated. First, continuance would facilitate completion of the impressive gains thus far made; and second, continuance would guard against backsliding. Those assessments were well within Congress' province to make and should elicit this Court's unstinting approbation.[18]

Alas, a majority of the super-legislature did not offer approbation to the actual legislature's assessment, instead substituting its judgment on the policy merits for Congress's. If *Shelby County* were anomalous, this might not be notable, but the point is that it is fairly typical of what happens in the public law domain.

The problem is exacerbated, of course, because the US Supreme Court *selects* its docket—it picks the cases it wants to hear. Unsurprisingly, it picks the cases where the federal circuits conflict or where the law is up for grabs, "up for grabs" in precisely the sense that the rule of recognition does not clearly settle what should be done. Of course, the Supreme Court, having claimed for itself—without any basis in the constitutional text—final authority to adjudicate constitutional questions two centuries ago in *Marbury*[19] (one of the more successful [eventual] revisions of the American rule of recognition in our history) sometimes takes cases that might appear to be settled, a clear indication that the Court intends to exercise its super-legislative authority. Recall *New York v. United States* from 1992,[20] one of the early cases[21] that signaled the intent of some members of the super-legislature to redraw the boundaries of federal power after an earlier super-legislature appointed by President Franklin Roosevelt redrew them in the late 1930s and early 1940s to make the New Deal possible. *New York* concerned the Low-Level Radioactive Waste Policy Amendments Act of 1985, which the

[17] Ibid., 2629, 2630–31.
[18] Ibid., 2632–33.
[19] Marbury v. Madison, 5 U.S. 137 (1803).
[20] New York v. United States, 505 U.S. 144 (1992).
[21] Earlier, see Gregory v. Ashcroft, 501 U.S. 452, 461 (1991).

State of New York now challenged as betraying federalism values by violating state autonomy. Under what one might have thought the controlling precedent, *Garcia v. San Antonio Metropolitan Transportation Authority*[22] just seven years earlier, this should have been an "easy" case (i.e., one in which the law clearly dictated that New York lose). *Garcia*, which concerned federal regulations about wages and working hours, held (or so it seemed at the time!) that the only protection for federalism values, like state autonomy, came from the political process itself, that is, from the fact that the states were all represented in Congress; only if there were a breakdown in the political process, so the *Garcia* court suggested, would the US Supreme Court intervene. *New York v. United States* was a clear case from the standpoint of *Garcia*: The Federal Radioactive Waste Management Act had been enacted by Congress *after being drafted by the various states*: the states, in effect, wanted Congress to bind them to the agreement they had reached among themselves. This would seem to be a paradigmatic case of federalism values in action: Autonomous states strike a bargain about how to dispose of their radioactive waste, and then ask Congress to enforce the bargain.

Once the super-legislature, known as the Supreme Court, granted cert in the matter, everyone was on notice, of course, that the super-legislature planned to act. And act it did: In its majority opinion, Justice O'Connor took a page from the great American Legal Realist Karl Llewellyn's explanation of the malleability of precedent from his 1930 book *The Bramble Bush*.[23] In Llewellyn's famous rendering, appellate courts approach precedents in one of two ways: They read "unwelcome" precedents strictly; that is, they characterize their holding in a way that is highly specific to the facts of the earlier case to distinguish it from the case currently before the court. In Llewellyn's obviously facetious example, a strict reading of an earlier court's holding might be, "This rule holds only of redheaded Walpoles in pale magenta Buick cars."[24] By contrast, a "loose" reading of a precedent abstracts away from the particular facts of the case in favor of a generic rule of law that the court would like to treat as binding in the present instance. Not every "strict" or "loose" reading is going to be plausible, but Llewellyn, as the smart and experienced lawyer he was, is plainly correct that the doctrine of precedent affords courts enough latitude in construing the holdings of earlier cases to make precedent a feeble constraint on present decision in many cases. And that is precisely what happened in *New York v. United States*.

Justice O'Connor, in the majority opinion, faced an obvious problem as I mentioned: Under *Garcia*, the Federal Radioactive Waste Act looked like a clear case of the political process operating to protect the interests of the

[22] 469 U.S. 528 (1985).
[23] Karl Llewellyn, *The Bramble Bush* (Oceana, 1930), 68–71.
[24] Ibid. at 68.

states—after all, the states had drafted the Act in negotiations with each other, and then asked Congress to enact it. Presumably O'Connor lacked the votes to overrule *Garcia*—a move that would have been unseemly, in any case, given that *Garcia* had overruled another case, *National League of Cities*,[25] from less than a decade before!—and so, taking a page from Llewellyn, she set out to *distinguish* *Garcia* by reading it strictly. According to Justice O'Connor's majority opinion,[26] the rule in *Garcia*—the rule that the only protection for federalism values comes from the political process itself—applies *only* in cases where the federal regulation applies to *both* public and private entities, as was true of the wage and hour regulations at issue in *Garcia*. *Garcia* itself did not make an issue out of this, but now, seven years later in *New York*, Justice O'Connor did: for the Federal Radioactive Waste Management Act applied only to public entities, namely, states, and so, according to Justice O'Connor, presented a different issue than in *Garcia*. With *Garcia* distinguished, Justice O'Connor proceeded into a historical analysis and ultimately invalidated a portion of the Act. Those details do not matter for our purposes.

The dissenting opinion by Justice White[27] also took a page from Llewellyn: He effectively accused the majority of distinguishing *Garcia* on the basis of factual differences that did not make a difference—in effect, Justice White complained, the majority opinion said the rule in *Garcia* applies only to "redheaded Walpoles in pale magenta Buick cars."[28] From Justice White's perspective, the difference between a federal regulation that reached public and private entities as opposed to only public ones was irrelevant; *New York v. United States* was an easy case, and *Garcia* should have controlled the result.

I want to be clear that I do not think either majority or dissent was right "as a matter of law" in this case. Justice O'Connor did a poor job, to be sure, of explaining why the factual difference between *Garcia* and *New York* actually mattered, but an explanation is not hard to come by: Surely it is not crazy to think state autonomy might be more at risk when a federal regulation *only applies to the states*, as opposed to regulating state and private actors equally. At the same time, Justice White's view was equally plausible as a matter of law: The *Garcia* rule emphasized the importance of the political process as a safeguard for state autonomy, and the underlying facts in *New York* seemed to indicate a political process functioning well, indeed, driven by the states themselves, until the state of New York had some buyer's remorse.

If the preceding is correct, then we should ask what really happened in *New York v. United States*? *New York*, as students of federalism know, was near the

[25] Nat'l League of Cities v. Usery, 426 U.S. 833 (1976).
[26] New York v. United States, 505 U.S. 144, 149–88 (1992).
[27] Ibid., 188–211.
[28] Llewellyn, *Bramble Bush*, 68.

beginning of a series of Supreme Court cases in which, for the first time since the triumph of the New Deal, the Court began placing some limits on the exercise of federal power. President Reagan, who appointed Justice O'Connor a decade earlier, ran partly on this issue, the issue of state autonomy from federal overreach. And so for Justice O'Connor, a newfangled conservative in the Reagan mold, *New York* presented an opportunity to state loud and clear that there really are limits on federal power. By contrast, for Justice White, an oldfangled conservative, appointed by President Kennedy in the early 1960s, the New Deal revolution had settled all the questions about the scope of federal power; Justice White was a law-and-order conservative, skeptical of the expanding rights of criminal defendants, as well as of abortion rights, but he was fully accepting of the transformation of the constitutional system effected by the New Deal. The federal legislature voted to bind the states to a proposal for disposing radioactive waste that they themselves had drafted; in *New York v. United States*, the super-legislature known as the Supreme Court voted to overturn part of that plan. In doing so, they did not act as the law requires: Only a naif could believe that. Instead, they exercised moral and political judgment and acted accordingly.

Let us now fast forward to the decision in *Burwell v. Hobby Lobby*.[29] In *Hobby Lobby*, the Supreme Court upheld a challenge by closely held corporations to a requirement of the Affordable Care Act—more precisely, the mandate imposed by the Department of Health & Human Services under that Act—that employers (of a certain size) pay for employee health insurance that covers, among other things, four kinds of (allegedly) post-conception contraceptive drugs and devices. The challenge was based on the Religious Freedom Restoration Act (RFRA), a 1993 law which attempted to restore the constitutional protections for "free exercise" of religion that had existed prior to Justice Scalia's majority opinion in *Employment Division v. Smith*.[30] That 1990 decision held that the state need not grant religious exemptions for neutral laws of general applicability—neutral in the sense that their purpose was not (facially or otherwise) to substantially burden a particular religious faith. Thus, under *Smith*, the federal government did not need to find a less burdensome alternative to a law that imposed incidental but substantial burdens on free exercise of religion.

The *Hobby Lobby* decision found, plausibly, that the owners of the closely held corporations challenging the mandate genuinely believed that life begins at conception, so that they genuinely believed that post-conception contraception was akin to murder.[31] I want to emphasize that three aspects of the *Hobby Lobby*

[29] 134 S. Ct. 2751 (2014).

[30] Employment Div., Dep't of Human Res. of Oregon v. Smith, 494 U.S. 872 (1990). Congress, and many states, reacted against this decision, and Congress subsequently passed RFRA, which now binds the federal government not to substantially burden religion when alternatives are available.

[31] *Hobby Lobby*, 134 S. Ct. at 2764–65, 2766, 2775.

decision seem to me fairly banal, given the existence of RFRA: first, that the free exercise of religion of a closely held corporation is not meaningfully distinguishable from the free exercise of religion by the individuals who closely own the corporation (in other words, closely held corporations are "persons" for purposes of RFRA); second, that since the federal government had already provided an opt-out provision from the mandate for nonprofit entities with religious objections (like the University of Notre Dame), one that did not shift costs to the employees seeking contraceptive coverage, then it was clear that there were regulatory alternatives available to the federal government to insure that contraception was available to female employees that did not impose a substantial burden on religious belief; and third, that under our constitutional regime of religious liberty, courts must take seriously someone's religious belief that life begins at conception. I, myself, disagree with this latter aspect of our constitutional system, just as I also think RFRA is a bad law,[32] but that is not at issue in my doubts about *Hobby Lobby*. My doubts lie elsewhere.

The crucial legal question presented in *Hobby Lobby*—granting the points I have just conceded—is whether requiring a closely held corporation to pay for health insurance that an employee *might* use to access medical services of which her employer disapproves constitutes a "substantial burden" on the free exercise of the employer's religion in a society which is not a theocracy, that is, in a society in which, for example, employees need not subscribe to the religion of their employers. The idea that it would constitute a substantial burden ought to have seemed preposterous on its face. Yet in the majority opinion of the super-legislature by Justice Alito, a conservative Catholic, we are told that the belief of the owners of the closely held corporations that their paying for insurance which their employees could use to secure contraceptive services of which their employers disapprove "implicates a difficult and important question of religion and moral philosophy, namely, the circumstances under which it is wrong for a person to perform an act that is innocent in itself but that has the effect of enabling or facilitating the commission of an immoral act by another."[33] It is not for the courts, Justice Alito asserts, to tell "the plaintiffs that their beliefs are flawed."[34] The job of the courts is only to determine whether the beliefs are sincere religious beliefs, which everyone, including me, grants that they are.

This sounds reasonable until one considers a scenario in which the religious plaintiffs profess the following putatively religious belief: "This law substantially burdens our free exercise of religion." That looks rather like a legal conclusion masquerading as a religious belief, but now we need to ask how such a scenario is

[32] *See* Brian Leiter, *Why Tolerate Religion?* (Princeton University Press, 2013).
[33] *Hobby Lobby*, 134 S. Ct. at 2778.
[34] Ibid.

any different from the position of the challengers in *Hobby Lobby*? If you believe that paying for medical insurance that can be used by your employees to access medical procedures of which you disapprove violates your free exercise rights, that's a legal question for the courts: the courts can grant that *you really believe this*, indeed, that you hold a particular philosophical or religious view about "the circumstances under which it is wrong for a person to perform an act that is innocent in itself but that has the effect of enabling or facilitating the commission of an immoral act by another." But calling it a "philosophical" or religious view does not change the fact that it states a legal conclusion, namely, that the law requiring you to pay for the medical insurance substantially burdens your religion.

In short, we can agree with Justice Alito that the Supreme Court has long held that it will not adjudicate whether religious beliefs are sensible, only whether they are *religious* and *sincerely held*. But that does not mean that the courts must defer to the religious person's beliefs about whether the law substantially burdens their religion: That has to be a legal question for the courts, or the courts are out of business. The super-legislature should have acted like an actual court and found there was no "substantial burden" on *Hobby Lobby*.[35]

It is important to notice that the mistake in Justice Alito's reasoning was, in fact, a *legal* mistake, not in the sense that he failed to recognize the relevant sources of law but in the sense that he failed to understand the conceptual or logical entailments from those sources. More precisely, Justice Alito failed to correctly distinguish the *legal* question whether a particular law actually imposes a "substantial burden" on religious exercise from the nonlegal question that courts are not supposed to adjudicate, namely, whether the claimant's religious beliefs are reasonable. If it were really the case that courts must defer to claimants' allegedly *religious beliefs about substantial burdens—that is, about whether their legal rights are violated*—then there is nothing for the courts to do. Since that is absurd, Justice Alito obviously made a serious mistake in his reasoning.

Even if the super-legislature's mistake in *Hobby Lobby* was a *legal* mistake, it still calls attention again to the importance of moral and political judgment by the members of this super-legislature, since their moral and political values may explain their propensity to make certain kinds of mistakes. Remember that the Supreme Court, two hundred years ago in *Marbury v. Madison*, first claimed for itself the power to settle *constitutional* questions, meaning that the actual legislature cannot easily undo the mistakes that are motivated by the moral and political beliefs of the Justices—in this case, the desire of the conservative majority of the super-legislature to signal their fundamental sympathy with religious conservatives. To be sure, *Hobby Lobby* concerns RFRA, not the First

[35] Justice Ginsburg makes this point in dissent. Ibid. at 2798.

Amendment, though RFRA was, at a minimum, purporting to reestablish an earlier constitutional regime. But it is a reasonable prediction that Congress will not revisit RFRA to undo the *Hobby Lobby* decision. Thus, even the plain legal mistakes of the super-legislature give us further reason to want to know the moral and political views of the Justices before they are appointed, since those views will illuminate precisely the domains in which they are likely to make errors.

IV. The Truth about the Supreme Court

Alas, the only people who are led to believe that Supreme Court Justices are appointed based simply on their legal skill and knowledge are the American people (i.e., the electorate).[36] Every American president, from at least Roosevelt to Reagan to the present, understands that the US Supreme Court often acts as a super-legislature, and therefore one had better try to appoint legislators (i.e., Justices) who share the moral and political views of the appointing president. Let me share an amusing, but revealing, story my colleague, Judge Richard Posner, told me, and which he has shared with many others, so I am not betraying any secrets here. Posner was appointed to the US Court of Appeals for the Seventh Circuit in 1981, when, as he said to my jurisprudence class one year, people did not realize Reagan was "stacking" the courts with "right-wingers like me." Those are Judge Posner's words, though as all lawyers know, he proved to be far less of a right-winger than the current Republican Party might have hoped. In any case, Judge Posner's point was that the media did not pay much attention to Senate confirmation hearings then. Posner's hearing was presided over by Senator Strom Thurmond of South Carolina, even then (in the early 1980s), a nearly octogenarian segregationist trying to pass as a member of the modern world. Senator Thurmond, reading from his prepared script, asked, "Mr. Posner, if appointed to the Court, will you regard it as your obligation to apply the law as written rather than make new law?" Posner, being a smart lawyer and scholar, explained that the choice was a false one: Appellate courts are repeatedly asked to decide cases in which the law is not settled—that is one reason the cases are litigated through the stage of appellate review, after all—and in those cases, the courts must provide authoritative resolution, essential to a civilized society. So,

[36] The public is not wholly ignorant, to be sure. A CBS News poll in 2012 found that three quarters of Americans believe that Supreme Court Justices "sometimes let their personal or political views influence their decisions." See http://www.pollingreport.com/court.htm. The Public Religion Institute in 2013 found that 55 percent of those surveyed thought Supreme Court Justices were influenced by their own political views "a lot," while 32 percent thought they were influenced only "a little," and 8 percent "not at all." Despite these suspicions, when Supreme Court Justices are confirmed in public by the Senate, inquiry into their personal or political views is treated as off-limits. (Thanks to Mike Seidman for help on this topic.)

of course, appellate judges must sometimes make new law, since no legislature—as H. L. A. Hart observed a half-century ago—could possibly anticipate all the problems that will arise. In other words, appellate judges must exercise moral and political judgment, an unavoidable part of their job. Senator Thurmond, already well into his dotage, did not respond to the actual answer, but moved on to the next question in his script. Now we come to the punchline of this curious story: when Judge Posner received the transcript of his confirmation hearing several weeks later, Senator Thurmond's initial question was correctly recorded, namely, "Mr. Posner, if appointed to the Court, will you regard it as your obligation to apply the law as written rather than make new law?" But instead of Posner's actual answer, the transcript read that Posner simply replied, "Yes."

Now this is America in 1981, not Stalinist Russia, yet a federal judicial nominee's *actual* answer to a silly question by a political hack was *erased* from the historical record in order to comport with the political agenda of a president—Ronald Reagan—who liked to claim that he only wanted to appoint judges who apply the law rather than make the law. But Reagan and his advisors knew this was nonsense, just like Judge Posner: They knew that appellate judges must inevitably exercise moral and political judgment beyond the issues settled by the law to resolve the actual disputes that come before the appellate courts. How, in a democratic society, can such secrecy be justified?

In my view, it cannot. We should tell the truth to the electorate: Lawmakers cannot anticipate all problems that will arise, but in a civilized society, we need courts to provide authoritative resolutions of disputes that are left unsettled by the existing sources of law. Courts play that role, and the "higher" the court, the more likely it is that the court will be asked to exercise circumscribed moral and political judgment, akin to what we expect from honest legislators, assuming that term is not an oxymoron in America these days. Therefore, when such judges are to be appointed, the nominal representatives of the people should evaluate the quality of moral and political judgment the nominee would exercise. Will the nominee reflexively side with markets against state regulation, with majorities against minorities, with the religious against the nonreligious, with color-blindness against sensitivity to the role of race in society, with the police against criminal defendants, with the current ideological fixations of the Republican Party against the current ideological fixations of the Democratic Party? Is the nominee sensitive to injustice, to the powerless, to the losers in the political process, or does he or she side reflexively with those in power, with the status quo? These questions should be central to the confirmation process of members of the super-legislature—or rather, they should be central *in public* to that process, since they are obviously central to the actual nominators. They are also, to be sure, the subject of speculation, rumors, and gossip, but that is not the same as making them central to the actual proceedings in which the Senate confirms a nominee. There are, certainly, many issues in which legal expertise is essential, but there is no shortage of candidates with the requisite expertise to parse technical points of law, and it is rare indeed that a president puts forward a candidate for the super-legislature lacking that competence. What is not rare, unfortunately, is for presidents to put forward candidates for the super-legislature whom they choose based on their moral and political views, but then fail to acknowledge that fact to the rest of the polity, indeed, to object when the Senate even asks about those views.

There is, one must acknowledge, a serious worry about encouraging candor on these matters. The worry, simply put, is that it will embolden judges to overreach the legal limits *even more* than they already do.[37] This is a serious concern, but let us remember that the status quo is that elected officials appoint super-legislators because of their moral and political views, but no one is permitted to discuss that fact in public. If, in fact, we had a public discussion of what all the insiders know—namely, that appellate judges at the highest levels *must* exercise moral and political judgment—then perhaps those judges who actually survive the process will be those whose moral and political judgments comport more closely with those of the polity at large?[38] A polity that might welcome a liberal one decade might not welcome her a decade later, and so that is yet another reason to abolish lifetime tenure for federal judges in favor of fixed-term appointments, as other scholars have proposed.[39] But even before that happens, I do not see how in a democratic society where transparency in the exercise of public power (outside a select realm of areas, such as national security) is a fundamental value we can continue to tolerate the current charade of nominating lawyers to the US Supreme Court without vetting, fully and in public, their moral and political views which will determine their decisions in a range of momentous constitutional matters, and sometimes not only there.[40]

[37] My colleague Adam Mortara, a conservative lawyer, pressed this worry on me, pointing to some "lawless" conservative judges.

[38] I assume, for the sake of argument here, that majority approval suffices to "legitimate" the moral and political views of the judges. For independent reasons, this strikes me as dubious, but that would require a separate argument.

[39] See, e.g., Roger Cramton and Paul Carrington (eds.), *Reforming the Court: Term Limits for Supreme Court Justices* (Carolina Academic Press, 2006); Letter from Paul Carrington, Professor, Duke Univ. Sch. of Law, et al. to Vice President Joseph Biden et al. (Feb. 2009) (available at http://www.scotusblog.com/ 2009/ 02/ groups-proposals-for-supreme-court-reform).

[40] I am grateful to Aziz Huq and Nicholas Stephanopoulos for very helpful and detailed comments on a much earlier draft; to Mike Seidman for shrewd and illuminating advice on the penultimate draft; and to Phil Smoke at the University of Chicago Law School for excellent research assistance. Finally, my thanks to the audience at the Tobriner Lecture in San Francisco, and especially Judge Joseph Grodin, for a helpful correspondence afterward.

13

The Roles of Judges in Democracies

A Realistic View

I. Introduction: Judges and Their Obligations

What should the role of a judge be in contemporary democracies? That is our topic, but it has two important component parts that we should examine separately: a judge's role and democracy. Let us begin with a few introductory words about the former.

On one sensible view, succinctly articulated by Leslie Green, judges "settle disputes by applying pre-existing standards."[1] Preexisting standards need not be codified, and they need not be legally authoritative, though most will be. The central thought is that a judge in a legal system assesses disputed conduct relative to a norm that (usually) predates the conduct and thus was not created by the judge. Sometimes, of course, those denominated judges make retroactive decisions, holding actors accountable to standards that they never would have (or even could have) recognized at the time, and sometimes the judges also themselves create the standard, but these are not the normal cases for the judicial role, though they may be among the most important roles: Authoritative resolution of disputes is central to civic peace. In any case, let us call making decisions according to preexisting standards the *Minimal Role* of a judge.

Green proposes three further "obligations" of judges, following H. L. A. Hart:

(1) "Judges have an obligation to apply valid law in making rulings, and . . . to make correct findings of fact, to know what the law is, to keep their knowledge of the law up to date . . .";
(2) "Judges have an obligation to keep the law 'legally in good shape'" (quoting John Finnis, and meaning judges should resolve unclarity and conflicts);

[1] Leslie Green, "Law and the Role of a Judge," in *Legal, Moral, and Metaphysical Truths: The Philosophy of Michael S. Moore*, ed. Kimberly Kessler Ferzan and Stephen J. Morse (Oxford University Press, 2016), 323.

From a Realist Point of View. Brian Leiter, Oxford University Press. © Brian Leiter 2026.
DOI: 10.1093/9780197749852.003.0015

(3) "Judges have obligations to regulate their own processes and the conduct in their courts, and to protect the rule of law and the integrity of their jurisdiction from those who would attack it . . . ."[2]

I shall call these the *Minimal-Plus Roles.* Probably judges should do all these things too, though no legal positivist, including Green, thinks that judges have a nondefeasible moral obligation to apply valid law (as (1) suggests).[3] The hard issues about the role of judges in democracies are threefold: What are the obligations of judges in determining what the applicable preexisting standards are and their meaning; when should judges not apply valid law, per their *Minimal-Plus Role*; and what further "obligations" do judges have beyond the Minimal and Minimal-Plus roles?

In the realistic spirit suggested by my title, let me be clear at the start that "obligations"—understood as *moral* obligations—do not really exist[4]: when we speak of moral "obligations" (or "rights" or "duties") we are expressing certain attitudes, often very intense and insistent attitudes, about what we feel other people should or should not do.[5] Expressing such attitudes is central to human life: as Nietzsche put it, "all of life is a dispute over taste and tasting," and there is value in distinguishing between the strength and character of different tastes, as talk of "obligation" nicely does.[6] Like other people who are products of the post-Enlightenment, post-World War II consensus, my "tastes" run toward individual rights and freedom and the rule of law, in which judges can play a crucial role in constraining behavior by other state actors, since such institutional practices seem to enhance aggregate human well-being.[7]

[2] Ibid., 334–35.

[3] Elsewhere, Green himself endorses the view that in some circumstances, "judges should violate their judicial obligations . . . . This suggestion elicits horrified reactions from those so devoted to the ideal of legality that they think judges should always apply existing law no matter what. But that view is unacceptable, and pretence of accepting it is sustained only by fancy arguments that purport to show that, properly interpreted, the law is always worth applying. A more plausible view is that legality is one value among others, not to be discarded lightly, but neither to be pursued at the expense of all other things law should attend to. If judges did not accept that we would not want them on the bench." Leslie Green, "Should Law Improve Morality?" in *The Germ of Justice* (Oxford University Press, 2023), 270.

[4] *Legal* obligations, rights and duties do exist: They are certain kinds of social artifacts (like "money" and "stocks"), produced by legal systems, and whether or not they obtain depends on whether they satisfy the existence-conditions for such legal norms in that system (see Brian Leiter, "Legal Positivism about the Artifact Law: A Retrospective Assessment," in *Law as an Artifact*, ed. Luka Burazin, Kenneth Einar Himma, and Corrado Roversi (Oxford University Press, 2018), 3–28). Alf Ross's well-known skepticism about moral obligations was quite correct.

[5] See esp. Charles L. Stevenson, *Ethics and Language* (Yale University Press, 1944).

[6] Friedrich Nietzsche, *Thus Spoke Zarathustra*, in *The Portable Nietzsche*, trans. Walter Kaufmann (Penguin Books, 1976), II.13.

[7] Talk of "taste" like the economists' talk of "preferences" runs the risk of flattening the important differences between our attitudes about what others ought to do. I "prefer" chocolate to vanilla, but I do not simply "prefer" toleration to Genocide: those who "prefer" vanilla are not my mortal enemies; those who "prefer" genocide are.

Not having illusions about talk of obligation, however, is not simply a matter of being strict about philosophical concepts: imagine if theorists who said judges have "obligations" to do X said, instead, judges are "required by God" to do X? Recognizing that the latter is false—God does not exist, and so, unsurprisingly, has no views about anything, let alone the obligations of judges—would be liberating. One could express contrary attitudes without violating any moral or rational norm, let alone the will of God! Skepticism about "obligation" talks opens the conceptual and practical space for contrary recommendations. This is a more important point, I think, than is usually recognized in recent academic writing. Assumptions *about what is the case* exercise a powerful normative force on human behavior and thought—sometimes for very good reason, to be sure. For example, *that it is the case that the door is closed and locked* gives me a very powerful prudential reason not to try to march straight through the doorway. Let us call this *the normativity of fact*: that something is taken to be factual or real, *to be the case*, influences, sometimes quite profoundly, what people think is possible, permissible, and so on.[8] Sometimes, as in the case of locked doors, that's a good thing, but other times, it is not. So when we deny, in a realistic spirit, that moral obligations are metaphysically real, we are making both a true metaphysical claim (the ontology of the world includes no moral obligations[9] even if it includes some locked doors), and, at the same time, we are defeating the normativity of fact where its normativity has no real justification.[10]

When humans speak of moral "obligations," they are speaking of what they *really want or expect* certain people to do, perhaps *no matter what*. This is certainly revealing about the feelings of those engaged in such talk, and perhaps also revealing about their social and economic circumstances: Nazis, for example, thought of their actions in terms of obligations,[11] and this included judges—not surprising, since, as Hart argued sixty years ago, where there is a legal system, judges take themselves to have obligations to apply the valid legal norms, even when others might reasonably deem them catastrophically wrong to feel that way.[12] What this should remind us of is that speaking about "obligation" is an important feature of human social existence, but it is also compatible with a radical revision of human attitudes and thus a different set of attitudes about

[8] This is related to one of the central cases of ideology for Marx, namely, where some contingent and optional practice is treated as natural or necessary. See Jaime Edwards and Brian Leiter, *Marx* (Routledge, 2025), 160–61.

[9] See Brian Leiter, "Moral Facts and Best Explanations," *Social Philosophy & Policy* 18, no. 2 (2001): 79–101 (repr., in Leiter, *Naturalizing Jurisprudence* [Oxford University Press, 2007]; chs. 15 and 16 in this volume.

[10] Of course, "justification" itself is normative, but normativity has a "justification" in my deflated sense when it comports with instrumental desires like not walking into closed doors.

[11] See Herlinde Pauer-Studer and J. David Velleman, *Konrad Morgen: The Conscience of a Nazi Judge* (Palgrave Macmillan, 2015).

[12] H. L. A. Hart, *The Concept of Law*, 3rd ed. (Oxford University Press, 2012), 116.

what our "obligations" are. Suitably deflating the idea of "obligation" is important if we are to think clearly about the roles of judges: For example, even in cases where judges "promise" through an oath of office to do certain things, it may be that they should sometimes act otherwise.[13] We return to that issue, also, below, pp. 284–86.

So, can we generalize about the "roles of judges in democracies"? We can, though, subject to some constraints, since judges and democracies seem to differ along various dimensions. For example, there are "civil service" judiciaries in which appointment and promotion depend on evaluation by other judges, as in Britain; there are "political" judiciaries in which appointment depends on political connections and affiliation, as in the United States; and there are mixed models in which, for example, purportedly "peer" evaluation of judges for appointment and promotion is, in fact, influenced by political partisanship (I am told Italy is such a case). Democracies differ in many respects as well: Some are plutocracies masquerading as democracies (e.g., the United States); some are incipient authoritarian societies masquerading as democracies (e.g., Hungary, maybe the United States, and, not long ago, Poland, though it seems to have recovered); and some are more conventional representative democracies with all their pathologies of class conflicts and political personalities (e.g., the current United Kingdom and France).

A serious discussion about the roles of judges in democracies has to be *realistic* both about judges and about democracies. It has to acknowledge what judges really do and how democracies actually function, and it has to be clear about what judges can do against those backgrounds. It also has to be explicit about our normative aspirations and ideals (and also whether judges can realize them). Normative aspirations and ideals tend to be inchoate and not wholly consistent, though in their broad outline in the present historical moment they are clear: No one needs a moral *theory*, after all, to know whether they are against racism or in favor of racial equality, against chattel or wage slavery or in favor of human freedom, against cruelty or in favor of treating people in a dignified way, against human misery or in favor of human happiness. (The problem, after all, with academic friends of Jobbik in Hungary, the National Rally in France, or Donald Trump in America is not that they failed to appreciate the "correct" moral theory![14]) Judges—like other psychologically normal post-Enlightenment people—should try to promote human well-being on some

[13] A promise might be thought to generate a *moral obligation* to fulfill certain functions in an institutional role. Whether those functions are obligations of the role is separate from the question of whether there is a real moral obligation to fulfill those functions simply because of a promise.

[14] Remember that normative theory delivers no decisive conclusions about what ought to be done, being hostage to "intuitive" starting points that are ethnographic data and that themselves can never be defended. See ch. 17 in this volume, "The Paradoxes of Public Philosophy."

reasonable understanding (the theoretical differences between extant accounts rarely matter given the constraints imposed in practice on judicial power)—though the role of judges in helping to promote human well-being will vary quite a bit depending on the nature of the judiciary and the nature of the democracy. My main topic will be the kinds of realistic variations and constraints on the exercise of this judicial role. I thus hope this essay will be a contribution to the ongoing revival of realist political and legal theory against the moralizing fantasies of so much academic writing about these matters over the last half-century.[15] *Theory* will be important in what follows—for example, empirical theories about voting behavior in democracies, as well as philosophical claims about the nature of law—but *normative* theory will not be.

I start with a realistic view of democracies, and then turn to judges.

II. A Realistic View of Democracy

Democracies typically have two features: Individuals have *the right to vote* for some number of those who hold political power, and citizens also enjoy *rights to certain individual freedoms.* So, on the one hand, democracies hold elections in which some significant portion of the citizenry can vote for some range of candidates or parties (perhaps two or three or four), the elections are fair, and incumbents can actually be voted out of office: This is the crux of the democratic ideal that "the people rule." On the other hand, democracies also typically, in the post-World War II era, protect some range of individual rights—rights to expression, privacy, and fair legal process most prominently, though again to varying degrees.[16] Call the combination of electoral rights and rights to individual freedom "Democratic Values." Debates about the role of judicial review of legislation in democracies typically focus on the electoral aspect, and how that is consistent with judicial invalidation of legislation when it violates individual rights: In the United States, this is called the "countermajoritarian" difficulty,[17] though in parliamentary systems, it could also be called the "counterdemocratic" difficulty, since judges, once again, defy the will of a democratic legislature,

[15] See ch. 1 in this volume for a more extended discussion, and also ch. 11, "In Praise of Realism."

[16] The protection of individual freedoms is typically dependent on allegiance to the family of "rule of law" virtues, such as an independent judiciary, the principle that no one is above the law, the requirement to treat like cases alike, the publicity of legal standards, etc. It is not wholly dependent—*contra* Lon Fuller and other antipositivists—since the *substantive content* of the law matters crucially, even if all the different rule-of-law virtues are honored.

[17] Alexander M. Bickel, *The Least Dangerous Branch: The Supreme Court at the Bar of Politics* (Bobbs-Merrill Company, Inc., 1962). Bickel himself was silent on the moral question of why democracy conferred legitimacy on legislation.

though less often a majoritarian one.[18] A realistic view of democracy should help us see why this latter concern is without merit, and why the real question for judges who embrace "Democratic Values" should be whether laws really protect the individual rights that are equally central to democratic values.[19]

The reason we should disregard the supposed countermajoritarian or counterdemocratic difficulty is that there is almost never a plausible sense in which the particular laws passed by a legislature represent the views of an electorate, whose will is then thwarted. That laws reflect the view of the electorate would be true only if two further claims were true:

(1) The majority of the legislature intended the legislation to achieve purpose X.
(2) The majority (or plurality) of people who elected the legislature (the "electorate") wanted them to pass legislation which achieved purpose X, or, less demandingly, wanted them to enact general policies related directly or indirectly to purpose X.

The first claim has been subjected to various kinds of critique by economists and public choice theorists,[20] who emphasize that collective intentionality in a legislature is a fiction, and a misleading one.[21] The more serious problems arise, however, for the second claim, which presupposes something doubtful: that lawmakers are elected because of commitments to pass particular kinds of legislation to achieve particular policy goals. Even in its most plausible form, known as the "spatial theory of voting" in the empirical political science literature, it supposes only that people vote for the party that is closest (in ideological space, as it were) to their ideological "preferences." Even if voters really did that, this would rarely license the conclusion that any particular piece of legislation that achieved purpose X reflects the will of the voters. There are, of course, the

[18] The US Congress is not a majoritarian institution either, as it happens—its Senate is obviously not, and its House of Representatives, due to gerrymandering, is not either. The United Kingdom is a special case, since the courts cannot invalidate acts of Parliament on grounds of violating individual rights, but they can declare them incompatible with such rights, and thus prompt a legislative reevaluation.

[19] I assume, with Mill among others, that protection of individual rights generally promotes human flourishing and well-being. Perhaps this is false, but as of now, we have no reason to think it is, although we could quibble about the scope of individual freedoms that are needed.

[20] Public choice theorists believe that legislators simply pursue their self-interest in remaining in power, and so their voting behavior depends only on who will give them money to run for reelection. Public choice theory has flourished in the United States, for perhaps obvious reasons.

[21] See Frank H. Easterbrook, "Statutes' Domains," *University of Chicago Law Review* 50, no. 2 (1983): 547–48; Frank H. Easterbrook. "Text, History, and Structure in Statutory Interpretation," *Harvard Journal of Law and Public Policy* 17, no. 1 (1994): 68. But for a different view, see Richard Ekins, *The Nature of Legislative Intent* (Oxford University Press, 2012). However, even the defenses of intention do not really establish the requisite level of specificity of intention that would make the countermajoritarian difficulty meaningful.

fundamental theoretical difficulties with this view due to Arrow's Theorem,[22] but even more worrisome for the spatial theory is the overwhelming evidence that voters do not have clear ideologies. For example, in the 1980s—the height of the reactionary Reagan Era in the United States, when the social welfare state was under sustained attack[23]—nearly 65 percent of Americans thought the government was spending too little on "assistance to the poor," but at the same time only 25 percent thought too little was spent on "welfare,"[24] a term that had been demonized by Reagan, even though it means "assistance to the poor"![25] What this shows is that expressions of purported "ideology" by the population are sometimes nothing of the kind, unless by "ideology" one does not mean what voters actually believe about policy.

This is surprising to university professors, of course, who are disproportionately "ideologues" in the sense defined by the American political scientist Philip Converse in 1964, namely, those who have well-defined views about policy questions (such that, e.g., they realize that "assistance to the poor" is the same as "welfare," and either favor or oppose both). In Converse's study, these "ideologues" were 3 percent of the population, while 85 percent of the voting population "seemed to think about parties and candidates in terms of group interests or the 'nature of the times' or in ways that conveyed 'no shred of policy significance whatever.' "[26] Ironically, academic interest in the United States in the "countermajoritarian" difficulty about judicial review of legislation flourished precisely after the period studied by Professor Converse.

If the spatial theory of voting fares poorly in showing why we should worry about judicial invalidation of democratically enacted laws that violate individual

[22] Christopher H. Achen and Larry M. Bartels, *Democracy for Realists: Why Elections Do Not Produce Responsive Government* (Princeton University Press, 2016), 23–30. Achen and Bartels reprise, with new evidence, arguments first made by Elmer Schattschneider. See Elmer E. Schattschneider, *The Semisovereign People: A Realist's View of Democracy in America* (Holt, Rinehart and Winston, 1960). Spatial voting theorists, in turn, have produced new evidence in the last twenty years to try to resist the realist conclusions. An important example is Stephen A. Jessee, "Spatial Voting in the 2004 Presidential Election," *American Political Science Review* 103, no. 1 (2009): 59–81, https://doi.org/10.1017/S000305540909008X. The problem with this latter literature is that its results are compatible with the realist hypotheses about the role of group identity in driving party identification, and the way in which voters conform their views to the party leaders rather than the other way around.

[23] America always had more limited social welfare programs than Western European countries, but Ronald Reagan led an attack even on those programs.

[24] Achen and Bartels, *Democracy for Realists*, 30.

[25] We don't know how clarification about the terms would have shifted preferences, of course, but it is easy to see how it could have gone either way: Some of the anti-welfare folks would have realized that "assistance to the poor" was meant to incorporate all the putatively bad aspects of welfare; similarly, some of the pro-"assistance to the poor" folks might have been horrified to learn that what they favored really had the putatively bad aspects of welfare. And, of course, we can imagine the converse.

[26] Achen and Bartels, *Democracy for Realists*, 32. Further references will be included in the body of the text by page number. See Donald R. Kinder and Nathan P. Kalmoe, *Neither Liberal nor Conservative: Ideological Innocence in the American Public* (University of Chicago Press, 2017) for an updated and concurring investigation of ideological identification in the American public.

rights, the alternatives fare even worse. The "retrospective theory" of democracy suggests that voters express their judgment of the past performance of those they vote for (or against). That sounds somewhat promising, but in fact voters primarily respond to economic events only in the several months preceding an election (Achen and Bartels, 148–58) and, more importantly, they do not discriminate between events for which elected officials bear some plausible causal responsibility and those events which are basically natural disasters: floods, droughts, even shark attacks (on one occasion) have all influenced voters in past elections (118–35).[27] Simply put: If voters are miserable in the months before an election, often regardless of the cause of the misery (122–37),[28] they generally take out their unhappiness in their voting behavior. If there are reasons for

[27] Achen and Bartels's shark attack claim has been challenged in Anthony Fowler and Andrew B. Hall, "Do Shark Attacks Influence Presidential Elections? Reassessing a Prominent Finding on Voter Competence," *The Journal of Politics* 80, no. 4 (2018): 1423–37, https://doi.org/10.1086/699244. The first half of Fowler and Hall's critique is irrelevant, since it tests a hypothesis that Achen and Bartels do not defend, namely, that shark attacks influence presidential elections. Achen and Bartels focus on a rather singular case—the multiple shark attacks in 1916 along the New Jersey coast, which attracted national and international attention, and which were utterly unprecedented. Their finding was that in the coastal counties closest to the site of the widely covered attacks, Woodrow Wilson's share of the presidential vote declined markedly by comparison to both his 1912 results *and* his results in New Jersey counties farther removed.

The relevant part of the Fowler and Hall critique centers on disputing choices by Achen and Bartels about the various comparison classes, and most of those critiques simply show that, if you redraw the comparison classes, the statistical effect on election outcomes of the shark attacks is reduced. The notion of "statistical significance" is epistemically vexed, to put it mildly, but what is missing from the Fowler and Hall critique is any serious attention to the question of "mechanism," that is, the causal processes by which a certain event X brought about an outcome Y. Only with a plausible story about mechanism can we really rule out or in "statistically significant" or "statistically insignificant" correlations, since the *P* value of greater than 95 percent is both arbitrary and largely meaningless (see David Colquhoun, "An Investigation of the False Discovery Rate and the Misinterpretation of *p*-Values," *Royal Society Open Science* 1, no. 3 (2014). https://doi.org/1098/rsos.140216). (The basic problem is that 95 percent confidence that an effect is not random compared to the null hypothesis does not guarantee it is a *real* effect (a real cause-effect relationship). What we need to know *in addition* is how good our test is for detecting *real effects* and how many real effects there are in the sample studied (the latter, of course, is hard to estimate). But consider: even with the standard $p = .05$ standard of statistical significance, if our measures only capture 80 percent of *real effects*, and real effects are only 10 percent of our sample, then one-third of our positive results will turn out to be false positives even with the standard *P* value. Colquhoun, "Investigation of the False Discovery rate," 4–5.

Achen and Bartels are aware of the need for a story about causal mechanisms (see their discussion of narratives at 138–42), and the shark attack case, while amusing and memorable, is only one small data point for their general hypothesis that voters are terrible at assigning causal responsibility for events that affect them adversely. If the underlying causal mechanism in their explanatory story is that ordinary voters have little understanding of causal responsibility, and yet unpleasant experiences influence their voting behavior regardless of causal responsibility, then they have a story about mechanism which Fowler and Hall lack.

[28] Caveat: Sometimes voters need a narrative before assigning blame. Achen and Bartels discuss the case of the catastrophic Spanish influenza pandemic of 1918, which felled half a million Americans yet did not translate into losses at the polls for incumbents: "[N]o thread of elite rhetoric or popular discourse seems to have suggested any attribution of responsibility to President Wilson or other public officials. As long as no one supplied a convincing argument that the government did control or should have controlled the spread of the pandemic or its horrific consequences, the pain of millions failed to have any electoral impact" (142).

judges committed to individual rights and human well-being to hesitate to invalidate legislation produced by such a process, those reasons can have nothing to do with the moral importance of democratic voting.[29]

I acknowledge that there may be other reasons for judges to hesitate before invalidating legislation.[30] Most importantly, settled law creates settled expectations, and unsettling those have costs that judges must consider. In addition, and as we will return to below, invalidating legislation may affect the legitimacy of the courts, and it may also provoke backlash from other branches of government.[31] But what is important to notice is that both these reasons for judicial restraint have nothing to do with the moral significance of how the population voted.

An alternative account of voting behavior recently defended most vigorously by self-described "realists" about democracy, Christopher Achen and Larry Bartels, does nothing to restore the moral importance of democratic voting. On their view, it is "group identity" that best explains voting behavior in democracies.[32] By group identity, they mean the religious, racial, ethnic, occupational, and cultural identities[33] that are important to people: their "tribes" for short. On their "group theory of politics—the powerful tendency of people to form groups, the ensuing construction of 'us' and 'them,' and the powerful role of emotion rather than reason in directing group activity"—"group attachments are easily generated and profoundly felt" (215).[34] What Achen and Bartels argue is that the group identity largely explains the political party with which individuals identify, and we know that, as Professor Converse put it, "expressions of party identification were much more stable" over time than ideological convictions (34). In other words, for most voters, their *tribal loyalties* drive party identification, and party identification then drives voting behavior.[35]

[29] Might there be other theories of why legislation deserves deference, quite apart from the pragmatic virtues of deference? There might be, although in many years of presenting this paper, I have yet to hear a convincing one.

[30] This is important to emphasize because many of my ultimate recommendations could apply to other official actors, albeit in slightly different terms. But there are aspects of institutional role and public expectations that caution restraint in all cases, including the judicial, but they vary with institutional role.

[31] This is a central theme in French legal realism. See Michel Troper, "Legal Realism in France," in *Oxford Studies in Philosophy of Law, Volume 5*, ed. Leslie Green and Brian Leiter (Oxford University Press, 2025).

[32] Caveat: The majority of their evidence comes from the United States, but they also include case studies from France, Germany, Ireland, and Sweden, among other countries.

[33] The "cultural" identities are often geographically bounded: see Achen and Bartels ch. 9.

[34] Note that there is no reason that voting in accordance with one's group identity means voting in accordance with one's "interests" or well-being. Achen and Bartels do not claim otherwise. On any plausible view of human interests or well-being, voting in the pattern described by Achen and Bartels would stand in only an accidental relationship to the interests or well-being of the voters.

[35] Crucially, tribal loyalty does not drive party identification based on party ideology, except at the margins.

In some measure, popular commentary on the political process in America has registered this fact. In America, we all know that African-Americans vote Democratic by overwhelming majorities, and that white men do not. But this also explains another important empirical finding, namely, that voters typically adjust their views to fit the ideology of their party (or its most visible representatives), rather than choosing parties based on how well they fit the voter's own views (Achen and Bartels 41–45, 258–64, ch. 10)![36] That fact helps make sense of the peculiarity of the Trump phenomenon in the United States, since he, in fact, rejected many staples of the "Republican brand" since the Reagan Revolution of the 1980s, though he won an overwhelming percentage of Republican voters in the end (I return to Trump below, p. 281).

Ideology of a party can matter at the margins, of course: At some point, a particular "tribe" registers that a particular party is clearly friendly or hostile to the tribe. African Americans in the United States supported Republicans from the end of the Civil War through the 1920s (at least when they could vote) since, after all, it was a Republican president who freed them from chattel slavery. (Unsurprisingly, a group freed from chattel slavery noticed that fact.) Although Franklin Delano Roosevelt began capturing a large share of the African American vote in the 1930s, it was not until Harry Truman desegregated the armed services in 1948 that a majority of African Americans began to identify as Democrats (though Republicans still got a third or more of the African American vote throughout the 1950s). It was, however, a Democratic president, Lyndon Johnson, who ended de jure [legal] segregation in America in 1964, and he went on to win 94 percent of the African American vote that year, and since then African Americans have voted overwhelmingly for Democrats[37] (though, strikingly, as Achen and Bartels document, Southern whites were moving to the Republicans before the 1960s (246–58)). The shift of tribal loyalty to Democrats may explain why African Americans continued to support Democrats into the 1990s and 2000s—including the Clintons (Bill and Hillary) —despite the evidence that they were not very good for the African American community.[38] Of course, it will be fairly noted that the Clintons were always less hostile to the interests of the African American community than the Republicans, but even

[36] This was true in the case of Hitler, too. For one of the most chilling discussions in the book, see Achen and Bartels, 314–16, which argues that the 1932 electoral success of the Nazis was almost entirely due to Protestant voters switching from the traditional Protestant parties (discredited by the crisis of capitalism beginning in 1929) to the National Socialists, while Catholics continued to vote as before. As Achen and Bartels note, the National Socialists did not emphasize antisemitism at all in the 1932 campaign.

[37] David A. Bositis, *Blacks and the 2012 Democratic National Convention* (Joint Center for Political and Economic Studies, 2012), 9, accessed December 28, 2024, https://jointcenter.org/wp-content/uploads/2020/10/Blacks-and-the-2012-Democratic-National-Convention.pdf.

[38] See, e.g., Michelle Alexander, *The New Jim Crow: Mass Incarceration in the Age of Colorblindness* (The New Press, 2012).

so, it hardly explains the failure of African Americans to rally to Senator Bernie Sanders, a Roosevelt New Dealer, in the 2016 Democratic primaries.[39] Reflexive loyalties do seem to explain it.[40]

Ironically, in the end, the absence of a member of their tribe on the ticket also helps explain the fact that African American turnout was depressed in the 2016 presidential election compared to elections when Obama was the candidate:[41] African Americans, highly motivated to turn out to vote when one of their own was a candidate, were not nearly as enthusiastic about voting for a white woman and a white man in 2016. At the same time, some modest number of white working-class voters (not more than 100,000 in the three crucial states of Pennsylvania, Michigan, and Wisconsin), some of whom had supported Obama in 2012, flipped to Trump in 2016.[42] This indicates that at least some *highly salient* parts of *expressed* ideology are relevant to some voters (Achens and Bartels do not deny this, but they are sloppy in their analysis, which is typical of this literature: They effectively acknowledge the point with their endless qualifications about what "mostly" or "often" explains voting behavior). As the rabble-rousing filmmaker Michael Moore observed, when Trump came to Detroit, Michigan (the center of the American auto industry) and threatened auto executives in vulgar terms that they had better not move their plants outside the United States, he did something no other candidate of the two ruling class parties in the United States had done in living memory.[43] "Free trade" has become a mantra of the ruling class and its intellectual apologists like Paul Krugman in America, but when a presidential candidate repudiated it in the Mafioso terms in which Trump specializes, some number of voters took note, perhaps contributing to his victory in states with lots of industrial working-class voters like Pennsylvania, Michigan, and Ohio. And yet this result still confirms the main point of the realist theory of democracy. The working-class voters who flipped to Trump were

[39] African American support for Barack Obama is easier to explain in tribal loyalty terms.

[40] Trump's 2024 victory involved some small erosions into the African American vote, although as with his other gains, these seem mostly attributable to deep unhappiness about substantial inflation since he left office, together with the kind of "magical" thinking that characterizes those voters who are not loyal to a party's candidates: "The economy was good under Trump, Trump caused that, and he will cause it again."

[41] Nate Cohn, "How the Obama Coalition Crumbled, Leaving an Opening for Trump," *New York Times*, December 23, 2016, http://www.nytimes.com/2016/12/23/upshot/how-the-obama-coalition-crumbled-leaving-an-opening-for-trump.html. Note that the decline in African American turnout was consistent across states that had recently enacted new voter suppression rules and those that had not.

[42] Ibid. See also Nate Cohn, "The Obama-Trump Voters Are Real. Here's What They Think," *New York Times*, August 15, 2017, https://www.nytimes.com/2017/08/15/upshot/the-obama-trump-voters-are-real-heres-what-they-think.html.

[43] *Michael Moore in TrumpLand*, directed by Michael Moore (Dog Eat Dog Films and IMG Films, 2016).

largely union members,[44] their loyalty to their class based on union membership (an increasingly uncommon loyalty in America) having a decisive effect on their votes. If we are realists about democracy, then we need to acknowledge, as Achen and Bartels document, that tribal loyalties explain a frightening amount about voting behavior, while moral or ideological commitment generally does not, except in the extreme cases or among a small segment of the electorate.[45]

It is worth quoting at some length Achen and Bartels's own summary of their research findings, since it makes clear the extent to which the popular, and theoretical, conceptions of democracy bear little relationship to any reality. In the summary that follows, they presuppose that party identification drives most voting behavior, and then focus on the case of the "pure" independent voters[46] in the American context, those who do not lean to either the Democrats or Republicans:

> While they, too, have group ties and social identities, they are often quite unclear about which groups "belong" in which party. Typically less-informed, they may fail to grasp what is at stake in the choice of one party or another, much less where their overall interests lie. Thus, they are often swept along by the familiarity of an incumbent, the charisma of a fresh challenger, or a sense that it is "time for a change," even when the government did not cause the current unsatisfactory situation and cannot greatly alter it. When the party balance is close . . . election outcomes turn on how these "swing voters" happen to feel when they go to the polls. As Philip Converse [citation omitted] put it, "Not

[44] See, e.g., Philip Bump, "Donald Trump Got Reagan-Like support from Union Households," *Washington Post*, November 10, 2016, https://www.washingtonpost.com/news/the-fix/wp/2016/11/10/donald-trump-got-reagan-like-support-from-union-households; and David Weigel, "How Voters Who Heavily Supported Obama Switched over to Trump," *Washington Post*, November 10, 2016, https://www.washingtonpost.com/politics/how-voters-who-heavily-supported-obama-switched-over-to-trump/2016/11/10/65019658-a77a-11e6-ba59-a7d93165c6d4_story.html.

[45] Achen and Bartels are particularly critical of "highly idealistic models of *participatory* or *deliberative* democracy" (301). They write: "These models of democracy emphasize—indeed, they often simply assume—rationality, mutual consideration, and the patient exchange of publicly justified reasons for supporting specific policies. Thus, they rest on essentially the same unrealistic expectations about human nature embodied in the folk theory [of democracy]" (301). Although I think Achen and Bartels are right to be dismissive of deliberative democracy theories, their reification of "human nature" cannot go unchallenged: None of the evidence supports the claim that the unrealistic character of deliberative democracy has anything to do with essential biological and psychological facts about human beings. The evidence they adduce only supports the view that *under the conditions in which most people live*, they have neither the time nor the interest to engage in deliberative democracy fantasies.

[46] They here mean to exclude the "independents" who, in fact, on further questioning, lean to one party or the other. They also mean to exclude quite clearly a category they don't mention, namely, "academic independents," who, as ideologues, have such well-defined views on policy questions that no existing party could be adequate to their excruciatingly "nuanced" conception of what should be done. As Nietzsche would say, "the rule is more interesting than the exception." Friedrich Nietzsche, *Beyond Good and Evil: Prelude to a Philosophy of the Future*, trans. Walter Kaufmann (Vintage Books, 1989), II.26.

only is the electorate as a whole quite uninformed, but it is the least informed members within the electorate who seem to hold the critical balance of power, in the sense that alternations in governing party depend disproportionately on shifts in their sentiment."

The result is that, from the viewpoint of governmental representativeness and accountability, election outcomes are essentially random choices among the available parties—musical chairs. Elections that "throw the bums out" typically do not produce genuine policy mandates, not even when they are landslides. *They simply put a different elite coalition in charge* [emphasis added]. This bloodless change of government is a great deal better than bloody revolution, but it is not deliberate policy change. The parties have policy views and they carry them out when in office, but most voters are not listening, or are simply thinking what their party tells them they should be thinking. This is what an honest view of electoral democracy looks like (Achen and Bartels 312).

The topic unaddressed by Achen and Bartels is the mechanism by which a particular "elite coalition" emerges from the "musical chairs" electoral process. Marx had an account of how elite consensus emerges,[47] but an adequate account of the emergence of a particular "elite coalition" would no doubt turn on the mechanisms by which control of extant political parties can be seized. On this Achen and Bartels are silent, but it is the really crucial research question suggested by their realism about democracy.

Back, now, to our main topic: Given realism about democracies, what does it mean to say, as I said earlier, that some democracies are merely "masquerading" as such, concealing in reality plutocracies or incipient authoritarian societies? The answer, I believe, is, in one sense, rather simple. It means that the tribal loyalties operate in such a way that actual decisions about policy are taken either by (a) economically dominant groups in accord with their interests, not the interests of the tribal groups that support them; or (b) authoritarian groups in accord with their interests, and not the interests of those tribal groups that support them.[48] The former was true in the Clinton Administration of the 1990s, and the first Trump Administration, despite meaningless "populist" rhetoric, fit both models, with tax cuts for the rich as well as demonization of minorities and immigrants in the name of "jobs" and "national security." How that came to be the case in the United States is the hard question, but beyond the scope of this paper.[49] But the descriptive generalization still stands.

[47] See Edwards and Leiter, *Marx*, 66–69.

[48] The interests of authoritarian elites often track those of economic elites, but not always.

[49] A useful documentation of the fact that it is the case is Martin Gilens and Benjamin I. Page, "Testing Theories of American Politics: Elites, Interest Groups, and Average Citizens," *Perspectives on Politics* 12, no. 3 (2014): 564–81, https://doi.org/10.1017/S1537592714001595. The standard Marxist theory of the state under capitalism—as the committee that organizes the affairs of the ruling

So if electoral democracy is, as the realists portray it, a matter of tribal loyalties translating into party identification, and then electing representatives, who may or may not even represent the views of the tribes that elected them, how should that affect our conception of the roles of judges?

III. A Realistic View of the Judicial Role

Everywhere judges—consistent with what I earlier dubbed their familiar "Minimal Role"—are expected to apply preexisting standards, meaning usually "the law," though as judicial oaths of office reveal, they are sometimes expected to do more, and often in terms that are not obviously consistent with the Minimal Role. Whether judges should keep those promises is an open question, but before we get to that, let us look at the promises they are actually asked to make when taking office in a variety of modern legal systems. These promises display some striking ambiguities and also reveal the extent to which even judicial promises leave much of the judge's role open.

In Serbia, for example, judges take the following (rather typical) oath: "I solemnly swear on my honour that I will perform my duties in compliance with the Constitution and the law, according to the best of my knowledge and ability and in the service of only truth and justice."[50] The promise of Serbian judges embodies the ambiguity in many such promises: namely, between loyalty to the law and then loyalty to "truth and justice." But how does one serve "truth and justice" if one is supposed to comply with laws that are unjust or contain actual falsehoods? It is unclear from the Serbian oath, though this oath is hardly atypical in this regard.

The German oath, pursuant to the German Judiciary Act,[51] is similar: "I swear to exercise judicial office in conformity with the Basic Law of the Federal Republic of Germany and with the law, to adjudicate to the best of my knowledge and belief, without distinction of person, and to serve the cause of truth and justice alone—so help me God." German jurists, who perhaps know better than most that God does not exist, are allowed to omit the "so help me God" bit at the end. The German oath also adds the interesting demand, one that is otiose on the Basic Law, namely, adjudication "without distinction of person," but that

class—would have predicted as much. See also Edwards and Leiter, *Marx*, 66–69. Two peculiar factors in the American case are the huge size of the country, which favors those with resources who can access the mass media, and the high level of religiosity, which capitalism usually destroys more effectively than it has in the United States. The latter complicates the economic elite story.

[50] Law on Judges, *Official Gazette of the Republic of Serbia*, No. 116, 2008, Art. 54.
[51] Deutsches Richtergesetz [German Judiciary Act], Apr. 19, 1972, BGBl. I at 713 as amended.

again perhaps reflects the special history of Germany in the last century. Like the Serbian oath, it poses the puzzle how fealty to false or unjust law is compatible with serving only "the cause of truth and justice."

An Egyptian judge must swear "by God Almighty that I shall adjudicate between people according to justice and respect the laws,"[52] which poses the same puzzle about how to resolve conflicts between justice and fealty to the positive law (unless justice is just a different way of saying "fealty to law," in which case it is otiose). Judges in Israel must pledge "allegiance to the State of Israel and its laws" and swear "to dispense true justice, not to pervert the law or to show favor."[53] This promise arguably implies that if "true justice" is at stake, then ignoring positive law would not be a "perversion" of such law but a requirement. In South Africa, judges of the Constitutional Court and Supreme Court promise to be "faithful to the Republic of South Africa," as well as "uphold and protect the Constitution and the human rights entrenched in it, and will administer justice to all persons alike without fear, favour or prejudice, in accordance with the Constitution and the law."[54] This oath has in it an interesting additional ambiguity: Is it the duty of judges to protect *actual* human rights or only the "human rights entrenched in" the Constitution? The latter is the more natural reading, but at the same time, it would seem an odd oath if it were rewritten to make that explicit ("I promise to uphold and protect the Constitution and only those human rights recognized by it, but other human rights—well, they get no protection").[55]

[52] See Alaa Shahine, "Egypt Women Sworn in as Judges Despite Opposition," *Reuters*, April 10, 2007, accessed January 28, 2024, for evidence of this oath being administered, https://www.reuters.com/article/world/egypt-women-sworn-in-as-judges-despite-opposition-idUSL10471860/.

[53] See State of Israel Judicial Authority (n.d.).

[54] S. Afr. Const., sched. 2 §6(2) as amended by Sixth Amendment Act of 2001 §18.

[55] South African judges frequently rule on whether or not a particular law or practice is consistent with "human rights," appealing to the principles underlying the Constitution. *S v Makwanyane and Another* (CCT 3/94), for example, struck down the use of the death penalty as inconsistent with the commitment to human rights enshrined in the South African Constitution. (Thanks to Cora True-Frost for calling this case to my attention.) Indeed, the South African Constitution refers to "human rights" without qualification, even though the requirements of human rights under the South African Constitution are not coextensive with those of international human rights law. *S v Makwanyane* says this directly, as it notes that international human rights law does not ban the death penalty, but holds that the South African Constitution requires otherwise. As the Court stated:

> Our Constitution expresses the right to life in an unqualified form, and prescribes the criteria that have to be met for the limitation of entrenched rights, including the prohibition of legislation that negates the essential content of an entrenched right. In dealing with comparative law, we must bear in mind that we are required to construe the South African Constitution, and not an international instrument or the constitution of some foreign country, and that this has to be done with due regard to our legal system, our history and circumstances, and the structure and language of our own Constitution. We can derive assistance from public international law and foreign case law, but we are in no way bound to follow it.

S v Makwanyane and Another (CCT 3/94) § 39, http://www.saflii.org/za/cases/ZACC/1995/3.html.

Perhaps the most interesting oath in the ones I surveyed is the one from Hungary:

> I hereby do solemnly swear that I shall assess the cases entrusted to me in fair proceedings, without bias, conscientiously, solely in accordance with the rules of law; in the fulfilment of my duties, I shall be driven by the desire to uphold justice and equity.[56]

In Hungary, judicial fealty is not to the country, its constitution, or its legal system but to impartiality in adjudication "in accordance with the rules of law" and to "justice and equity." This would appear to give a Hungarian judge ample grounds for going beyond the positive law—assuming they had the requisite desire "to uphold justice and equity"—something such a desire is likely to require under Viktor Orban, although there is little sign Hungarian judges are fulfilling their promise.

As the preceding examples make plain, judicial oaths leave it uncertain how judges should resolve conflicts between positive law, truth, and justice. But now, with our realist hats on again, we should remember that the idea that promises *actually bind* has the same status as the idea of "obligation" generally: Certainly many people, especially those who have been reading too much Kant, feel very strongly that promises create binding moral obligations. But the promises judges make, as the examples above illustrate, are various and at times vague about the relationship between judicial obligations and obligations to justice and truth. Should one feel that promissory obligations defeat the general "obligations" to do what is just, especially in cases where the promise is ambiguous about how to resolve the conflict between justice and law? Legal philosophers typically note that judges are also human, and insofar as we feel that humans ought to behave morally, then judges should too. From this it follows, as every legal positivist I know believes, that promises to uphold the law notwithstanding, sometimes judges ought to do what is "morally right" even if that is in violation of the Minimal and Minimal-Plus Roles of judges. When we remember what democracy is really like, that judges should sometimes do that should seem less worrisome (though it depends, of course, on the judiciary, a point to which we return below).

The central theoretical constraint in thinking about judicial roles has to do with the nature of law itself, since we would not otherwise know how to interpret the command to apply or follow "the law," so central to the various judicial oaths. There is a superficial, if popular, view that legislators create law and judges are

[56] See *Opinion on Act CLXII of 2011 on the Legal Status and Remuneration of Judges and Act CLXI of 2011 on the Organisation and Administration of Courts of Hungary*, European Commission for Democracy through Law, Op. 66 (Mar. 19, 2012).

the mere mechanical appliers of the law. Whether the society is authoritarian or democratic, this view is a gross simplification, as all lawyers and scholars know. Even if one agrees that norms are legally valid only by virtue of their source (e.g., legislative or judicial enactment), and even if one agrees that where there is a legal system, there exists Hart's naturalized version of a Kelsenian *Grundnorm*, namely, a practice of officials of treating certain criteria as obligatory criteria of legal validity, that still does not tell us the role of a judge, even on the assumption that judges should "apply the law." Statements of the law, whether by legislatures, courts, or any other lawmaker, must be *interpreted* so that their import with respect to particular facts is clear. Every serious scholar who has written about legal interpretation over the last century—from the American Karl Llewellyn to the Englishman H. L. A. Hart to the Italian Riccardo Guastini to the Frenchman Michel Troper, among many others—has recognized that interpretive norms in a given legal system accord judges latitude, perhaps great latitude, in saying what the law is. Even the most extraordinary sophist and moralist of the last century's legal philosophy, Ronald Dworkin, admitted that no one may really *know* what the right interpretation of the law is (though he, of course, believed there was one and he happened to know what it was). Dworkin's main focus was, ironically, the American constitutional order, in which its highest court is rather clearly—to realists—a super-legislature (see ch. 12 in this volume. What that means, of course, is that judicial decisions interpreting the other sources of positive law can be crucial sources of legally valid norms themselves—and not just for the parties before the court, at least in any legal system that treats judicial precedent as a valid source of law.

So what legal constraints are there on interpretation? Here, there is little of a general nature we can say, since norms of legal interpretation vary with legal systems just as Hartian rules of recognition do. Since rules of recognition are social rules in Hart's sense—that is, psychosocial artifacts arising from the actual interpretive practices of the judges that they endorse from an internal point of view—it follows that norms of interpretation can evolve and will vary with the nature of the judiciary and its interpretive practices: For example, civil service systems, where judges are promoted by peer evaluation, create more pressure toward adhering to the prevailing interpretive norms, while systems, like the American, which are political, do not.[57] If there are generalizations available about viable norms of interpretation, I suspect they derive more from sociological facts about how law interacts with society and human interests, and the practical constraints

[57] See the "explanation" of legal realism in Grant Gilmore, "Legal Realism: Its Cause and Cure," *Yale Law Journal* 70, no. 7 (1961): 1037–48; and Richard A. Posner, *Law and Legal Theory in England and America* (Oxford University Press, 1996) on the American vs. British judiciary.

that then emerge on interpretive practices, rather than from any true philosophical thesis about the nature of law. I consider only one example.

In the United States, a small number of judges, and many more legal scholars, have argued that the Constitution should be interpreted according to its "original" meaning. Bear in mind that the US Constitution was written in 1789, though amended in significant part after the American Civil War in the 1860s. Originalism in America has come in two varieties. One version is that constitutional provisions should be interpreted in accordance with the *intentions* of those who wrote the provisions. The other version, popularized especially by the late Justice Antonin Scalia of the US Supreme Court, is that constitutional provisions should be interpreted in accordance with the original "public meaning" of the provisions, the latter determined not by historical inquiry into the intentions of framers of the provisions but by old dictionaries and historical evidence about the circumstances and problems to which the provision was responsive.[58]

The first version of originalism famously confronted the problem of identifying meaningful *intentions* of collective bodies, especially about matters they never could have anticipated.[59] The second version was also afflicted by disputes about how one fixes the initial "public" meaning.[60] There is, however, a deeper practical problem afflicting both versions. The real issue is *not* that there is never any fact about the original intent or meaning of a constitutional provision (sometimes there is), but that serious commitment to original intentions or

[58] See, e.g. Justice Antonin Scalia's originalist opinion in *Crawford v. Washington*, 541 U.S. 36 (2004), reinterpreting the "Confrontation Clause" of the US Constitution as prohibiting the admission of certain kinds of "hearsay" statements against criminal defendants, statements that would otherwise have been admissible under traditional exceptions to the rule excluding hearsay. Because Justice Scalia's approach has created so many burdens for prosecutors, the one former prosecutor on the Supreme Court, Justice Sonia Sotomayor, has been doing her best to weaken the rule: e.g., Michigan v. Bryant, 562 U.S. 344 (2011).

[59] See, e.g., Paul Brest, "The Misconceived Quest for the Original Understanding," *Boston University Law Review* 60 (1980): 204–38. In the United States, a new originalist literature, inspired by the work of Keith Whittington, tries to dodge this problem by distinguishing "interpretation" (determining the ordinary, communicative meaning of the provision) and "construction" (determining its legal effect). The distinction is dubious, since in every legal jurisdiction I am aware of, there are rules of legal interpretation that make ordinary, communicative meaning irrelevant. (Take the United States: Is it "cruel and unusual" and thus unconstitutional to execute juveniles? As a matter of ordinary meaning, who knows? But it is clearly unconstitutional now given the rules of legal interpretation in the United States.) Proponents of the distinction, of course, think this is the way interpretation *ought* to be pursued, but most of them fail to articulate a normative reason for doing so; an exception is Randy Barnett, who thinks the *original* Constitution is morally superior from a moral and political point of view. See Randy E. Barnett, *Restoring the Lost Constitution: The Presumption of Liberty* (Princeton University Press, 2004). If that were remotely plausible, then this would be a good argument.

[60] See David M. Zlotnick, "Justice Scalia and His Critics: An Exploration of Scalia's Fidelity to His Constitutional Methodology," *Emory Law Journal* 48, no. 4 (1999): 1377–1429, esp. 1407–10 and accompanying notes.

meanings will inevitably undermine altogether "constitutionalism," that is, *the idea that political power should be constrained by a piece of legislation that no one living participated in enacting and that cannot be repealed or overridden in the manner of ordinary legislation.* "Originalism" makes for good rhetoric, but usually awful politics, something that most jurists in the United States recognized, whether explicitly or not, at least until recently.[61] Let us call this *the Real Problem of Constitutional Interpretation.*

The *Real Problem* is that constitutional restrictions on what current polities want to do always make the current polities deeply unhappy (the "dead hand of the past"). Now we must remember that, given realism about democracy, this is not the same as saying that constitutional restrictions are restrictions on democratic majorities. That is false, since elected officials who might find themselves constrained by a constitution do not represent the moral and political views of current democratic majorities (except sometimes by accident), for the reasons already discussed. That being said, there is a limit to how many political elites and perhaps even voters will tolerate frustration of their objectives by an old piece of legislation (i.e., the Constitution).[62] And constitutions are, as we all know, just old pieces of legislation with special prohibitions on their repeal by later legislators, often a degree of generality about political aspirations, and a certain positive moral valence attached to them. One need not be a historical materialist to recognize that the world changes continuously as its economic and productive power evolves, and that these changes affect the values, aspirations, and goals of human beings and their political associations.[63] (Historical materialists do have the theoretical advantage of explaining this!) What that means, of course, is that serious

[61] The late Justice Scalia famously said his originalism was "fainthearted," that he was an originalist but not a "nut" (i.e., he was willing to accept precedent). See, e.g., Antonin Scalia, "Originalism: The Lesser Evil," *University of Cincinnati Law Review* 57, no. 3 (1989): 864. On the current US Supreme Court, Justice Thomas is a "nut," and he may not be alone. See his dissents in *Dobbs v. Jackson Women's Health Organization*, 597 U.S. 215 (2022), and *United States v. Rahimi*, 602 U.S. 680 (2024).

[62] The Trump-appointed judges, especially on the US Supreme Court, may soon make that clear.

[63] See not only Marx's corpus, but more recently Ian Morris, *Forages, Farmers, and Fossil Fuels: How Human Values Evolve* (Princeton University Press, 2015) and, a bit longer ago, Marvin Harris, *Cows, Pigs, Wars and Witches: The Riddles of Culture* (Random House, 1974). While Marx treated the level of development of a society's productive powers as a whole as the crucial explanatory variable, Morris (a classical archaeologist) focuses specifically on the degree of energy extraction from nature, while Harris (an anthropologist) looks at short-term material incentives, such as the ability to have enough food to eat in the year ahead. Morris and Harris are, as it were, "micro"-Marxists, accepting the basic Marxist thesis that how people produce the conditions of their material existence determines their beliefs and values, but filling in the micromechanisms that explain the patterns we find. Harris is better than Morris in this regard, since Harris is more alert to what would motivate individuals to act as they do, while Morris operates largely at the level of striking correlations, without sufficient attention to psychological mechanisms that would explain the correlations.

originalism, of either variety (intentionalist or public meaning), endangers the idea of constitutionalism, of the attractiveness of being bound at all by old pieces of legislation. Constitutionalism as an ideal survives only because incremental adjustments to constitutions by courts are possible in every jurisdiction I am aware of, and so the most offensive aspects of being bound by the will of long-dead people—sometimes rather unappealing long-dead people!—are removed or mitigated. Perhaps constitutionalism has no value, though on the limited evidence we have (after all, only the United States and Sweden have constitutions that span four centuries), it seems that constitutions may exercise a constraint on political power that maximizes human well-being.[64]

Canada, which has a more European-like social democracy, is an interesting case study in this regard. The Canadian Charter, or "constitution," was adopted only in 1982, but the courts moved quickly to repudiate the idea that the intentions of its framers controlled its interpretation. In 1985, the Supreme Court of Canada in *Re B.C. Motor Vehicle Act*[65] made clear that the intention of the framers did not control how the "principles of fundamental justice" should be interpreted. A bit of realistic context is important. The US Supreme Court claimed authority for itself to settle the meaning of the US Constitution some two hundred years ago,[66] a point that could not have been lost on the Canadian High Court. Also not lost on them was the fact that the framers of the 1982 Canadian Charter were quite alive, and would be for a long time. In order not to have its authority usurped, it was important to make clear, and make clear quickly, that having written the Charter, the authors were done. What that Charter meant was now in the hands of the courts and the polity. This was, however, not simply a "power-grab" but a clear-headed recognition of the fundamental fact of "constitutionalism": namely, that a polity (e.g., its political elites) will not tolerate being constrained by its predecessors unless there is substantial room for adjustment. This is why America's most notorious originalist, the late Justice Antonin Scalia, attracted so few judicial adherents for his radical originalism over nearly forty years until fairly recently.[67] Most American lawyers and judges are tacit realists, whatever their professed views about constitutional interpretation.

[64] Mao's Premier and Minister of Foreign Affairs Zhou Enlai, when asked about the effects of the French Revolution, famously replied, "It's too early to say." Perhaps the same is true of constitutionalism. Indeed, from the materialist perspective, even the constitutions may turn out to be epiphenomenal. What is happening in the United States currently may provide useful evidence.

[65] [1985] 2 S.C.R. 486.

[66] Marbury v. Madison, 5 U.S. 137 (1803).

[67] Since his death, and thanks to Trump, Justice Scalia has attracted more support for his views on constitutional interpretation on the US Supreme Court. This may yet precipitate a crisis in the American rule of recognition, in which other political actors once again reject the idea that the Supreme Court has final authority to say what the Constitution means.

IV. The Roles of Judges in Democracies

So if we are realistic about democracies and about judges, what conclusions can we draw from the preceding observations?[68] I am not interested in the banal "obligations" partly captured by the *Minimal* and *Minimal-Plus* views. I want to focus only on the key issues, as stated earlier: what are the obligations of judges in determining the existence and meaning of the preexisting standards, when they have latitude within the rule of recognition about how to determine it, and what are the obligations of judges when the meaning of the preexisting standards is determinate? Since, on a realistic view of the judicial role, it involves inherently moral and political judgment (see ch. 12 in this volume), I see no way to answer these questions about the "obligations" of judges without regard to their moral and political views.

Let me introduce some categories that will help us conceptualize the options. The categories are admittedly crude, but their crudity may highlight what is at stake. I use the terms "progressive," "reactionary," and "status quo" in descriptive senses in what follows, though the terms often have moral valences. "Progressive" may seem the least descriptive of the three, but I use it here in what we can call the descriptive "Hegelian sense." Hegel thought that the history of humanity was a matter of God (or "Absolute Spirit") achieving self-knowledge (with the help of Hegel's philosophy, of course). What we learn is that there has been a general tendency in human history for the domain of "freedom" to expand (see, e.g., ch. 14 in this volume). Think only of democratic voting rights in America: first, it was only propertied white men; then men without property, then women, then non-whites, and so on. The history of humanity, for Hegel, is the history of the expansion of freedom.[69] *Progressive* means—as a shorthand for its clearly Hegelian background[70]—*increasing the range* of people who enjoy freedom. (Many "progressives," of course, think the range should extend to nonhuman animals and even non-animal nature. Other "progressives"—I think I am one—are more skeptical.) The boundaries of such freedom are contestable, but the basic pattern is crystal clear: More and more humans (and maybe even nonhumans) are entitled to the same moral concern, and the same moral rights, as others. This is the central ideology of post-Enlightenment modernity—shared by Kant and Marx, as well as Rawls and Hayek—and one opposed only by Nazis, fascists,

[68] I think the view I defend below is not that far away from the view articulated by Judge Posner originally in Richard A. Posner, *The Problematics of Moral and Legal Theory* (Harvard University Press, 1999), though I eschew his terminology about "pragmatism" which conceals more than it explains. See also ch. 11 in this volume.

[69] Hegel, rather notoriously, seemed to think this expansion reached its perfection with the Prussian state circa 1820, but that tells us more about the parochialism of philosophy than about freedom.

[70] I see no way to understand talk of "progress" except against the Hegelian/Christian background and its normative assumptions.

reactionaries, and religious traditionalists of all stripes.[71] A different view might insist that the real metric of progress is improvement in "well-being," but that is compatible with the point just made: freedom, in the relevant sense here, stands in a constitutive relationship with "well-being"—you cannot be well-off unless free, and vice versa—so for ease of discussion I will speak strictly in the former terms.

The other two terms again have descriptive content, though also normative connotations, depending on who is using the terms. Those who favor the "status quo" are those who favor, obviously, the way things are. This can have a pejorative connotation when the status quo is not very attractive in the opinion of the speaker, but it need not have such a connotation, since sometimes the status quo is morally preferable to the available alternatives, even in the opinion of the speaker. Those who are "reactionary" would like to return society to an earlier state of affairs, especially in terms of the legal and political status of citizens: A reactionary opposes the expansion of the freedom that the progressive favors.

Debates between so-called conservatives and liberals are not necessarily debates between reactionaries and progressives in my sense, but rather intramural debates between progressives in the Hegelian sense, that is, those who disagree either about *the means* or about *the extension* of the relevant concepts of freedom. This explains why it seems perplexing to libertarians (or "liberals" in the European context) when they are placed on the right (i.e., when they are placed among "the conservatives"). Libertarians contest the kind of freedom that modernity should progress toward, and so are often at odds with actual reactionaries. Libertarians are, in my view, much closer to reactionaries because of their naivete about how so-called economic freedom operates in practice, that is, how it operates to reduce the sphere of freedom for most people.[72] (To be sure, to the extent Hegel is right about the progressive tendency of modernity, we should hardly be surprised to find actual reactionaries trying to obscure their position by framing it, for rhetorical reasons, in "progressive" terms.)

In talking about the roles of judges in democracies, I assume—without argument, since there is no useful argument that can be given[73]—that judges should

[71] On "traditionalism," see the twentieth-century Italian fascist philosopher Julius Evola, cited favorably by Trump's former advisor Stephen Bannon. Jason Horowitz, "Steve Bannon Cited Italian Thinker Who Inspired Fascists," *New York Times*, February 10, 2017, https://www.nytimes.com/2017/02/10/world/europe/bannon-vatican-julius-evola-fascism.html.

[72] Libertarians, most importantly, do not recognize coercion by the market as an infringement on freedom, whereas starting with Marx, left progressives see that the most omnipresent form of coercion, and thus violation of freedom, results from the fact that most people must devote their productive lives to working for a wage that will support their survival: They are, for good reason, described as "wage slaves." See generally Edwards and Leiter, *Marx*, chs. 3 and 4.

[73] It is a standing problem in moral and political philosophy that no arguments can be given for "first principles" that can persuade opponents. All arguments about *what ought to be done* depend on intuitions about first principles, and such intuitions admit of psychological and sociological explanations but cannot be defended rationally against those with opposing intuitions. See ch. 15 in this volume.

facilitate progress, rather than protect the status quo unreflectively or move us backward. If the reader grants me that assumption, then the question about the roles of judges in democracies becomes clearer, though it has to be relativized to the background facts about the judiciary and the democracy. Here are, I believe, the relevant parameters.

A *Progressive Judiciary* is one that wants to expand freedom, and so exercises its interpretive latitude in service of that end.[74] A *Status Quo Judiciary* takes its promise to uphold the positive law very seriously, and even where there is interpretive latitude, interprets it in favor of the status quo. A *Reactionary Judiciary* is antiprogressive, so it exercises its interpretative latitude in service of that end, looking always to restrict freedom to the elite classes or races or sects who had enjoyed its exclusive prerogatives in the past.

A *Progressive Democracy* is one in which tribal loyalties have converged upon legislation that expands freedom. Canada and Germany are arguably examples today. A *Middling Democracy* is one in which tribal loyalties entrench a status quo that is neither progressive nor reactionary. The United States is arguably an example today, though perhaps we are about to enter a reactionary era. Finally, a *Reactionary Democracy* is one in which the tribal loyalties have converged upon legislation that restricts freedom, aiming to bestow its benefits only on select elites or groups. Hungary is an obvious example. Poland was until recently, but it has reversed course.

Finally, we need some way of characterizing the effect of judicial invalidation (or reinterpretation) of legislation in different systems.[75] Let us call a *Judge-Centered System* one in which judicial decisions invalidating legislation are generally accepted and are absorbed with little resistance by political elites and popular constituencies. Let us call a *Legislature-Centered System* one in which legislation has prima facie popular and elite legitimacy, and judicial invalidation of such legislation is typically met with skepticism or resistance by elites and perhaps popular constituencies. *Mixed Systems* are ones in which judicial invalidation of legislation sometimes looks like a Judge-Centered system, sometimes like a Legislature-Centered system.

Given these rough categorizations, here is how I suggest we think of the "obligations" of judges in contemporary democracies.

Progressive Judiciaries in Progressive Democracies should exercise minimal interpretive latitude with respect to positive law. They should honor the

[74] Note that I assume that a progressive *judiciary* can only promote freedom and equality within the constraints of its institutional role. Other progressives will, of course, pursue progressive ends within the parameters of their roles.

[75] Of course, there are legal systems in which courts officially lack the power to *invalidate* legislation—Britain, with its doctrine of parliamentary sovereignty, may be the most important case, though there is a clear tradition of parliament revisiting legislation when the courts find an "inconsistency" with fundamental rights.

Minimal Role of judges, scrupulously in Legislature-Centered Systems, since this will both promote progressive ends and honor public expectations and sustain the legitimacy of judicial review. Progressive Judiciaries in Middling Democracies should exercise their interpretive latitude in order to move the law in a progressive direction—aggressively in a Judge-Centered System, less aggressively in a Legislature-Centered system. Progressive Judiciaries in Reactionary Democracies should exercise their interpretive latitude aggressively, even in a Legislature-Centered system. The loss of legitimacy for the judiciary in aggressive judicial review is worth the risk given the pernicious character of a Reactionary Democracy.

Now the preceding admittedly simplifies how a Progressive Judiciary should think about its obligations, especially in Middling and Reactionary Democracies. A judge who thinks she has an obligation to exercise interpretive latitude in the service of progress (perhaps even to disregard settled law in the service of progress) must also take into account the ramifications of doing so—for example, the likelihood of provoking a reactionary legislature to revisit a question where the judge has ruled in a different direction. The pursuit of progress must, of course, be strategic, within the parameters in which an agent of progress can operate. A progressive judge who disregards the "backlash" effect of her decisions is not a reliable friend of progress.

With that important caveat in mind, we can proceed to the other cases. A Status Quo Judiciary should honor the positive law and exercise minimal interpretive latitude in a Progressive Democracy, whether its culture is Legislature-Centered or Judge-Centered. In a Middling Democracy, a Status Quo Judiciary in a Legislature-Centered System should probably act similarly, since it is unlikely to exercise interpretive latitude for progressive ends, and even if it did so, little good would likely result. If the Middling Democracy is Judge-Centered, then a Status Quo Judiciary should exercise its interpretive freedom in progressive directions, to the extent it is able to do so. In a Reactionary Democracy, the obligation of a Status Quo Judiciary is to try to be Progressive!

You can infer from the preceding how my account of obligations will go in the other cases. But let me address one case explicitly, namely, that of Reactionary Judiciaries in Reactionary Democracies. These judges have only one obligation in my view: to resign their position or, equally unlikely, reform their moral views and become more progressive.

The preceding has focused only on the judicial role vis-à-vis legislation, but a similar set of recommendations could be generated for the judicial role in interpreting prior court decisions or constitutional provisions or the edicts of administrative agencies.[76] A Progressive Judiciary will generally produce

[76] Thanks to Jennifer Nou for pressing me on this point.

progressive precedents, though judiciaries are not univocal, and there may be outliers of course. In that case, Progressive Judges should utilize their interpretive latitude in much the same ways as they do with respect to nonprogressive legislation. Here, the risks are likely to be different than in the legislation case: That is, the risk is not provoking legislative backlash, but judicial backlash from less progressive colleagues. Once again, the same kinds of considerations apply as in the legislation case: progressive lower courts need to be mindful of their status quo or reactionary higher courts, and so on. But the basic idea is the same: progressive judges ought to pursue, strategically, progressive outcomes, with due attention to context and ultimate outcome.[77]

Some readers may think the preceding recommendations are too facile. Surely, these skeptical readers will say, the *obligations* of judges should not depend on the quality of their moral and political views, or the moral and political quality of the legislation they must review. It is true that the question is typically approached in academic writing without regard to these kinds of distinctions, but such an approach is unrealistic both about the judicial role and about democracies in my view. Judges should generally honor their *Minimal Role*, but not always. And their *Minimal Role* affords them considerable freedom, and how they exercise that freedom has to depend on the quality of the judges (i.e., the quality of their moral and political judgment). Insofar as moral and political judgment is essential to exercise of the judicial role, especially at the highest levels of appellate review, and insofar as democracies differ in their moral and political character (as they obviously do), I see no way of discussing what judges should do without regard to their moral and political judgment and the nature of the democracy in which they serve.

To another kind of skeptic of my account, my way of thinking about the judicial role will seem to presuppose that we really know what kinds of decisions protect and expand freedom and well-being. Clearly we do not know with

[77] A nice example of strategic thinking by progressive judges comes from cases in Ohio in the 1840s and 1850s, in which judges were confronted with the question of whether to return escaped slaves to the slave-holding American South. Considerations of comity first dominated, but by the 1850s receded. Compare Birney v. State, 8 Ohio 230, 238 (Ohio 1837) (holding the indictment for harboring an escaped slave defective for not charging scienter, thus not reaching the question whether a slave who escaped while in transit through Ohio was free ("it thus becomes unnecessary to decide upon the other points, . . . of a character too important in their bearing upon the whole country to be adjudicated upon without necessity")), and State v. Hoppess, 2 West. L.J. 279 (Ohio 1845) (holding a slave escaped from a boat docked to the Ohio shore of the Ohio River was a fugitive and thus subject to recaption under federal law, but noting that a slave brought voluntarily into Ohio would be emancipated), with Anderson v. Poindexter, 6 Ohio St. 622, 630–31 (Ohio 1856) ("There has never been a period during our state government, when a slave could for one single moment, by the consent and act of its owner, be placed and continued in bondage here. . . . Kentucky can not, by the law of comity, demand of this state an abrogation of its constitution and municipal laws, to promote any of its own peculiar institutions . . . ."). For a thorough account of the Ohio slave transit and fugitive slave cases of this period, see Paul Finkelman, *An Imperfect Union: Slavery, Federalism, and Comity* (The University of North Carolina Press, 1981), especially ch. 6. (Thanks to Todd Henderson for calling my attention to these cases.)

certainty what state of affairs would actually maximize real human freedom and well-being. In the actual democratic capitalist world as it currently exists, however, we often do know, even allowing that there will be controversial cases. Decisions that protect the freedom of individual choice, within the limits set by some reasonable understanding of the Millian Harm Principle, and decisions which support social-economic policies that protect people from misfortune and encourage productive activity within capitalist relations of production (the current benchmark, of course) are good decisions. All complications to one side, the preceding basically describes the neoliberal consensus of the past half-century.[78] There may be hard cases, of course, where it is unclear, and so the obligation of judges will be less clear. The only theory of judicial obligation, however, that avoids such problems is one that would be morally ridiculous (e.g., judges should defer to whatever the legislature or executive says, regardless).

In any case, the genuinely hard cases, from a progressive point of view, are few and far between. The Affordable Care Act (ACA) honored the Hegelian impulse to maximize freedom by extending access to healthcare—essential to well-being—and the US Supreme Court correctly upheld it,[79] albeit in a way designed to appease the ideological deformities of the current moment in American political life. If there is an argument against the ACA, it has to be that its means were inadequate to its objective—and to the extent they were, it seems to have been because of the need for political compromise with reactionaries in its passage. Legalizing same-sex marriage[80] obviously expanded freedom, with the arguments against it turning on religious and metaphysical fantasies about the alleged "nature" of marriage[81] that bore no relation to the role of marital union in capitalist modernity. American free speech doctrine is a notorious moral catastrophe,[82] shielding Nazi sociopaths and pathological defamers in a way no other democracy does. That the US Supreme Court has gone so wrong in the latter cases, as it has on decisions about the financing of political campaigns,[83] is easily explicable by the pathologies of American plutocracy (people with money to spend to promote their economic interests under the guise of "freedom" drown out other voices, and shape the public discourse).[84] But the important point is that these kinds of decisions are pretty obviously wrong from the standpoint of progressive judges. The disagreements on these issues between progressive judges and others

[78] The neoliberal consensus is wholly wrong, of course, at least for the long haul; for now, it may be fine. This is normative advice for the present; the advice for the future will change.

[79] National Federation of Independent Business v. Sebelius, 567 U.S. 519 (2012).

[80] Obergefell v. Hodges, 576 U.S. 644 (2015).

[81] See, e.g., Sherif Girgis, Ryan T. Anderson, and Robert P. George, *What Is Marriage? Man and Woman: A Defense* (Encounter Books, 2012).

[82] For doubts, see Jeremy Waldron, *The Harm in Hate Speech* (Harvard University Press, 2012) and Brian Leiter, "The Case against Free Speech," *Sydney Law Review* 38, no. 4 (2016): 407–39 (2013 Julius Stone Address in Jurisprudence).

[83] See, e.g., Citizens United v. Fed. Elec. Comm'n, 558 U.S. 310 (2010).

[84] See Leiter, "The Case against Free Speech."

who are not explicitly reactionaries are disputes about the empirical facts. If the facts were otherwise, progressive judges should yield, of course.

In this regard, I should emphasize that my proposed template for thinking about judicial obligations is easily applicable as well by jurists and theorists who dispute the empirical facts. A libertarian—that is, someone who disputes the extension of "freedom" and especially the facts about state regimes that maximize it—can accept the preceding framework, but maintain that, for example, the ACA should have been invalidated, since it did not *really* maximize human well-being. On this interpretation, invalidation of the ACA is the "progressive" decision, because of a dispute about the nature of freedom and facts about the legislation in application. This view is wrong, but at least we have now located the dispute in the right place, rather than in nonsense about the act/omission distinction as the US Supreme Court did. So, too, an actual reactionary, one who does not think human freedom and well-being without regard to rank or status matters, can also think the ACA should be invalidated, since maximizing the freedom of *all* human beings has no value—not because such a decision is progressive but because a reactionary decision is preferable. (Obviously, reactionaries will be loath to acknowledge this as the *real* reason!) In both cases, it is dubious that the interpretive freedom afforded judges, even in America, would have licensed that outcome *on those reasons*, but that might not matter if judges at the highest appellate levels choose outcomes that are legally permissible on the basis of their moral and political views, and the boundaries of permissibility are fluid and wide.[85]

In short, I think it is a virtue of my account that it locates the dispute at the right place: not about some putatively "general" judicial obligation but at the level of substantive disputes about the facts about how particular policies affect human beings. Counting against my approach, however, is the fiction that judges are politically neutral and mere mechanical appliers of the law. I do not want to deny that this fiction is taken very seriously in most societies that honor Democratic Values and that it may turn out to be of crucial importance to human freedom and well-being in some circumstances: Realism demands as much. But I am not aware of a legal system that has really tested the relevant hypothesis about the fiction. In that system, the polity would actually understand that preexisting legal standards can never be adequate to the array of problems that courts are asked to address and would, with H. L. A. Hart, renounce the desire for it to be otherwise:

> [W]e should not cherish, even as an ideal, the conception of a rule so detailed that the question whether it applied or not to a particular case was always settled in advance, and never involved, at the point of actual application, a fresh choice

[85] I am skeptical they are wide enough for the reactionary, but if, following Karl Llewellyn, the boundaries of legitimate interpretation are defined by a sociological fact—current opinion among lawyers and jurists—then we can hardly be confident.

> between open alternatives. . . . [T]he reason is that necessity for such choice is thrust upon us because we are men, not gods. It is a feature of the human predicament (and so of the legislative one) that we labour under two connected handicaps whenever we seek to regulate, unambiguously and in advance, some sphere of conduct by means of general standards to be used without further official direction on particular occasions. The first handicap is our relative ignorance of fact: the second is our relative indeterminacy of aim. . . . [H]uman legislators can have no such knowledge of all the possible combinations of circumstances which the future may bring. This inability to anticipate brings with it a relative indeterminacy of aim. When we are bold enough to frame some general rule of conduct (e.g. a rule that no vehicle may be taken into the park), the language used in this context fixes necessary conditions which anything must satisfy if it is to be within its scope, and certain clear examples of what is certainly within its scope may be present to our minds. They are the paradigm, clear cases (the motor-car, the bus, the motor-cycle). . . . We have initially settled the question that peace and quiet in the park is to be maintained at the cost, at any rate, of the exclusion of these things. . . . But] [w]e have not settled, because we have not anticipated, the question which will be raised by the unenvisaged case when it occurs. . . . [W]hen [it] . . . does arise, we confront the issues at stake and can then settle the question by choosing between the competing interests in the way which best satisfies us.[86]

If there were a legal system that embraced Hart's realism and then produced catastrophic results for human freedom and well-being, we should all pause. We can put the point more starkly: If the fiction is really essential to maximizing human freedom and well-being, then this paper should be censored! But if the fiction is what Hart and I suspect it is, and recognizing it as such would be salutary, then our public discourse about judges in democracies must change accordingly.[87]

[86] Hart, *Concept of Law*, 128–29.

[87] The earliest version of this essay was presented as the keynote address at an international conference on "Interpreting Law: The Role of Judges in Contemporary Democracies" at the University of Belgrade in Serbia on October 14, 2016. I am grateful for comments and questions on that occasion, especially from Michel Troper. A later version was presented in December 2016 at the University of Chicago Law School work-in-progress luncheon, and elicited many helpful questions and comments; I recall with gratitude those from Omri Ben-Shahar, Dhammika Dharmapala, Lee Fennell, Todd Henderson, William Hubbard, Jennifer Nou, Eric Posner, Julie Roin, and David Weisbach (with apologies to those I forgot). Later versions benefited from questions and comments, both before and after, at a workshop at Syracuse University College of Law in February 2017 (thanks especially to Keith Bybee, David Driesen, and Cora True-Frost, with apologies again to those I forgot); at the University of Surrey Centre for Law & Philosophy (thanks especially to Stephen Bero, Ken Ehrenberg, Diana Richards, and Alex Sarch, with the same apologies); and a workshop at the National University of Singapore (with thanks especially to James Penner). The penultimate draft that appears here benefited from workshops at Wayne State University and the University of Wisconsin, Madison; particular thanks to Joshua Braver, Anuj Desai, Sebastian Lewis, Will Ortman, Nina Varsava, and Jon Weinberg for good questions that led to revisions. I also thank Taylor Coles and Aaron Graham for valuable research assistance.

14
The Boundaries of the Moral (and Legal) Community

I. The Expanding Moral Community

Let me invite you to step back from the parochial political disputes that dominate public life in America and most other modern democracies, as well as from the internecine academic quarrels characteristic of so much professionalized scholarship in the modern academy, and reflect, instead, on the broader sweep of moral and political thought, in both the philosophical and practical realm, over the past two or three hundred years. What must immediately strike any observer of this period is the remarkable expansion it has witnessed of what I will henceforth call "the moral community,"[1] that is, the community of creatures that are thought entitled to equal moral consideration, whatever the precise details of what such consideration involves—that is, whether it is a matter of showing "respect," recognizing the "dignity" of each, or "maximizing the utility or well-being of each, or some other formulation.[2] I am speaking here about our official ideologies and discourse, not necessarily all our actual practices and laws, though they gradually followed suit over the course of a century or so. But at the level of ideology, reflected in both ordinary moral opinion and in the work of philosophers, we in the West—ignorance of the relevant philosophical and legal traditions requires me to remain agnostic on the proverbial "East," though the trends seem to be similar—have largely abandoned the ideas that gender, race, ethnicity, religion, class, and now even sexual orientation are *morally relevant* attributes in the sense that they are attributes that determine the basic moral consideration to which one is entitled. To be sure, *in particular contexts,*

[1] Peter Singer described a similar phenomenon with a different metaphor—"the expanding circle"—although he was mainly concerned to argue for a normative conclusion about adding nonhuman animals to the circle. See Peter Singer, *The Expanding Circle: Ethics and Sociobiology* (Clarendon Press, 1981).

[2] To be sure, it is equally notable the extent to which the community of creatures entitled to *some*—if not necessarily *equal*—moral consideration has also expanded. But the press on many fronts has been toward *equality* of moral consideration, a fact particularly important in the case of nonhuman animals, to which we will return.

From a Realist Point of View. Brian Leiter, Oxford University Press. © Brian Leiter 2026.
DOI: 10.1093/9780197749852.003.0016

these characteristics may matter *because of the context*. So, for example, I take it most would still think it morally unproblematic to consider race in casting the lead role in Shakespeare's *Othello*, and most of us would still think it morally unproblematic that a man contemplating marriage gives some consideration to the gender or religion of his potential mate.[3]

Where the remarkable modern consensus emerges is with respect to what I will refer to henceforth as *basic moral consideration*. To say that everyone is now thought equal in terms of their entitlement to *basic moral consideration* means that no one can be treated differently based on their gender, race, ethnicity, religion, class, and increasingly sexual orientation *unless* there is a *further* reason beyond simply the fact of having those characteristics for doing so, and that additional reason itself does not offend against our sense of what is morally right and wrong. In the case of casting *Othello*, for example, there is an *artistic* reason, related to the conditions for a successful staging of the play given its setting and the description of its characters, for taking race into account. And in the case of choosing a mate, there are reasons related to the value of individual autonomy in private affairs for thinking it appropriate that in intimate relationships persons may weigh gender, religion, and race. But it will no longer suffice to say that the reasons for treating Jews differently than Christians *is that they are Jews*, or that the reason for treating Blacks differently than whites *is that they are Blacks. Being a human being is now enough to trigger basic moral consideration*. That sentiment is, of course, enshrined in the Universal Declaration of Human Rights adopted after World War II.[4] It is one of the cruel ironies of history that we quite clearly have Hitler and his atrocities to thank for producing this most recent, stunning shift in moral consciousness—that is, the one reflected in the Universal Declaration—even though it is one that he himself certainly did not intend.

With regard to this equality of basic moral consideration among human beings, it bears emphasizing that almost all the major moral and political theorists of modernity converge, though they have very different reasons for doing so and very different ideas about what *basic moral consideration* requires. But with respect to the entitlement to basic moral consideration, Bentham and Kant, Marx and Hayek, Rawls and Nozick all agree.[5] Bentham's slogan, recall,

[3] There are, of course, those in the academy, and to some extent outside it, who would dispute both points. To some extent, they are following the "logic" of the expanding moral community, and its egalitarian impulse, where it may lead.

[4] See generally Hurst Hannum, "The Status of the Universal Declaration of Human Rights in National and International Law," *Georgia Journal of International and Comparative Law* 25 (1996): 287–397.

[5] To be sure, philosophers like Kant often endorsed the parochial prejudices of their day, especially about non-whites, but that was almost always due to their endorsement of false factual claims about racial differences. I should add that my list of juxtaposed philosophers in the text is only meant to be representative of thinkers from different ends of the ideological spectrum, and not to imply that

was that each counts for one, and not more than one, in the utilitarian calculus.[6] Kant's formalization of the Golden Rule eschewed consequential calculations, but still issued in the same edict about moral consideration: No one was to be treated merely as a *means*, but rather as an end, a standard even more demanding than Bentham's, but one that accepts the entitlement to basic moral consideration—at least among rational persons, a caveat to which we will need to return. Marx's famous formulation—"from each according to his ability, to each according to his need"—made no reference to race or gender, just to human abilities and needs.[7] What Hayek calls the moral ideal of "individualism" involves "the respect for the individual man *qua* man, that is, the recognition of his own views and tastes as supreme in his own sphere . . . and the belief that it is desirable that men should develop their own individual gifts and bents."[8] Nothing in Hayek's argument suggests that the reference to "man" should be taken semantically rather than syntactically.

In this pantheon of well-known moral and political theorists of modernity, the case of Bentham is particularly instructive, because the increasing moral importance assigned to the experience of pain and suffering (which was his great innovation in Western moral thinking) is also one of the stunning changes in the moral sensibility of modernity. One need only recall the Homeric epics to realize that there were eras of humanity in which pain was not deemed an overriding practical consideration compared to, say, honor or glory. And as Nietzsche emphasizes, there are large swaths of human history in which the cruel infliction of pain on others was an occasion for festivities and celebration.[9] But Benthamite hedonism—though it has few explicit adherents these days—has in one very important respect now carried the day in ordinary and even philosophical thought, so that even nonutilitarians and non-Benthamites avert to, indeed take for granted, the moral salience of suffering. The "intuitive" moral salience of suffering is certainly central to the rise of vegetarianism on so-called moral grounds in the affluent capitalist societies over the last generation. We shall return to that astonishing phenomenon and the efforts to add "species" to the list of morally irrelevant attributes later in this lecture.

they are philosophical peers: Hayek is obviously not a thinker on a par with Marx, nor Nozick on a par with Rawls.

6 John Stuart Mill, *Utilitarianism*, 7th ed. (Longmans, Green, and Co., 1879).

7 Karl Marx, *Critique of the Gotha Programme* (International Publishers, 1966).

8 Friedrich Hayek, *The Road to Serfdom*, ed. Bruce Caldwell (University of Chicago Press, 2007). The book was originally published in 1944.

9 Friedrich Nietzsche, *On the Genealogy of Morality*, trans. Maudemarie Clark & Alan Swensen (Hackett, 1998), Essay II, sections 5–7. Cf. Michel Foucault, *Discipline and Punish: The Birth of the Prison*, trans. Alan Sheridan (Pantheon, 1977).

I should emphasize again that my thesis about the expansion of the moral community—the community in which equal basic moral consideration is due—does not involve denying that there remains pernicious hostility based on gender, race, ethnicity, and class. The striking fact, however, is that such hostility must now generally travel in disguise, since only Klansman and Nazis and misogynistic sociopaths talk *openly* any longer about moral status depending on one's race or religion or gender. Opponents of gay marriage are now under enormous moral pressure for precisely this reason. Once marriage among elites, especially over the course of the nineteenth century, ceased to be arranged for social and economic advantage and became instead a relationship based on such mercurial considerations as "love" and "compatibility," then the explanation for why two men, or two women, or one woman and three men, should not be "married" ceased to make any sense. More than a century later, this development now draws its obvious consequence. More generally, laws have gradually come to reflect these changes in the conception of the moral community, from the Universal Declaration of Human Rights (already mentioned) to the Civil Rights Act of 1964, to the Americans with Disabilities Act, to the constitutions of all the Western countries that emerged from the horrors of World War II.

This kind of emerging moral consensus poses a stark challenge to a meta-ethical view that was dominant for much of the twentieth century, and one that I will be defending in this lecture: what is called, in contemporary philosophical terminology, "moral anti-realism." Moral antirealists deny that there are any objective facts about what is morally right and wrong, that judgments about such facts are either mistaken *in toto* or really devices for doing something else, for example, expressing feelings and noncognitive attitudes, perhaps as a way of cajoling our compatriots to feel similarly.[10] Our world, says the moral antirealist, contains many different things: rivers and mountains, chairs and tables, oxygen and quarks, human minds and human bodies, gold and other metals. But one thing it does not contain is any objective fact about what is morally right and wrong. Just as the scientific revolution and its legacy purged the world of gods and ghosts, of the ether and of phlogiston, so too it has rendered explanatorily otiose the idea that the world contains any objective moral facts that explain our moral attitudes.[11] To be sure, events in the world induce powerful emotive and affective responses in humans, and at least some of those responses are then reified as "moral truths," rather than being recognized as the psychological and anthropological artifacts they are—artifacts that are of theoretical interest to

[10] Brian Leiter, *Nietzsche on Morality* (Routledge, 2002; 2nd ed. 2015).

[11] See Brian Leiter, "Moral Facts and Best Explanations," *Social Philosophy and Policy* 18, no. 2 (2001), repr. Brian Leiter, *Naturalizing Jurisprudence* (Oxford University Press, 2007). And see also ch. 15 in this volume.

observers, to be sure, as well as of practical importance to "insiders," but which do not pick out any independently existing features of our world.

But how, then, is such moral anti-realism to be squared with the apparently remarkable consensus about the contours of our expanding moral community? Why not think this convergence in moral (and gradually, legal) opinion over the past two centuries is really just convergence on an objective fact, just like the massive scientific convergence on the laws of Newtonian mechanics regarding observable physical objects, or on the evolution of species by the mechanism of natural selection? That is the central philosophical question about the expanding boundaries of the moral and legal community that will be my focus here.

II. Explaining the Expanding Moral Community: The Whig Histories

One attractive—and decidedly anti-anti-realist—way to explain this quite extraordinary development in human consciousness—namely, our expanding conception of who counts *morally*—is by appeal to what I will call "Whig Histories," according to which these changes really are just a story of expanding moral *knowledge*. Just as we discovered that the movement of mid-size physical objects is governed by the laws of Newtonian mechanics, and that those same laws do not describe the behavior of quantum phenomena, so too we have discovered that chattel slavery is a grave moral wrong and that women have as much moral claim on the electoral vote as men.

We have not, however, "discovered" all these claims in quite the same way, and that requires some notice. The justification of (many) scientific propositions turns on their predictive, empirical success and when they are, in fact, deemed successful they are thought to have illuminated some aspect of the causal structure of the world.[12] By contrast, the *justification* of moral beliefs turns neither on their empirical predictive success nor on their illuminating the causal structure of the world.[13] One justifies, for example, the belief that eating meat is morally wrong by appeal to a principle thought to be intuitively (not empirically!) plausible like, "unnecessary suffering is morally wrong," conjoined with empirical beliefs like "animals are sentient creatures capable of suffering" and "the way animals are raised and killed in preparing meat causes them unnecessary suffering."

[12] On the centrality of causation to understanding what it is scientific theories do in explaining phenomena, see Nancy Cartwright, "From Causation to Explanation and Back," in *The Future for Philosophy*, ed. Brian Leiter (Oxford University Press, 2004), 230.

[13] Even moral realists who think moral facts are part of the best causal explanation of experience do not believe that this fact is part of the *justification* of their being morally true. See, e.g., Peter Railton, "Moral Realism," *Philosophical Review* 95, no. 2 (1986): 1963.

This kind of argument licenses no empirical predictions and illuminates naught about the causal structure of the world. By contrast, we now accept that a scientific proposition like $e = mc^2$ is true not for the kinds of reasons offered against the morality of eating meat, but because the mass-energy equivalence Einstein proposed was experimentally confirmed (the first time was in 1932 by J. D. Cockcroft and E. T. Walton).

It would be too quick, however, to draw such a purportedly clean line between empirical and moral propositions. The striking fact about the history of inegalitarian thought is that it has regularly traded on empirical claims that are amenable to investigation in accord with the canons of epistemic warrant (i.e., the standards of evidence and justification) we deploy in the sciences. Aristotle is only the most notorious case—he thought, for example, that women and slaves were cognitively incapable of managing their lives, so were actually *better off* ceding control to free men so capable[14]—-but Aristotelian reasoning was also invoked to justify the treatment of African slaves in the modern era, who were variously deemed to "suppl[y] the missing link between human beings and chimpanzees"[15] and, according to some scientists "were a separate species," with more in common with monkeys than Europeans.[16] As the historian Annette Gordon-Reed notes, in discussing the profound impact of Harriet Beecher Stowe's 1852 novel *Uncle Tom's Cabin*, "[H]er story was effective because it directly assaulted Southern pretensions. Pro-slavery Southerners had been propagating a narrative of their own: slavery was a benevolent institution in which mentally inferior slaves were watched over by owners who treated them as part of their family."[17] Stowe's novel exploded that ludicrous narrative. The Nazi characterization of the Jews was similar to the characterizations of Africans by slavery apologists. Heinrich Himmler produced an entire magazine, in 1942, about "The Subhuman," warning Germans against being deceived by appearances, by—as he put it— "beasts in human form."[18] Jews were his prime examples, of course, but failures to pinpoint the "blood" differences between Jews and "real" humans led Hitler to recruit "literary and legal scholars, linguists,

[14] Aristotle's view exerted influence well beyond his own time. As David Livingstone Smith writes in his gripping book *Less Than Human: Why We Demean, Enslave, and Exterminate Others* (St. Martin's Press, 2011), even in the sixteenth century, Spanish scholars were arguing "that there is almost as great a difference between Indians [in the New World] and Spaniards as between monkeys and men," and that "although the natives are not 'monkeys and bears,' their mental abilities are like those of 'bees and spiders.'" Ibid., 77–78. "Why bees and spiders?" As Professor Smith notes, Aristotle thought some animals were capable of "purposive behavior" that still was irrational, since it did not involve practical reason and thought. "Aristotle believed that only humans can think. So, in comparing the behavior of Indians to that of spiders and ants, [one] implicitly denied that they are rational—and therefore human—beings." Ibid., 78.

[15] Ibid., 114.

[16] Ibid., 119

[17] Annette Gordon-Reed, "The Persuader," *New Yorker*, June 13, 2011, 120, 122.

[18] Smith, *Less Than Human*, 155.

historians, geographers, and anthropologists" to make the case for the "subhuman" character of Jews.[19] Though biology did not deliver the alleged "factual" component for Nazi racism, the social sciences complied.

Moral antirealists like me of course recognize that moral attitudes tend to be responsive to nonmoral facts—even the most subjective evaluative attitudes are so responsive, after all. The judgment, "We shouldn't eat at *La Bistro Francais Pretense*," will typically give way before a satisfying gustatory experience there. More importantly, the evaluative judgment, "Don't eat the pork dishes at *Szechuan West*, they're made from cat," is quite plainly defeated by the revelation that this is a slander on the restaurant's proprietor. Changes in our understanding of the facts have surely played some role in changes in our moral attitudes, yet this just pushes the explanatory question back one step: namely, why were people so slow to cognize correctly the nonmoral facts, why were they so ready to accept factual claims that could not, in fact, withstand scrutiny in light of the canons of epistemic warrant otherwise operative in contemporaneous scientific investigations? Canons of epistemic warrant and justification are, after all, themselves norms or values, and yet they were rendered inert in certain domains by countervailing inegalitarian moral attitudes. Some other evaluative attitude (disgust with, contempt for, antipathy toward, e.g., Africans or Jews) was itself an obstacle to responsible investigation of the nonmoral facts. That phenomenon should hardly be surprising in light of recent work in social psychology. In an influential paper that synthesized a wide body of empirical research,[20] Jonathan Haidt argued that moral judgments in most ordinary contexts arise from powerful emotional responses, not rational reflection, and that while reasons and evidence are often supplied post hoc, commitment to the evaluative judgment typically survives the failure of the reasons and evidence to support them! Haidt suggested that "the mere fact that friends, allies, and acquaintances have made a moral judgment" was more important to understanding someone's commitment to it than the actual rational support for the judgment.[21] That suggests the best explanation for the prevalence of a moral judgment will be psychosocial in character—whatever it is that explains the community convergence—rather than something epistemic or cognitive.

In light of these findings, then, we may still wonder: Why did the racist evaluative attitudes yield at the time they did, such that reliable empirical knowledge

[19] Ibid., 161.

[20] Jonathan Haidt, "The Emotional Dog and Its Rational Tail: A Social Intuitionist Approach to Moral Judgment," *Psychological Review* 108, no. 4 (2001): 814.

[21] Ibid., 819. A moral intuitionist, who thought correct moral judgment was just a matter of "intuiting" the moral properties of a situation, might think that the judgments of "friends, allies, and acquaintances" constitute testimony that does *justify* making the same judgment. I assume throughout that moral intuitionism is false, for the kinds of reasons P. F. Strawson adduced a half-century ago in "Ethical Intuitionism," *Philosophy* 24, no. 88 (1949): 23.

about racial or ethnic differences could come to light and the moral community begin to expand accordingly? If, on the Whig history, "moral knowledge" flowed from a correct appreciation of nonmoral factual knowledge, we still need to know why such nonmoral factual knowledge became possible when it did, that is, why it became possible to overcome the inegalitarian evaluative attitudes of "friends, allies, and acquaintances" and discover the facts about different races, different ethnic groups, and so on when we did? "Factual knowledge" is, to repeat, a value-laden notion, one dependent on the acceptance of certain epistemic values that license judgments about what the facts are. Yet one striking feature of the changing conceptions of the moral community is that there was widespread agreement on the relevant epistemic values long before there was widespread agreement, for example, on the fact that African Americans were not, in fact, cognitively or biologically different from European Americans, and were equally capable of governing their affairs autonomously. The key challenge for the Whig histories is to explain the delay in recognizing the "facts" that shared epistemic values should have revealed. If the expanding moral community was really just a case of expanding *knowledge*, then why was such knowledge retarded by inegalitarian moral attitudes?[22]

Someone might object: Surely the fact that the Catholic Church once rejected Galileo's heliocentrism on religious grounds does not show that it is not an objective fact that the sun is the center of our solar system? And, indeed, even a moral antirealist like me must agree it does not. But remember that the dispute between Galileo and the Church was a dispute about different *epistemic* criteria, with Galileo appealing to systematic observational evidence and the Church appealing to scripture. The puzzle about the persistence of inegalitarian moral attitudes is that many, perhaps most, of those who embraced them accepted the *exact same standards of evidence* as their opponents. What is the Whig historian to say about this?

We must, of course, be sensitive to the possibility that in some cases the inegalitarian attitudes were just, as it were, *brute*; that is, they did not depend upon nonmoral factual claims that might themselves be amenable to empirical refutation in the ordinary course of scientific investigation. One can accept, as most philosophers do, the supervenience of evaluative facts on descriptive ones (in other words: No difference in the value of X is possible without some difference in the underlying descriptive facts about X) and still think it possible that many

[22] To put the point differently: If you think that increasing knowledge about moral facts is like increasing knowledge of physical facts, then you have to explain why epistemic values wholly adequate to knowledge of certain physical (or psychophysical) facts are not wholly adequate to knowledge of the moral facts that depend on those physical facts. That is, convergence on epistemic values (those that license conclusions about what we know in the physical or psychophysical realm) has turned out to be insufficient to guarantee convergence on moral values. So something else must explain that convergence (when it finally occurs), something nonepistemic.

evaluative judgments are *brute*; that is, they depend on no claims beyond the judgment that certain descriptive characteristics obtain. Think of the evaluative judgment, "I will not eat the tofu pizza, it is awful." This judgment is *brute* in the sense that we demand no more from the judger than that he be correct that it is tofu pizza he is asked to eat *and* that he sincerely reports his response to that. He needn't supply any additional justifications to explain the judgment; that is, he need not make any further descriptive claims about tofu pizza: His evaluative response is just *brute*. We must, alas, countenance the possibility that some inegalitarian evaluative attitudes are like that too (i.e., they are *brute*).

Among contemporary philosophers, Jeremy Waldron is unique in giving explicit attention to something like the last phenomenon: namely, someone who, in "brute" fashion, tries to deny what Waldron calls "basic equality."[23] How can we respond to such an inegalitarian, someone who simply denies that Jews or Blacks or women are of equal moral worth, deserving of equal basic moral consideration? The conclusion of Waldron's argument should give the Whig historian of moral knowledge pause. Waldron correctly notes that contemporary bourgeois philosophers[24] in the capitalist societies (like Ronald Dworkin, John Rawls, and Bernard Williams) take for granted that *all human beings* are entitled to equal moral consideration,[25] but that they offer no satisfactory account of why this is so.[26] Waldron turns to John Locke, who does have an account of why human beings are all entitled to equal moral consideration, however that moral consideration is construed. But on Waldron's reading—a *very* plausible reading of Locke, I want to emphasize—the defense of "basic equality" is "an axiom of theology, understood as perhaps the most important truth about God's way with the world in regard to the moral and political implications of His creation of the human person."[27] Or as Waldron puts it later: "Lockean [basic] equality . . . is a conception of equality that makes no sense except in the light of a particular of the relation between man and God."[28] But if the only explanation in the offing as to why human beings are entitled to equal moral consideration depends on religious premises, including a belief in a certain kind of God, then defenders of moral equality in the twenty-first century should, perhaps, be worried, at least if they think their egalitarianism requires a true or at least rational foundation.[29]

[23] Jeremy Waldron, *God, Locke, and Equality: Christian Foundations in Locke's Political Thought* (Cambridge University Press, 2002).

[24] I use the term "bourgeois" in the traditional Marxian sense, to connote both the class position of these philosophers and the scope and character of their moral concern and moral advocacy. It is not meant to prejudge the merits of their views.

[25] They are not, I hasten to add, all moral realists—indeed, Williams is explicitly an antirealist.

[26] Waldron, *God, Locke, and Equality*, 2–4.

[27] Ibid., 6. The key argument for this reading comes in ch. 3.

[28] Ibid., 82.

[29] Nietzsche was famously hopeful that a decline in belief in God would lead to a repudiation of moral egalitarianism. See Brian Leiter, "The Death of God and the Death of Morality," *The Monist* 102 (2019): 386–402.

So where does that leave the Whig histories of the expanding moral community? They can appeal to discoveries about the facts that underlie the egalitarian evaluative judgments, but they cannot explain that process in solely epistemic terms, that is, solely in terms of greater sensitivity to considerations relevant to the truth or warrant of particular claims about what the world is like.[30] That, by itself, does not defeat the Whig histories, since we have examples, even in the history of science, of the way in which nonepistemic interests (i.e., interests unrelated to truth or knowledge) yield epistemically sound results. As Marxists like to point out, the capitalist class has a strong interest in figuring out the *actual* causal structure of the world, since without such knowledge, profit cannot be extracted from nature.[31] But in the case of the Marxian explanation of scientific progress, we can see why nonepistemic considerations would have yielded epistemically privileged outcomes: If you do not know the actual causal mechanisms by which oil can be removed from the earth, then you cannot realize your nonepistemic interest in profit from the recovery and sale of oil. Can we tell such a story in the case of the expanding moral community? Can we explain why *human* suffering matters morally, regardless of the kind of human who suffers? More problematically, the Whig historian, if Waldron is right, can only justify the abandonment of brute inegalitarian attitudes by relying on theological premises that are now wholly incredible in light of the canons of epistemic warrant otherwise operative in scientific investigations.[32] In that case, one would expect a massive rise in inegalitarian attitudes and a contraction of the moral community in parts of the world, like Europe, increasingly dubious of theological premises. But what we see, in fact, in most of Europe is just the opposite.

III. Explaining the Expanding Moral Community: the Non-Whig Histories

There must, of course, be non-Whig explanations possible for the phenomenon of the expanding moral community, and it is to those that I want to turn my attention. These explanations have in common that they do not need to suppose that our sense of the expanding moral community is a matter of *knowledge*

[30] Once again, I assume that moral intuitionism is not a serious position. Admittedly, there has been a revival of intuitionism (under different names) in academic philosophy, but this is, it seems to me, more an embarrassment for the discipline than a serious intellectual development.

[31] See Peter Railton, "Marx and the Objectivity of Science," reprinted in *The Philosophy of Science*, ed. Richard Boyd et al. (MIT Press, 1991), 763.

[32] Of course, one might abandon a brute inegalitarian attitude because of a competing brute egalitarian attitude, but that is wholly compatible with the moral antirealist account, since there are no objective facts about the world that command one attitude or the other: It is just the clash of brute attitudes.

or *discovery* of some objective facts. Let me start with the most familiar form of non-Whig, or debunking explanation, namely, evolutionary explanations, which are all the rage these days in philosophy and the social sciences.[33] By evolutionary explanations, I mean explanations that appeal to evolution by natural selection, as opposed to all the other evolutionary mechanisms (e.g., genetic hitchhiking or genetic drift) that affect the evolution of species. Such explanations are of somewhat limited help to the non-Whig stories about the expanding moral communities, though they certainly contribute to them. First, the explanatory stories on offer concern only the evolutionary explanation of *altruism*, that is, concern for others, a kind of concern that can, of course, be far more tepid than considering the "other" to be a full-fledged member of the moral community, whose suffering, for example, has as much moral salience as the suffering of anyone else. Second, the only well-confirmed and generally accepted evolutionary hypothesis in the literature—deriving from the work of W. D. Hamilton—involves altruistic concern for *kin*, that is, for organisms that share some of the genetic make-up of the altruist. From a selectionist point of view, so the Hamiltonian argument goes, altruistic concern for kin can be highly effective in passing on genetic material to the next generation as long as that concern is directed toward kin, such as sisters or cousins or aunts who have some of the same genetic material. Thus, natural selection will select for a genetic predisposition to nurture and sustain kin, since they too can pass the genetic inheritance on. Yet that is, of course, a very far cry from viewing non-kin, indeed utter strangers, regardless of race or religion, as entitled to basic moral consideration. Third, even the more ambitious selectionist arguments for "group selectionism," associated with Elliott Sober and David Sloan Wilson, would still fail to explain the elastic boundaries of the moral community in the contemporary era, since, at best, these arguments tell us why individuals might develop altruistic concern for *members of their group* who are not kin; they do not explain why communities might come to adopt laws that give equal moral consideration to persons outside the group. In the end, then, evolutionary explanations inspired by Darwin do not fully explain the actual phenomenon at issue, namely, the expansion of the boundaries of the moral community beyond kin and group members over the past two centuries.

If Darwin cannot fully discharge the task, then perhaps we should turn our attention to those other two giants of nineteenth-century thought, Marx and Nietzsche.[34] Let us call the first family of explanations we will consider "Marxish,"

[33] Evolutionary explanations are not necessarily debunking, and some writers have thought, quite mistakenly in my view, that an evolutionary account lends support to the objectivity of morality. For a recent, contrary view, see Sharon Street, "A Darwinian Dilemma for Realist Theories of Value," *Philosophical Studies* 127, no. 1 (2006): 109.

[34] A PhD social psychologist once suggested to me that the focus should be on the "empirical" results of social psychology of the last forty or fifty years. To the extent this work helps answer the

in the hopes of being accorded some textual latitude about Marx interpretation. On these Marxish accounts, very crudely, our expanding moral sympathies are explicable in terms of economic developments. So, for example, even as the nations in the vanguard of capitalist development, like much of Europe and the United States, ravaged other parts of the globe in the nineteenth and twentieth centuries, in pursuit of capitalist profit, it is striking that their moral sensibilities rose to new heights: gruesome executions, the suffering of the poor, even the suffering of nonhuman animals, gradually became either *verboten* or objects of moral concern. Such new moral attitudes served an obvious ideological function, obscuring the actual practices of the capitalist ruling classes behind a veneer of high-minded moral concern. Yet one imagines something more was at work as well. Capitalism, as it expands the productive capacity of humanity to heretofore unimagined heights, increasingly ameliorates the base needs of our bodily existence: for food, for shelter, for protection from physical harm. As the sensitivity of the capitalist class to pain, even discomfort becomes more refined—a fact familiar to anyone who spends time in the company of representatives of the ruling class—it should hardly be surprising that a moral distaste for the infliction of suffering becomes prevalent. We quite naturally project our own sensitivities onto those we recognize as similar to us. Of course, the key notion is "similar to us," and the capacity for the capitalist class to deceive itself about relevant similarities has been as great as that of most other ruling classes in history. Yet the gradual rise in living standards that follows upon most successful cases of capitalist development typically ensures the spread of such sensitivity in the population at large, making it harder for social orders to remain stable without becoming more responsive to the increasingly refined needs of the broader population.

Perhaps more important is that in capitalist societies all persons are evaluated first and foremost along a single dimension—namely, their market value. Thus, corporate executives are ranked by compensation, artworks make the news based on the price they command at auction, and even university professors carefully scrutinize their compensation relative to their perceived peers. Notice, however, that if every person's worth is ultimately resolvable into an economic value, then almost all other possible bases of worth and consideration (e.g., race or gender) should really be foreclosed as relevant data points.[35] The logic of value in capitalist societies is quite plainly one in which the moral community ought to expand to include anyone who can establish their value in the marketplace. This

questions, its contributions would be relevant. See Brian Leiter, *Moral Psychology with Nietzsche* (Oxford University Press, 2019), ch. 3; Jaime Edwards and Brian Leiter, Marx (Routledge, 2025), esp. ch. 5.

[35] Gary Becker, an important "neoliberal" ideologist of capitalism, made this point decades ago. See Gary Becker, *The Economics of Discrimination* (University of Chicago Press, 1971).

is obviously not to deny that capitalist societies have been rife with invidious prejudice—the United States is an obvious example[36]—or that the logic of the market will yield the ideally inclusive moral community. It is, however, to claim that capitalism itself puts pressure on attempts to limit the moral community (as Marx himself recognized, and as historical experience has repeatedly borne out).[37]

Our other family of non-Whig explanations is associated with another German philosopher, Friedrich Nietzsche, though it finds some obvious echoes in the work of Freud. Nietzsche is, in one sense, a materialist: he thinks the moral attitudes of individuals often admit of a physiological explanation. But he is not a materialist in the Marxist sense of appealing to the economic circumstances of societies as explanatory factors; Nietzschean explanations operate at the level of individual psychology, not socio-economics, though their targets are often large-scale cultural transformations, such as the triumph of Christianity in the Roman Empire. Nietzsche thinks that *ideas and values*, once let loose in the world, have the potential to take advantage of the pre-existing dispositions of individuals and wreak world-historic changes. In *On the Genealogy of Morality*, Nietzsche suggests that three profound psychological events laid the foundation for modern moral consciousness.

First, there was the resentment tinged with envy of the oppressed classes in the late Roman Empire (the "slave revolt in values" as Nietzsche calls it), the period when Christianity was born, which led to a revaluation of existing Roman values, such that "the aristocratic value-equation (good=noble=powerful=beautiful=happy=beloved of God)" was inverted into a very different valuation, according to which "'the wretched alone are the good; the poor, impotent, lowly alone are good; the suffering, deprived, sick, ugly alone are pious, alone are blessed by God."[38] Second, there was the primordial fact that creatures like us, once forced into civilization, had to find new outlets for our instinctive cruelty,

[36] In both the United States and South Africa, it was, of course, white communists who were the early organizers of opposition to racial segregation. But communism was, of course, also predicated on an expansive idea of the moral community, of all human beings *qua* members of a species with certain distinctive characteristics conducive to their flourishing.

[37] Essentially Marxian explanations—ones that treat technological progress as the primary driving force—can be cashed out in the language of contemporary economics as well, as my colleague Anup Malani reminds me. Humans have certain basic needs—food, clothing, shelter, some basic forms of culture—and technological improvements (that are partly exogenous, though can be influenced endogenously by factors like intellectual property regimes) enable us to meet those needs in new ways, without the need for slaves, for example, or without the need for women to work only in the home. To the extent such neoclassical economic explanations can be filled out, they just strengthen the case for the non-Whig histories.

[38] Nietzsche, *Genealogy of Morality*, 16. Obviously, the triumph of Christianity can be explained by reference to a variety of causes, but Nietzsche is primarily interested in facts about individual psychology, which better suit his polemical aims. Of course, if one accepts the demand of methodological individualism in historical explanation, then any candidate explanation had better be explicable ultimately in terms of the motives individuals would have had for taking certain actions.

and found those outlets in *self*-cruelty, namely, the strictures of conscience and guilt. (Freud made this idea famous in *Civilization and Its Discontents*[39].) Third, and finally, there was the existential need to make sense of suffering, of the fact that suffering is an inescapable feature of human existence, yet one that can only be tolerated if it *makes sense, if it has a meaning*—that is, if it is understood as punishment for sin, for transgressing moral ideals of self-denial that no *actual* individual can live up to for long.[40] Out of this complicated psychological and historical brew of envy, cruelty, and existential need emerged our modern moral consciousness characterized most distinctively by its hypersensitivity to suffering, as reflected in both Christianity and its concern to reconcile its followers to suffering, and, as a later consequence, Benthamite utilitarianism, with its reduction of all normative questions to questions of pleasure and pain.[41] Since, on Nietzsche's rather plausible view, there was no way, given the existential facts about the human situation, that pleasure could prevail in such a competition, it seemed to him clear that a utilitarian perspective on life would yield the conclusion that life was not in fact worth living. Nietzsche's way of resisting that conclusion was to resist the idea that suffering was prima facie objectionable from a moral point of view.[42] It is worth noting that this was not idle posturing on his part, since he himself endured extraordinary physical maladies throughout his productive life, yet never gave up on life or work during his years of hardship. But from a Nietzschean perspective, the modern conception of the expanding moral community, which has its roots in the Christian idea of the equality of all who suffer, is fundamentally an artifact of the historical and psychological forces that have elevated suffering to its overriding importance in practical thought.

I suspect that the best explanation for the emerging consensus about basic moral consideration among Western theorists involves the kinds of considerations adduced by non-Whig histories, of which I have given only a truncated survey. One cannot claim, of course, that there is overwhelming empirical evidence in support of the evolutionary, Marxian, or Nietzschean explanations, though each has plenty of evidence in its favor. The holistic character of all justification

[39] Sigmund Freud, *Civilization and Its Discontents*, trans. Joan Riviere (Martino, 2016).

[40] See Leiter, *Nietzsche on Morality*, esp. chs. 6–8 for a systematic account.

[41] Even contemporary moral philosophers who are not hedonists, like Derek Parfit, assign a central role to the moral significance of *suffering*. See, e.g., Derek Parfit, *On What Matters: Volumes 1 and 2* (Oxford University Press, 2011). Ironically, Parfit thinks the kind of systematic moral theory he and his followers pursue is one that somehow purges ethical thinking of its religious prejudices.

[42] I do not want to ascribe the view in the text to Tamsin Shaw, but her paper, "The 'Last Man' Problem: Nietzsche and Weber on Political Attitudes to Suffering," in *Nietzsche as Political Philosopher*, ed. Manuel Knoll and Barry Stocker (De Gruyter, 2014) helped me in thinking about these issues in Nietzsche. For related discussion, see Brian Leiter "The Truth Is Terrible," *Journal of Nietzsche Studies* 49 (2018): 151–73. (Note that while Benthamite hedonism entails that suffering is prima facie objectionable, one might reject the former and still embrace the latter on some other grounds.)

requires us, of course, to consider the costs of alternatives, and here I think it is crucial that the costs to a plausible metaphysics and epistemology that admits the existence of objective moral facts into our overall picture of what the world is like are too great, on a par with admitting the objective reality of gods and spirits. I do not intend the preceding considerations to be convincing to the arch moral realist (someone committed to the objectivity of moral truths), but grant me, for the sake of the remainder of the argument, that the non-Whig histories tell us quite a lot, perhaps all, about our expanding sense of the moral community.[43]

IV. How Far Will (Should?) the Community Expand?

If we may be permitted some simplification, we can say that in roughly the last two hundred fifty years in the West, the moral community has expanded from propertied Christian white men to include women, people of all races, and people of all religions. We are now, presently [2011], engaged in the concluding stages of a struggle—symbolized by the battle over gay marriage—between those who would expand the moral community to include gay men and lesbians, and those who would resist, though it now seems certain that the community will expand to include them, even in the United States. No one is in doubt any longer about either their sentience or their economic value in capitalist societies; in many respects gay men and lesbians are already full members of the legal community. Since marriage, in capitalist societies, is now purely an affair of individual desire, it is almost inconceivable that legal restrictions on marriage to (professed) heterosexuals of opposite sexes will survive much longer.

But how far will the expansion of the moral community go? Will it come to include trees and plant life? Insects? The earth itself? You may think those cases far-fetched, and perhaps they are, but what has seemed "far-fetched" in moral matters at one time is often a poor guide to what comes to seem important at a later date. Right now, one of the central battles over the contours of the moral and legal community in the advanced capitalist societies concerns nonhuman animals, and it is to their status I would like to turn. The Western moral community may increasingly renounce discrimination among religions, genders, class, and race, but it still takes species differences quite seriously, as the menu of almost any restaurant immediately reveals.

[43] Whig and non-Whig histories aren't the only possibilities: it could also just be "luck." Suppose Hitler had won World War II: It seems very likely that our conception of the moral community might have been very different from what it is, unless we are confident that other historical forces would have pressed even a Nazified Europe in the same direction. (Thanks to Anup Malani for pressing a version of this worry.)

We may ask two kinds of questions about the moral status of nonhuman animals: a predictive one about whether the moral community will expand to include them, and a moral question about whether it should. As a moral antirealist, I think the latter question has no rational answer, once we clear up any disagreements about the nonmoral facts.[44] We can agree that nonhuman animals are sentient, and that they suffer, and still "reasonably" believe that their suffering is justifiable or defensible, given our other moral attitudes. That this is so is brought out clearly by the work of the moral philosopher Peter Singer, our leading contemporary heir of Bentham and advocate for vegetarianism. He has argued, on the one hand, that our treatment of nonhuman animals is morally indefensible, since the suffering of a sentient creature is what is morally salient,[45] not the species of the sufferer. Yet, on the other hand, he has argued that it can be morally justifiable to kill human infants afflicted with various kinds of cognitive and physical defects, since to allow them to live would, over the long term, produce more suffering than happiness.[46] If one thought infanticide was morally abhorrent—as a matter of brute moral attitude—then one might take Singer's position as a simple *reductio* of the idea that *suffering* per se is the only thing that is morally relevant, since it leads to an absurd and heinous conclusion. Singer has no actual argument against such a response, since his entire position rests simply on an equally brute, and unexplained, attitude, namely, that *suffering* per se *is abhorrent*.[47] But if the consequence of believing that *suffering* per se (*regardless of species*) is the only thing that is morally salient leads to the conclusion that it is permissible to kill human babies with defects, it is equally reasonable to take that to show that species membership (namely, being human) is morally salient, since it explains why killing human babies is wrong, even when their cognitive and physical defects will impose burdens on others.

It should hardly be surprising that it is not rationally obligatory to think the suffering of nonhuman animals is on a par with that of humans, given more general lessons of twentieth-century philosophy, which show that no belief about *any* subject matter is rationally obligatory for all agents regardless of their ends. First, from the famous Duhem-Quine thesis[48] about the underdetermination of scientific theories by evidence, we know that there are not even any scientific hypotheses that are rationally obligatory, in the sense of required by

[44] See ch. 15 in this volume.

[45] There are nuances of Singer's views I am ignoring here: For example, he talks in terms of desire-satisfaction, rather than pleasure and pain, though this comes to the same thing in the case of nonhuman animals. Singer also thinks *sapience* can be morally salient, insofar as it affects the experience of pleasure and pain (or the satisfaction of desires).

[46] Peter Singer, *Practical Ethics*, 3rd ed. (Cambridge University Press, 2011), 158–76.

[47] He sometimes derides responses like this as failures to follow through a principled and rational argument, but such a rejoinder is obviously question-begging.

[48] Named after French chemist Pierre Duhem and American philosopher W. V. O. Quine.

logic and evidence. This is because any recalcitrant evidence elicited in a test of a hypothesis is compatible with the hypothesis as long as we are willing to give up the background assumptions such a test requires. In choosing among competing hypotheses and background assumptions, we must always fall back on nonrational considerations, such as theoretical simplicity, methodological conservatism, and consilience.[49] Second, unless there were a plausible *substantive* conception of rationality (there does not appear to be one, alas), then rationality itself is instrumental, imposing normative constraints only on the means chosen to realize our ends, whatever they may happen to be. Thus, even norms for belief are hostage to ultimate ends, and so particular beliefs are "irrational" only relative to the believer's ends.[50] Neither Singer nor anyone else can show that one is rationally required to rule out ends (like forbidding infanticide) that require as a matter of instrumental reasoning the repudiation of the moral salience of suffering without regard to species.

Given our general epistemological predicament—namely, that no belief is rationally obligatory—it becomes even more interesting to ask the causal-predictive question, namely, whether it seems likely that the moral community *will* expand to include nonhuman animals? The answer to this question turns, in significant part, on the question of what *features* of living things will come to seem morally significant. Even Peter Singer has acknowledged[51] that one of the most influential parts of his 1975 book *Animal Liberation* was not the Benthamite argument mentioned already but rather the emotionally evocative description of factory-farming practices in chapter 3 of his book. These descriptions evoked the *suffering* of sentient creatures and so elicited feelings of compassion from readers quite effectively. But from Singer's perspective, the moral salience of suffering also entails the moral permissibility of infanticide, and it is easy enough to see that even a rather discreet description of infanticide factories or hospices (call them what you want) would immediately elicit a very different set of moral intuitions and feelings. Clearly, our emotional responses to vivid descriptions of *factory-farmed chickens* and *the painless killing of defective human babies* are not going to yield a rational verdict about the moral propriety of either practice.[52]

Despite the best efforts of Bentham and Singer, sentience can hardly claim pride of place in our moral thinking these days. Let me ask you to recall, for a moment, the old *Planet of the Apes* movie and its successors—not the 2001

[49] See, e.g., W. V. O. Quine and J. S. Ullian, *The Web of Belief* (McGraw-Hill, 1978).

[50] See, e.g., Peter Railton, "Facts and Values," *Philosophical Topics* 14, no. 2 (1986): 5.

[51] See his reply to Judge Richard Posner at Peter Singer, "Animal Rights," *Slate*, June 13, 2001, http://www.slate.com/id/110101/entry/110236/.

[52] The antiabortion forces in the United States have always employed a Singerian strategy of describing the disgusting particulars of abortion to motivate "moral" opposition to it. It strikes me as curious that philosophers skeptical of the latter fail to notice the similarity to the most successful bits of rhetoric in support of the rights of nonhuman animals.

remake,[53] but the original 1968 movie and progeny—which illustrate very clearly that it is not sentience but the *ability to speak and reason* that is thought to be the morally significant feature of persons. In this story, American astronauts travel into Earth's future, only to discover that speaking and intelligent apes now rule, while mute humans are treated essentially as slaves. The creators of the movie assume, quite safely, that viewers will find the treatment of the mute humans shocking, but that at the same time they will be forced to recognize that it is not really different from the current treatment of nonhuman animals, including apes. The movie, then, might be thought to raise the question: Is the only morally relevant difference between humans and nonhuman animals the capacity for speech and reason? Is that really enough to justify differential treatment?

Let us appreciate for a moment the emotional force of this position. Imagine if, all of a sudden, the pigs, cows, and chickens on factory farms began to speak cogently and intelligibly to us: to complain of their discomfort, to express their aspirations, to query after the fate of their offspring, and so on. Is it not inconceivable that factory farming could survive in such circumstances? Recall that in a later episode of *Planet of the Apes*, when nonspeaking apes have been turned into slaves, the great fear of their human masters is that the last remaining speaking ape will reproduce. The immediate concern of the slave owners is a prudential one, namely, that a speaking ape could organize effective resistance to ape slavery. But surely another consideration is at play, too. It is one thing to treat living creatures as mere slaves and instruments if they cannot articulate in language their reasons, if they are "mere brutes," fit to serve. But if your ape slave talks and reasons *just like you*, and if the object of your carnivorous desire also talks and reasons *just like you*, then the situation changes. No one listening to this lecture, I may safely assume, would gladly consume the person next to him for dinner. But if the creature to your left or right were a chicken or sheep similarly engaged cognitively and discursively in my lecture, would you feel differently?

To be sure, even the moral significance we now instinctively and affectively accord to being able to speak and reason is of very recent vintage, as the history of chattel slavery of humans shows all too clearly. As the philosopher David Livingstone Smith points out, the treatment of European slaves was generally akin to the treatment of nonhuman animals, like sheep and cattle, and the fact that these slaves could not speak the language of their master " 'made them appear less than fully human,' "[54] and thus was crucial to rationalizing their servitude.

[53] The remake essentially misunderstands the deep moral message of the original 1963 novel by Pierre Boulle, most centrally by presenting the human slaves as capable of speech.

[54] Smith, *Less Than Human*, 107 (quoting historian Karl Jacoby). Smith goes on to argue that the European slaveowners must have realized, at some level, that their slaves simply spoke *other* languages (ibid., 108), which seems plausible but is probably irrelevant to their ability to rationalize away the humanity of the slaves.

Perhaps most remarkable is the story recounted by Smith about Ota Benga, a nineteenth-century African pygmy and resident of the Congo Free State, who was sold into slavery by the Belgians after his family was murdered. He was then acquired in the early 1900s by an American zoo proprietor, who befriended him and then brought him to the United States. Professor Smith recounts what happened next:

> After a brief stint in New York's Museum of Natural History, Ota Benga was given a home at the newly opened Bronx Zoo [circa 1906], where he soon became an exhibit, sharing a cage with an orangutan. "Few expressed audible objection to the sight of a human being in a case with monkeys as companions," *The New York Times* wrote the next day, "and there could be no doubt that to the majority the joint man-and-monkey exhibition was the most interesting sight in Bronx Park."[55]

This no doubt seems utterly shocking to us *because a human being was put in a cage with an ape as an exhibit.* It does not shock most of us, I suspect, in the first instance that an ape was also in a cage for the amusement of humans. That it is the former, and not the latter, that is so disturbing is, of course, testament to our deeply engrained moral speciesism, our continuing sense that the boundaries of the moral community do stop at the species line.

Should we take comfort in the fact that Kantians can give us a purportedly principled justification for such a stopping point? After all, moral standing, for Kantians, turns on rational capacity, on the ability to respond to reasons and thus to conform one's conduct in accordance with the demands of practical reason (i.e., reasoning about what one ought to do). Nonhuman animals cannot do that, and so have no real moral standing at all. Kant's best argument against their mistreatment is that it might encourage immoral behavior in rational agents, not that mistreatment of nonhuman animals is intrinsically offensive to morality.[56] But, of course, Kant's position, like the Benthamite Singer's position, entails morally shocking conclusions about the moral status of those with severe cognitive deficiencies, the comatose, and so on.[57] It will come as no surprise to social psychologists, but it seems clear that rational reflection does not track very well our actual, or even imaginable, moral attitudes.

[55] Ibid., 122.

[56] Some contemporary Kantians, being fond of nonhuman animals like cats and dogs, have tried to resist that conclusion. Their efforts are a bit tortured, and would, I suspect, be unrecognizable to Kant. An instructive example is the work of Christine Korsgaard. See, e.g., Christine Korsgaard, "Interacting with Animals: A Kantian Account," in *The Oxford Handbook of Animal Ethics*, ed. Tom Beauchamp and R. G. Frey (Oxford University Press, 2011).

[57] Kantians often adduce ad hoc considerations to block these conclusions, such as appealing to *potential* rationality and so on. These efforts do not really warrant sustained attention.

I thus shift back to predictive mode: Will the moral, and ultimately legal, community expand to include nonhuman animals as full members? As a colleague of mine quipped,[58] if soy or tofu could be made as tasty as prime rib, then it seems easier to imagine that our negative emotional response to the suffering of sentient beings would carry the day, notwithstanding their lack of reason and language, and notwithstanding the fact that the moral judgment implicit in the prioritization of such sentience would entail results that strike most of us as morally abhorrent. That tofu might actually taste good (and thus be integrated into all the cultural and religious traditions in which food figures) is far more likely, of course, than that cows and chickens will talk and reason. That this seems relevant to predicting human attitudes is itself instructive: for it means that sentience matters practically along many dimensions beyond suffering, that the multifold pleasures attendant upon our consumption of nonhuman animals occupy an important place in our thinking about how to live.

In predicting the evolution of moral attitudes, however, we must also take into account the "materialist" lesson of much history and anthropology,[59] namely, that moral attitudes are shaped by the economic and material circumstances in which people find themselves. Advanced capitalist societies, for example, continue to employ moral notions of "desert" that, in practice, justify the denial of basic moral consideration along class lines, though without saying as much: consider the role that notions of "individual responsibility" and "hard work" continue to play in moral discourse. Economically undeveloped societies, by contrast, in which the struggle for daily survival is the basic fact, are plainly not societies that will generally find at all cogent the moral impropriety of eating the nonhuman animals that are available for basic sustenance. Because the advanced capitalist societies are ones in which the option of *not* consuming nonhuman animals is, for the first time in human history, a live option for large numbers of people, it is now possible to treat this question as one of moral concern. Whigs regard this as a discovery of a morally salient fact; non-Whigs regard it as an artifact of socioeconomic circumstances. My own, non-Whig prediction is that *sentience* per se is unlikely ever to become an overriding moral consideration in wealthy societies (which are all basically capitalist societies at present) for a variety of reasons, some causal or explanatory, and some rationalizing or justificatory. First, on the explanatory side, the market value of nonhuman animals is realized primarily in their availability for consumption in one form or another by humans, and thus the kind of pressure markets can exert on intraspecies prejudice is largely absent in the interspecies case. Second, and again on the causal/explanatory

[58] My thanks to Anup Malani for the quip.

[59] See, e.g., Marvin Harris, *Cows, Pigs, Wars, and Witches: The Riddles of Culture* (Random House, 1974).

side, part of the "improved" standards of living that capitalist societies deliver everywhere, albeit in fits and starts, includes the availability of the nutritional and gustatory rewards of consuming nonhuman animals; that these are often tied up with cultural and religious tradition makes them especially resilient, though such traditions have often yielded, over time, before the demands of the global market, a fact we should not forget. Third, and finally, there is a justifying reason—not simply causal—for thinking that the species boundary is unlikely to be fully crossed when it comes to basic moral consideration. For the theoretical reasons, like Bentham's or Singer's, for doing so entail shocking conclusions—the permissibility of infanticide, for example—conclusions that reveal the ethical peculiarity of the perspective of thinkers like Bentham or Singer. There is more to life than the avoidance of suffering, and there is also more to life than the pursuit of pleasure, but we can agree that if one were as morally blinkered as Singer is, then eating hamburger could sometimes be worse than infanticide. All the world's cultures and literatures reject the Benthamite/Singerian calculus, which is an artifact of a particular moment in capitalist development, and it is a reasonable abductive inference over this vast mountain of evidence that it reveals something important about human moral attitudes, including the fact that they appear to be deeply anthropocentric. And since there is nothing more to ethics than these attitudes, there seems little reason to expect that the moral community will expand to include nonhuman animals as fully equal members.[60]

[60] I am grateful to Jaime Edwards, Anup Malani, Richard Posner, and, especially, Matt Evans for helpful comments on an early draft of this lecture. I was helped by comments on a later draft from Roger Clarke, Anuj Desai, Guy Elgat, Harold Langsam, and Joshua Sheptow; by questions and comments at a work-in-progress luncheon at the University of Chicago Law School; and by questions and comments from members of the audience at the Meador Lecture at the University of Alabama on September 30, 2011.

15

Disagreement, Anti-realism about Reasons, and Inference to the Best Explanation

I. Explaining Philosophical Disagreement: The Explanandum

I will argue that the best explanation of one important kind of intractable disagreement about reasons for action—namely, the disagreement among philosophers which defines the entire history of moral philosophy—includes the fact that realism about reasons is false. By realism about reasons, I will mean the view that what an agent has reason to do is "mind-independent," that is, it does not depend on anyone's beliefs or attitudes about the reasons for acting, even under ideal epistemic conditions.[1]

[1] See Sharon Street, "A Darwinian Dilemma for Realist Theories of Values," *Philosophical Studies* 127 (2006): 109–66; David Enoch, "How Is Moral Disagreement a Problem for Realism?," *The Journal of Ethics* 13 (2009): 16 for "robust realism."

A threshold objection to this strategy of argument deserves brief consideration. Enoch notes that "[n]ot every phenomenon calls for explanation—we are inclined to take some facts as brute." Enoch, "How Is Moral Disagreement a Problem," 23. That seems right, but is disagreement a "brute fact" that does not "call" for explanation? Enoch notes that a "full answer . . . would have to determine first what makes a phenomenon explanatorily interesting," and confesses, "I know of no satisfactory answer to this question." Ibid. We do not need, of course, a full answer to that question, just an answer to the question whether intractable disagreements should be treated as "brute." Enoch admits that "declaring all cases of moral disagreement as explanatorily uninteresting is a rather desperate (and dogmatic) move." Ibid.

Let us distinguish between the metaphysical claim that some facts are brute (i.e., that they do not admit of further explanation) and the epistemological or practical claim that a phenomenon does not "call" for or warrant an explanation. Many phenomena are brute in the latter sense, but not in the former—for example, that my bread toasts in the toaster each morning, that the car starts when I turn it on, that my daughter Celia is a terrific cook. None of these phenomena are metaphysically brute, of course, and they all can be explained, but except in unusual circumstances we have no reason, epistemic or practical, to seek out such an explanation: They do not "call for" explanation. Metaphysically brute facts simply do not admit of any further explanation. There may not be many such facts, though this will likely depend on one's metaphysics. That we experience time as moving forward not backward, that fundamental physics gives us the best account of matter in motion, that death awaits all living organisms, may all be metaphysically brute facts. The phenomenon of disagreement is obviously not metaphysically brute in any similar sense.

So Enoch's challenge should be understood as the demand that we need to articulate when, for epistemic or practical reasons, we should seek an explanation of a phenomenon. We do not, as noted, need a general account of "what makes a phenomenon explanatorily interesting," since it will suffice if we can identify some features that make a phenomenon explanatorily interesting, and show that disagreement has those features.

From a Realist Point of View. Brian Leiter, Oxford University Press. © Brian Leiter 2026.
DOI: 10.1093/9780197749852.003.0017

When people take themselves to be trying to discover some objective fact[2] about the world but fail to converge on an answer despite trying for a long time, it is natural to wonder what explains their failure. Imagine: You and your neighbors spend hours looking in the backyard for a lost ball; you all think you know what the ball looks like, and you all profess sincerely wanting to find it. Yet, after fruitless hours of searching, there is no agreement that it has been found. While some neighbors produce ball-like objects, others disagree that that is the ball; still others deny that any candidate "balls" have even been found. Is it not quite appropriate to ask what the explanation is for this strange state of affairs? Perhaps the ball is not in the yard; or perhaps there is no ball at all; or perhaps some of the ball hunters are blind; or perhaps some of the ball hunters have been bribed by those who hid the ball to assist in their scheme. All of these could be possible explanations for the disagreement among the ball searchers, but what seems clear is that some explanation is "called for."

The situation is the same, I suggest, with regard to trying to figure out the reasons for action we have. "Reasons for action" may be the *au courant* philosophical lingo,[3] but the entire history of Western philosophy has been devoted to this question under various descriptions. Consider:

(1) Are reasons for acting culturally relative (the Sophists) or absolute (Plato)?
(2) Are reasons for acting deontological (Kant) or consequentialist (too many to list) or derived from some other source (Aristotle et al.)?
(3) If reasons for acting are consequentialist in justificatory structure, do they appeal to what maximizes pleasure (Bentham), happiness (Mill), informed desire-satisfaction (Brandt, Railton), or something else?
(4) If reasons for acting are deontological in justificatory structure, do they require acting from the motive of duty, or acting in accordance with the categorical imperative, or showing respect for persons (a vast literature of intrasectarian disputes among Kantians)?
(5) Are moral reasons for acting overriding, or do nonmoral reasons sometimes (or often) trump moral reasons (Philippa Foot, Bernard Williams, Nietzsche, maybe Susan Wolf) or are moral and egoistic reasons for acting locked in irresolvable conflict (Sidgwick)?

After more than two thousand years, philosophers still cannot find the "ball," as it were: They do not agree about what our reasons for acting really are. That

[2] An "objective fact" is a mind-independent fact in the following sense: Its existence and character do not depend on the epistemic states of other persons, even under epistemically ideal conditions.
[3] Derek Parfit and Joseph Raz seem to be most responsible for this way of talking.

is our explanandum. This calls for an explanation: More precisely, we want to know what the best explanation is.

II. The "Best" Explanation

The "best" explanation of some phenomenon satisfies a variety of epistemic and pragmatic desiderata,[4] ones derived from the successful empirical sciences, which remain our paradigms of fruitful ways of explaining observable phenomena. These desiderata include: (1) simplicity (especially ontological simplicity), as opposed to *gratuitous* complexity (i.e., the gratuitous positing of entities that satisfy no other epistemic or pragmatic desiderata); (2) consilience, that is, the ability to show how seemingly disparate phenomena have common causes and thus are not really independent, but causally dependent on the same underlying facts; and (3) conservativism, that is, being consistent with, and thus not unsettling, other beliefs about the world that have been well-confirmed. This is a nonexhaustive list, to be sure, but it is on these that I will focus.

Consider: sitting at home, watching a movie on your computer, suddenly the computer goes off, as do all the lights in the house. What is the best explanation of this phenomenon? Here's a first hypothesis: mischievous leprechauns have invaded the house, discovered the circuit breakers, and flipped them all simultaneously, cutting power to all electrical devices. This explanation does complicate our ontology: It posits leprechauns, beings who are capable of mounting mischievous attacks, for example. That would not be objectionable if, for example, there were other observable phenomena that were satisfactorily explained by such an expansion of our ontology: for example, finding little green hats in the backyard, or pots of gold at the end of rainbows, or, even better, the corpses of very small persons dressed in green. But absent that, this first hypothesis would be quite radical: It would add to our ontology a class of little creatures (are they humans? They seem to have complex cooperative planning capacities!) that, heretofore, we had no reason to think existed.

Our first hypothesis, in short, is not a good candidate for the best explanation of the phenomenon that demands explanation. So let us turn to a second hypothesis: There has been an electrical power failure in the neighborhood. This hypothesis would win additional support from observable facts like (1) all items powered by electricity went off simultaneously; perhaps (2) lights and other electrically powered items went off in neighboring properties; and perhaps

[4] See Brian Leiter, "Moral Facts and Best Explanations," *Social Philosophy and Policy* 18 (2001): 79–101, repr., Brian Leiter, *Naturalizing Jurisprudence* (Oxford University Press, 2007).

(3) there was a thunderstorm or an electrical explosion that would explain the sudden cessation of electricity to homes in the area. This explanation, assuming the observable evidence confirms it, would be simple (no new ontological entities), consilient (it would explain what happened in the house and in neighboring properties), and conservative (electricity, power outages, and the role of storms in causing them are all part of our familiar and going theory of how the world works).

I use this silly example to motivate an answer to the question: What is the best explanation of why philosophers cannot agree on our reasons for action? The analogy is not exact in lots of ways. But the same kind of "best explanation" phenomenon presents itself. There is a fact in both cases that everyone agrees upon: In the power outage case, there is suddenly no electrical power; in the reasons for action case, there is no agreement among philosophers about what our reasons for action *really* are. What is the "best explanation" of that agreed-upon phenomenon? The power outage case illustrates, in simple form, some of the relevant considerations.

Let us take, however, a different hypothetical case, with even more structural analogies to our real topic. A parent takes a group of young children—five or six years old, suppose—to a restaurant to celebrate a child's birthday. The children are served a cake with a rich vanilla icing and strawberry and chocolate filling. Some children think it delicious, the best cake they have ever had; others think it disgusting, indeed inedible; still others eat it, without enthusiasm. Now these are children, prone to stubborn opinions, convinced of their rectitude and good sense (not like philosophers, of course). The enthusiastic cake eaters are denounced by their repulsed cake-eating compatriots: "That's disgusting, how could you eat that"? The cake enthusiasts are appalled, "What's wrong with you? This is a great cake!" The "neutral" consumers are mystified: "Don't fight," they say.

I have hosted children's birthday parties, and I exaggerate only a bit the extremities of reaction, though that is to be chalked up to bourgeois social norms of politeness that are often inculcated even in younger children. But the "best explanation" of the birthday party cake is easy: None of the children are "wrong," tastes differ, and add to that oddities of child psychology, and the drama is easy to explain. There is no objective fact about whether or not the birthday cake is good; there are different gustatory sensibilities, together with facts about child psychology, that explain the conflagration that ensues.[5]

[5] To preempt confusion: I think disagreement among philosophers is more like the birthday cake example than the missing ball example. The latter was meant only to motivate the thought that an explanation was "called" for.

III. An Inference to the Best Explanation of Disagreement among Moral Philosophers

Now let us return to the philosophers. Everyone knows they disagree about the nature of our reasons for action in the sense that there is no consensus about propositions 1–5 mentioned earlier.[6] One contemporary, the late Derek Parfit, thought this a scandal, an indictment of the *bona fides* of all moral philosophy, including his own. (Here I agree with him.) His final work was devoted to demonstrating that all "major" moral philosophers (or at least his friends, plus Nietzsche![7]) agreed with his views (or were not *really* disagreeing), appearances notwithstanding. Almost no one was convinced,[8] though the details do not matter for my purposes. What I want to emphasize is that even some realists about reasons think that the failure of philosophers to agree impugns the objectivity of the results.

But why should it? Here is where we come back to inference to the best explanation (IBE) considerations.[9] If two epistemic agents are equally well-situated to cognize certain objective facts, yet neither one can agree on what those facts are,

[6] Philosophers (i.e., employed teachers of philosophy in universities) do largely agree about trivial applied propositions that no one has ever disputed—for example, "No one has a reason to torture babies for fun." (As an aside, it's not clear that certain kinds of internalists about reasons, like Sharon Street, do agree with this, but put that worry to one side.) Convergence on applied claims about reasons for action typically belies deeper disagreements about *why*, say, torturing babies for fun is wrong. (Even where the applied judgments are just brute, the fact of convergence on them admits of other explanations that do not require realism about the matters agreed upon: See the discussion about whether causing suffering is wrong, below.) Philosophers also like to claim, without evidence, that the "folk" generally agree that we should honor agreements, promote the good, and not harm others. But such armchair assertions about what the folk believe are belied by several considerations. What the "folk" actually do is inconsistent with these alleged agreed-upon reasons for acting, which raises a question about whether the folk really accept these reasons. Even worse, the folk are fairly explicit about the *ceteris paribus* conditions that attach to these reasons: e.g., "do not harm others, *unless* they deserve it" or "honor agreements, *unless* the other party is an asshole," or "it is wrong, other things being equal, to cause severe suffering to an innocent." Is there agreement, among the folk even, about who *deserves* harm, or who the *assholes* are? I am not aware of any evidence in support of such armchair fantasies. Philosophers affirm from the armchair that folk agreement does not exist in reality. Of course, as soon as we move to the level of philosophical grounds for the particular reasons, the disagreement becomes even more apparent. And philosophers replicate the same problem: E.g., many philosophers might affirm that "it is wrong, other things equal, to cause severe suffering to an innocent being," but everything turns on what "other things equal" means, and here again philosophers differ. Often, in the literature, agreement about "pro tanto" reasons or "pro tanto" wrongness operates the same way: It obscures the real disagreement by bracketing it.

[7] Parfit's chapter on Nietzsche is not good, but as a matter of academic sociology, those of us in the boring Anglophone world interested in Nietzsche can only be grateful that he thought it worth the bother. He sent me an early version, and I sent him comments, but it did not salvage the published version. For criticisms, see Christopher Janaway, "Attitudes to Suffering: Parfit and Nietzsche," *Inquiry: An Interdisciplinary Journal of Philosophy* 60 (2017): 66–95.

[8] See, e.g., Mark Schroeder, "Review, On What Matters, Volumes 1 and 2," *Notre Dame Philosophical Reviews* (2011), https://ndpr.nd.edu/reviews/on-what-matters-volumes-1-and-2/.

[9] This is a version of option #4 in Enoch, "How Is Moral Disagreement a Problem," 21–29; I'll have more to say about some of his objections in the text.

we may appropriately ask: why do they not agree? One possible (antirealist) explanation is that (1) there is no objective fact to be cognized, and (2) judgments about that putative fact are better explained by nonepistemic features of agents. (I return to possible realist hypotheses below, pp. 328–29.)

That seems to describe, nicely, the situation in philosophy regarding our real reasons for acting. Sentimentalists—Hume, Herder, Nietzsche, for example—claim that moral judgments result from the arousal of emotions in response to certain states of affairs, and that the emotions aroused are not to be explained by their "cognitive detective" capacities (i.e., their ability to pick out features of the world warranting a particular response) but by psychological facts about persons that are epistemically insensitive to the "real" moral (or reason-giving) qualities of states of affairs. When sentimentalists observe a two-thousand-year-long intractable debate among moral philosophers, they are hardly surprised: Even moral philosophers are hostage to their psychology, which determines their affective responses, which determine their intuitive moral judgments, which ultimately determine their moral philosophies.

Let us now state the argument more precisely:

(1) If there were objective reasons for action, epistemically well-situated observers would probably converge upon them after two thousand years.[10]
(2) Contemporary philosophers, as the beneficiaries of two thousand years of philosophy, are epistemically well-situated observers.
(3) Contemporary philosophers have not converged upon reasons for action.
(4) Conclusion: There are no objective reasons for action (IBE from the first three premises; the details of the IBE will be spelled out below).

This argument makes two key assumptions about epistemic access and epistemic capacities: first, it assumes that *if* there were objective facts about reasons for action, they would be knowable in principle by epistemically well-situated agents; and second, it assumes that two thousand years of moral philosophy should have rendered us epistemically well-situated observers (if it has not, why not?).

An easy way for the realist about reasons to defeat the argument is to deny one or both of the epistemic assumptions. There are, of course, serious costs to doing so. If one denies the first assumption, and allows that *real* reasons for action can be wholly evidence-transcendent, even under ideal conditions, then one has to admit that we can never really know if we have made a genuine mistake about

[10] Someone could deny this, of course, but far less than two thousand years has sufficed for massive progress and convergence in most other cognitive domains. Cf. the discussion of the supposed "youth" of moral philosophy, below, pp. 339–40.

reasons for acting. One need not agree with Marx's second *Thesis on Feuerbach* ("The dispute over the reality or non-reality of thinking which is isolated from practice is a purely scholastic question") to nonetheless agree that it is a high cost for the realist to allow that there are practical truths, but, alas, they remain beyond our cognitive capacities.[11]

If the realist denies the second assumption, then the realist must consign to irrelevance some (or perhaps all) of two thousand years of moral philosophy as epistemically inadequate to what our reasons for action really are. But what could justify doing so? Is there some other method for discovering the real reasons for acting? Holy texts, divine revelations, the words of prophets, and the advice of poets appear to be as deeply in conflict as the views of moral philosophers, but even if they were not, there is so much other evidence that these sources are epistemically unreliable that they seem poor contenders as alternatives. If that is right, then this second realist response appears simply ad hoc.

With respect to the possible realist repudiation of the first assumption, we may also ask: What could justify it, beyond the desire to salvage realism about reasons? Put differently, we may ask whether the existence of evidence-transcendent practical truths would survive IBE?[12] Is there an IBE of intractable disagreement about reasons for action among philosophers that would include as a premise the existence of evidence-transcendent practical truths? I am not aware of any, but I invite the realist who wants to opt for this route to supply one.[13]

This is a natural point at which to spell out the IBE involved in the fourth proposition above: Why is the nonexistence of objective reasons for action part of the best explanation of intractable disagreement among philosophers? Answering this question requires proffering a full explanation for this disagreement, which I now set out in terms of the premises to which it is committed.

First premise: *Sentimentalism.* Basic intuitive moral judgments (e.g., about the right-making or good-making features of situations or actions) are best explained, causally, by basic emotional or affective responses.

[11] See Folke Tersman, *Moral Disagreement* (Cambridge University Press, 2006), especially ch. 44 discussing arguments in Crispin Wright, *Truth and Objectivity* (Harvard University Press, 1992).

[12] Rach Cosker-Rowland, "The Epistemology of Moral Disagreement," *Philosophy Compass* 12 (2017), offers one argument why there cannot be such practical truths. Arguably Nietzsche does too with his quip about Kant: "[H]ow could something unknown obligate us?" (*Twilight of the Idols*). My argument can proceed without defending either of theirs.

[13] Professor Rowland suggests to me that such an argument would parallel that for thinking there are historical truths we cannot know because (e.g., they depend on evidence unavailable to us). But this case is crucially different from the disagreement about reasons-for-acting case: in the former, but not the latter, we know exactly what kind of evidence would settle matters, we just do not, in fact, have access to it. (This is often true in the natural sciences, especially physics.) In the latter case, we don't even know what the relevant evidence would be, precisely because, as the antirealist would say, there is no fact of the matter!

Second premise: *Noncognitivism about affects.* The affects involved in basic intuitive moral judgments have no cognitive component: They have no cognitively evaluable belief component, but rather a distinctive phenomenal feel. (I will assume, following Nietzsche,[14] that these affects are primarily ones of *inclination* and *aversion*; more on that below, pp. 330–33.)

Third premise: *Philosophical arguments for what our reasons for action* are always involve a premise that depends on a basic intuitive moral judgment.

Fourth premise: *Philosophers have not converged on our real reasons for acting.*

Conclusion (by IBE): *The best explanation for the views philosophers defend* are the psychological and sociological facts that explain their basic affects; objective facts about reasons are explanatorily otiose.

IV. A (Metaphysically) Realist Rejoinder?

But why is this the *best* explanation? IBE is a comparative test, so we must have some competitor explanation for moral disagreement on offer if we are to evaluate the relative merits. Here is moral realist David Enoch's explanation of nonphilosophical moral disagreement[15] which I quote at some length:

Many moral matters are complex and not at all straightforward; people are the victims of any

> number of cognitive shortcomings . . . and so that some may be more likely to make moral mistakes than others; many find it hard—or do not want—to sympathize and imagine what it is like to occupy a different position in the relevant interaction, and different people are sensitive to the feelings of others to different degrees; we let our interests influence our beliefs (moral and otherwise); we are subject to the manipulation of others, and so to the distorting effects also of their self-interests. . . .
>
> Let me draw special attention to one of these kinds of alternative explanation: that in terms of the distorting effects of self-interest. This kind of explanation is especially important for at least two reasons: It is extremely powerful, and it helps explain the difference in the scope of disagreement in morality and in other discourses.[16]

[14] Brian Leiter, "Moralities Are a Sign-Language of the Affects," *Social Philosophy & Policy* 30 (2013): 237–58; Brian Leiter, *Moral Psychology With Nietzsche* (Oxford University Press, 2019).

[15] I agree with David Enoch, "How Is Moral Disagreement a Problem," and many others (e.g., David Owen Brink, *Moral Realism and the Foundations of Ethics* (Cambridge University Press, 1989)) that some moral disagreements really mask empirical disagreements, but I do not see that as being at issue in the case I am interested in (i.e., intractable disagreement among moral philosophers). Benthamites and Kantians disagree, but they are not disagreeing about any empirical facts.

[16] David Enoch, "How Is Moral Disagreement a Problem," 25–26.

Since a central part of what is in dispute in the history of philosophy is whether our real reasons for action are self- or other-regarding, Enoch's last point is question-begging, so I will put it to one side. But even if we discount Sidgwick (who thought the conflict between self-regarding and other-regarding reasons intractable), as well as the various opponents of Plato who defended obviously self-regarding reasons for acting,[17] how would the considerations Enoch adduces fare as an explanation of the disagreement among *the other philosophers for* two thousand years about our reasons for action? What cognitive shortcomings, for example, did Bentham suffer from that Kant did not? What "interests" influenced Kant that led him to disagree with Bentham? Who "manipulated' Mill and Aristotle? (And, as Kant would instruct us, "sympathizing" with someone is not a sound basis for determining one's moral obligations anyway!)

Enoch's points seem unlikely candidates to explain away the intractable disagreement about reasons for action that characterize the history of Western philosophy (even if they have some purchase in the case of nonphilosophical disagreement). But does the antirealist explanation sketched above, 325–28, fare better? I shall argue it does.

V. In Defense of the Antirealist IBE

First, the empirical evidence in support of sentimentalism (the first premise) is very strong. As a recent literature survey notes, individuals "with selective deficits in emotional processing" due to disease or injury to the brain render different moral judgments about hypothetical situations like the Trolley cases than most emotionally normal subjects do about hypothetical situations,[18] suggesting that the affective responses are causes of the moral judgments. Psychologist and philosopher Joshua Greene has argued that emotional responses loom larger in deontological than consequentialist moral judgments,[19] the latter demanding more "controlled cognition,"[20] but in more recent work, even Greene has acknowledged that "affect supplies the primary motivation to view harm as a bad thing" in the first place, so that even consequentialist reasoning has "an affective

[17] Plato, of course, thought that moral (e.g., justice-based) reasons for acting were actually in the agent's interest, but that is so far from obvious that it demands the famous dialectical efforts of Plato to try to render it plausible.

[18] Fiery Cushman, Liane Young, and Joshua Greene, "Multi-System Moral Psychology," in *The Moral Psychology Handbook*, ed. John Doris and the Moral Psychology Research Group (Oxford University Press, 2010), 53–54.

[19] Joshua Greene, "Why Are VMPFC Patients More Utilitarian? A Dual-Process Theory of Moral Judgment Explains," *Trends in Cognitive Sciences* 11 (2007): 322–23.

[20] Cushman et al., "Multi-System Moral Psychology," 54.

basis."[21] In another recent review of the empirical literature, Timothy Schroeder, Adina Roskies, and Shaun Nichols found that the view they dub "sentimentalism"—namely, the view that "the emotions typically play a key causal role in motivating moral behavior"[22]—is well-supported by the "evidence from psychology and neuroscience,"[23] and that while "motivation derived [exclusively] from higher cognitive centers independently of desire is possible . . . the only known model of it is pathological" involving Tourette syndrome.[24] In sum, the empirical evidence supports the claim that sentimentalism is part of a consilient explanation of the phenomenon of moral judgment.[25]

Second, noncognitivism about basic affects (the second premise) is also highly plausible, psychologically and philosophically. Here, let me focus on Nietzsche's version of this view. In *Daybreak*, Nietzsche says "moral feelings" (*Moralische Gefühle*) are inculcated when "children observe in adults inclinations for and aversions to certain actions and, as born apes, *imitate* these inclinations [*Neighungen*] and aversions [*Abneighungen*]; in later life they find themselves full of these acquired and well-exercised affects [*Affekten*] and consider it only decent to try to account for and justify them" (*Daybreak*, section 34). We may bracket the astute concluding observation—about the impulse to supply post hoc rationalizations for evaluative judgments produced by a nonrational mechanism—to focus on its picture of basic affects. Moral feelings or affects are equated with "inclinations for and aversions to certain actions," or, more precisely, with the mental state, whatever it is, that motivates one to perform certain actions or avoid certain other actions. It is surely plausible that any credible ontology of the mind includes mental states that are *motivationally effective*, at least in the sense that they produce what I will call henceforth, *motivational oomph* (or *push*), that is, they incline toward or avert away from certain acts, even if they are not ultimately successful in producing action. We typically presume, of course, that *affects* or *feelings* are characterized, in part, by their ability to produce *motivational oomph*, and, indeed, the fact that they do so is one of the main

[21] Ibid., 62. More precisely, "affect supplies the primary motivation to regard harm as bad. Once this primary motivation is supplied, reasoning proceeds in a currency-like manner (currency emotions are designed to participate in the process of practical reasoning)." Ibid., 63. "[A]larm-bell emotions are designed to circumvent reasoning" (ibid., 62) and, arguably, this is "the origin of the welfare principle," as "Parkinson's disease appears to show that intrinsic desires are necessary to the production of motivation in normal human beings, and this would seem to put serious pressure on the cognitivist position." Ibid., 93.

[22] Timothy Schroeder, Adina L. Roskies, and Shaun Nichols, "Moral Motivation," in *The Moral Psychology Handbook*, ed. John M. Doris and The Moral Psychology Research Group (Oxford University Press, 2010), 77.

[23] Ibid., 98.

[24] Ibid., 94.

[25] Note that sentimentalism could be true and well-supported by empirical evidence, but that could be compatible with moral realism.

points thought to count in favor of views, like sentimentalism, that understand moral judgments to involve essentially the expression of feelings.

It is equally a part of ordinary usage to take feelings to have another crucial characteristic: namely, that they are phenomenologically distinctive. There is something *it feels like* to be inclined to stop the child from sticking his hand in the fire, and there is something *it feels like* to be inclined to avoid killing a child. A *noncognitivist* view of affects claims that they can be fully individuated by their distinctive phenomenal feel; a cognitivist view denies that, claiming, instead, that to individuate the affect one also needs to consider some aspect of its *cognitive* (i.e., truth-evaluable) content, such as a belief. Cognitivist views of emotions, notoriously, are forced to deny that human infants can have emotions, since they lack the concepts necessary for having truth-evaluable judgments.[26] That infants cannot have emotions is, by my lights (as someone who has cared at length for three infants!), a *reductio* of the cognitivist position. But less anecdotally, cognitivism about the emotions runs up against a large body of psychological research showing that, as Jesse Prinz puts it, "emotions can arise without judgment, thoughts, or other cognitive mediators."[27] While it may be doubtful that qualitative feel can distinguish all emotional states (Prinz's example is differentiating "anger" from "indignation"[28]), that is not relevant here: The question is, following Nietzsche's proposal, that the *affective* source of moral judgment, in the first instance, consists of fairly basic or simple mental states of *inclination* and *aversion*, and it seems quite plausible that there is something it feels like to be *inclined toward* X or *averted away from* Y, even if the relevant *qualia* might be thought inadequate to pick out all conceptual nuances we might want to apply to such cases. It is also possible, of course, that our conceptually nuanced distinctions between, say, *anger* and *indignation* are explanatorily otiose with respect to the *motivational oomph* associated with the feeling in question.

But what about the most common worry about noncognitivist views of feelings or affects, namely, how can they account for our propensity to think emotional responses can be assessed as warranted or not?[29] Even in infants, of course, emotional responses have causal triggers: The infant *sees* a scary "monster" and reacts by crying in fear. The infant's *fear* has an *intentional content*: It is *about*

[26] See John Deigh, "Cognitivism in the Theory of Emotions," *Ethics* 104 (1994): 824–54. Views according to which emotions are like perceptions of evaluative properties (e.g., Christine Tappolet, *Emotions, Value, and Agency* (Oxford University Press, 2016)) have responses to these sorts of worries, but face many different problems: for one thing, they have to presuppose exactly one of the points in dispute here, namely, whether there are evaluative properties there to be perceived. Some other problems (pertaining to the way in which the analogy between emotional responses and perception breaks down) are usefully reviewed in Benjamin De Mesel, "Review: Emotions, Values, and Agency," *Notre Dame Philosophical Reviews* (2017).

[27] Jesse Prinz, *The Emotional Construction of Morals* (Oxford University Press, 2007), 57.

[28] Ibid., 52.

[29] See ibid., 60.

something, namely, the scary monster. We might believe the infant is wrong to be afraid (i.e., what the infant sees is not dangerous, since it is only make-believe), but that does not change the fact that the infant experiences upset and fear. I believe that a child is about to stick his hand in the flame, and so I *feel inclined* to stop him. "Feel inclined" understates the character of the feeling, of course: *I feel I must* stop him. But the fact that there is a causal relationship between a mental state with cognitive content and an affective response does not show that to *identify* the affect, one must understand it to be constituted, in whole or even in part, by a *cognitive* component. We need to account for the *intentionality* of emotions, to be sure, but that does not mean we have to identify emotions with *judgments*. It might suffice to introduce a kind of explanatorily primitive mental state, as Peter Goldie famously proposes,[30] like "feeling toward," one that captures both the *intentionality* of emotional states *and* their distinctive qualitative character.

So, feeling inclined to do X or averse to doing Y can have a distinctive phenomenal character, even if the causal trigger for the feeling is a false belief of the agent with the distinctive feeling. When we criticize the resulting emotion, perhaps, then, we are making a different normative judgment, something like: a correct belief about the facts is not likely to cause such an affective response. Consider: The infant falsely perceives (without any conceptual content) the family dog as dangerous, and so bursts into tears. We think the infant is *mistaken*, because we know that the family dog is not dangerous. But we don't criticize the infant for having an unwarranted affective response; rather, we console the infant. Why? Perhaps because we don't think the infant is *epistemically responsible* for its false cognition of the family dog as dangerous. But when I react with anger to a perceived slight by the store clerk that, in reality, was nothing of the kind, I can be criticized not because anger is anything other than noncognitive, and not because my "belief that I've been slighted" is a causal trigger for my anger, but because I am epistemically culpable for having a false belief, one that produces unhappy consequences (my anger, a fight with the clerk at the store, an unpleasant scene, etc.). (Note that anti-realism about epistemic judgment is a live option.[31])

Yet it seems I can also be criticized for responding with anger even when my belief was correct (i.e., when the store clerk *really was* rude). How can that criticism make sense if the cognitive belief is just a causal trigger for an evaluative/affective response that has no cognitive content? The obvious answer is that such judgments are, themselves, the expression of other non-cognitive attitudes

[30] Peter Goldie, *The Emotions: A Philosophical Exploration* (Oxford University Press, 2002), 19.
[31] See Hartry Field, "Epistemology without Metaphysics," *Philosophical Studies* 143 (2009): 249–90.

or feelings, such as an inclination toward nonaggressive responses to insults or an aversion to aggressive ones (we might call the latter the "Christian attitude"). Of course, if we view such criticism as making a cognitive, rather than noncognitive, statement, then we will be forced toward an error-theoretic interpretation of such judgments (i.e., we will have to interpret all such judgments as false) or some more complicated noncognitive (in the semantic sense) interpretation of them. Thus, the noncognitivist about basic affects of inclination and aversion can claim that a distinctive conscious, qualitative feel marks our basic affects of inclination and aversion; that these feels are the causal root of our moral judgments; and the social practice of assessing such feelings as warranted or unwarranted can be compatible with the noncognitive character of the feeling because to deem them warranted or unwarranted is either (1) to render an epistemic judgment (perhaps itself amenable to antirealist treatment) about the cognitive judgment that is the causal trigger for the noncognitive state, or (2) to express a meta-affect (i.e., an affect *about* an affect) about someone else's affective response to a causal trigger. In sum, noncognitivism about basic affects offers a simple and conservative explanation of the crucial claims in the sentimentalist hypothesis about moral judgment.[32]

The third premise makes a claim about the logical structure of arguments for reasons for action that seems hard to dispute: Such arguments depend on a premise that appeals to what is supposed to be intuitively plausible. Now the "Kantian" loosely construed—that is, someone who thinks rational action itself, either as a matter of logic (e.g., arguably Kant or Gewirth) or its constitutive character (e.g., Korsgaard or Velleman), supplies the crucial normative premise—will deny that intuition is at issue, as opposed to the demands of rationality or action. I shall simply record my view that these arguments are implausible, so much so that Gewirth's has no defenders anymore, and Korsgaard's and Velleman's constitutivism will, one hopes, go the same way.[33] With apologies to members of this particular Kantian sect, I will say nothing further about these views.

The fourth premise notes the key explanandum we have been discussing throughout: Philosophers do not agree about reasons for acting.

Now we are ready for the antirealist inference to the best explanation. Since philosophers develop arguments that depend on key intuitive premises, that are

[32] Someone might worry that it is not at all "conservative," but radically revisionary of ordinary "folk" beliefs, to tell people that there is (as Nethanel Lipshitz aptly put it to me) "no such thing as good and evil," and that there is nothing they *objectively* have a reason to do or not do. But this kind of worry involves a misunderstanding of conservativism as a demand on choosing better and worse explanations. We should be conservative with our explanations vis-à-vis well-confirmed theories and beliefs about the world, not about folk beliefs and intuitions, which are (outside, say, judgments about midsize physical objects) a notorious hodgepodge of falsehood, delusion, and wish fulfillments.

[33] See David Enoch, "Agency, Schmagency: Why Normativity Won't Come from What Is Constitutive of Action," *Philosophical Review* 115 (2006): 169–98.

noncognitive, but explicable in terms of facts about the psychology and sociology of those who make the judgments, it should hardly be surprising that their philosophical systems are locked in intractable conflict, since their arguments depend, both logically and causally, on views that are psychosocial artifacts that vary with person, time, and place.[34] Bentham thinks it intuitively obvious that the experience of pain is the most morally salient fact; Kant (on certain readings) thinks it intuitively obvious that the motive for action is the most morally salient fact. What would an argument for either premise look like that did not already presuppose the intuition?

Recall the children at the birthday party. Child A says, "The cake is disgusting, you ought not eat it!" Child B says, "The cake is delicious, eat it!" Child A, with some help from a philosopher, explains that (1) chocolate and strawberry are a revolting combination of flavors; (2) any combination of flavors that is revolting ought not be eaten; therefore (3) the cake should not be eaten. Child B, with the help of another philosopher, retorts: (1) chocolate and strawberry are a delightful combination of flavors; (2) any combination of flavors that is delightful ought to be eaten; therefore (3) the cake should be eaten. Their debate is intractable because a crucial premise in their argument—the first premise—is determined by their gustatory sensibilities, an artifact of each child's psychology (perhaps also biology) and upbringing. There is no objective fact of the matter about whether chocolate and strawberry combined are delicious or not.

The intractable debate among philosophers about reasons for action has the same explanatory structure.[35] The disputants depend on a premise that is determined not, of course, by their gustatory sensibilities, but by facts about their psychology and sociology: their sensitivity, their stamina, their openness, their neuroticism, their upbringing, their peer environment, etc. That premise (the basic moral intuition) is typically nonnegotiable in reality, but itself has no cognitive status, and so cannot be refuted by logic or evidence. Let us recall, for example, that Derek Parfit's parents were doctors and Christian missionaries

[34] Max Etchemendy points out to me that there is another IBE in the offing here, which accepts my first three premises but adds one more, namely, that basic affective responses are not amenable to change through argumentation in seminar rooms or in the pages of philosophy journals. That, too, would explain the failure of convergence among contemporary philosophers, but without taking a position on realism versus anti-realism about reasons. It would, of course, entail that moral philosophy is irrelevant, and so, in that regard, is a version of the first realist rejoinder considered earlier (i.e., affirming that the truth about reasons for acting transcends what we can know about them). But that raises the question of why we should think *that* is the explanation for the failure of convergence.

[35] The realist may here object that a key difference is that while adult observers will agree that the children are wrongly disputing mere matters of taste in the cake case, they will not so view their moral disagreements. Assuming that is true (the evidence is mixed—consider the economists' talk of "preferences," which is ubiquitous in the neoclassical tradition), that simply raises the question what best explains such a metaview about the status of moral disagreements. It is not clear to me that the explanation is really that different in either case, though the habit of academic philosophers of talking only to each other perhaps encourages a different judgment.

in China and he was raised a theist; that John Rawls had planned to be an Episcopal priest; and, more recently, that Rae Langton's parents were Christian missionaries. Are these facts about some contemporary moral philosophers *really* irrelevant to their moral philosophies?

Presumably, even the realist will admit these psychosocial facts are relevant; the question is whether these facts about the prosaic origins of philosophers' central moral intuitions are part of the best explanation of why they end up disagreeing with each other. Of course, the disagreements among products of Judeo-Christian indoctrination can look like the narcissism of small differences compared to the disagreement between recent Western moral philosophy and Nietzsche or Homer or the rest of the world, so perhaps we should pause for a moment to mention the more dramatic cases of disagreement.

VI. A Dramatic Case of Disagreement: Is Causing Suffering Wrong?

Standard-issue academic Anglophone philosophers in recent years think it intuitively obvious that "suffering is bad," even if they often disagree about whether this judgment admits of further explanation or what that explanation would be.[36] My argument is that, however much affection readers have for this premise, it is nothing more than an affectively induced intuition that tells us more about "socialization"[37] than about reality. The contemporary agreement can be explained without assuming realism, a fact we can bring out by noting the disagreement with it outside the confines of recent moral philosophy.

Someone part of the Homeric world—or perhaps the Mafia more recently?—would find these purportedly intuitively obvious claims bizarre. Suffering is essential to glory and honor; it is not objectionable but welcome.[38] Loyalty and the ability to exact revenge are far more important than suffering, and individuals can be harmed when honor, glory, or revenge demands it. It is not simply that all of human history reveals the powerful role of this competing set of norms,

[36] A Kantian might think this follows from a more fundamental principle about the dignity of persons, while a utilitarian might take this as a brute starting point, or as following from some principle of utility defended on other grounds.

[37] I use "socialization" very loosely to capture all those psychosocial facts about persons that explain their moral judgments per the IBE sketched earlier.

[38] Someone might object that even those committed to the view that suffering is bad and that inflicting suffering is wrong can allow that those are defeasible normative considerations. Thus, the Homeric hero is not disagreeing. That could be true if there were evidence that the Homeric hero's "practical reasoning" worked this way: But, first, Homeric heroes don't engage in much practical reasoning (at least not as Homer presents them), and second, there is no indication that Homeric heroes are committed to the wrongness of suffering being a normative consideration that needs to be defeated.

but that there is no refutation of commitment to them that does not presuppose a premise involving a different affective commitment. These norms can be coherently formulated and applied, and they play,[39] as much as we observers might regret it, an enormous role in human affairs.

Most academics have a profound affective identification with the intuitions at the foundation of both the Kantian and utilitarian traditions (I find myself moved by aspects of both).[40] Glory, honor, revenge, and loyalty lack academic defenders, but that is not to be regretted, since those normative ideals thrive and structure lives without academic philosophers writing in support. But calling attention to them indicates the diversity of views about reasons for action that have gripped human minds.

To be sure, the realist might retort that the appeal of glory or revenge as a reason for acting is vulnerable to being explained away, perhaps along precisely the lines Enoch proposed originally. Recall Enoch:

> Many moral matters are complex, and not at all straightforward; people are the victims of any number of cognitive shortcomings . . . and so that some may be more likely to make moral mistakes than others; many find it hard—or do not want—to sympathize and imagine what it is like to occupy a different position in the relevant interaction, and different people are sensitive to the feelings of others to different degrees; we let our interests influence our beliefs (moral and otherwise); we are subject to the manipulation of others, and so to the distorting effects also of their self-interests.[41]

Remember that our topic is reasons for action, not simply "moral" reasons for action as conceived within a particular parochial tradition, say, the Kantian or utilitarian. But to evaluate Enoch's alternative, let us take as an example Odysseus, who is celebrated by Homer for his talents at deception and his capacity to exact revenge. Odysseus, recall, returns after his long journey to find suitors in his home trying to seduce his faithful wife Penelope. Disguised as a beggar, Odysseus is the only one strong enough to string his old bow (the challenge put to the suitors by Penelope), at which point he slaughters the other suitors in revenge.

Has Odysseus made a mistake about his reasons for acting? Did he fail to "sympathize and imagine what it is like to occupy a different position in the

[39] Commitment to logical consistency is also an affective commitment, not that widely shared, it seems, given the history of the world.

[40] I put to one side Aristotle and the neo-Aristotelians with their fanciful assumptions about what it means to be human: They have the distinct advantage of not regarding empirical evidence from the natural and human sciences of what humans are actually like as having any bearing on their ideas.

[41] Enoch, "How Is Moral Disagreement a Problem," 25.

interaction"? Let us grant that this is, in fact, a legitimate demand on reasons for acting, though it looks dangerously close to assuming, without argument, that possibly self-regarding reasons (like honor) are out of bounds. But it is easy enough to imagine that Odysseus would reason as follows: "Were I to be found out trying to seduce another man's wife during his absence, he would be right to slaughter me." Was Odysseus insufficiently "sensitive to the feelings of others"? Again, let us grant that this consideration is even relevant to his reasons for acting. Has he really failed to be "sensitive to the feelings of others"? The feelings of others are, presumably on any view about reasons for action, a defeasible consideration: It no doubt hurt Donald Trump's feelings that residents of London flew a giant balloon of a "Baby Donald" over the city during his recent visit to the country, yet his feelings were not a serious reason for the protesters not to do that. Even if Odysseus does not give much weight to the suitors' strong preference not to be slaughtered, this does not mean he gave it no weight: Odysseus surely knows his suitors would prefer not to be victims of his revenge. Yet he could reason, without error, as follows: "[T]o try to marry a man's faithful wife while he is away engaged in an arduous life-and-death struggle for a worthy cause is an offense to honor and decency, and anyone who embarks on such a path has forfeited his claim to have his wish to live respected."

Of course, that reasoning would be in error *if* one granted a premise like "inflicting death on others for the sake of revenge is always wrong" or, alternatively, "inflicting death on others to avenge their wrongful actions is always wrong." But Odysseus accepts neither premise, not because either is false but because the psychology and sociology of his own upbringing leave him with no affective inclination toward accepting these premises such that they should influence his practical reasoning.[42] Odysseus disagrees with the reasons for acting that seem decisive to we moderns because his psychology and sociology are different, not because there is an objective reason for him not to slaughter the suitors of Penelope—or, for that matter, an objective reason for him to slaughter them.

A realist might protest that the *best* explanation of why we judge Odysseus's reasons for acting mistaken is precisely that we are sensitive to the infliction of death on sentient beings for trivial reasons, and that any action with that attribute is a token instance of "moral wrongness": Yes, we were brought up to be sensitive to that, but in so being raised, we were raised to be sensitive to actual moral wrongdoing! Now, in order not to beg the question, we have to ask whether the thesis that "moral wrongdoing" is identical with or supervenient upon, among other things, inflicting death on sentient beings for revenge, would be part of the

[42] As noted previously, I do not think Odysseus actually engages in "practical reasoning," rather than acting instinctively. But this is a separate debate: For skepticism about practical reason, see my discussion of Nietzsche's view in Brian Leiter, *Moral Psychology with Nietzsche* (Oxford University Press, 2019).

best explanation of the Odysseus/contemporary dispute? The antirealist explanation, recall, appeals to psychological and sociological facts, and their historical, cultural, and temporal variation; the realist explanation presumably does not deny any of those facts *but then adds a further fact,* namely, that killing for revenge is a case of objective moral wrongness. Does that additional metaphysical thesis, which certainly makes our ontology less simple, make the explanation more consilient? *What else does it help us explain*? I have argued elsewhere that such an assumption has no consilience benefits at all.[43] Is it a methodologically conservative assumption? It would be if our best-going theory of the world already required that there be objective facts about reasons, but there is no evidence I can see that it does.[44] Anti-realism about reasons for acting is rampant in all the social (as well as physical) sciences; it is only some philosophers (and theologians) who think there are objective reasons for acting.

VII. A Final (Metaphysically) Realist Rejoinder

Realists about reasons have developed many "defusing explanations"[45] to block the abductive inference from apparently intractable disagreement about our reasons for acting to skepticism about objective reasons. Disagreement, as I have acknowledged throughout, is an epistemic phenomenon, from which we propose to draw a metaphysical conclusion. The "defusing" explanations of such disagreement propose to exploit that fact by suggesting alternate epistemic explanations for the disagreement, many of which I have already touched upon. Here, I want to comment on one residual defusing explanation.

Perhaps, this defusing argument goes, disagreements about reasons for action are not *really* intractable but resolvable in principle. This has been the standard optimistic refrain from philosophers ever since "moral realism" was revived as

[43] Leiter, "Moral Facts and Best Explanations" argues at length that the ontological complexity produces no explanatory payoffs and so fails by IBE standards: I there criticize in detail proposals by Brink, J. Cohen, and Sayre-McCord, among others.

[44] Enoch mischaracterizes the issue when he says (correctly) that "[c]ompeting explanations are evaluated holistically and against a background of prior beliefs," but then says (falsely) that competing explanations of moral disagreement will "depend on whether we were metaethical realists to being with." Enoch, "How Is Moral Disagreement a Problem," 27. But holistic forms of justification, informed by conservativism, do not assume that just any "prior beliefs" count: It is the "prior beliefs" that we already have good IBE reasons to think are true (i.e., those that are already part of a well-confirmed theory of the world)! But our prior beliefs about realism about reasons for action are precisely what is at issue in the IBE argument, so we cannot presuppose such beliefs in evaluating competing explanations.

[45] John M. Doris and Alexandra Plakias, "How to Argue about Disagreement: Evaluative Diversity and Moral Realism," in *Moral Psychology, Vol. 2: The Cognitive Science of Morality: Intuition and Diversity*, ed. W. Sinnott-Armstrong (MIT Press, 2008), 311, 320–21; see also Don Loeb, "Moral Realism and the Argument from Disagreement," *Philosophical Studies* 90 (1998): 281–303 for a useful survey and rebuttal of various strategies.

a serious philosophical position in Anglophone philosophy in the 1980s. With respect to very particularized moral disagreements (e.g., about questions of economic or social policy) which often trade on obvious factual ignorance or disagreement about complicated empirical questions, this seems a plausible retort. But for over two hundred years, Kantians and utilitarians have been developing increasingly systematic versions of their respective positions. The Aristotelian tradition in moral philosophy has an even longer history. Utilitarians have become particularly adept at explaining how they can accommodate Kantian and Aristotelian intuitions about particular cases and issues, though in ways that are usually found to be systematically unpersuasive to the competing traditions and which, in any case, do nothing to dissolve the disagreement about the underlying moral criteria and categories. Philosophers in each tradition increasingly talk only to each other, without even trying to convince those in the other traditions.[46] And while there may well be "progress" within traditions—for example, most utilitarians (but not all) regard Mill as an improvement on Bentham—there does not appear to be any progress in moral theory, in the sense of a consensus that particular fundamental theories of right action and the good life are deemed better than their predecessors. What we find now are simply the competing traditions—Kantian, Humean, Millian, Aristotelian, Thomist, perhaps now even Nietzschean—which often view their competitors as unintelligible or morally obtuse but don't have any actual arguments against the foundational premises of their competitors. There is, in short, no sign—I can think of *none*—that we are heading toward any epistemic *rapprochement* between these competing moral traditions. So why exactly are we supposed to be optimistic?

As grounds for optimism, many philosophers appeal to the thought (due to Derek Parfit) that secular "moral theory" is a young field, so of course it has not made much progress. This strikes me as implausible for several reasons. First, most fields with objective subject matters have usually managed to make progress, as measured by convergence among researchers, over the course of a century—and especially the last century, with the rise of research universities. Moral theory is, again, the odd man out when compared to physics, chemistry, biology, or mathematics.[47] Even psychology, the most epistemically robust of

[46] The one partial exception is Parfit's last work, though the extent to which it really engages the competing views is open to some doubt. See Schroeder, "Review, *On What Matters*."

[47] It is natural to worry that the problem of intractable disagreement is not limited just to moral philosophy: Isn't the same apparently intractable disagreement mirrored in many other parts of our discipline? Are not metaphysicians and epistemologists also locked in intractable disagreements of their own? Think of debates between internalists and externalists in epistemology, or between presentists and four-dimensionalists in the philosophy of time. If disagreement among moral philosophers supports an abductive inference to denying the existence of moral facts, what, if anything, blocks that inference in all these other cases? Some writers think this kind of "companions in guilt" consideration counts in favor of moral realism, notwithstanding the disagreement among moral philosophers. It is not entirely clear why they rule out, however, the other natural conclusion. Of course, we would need to think carefully about individual cases of philosophical disagreement,

the "human" sciences, managed to make progress: for example, the repudiation of behaviorism and the cognitive turn in psychology in just the last fifty years. Second, Spinoza, Hume, Mill, and Sidgwick (among many others) may not have advertised their secularism, but the idea that their moral theories are for that reason discontinuous with the work of the past hundred years does obvious intellectual violence to the chains of influence of ideas and arguments. Third, and relatedly, so-called secular moral theory regularly conceives itself in relation to a history that stretches back in time (sometimes back to the Greeks)—contrast that with the relative youth of modern physics!—so that it becomes unclear why the bogeyman of the deity was supposed to have constituted the insuperable obstacle weighing down intellectual progress. Most contemporary deontologists may be atheists, for example, but it is not obvious that their atheism enabled them to make stunning intellectual progress beyond Kant.[48]

Psychological and sociological facts are part of the ontology of the social sciences already; objective facts about reasons for acting are a significant addition. Unfortunately, it is unclear that adding such facts offers any explanatory advantages. Such an ontological add-on seems to fare especially poorly in helping us understand the history of philosophy, which is the history of intractable disputes about reasons for acting.[49]

since not all of them, in all branches of philosophy, are as intractable or as foundational as they are in moral philosophy. Some philosophical disagreements can, in fact, be defused fairly easily. Thus, to take an example from one of my other fields, the debate in legal philosophy between natural law theorists and legal positivists about the nature of law both has an element of tractability (natural law theorists like John Finnis have, in fact, conceded most of the claims that actually matter to legal positivism) and admits, in the intractable parts, of defusing by reference to the obvious religious commitments of natural law theorists on the remaining issues they refuse to cede. In sum, the skeptical argument from disagreement among philosophers may have implications beyond moral philosophy, but what precisely they are will have to be decided on a case-by-case basis. For discussion, see Brian Leiter, "Moral Skepticism and Moral Disagreement in Nietzsche," *Oxford Studies in Metaethics* 9 (2014): 126–51.

[48] Alastair Norcross suggests to me that the real problem is that ethics requires reliance on "intuitions," and our intuitions are still strongly tainted by our religious traditions. That seems a more plausible point, though it is unclear what criteria we can use to distinguish between "tainted" and "untainted" intuitions. As Nietzsche would be the first to point out, the utilitarian obsession with sentience and suffering is, itself, indebted to Christianity—an ironic fact, given the centrality of the wrongness of suffering to Parfit's own moral philosophy (e.g., Derek Parfit, *On What Matters, Vol. 2* [Oxford University Press, 2011], 565).

[49] I received helpful comments on an early draft of this paper from Thomas Adams, Max Etchemendy, and Nethanel Lipshitz. The current version benefited from comments by participants at the Australian Catholic University conference in Rome in September 2018 on "Moral Disagreements." I should acknowledge, in particular, David Enoch, Don Loeb, Rach Cosker-Rowland, and Folke Tersman. I also received excellent comments on that version from Paul Boswell.

16
Normativity for Naturalists

I. Naturalism and Normativity: The Problem

By "naturalists" I mean philosophers who think that what there is and what we know are questions reliably answered by the methods of the empirical sciences; "speculative naturalists," like Hume and Nietzsche, are philosophers who think that we can try to answer those questions by extending existing scientific explanatory paradigms to questions of philosophical interest that the sciences have not gotten around to addressing.[1] Some professed naturalists, Quine most notoriously, are better in theory than practice: Quine maintained allegiance to an ontology (physicalism) and a psychology (behaviorism) decades after both were discredited as a matter of actual scientific practice. (Quine, sadly, never got much past the science of the 1930s and 1940s.) Ironically, speculative naturalists like Hume and Nietzsche often do better: They extended their ontology to include the nonreducible mental states necessary to make causal sense of human phenomena long before the general cognitive revolution in psychology. And Nietzsche does better than Hume: first, because he extends psychological causes to the unconscious, and second, because he does not assume that the most plausible psychology will vindicate prevailing moral opinions.

"Normativity" picks out a number of philosophical problems, but I take the central one posed for naturalists to be this: What is a naturalist to say about ubiquitous normative claims like "You ought to believe in the theory of evolution given the evidence," or "You ought not eat beef given the cruelty of factory farming of cows"? These normative claims are in the deontic mode, but they need not be: one can just as well ask what naturalists should say about normative claims like "You're a damn fool if you don't believe in the theory of evolution," and "You're a moral reprobate if you still eat beef given all we know about factory farming." How do we locate claims about *what you ought to believe* or *what you ought to do*, or about *which claims deserve credence* or about *what your moral worth is given your conduct* in a world conceived naturalistically? Following Stephen Finlay among many others,[2] we will say that the central problem is about

[1] See Brian Leiter, *Nietzsche on Morality*, 2nd ed. (Routledge, 2015), 4–9.
[2] See Stephen Finlay, "Recent Work on Normativity," *Analysis Reviews* 70 (2010): 334.

From a Realist Point of View. Brian Leiter, Oxford University Press.
DOI: 10.1093/9780197749852.003.0018

understanding the property of *being a reason*, whether for action or belief.[3] It is important to emphasize at the start that the problem for naturalists is not simply about *moral* or *practical* normativity but about normativity *tout court*. Reasons for belief are normative too, and it was the primary mistake of twentieth-century naturalists and moral skeptics like A. J. Ayer and C. L. Stevenson to ignore the epistemic case—a mistake that can be remediated, I will suggest, in what follows.

Why are these kinds of normativity a problem for the naturalist? The central worry, I take it, is that the explanatory modalities of the empirical sciences do not make any reference to deontic or normative properties related to *reasons*, as distinct from nomic or descriptive ones. Naturalistic explanations operate in the idiom of *causes*, not *norms*. Casual mention of norms in such explanations are always shorthand for causal explanations that are norm-free: For example, "Oedipus gouged out his eyes when he discovered the wrongful things he had done" is really shorthand for "Oedipus gouged out his eyes when he *came to believe* he had married his mother and killed his father, because he *felt* these actions were shameful." An adequate naturalistic explanation does not depend on it being a fact (or true) that it was wrongful to murder one's father and marry one's mother; it does not depend on it being a fact (or true) that one has a reason not to murder one's father or marry one's mother.[4] An adequate naturalistic explanation depends only on facts about the psychological states in which Oedipus found himself and the facts about human behavior in the world; it might also depend on psychosocial or anthropological facts about the beliefs and attitudes of others in the relevant community in which Oedipus lived. But what it does not depend on is that it is *shameful*, independent of how Oedipus or his compatriots feel, to marry your mother and kill your father, or that it is wrongful, independent of how Oedipus and others feel, to marry your mother and kill your father.

Why then is normativity a puzzle for the naturalist? It seems the naturalist has a straightforward account of normativity: What we call "normativity" just picks out the psychological properties of certain biological organisms—that is, what they *feel* or *believe* or *desire* (or are *disposed to feel, believe, or desire*). As long as the posited organisms are naturalistically respectable, and the mental states invoked are as well, then that is the end of the naturalist's story. What's all the fuss?

One kind of philosophical fuss pertains to the semantics, to how we are to understand the *meaning* of the normative talk in the naturalist's world. I do not plan to discuss that at length here, since I think it represents a wrong turn in

[3] For a similar view, see T. M. Scanlon, *Being Realistic about Reasons* (Oxford University Press, 2014), 1–2.

[4] See Brian Leiter, "Moral Facts and Best Explanations," in *Naturalizing Jurisprudence: Essays on American Legal Realism and Naturalism in Legal Philosophy* (Oxford University Press, 2007), 203–24.

philosophical discussion of normativity. Naturalists have usually (John Mackie is the most famous exception) opted for noncognitivist interpretations of the semantics, and this has led them into the abyss of the Frege-Geach problem, the problem of how to explain the truth-preserving properties of inferences involving moral propositions embedded in the antecedents of conditionals (e.g., "If stealing is wrong, then it is wrong to encourage John to steal"; but "stealing is wrong"; so "it is wrong to encourage John to steal"). My view is that we should not let our metaphysics—our most plausible account of what really exists—be driven by linguistic practices: Why let the semantic tail wag the metaphysical dog? As Crispin Wright observed a quarter-century ago, if metaphysical anti-realism about moral facts conjoined with noncognitivism about the semantics of moral judgments had "absolutely no prospect of a satisfactory construal of conditionals with moral antecedents that could hardly be decisive. Rather, whatever case there was for [this kind of antirealist view] would become potentially revisionary of our ordinary and moral linguistic practice."[5] But we don't even have to "bite the bullet" on such "radical revisionism" (as Wright aptly calls it), when there remain other options on the semantic front: First, there are highly technical noncognitivist solutions to the Frege-Geach challenge, like Allan Gibbard's; second, we can adopt a minimalist approach to truth, such that the propriety and intelligibility of certain assertoric idioms in evaluative language is enough to warrant cognitivism, with the issue between moral realists and anti-realists located elsewhere (e.g., in the conception of objectivity);[6] and third, we can simply eschew the representationalist framework for understanding language, opting for inferential views which take seriously that "meaning is use," and thus are quite compatible with a naturalistic metaphysics in which normativity does not exist.

Putting the semantics to one side, I want to focus on an interlocking set of metaphysical, epistemological, and, for want of a better word, "practical" or first-personal worries about normativity for naturalists. We may summarize them as follows. First, naturalism is self-refuting, since the naturalistic outlook itself presupposes *epistemic* norms whose status is not naturalistically vindicated. Second, naturalism imposes domain-specific standards on domains of thought where they do not belong. Third, naturalism fails to do justice to the real, practical nature of normativity: it can explain what we *call* normativity, but it cannot explain *real* normativity (i.e., how normative demands are experienced by the agent confronting them).[7] I shall take these up in turn.

[5] Crispin Wright, "Realism, Antirealism, Irrealism, Quasi-Realism," *Midwest Studies in Philosophy* 12 (1988): 31.

[6] See, e.g., Crispin Wright, *Truth and Objectivity* (Harvard University Press, 1992).

[7] I take it that "real normativity" means standards of what one ought to do or believe that are not dependent for their binding force on the attitudes, feelings, or beliefs of persons.

II. Naturalism Is Self-Refuting

The naturalist supposes that we should treat the methods and thus the results of the empirical sciences as arbiters of what is true and what is knowable. Why do so, however, unless those methods and results are themselves *normatively sound*, that is, justified by epistemically relevant considerations? Yet we may then ask: Are those "epistemically relevant considerations" themselves to be interpreted as results of the empirical sciences? Clearly not, on pain of circularity, but even apart from worries about circularity, it is not at all clear that these norms constitute scientific results as opposed to being presuppositions of scientific method. So that means the naturalist commends epistemic norms that are, themselves, not vindicated naturalistically: hence self-refutation.

This objection would be correct if the defense of naturalism were that epistemic norms favored it. *This, however, is not and cannot be the defense of naturalism.* Quine, the leading Anglophone naturalist, was not ideally clear on this issue, sometimes being rather glib about the circularity problem, but I take it the right response to the worry is apparent in the famous closing observations in his "Two Dogmas of Empiricism":

> As an empiricist I continue to think of the conceptual scheme of science as a tool, ultimately, for predicting future experience in the light of past experience. Physical objects are conceptually imported into the situation as convenient intermediaries—not by definition in terms of experience, but simply as irreducible posits comparable, epistemologically, to the gods of Homer. Let me interject that for my part I do, qua lay physicist, believe in physical objects and not in Homer's gods; and I consider it a scientific error to believe otherwise. But in point of epistemological footing the physical objects and the gods differ only in degree and not in kind. Both sorts of entities enter our conception only as cultural posits. The myth of physical objects is epistemologically superior to most in that it has proved more efficacious than other myths as a device for working a manageable structure into the flux of experience.[8]

The interest in predicting the future course of experience is necessarily a widely shared interest, one that facilitates crossing the street, eating a meal, and living a life. On this kind of view, we should be naturalists because *naturalism works*, not because it is "true" or "justified" in some sense either independent of or dependent upon naturalistic criteria: It works because it answers

[8] W. V. O. Quine, "Two Dogmas of Empiricism," *The Philosophical Review* 60 (1951): 41.

to fundamental and universally shared human interests in predicting the future course of experience.[9]

"Naturalism works" may sound like a slogan, but it is a slogan with real significance. Consider: Thanks to the warranted beliefs of aerospace engineers (and, behind them, physicists and chemists), the plane that brought me to Rome *actually brought me here,* that is, several tons of metal tubing and associated electronics rose tens of thousands of feet into the sky, with me strapped inside, and moved faster than any natural thing can on the ground, and deposited me in the place I was aiming to go—and not in the middle of the ocean or the middle of a desert—and did this without incinerating, mutilating, or otherwise killing me. Imagine telling a Homeric era farmer that "[i]n the future, farmers like you will be able to travel through the clouds in special tubes to faraway places you have heard of in stories, and do that in the time it takes you to ride a horse to the neighboring village." To be sure, the ontology of Homeric gods licenses telling stories about such magic, but the ontology of aerospace engineers allows the farmers and the professors to actually experience it. That airplanes work is not an epistemic warrant, but it gives us the pragmatic explanation for why creatures like us are disposed to treat the epistemology that underlies aerospace engineering as the benchmark of the true and the knowable. The reasons for being a naturalist in the first place are not question-beggingly epistemic reasons; they are pragmatic ones, that almost everyone—including the antinaturalists—actually accept in practice.[10] Naturalism thus makes its claim on us in virtue of its resonance with our attitudes, our practical interests in coping with the future course of our experience in the world.[11]

[9] There may be other universally shared human interests: in self-preservation, in power, and so on. But all of these depend on satisfying the interest in predicting the future course of experience. In that sense, naturalism is basic for creatures like us.

[10] Other kinds of apparent self-refutation objections have appeared in the literature: Jaegwon Kim, for example, argues that the notion of "belief" itself is normative, in the sense that a Quinean naturalized psychology of belief-formation must help itself to normative views to individuate those mental states that arise in response to sensory input as instances of "belief." See Jaegwon Kim, "What Is Naturalized Epistemology?" *Philosophical Perspectives* 2 (1988): 381–405. More recently, Ralph Wedgwood has argued that the "intentional" is an inherently normative notion, so to the extent naturalists help themselves to intentional explanations (as all the great naturalists from Hume to Nietzsche do), they necessarily presuppose normative standards for individuating intentions. See Ralph Wedgwood, *The Nature of Normativity* (Clarendon Press, 2007). The mistake of both Kim and Wedgwood is in thinking that a naturalist must eschew normative concepts; to the contrary, the naturalist can help himself to any normative concepts that do useful naturalistic work. What the naturalist denies is that any of these pick out real instances of normativity not dependent on their usefulness.

[11] Naturalism "works" in the sense described in the text might seem like too lax a criterion. Why not think, for example, fictionalist naturalism—act as if we believe, rather than actually believe, whatever best explains our experience—would be just as good as actual naturalism? The only colorable answer is that it would not be: Maintaining a make-believe posture is much harder than believing (one can voluntarily choose make-believe, unlike believing), which is why make-believe occupies so little of our lives. Skepticism about "naturalism works" usually trades, I suspect, on understating how well a naturalistic view really works in both ordinary and theoretical life.

Notice that the locution "reasons for being a naturalist" really means "what explains why creatures like us are affectively disposed to take naturalistic epistemic criteria seriously." Someone could "reasonably" reject these reasons, but "reasonably" is, itself, a pro-attitude term of endorsement, meaning only that someone could feel indifferent to epistemic norms that, when applied, produce certain outcomes—outcomes like planes taking off and landing where they are supposed to. That epistemology bottoms out in practical interests should hardly be a surprising conclusion for a naturalist. Let us recall two important lessons from naturalistically minded twentieth-century philosophy. First, from the famous Duhem-Quine thesis[12] about the underdetermination of scientific theories by evidence, we know that there are not even any scientific hypotheses that are epistemically obligatory, in the sense of required by logic and evidence.[13] This is because any recalcitrant evidence elicited in a test of a hypothesis is compatible with the hypothesis as long as we are willing to give up the background assumptions such a test requires. In choosing among competing hypotheses and background assumptions, we must always fall back on evaluative considerations that "nature" does not adjudicate among, considerations such as theoretical simplicity, methodological conservatism, and consilience.[14] Second, unless there were a plausible *substantive* conception of rationality (there does not appear to be one, alas), then rationality, including any internalist norm of epistemic warrant, is itself instrumental, imposing normative constraints only on the means chosen to realize our ends, whatever they may happen to be. Thus, even norms for belief are hostage to ultimate ends, and so particular beliefs are unwarranted (i.e., irrational) only relative to the believer's ends, a point Peter Railton pressed twenty years ago against those who thought there was a firm fact/value distinction.[15] That conclusion would also hardly be surprising to a naturalist like Nietzsche, who clearly appreciated the extent to which practical ends and interests drove theoretical questions.[16]

[12] See Pierre Duhem, *The Aim and Structure of Physical Theory*, trans. Phillip Wiener (Princeton University Press, 1954); W. V. O. Quine, "On Empirically Equivalent Systems of the World," *Erkenntnis* 9 (1975): 313–28; W. V. O. Quine, *Pursuit of Truth* (Harvard University Press, 1990).

[13] I acknowledge that the inveterate dogmatic realist may think this is merely an *epistemic* point, not a metaphysical one: There could still be *real epistemic values*; after all, we just do not know what they are or how to apply them. That is a logically possible position, but I am with Quine in thinking that if the *actual successful sciences* do not disclose such epistemic values, then it is dubious that reality demands any particular set of them.

[14] See W. V. O Quine and Joseph Ullian, *The Web of Belief*, 2nd ed. (Random House, 1978). Scientific theories are none the worse for the naturalist in depending on logic, evidence, and nonepistemic evaluative considerations: If the resulting theories work well for creatures like us, what more is there to expect?

[15] See Peter Railton, "Facts and Values," *Philosophical Topics* 14 (1986): 5–31.

[16] See, e.g., Friedrich Nietzsche, *Beyond Good and Evil: Prelude to a Philosophy of the Future*, trans. Walter Kaufmann (Vintage Books, 1989), 11–16.

Naturalism is, then, not self-refuting, since what commends naturalistic norms is not their warrant but their resonance with our practical interests and attitudes.

III. Naturalism Imposes Domain-Specific Standards Where They Do Not Belong

Someone who acknowledged the resonance of naturalistic epistemic norms with our practical attitudes might nonetheless object that such norms, while great for air travel and crossing the street, do not really help when it comes to coping with the prospect of death and suffering, or figuring out how to treat their neighbors. Why think naturalistic norms for belief should dominate the epistemic field, especially since, as we have just conceded, naturalism is not epistemically or, more broadly, rationally obligatory? Why think it should govern our talk and thought about norms outside the domain of phenomena for which we seek causal explanations? Maybe naturalistic norms "work" in certain domains, and that's enough, but why treat them as binding in other domains? That is the objection I wish to consider now.

The late Ronald Dworkin posed an extreme version of this challenge in 1996,[17] but since then it has been taken up by his friends, including Thomas Nagel,[18] Derek Parfit,[19] and T. M. Scanlon.[20] The core thought that animates the antinaturalists is this: Even if causal or explanatory power is the criterion of the real and the knowable in the domain of the natural sciences, there is no reason to treat it as the arbiter of the real and the knowable in other domains of thought and inquiry. Call this view Domain Separatism. Domain Separatists hold that metaphysical and epistemological criteria vary with the subject matter of cognitive domains and that it is an error to impose naturalistic criteria, appropriate, for example, in empirical scientific inquiries, onto other domains. Domain separatists thus endorse a version of the doctrine of "separate but equal": separate metaphysical and epistemic criteria for each domain, but all the domains are equal in terms of cognitive status (i.e., stating truths and generating knowledge).

The crucial question, obviously enough, is how we demarcate domains as the Domain separatist would have us do? Dworkin said that while causal explanatory power "does seem appropriate to beliefs about the physical world," it makes no sense for moral beliefs "[s]ince morality and the other evaluative domains

[17] Ronald Dworkin, "Objectivity and Truth: You'd Better Believe It," *Philosophy & Public Affairs* 25 (1996): 87–139.

[18] Thomas Nagel, *The Last Word* (Oxford University Press, 1997).

[19] Derek Parfit, *On What Matters: Volumes 1 and 2* (Oxford University Press, 2011).

[20] T. M. Scanlon, *Being Realistic about Reasons* (Oxford University Press, 2014).

make no causal claims."[21] But that is plainly false: the moral explanations literature from the 1980s onward—recall Brink, Railton, Sayre-McCord, Sturgeon, and others—is replete with examples of the role of causal claims in ordinary normative discourse (e.g., "Of course he betrayed them, he's an evil person"). It is perfectly reasonable, then, even on the terms established by normative discourse itself, to inquire whether these explanations are *good* ones, let alone *best* explanations for the phenomena in question.[22]

Scanlon's recent view is more nuanced than Dworkin's.[23] Scanlon allows that there are "mixed" normative claims, ones that involve or presuppose claims about natural facts (and presumably could involve or presuppose causal claims in particular). However, at the same time he affirms the core of Domain separatism, namely, that it "makes most sense" to "not privilege science" but instead to endorse a view that

> takes as basic a range of domains, including mathematics, science, and moral and practical reasoning. It holds that statements within all of these domains are capable of truth and falsity, and that the truth values of statements about one domain, insofar as they do not conflict with statements of some other domain, are properly settled by the standards of the domain that they are about.[24]

I note in passing that Scanlon gives no real argument for demarcating domains other than saying he thinks it "makes most sense"[25] to think of things his way. This betrays, I think, a deep peculiarity of much philosophy, including most Anglophone philosophy of the past half-century, namely, that it treats subjective reports of what "makes most sense" as data points with epistemic weight, as opposed to psychosocial artifacts that admit of explanation. But I will bracket that skeptical doubt here, even though a thorough-going naturalist should not: The psychology and sociology of inquirers, especially in a field as devoid of clear cognitive standards as philosophy, is an apt topic for systematic empirical investigation.

Let us return to Scanlon's version of domain separatism. Prior to saying it "makes most sense" to demarcate domains, Scanlon does note one consideration that might favor domain separatism, namely, the difficulties naturalists like Quine have in accounting for certain abstract mathematical truths, ones that do

[21] Dworkin, "Objectivity and Truth," 119–20.

[22] For a negative answer to this question, see Brian Leiter, "Moral Facts and Best Explanations," *Social Philosophy & Policy* 18 (2001): 79–101, repr. Leiter, *Naturalizing Jurisprudence* (Oxford University Press, 2007).

[23] See Scanlon, *Being Realistic about Reasons*, 21–22.

[24] Ibid., 19.

[25] Later, Scanlon says the idea of "domains" is just "common sense" (ibid., 23), but that common sense embraces falsehoods is, from my philosophical standpoint, neither probative nor surprising.

not seem indispensable for our best scientific theories. The latter kinds of abstract mathematical truths are worrisome for precisely the reason that domain separatists like Dworkin and Scanlon hope to invoke against the naturalist in the moral or practical case: namely, that it seems there are *clear* truths in this domain, which we should be loath to give up. If the Quinean naturalist cannot capture all the abstract truths of mathematics with his causal/explanatory criterion for the real and the knowable, then so much the worse for the Quinean, so the domain separatist suggests.

That intuition is prima facie plausible in the mathematical case, but precisely for the reasons it is dubious in the moral case, a point that requires emphasis. Remember: The fact that there is massive cross-cultural and cross-temporal convergence on mathematical truths among inquirers, a kind of convergence that seems hard to explain away sociologically or psychologically, is precisely what makes it tempting to reject any metaphysical or epistemological criteria that made the convergence inexplicable on epistemic grounds (i.e., as manifesting insensitivity to the mathematical truths in question). (In fact, convergence, like divergence, demands an explanation, and truth is not the only candidate even in cases of convergence, but we may bracket that here.) Importantly, nothing comparable is true in the moral case: We do not even have the requisite convergence in moral opinions that might create a defeasible presumption in favor of truth.[26] Indeed, as I have argued elsewhere, drawing on Nietzsche, the most striking fact about inquirers in the moral domain is that they agree about almost nothing, not about the priority of the right versus the good, or about the criterion of right action, or the criterion of goodness, or about whether the right and the good are even the fundamental ethical categories.[27] Massive failure of convergence in the ethical domain ought to worry the moral realist.[28] Scanlon is certainly sensitive to this concern and so appeals to such purportedly uncontroversial truths about practical reason like "[t]he fact that a person's child has died is a reason for that person to feel sad,"[29] which is, unfortunately for Scanlon, almost precisely the thesis that the Stoics quite intelligibly denied.[30] We should allow, however,

[26] See the discussion in Brian Leiter, "Realism, Disagreement, and Explanation," *Philosophy & Phenomenological Research* 107 (2023): 803–09.

[27] See Brian Leiter, "Moral Skepticism and Moral Disagreement in Nietzsche," in *Oxford Studies in Metaethics, Volume 9*, ed. R. Shafer-Landau (Oxford University Press, 2014), 126–51, and also ch. 15 in this volume.

[28] It worries Parfit, of course, in *On What Matters,* and he tries to argue that, in fact, all major theories converge. For some doubts, see Simon Blackburn, "Morality Tale," review of *On What Matters: Volumes 1 and 2*, by Derek Parfit, *Financial Times*, August 6, 2011, http://www.ft.com/intl/cms/s/2/2bf7cf30-b9e1-11e0-8171-00144feabdc0.html#axzz3VXVu0KhG; see also Constantine Sandis, "Review of *On What Matters, Volumes I and II*," *The Times Higher Education*, June 9, 2011, https://www.timeshighereducation.com/books/on-what-matters-volumes-i-and-ii/416411.article?sectioncode=26&storycode=416411&c=1.

[29] Scanlon, *Being Realistic about Reasons*, 2.

[30] See, e.g., Cicero, *Tusculan Disputations*, Book 3 ch. XIV. (Thanks to Martha Nussbaum for this reference.)

that there might well be some odd practical claims that strike most creatures like us as correct (e.g., don't torture babies for fun) but such irrelevant outliers do not come close to the enormous cross-cultural convergence in the mathematical case.

So how, then, do we ultimately demarcate domains on Scanlon's view? Scanlon makes a variety of comments regarding how to think of "domains"—for example, that a domain should be "understood in terms of concepts that it deals with, such as number, set, physical object, reason, or morally right action"[31]—and he even purports to allow that "there can be meaningful 'external' questions about the adequacy of reasoning in a domain."[32] In the end, though, Scanlon echoes Dworkin in his own discussion of Gilbert Harman's "best explanation" argument for moral anti-realism.[33] Harman, recall, argued that since the best explanation of why we might judge it wrongful for a bunch of young hoodlums to douse a cat with lighter fluid and set it aflame need not refer to it actually being wrong to do so, only to facts about our psychology and our socialization, that we, therefore, have no reason to think it is *really* or *objectively* wrongful. Against Harman's view, Scanlon writes:

> [T]here is no reason to accept Harman's [best explanation] requirement as he formulated it—as a perfectly general requirement applying to all domains—since they do not all aim at the same kinds of understanding (e.g., at the best causal explanations of the world that impinges on our sensory surfaces).[34]

We may grant that moral talk and "understanding," assuming there is such a thing, does not aim primarily at causal explanation, even if, as we remarked earlier, moral talk sometimes helps itself to causal explanations—but Scanlon is more cautious than Dworkin, since he does not deny *outright* the relevance of causal explanation to moral thought, claiming only that moral thought has other primary aims. Does it follow, however, from this concession that there really is, as Scanlon claims, *no reason* to accept causal explanatory power as a marker of the real and the knowable even in the moral domain? That strong claim seems to overstate the case. Causal explanatory power has exercised pressure on attempts to make sense of the world precisely because, since the scientific revolution, our understanding of the world was purged of nonmaterial causes, teleologies, and gods and ghosts, because such entities have no causal explanatory power. We seem to know and understand more as a result of this epistemically motivated cleansing. Why not say, then, that *all* domains that aim at *understanding* have

31 Scanlon, *Being Realistic about Reasons*, 19.
32 Ibid., 21.
33 See Gilbert Harman, *The Nature of Morality* (Oxford University Press, 1977).
34 Scanlon, *Being Realistic about Reasons*, 27.

a reason to take seriously the most successful markers of actual knowledge we have? Indeed, the history of human inquiry since the scientific revolution is the history of purportedly domain-specific reasoning being subjected to scrutiny from scientific domains whose concepts and ontologies seemed to warrant more epistemic credence. Perhaps there is only *one* domain, the domain of human attempts to make sense of the world in all its baroque complexities, and to do so in terms that warrant some degree of epistemic confidence?

We may put the challenge to the domain separatist more precisely. Domain separatists maintain that metaphysical and epistemological criteria vary with the subject matter of purportedly "cognitive" domains and that it is an error to impose naturalistic criteria, appropriate, for example, in natural scientific inquiries, onto other domains. But in what domain do we locate the domain separatist thesis itself? What domain determines that a particular domain is, in fact, "cognitive"? By what domain's criteria is it supposed to be an error to ask whether practical reasoning satisfies naturalistic criteria? I suppose it will be tempting to say at this point that these claims are located in the domain of philosophy, that it falls to something called "philosophical reasoning" to adjudicate overreaching by one domain against another. Naturalists, however, deny that there is something called "philosophical reasoning" that stands apart from the kinds of reasoning that work in the various sciences, so that response either begs the question against the naturalist *or* amounts to an admission that there is a meta-domain of reasoning, something the naturalist accepts, and which is precisely what the naturalist relies on in adjudicating the metaphysical and epistemological *bona fides* of all other domains. Either way, it seems, the domain separatist loses.

Or does she? Even if the domain separatist eschews the question-begging response of invoking the nonnaturalist philosophical domain as the one that adjudicates the boundaries between domains, she can still ask the naturalist: Why think the meta-domain of reasoning about which domains are cognitive should be governed by naturalistic standards of reasoning? That question is especially pressing because naturalistic standards of reasoning are, as I have already conceded, not rationally obligatory, but commended, instead, by our practical attitudes and interests.

Here, I think there is no better answer to the domain separatist than the one we considered in the prior section: The deliverances of naturalistic norms generally work well for creatures like us. No one finds it surprising, after all, that if we relax naturalistic constraints, we will get a promiscuous ontology, replete with moral facts, spirit facts, gustatory facts, aesthetic facts, theological facts, and so on. Someone might, of course, prefer more moral, spiritual, and gustatory facts, and the like, in their ontology, but that is not, by itself, an argument against naturalism, unless one thinks the epistemic norms that license belief in such facts answer to equally or more important practical attitudes of creatures like us. The naturalist, to be sure, noting the extent to which *all of us* are invested in naturalistic norms because they work so well in coping with the future course of experience, might then point out the pressures created by consistency—though that, too, is an epistemic attitude that is also not epistemically obligatory. And consistency in application of epistemic norms across domains might well yield in the face of the practical need for certain kinds of facts, such as facts about reasons. This brings us to what, I take it, has to be the real objection to the naturalist about normativity: namely, that he has not explained "real" normativity—that is, the bindingness of standards independent of our attitudes—and that explaining the real normativity of reasons is indispensable for creatures like us when we are trying to figure out what to do (or believe).

IV. The Naturalist Has Not Explained "Real" Normativity

Perhaps the naturalist can explain our normative talk and judgments in terms of certain psychological states of inclination and aversion, and complicated variations on those, but that does not explain *normativity*, since it does not explain why it is actually wrong to do X or why there is an overriding reason to do Y. Explaining the existence of normative talk in terms of normative attitudes is not the same as explaining normativity, and the former is all my naturalist has offered.

On this issue, I want to begin by noting my agreement with the antinaturalists and my disagreement with certain kinds of contemporary Humean naturalists. Many contemporary Humean naturalists think they can give a naturalistic account of "real" normativity in terms of psychological states like desire and thus deflect the antinaturalist's worry about the status of real normativity. But here I think an arch antinaturalist like Scanlon gets it exactly right: There is, he says, an "evident lack of intrinsic normative significance of facts about desires."[35] The significance of desire is, as Scanlon says, merely causal. Here is how Scanlon puts it at greater length:

> The question [for the Humean] . . . would be whether identifying facts about reason with non-normative facts would explain reasons or eliminate their normativity. The 'action guiding' force of reasons, on such a theory, would seem to be purely causal and explanatory. If the fact that one has a strong reason to do *a* (and no countervailing reason to do *a*) is just a natural fact about what will satisfy one's desires, then this fact might explain one's failure to do *a*. But it does

[35] Ibid., 6.

> not explain why believing that one has such a reason (believing that this natural fact obtains) can make it irrational for one to do *a*.[36]

The problem is that the claim that it is "irrational for one to do *a*" means, for the naturalist, nothing more than that some people, or even all people, might *feel* that you should not do *a*. The failed neo-Humean response to the problem of normativity underlines what it means to *really* be a naturalist about normativity. Of course, the neo-Humean naturalist has not explained *real* normativity, as Scanlon complains, because real normativity does not exist: *That is the entire upshot of the naturalist view.* There are no *reasons* whose existence and character are independent of human attitudes; there are only human attitudes which lead us to "talk the talk" of reasons that do not exist apart from our attitudes. And if *real* normativity does not exist, if only *feelings* of inclination and aversion, compulsion and avoidance, actually exist, then that means that all purportedly normative disputes bottom out not in reasons but in the clash of will or affect. That is why, as A. J. Ayer correctly observed some eighty years ago, "[W]hen we come to deal with pure questions of value, as distinct from questions of fact . . . we finally resort to mere abuse."[37] Rhetorically, abuse has many uses, but its predominant role in moral discourse, including among philosophers,[38] should be a red flag that we are far removed from the fabled "space of reasons" in this arena.

Now what about the person deciding what she ought to do? If the naturalist is right, how does this view help her? The answer has to be that it does not. The naturalist about normativity gives us a third-person account of what normativity

[36] Ibid.

[37] A. J. Ayer, *Language, Truth and Logic* (Victor Gollancz Ltd., 1936), 147.

[38] Anscombe is notorious in this regard. See her two-sentence paper in *Analysis*: "The nerve of Mr. Bennett's argument is that if A results from your not doing B, then A results from whatever you do instead of B. While there may be much to be said for this view, still it does not seem right on the face of it." Elizabeth Anscombe, "A Note on Mr. Bennett," *Analysis* 26 (1966): 208. Anscombe does not always treat her interlocutors as generously as she does Bennett: "But if someone really thinks, *in advance*, that it is open to question such an action as procuring the judicial execution of the innocent should be quite excluded from consideration—I do not want to argue with him; he shows a corrupt mind." Elizabeth Anscombe, "Modern Moral Philosophy," *Philosophy* 33 (1958): 17. Among consequentialists too, rhetorical abuse sometimes presents itself as an offer to self-approbation. Consider Smart: "Or would you, as a humane and sympathetic person, give a preference to the second universe? I myself cannot help feeling a preference for the second universe. But if someone feels the other way I do not know how to argue with him." J. J. C. Smart, "An Outline of a System of Utilitarian Ethics," in *Utilitarianism: For and Against*, ed. B. Williams and J. J. C. Smart (Cambridge University Press, 1973), 28. Consider also Wolf's use of "scare-adjectives" (remarked upon in Tamler Sommers, "The Objective Attitude," *The Philosophical Quarterly* 57 [2007]: 327): "A world in which human relationships are restricted to those that can be formed and supported in the absence of the reactive attitudes is a world of human isolation so cold and dreary that any but the most cynical must shudder at the idea of it." Susan Wolf, "The Importance of Free Will," *Mind* 90 (1981): 391. Della Rocca's epigraph to "The Taming of Philosophy" is here apt: "Don't mistake the fact that you don't like my view for an argument against it." Michael Della Rocca, "The Taming of Philosophy," in *Philosophy and Its History: Aims and Methods in the Study of Early Modern Philosophy*, ed. M. Laerke, J. Smith, and E. Schliesser (Oxford University Press, 2013), 178.

is, namely, certain kinds of psychological states that grip certain kinds of biological organisms, and move them to action or inaction. From the standpoint of the person thinking about what she ought to do, all this is irrelevant. She will act on the feelings of inclination and aversion she has, subject to the constraints they impose upon her beliefs about what is the case. In thinking about whether she should act upon any particular inclination or aversion, she will be influenced by her other inclinations and aversions, including the inclinations and aversions common in her community. The only so-called normative guidance that could follow from these facts would be the guidance that follows from a plausible psychosocial account of the relevant attitudes, which itself she might, of course, repudiate, unless she has, like most people, a strong inclination not to deviate too far from approved behavior in her locale.

Those who think practical philosophy is a cognitive subject—as opposed to what it actually is, namely, a kind of armchair sociology of the moral etiquette of bourgeois philosophy professors—typically object to the naturalist at this point by noting that an agent faces comparable questions of *theoretical normativity*, questions about what she ought to believe.[39] Here I differ from twentieth-century naturalists and moral skeptics like Ayer and Stevenson, who ignored this problem, and agree with naturalists and moral skeptics like Nietzsche, who did not: I think the issue is the same.[40] Even in the theoretical domain, there is no real normativity, that is, no norms of belief or epistemic value the agent *must* adhere to, as I argued earlier. If epistemology proper, the systematic account of what one "ought" to believe, gives the appearance of a more robust discipline, it is only because its primary data points—namely, the claims of the successful empirical sciences—are clearer and more widely accepted, precisely because of their resonance with our universally shared practical interests. But that also means that epistemology proper is also a kind of armchair sociology, though one that can be discharged more responsibly from the armchair since its data points—the epistemic norms manifest in the practices of the successful sciences—are ones that can be studied in illuminating ways by reading books and journals.

[39] See, for example, Christine Korsgaard's *3AM* interview:

> [T]here is no more reason to doubt that reason plays a role in guiding human actions than there is to doubt that reason plays a role in forming human beliefs. In fact there is less, since people believe much crazier things than they do. And all of [Alexander Rosenberg, Patricia Churchland, and Brian Leiter] are dedicated to the project of working out what we have good reason to believe. If they came to the conclusion that reason doesn't play much of a role in forming most people's beliefs most of the time, they wouldn't give up that project themselves. They are interested in the kinds of questions that arise when we are trying to use reason to figure out what to believe. As a moral philosopher, I'm interested in questions that arise when we are trying to use reason to figure out what to do.

Christine Korsgaard, "Treating People as Ends in Themselves," interview by Richard Marshall, *3:16AM*, 2012, https://www.3-16am.co.uk/articles/treating-people-as-ends-in-themselves.

[40] See Brian Leiter, "Moralities are a Sign-Language of the Affects," *Social Philosophy & Policy* 30 (2013): 237–58.

For my kind of naturalist, there is no metaphysical difference *in kind* between moral and epistemic values—both are artifacts of attitudes common among creatures like us—but that latter point is still compatible with a radical difference in *degree* between them. Let us call a "Global Humean" about epistemic values someone who notices that creatures like us generally converge in our epistemic attitudes because the norms those attitudes endorse do so well at meeting universally shared human needs and interests, such as predicting the future course of experience, as I argued earlier. Consider epistemic norms like the following: Treat normal perceptual experience as prima facie veridical, honor logical inferences, and employ the inductive method in empirical inquiry. These epistemic norms do, indeed, seem to facilitate successful navigation of the world and prediction of the future course of experience. Something like this, I suspect (or hope), was Hume's own view, though unlike Hume, the other great modern naturalist Nietzsche does not think natural dispositions converge as well in the ethical case. That would explain why the great insight Nietzsche attributes to the Sophists concerns "the multiplicity (the geographical relativity) of the moral value judgments [*Moralischen Werthurtheile*]."[41] Not *all* value judgments, in other words, but the distinctively moral ones. The key difference in the case of theoretical normativity is that creatures like us share enough attitudes and interests to allow meaningful debates about warrant and justification. Global Humeanism in the domain of theoretical norms gives the appearance of "real" normativity; if the same were true in the practical domain, we would not get *real normativity* there, just Global Humeanism about the practical. But *contra* Humean optimism, that is not what we find.

If we have no *real* reason to believe the same or act the same, and thus we may not believe the same or act the same, given that our underlying psychological states (our attitudes) vary, what follows? What follows is basically what Ayer and Stevenson correctly diagnosed not quite a century ago: Where people share attitudes, reasoning about what one ought to do and what one ought to believe is possible; where people do not share attitudes, reasoning is not possible and only force prevails in a dispute, whether that is the rhetorical force of producing a change in attitudes by whatever means are effective or the physical or lawful force of suppressing contrary attitudes.[42] An agent deciding what to do or what to believe is in the grips of particular normative attitudes, some practical and some theoretical, and has no reason to discount them since after all *they are her attitudes*—although, as Nietzsche noticed, she might discount them if she were in the grips of a nonnaturalistic view of what had to be true of her attitudes for

[41] Friedrich Nietzsche, *The Will to Power*, trans. Walter Kaufmann and R. J. Hollingdale (Vintage Books, 1967), 233.
[42] If philosophers were more attuned to reality, they would investigate the differing kinds of *force* operative in human affairs.

them to move her, that is, if she thought they had to be something more than *her attitudes*. That I like Japanese food better than Thai food is a fact about my gustatory attitudes, yet it seems none the worse for that: Why wouldn't I eat Japanese food if *that's my gustatory attitude*? My moral and epistemic attitudes are more ambitious in their scope—for example, they are not indifferent to *your* attitudes on similar questions—but they are not, on the naturalistic view, different from the gustatory attitudes in their metaphysical or epistemological status. We can easily imagine a world—since such worlds have existed—in which perceptual evidence is not treated as even defeasibly veridical, in which the so-called scientific method is dismissed, and in which the dominant epistemic values are what the holy book says or what the holy leader declares. Worlds governed by such epistemic norms tend to have features we modern, post-Enlightenment folk find unpleasant, but that is, itself, another attitudinal response. If enough of our fellows share our attitudes, then darkness recedes, and Enlightenment triumphs. Those are simply facts about people's attitudes, as influenced by their pleasures and pains, their inclinations and aversions, their loves and hatreds, and not about real normativity. For naturalists, there is no real normativity, but normative judgment, and its role in the lives of creatures like us, is easy enough to explain.[43]

[43] Thanks to Ram Neta and audiences at the University of California, Riverside and the University of Miami for helpful questions and comments. Special thanks to Justin Clarke-Doane for, as usual, incisive comments on an earlier draft. I am also grateful to Daniel Telech for excellent research assistance.

17

The Paradoxes of Public Philosophy

What Philosophers Can Learn from Lawyers

I. Public Philosophy

Philosophy has long been part of the public life of human societies: One need only mention Socrates in Greece or Confucius in China, or, to leap forward a couple of thousand years, Rousseau in France and Hegel in Germany, to recognize that philosophers can be taken *very seriously* by the politicians, the journalists, and sometimes the ordinary citizens of their eras.[1]

The idea of "public philosophy" as I will be discussing it here, however, is an artifact of the professionalization of the discipline over the past two hundred years, with the rise of research universities and, especially in the Anglophone world after World War II, the rise of a professional class of philosophers—"professional" in the precise sense that they earn their living by teaching and writing about philosophy, paid either by private or mostly public universities to do so. There are now numerous organizations that promote "public philosophy," that seek to make philosophy "relevant" and "significant" to the broader culture. These locutions are themselves striking, since philosophy is relevant and significant to anyone—including presumably members of the "public"—who want to know what is true or to know what they do and do not know, but that is obviously not what is meant by "public philosophy." Rather, the special purview of so-called public philosophy is to contribute philosophical insight, knowledge, or skill to questions of moral and political urgency in the community in which it is located. So conceived, public philosophy is an artifact of what is usually called the "neoliberal" way of thinking that has dominated the capitalist world completely since the 1980s, in which every human activity justifies itself by its contribution to something for which there is demand in the marketplace. The most extreme form of this pathology in a country with a formerly preeminent but now declining university system is England, where philosophers are asked to adduce

[1] This is compatible with the fact, noted in chapter 1 in this volume, that their influence is negligible to non-existent. As Hegel says, "[T]he owl of Minerva [i.e., philosophical wisdom] flies only at dusk"—that is, the influence is often a sign that these philosophers are giving expression to inchoate ideas in the culture at large not produced by philosophy.

From a Realist Point of View. Brian Leiter, Oxford University Press. © Brian Leiter 2026.
DOI: 10.1093/9780197749852.003.0019

evidence of their "impact" to justify the funding of their work.[2] "Impact" here does not mean influencing how other scholars or students think about issues but rather such ephemera as appearing on television or having one's research discussed in a newspaper.

II. The First Paradox: What Knowledge?

The idea of "public philosophy" so conceived—that is, philosophy as contributing to questions of moral and political urgency in the community in which it is located—is paradoxical, however, for reasons that I propose to discuss. The first puzzle may be simply put: Normative philosophy has no well-established substantive conclusions about the right and the good—literally, none!—that could possibly dictate to the polity at large what should be done. All biologists agree that the theory of evolution by natural selection is crucial to understanding the diversity of life on the planet; all physicists agree that Newtonian mechanics gives a correct description of the movement of mid-size physical objects; all moral and political philosophers agree about nothing, except perhaps the very modest claim that all human beings have equal moral standing. And they do not even really agree about that, since some major philosophers, like Nietzsche, deny it; others deny that equality of moral standing attaches to species membership at all; and all the rest differ so dramatically on what is required for or because of "equal moral standing" that the apparent agreement is wholly illusory (consider: for Kantians, equal moral standing requires something like rational personhood; for some utilitarians, something like sentience; for some Marxists, something like needs).[3] Moral and political philosophers cannot agree about whether the right has priority over the good or vice versa; they cannot agree about what the criterion of human well-being is; they cannot agree about the correct formulation of Kant's categorical imperative; they cannot agree whether agents in the Rawlsian original position would choose deontological or utilitarian principles; and so on.

[2] This is not the first time, of course, since the birth of the research universities, that philosophers have had to justify their place in it. But during prior iterations, the question was an intellectually and epistemically serious one. As Frederick Beiser writes regarding German academia a bit before mid-nineteenth century, "To receive funding, a faculty had to demonstrate that its discipline was legitimate, that it had its own 'scientific' methods, and that it occupied a necessary place in the academic division of labor." Frederick Beiser, *After Hegel: German Philosophy, 1840-1900* (Princeton University Press, 2014), 18. Demonstrating the existence of a *Wissenschaft*, of reliable and rigorous methods for ascertaining knowledge, is quite a bit different than adducing evidence that *The Daily Mail* noted one's research.

[3] See generally Brian Leiter, "Moral Skepticism and Moral Disagreement in Nietzsche," in *Oxford Studies in Metaethics: Volume 9*, ed. R. Shafer-Landau (Oxford University Press, 2014), as well as chs. 14 and 15 in this volume.

Agreement may not secure the reliability of the claims agreed upon, of course,[4] but such agreement does seem a prerequisite for successful influence on questions of public interest. Consider a dubious science like economics,[5] which in the United States has had considerable influence on public policy. That economists could present fairly unified fronts for significant periods of time—first, under the Keynesian umbrella, subsequently under the "Chicago School" umbrella—no doubt lent credence to their claimed epistemic authority. (Even there, one suspects that nonintellectual factors, such as the extent to which economic theory tracked the interests of ruling elites, played a decisive role in the triumph of various economic orthodoxies at the level of policy.) In the United States, at least, that apparent authority may now be ending, due partly to the very public nature of the disagreements—a result primarily of the prominent polemics of the neo-Keynesian Paul Krugman—and partly to what is increasingly apparent, namely, that macroeconomists, in either camp, have almost no ability to predict any significant economic events. Putative sciences with no significant predictive power eventually lose credibility.

But let us return to philosophy. No philosopher can even pretend to enter the fray of public debate by reporting, "Philosophers have discovered that rule utilitarianism is the only correct way to assess questions of public policy." Nor can any philosopher intervene in a dispute by noting that "such a policy would be unjust given the Rawlsian difference principle." The "difference principle"—the idea that economic rewards should be distributed in such a way as to maximize the position of the economically worst-off in a society—is not a result or a discovery but an intuition, the formalization of some feelings (allegedly widely shared feelings) about what justice involves. If a society ignores the difference principle—as essentially all do—there is no discernible consequence. If someone tries to ignore the laws of Newtonian mechanics, the consequences are immediate!

In short, the first paradox of public philosophy is that philosophers enter moral and political debate purporting to offer some kind of expertise, but the expertise they offer cannot consist in any credible claim to know what is good, right, valuable, or any other substantive normative proposition that might be decisive in practical affairs.

[4] Derek Parfit, a leading contemporary moral philosopher, does think such agreement is essential to secure the objective truth of moral conclusions. See Derek Parfit, *On What Matters* (Oxford University Press, 2011).

[5] On the failures of neoclassical macroeconomics, see Alexander Rosenberg, *Economics: Mathematical Politics or Science of Diminishing Returns?* (University of Chicago Press, 1993).

III. The Second Paradox: Discursive Hygiene

That brings us to the second paradox of public philosophy. If it is not substantive normative knowledge that philosophers bring to debate, then perhaps it is a *method* or *way of thinking* about contested normative questions that they offer. And this strikes me as a far more plausible suggestion. Starting with certain normative intuitions, public philosophers work out their logical entailments demonstrating claims of the form, "If you believe X, then you ought to believe Y," and "If you believe Y, you should not do Z." What philosophers—at least those in the broadly Socratic traditions—are good at is parsing arguments, clarifying the concepts at play in a debate, teasing out the dialectical entailments of suppositions and claims, and so on. Socratic philosophers are, in short, purveyors of what I will call "discursive hygiene."

Although this constitutes a detour from my main claims, I want to emphasize that this conception of moral and political philosophers as purveyors of discursive hygiene is compatible with the emotivist (noncognitivist) theory of normative discourse defended by A. J. Ayer and Charles Stevenson in the middle of the twentieth century. However, their metaethical views tend to be reviled today by those who think they somehow distracted philosophers from important normative questions for a long period.[6] Recall that for Stevenson, ethical judgments express, roughly, an attitude like, "I disapprove of X, do so as well." So they express pro and con (favorable and unfavorable) attitudes, plus a meta-attitude about the attitudes others should have. Stevenson thought, correctly, I believe, that the emotive meaning of ethical terms was essential to understanding their centrality to social life. Ethical disagreements are at bottom a function of disagreement in attitudes, rather than disagreements in beliefs (here he follows Ayer): "[E]thical argument usually terminates when disagreement in attitude terminates, even though a certain amount of disagreement in belief remains."[7] (He thinks this counts in favor of explaining what we observe about moral disagreements, namely, that they often end when we secure agreement in belief, but seem interminable when they involve disagreements in attitudes.) But this does not mean that all ethical disagreement is just a *brute* clash of attitudes. As Stevenson writes, "since attitudes are often functions of beliefs, an agreement in belief may lead people, as a matter of psychological fact, to agree in attitude" (put another way, there is "the psychological fact that altered beliefs may cause altered attitudes"[8]). Notice, though, that on Stevenson's account, the connection

[6] The irony, of course, is that those philosophers who did address "normative" questions only rarely addressed important ones! See ch. 17 in this volume.

[7] Charles L. Stevenson, "The Nature of Ethical Disagreement," in *Foundations of Ethics: An Anthology*, 3rd ed., ed. R. Shafer-Landau and T. Cuneo (Blackwell, 2007), 373.

[8] Ibid.

between particular facts and our attitudes is just a contingent *psychological/causal fact*: It is just a psychological fact about many creatures like us that if our beliefs change, our attitudes often change too.[9] Philippa Foot, a famous critic of emotivism, emphasized this point: on Stevenson's view, she complains, "[T]here are no rules validating particular inferences [from beliefs to evaluative attitudes], but only causal connections between the beliefs and attitudes concerned."[10]

Was Stevenson wrong in thinking that normative theory operates mainly by exploiting the fact that creatures like us—or at least some of those creatures—are psychologically disposed to be moved by certain kinds of inferential connections between our attitudes or between our attitudes and our beliefs? Around the same time as Foot leveled her critiques of Stevenson's emotivism, Richard Brandt, in his 1959 textbook *Ethical Theory* (a crucial book for anyone who wants to understand the sociology of Anglophone moral theory in the last half-century), offered a similar challenge. Brandt asks us to imagine the case of Mr. A and Mr. B, who disagree about whether colleges should accept direct grants of money from the government, Mr. A holding a favorable attitude, Mr. B an unfavorable attitude. Brandt writes:

> We do *not* consider an argument relevant or well-taken *just* because it is successful in influencing attitudes. If Mr. B. is a legislator and Mr. A wants to influence his vote, there are various "arguments" he might use that no one would think ethically relevant. Mr. A might say: "Your alma mater will surely go bankrupt unless this bill is passed." Or, perhaps better, he might say, "Your daughter will be admitted to ____ College, if you vote for this bill; otherwise she won't be." These arguments may be of wonderful effect in changing Mr. B's attitudes, but they are not ethically relevant. On the contrary, suppose Mr. A argues about the importance of having independent educational institutions, where absolutely uncensored thinking and discussion can occur. In this case, Mr. A will have argued relevantly, irrespective of whether Mr. B is interested.[11]

Unnoted by Brandt is that the judgment that an attitude-altering argument is not "ethically relevant" is itself an evaluative judgment, so the expression of another attitude, according to the emotivist. So what Brandt's example really illustrates is that we also have pro and con attitudes about the kinds of arguments that influence attitudes, which is hardly surprising. In other words, sometimes we not

[9] Emotivism and noncognitivism got sidetracked into the Frege-Geach problem. For an overview, see Mark Schroeder, "What Is the Frege-Geach Problem?" *Philosophy Compass* 3, no. 4 (2008): 703–20.

[10] Philippa Foot, "Moral Arguments," *Mind* 67 (1958): 503.

[11] Richard Brandt, *Ethical Theory: The Problems of Normative and Critical Ethics* (Prentice Hall, 1959), 219.

only want someone to change their attitude, but we also want them to do so for a non-self-interested reason, because we have an unfavorable attitude toward self-interested considerations and a favorable attitude toward those we denominate "ethical" considerations.[12]

I believe that Stevenson had it exactly right. Changes in belief do influence changes in attitude, but only as a contingent, psychological fact: This includes changes in belief about the logical or inferential relations between beliefs or between beliefs and attitudes. This brings us to the second paradox of public philosophy. Although philosophers can contribute no substantive knowledge about the good and the right, they can contribute *discursive hygiene*. Discursive hygiene, however, plays almost no role in public life, and only an erratic and highly contingent role in how people form beliefs about matters of moral and political urgency. Both points deserve notice, but they are distinct.

The absence of discursive hygiene in public life should be familiar to any reflective observer. Public debate, including in democracies, is awash in fallacious inferences, non sequiturs, and arguments based on obviously false premises. This was true long before Trump, and he certainly did not change that; indeed, no political leader has. I shall give just one example, chosen only because it is recent and I know a lot about it because I was involved in the public debate. The University of Illinois at Urbana-Champaign, a major public research university in my home state in America, offered a tenured position on its faculty to a man named Steven Salaita. Dr. Salaita writes about colonialism and the experiences of colonized peoples, including the Palestinians in the Middle East. (Salaita himself is a Palestinian American.) He was offered a tenured position at the University of Illinois in October 2013, accepted it fairly quickly, and the university began making arrangements for his arrival and for his teaching to start in late August 2014. Dr. Salaita is also an active user of social media, including Twitter. In response to the Israeli attack on Gaza in the spring and summer of 2014, Dr. Salaita began "tweeting" vigorous moral outrage at the slaughter of children and civilians, and at the apologists for these crimes, and began expressing himself in increasingly vulgar and hostile terms. I will give just one example. Dr. Salaita reposted on his Twitter page a comment someone else made about an American journalist named Jeffrey Goldberg, who is an apologist for any crimes committed by Israel. Here is the statement that Dr. Salaita "retweeted": "Jeffrey Goldberg's story should have ended at the pointy end of a shiv." A "shiv," for those who do not know, is a sharp knife, like the kind that might also be known as a "bayonet" attached to a rifle. The most natural reading of this tweet—contrary to some defenders of Dr. Salaita—was that he wished Goldberg dead. That's not a

[12] The point extends to our epistemic attitudes on my view, though I do not discuss that here. See Brian Leiter, *Moral Psychology with Nietzsche* (Oxford University Press, 2019), chs. 3, 4.

nice sentiment, but it is not illegal in the United States to express such a wish on your Twitter account, and far more illustrious writers than Dr. Salaita have made the same point. We need only recall Heinrich Heine, one of the great German writers of the nineteenth century, who famously expressed the wish that "if God wants to make my happiness complete, he will grant me the joy of seeing some six or seven of my enemies hanging from [the] trees" in front of his cottage.[13] It is easy enough to understand how someone who believes his people are the victims of violent oppression might wish apologists for this oppression dead.

We only know about this "tweet" because, in the United States, there are a large number of so-called conservative—mainly reactionary and crypto-fascist—websites and media outlets devoted to monitoring and harassing university professors who deviate from what they regard as "acceptable" opinions. These websites began publicizing other examples of offensive, sometimes vulgar "tweets" by Dr. Salaita in July 2016. Soon, alumni and wealthy donors to the University of Illinois began complaining to the university about this prospective hire. Although the tenured appointment had been approved by the department, by the dean, and by the provost a year ago, the chancellor, on August 1, 2016, notified Dr. Salaita that she would not forward the appointment to the Board of Trustees for final approval (ordinarily pro forma in every prior case).

From a legal point of view, the issues here are fairly clear-cut. In the United States, it is illegal for a public university to deny employment to someone because of their political point of view: that violates their constitutional right to free speech and freedom of association. Citizens also have a well-established constitutional right in the United States to express their political views in vulgar and offensive terms.[14] From a constitutional point of view, these claims are banal and familiar to lawyers and scholars. Yet the chairperson of the university's Board of Trustees, in justifying the firing of Dr. Salaita, declared that "there can be no place for [disrespectful and demeaning speech] in our democracy, and therefore, there will be no place for it in our university."[15] As a factual matter, there is quite a lot of disrespectful and demeaning speech in American democracy. More importantly, the University of Illinois, as a public university, and thus subject to constitutional limits, *must* permit such speech, at least to the extent it takes place outside the classroom. (Inside the classroom, it likely would disrupt

[13] Heinrich Heine, *Gedanken und Einfälle,* ch. 1, cited in Sigmund Freud, "Civilization and Its Discontents," in *The Standard Edition of the Complete Psychological Works of Sigmund Freud* (Hogarth Press, 1930), 21:110n.

[14] A federal court in the United States has since rejected an attempt by the University of Illinois to dismiss Prof. Salaita's lawsuit, affirming that he clearly had valid legal claims. Salaita v. Kennedy et al., 1:15-cv-00924, No. 59 (N.D. Ill. Aug. 6, 2015). The university subsequently paid out nearly a million dollars to settle his claim.

[15] Before the Committee on Academic Freedom and Tenure (CAFT) of the University of Illinois at Urbana-Champaign, *Report on the Investigation into the Matter of Steven Salaita,* 8. https://www.senate.illinois.edu/af1501.pdf.

the university's pedagogical mission, and so could be regulated, but that was not at issue here.) The chairperson went further, saying that he believes only in "free speech tempered in respect for human rights."[16] There are some countries where this statement would make sense: In Germany, for example, human dignity is the fundamental constitutional value, which can trump freedom of expression. But American constitutional law is the opposite of German constitutional law. There is no doctrine of "free speech tempered in respect for human rights," and what is called in other jurisdictions "hate speech" is fully protected under American law.[17] Anyone interested in the prospect of public philosophy should think hard about this case: We have a public official, the chairperson of the Board of Trustees of a major public university in the United States, who is completely ignorant of the basic facts of American constitutional law, making assertions that are both false and, if implemented, wholly illegal. Can one imagine the travesty that would result were there to be subtle issues of philosophical argumentation at stake?

Alas, this public stupidity was not anomalous in this affair. Chicago's leading newspaper, the *Chicago Tribune*, defended the decision[18] to fire Salaita on the grounds that his critical comments constituted "hate speech." I want to emphasize that Chicago is the third largest city in the United States, and this newspaper serves a community of more than nine million people: After *The New York Times*, the *Tribune* is one of the three or four most significant newspapers in my country. Yet nowhere does the editorial defending the obviously illegal firing of Salaita even mention that "hate speech" is constitutionally protected in the United States. The editorial does not even mention that under most "hate speech" legislation in other countries that I have seen, nothing Salaita said would qualify.

I must underline that I am here talking about *clear points of law*, not hard philosophical questions. Yet the editors of a major American newspaper and the public official chairing a major American university's Board of Trustees do not even understand simple legal points, and so make claims and arguments that are false and fallacious. I wish this problem were only confined to the United States, but I am sure it is not. So what hope is there for public philosophy—for the discursive hygiene that philosophers can offer—in a world like this?

[16] Ibid.

[17] See, for instance, R.A.V. v. City of St. Paul, 505 U.S. 377 (1992); Matal v. Tam, 582 U.S. 218, 246 (2017) ("Speech that demeans on the basis of race, ethnicity, gender, religion, age, disability, or any other similar ground is hateful; but the proudest boast of our free speech jurisprudence is that we protect the freedom to express 'the thought that we hate.' ").

[18] Chicago Tribune Editorial Board, "U. of I. Right to Reject Prof's Hate Speech," *Chicago Tribune*, September 11, 2014, https://www.chicagotribune.com/2014/09/11/u-of-i-right-to-reject-profs-hate-speech/.

IV. Moral and Political Attitudes and Emotions

That discursive hygiene should be almost wholly absent from public debate is not surprising given the psychological evidence that people's beliefs about matters of moral and political urgency—and, perhaps, more important, what they do based on those beliefs—are only slightly influenced by a regime of discursive hygiene; instead, their emotional and affective responses mostly determine their moral attitudes. Consider the psychologist Jonathan Haidt's famous work on the "social intuitionist" model of moral judgment,[19] according to which in most ordinary situations, moral judgments are produced by emotional or affective responses, the reasons adduced in their support being post hoc: They do not explain the judgment, as evidenced by the resilience of the judgment even in the face of the defeat of the proffered reasons. Thus, in one famous case, Haidt describes to experimental subjects the case of a brother and sister who decide, after discussion, to experiment with incestuous sex. All the experimental subjects think this is wrong, but the scenario, as described by Haidt, rules out *all the reasons for thinking it wrong*: The brother and sister only do it once, they do it voluntarily and are happy with the experiment, they use birth control to ensure no pregnancy results, no one knows what they did, and so on. But people's visceral reaction remains powerful and unshakeable, even when the facts of the hypothetical defeat the reasons they give for their judgment. In the realm of ordinary moral judgment, emotion trumps reason.

We also know from work in empirical psychology that individuals "with selective deficits in emotional processing" due to disease or injury to the brain render different moral judgments about hypothetical situations like the Trolley cases than most emotionally normal subjects,[20] suggesting that the emotional responses are the real causes of the moral judgments. Psychologist and philosopher Joshua Greene has argued[21] that emotional responses loom larger in deontological than consequentialist moral judgments, the latter demanding more "controlled cognition,"[22] but in more recent work even Greene has acknowledged that "affect [or emotion] supplies the primary motivation to view harm as a bad thing" in the first place, so that even consequentialist reasoning has "an affective basis."[23] More precisely, according to Greene et al., "affect supplies the

[19] Jonathan Haidt, "The Emotional Dog and Its Rational Tail: A Social Intuitionist Approach to Moral Judgment," *Psychological Review* 108 (2001): 814–34.

[20] Fiery Cushman, Liane Young, and Joshua Greene, "Multi-System Moral Psychology," in *The Moral Psychology Handbook*, ed. J. M. Doris and the Moral Psychology Research Group (Oxford University Press, 2010), 53–54.

[21] Joshua Greene, "The Secret Joke of Kant's Soul," in *Moral Psychology*, Volume 3, ed. W. Sinnott-Armstrong (MIT Press, 2007): 35–117.

[22] Cushman, Young, and Greene, "Multi-System Moral Psychology," 54.

[23] Ibid., 62.

primary motivation to regard harm as bad. Once this primary motivation is supplied, reasoning proceeds in a currency-like manner ['currency emotions are designed to participate in the process of practical reasoning']."[24] "[A]larm-bell emotions are designed to circumvent reasoning" and, arguably, this is "the origin of the welfare principle."[25]

In a recent review of the empirical literature, Timothy Schroeder, Adina Roskies, and Shaun Nichols found that the view they dub "sentimentalism"—namely, the view that "the emotions typically play a key causal role in motivating moral behavior"[26]—is well-supported by the "evidence from psychology and neuroscience"[27] and that while "motivation derived [exclusively] from higher cognitive centers independently of desire is possible . . . the only known model of it is pathological," involving Tourette syndrome.[28] Such empirical findings do not rule out the possibility that moral judgments can be influenced by what I have been calling discursive hygiene, but they certainly explain why so much of public discourse is manifestly irrational and emotion-driven.

But the research on the role of irrational emotional responses to moral questions is just the tip of the iceberg. The real problem, of course, is that prejudice and bias are dominant forces in human life. What I will call Tribalism—the propensity of creatures like us to identify with those "like themselves," and to view others as unacceptably different, deficient, depraved, and perhaps dangerous[29]—is, as any realistic appraisal of human affairs will reveal, a dominant force in public life. Tribalism—whether it is Irish Catholics killing Irish Protestants, Sunni Muslims terrorizing Shia Muslims, or working-class American whites hating working-class American Blacks—is the curse of our species, against which discursive hygiene is the feeblest of weapons. As Nietzsche observed, "Nothing is easier to wipe out than a dialectical effect," and he was only thinking of Socrates's argumentative harassment of the rich youth of Athens.[30] Given that tribalist prejudices engage a range of powerful emotions—pride, self-respect, resentment, and others—how can discursive hygiene make an impact?

It may be said that tribalism's terrain has receded, especially in the last two hundred years, and that certainly seems to be true in various parts of the world.

[24] Ibid., 63.
[25] Ibid., 62, 63.
[26] Timothy Schroeder, Adina L. Roskies, and Shaun Nichols, "Moral Motivation," in *The Moral Psychology Handbook*, ed. J. M. Doris and the Moral Psychology Research Group (Oxford University Press, 2010), 77.
[27] Ibid., 98.
[28] Ibid., 94.
[29] For a striking catalogue of the extreme version of this phenomenon, see David Livingstone Smith, *Less Than Human: Why We Demean, Enslave, and Exterminate Others* (St. Martin's Press, 2011).
[30] Friedrich Nietzsche, "The Problem of Socrates," section 6, in "Twilight of the Idols," in *Sämtliche Werke: Kritische Studienausgabe*, eds. G. Colli and M. Montinari (Taschenbuch Verlag, 1980).

We may, however, reasonably ask what role discursive hygiene actually played in this process. Consider that the post-World War II consensus that emerged in many democracies about the importance of "universal human rights" only emerged after the ghastly slaughters that resulted from the extreme tribalism of German and Japanese fascists and racists. Argument played little or no role; emotional revulsion at barbarity did. Yet tribalist loyalties and prejudices remain ferocious, in America, in Iraq, in Israel, in India, in Pakistan, and elsewhere. The great cosmopolitan ideal of the nineteenth century, famously expressed by Karl Marx, was that, "Human emancipation will only be complete when the real, individual man has . . . in his everyday life, in his work, and in his relationships . . . become a *species-being* [*Gattungswesen*],"[31] that Marxian ideal of human beings who recognize their social and existential interdependence in producing the conditions of their existence *qua* human beings, but who no longer identify as simply the self-interested members of their tribes. That Marxian ideal remains an aspiration, even as *some* tribalist loyalties have receded over the last century.

The key point, however, is that we philosophers must recognize that moral change depends fundamentally on the emotional attitudes of people, and that these attitudes tend in a strongly tribalist direction. And the most plausible explanations for the evolution of such attitudes do not, alas, assign much role to discursive hygiene.[32] Consider selectionist explanations, which are all the rage these days in philosophy and the social sciences. These explanations appeal to evolution by natural selection, as opposed to all the other evolutionary mechanisms (e.g., genetic hitchhiking or genetic drift) that affect the evolution of species. Such explanations have serious limitations,[33] but they do help explain the persistence of tribalist tendencies. First, these explanations concern only the evolutionary explanation of *altruism*, that is, concern for others, a kind of concern that can, of course, be far more tepid than considering the "other" to be a full-fledged member of the non-tribal moral community, whose suffering, for example, has as much moral salience as the suffering of anyone else. Second, the only well-confirmed and generally accepted evolutionary hypothesis in the literature—deriving from the work of biologist W. D. Hamilton—involves altruistic concern for *kin*, that is, for organisms that share some of the genetic makeup of the altruist. From a selectionist point of view, so the Hamiltonian argument goes, altruistic concern for kin can be highly effective in passing on genetic material to the next generation as long as that concern is directed toward kin, such

[31] Karl Marx, "On the Jewish Question," in *The Marx-Engels Reader*, 2nd ed., ed. R. Tucker (W.W. Norton, 1978), 46.

[32] See, e.g., Kwame Anthony Appiah, *The Honor Code: How Moral Revolutions Happen* (W.W. Norton, 2010).

[33] See, e.g., Brian Leiter and Michael Weisberg, "Why Evolutionary Biology Is (So Far) Irrelevant to Legal Regulation," *Law and Philosophy* 29 (2010): 31–74.

as sisters or cousins or aunts who have some of the same genetic material. Thus, natural selection will select for a genetic predisposition to nurture and sustain kin, since they too can pass the genetic inheritance on. That, of course, is a far cry from viewing non-kin, indeed, utter strangers, regardless of race or religion or tribe, as entitled to basic moral consideration, but it is certainly consistent with the tribalism we observe. Third, even the more ambitious selectionist arguments for "group selectionism," associated with Elliott Sober and David Sloan Wilson,[34] would still fail to explain the evolution of moral sensibilities beyond tribalist ones, since, at best, these arguments tell us why individuals might develop altruistic concern for *members of their group* who are not kin; they do not explain why human communities might come to adopt non-tribalist moral ideals.

Doubts about the prospects of discursive hygiene are strikingly illustrated by considering the case of Peter Singer, undoubtedly the most successful "public philosopher" in the Anglophone world in recent years, though in a somewhat schizophrenic way: He is lauded for his defense of the rights of nonhuman animals, but also denounced (indeed, sometimes banned from speaking—in Germany, for example[35]) for his willingness to approve of the killing of defective human beings. Singer is, however, a paragon of consistent discursive hygiene. He has argued, on the one hand, that our treatment of nonhuman animals is morally indefensible, since the suffering of a sentient creature is what is morally relevant,[36] not the species of the sufferer. Yet, on the other hand, he has argued that it can be morally justifiable to kill human infants afflicted with various kinds of cognitive and physical defects, since to allow them to live would, over the long term, produce more suffering than happiness. If one thought infanticide was morally abhorrent—as a matter of brute moral attitude—then one might take Singer's position as a simple *reductio* of the idea that *suffering* per se is the only thing that is morally relevant, since it leads to an absurd and heinous conclusion. Singer has no actual argument against such a response, since his entire position rests simply on an equally brute, and unexplained, emotional attitude, namely, that *suffering* per se *is abhorrent*.[37] But if believing that *suffering* per se

[34] Elliott Sober and David Sloan Wilson, *Unto Others: The Evolution and Psychology of Unselfish Behavior* (Harvard University Press, 1998).

[35] "Umstrittener Philosoph wieder ausgeladen," *Deutschlandfunk*, May 30, 2015, http://www.deutschlandfunk.de/phil-cologne-umstrittener-philosoph-wieder-ausgeladen.1818.de.html?dram%3Aarticle_id=321259. For coverage in English, see Michael Cook, "Peter Singer 'Disinvited' from German Philosophy Festival," *BioEdge*, June 20, 2015, http://www.bioedge.org/bioethics/peter-singer-disinvited-from-german-philosophy-festival/11491.

[36] There are nuances of Singer's views I am ignoring here: For instance, he talks in terms of desire-satisfaction, rather than pleasure and pain, though this comes to the same thing in the case of non-human animals. Singer also thinks *sapience* can be morally salient, insofar as it affects the experience of pleasure and pain (or the satisfaction of desires).

[37] He sometimes derides responses like this as failures to follow through a principled and rational argument, but such responses are obviously question-begging.

(regardless of species) is the only thing that is morally salient leads to the conclusion that it is permissible to kill human babies with defects, it is equally reasonable to take that to show that species membership (namely, being human) is morally salient, since it explains why killing human babies is wrong, even when their cognitive and physical defects will impose burdens on others. That this rather obvious point is not much acknowledged in the philosophical literature should make even philosophers wonder what role *discursive rationality* as opposed to other forces are playing in their arguments.

From a serious philosophical point of view, of course, it should hardly be surprising that it is not rationally obligatory to think the suffering of nonhuman animals is on a par with that of humans. More general lessons of twentieth-century philosophy, I believe, show that no belief about *any* subject matter is rationally obligatory for all agents, regardless of their ends. First, from the famous Duhem–Quine thesis[38] about the underdetermination of scientific theories by evidence, we know that there are not even any scientific hypotheses that are rationally obligatory, in the sense of required by logic and evidence. This is because any recalcitrant evidence elicited in a test of a hypothesis is compatible with the hypothesis as long as we are willing to give up the background assumptions such a test requires. In choosing among competing hypotheses and background assumptions, we must always fall back on nonrational considerations, such as theoretical simplicity, methodological conservatism, and consilience.[39] Second, unless there were a plausible *substantive* conception of rationality (there does not appear to be one, alas), then rationality itself is instrumental, imposing normative constraints only on the means chosen to realize our ends, whatever they may happen to be. Thus, even norms for belief are hostage to ultimate ends, and so particular beliefs are "irrational" only relative to the believer's ends.[40] Neither Singer nor anyone else can show that one is rationally required to rule out ends (like forbidding infanticide) which require as a matter of instrumental reasoning the repudiation of the moral salience of suffering without regard to species.

Given our general epistemological predicament—namely, that no belief is rationally obligatory—it becomes even more interesting to ask what role discursive hygiene can play in public life. Even Peter Singer has acknowledged[41] that one of the most influential parts of his 1975 book *Animal Liberation*[42] was not the Benthamite argument mentioned already but rather the emotionally

[38] Named after French physicist Pierre Duhem and American philosopher W. V. O. Quine.

[39] See, e.g., W. V. O. Quine and Joseph Ullian, *The Web of Belief*, 2nd ed. (Random House, 1978).

[40] See, e.g., Peter Railton, "Facts and Values," *Philosophical Topics* 14 (1986): 5–31.

[41] See his reply to Judge Richard Posner in Peter Singer and Richard Posner, "Animal Rights," *Slate*, June 13, 2001, http://www.slate.com/articles/news_and_politics/dialogues/features/2001/animal_rights/_4.html.

[42] Peter Singer, *Animal Liberation: A New Ethics for our Treatment of Animals* (Random House, 1975).

evocative description of factory-farming practices in chapter 3 of his book. These descriptions evoked the *suffering* of sentient creatures, and so elicited feelings of compassion from readers quite effectively. But from Singer's perspective, the moral salience of suffering also entails the moral permissibility of infanticide, and it is easy enough to see that even a rather discreet description of infanticide factories or hospices (call them what you want) would immediately elicit a very different set of moral intuitions and feelings. Clearly, our emotional responses to vivid descriptions of *factory-farmed chickens* and *the painless killing of defective human babies* are not going to yield a rational verdict about the moral propriety of either practice.[43]

V. What Is to Be Done? Learn from the Lawyers!

So if tribalism and emotion dominate most moral thinking in the public sphere, should we simply not bother with "public philosophy"? That is not, in fact, the skeptical conclusion I draw, and it is important to emphasize why. First, of course, some of us, both citizens and philosophers, want to try to reason our way to sound views of moral and political questions of public significance, despite the irrational and Tribalist tendencies of most public discourse. That may effectively render "public philosophy" private, defeating its originally neoliberal rationalization, but perhaps that needs to be acknowledged. The *primary* reason for trying to figure out what is right and wrong in public affairs is to determine what is right and wrong (assuming there might be facts of the matter about this), not necessarily to influence public policy. Second, let us also remember that we do not understand well the conditions under which discursive hygiene matters to public policy over the long haul, and that is an additional reason for philosophers to continue trying to cleanse public debate and reasoning of its fallacies and non sequiturs: discursive hygiene may lead philosophers to satisfactory conclusions about the right and the good, but it also may, through causal channels we do not yet understand very well, lead society to similar conclusions.[44]

Finally, and perhaps most significantly, we do know that the discipline closest to philosophy—namely, law—is grounded in a commitment to discursive hygiene as well, albeit less rigorously and formally. Judges give reasons for their decisions, and those reasons are based on premises, from which inferential steps

[43] The antiabortion forces in the United States have always employed a Singerian strategy of describing the disgusting particulars of abortion to motivate "moral" opposition to it. It strikes me as curious that philosophers skeptical of the latter fail to notice the similarity to the most successful bits of rhetoric in support of the rights of nonhuman animals.

[44] As many other essays in this book make clear, I am skeptical about this possibility, but it is, nonetheless, a possibility.

purportedly follow. Judges are influenced by myriad nonlegal factors, but discursive hygiene matters to them, as even those great skeptics of twentieth-century Anglophone jurisprudence, the American Legal Realists, repeatedly emphasized. Let us recall the anecdote invoked by Jerome Frank, one of the two most important American realists and the most skeptical of the group. He observed:

> A century ago a great American judge, Chancellor Kent, in a personal letter explained his method of arriving at a decision. He first made himself "master of the facts." Then (he wrote) "I saw where justice lay, and the moral sense decided the court half the time. I then sat down to search the authorities . . . I might once in a while be embarrassed by a technical rule, but I *almost always found principles suited to my view of the case.*[45]

Frank took this to be illustrative of the general form of legal decision-making by judges, namely, that they arrive at their decision based on their "moral sense" about what would be a fair outcome given what happened. In this regard, Frank's picture is still consistent with Haidt's "social intuitionist" model of moral judgment. But notice that the account Frank endorses has two other striking features. First, judges, on Frank's picture, still want to find *legal principles* that will justify deductively the conclusion they find morally attractive. Second, judges can still be "embarrassed by a technical rule," that is, they can come to recognize that the result they deem fair is not permissible *discursively* because of the logical entailments of the controlling legal rules. Those concessions by a radical skeptic like Jerome Frank about rational decision-making about practical questions should remind us that even in the sphere of emotional reaction and tribalism, discursive hygiene can still exert pressures. Perhaps public philosophy can contribute to those pressures.

This will no doubt seem too tepid a conclusion to those whose vision of philosophy is different than mine. Like the Skeptics of antiquity, and like the great modern skeptics about reason, namely, Hume and Nietzsche, I think we must recognize that reason underdetermines what to believe, even in the best of circumstances, and that, unsurprisingly, in the worst of circumstances—such as public discourse—nonrational factors overwhelm all others. We philosophers labor at the margins of public life, public life being dominated by irrational emotion and tribalist prejudice. But in ways we cannot always anticipate, our labors in the service of discursive hygiene may matter. Law is our ally in this regard, because lawyers are the practical torch-bearers of discursive hygiene. But lawyers understand something that most philosophers—the Sophists, Marx, and Nietzsche are prominent exceptions—do not, namely, that rhetoric—the art of

[45] Jerome Frank, *Law and the Modern Mind* (Brentano's, 1930), 112.

persuasion apart from appeal to what follows from discursive hygiene—matters, and often matters decisively, in what the public believes. "Belief fixation," the process by which certain beliefs take hold in the cognitive and affective economy of the mind and thus yield action, does not necessarily track evidential, inferential, and logical relations that interest philosophers: The empirical evidence for that is, by now, overwhelming. Rhetoric was always, from the Sophists onward, the art of producing belief fixation, and it is not taught sufficiently either in law or philosophy faculties.

Of course, rhetoric does not tell us what *beliefs* we should try to produce with our rhetorical tools, but for reasons I have already discussed, it is doubtful that discursive hygiene will help us on this score. The two great polemicists of modern philosophy, Marx and Nietzsche, understood this, despite their differences in moral attitudes. Marx did not engage in public philosophy in the sense now fashionable in professional philosophy: He did not offer reasons why the abolition of capitalism was just or morally obligatory.[46] Instead, Marx offered a causal-explanatory theory of historical and economic change, taking for granted that if capitalism immiserated the mass of humanity, the understanding of *how things really work* would suffice to produce action, since the motivations of the vast majority to change things could be taken for granted on self-interested grounds. Nietzsche, by contrast, viewing almost all philosophy in the Socratic tradition as a kind of fraud, the attempt to rationalize the emotional prejudices of particular cultures, or particularly sick individuals (as Nietzsche viewed most philosophers), wanted to displace it with a self-conscious "legislation of values," values in the service of making life worth living.[47] For Nietzsche, this meant living in a world in which genius and its aesthetically pleasing products prevailed, something to which he thought the ascetic moralities of the last two thousand years constituted obstacles. Marx and Nietzsche both were "public philosophers"—Marx during his lifetime in some measure, Nietzsche only afterward—and both on a scale undreamed of by any academics of the last hundred years, yet neither was primarily a practitioner of discursive hygiene in the sense of neoliberal "public philosophy." There may be an important lesson in this fact for aspiring "public philosophers," who should give at least as much attention to rhetoric as to discursive hygiene. We need discursive hygiene for the study and the seminar room, but in public, we need something else, something much more important, namely, rhetorical skill that will make our academic conclusions salient to a public too often influenced by emotion and tribalist sympathies.[48]

[46] See ch. 18 in this volume.

[47] See Brian Leiter, *Nietzsche on Morality*, 2nd ed. (Routledge, 2014).

[48] The earliest version of this essay was given as a public lecture at the Jindal Global Law School near Delhi in November 2014.

18

Why Marxism Still Does Not Need Normative Theory

A Polemic

I. Introduction

Marx, early and late, had normative opinions, opinions about what was good and bad, right and wrong, and valuable and disvaluable. What he did not have, except inchoately in the *1844 Manuscripts*,[1] was a *normative theory*, that is, a theory that purported to justify, discursively and systematically, his normative opinions, to show them to be rationally obligatory or objectively valid. In this regard, Marx was obviously not alone: Almost everyone, including those who lead what are widely regarded as exemplary "moral" lives, decides and acts based on normative intuitions and inclinations that fall far short of a theory. The one candidate for a normative theory in Marx, in the *1844 Manuscripts*, is not a very promising one, involving as it does dubious speculation about the essential nature of human beings and normative claims that run counter to the mature Marx's views about morality and value, in particular, the view he shared with Engels that because the existing relations of production determine moral opinions, we cannot know what morality would be characteristic of a society that did not have capitalist relations of production. Later, Marx's insight should temper enthusiasm for the speculations of the early Marx.[2]

[1] Karl Marx, *Economic and Philosophic Manuscripts of 1844*, trans. Martin Milligan (Progress Publishers, 1959).

[2] The early Marx held that under capitalism, individuals suffered from alienation (*Entfremdung*) from their essential nature. While alienation might have distinctive phenomenological markers, these have only evidential significance: Alienation is fundamentally an objective failure to realize one's essential nature. But does man really have an essential nature, and if so, what is it? The core idea in the *1844 Manuscripts* is that humans only flourish when they freely engage in productive activity (rather than engaging in it to meet basic human needs), recognize their own dependence on cooperative productive activity, and recognize that it is essential to the very nature of the species to which they belong that they engage in such self-aware productivity activity. Marx's characterization of the "species-being" of humans is, to put it gently, a claim of dubious epistemic status. It is certainly no part of serious biology, either then or since, and it is not clear it does any explanatory work in making sense of historical transformation. It has attracted, to be sure, the attention of the worst kind of bourgeois armchair moral theorists, neo-Aristotelians like Philippa Foot and Michael Thompson who, like Aristotle (but less forgivably), simply make up the facts about human beings to suit their moral

From a Realist Point of View. Brian Leiter, Oxford University Press. © Brian Leiter 2026.
DOI: 10.1093/9780197749852.003.0020

Putting the early Marx to one side, what is clear is that in almost all his mature work, even when he expresses normative opinions in passing, his primary concern is to offer a sound causal-explanatory theory of socioeconomic change and its possibility. Marx takes for granted that, *at the right historical moment*, circumstances will be such that large numbers of people will be motivated to undertake revolutionary change; they do not require a normative theory to help them. What they will find useful is a correct understanding of their historical situation and the causal mechanisms at work that explain its potential, precisely the theory Marx purports to offer.[3] Thus, I shall argue that a familiar complaint about Marx—that he lacked an adequate individual psychology that would explain why people act as his theory predicts—is sound, but that we have every reason to supplement the Marxian causal-explanatory theory of historical change with a psychology that shows why normative theory is entirely irrelevant. This is the subject of section II of this chapter.

Events in the twenty-first century continue to confirm the basic correctness of Marx's causal-explanatory theory (e.g., developed capitalist societies tend toward widening inequality; capitalism continues to conquer the globe, and where it does so, it erases local cultures and customs in favor of homogeneity and capitalist values; the dominant moral and political ideas are those of the ruling classes, those with control over the main forces of production), as do the major currents of historical explanation in the scholarly literature, even if we no longer have reason to accept the teleological view of history Marx inherited from Hegel.[4] Yet in the last half-century, many self-identified Marxists in the West have increasingly taken up the sort of normative theory Marx eschewed.

prejudices. But is it not equally plausible that human beings are "essentially" locked in a struggle between their erotic and aggressive impulses (as Freud had it), such that no stable, flourishing compromise will be possible? And perhaps it is possible, as Nietzsche believes, that the essential nature of humans is not uniform, such that the conditions of flourishing for most humans has little to do with the conditions of flourishing for the exceptional cases? Even if Marx is wrong, his *1844 Manuscripts* remain deeply evocative of the phenomenology of alienation of labor under capitalism. For an assessment (including doubts), see Jaime Edwards and Brian Leiter, *Marx* (Routledge, 2025), ch. 6.

[3] Most of the professed Marxist revolutionaries of the twentieth century—Mao, Castro, Pol Pot, others—clearly had no understanding of the explanatory theory, or every one of them would have instituted a free market economy in their agrarian and preindustrial societies. Why they were such incompetent readers of Marx is a topic for a different day. (Lenin had a better understanding, hence his short-lived experiment with capitalism after the Bolshevik Revolution--derailed, alas, by the need to fight the war against the capitalist invaders.)

[4] See, e.g., Eric Hobsbawm, *The Age of Extremes: A History of the World, 1914-1991* (Penguin, 1994); Marvin Harris, *Cows, Pigs, Wars and Witches: The Riddles of Culture* (Random House, 1974); Robert Brenner, "The Capitalist Economy, 1945-2000", in *Varieties of Capitalism, Varieties of Approaches*, ed. David Coates (Palgrave Macmillan, 2005); Ian Morris, *Foragers, Farmers, and Fossil Fuels: How Human Values Evolve* (Princeton University Press, 2015); and, in his fashion, Thomas Piketty, *Capital in the Twenty-First Century* (Harvard University Press, 2014). See also Edwards and Leiter, *Marx*, ch. 2.

That such theory arose is hardly surprising from a Marxian point of view which understands that intellectual labor, even intellectual labor by people of good intentions, is structured by the economic and political circumstances in which such labor takes place. The two key figures in this regard are G. A. Cohen and Jürgen Habermas. Their betrayal of Marx deserves to be understood, since in neither case can it be explained by ulterior reactionary motivations. In both cases, the structure of the postwar academic labor system and prevailing ideological currents may help make sense of the wrong turn their work took. That is the subject of Parts II and III.

II. Why Do People Revolt?

Why do people revolt? Why do they undertake any actions, drastic or otherwise? Is it because they are moved by reason, or is it, rather, that they are moved by the nonrational parts of the soul, their desires, and passions? The Humean view that agents are only moved to act by the nonrational parts of the mind—desires, drives, wishes, and so on—has won such a decisive victory in the empirical psychology of the past century that the persistence of the Kantian alternatives (in which reason alone might be the source of motivation) seems only an artifact of Christianity ("Platonism for the people," as Nietzsche says in the Preface to *Beyond Good and Evil*) and the division of labor in the university system in which some people are paid to tell edifying but incredible stories about human motivation. In a recent review of empirical literature on so-called moral action, for example, Timothy Schroeder, Adina Roskies, and Shaun Nichols found that the view they dub "sentimentalism"—namely, the view that "the emotions typically play a key causal role in motivating moral behavior"[5] —is well-supported by the "evidence from psychology and neuroscience"[6] and that while "motivation derived [exclusively] from higher cognitive centers independently of desire is possible . . . the only known model of it is pathological" involving Tourette syndrome.[7]

Was Marx a Humean about motivation? He plainly should have been, given what he tells us, quite explicitly, about the conditions under which revolutionary transformation takes place. In a famous passage from *The Germany Ideology*, for example, Marx claims that capitalism will collapse only under certain rather extreme circumstances:

[5] Timothy Schroeder, Adina Roskies, and Shaun Nichols, "Moral Motivation," in *The Moral Psychology Handbook*, ed. John Doris (Oxford University Press, 2010), 77.
[6] Ibid., 98.
[7] Ibid., 94.

> [I]t [capitalism] must necessarily have rendered the great mass of humanity "propertyless," and produced, at the same time, the contradiction of an existing world of wealth and culture, both of which conditions presuppose a great increase in productive power, a high degree of development. . . . [T]his development of productive forces . . . is an absolutely necessary practical premise because without it *want* is merely made general, and with *destitution* the struggle for necessities and all the old filthy business would necessarily be reproduced; and furthermore, because only with this universal development of productive forces is a *universal* intercourse between men established, which produces in all nations simultaneously the phenomenon of the "propertyless" mass . . . Empirically, communism is only possible as the act of the dominant peoples "all at once" and simultaneously, which presupposes the universal development of productive forces and the world intercourse bound up with communism.[8]

On this account, there are three necessary conditions for communist revolution: first, *mass* (i.e., wide-scale) immiseration; second, truly *global* capitalism (which is precisely what produces mass immiseration: "the mass of *propertyless* workers . . . presupposes the *world market* through competition" [Marx and Engels, *German Ideology* 162]); and third, an enormous increase in productive power. As G. A. Cohen aptly puts it, the transition from capitalism to communism is brought about by "the problem . . . of massive power to produce, alongside massive poverty. As that problem deepens, its solution looms, as and because the problem deepens."[9] It is not a condition for revolution that people have the correct normative theory of justice or fairness; as even Cohen's gloss acknowledges, misery, privation, and need are quite sufficient to motivate behavior. Marxists, in the grips of the extravagant metaphysician Hegel,[10] speak about a "contradiction," in which capitalist relations of production "fetter" the development of the forces of production. But what Marx has in mind is far more prosaic, and plausible. As Marx writes at the end of the *German Ideology*: "The contradiction between the individuality of each separate proletarian and labor, the condition of life forced upon him, becomes evident to him, himself, for he is sacrificed from youth upwards and, within his own class, has no chance of arriving at the

[8] Karl Marx and Friedrich Engels, *The German Ideology (Part 1)*, in *The Marx-Engels Reader*, 2nd ed., ed. Robert Tucker (W.W. Norton, 1978)(originally, 161–62. Further references will be included in the body of the text by page number.

[9] G. A. Cohen, *If You're an Egalitarian, How Come You're So Rich?* (Harvard University Press, 2000), 63. Further references will be included in the body of the text by page number.

[10] A large literature has arisen devoted to trying to obscure the fact that Hegel was a purveyor of the worst kind of theologically motivated metaphysical nonsense that the best tendencies in philosophy of the last two hundred years have tried to eradicate. Marx is to be included in that effort, though his proximity to the virus no doubt limited his ability to do it. On the *real* Hegel, Frederick Beiser, *Hegel* (Routledge, 2005) is admirably candid and clear.

conditions which would place him in the other class" (Marx and Engels, *German Ideology* 200). In other words, at a certain point capitalist relations of production evolve in such a way that those who labor for survival wages realize there is no hope of a better future. Such people, unsurprisingly, will agitate for change, especially if they have a correct understanding of the causes of their situation and the alternatives, precisely what Marx tries to provide.

It is important to emphasize that the agent of revolutionary transformation in the official Marxian view is largely indistinguishable from the agent of bourgeois economics in the twentieth-century neoclassical tradition: He has certain basic desires, and he is instrumentally rational in pursuit of their satisfaction. The genius of neoclassical economics was to diagnose the only kind of "thinking" that could count as rational under capitalism, namely, figuring out what means would satisfy one's ends, the latter immune to rational adjudication. It is precisely that fact on which the most plausible Marxian theory of revolutionary motivation depends.[11] In a communist revolution, Marx says, "individuals must appropriate the existing totality of productive forces, not only to achieve self-activity, but, also, merely to safeguard their very existence" (Marx and Engels, *German Ideology*, 191). The desire to "safeguard" one's "very existence" is a basic motivation for those who revolt.

When writing for a more popular audience, in the 1848 *Communist Manifesto*, Marx is quite clear on the relevant psychological story:

> The modern laborer . . . instead of rising with the progress of industry, sinks deeper and deeper below the conditions of existence of his own class. He becomes a pauper, and pauperism develops more rapidly than population and wealth. And here it becomes evidence, that the bourgeoisie is unfit any longer to be the ruling class in society . . . It is unfit to rule because it is incompetent to assure an existence to its slave within his slavery. . . . Society can no longer live under this bourgeoisie . . . its existence is no longer compatible with society.[12]

The laborer's motivation to revolt under these circumstances is not some quasi-Hegelian interest in his species being; it is that he works and works, and his life gets worse and worse. It not only gets worse and worse, but it does so under

[11] This also marks one of the dramatic breaks from Marx in the writings of the Frankfurt School theorists. As Anton Leist aptly observes: "Horkheimer early on (and in contrast to Marx) favored a Kantian rationality that was to be held as an ideal over and above the instrumental rationality present in existing society." Anton Leist, "The Long Goodbye: On the Development of Critical Theory," *Analyse & Kritik* 30 (2008): 335. Habermas then exacerbates this break, as I discuss below, pp. 395–98.

[12] Karl Marx and Friedrich Engels, *Communist Manifesto*, in *The Marx-Engels Reader*, 2nd ed., ed. Robert Tucker (W.W. Norton, 1978), 483. Further references will be included in the body of the text by page number.

circumstances in which the productive capacity of humanity is so great that, *if things were otherwise*, his life would be better in its material respects.[13] Marx, again reflecting the baneful influence of Hegel, thought he had to explain how capitalism eventually becomes a "fetter" on the development of the productive forces, for which he offered the famous theory of the falling rate of profit, which depended, alas, on the false labor theory of value.[14] Marx, in fact, also had on offer a much better explanation for the instability of capitalism, one that did not depend on the labor theory of value. Capitalism incentivizes technological innovation that displaces human labor power. As even mainstream capitalist economists have noticed, technological innovation in the twenty-first century has increasingly displaced labor power without reinstatement of human labor needs elsewhere in the economy.[15] Since the logic of capitalism requires endless cost reduction, including through technological innovation and reduction of labor costs, the endpoint would seem to me to be the increasing elimination of human labor. But since most humans have only their labor power to sell, their loss of income will result in a collapse in consumption, meaning, in the end, production produces very little that can generate profit. The endpoint of this process might be communism, but it also might be despotism on behalf of the owners of productive power.[16]

In short, people revolt when they are miserable, see no alternative, and understand that radical action holds out the promise of an alternative given the level of development of the productive forces. What constitutes misery is set by actual biological and psychological facts about creatures like us: that we need food, clothing, shelter, but also that we typically want and perhaps need opportunities to engage in productive and creative activity.[17] Capitalism, as Marx understood,

[13] Jaime Edwards has pointed out to me, correctly, that much Marxist theory after Marx, including importantly the Frankfurt School theorists, has been devoted to trying to understand why communism has not overtaken capitalism in a "timelier" fashion, as it were: The worry, of course, has been that the immiserated, due to false consciousness, are quite tolerant of their misery. Ideological delusion is real, to be sure, and it is part of the task of Marxist political advocacy to shatter it. But the basic mistake of much Marxism after Marx was failure to realize that capitalism has yet to runs its course: there is both more productive power and more misery in the offing. And the misery must be sufficient to motivate the counterfactual thought *that if things were otherwise*, everything would be better. In the United States, for example, we are probably a century or more away.

[14] For a detailed discussion, see Edwards and Leiter, *Marx*, ch. 4.

[15] For references to the recent economic literature and discussion, see ibid., 136–38.

[16] See, again, ibid., 139–42. In the despotism scenario, we are back in the dystopian world of the *Manifesto*, in which productive power is immense, but those who manage it, the bourgeoisie, use none of it to meet the needs of the vast majority of humanity. This seems an inherently unstable scenario, as the experience in despotic capitalist and nominally communist regimes from Nicaragua to Romania suggests.

[17] The *1844 Manuscripts* are naturally read as an evocative account of the other things humans might want and need to live well. Even then, the claims therein are debatable, but they are at least inspiring. On the "thin" conception of human nature that is important to the later Marx, see Brian Leiter, "How Are Ideologies False? A Reconstruction of the Marxian Concept," *Social Philosophy & Policy* 41 (2024): 223–40.

unleashes the productive power and ingenuity of humanity like no other economic system, but unlike the apologists for capitalism, Marx saw that the structure of the entire system guaranteed the misery of the vast majority. If agents' basic needs and desires are frustrated, and you can explain to them both why and what the alternatives are, you can be confident that those agents will be motivated to change things. Instrumental rationality and some assumptions about human desires are all one needs by way of a psychology of revolution. Agents do not need to know what justice is, or fairness, or morally right action. To be sure, they may express their desires in normative language (we all use normative language, all the time), but that is not the same as saying they need a discursive justification or theory of those concepts to be motivated to act. They do not, in short, need a normative theory to explain why they should revolt if Marx's descriptive claims about the tendencies of capitalist development are correct.[18] Even if Marx's qualitative predictions about the tendencies of development in capitalist societies are incorrect, there is, alas, no evidence that philosophical arguments meant to induce purportedly true beliefs about "justice" or "fairness" are effective in motivating behavior.[19] Marx had the right psychology for creatures like us under the conditions in which we live. If it turns out that the empirical claims central to his theory are wrong, then Marxism truly is dead, and no one should pretend otherwise. But so far we have no reason to think that.

III. Bourgeois Practical Philosophy and the Marxian Tradition

Bourgeois practical philosophy—broadly speaking, philosophizing about "what ought to be done" that poses no threat to capitalist relations of production or to the perquisites of the capitalist class—is now almost the only practical philosophy we have in the Western capitalist democracies, apart from the often unintelligible and juvenile posturing of products of the "intellectual entertainment industry" like Zizek or, a generation ago, Derrida.[20] The genealogy of how we arrived at

[18] Would individuals who lived under conditions in which competition for economic survival was not the central fact of existence have need of a normative *theory*? Perhaps so, but as with the shape of morality under such circumstances, we can only speculate about what it might be. What is clear is that, according to Marx, under capitalist relations of production, a normative *theory* is otiose with respect to revolutionary action.

[19] See the discussion of G. A. Cohen and Thomas Nagel, below, pp. 390–95.

[20] The "intellectual entertainment industry" is an offshoot of the "culture industry" diagnosed by Horkheimer and Adorno in the 1940s, though the former is not quite as profitable as the latter. But like the latter, its themes are repetition and superficial amusement, with originality or genuine demandingness of thought forbidden. The gradual collapse of the *wissenschaftlich* ideal that animated the modern research university two hundred years ago has created considerable room for the intellectual entertainment industry to operate in the more obviously feeble parts of the humanities and social sciences. Although much Anglophone philosophy is, in my view, worthless, it is not because of its betrayal of the *wissenschaftlich* ideal that justifies the university and animated, for example, Marx's *Das Kapital.*

such a state of affairs in the Anglophone context is worth brief notice, though its trajectory is different in the two main centers of Anglophone philosophy, Britain and America—which were also, of course, the two main Anglophone imperial powers of the last century.

A. Normative Theory and Intuitions in the Anglophone World

In Britain, normative theorizing by philosophers had a lively history going back to Bentham, Mill, and Sidgwick in the nineteenth century, and continuing through to figures like G. E. Moore and W. D. Ross in the early decades of the twentieth century.[21] Bentham and Mill were methodologically un-self-conscious, content with armchair empirical psychology about human motivation to lay the putative foundation for their normative utilitarian conclusions. Sidgwick marks the shift to the preferred form of twentieth-century armchair sociology in Anglophone philosophy, namely, to claims about what "ordinary" or "common people" believe, though Sidgwick had the intellectual decency to allow that even if ordinary practical thought is "unconsciously utilitarian," it is equally egoistic, thus leaving individual "practical reason" in an irresolvable deadlock. In so arguing, Sidgwick had acutely diagnosed the ideological peculiarity of conjoining Christianity and capitalism, that is, of trying to reconcile a Christian "morality"—one demanding altruistic concern for the welfare of others—with the economic system of capitalism, in which the only imperative of economic life is to promote one's own interests, others be damned. In describing this as a "duality of practical reason," Sidgwick was, in effect, diagnosing the fundamental tension in so-called practical reason under capitalism.

By the early twentieth century in Britain—with the country now the preeminent Western imperial capitalist power—its leading academics could put aside worries about the duality of practical reason in favor of utter confidence that members of their class would simply "intuit" all the morally significant features of states of affairs, none of which involved, for example, the wrongness of exploitation or the injustice of plundering the resources of nonwhite populations. The British intuitionists, however, also set the stage for the paradigm of bourgeois moral philosophy over the last century by limiting its domain to allegedly obvious "intuitions" shared by members of the same socioeconomic class about matters that never had systemic import.

[21] On the latter, see esp. the sympathetic accounting by Thomas Hurka, "Normative Ethics: Back to the Future," in *The Future for Philosophy*, ed. Brian Leiter (Oxford University Press, 2004). Earlier British figures, like David Hume and Adam Smith (and excluding the Christian preachers masquerading as philosophers), were more concerned with explaining how proto-bourgeois morality arose or could arise.

The extreme to which British moral philosophy went in the first half of the twentieth century—in which, essentially, the etiquette manuals of the "Bloomsbury Group" constituted "ethics"—was put in check by a variety of developments. At the material level, the collapse of global capitalism in the 1930s and the rise of fascists, who did not intuit the "good" as G. E. Moore did, surely highlighted the ridiculousness of intuitionism as an explanation of putative moral knowledge.[22] The rise of logical positivism—itself enabled by the triumph of capitalism that the modern sciences made possible and that, in return, rationalized its hegemony—resulted in a collapse of practical philosophy in the Anglophone countries, especially America. Practical philosophy was now consigned to the realm of emoting about what ought to be done, its criteria for cognitive adequacy so clearly lacking by comparison to the standards of confirmation in the various natural sciences. Logical positivists were, to be sure, not shy about emoting, as their opposition to Nazism makes clear. But they did not think that a normative philosophy was required, or even possible, to explain why they did not want complicity with Hitler's thugs and murderers.

The complete irrelevance of Anglophone bourgeois practical philosophy in the first half of the twentieth century—its irrelevance to the horrific crimes and atrocities of two world wars, as well as the horrific crimes and atrocities perpetrated by imperialist capitalist powers between and during those wars—might have been thought an indictment of its *bona fides*, quite apart from the epistemic worries of logical positivists. Bourgeois practical philosophy, alas, has returned with a vengeance, precisely during the time when the university system expanded dramatically—in enrollments and funding—after World War II. The massive expansion of university faculties after World War II, especially in America, created a demand for people to fill positions. The political purge of anticapitalists in American universities in the 1950s ensured that *if* anyone were interested in questions about *what ought to be done*, it would be strictly in terms that did not challenge the prerogatives of the now dominant capitalist systems (a point to which I return, below, pp. 399–401).

John Rawls, the most important manifestation of this transformation, applied essentially the same "method" as G. E. Moore, but with a small modification:[23]

[22] After the war, P. F. Strawson delivered the dialectical deathblow to intuitionism. See P. F. Strawson, "Ethical Intuitionism," *Philosophy* 24 (1949): 23–33. Intuitionism has returned more recently, under similar economic circumstances brought about by the "neoliberal" revolution from the right in the 1980s led by Margaret Thatcher in Britain and Ronald Reagan in America; as economic inequality in these capitalist democracies reached 1920s levels, it should hardly be surprising that "elite" academics once again became confident in their own moral opinions to such an extent that they view their confidence as having epistemic status.

[23] Rawls loyalists insist that the official method is more demanding, requiring consideration of all "reasonable" intuitions across history, usually meaning the history of Western philosophy. Of course, Rawls himself did not practice this approach, nor does the huge literature inspired by the "method" of "reflective equilibrium." To be sure, if we raise the evidential bar as the loyal Rawlsians propose, no conclusions at all can be drawn.

On the Rawlsian view, we should seek an equilibrium between our intuitions about particular cases and the theory that seems to explain those intuitions, once we consider that theory's other implications. The "method," appropriately enough, was dubbed "reflective equilibrium," which a contemporary of Rawls, the Oxford philosopher R. M. Hare, correctly dismissed because:

> It is certainly possible, as some thinkers even of our times [i.e., Rawls] have done, to collect all the moral opinions of which they and their contemporaries feel most sure, find some relatively simple method or apparatus which can be represented, with a bit of give and take, and making plausible assumptions about the circumstances of life, as generating all these opinions; and then pronounce that that is the moral system which, having reflected, we must acknowledge as the correct one. But they have absolutely no authority for this claim beyond the original convictions, for which no ground or argument was given. The "equilibrium" they have reached is one between forces which might have been generated by prejudice, and no amount of reflection can make that a solid basis for morality.[24]

Hare was no Marxist, to be sure, and he thought there were other more epistemically sound methods available—though his views on that score enjoyed little influence even in Anglophone practical philosophy—but his basic criticism of Rawlsian intuitionism was sound, and never received a serious rejoinder since the sociology of the academic profession guaranteed that the major universities were now populated with Harvard graduates and often Rawls's students.

B. The Characteristics of Bourgeois Practical Philosophy

So far, I have used the epithet "bourgeois" practical philosophy to refer to normative theory that does not challenge capitalist relations of productions and does not directly threaten the perquisites of the capitalist class. Thus, while Rawls, unlike Moore or Ross, endorsed intuitions that had implications for basic social and economic policy in capitalist societies, his theory was neither presented nor understood as threatening capitalist relations of production, a fact surely central to any explanation of how it could become so influential in capitalist democracies, at least in the universities. But Rawls appears as a paragon of moral seriousness by comparison to most bourgeois practical philosophy in the Anglophone world, which has three further attributes that ensure its irrelevance to the economic system and the priorities of the ruling class. First, such a theory primarily

[24] R. M. Hare, *Moral Thinking: Its Levels, Method, and Point* (Oxford University Press, 1981), 12.

addresses questions of correct action in terms of what individuals ought to do, taking the systemic features of capitalism as fixed.[25] Second, its primary focus is on what bourgeois academics (academics whose class position is such that they are either members of the capitalist class or largely dependent on the needs of the capitalist class for their livelihood[26]) ought to believe, not on what ought to be done—once again, guaranteeing the irrelevance of its conclusions to the perquisites of the capitalist class. Third, it increasingly and disproportionately focuses on moral trivialities, a feature related to the first point. I take these up in turn.[27]

(i) The Focus on Individuals

In this expanded sense, Peter Singer is quite clearly the preeminent bourgeois moral philosopher of our time, with his relentless focus on individual action and its individual impact, holding constant (indeed ignoring) the systemic status quo. Thus, Singer argues that people have an obligation to give to charity (akin to their obligation to rescue, at low cost, someone in immediate distress), as well as obligations to refrain from eating nonhuman animals and to sometimes kill (or at least to permit the killing of) disabled human beings—all following from allegedly simple utilitarian premises.[28] Singer nowhere argues, for example, that people have an obligation to overthrow the capitalist system or to pursue, first and foremost, systemic reform, even though systemic harms to human well-being are the most significant. Marx is, arguably, a kind of consequentialist welfarist in the normative opinions he expresses: that is, he objects to capitalism because, at a certain point in its development, it fails to maximize the well-being (especially the freedom) of the vast majority. Marx's conception of well-being is obviously not a hedonic or desire-based one, but that is orthogonal to the main point: From a consequentialist, welfarist point of view—of which Singer's is putatively an instance—Singer's kind of moral reasoning should be suspect. This

[25] Rawls, in focusing on the "basic structure" of society, is a slight departure from this tendency, but only slight: the basic structure does not include capitalist relations of production.

[26] I am such an academic, so the point of the characterization is not that there is a crude determination relation between class position and thought, though there often is. In my own case I suppose it helps that I come from a labor union family, so have a more vivid sense of the competing class interests, even though I now occupy a position closer to that of the dominant economic class.

[27] Cf. Leist, "The Long Goodbye," 331, where he observes that in moral and political philosophy "[t]oday statements about how to improve society are typically suggestions for small-scale improvements to special institutions within society, backed up by reference to 'our' moral intuitions, a common moral knowledge taken as given among a representative part of the citizens, or, even more abstractly, among humans." Or similarly: "Moral philosophers frequently get bogged down in details of moral theory that have no clear connection to the trends that dominate social life; and those working in applied ethics are often unaware of the larger institutional framework necessary to put their normative contributions in perspective." Ibid., 332.

[28] See, for instance, Peter Singer, "Famine, Affluence, and Morality," *Philosophy & Public Affairs* 1, no. 3 (1972): 229-243; Peter Singer, *Animal Liberation: A New Ethics for Our Treatment of Animals* (HarperCollins, 1975).

should be obvious, but it seems to have eluded bourgeois moral philosophers in recent years.[29]

If harm to human well-being is primarily a product of systemic problems, as Marxists (correctly) believe, then focus on individual decision against a fixed systemic background will have pernicious consequences in both the long-term and even the medium short-term. Insofar as bourgeois moral philosophers like Singer are concerned with consequences (whether short- or long-term) they would have to acknowledge these possibilities. First, individual acts of charity encourage moral complacency about systemic harms to well-being among charitable givers, in large part because it obscures from serious consideration systemic causes of human misery.[30] Second, those pernicious consequences are only enhanced when the capitalist media seize, as they predictably do, on

[29] Singer's own engagement with Marx is replete with misreading and dismissive commentary. See, for example, Peter Singer, "On Your Marx," *The New York Review of Books,* December 20, 1979, http://www.nybooks.com/articles/archives/1979/dec/20/on-your-marx/, where, in reviewing Cohen's 1978 book, Singer concludes that "Marx's theory, like Hegel's cannot be classed as science," something Cohen "fails to realize" because his analogy between functional explanation in Darwinian theory and historical materialism "falls into a popular misconception" of Darwin's theory of evolution. Singer elucidates: "That long necks help giraffes survive was not new with Darwin. Darwin's distinctive insight was into the mechanism by which the forces of evolution operate, namely natural selection of varying types . . . but Darwin did not explain long necks by saying that the neck has the function of enabling giraffes to survive." (Of course, Cohen's book indicates no need for this lesson, cf. Cohen's reply to Singer in G. A. Cohen, "Marx and the Giraffe," *The New York Review of Books*, February 21, 1980, http://www.nybooks.com/articles/archives/1980/feb/21/marx-and-the-giraffe-1/.)

See also his endearingly titled, Peter Singer, "Dictator Marx?" *The New York Review of Books,* September 25, 1980 http://www.nybooks.com/articles/archives/1980/sep/25/dictator-marx/. There Singer tells us that "[f]or readers interested in a general discussion of Marxism, none of the books so far reviewed is really suitable: McLellan's is too superficial, Gouldner's too long-winded, and Moore's and Thomas's too specialized." Then Singer proceeds to praise a book invulnerable to such criticism, at least to the extent that its author (Robert Heilbroner) "admits that people like himself might well decide to be content with Swedish-style democratic socialism, thus avoiding the dangers of ridding themselves completely of capitalism." However, Singer's praise cannot extend itself to Heilbroner's challenge of "our preference [sic] for individual liberty": "to the extent that Heilbroner endorses the idea that our preference for individual liberty is a result of our bourgeois perspective, he owes us an account of the ethical basis on which one might accept socialism despite its antipathy to individual liberty. And he owes us a demonstration that this decision is somehow deducible from objective or universal moral considerations in a way that the decision to support individual liberty is not. *Without this, it is nonsense, or worse, to talk of socialism as "a new social order"*" (emphasis added). A number of philosophers have critiqued the logic of Singer's moral argument, from both the Marxist left (see Paul Gomberg, "The Fallacy of Philanthropy," *Canadian Journal of Philosophy* 32 (2002): 29–66) and the libertarian right (see David Schmidtz, "Islands in a Sea of Obligation: Limits to the Duty to Rescue," *Law & Philosophy* 19 (2000): 683–705). (Thanks to Chris Morris for guidance on this literature.)

[30] For an intelligent expression of this point, by an "insider," see Peter Buffet, "The Charitable-Industrial Complex," *The New York Times*, July 26, 2013, http://www.nytimes.com/2013/07/27/opinion/the-charitable-industrial-complex.html?_r=1:

> Inside any important philanthropy meeting, you witness heads of state meeting with investment managers and corporate leaders. All are searching for answers with their right hand to problems that others in the room have created with their left . . .
>
> As more lives and communities are destroyed by the system that creates vast amounts of wealth for the few, the more heroic it sounds to "give back." It's what I would call "conscience

instances of bourgeois morality as ideals to which others should aspire—for example, in the celebration of a young man who works in the "financial" industry and, influenced by Singer, gives half his income (US$100,000) to charities helping people in impoverished nations.[31] Yet we know with certainty that a Wall Street youngster giving US$100,000 per year to various charities will not actually eliminate (or even significantly reduce) poverty, human misery, or suffering—in either the third world or in the first world. The actual effects on well-being of charitable giving are hotly contested by economists,[32] but even when they make small short-term contributions to alleviating diseases or disabilities, we have little or no evidence that they actually contribute to flourishing human

> laundering"—feeling better about accumulating more than any one person could possibly need to live on by sprinkling a little around as an act of charity.
>
> But this just keeps the existing structure of inequality in place. The rich sleep better at night, while others get just enough to keep the pot from boiling over. Nearly every time someone feels better by doing good, on the other side of the world (or street), someone else is further locked into a system that will not allow the true flourishing of his or her nature or the opportunity to live a joyful and fulfilled life... People will rise above making $2 a day to enter our world of goods and services so they can buy more. But doesn't all this just feed the beast?

[31] Nicholas Kristof, "The Trader Who Donates Half His Pay," *New York Times*, April 4, 2015, http://mobile.nytimes.com/2015/04/05/opinion/sunday/nicholas-kristof-the-trader-who-donates-half-his-pay.html?_r=1.

[32] See, e.g., the contributions by the economists Acemoglu and Deaton responding to Singer's so-called effective altruism. Daron Acemoglu, "Response to Effective Altruism," *Boston Review*, July 1, 2015, https://www.bostonreview.net/forum_response/response-daron-acemoglu/ observes:

> [W]e cannot measure accurately which organizations use resources most effectively. More evidence is always preferred, but precise measurement of the social value of a donated dollar may be impossible. What is the social value of a dollar given to Amnesty International as opposed to Oxfam or an NGO providing vaccines or textbooks? Every measurement involves value judgments. How much more valuable is it to save the life of a one-year-old than to send a six-year-old to school?

And even more damningly, see Angus Deaton, "Response to Effective Altruism," *Boston Review*, July 1, 2015, https://www.bostonreview.net/forum_response/response-angus-deaton/:

> It is an illusion that lives can be bought like cars. For a start, the evidence is nearly always in dispute. The alleged effectiveness of the Deworm the World Initiative—which, at the time of this writing, ranked fourth in GiveWell's list of top charities—runs contrary to the latest extensive review of the evidence by the Cochrane Collaboration, an organization that compiles medical research data. Maybe Cochrane is wrong, but it is more likely that the effectiveness of deworming varies from place to place depending, among many other things, on climate and on local arrangements for disposing of human waste....
>
> [T]he evidence for development effectiveness, for "what works," mostly comes from the recent wave of randomized experiments, usually done by rich people from the rich world on poor people in the poor world, from which the price lists for children's lives are constructed. How can those experiments be wrong? Because they consider only the immediate effects of the interventions, not the contexts in which they are set. Nor, most importantly, can they say anything about the wide-ranging unintended consequences.
>
> However counterintuitive it may seem, children are not dying for the lack of a few thousand dollars to keep them alive. If it were so simple, the world would already be a much better place. Development is neither a financial nor a technical problem but a political problem, and the aid industry often makes the politics worse....

lives—primarily because those to whom aid is so often directed for discreet problems live under systemic conditions that thwart human flourishing along many other dimensions, to which charity is never responsive.[33]

What if instead of picking worthy charities in accordance with Singer's bourgeois moral philosophy, those with resources committed all of it to supporting radical political and economic reforms in powerful capitalist democracies like the United States, perhaps even committing their time and resources to helping other well-intentioned individuals with resources organize themselves collectively to do the same? Is it implausible that if all those in the thrall of Peter Singer gave all their money, time, and effort to challenging, through political activism or otherwise, the idea that human well-being should be hostage to acts of charity, then the well-being of human beings would be more likely to be maximized even from a utilitarian point of view? Do Singerites deny that systemic changes to the global capitalist system, including massive, forced redistribution of resources from the idle rich to those in need, would not dwarf all the modest improvements in human well-being achieved by the kind of charitable acts Singer's bourgeois moral philosophy commends?[34] The question is not even seriously considered in the bourgeois moral philosophy of Singer. Although purporting to be concerned with consequences, like most utilitarians they set the evidential bar so high, and the temporal horizon so short, that the *actual* consequences of particular courses of action, including the valorization of charity over systemic change, are never really considered.

(ii) What to Believe, Not What Ought to Be Done

Contemporary moral and political philosophy is bourgeois in a second, and different sense, namely, that its main aim is only to revise belief, not practice.[35] G. A. Cohen, the leading bourgeois Marxist of our time, put it clearly: "[T]he question for political philosophy is not what we should do but what we should think, even when what we should think makes no practical difference."[36] The contrast

[33] I am even bracketing here the costs to human well-being of someone working in a socially parasitic industry like finance, costs which are borne both by the worker and others.

[34] In fact, in conversing with Singerites, it seems many would deny this for classic rational choice reasons: namely, the marginal contribution of any individual to the transformation of unjust systems is negligible, by comparison to the "clear" impact of buying mosquito nets for people in Africa. This way of "calculating" what is worth doing of course guarantees that the existing socioeconomic system will remain untouched. The irony is that the "calculations" of Singerites, while purporting to be evidence-based and rational, are neither. See the critical discussion of the use of "evidence" in Emily Clough, "Effective Altruism's Political Blind Spot," *Boston Review*, July 14, 2015, http://bostonreview.net/world/emily-clough-effective-altruism-ngos. The Singer-inspired "effective altruism" movement is better-described as the "short-term measurable altruism" movement.

[35] Singer, to be sure, would revise discretionary spending by individuals who take him seriously, but that's about it.

[36] G. A. Cohen, "Facts and Principles," *Philosophy & Public Affairs* 31 (2003): 243.

with Marx's conception of intellectual inquiry is striking: As Marx wrote, in the second *Thesis on Feuerbach*, any "dispute over the reality or non-reality of thinking that is isolated from practice is a purely *scholastic* question."[37] He was here dismissing the preoccupation of post-Kantian idealists with the question of whether or not there is a world that exists independent of our conceptualization of it, but that is surely because it never would have occurred to Marx that philosophers would engage questions of practical import simply to figure out "what we should think," even though it makes no "practical difference."[38]

The ability to engage in intellectual inquiry simply to figure out what to believe is itself a luxury possible only in very particular economic circumstances, namely, ones in which all basic needs are met so effectively that some individuals can withdraw entirely into the realm of reflection without regard for its import. The value of such a possibility is a premise of the modern university, where insulation of inquiry from "practical value" is essential to research, including research that ultimately has practical import. But in the domain of practical reflection it seems perverse, given that its subject is *practical*, but most of its methods are without any epistemic standing—the intuitions or feelings of middle-class and often wealthier professors should be of no interest to anyone other than sociologists and anthropologists, perhaps—and its conclusions influence only, as Cohen puts it, "what to think."[39]

(iii) Moral Trivialities

This leads to the third problem, namely, the tendency of bourgeois moral philosophers to focus on moral trivialities and, to make matters worse, to do so with a "method," as we have already noted, that could hardly sustain serious

[37] Karl Marx, "Theses on Feuerbach," in *Marx/Engel Selected Works, Volume One*, trans. W. Lough (Progress Publishers, 1969): 13–15.

[38] Cf. Leist, "The Long Goodbye," 332: "[M]oral philosophers are eager to develop a technical vocabulary to capture their arguments—even though the distance that separates philosophical analysis and the practice it takes as its object is even greater in moral philosophy than elsewhere."

[39] It is often said by bourgeois practical philosophers that we need greater "clarity" about our practical thinking to lead our lives. But the evidence of those who led morally admirable lives—Martin Luther King, Jr., for example, or those who resisted Nazi terror—provides no support for the claim that "clear" practical reasoning was essential to what they did. This should hardly be surprising, since with respect to most ethically momentous decisions—should you cooperate in sending the Jews to their death? Should you treat other human beings like garbage because of their skin color?—the answers are either obvious or, to the extent they are not obvious, further moral philosophy is not what is needed. When I say the answers are "obvious," I am not endorsing intuitionism: I am only claiming that the problem with someone who thinks killing the Jews or the Blacks is reasonable is not that they lack moral knowledge or the right normative theory, it is that they are my enemies. Historically, communists, unlike others, understood these issues more clearly: Sometimes the problem with your opponents is not that they do not think clearly, but that they need to be stopped by force. Historically, of course, some self-described "communists" also misjudged both the historical situation and who the enemies were: but that, again, was not a failure of moral theory.

scrutiny. Let us use as a case study the work of a prominent young Anglophone moral philosopher, Hallie Liberto, whose "research" concerns promises and sex:[40]

> Consider a promise made by a college student, Jane, to another college student, John, that she will have sex with him tonight after the homecoming game. Call this case "Homecoming."
>
> We do not tend to take promises of this kind very seriously. We remind young people that they may change their minds about having sex at any time, no matter what they have said or done in the past, no matter what sort of expectations they have raised in their partners. We say they may change their minds at will, and without reasons. If we are correct when we issue these reminders, then that must mean that promises to have sex are very different from most other types of promises. After all, permissibly breaking a promise ordinarily requires a reason, at the very least —typically a very powerful one. But note that promises to engage in sexual activities are not the only sexual promises we make, nor are they the most common. We often make promises to refrain from having sex with other people. We take these promises *not* to have sex very seriously.

Put aside the triviality of the topic (promises by college students about whether to have sex[41]), though, admittedly, it observes the first requirement of bourgeois normative theory, namely, that it can treat capitalism as a fixed background, and no possible conclusion of the "inquiry" could affect the perquisites of the capitalist class! Even so, a natural question to ask about this analysis, if one is not already fully indoctrinated in the "method" of bourgeois normative theory, is, "Who is this 'we'?" Who is it that believes that promises to have sex can simply be broken, and who is it that believes promises to refrain from sex are more important? (Who is it that even believes breaking promises is of great ethical significance?) Much Anglophone "moral" philosophy has this "Emily Post" or "Dear Abby" quality, that is, armchair reports of what some suitably sensitive member of the relevant cultural and economic group feels ought to be done. ("Emily Post" and "Dear Abby" were influential American purveyors of popular advice in newspapers about "manners and morals," recording, often quite well, the prevailing informal norms of the American bourgeoisie in the mid- and

[40] Hallie Liberto, "Promising Sex," *Philosopher*, ed. M. Krishnamurthy, March 14, 2015, http://politicalphilosopher.net/2015/03/14/featured-philosop-her-hallie-liberto/. Further references will be included in the body of the text by parenthetical.

[41] Trivial, by comparison, say, to the fact of more than a billion humans living in poverty, or to wars of criminal aggression launched by countries that sponsor this kind of "moral philosophy," or to the billions of people who have little or no opportunity for human development due to the economic circumstances in which they find themselves.

later twentieth century. Their counterparts now populate university faculties of so-called ethics, though they generally write less well.) That there are no actual cognitive criteria for assessing the bits of moral etiquette advice proffered is obvious: The whole charade is sustained only by a system of "peer review" in which other Dear Abbys and Emily Posts participate.

Professor Liberto, correctly, situates her etiquette manual about sexual promises in the context of claims by other bourgeois normative philosophers:

> Tim Scanlon [a professor at Harvard] grounds promissory obligation in generated expectation. Promises promote a social practice that advances a human interest in knowing and planning for the future. Judith Thomson [a professor at MIT] grounds promissory obligation in reliance. For Thomson, a promise is an invitation to rely on the promisor (the person who makes the promise). A broken promise is wrong because it frustrates the expectations and/or reliance held by the promisee. A promise gives a promisee a map of some part of his or her future—a map to be used in planning. A broken promise renders that map inaccurate. (Liberto 2015)

Scanlon and Thomson take the moral etiquette manual to a higher level: They "explain" why members of the relevant class should deem promise-breaking wrong by appeal to other general normative considerations that some members of the class might think important, conjoined with the tendency of Kantians to engage in the psychological phenomenon known as "catastrophizing,"[42] that is, exaggerating the implications of particular events, in this case, inferring that breaches of a local etiquette norm on a particular occasion might have

[42] Catastrophizing is the "tendency to continuously think about how terrible a situation is and emphasize the negative implications for the future. Catastrophizing appears to be an extreme form of worry; this is important because evidence suggests that rumination and worry share a similar process, with rumination being a process of focusing attention primarily on current and past emotional stimuli, and worry being a process of focusing attention on the future implications of a current situation . . . Both catastrophizing and worrying have been shown to magnify negative affect in a similar manner as rumination, especially distress and anxiety related to future consequences of a situation. . . ." E. A. Selby and T. E. Joiner, Jr., "Cascades of Emotion: The Emergence of Borderline Personality Disorder from Emotional and Behavioral Dysregulation," *Review of General Psychology* 13 (2009): 221. The irrationality of catastrophizing is especially displayed by evidence that, "[d]espite attributing the same likelihood as nonworriers to their initial catastrophic events, worriers rated subsequent events in their catastrophizing sequences as much more likely to occur than nonworriers." M. W. Vasey and D. Borkovec, "A Catastrophizing Assessment of Worrisome Thoughts," *Cognitive Therapy and Research* 16 (1992): 516. As Vasey and Borkovec note, this may be an effect of the catastrophizer's being "able to imagine such threatening events more readily or vividly," though it is worth emphasizing—lest we make the "catastrophizer" too much of an aberrant— that there is strong evidence that we are generally more likely to come to believe a proposition in virtue of entertaining it. See Daniel Gilbert, Douglas Krull, and Patrick Malone, "Unbelieving the Unbelievable: Some Problems in the Rejection of False Information," *Journal of Personality and Social Psychology* 59 (1990): 601–13; and Daniel Gilbert, Romin Tafarodi, and Patrick Malone, "You Can't Not Believe Everything You Read," *Journal of Personality and Social Psychology* 65 (1993): 221–33.

far-reaching consequences (e.g., undermining "knowing and planning for the future"). The sheer silliness of such catastrophizing is obscured by a combination of the moral earnestness of their purveyors and the sociological effects of academic hierarchy in which nonsense must be treated seriously to advance professionally.

C. Anglophone Marxism and Bourgeois Practical Philosophy: The Case of G. A. Cohen

G. A. Cohen did not descend into the preceding kind of "etiquette" triviality. He was, as anyone who knew him[43] or has read his autobiography knows, animated by the normative opinions characteristic of Marxists: He wanted more human beings to flourish, and he believed that noncapitalist relations of production would bring that about. His famous 1978 book on Marx's historical materialism offered the most impressive articulation of the *functionalist* version of historical materialism, according to which growth in the productive forces was the motor of history and in which historical change was explicable.[44] This, unfortunately, was the least historically relevant and plausible form of historical materialism, obscuring the crucial causal role of class struggle.[45]

However, Cohen came to doubt the relevance of historical materialism.[46] As he wrote in later work, "Classical Marxism distinguished itself from what it condemned as the socialism of dreams by declaring a commitment to hard-headed historical and economic analysis: it was proud of what it considered to be the stoutly factual character of its central claims" (Cohen 2000, 102). Classical Marxism—including, clearly, Marx himself—had, in other words, a scientistic self-conception. The goal of theorizing was never to *justify* communism as morally desirable or just, but rather to construct an adequate descriptive and explanatory account of socioeconomic change that would have practical payoffs in

[43] I should add that none of the preceding criticisms are meant to suggest that any of these individuals are blameworthy. I also know T. M. Scanlon, an admirably kind, decent, and intellectually acute man for whom I have great affection and admiration; he is also a product of the upper class in America, which has undoubtedly influenced his moral sensibility. I do not know Thomson, except by her work, though her published thoughts on philosophy make clear her deeply conservative conception of philosophical inquiry, one appropriate for bourgeois practical philosophy (from Judith Jarvis Thomson, *Portraits of American Philosophy*, ed. Steven Cahn (Rowman & Littlefield, 2013), 54): "I came to think that the main, central problems [in philosophy] consist in efforts to explain what makes certain pre-philosophical, or nonphilosophical, beliefs true." That one sentence tells us quite a lot about analytic philosophy in the twentieth century, the logical positivists excepted.

[44] G. A. Cohen, *Karl Marx's Theory of History: A Defense* (Oxford University Press, 1978).

[45] For criticism, see Edwards and Leiter, *Marx*, 36–44.

[46] The discussion that follows borrows some material from Brian Leiter, "Marxism and the Continuing Irrelevance of Normative Theory," *Stanford Law Review* 54 (2002): 1129–51.

political organizing and revolutionary activity. As a result, as Cohen also notes, "Marxists were not preoccupied with, and therefore never examined, principles of equality, or indeed any other values or principles" (Cohen 2000, 103). Because Cohen believed that Marxism had now "lost much or most of its carapace, its hard shell of supposed fact," he concluded that, "[t]o the extent that Marxism is still alive . . . it presents itself as a set of values and a set of designs for realizing those values" (Cohen 2000, 103).[47] Of course, if Marx is right about human motivation under capitalism—this is where Marx and the Neoclassical economists agree—then it is a non-sequitur to say the falsity of Marxian factual claims means we should focus on "values."

Cohen's argument for the "falsity" of Marx's explanatory claims warrants some attention. Cohen claims, *contra* Marx, that

> [c]apitalism does not produce its own gravediggers. The old (partly real, partly imagined) agency of socialist transformation is gone, and there is not, *and never will be*, another one like it. Socialists have to settle for a less dramatic scenario, and they must engage in more moral advocacy than used to be fashionable. (Cohen 2000, 112)

That "capitalism does not produce its own gravediggers" is, to be sure, not an a priori truth; the only relevant question is what a posteriori requires us to reject it? That capitalism is presently flourishing is hardly evidence, unless one believes that history is over. Cohen has a somewhat unfortunate tendency to assume precisely this. He writes, correctly, that on the traditional Marxian view,

> [t]wo supposedly irrepressible historical trends, working together, guaranteed the future material equality [under communism]. One was the rise of an organized working class, whose social emplacement, at the short end of *in*equality, directed it in favor of equality. The workers' movement would grow in numbers

[47] There is an interesting question of Marx interpretation, however, regarding whether "equality" is really one of those values. Cohen assumes it is throughout the book (Cohen 2000), without ever specifying what is meant by Marxian equality. At one point, he equates "Marxist equality" with the famous slogan from *The Communist Manifesto*: "From each according to his ability, to each according to his needs." But the latter seems a slogan that contemplates vast amounts of inequality, making the exact content of the Marxist commitment to equality even more puzzling.

Now, in fact, it seems to me that Marx is committed to equality only in what is now the banal sense accepted by all post-Enlightenment thinkers: namely, that in moral deliberations, everyone's interests (well-being, dignity, autonomy, etc.) counts equally. I am not entitled to more or less moral consideration because I am an American, or a male, or white. At this level, however, equality as a doctrine does not do much to discriminate among possible positions. After all, Kant is an egalitarian in this sense, as is the arch-utilitarian, Bentham. As a matter of Marxology, it seems to me that, in fact, equality is not a Marxian value at all—except in the banal sense just noted—whereas freedom and well-being (human flourishing) are the central Marxian evaluative concepts. Marx is closer to consequentialism than deontology, the latter suggested by Cohen's employment of the egalitarian rhetoric.

> and in strength, until it had the power to abolish the unequal society which had nurtured its growth. And the other trend helping to ensure an eventual equality was the development of the productive forces, the continual increase in the human power to transform nature for human benefit. That growth would issue in a material abundance so great that anything anyone needed for a richly fulfilling life could be taken from the common store at no cost to anyone. (Cohen 2000, 104)

Cohen, writing once again as though he stands at the end of history, asserts that, "History has shredded each of the predictions that I have just sketched" (Cohen 2000, 104). We will turn, in a moment, to the surprisingly nonexistent empirical basis for these claims. But let us certainly grant Cohen this: Marx was spectacularly wrong about questions of timing. He thought, like many a giddy optimist of the nineteenth century, that the period of limitless abundance was almost at hand, and thus the end of capitalism near. No doubt his Eurocentric focus encouraged this way of thinking, since the industrial and technological progress there was stunning between 1750 and 1850. Yet Marx's qualitative predictions about the tendencies of capitalism have proven to be highly accurate in the 150 years since, *except with respect to the issue of timing* (i.e., Marx thought, wrongly, that capitalism was going to spread globally and fully realize the productive powers of humanity in the nineteenth century).

So how has history "shredded" the Marxian predictions noted above? Cohen is plainly correct that the proletariat did not become the "immense majority" (Cohen 2000, 104) and that, increasingly, the immiserated of the world are not producers like the classic working class; they are just miserable (Cohen 2000, 107–8). But Cohen thinks that a group, to be an effective agent of revolution, must have the four features that the classic nineteenth-century proletariat were supposed to have: They were the majority, they produced the wealth of society, they were exploited by the capitalist class, and they were needy (Cohen 2000, 107). It is true, as Cohen notes, that the second and third features made the cause of the proletariat particularly appealing: They *produced* society's wealth, yet it was taken from them. But what he never explains is why it would not suffice for revolution if the majority of humanity was needy *in conjunction with* there being enough productive power to meet their needs? Indeed, Cohen's whole discussion proceeds, somewhat oddly, without citation of any empirical evidence one way or the other!

My reformulation of the conditions for revolutionary change requires, to be sure, that Marx's abundance prediction be made good as well. And Cohen disputes this prediction also—though, once again, without citing empirical support. He says, "our environment is already severely degraded" such that "if there is a way out of the crisis, then it must include much less aggregate material consumption than what now prevails," meaning "unwanted changes of lifestyle" for those in the affluent West (Cohen 2000, 113). Thus, he concludes:

> It is certain that we cannot achieve Western-style goods and services for humanity as a whole, nor even sustain them for as large a minority as has enjoyed them, by drawing on the fuels and materials that we have hitherto used to provide them....
>
> We can no longer sustain Marx's extravagant, pre-Green, materialist optimism. At least for the foreseeable future, we have to abandon the vision of abundance. (Cohen 2000, 113–14)

Cohen affirms these empirical propositions without support, and apparently in indifference to, or ignorance of, the empirical literature that disputes them.[48] Technological innovations may yet solve, or ameliorate, the climate crisis; even more importantly, the global population is forecast to start declining in the next forty to sixty years, making it more realistic, within environmental constraints, that immense productivity will be possible. In any case, it seems inadvisable for Marxists to abandon the empirical claims of their theory without actual empirical evidence to the contrary.

Armchair political economy, of the kind Cohen practices, is an even less reputable discipline than armchair philosophy.[49] But bourgeois Marxists like Cohen should be given particular pause by the evidence that the "normative political philosophy" they embrace is motivationally inert (Cohen 2000, 117). In his later work, Cohen famously rejected the idea that the Rawlsian principles of justice apply only to "the basic structure" of society, arguing instead that

[48] See, e.g., Joel E. Cohen, *How Many People Can the Earth Support?* (W.W. Norton, 1995), 266, who wryly notes that

> [t]he Princeton demographer Ansley J. Coale observed that, in 1890 (when the U.S. population was 63 million), most reasonable people would have considered it impossible for the United States to support 250 million people, its approximate population in 1990; how would 250 million people find pasture for all their horses and dispose of all their manure?

See also *The Nation* (1997, 7): "From the annual U.N. Human Development Report: [D]elivering basic social services in all developing nations would cost $40 billion a year for ten years—less than 0.2 percent of total world income; the net worth of ten billionaires is 1.5 times the combined national income of the forty-eight poorest countries."

[49] Anton Leist, noting that much philosophy is armchair, asked me, "would you turn all [philosophy] into science"? The short answer is "yes," as long as we realize with serious historians and philosophers of science, like Larry Laudan in his *Progress and Its Problems: Towards a Theory of Scientific Growth* (University of California Press, 1977), that conceptual clarity and logical entailments (the kind of discursive contributions philosophers make), have always been part of scientific progress. I take this to be Marx's own conception of philosophy (i.e., as continuous with the empirical sciences). Even if all serious philosophy should aspire to *wissenschaftlich* status, rhetoric and advocacy should still loom large in human affairs.

> justice cannot be a matter only of the state-legislated structure in which people act but is also a matter of the acts they choose within that structure, the personal choices of their daily lives. I have come to think, in the words of a recently familiar slogan, that *the personal is political.* (Cohen 2000, 122)

This turn to very Protestant moralizing was, surprisingly, the distinguishing feature of Cohen's late work. Cohen became worried that on the Rawlsian Difference Principle, "inequalities are just if and only if they are necessary to make the worst off people in society better off than they otherwise would be" (Cohen 2000, 124). Yet this principle takes for granted that some people—those who can command more income for their work—are "acquisitive maximizers in daily life" (Cohen 2000, 140); that is, they want to get as much as possible for themselves, and thus the difference principle is necessary to insure that some "of the extra which they will then produce can be recruited on behalf of the worst off" (Cohen 2000, 124). Rawls here is closer to Marx than Cohen, ironically enough, for Cohen's objection is that the "talented" high earners have unjust motivations. Cohen writes:

> Why should we *care* so disproportionately about the coercive basic structure [of society], when the major reason for caring about it, its impact on people's lives, is *also* a reason for caring about informal structure and patterns of personal choice? To the extent that we care about coercive structure because it is fateful with regard to [the distribution of] benefits and burdens, we must care equally about the [informal social] ethic that sustains gender inequality, and inegalitarian incentives. (Cohen 2000, 140)

But a quasi-Marxian Rawls might reply (quite plausibly) that informal social ethics and personal choices are beyond the reach of institutional distributive reforms: they are hostage to economic circumstances which a theory of distributive justice cannot touch. Capitalist markets require individuals to be acquisitive maximizers, on pain of extinction in the marketplace. That philosophical arguments and Protestant moralizing might counteract this requirement of market societies is ludicrous.

Ironically, philosophical arguments cannot even affect the personal choices of those who purport to be egalitarian philosophers! Thomas Nagel, a decidedly egalitarian liberal philosopher and highly renumerated professor,[50] responded to Cohen's argument as follows:

[50] Just to make this concrete, I would guess that Nagel, by the end of his tenure in the late 2010s as a professor of philosophy and law at New York University was making in the vicinity of US$400,000 per year, perhaps quite a bit more if we factor in housing subsidies. He was, in short, in the same economic class as the wealthiest 1 percent of Americans.

> I have to admit that, although I am an adherent of the liberal conception of [justice and equality], I don't have an answer to Cohen's charge of moral incoherence. It is hard to render consistent the exemption of private choice from the motives that support redistributive public policies. I could sign a standing banker's order giving away everything I earn above the national average, for example, and it wouldn't kill me. I could even try to increase my income at the same time, knowing the excess would go to people who needed it more than I did. I'm not about to do anything of the kind, but the equality-friendly justifications I can think of for not doing so all strike me as rationalizations.[51]

Nagel, one of the preeminent bourgeois liberal philosophers of the day, understands and appreciates the force of Cohen's arguments and has no response to them, yet admits it will have no effect whatsoever on his behavior. One might think this rather dramatic evidence in favor of Marxian skepticism about normative theory. If high-quality bourgeois moral philosophy does not change the behavior of high-quality bourgeois moral philosophers, why think it is going to affect anyone else?

D. German Marxism and the Turn to Bourgeois Practical Philosophy: The Case of Jürgen Habermas

The descent into bourgeois moralizing in Continental European Marxism has a different intellectual genealogy than in the Anglophone case, since Western Marxism proceeded largely independent of logical positivism and other important philosophical movements of the twentieth century. The seed of the collapse into bourgeois moralizing is evident in Horkheimer and Adorno's famous *Dialectic of Enlightenment*,[52] which—its memorable critical cultural commentary to one side—locates a mistake in modern thought in its valorization of instrumental rationality, a theme it takes over from Horkheimer's 1937 essay on "Traditional and Critical Theory."[53] As we have noted already, Marx's critique of

[51] Thomas Nagel, "Getting Personal: Why Don't Egalitarians Give Away Their Own Money?," *Times Literary Supplement*, June 23, 2000, 6.

[52] Max Horkheimer and Theodor Adorno, *Dialectic of Enlightenment*, trans. John Cumming (Herder and Herder, 1972).

[53] Max Horkheimer, "Traditional and Critical Theory," in *Critical Theory: Selected Essays*, trans. Matthew J. O'Connell (Continuum, 2002), 188–243. Further references will be included in the body of the text by page number.

If the seed was planted by Horkheimer, it was certainly not cultivated by him or Adorno—it was left to Habermas to make explicit the implicit moralizing/Kantian critique of instrumental rationality in the early Frankfurt School. Horkheimer and Adorno's basic thesis—that Enlightenment rationality has led us to the fascist abyss—is a striking example of one kind of ideology Marx critiqued, namely, the false belief that ideas cause historical events. See Edwards and Leiter, *Marx*, 151–57.

capitalism, and the communist effort to mobilize the proletariat, takes no issue with instrumental rationality, indeed presupposes it: An instrumentally rational proletariat that understands how capitalism works, and what the alternatives are, will be motivated to undertake revolutionary acts.[54] The early Frankfurt School, wrongly in my view, sets out to challenge instrumental rationality in purely "ideal" or philosophical terms, and thus sets the stage for Habermas's complete transformation of the Marxian tradition into bourgeois practical philosophy.

"Traditional theory" for Horkheimer is a 1930s-style positivist conception of science, in which scientific methods of explanation and confirmation are uniform across all scientific domains, and in which science is marked by its somewhat austere empiricism and its commitment to mathematical formalizability.[55] (Almost all serious work in philosophy of science since has repudiated both the *unity* and the *uniformity* of methods of scientific inquiry and explanation characteristic of Horkheimer's conception of "traditional theory" and of logical positivism's conception of science.[56]) Critical Theory, in Horkheimer's rendering, eschews these characteristics,[57] instead aiming at "the rational state of society" and embracing "the idea of a future society as a community of free men" (Horkheimer 1937/2002, 217). Marx, of course, had such an end in mind as well, though there is no indication he thought his was anything but a "traditional theory"—that is, an empirically sound explanatory account of historical and economic change, minus the pretense of mathematical formulae. So why think the practical consequence of a good explanatory theory should be imported into the conception of the theoretical practice itself? That is the puzzle the Frankfurt School presents.

Here, I suspect, it is crucial to recognize the impact of György Lukács's reintroduction of Left Young Hegelianism into twentieth-century Marxism in *History and Class Consciousness* in 1923, especially in the chapter on "The Antinomies of Bourgeois Thought."[58] Marx, himself, had railed against the tendencies of Left

[54] Accepting the importance of instrumental rationality to human motivation under capitalism does not commit one to thinking that "collective action" problems pose a special problem for the Marxian theory of revolution, as Jon Elster claimed. For general discussion, see Edwards and Leiter, *Marx*, 46–47 and accompanying notes, as well as 134–35.

[55] The powerful impact of this essay on the Frankfurt School theorists is quite visible nearly forty years later, in Marcuse's polemic against "positivism" (essentially Horkheimer's "traditional theory") in Herbert Marcuse, *One-Dimensional Man: Studies in the Ideology of Advanced Industrial Societies* (Beacon Press, 1964), esp. 177.

[56] See, e.g., Richard W. Miller, *Fact and Method: Explanation, Confirmation and Reality in the Natural and the Social Sciences* (Princeton University Press, 1988); Philip Kitcher, *The Advancement of Science: Science Without Legend, Objectivity Without Illusions* (Oxford University Press, 1993).

[57] Horkheimer allows that "[e]ven the critical theory . . . derives its statements about real relationships from basic universal concepts . . . [B]oth kinds of theoretical structures [critical and traditional] are alike when it comes to logical necessity" (Horkheimer 1937/2002, 228).

[58] Georg Lukács, *History and Class Consciousness: Studies in Marxist Dialectics*, trans. Rodney Livingstone (MIT Press, 1972).

Young Hegelians to equate the critique of ideas with revolutionary critique, as though exposing the theoretical incoherence of a position would change the world. Lukács, alas, revived precisely that tradition in left-wing thought that Marx (and Engels) had so viciously lampooned 150 years earlier:[59]

> Since the Young Hegelians consider conceptions, thoughts, ideas, in fact all the products of consciousness ... as the real chains of men ... it is evident that the Young Hegelians have to fight only against these illusions of the consciousness. Since, according to their fantasy, the relationships of men, all their doings, their chains and their limitations are products of their consciousness, the Young Hegelians logically put to men the moral postulate of exchanging their present consciousness for human, critical or egoistic consciousness, and thus of removing their limitations. This demand to change consciousness amounts to a demand to interpret reality in another way, i.e., to recognize it by means of another interpretation. ... They forget, however, that to these phrases [constituting the old interpretation] they are only opposing other phrases, and that they are in no way combating the real existing world when they are merely combating the phrases of this world. (Marx and Engels, *The German Ideology* 149)

Although Horkheimer and Lukács had internecine disputes, Horkheimer followed Lukács, not Marx, on this fundamental theoretical issue.[60] Horkheimer explains that Critical Theory does not "consist[] in formulations of the feelings and ideas of one class at any given moment" (Horkheimer 1937/2002, 214), though that is, of course, *precisely* what Marx claimed the communist movement would do for the proletariat class at the moment of capitalism's impending collapse. In Horkheimer's conception, here echoing Lukács, what Critical Theory does is "take seriously the ideas by which the bourgeoisie explains its own order—free exchange, free competition, harmony of interests, and so on—and ... follow[s] them to their logical conclusion" in which "they manifest their inner contradiction and therewith their real opposition to the bourgeois order" (Horkheimer 1937/2002, 215). But this is precisely the practically irrelevant exercise that Marx and Engels lampooned in the *Manifesto*.[61]

[59] See especially the attack on Left Hegelians like "Saint Bruno" Bauer in Marx and Engels, *German Ideology*, 164–75.

[60] As did Marcuse, among others, and once again due to the pernicious influence of Hegel; cf. Marcuse's lamenting that in the wake of positivism the "metaphysical dimension [of reality], formerly a genuine field of rational thought, becomes irrational and unscientific." Marcuse, *One-Dimensional Man*, 1778. Marx would never have expressed such a lamentation, even if he would agree that instrumental rationality is a kind of rationality whose dominance is explained by capitalist relations of production.

[61] Ironically, Lukács was forced by Stalinists to repudiate this aspect of *History and Class Consciousness* as being insufficiently "scientific." In framing the criticism in terms of *Wissenschaft*, the Stalinist henchmen were just mouthing platitudes, but they were not wrong that

The return of "internal" critique of philosophical ideas to Marxism, especially the critique of instrumental rationality central to "reason" in capitalist societies, led naturally to Habermas's reintroduction of an essentially Kantian critique of instrumental reason into so-called Marxist theory.[62] Hegel was certainly right about the dialectical structure of history to this extent: Professors of philosophy do tend to excavate the contradictions in the most recently dominant philosophical ideas and subject them to dialectical critique. But as the un-Marxian Nietzsche famously quipped (regarding Socrates), "Nothing is easier to wipe out [*wegzuwischen*] than a dialectical effect,"[63] and though his reasons for doubt were different than Marx's,[64] it comes to the same thing: any dialectical critique of ideas, especially abstract theoretical ideas, which leaves the rest of reality intact, is only so much flotsam on the surface of the ocean. Habermas, over the last half-century, has increased the amount of flotsam by several orders of magnitude.

From his early work on an "ideal speech situation" to the later "communicative theory of action" (based on an implausible, linguistically and philosophically, theory of language use and meaning), Habermas has been relentless in his efforts to revive the Kantian project of providing an alternative to instrumental reason, in which ultimate ends (or desires) are to be subject to a putatively "rational" adjudication. Because of the proceduralism of his account, what ends are rational is never revealed by Habermas, but, once again, the appearance of a "method," and one utterly unthreatening to the bourgeois stability of post-World War II German economic prosperity, generated a whole "Habermas industry" to match the "Rawls industry" in academic disciples, Talmudic discipline, and practical irrelevance.[65] The withering criticisms of Habermas's arguments[66] have

this aspect of the book was a betrayal of Marx's theory. (Thanks to Brian O'Connor for calling this issue to my attention.)

[62] See Jürgen Habermas, *Erkenntnis und Interesse* (Suhrkamp Verlag, 1968), and especially Jürgen Habermas, *Theorie des kommunikativen Handelns* (Suhrkamp Verlag, 1981).

[63] Friedrich Nietzsche, "The Problem of Socrates," sect. 6, in "Twilight of the Idols," in *Sämtliche Werke: Kritische Studienausgabe*, ed. G. Colli and M. Montinari (Taschenbuch Verlag, 1980).

[64] Nietzsche recognized that affective, nonrational aspects of the psyche dominate belief fixation, and so overwhelm merely logical demonstrations.

[65] If there were any doubt about how far Habermas traveled from Marxism, his recent embrace of religious mysticism should eliminate it. See Jürgen Habermas, *An Awareness of What Is Missing: Faith and Reason in a Post-secular Age* (Polity Press, 2010).

[66] See, most potently, Raymond Geuss, *The Idea of a Critical Theory: Habermas and the Frankfurt School* (Cambridge University Press, 1981). Anton Leist, a friendlier critic, observes that Habermas's claim that communication "has built into it . . . a *telos* of reciprocal agreement" was supported by two main arguments: "the 'universal-pragmatics' conception of ethical presuppositions for every speech act, and the argument concerning a close link between truth and consensus. Both arguments have drawn an extensive amount of scrutiny, and it may be a fair summary of the debate that hardly anybody is convinced by either argument" (Leist, "The Long Goodbye," 343).

done little to dampen the enthusiasm of the workers in the industry. Why would it, given the current socioeconomic conditions of academic labor?

IV. Explaining the Collapse of Western Marxism into Bourgeois Practical Philosophy

It was central to Horkheimer's conception of Critical Theory that it had a reflexive dimension, that it aimed to understand "the functional role knowledge plays within the larger society" (Horkheimer 1937/2002, 334). In that spirit, we really must ask why and how Western Marxism in the academy, as exemplified by both G. A. Cohen in the Anglophone context and Jürgen Habermas in the German and, more broadly, European context, left Marx so far behind that it ended up generating an academic industry of normative theorizing that Marx would have regarded, correctly, as pointless, and perhaps even pernicious.

Here it seems there are two crucial factors at work. First, in both the United States and in West Germany in the 1950s, there was political repression of communism. In the United States, this took the form of formal and informal sanctions applied against anyone, including academics, with ties to, or even sympathies with, communist political groups, including the imprisonment of communists, which was repeatedly upheld by the courts during that period.[67] In West Germany, it culminated with the 1956 decision of the Constitutional Court declaring the German communist party, and any successor party, to be "unconstitutional."[68] With legal strictures and professional sanctions in place, it is hardly surprising that the primary Marxist intellectual movement in Germany, the Frankfurt School, should devolve into an academic Kantian exercise. Whatever criticisms one might make of Habermas, his work could not fall within the scope of the 1956 decision declaring communism unconstitutional.[69]

[67] Things were not as draconian in Canada and Britain, though the Canadian communist party was outlawed during World War II, initially because of its anti-interventionist stance.

[68] Aug. 17, 1956, 5 Entscheidungen des Bundesverfassungsgerichts [BVerfGE] 85. An English translation of the decision can be found in *Outlawing the Communist Party*, ed. Gerd Pfeiffer and Hans-Georg Strickert, trans. W.P. von Schmertzing (The Bookmailer, 1957), 225–27.

[69] Anton Leist presses on me that the situation in Germany was more complicated because of the background of East Germany, which was committed to the *wissenschaflitch* Marx in contrast to the Western Marxists, including Habermas, who took seriously the "early humanistic" and "life world" Marx. Leist also thinks that the Nazi background, against which Habermas responded as a robust defender of democracy, is important. In terms of the individual and social psychology, I suspect Leist is right: The East German totalitarians had little understanding of Marxism, and thus failed to realize that their country could not possibly be a successful communist society. But Habermas, instead of pressing the objection that the material conditions for Marxism were not possible, resorted to bourgeois moralizing about democracy and "free and equal" discourse. But "free and equal" discourse is impossible under capitalism, for reasons Marx diagnosed.

The second crucial factor involved both the massive expansion of the higher education sectors in both Europe and the Anglophone world after World War II[70] and the concurrent rise of the "new rigorism in the human sciences" as the historian Carl Schorske aptly dubbed it.[71] The huge increase in faculty positions, especially in America,[72] but also in Britain and Germany,[73] coincided not only with state repression of anticapitalist views, but also with the rise of Schorske's "new rigorism," a demand for well-defined methods of inquiry that would secure the epistemic validity of its results. This was simply a continuation of the phenomenon Max Weber diagnosed a century ago in "Science as Vocation," with the *wissenschaftlich* ideal firmly in command of the universities:

> [S]cience [i.e., *Wissenschaft*, meaning scholarly or method-based disciplines] has entered a phase of specialization previously unknown and . . . this will forever remain the case. Not only externally, but inwardly, matters stand at a point where the individual can acquire the sure consciousness of achieving something truly perfect in the field of science only in case he is a strict specialist. All work that overlaps neighboring fields, such as we occasionally undertake and which the sociologists must necessarily undertake again and again, is burdened with the resigned realization that at best one provides the specialist with useful questions upon which he would not so easily hit from his own specialized point of view. One's own work must inevitably remain highly imperfect. Only by strict specialization can the scientific worker become fully conscious, for once and perhaps never again in his lifetime, that he has achieved something that will endure. A really definitive and good accomplishment is today always a specialized accomplishment.[74]

Initially, the demand for "rigorous method" completely displaced "practical philosophy"—witness the rise of logical positivism and the demotion of practical philosophy to emoting—since practical philosophy was so clearly a feeble undertaking in a world that admitted of descriptive-explanatory treatment by

[70] See W. A. C. Stewart, *Higher Education in Post-war Great Britain* (Palgrave Macmillan, 1989); Martin Trow, *Problems in the Transition from Elite to Mass Higher Education* (Carnegie Commission on Higher Education, 1973).

[71] C. E. Schorske, "The New Rigorism in the Human Sciences, 1940-1960," *Daedalus* 126 (1997): 309. Further references will be included in the body of the text by page number.

[72] See Martin Trow, "The Expansion and Transformation of Higher Education," *International Review of Education* 18 (1972): 62.

[73] Barbara M. Kehm, "Germany," *International Handbook of Higher Education, Part One: Global Themes and Contemporary Challenges*, ed. J. Forest and P. Altbach (Springer, 2010), 731; David Greenaway and Michelle Haynes, "Funding Higher Education in the UK: The Role of Fees and Loans," *The Economic Journal* 113 (2003): 150.

[74] Max Weber, "Science as a Vocation," in *From Max Weber: Essays in Sociology*, trans. H.H. Gerth and C. Wright Mills (Routledge, 1917/1946), 134.

the sciences. But here again external events intervened. The student revolts of 1968, and the allied liberation movements for women, racial minorities, and gay people, created a demand for universities to be "relevant" to matters of practical concern, but within the constraints, of course, imposed by capitalist hegemony. The resulting bourgeois practical philosophy—as represented by Rawls and Habermas, and more recently Singer and Cohen—was an ideal response: It sometimes professed (no doubt earnest) sympathy with genuinely oppressed groups, it expressed moral concern with harms to well-being, it had its own "methods" and those who policed their application,[75] and it was utterly ineffectual with regard to and, indeed, almost entirely silent on, capitalist relations of production.[76] A Hollywood version of capitalist ideological domination of the universities would have hardly looked different than what happened. What are the mechanisms of capitalist ideological coercion in the academy? This is, I fear, less well understood than it should be. There is, of course, outright repression by force, as in the purge of anticapitalists in America and West Germany in the 1950s. But there are also the more subtle forms of intellectual coercion: who gets grants, what one's colleagues think is reasonable or acceptable, and so on. That elite Western academics, those who have the most influence on intellectual currents, are highly remunerated, sometimes members of the ruling class, but often on its cusp socially and economically, must surely have some impact on how they think about "what ought to be done." Academic opinion is also influenced by popular culture, even more so in an era in which the lines between the two are blurred, in which academics compete for recognition in the popular sphere, whether *The New York Times* or through *TED Talks*. I have the good fortune to work in one of the great academic centers of capitalist ideology, the University of Chicago, with colleagues who are admirable for their discipline, their hard work, and their commitment to ideas and argument. When, several years ago, I taught a kind of seminar with a colleague on "Capitalism: For and Against?" one colleague, a dialectically acute economist, wondered, sincerely, what could be said on the "against" side. The historian Schorske observed that "none of the 1960s movements—minority, feminist, or sexual—challenged the economic system" (Schorske 1997, 305). Like the economists themselves, the protest movements recognized, however tacitly, the capitalist free market as part

[75] The post-World War II academic labor system, with its emphasis on specialization, resulted in a whole series of academic industries, of which "the Rawls industry" was but one: the appearance of a "method," the presence of a canonical text, the enormous *A Theory of Justice*, and the stature of its author as a professor at what was then America's premier philosophy department at Harvard all fit perfectly the demands of the academy in this epoch.

[76] The German situation is more complicated because of the Nazi experience and Habermas's role as a proponent of democratic ideals. There can be no doubt that Habermas has been a powerful public voice for democracy and decency after the Nazi horror. The appearance of being an "important philosopher" has no doubt lent credibility, as a sociological matter, to these interventions.

of "the factual order of things" (Schorske 1997, 305). A debate of the form "The Factual Order of Things: For and Against?" is bound to seem incredible, and it is central to a kind of unconscious intellectual coercion that there are boundaries of what is "reasonable" and thus even discussable that have nothing, in the end, to do with reason or evidence.

Hume and Nietzsche, the two philosophical giants of modernity, both diagnosed the ways in which reason underdetermines belief, and both appealed to speculative psychological hypotheses to explain belief fixation even in the absence of rational evidence. Marx's important contribution to the sociology of knowledge was to identify, if not fully explain, how features of the economic system also supply the bridge between evidence that underdetermines belief and the phenomenon of rigid belief fixation among scholars and laypeople. One important task for a genuinely Marxist psychology and epistemology is still to understand the mechanisms by which this works (which entails, in part, a better understanding of the Marxian theory of ideology). One thing Marxists should not do, however, is waste time on normative theory for consumption by bourgeois academics.[77]

[77] I received extremely helpful and challenging comments on an earlier version of this essay from Jaime Edwards, Anton Leist, and Brian O'Connor, to which I have tried to respond, probably not adequately. I am also grateful to Daniel Telech for excellent research assistance, to Michael Magoulias for his careful editor's eye, and to Tes Hash for help with the bibliography.

19

Foucault as a Kind of Realist

Genealogical Critique and the Debunking of the Human Sciences

I. Foucault and Realism

Any reader of Foucault's corpus quickly recognizes that it is animated by an ethical or political impulse, namely, to liberate individuals from a kind of oppression from which they suffer. This oppression, however, does not involve the familiar tyranny of the Leviathan or the totalitarian state; it exploits instead values that the victim of oppression herself accepts, and which then leads the oppressed agent to be complicit in her own subjugation. Foucault's critique also depends, crucially, on a skeptical thesis about the epistemological authority of the social sciences that is supposed to be supported by his genealogies of those sciences. It is this conjunction of claims—that individuals oppress themselves by virtue of certain normative claims they accept because of their supposed epistemic merits—that marks Foucault's uniquely disturbing contribution to the literature whose diagnostic aim is, with Max Weber, to understand the oppressive character of modernity, and whose moral aim is, with the Frankfurt School, human liberation and human flourishing.

Foucault is also a kind of "realist" in his approach to the project of emancipation: He does not offer moral arguments to persuade people that they ought to behave differently than they do, but instead *shows* people the actual history of the institutions and norms to which they subjugate themselves. Realists, in my sense here, aim to diagnose, describe, and explain human beings and institutions, to cut through the self-serving stories people tell about their behavior, to reveal what is *really* going on. By contrast, moralists—the vast majority in the current academy—are fixated on creating a theoretical framework for the moral justification and evaluation of political institutions and individuals. Moralists especially like to scold people and institutions about how they should behave, making for an absurd spectacle, given that those to whom it is directed are, almost without exception, wholly indifferent to it. Of course, many academic moralists also specialize in offering rationalizations for the existing state of affairs, but when not performing that familiar ideological function, they instead sit in judgment,

From a Realist Point of View. Brian Leiter, Oxford University Press. © Brian Leiter 2026.
DOI: 10.1093/9780197749852.003.0021

wagging their fingers at the failure of states, institutions, leaders, and individuals to live up to the moralist's preferred theory of what is morally right and obligatory. Realism observes and diagnoses, moralism sits in judgment and scolds, even when its scolding is impotent, as it almost always is.[1] Some realists ground their diagnosis in claims about human nature (think of Thucydides, Machiavelli, Nietzsche, and Freud); Foucault is closer to Marx on this score, eschewing explanatory invocations of human nature in favor of broadly speaking "material" considerations (although not simply economic ones) to diagnose our institutions and norms.

The analogy with Marx is instructive, since no thinker (philosophical or otherwise) in the last 150 years has had a more profound influence on the "real world" than Marx, who was, of course, no philosophical moralist: He had no normative moral or political philosophy, although he flirted with some normative theory in early unpublished work. But in his maturity, Marx's emphasis was always on *diagnosis*: This is how capitalism works, and this is what will happen to most people given how it works. Marx took for granted that people would be motivated to act if they understood the causes of their misery and understood that those causes also promised an alternative. Foucault has been less influential, at least outside the academy, precisely because his diagnostic method is so different: he does not show us how the economy works, but how certain institutions (e.g., hospitals, including mental hospitals, and prisons) to which we regularly defer arose from dubious motives that should make us "skeptical" of the norms they try to impose. But Foucault shares with Marx the thought that a realistic appraisal of what's going on is important without a normative *theory* explaining what one "ought" to do.

Moralists, unsurprisingly, have the upper hand in capitalist academia these days:[2] Jürgen Habermas, Ronald Dworkin, Thomas Nagel, Peter Singer, even (tragically) G. A. Cohen, among many other contemporary and recent

[1] I hedge with "almost," but I can't think of an exception.

[2] Moralists have historically had the advantage for reasons Thucydides and Marx well understood: The ruling elites in every society have a vast appetite for justifications of their dominance. Some important historical figures are harder to place, depending on how one understands "realism." Bentham is a case in point. As David Runciman notes, it is tempting to see Bentham as "representative of a naïve form of moralism [in Runciman's slightly different sense], because he specified a single, pre-political value (utility) as the basis for assessing politics." David Runciman, "Political Theory and Real Politics in the Internet Age," *Journal of Political Philosophy* 25 (2017): 5. But Runciman says that this is a "caricature" since, "Bentham's writing exemplifies . . . the realist suspicion of the loose application of moralised language to politics, and in particular talk about rights, which for Bentham was meaningless in the absence of any underpinning in the terms of enforcement, or power." Ibid., 5. More importantly, he thought this moralized nonsense was "dangerous because it serves as a smokescreen for those engaged in the practice of politics." Ibid., 6. That is right as far as it goes—it shows that Bentham is not a "moralist" in Runciman's limited sense of someone who thinks politics is just applied moral philosophy. In other ways, Bentham is a moralist, though one, like Mill after him, with a finer talent for rhetoric than most contemporary moralists.

philosophers, are all moralists, while the realists can claim few recent allies. There is a characteristically tepid version of realism in writings by the late Bernard Williams,[3] and a less tepid version in the writings of Raymond Geuss, though one that is sometimes sophomoric, for example, in its polemics about Rawls.[4] Enzo Rossi and Matt Sleat, in their useful overview of what has been called "realism" in recent political theory, note that it has been disengaged from the "classical realism" of international relations (IR) scholars from earlier in the twentieth century, thinkers like Hans Morgenthau.[5] Rossi and Sleat aptly describe those earlier IR writers as showing "an appreciation of the political as a sphere of human activity that provides a context of disagreement which cannot be reduced to morality, a skepticism towards the power of reason and morality in political life and the difficulties in judging political action."[6] This is a useful characterization, but omits that the classical IR tradition, as well as much of the historical tradition (e.g., Thucydides and Machiavelli) was grounded in claims about what human beings are *really* like (i.e., broadly speaking, about human nature). Foucault, like Marx, stands in an ambivalent relation to that realist tradition, as mentioned earlier: Both are diagnosticians who eschew appeals to human nature, which they treat as another artifact to be diagnosed. Yet Foucault, and Marx, also differ from this recent "political realism" in another respect: They are not interested in *normative theory*, in justifying, from a moral or "political realist" perspective, what ought to be done, or in grounding their criticisms in such a perspective (they have normative opinions, rather obviously, and are critical of the status quo, but they invest no effort in constructing a moral theory that would justify those opinions and criticisms). Foucault and Marx, like realists such as Thucydides and Freud, abandon normative critique in favor of a realistic, empirically informed account of what is happening and what has happened—without moralizing illusions. It is this kind of realism that has become utterly foreign to most academic philosophy in the capitalist countries in recent decades.

[3] See Runciman, "Political Theory and Real Politics," 11 for a useful summary of Williams's view. As two other scholars note, in a survey piece on recent "realism" in political theory, Williams "does not give up on some justificatory standards for the exercise of political power," with the result that he is "too close to the mainstream approach he wants to reject." Enzo Rossi and Matt Sleat, "Realism in Normative Political Theory," *Philosophy Compass* 9 (2014): 692.

[4] See, e.g., Geuss's polemic against Rawls in Raymond Geuss, *Philosophy and Real Politics* (Princeton University Press, 2008). As Brian O'Connor points out to me, if the point is to get students and scholars to *read something else* than ridicule might be a sensible strategy—a point another realist, Nietzsche (who wrote much better than Geuss!), well understood.

[5] Rossi and Sleat, "Realism in Normative Political Theory." Some international realists think the behavior of states is due entirely to human nature, for example, the instinct for self-preservation or for power (Morgenthau was himself influenced by Nietzsche). The dominant strand of IR realism links the motive for self-preservation to the anarchic character of the international system: The international arena is the Hobbesian state of nature, so only the most powerful will survive. (Thanks to John Mearsheimer for discussing these issues with me.)

[6] Rossi and Sleat, "Realism in Normative Political Theory," 697.

II. "Bio-Power" and Self-Imposed Oppression

For Foucault, the modern era is marked by the emergence of a new kind of power—what he comes to call "bio-power"[7]—that differs from the classical, "juridical" models of power, captured so well by John Austin's (early nineteenth-century) view of law (and, ergo, state power) as a command of the sovereign backed by a threat of sanction. "We need to cut off the King's head," says Foucault, adding that "in political theory that still has to be done."[8] The agents of power and repression are no longer (or no longer *only*) the agents of the "King" or the state, and so the exclusive questions of political theory should no longer concern the justifications for and limits upon the exercise of centralized power by "the King." Rather, in the era of "bio-power," repression and regulation operate far more insidiously, for now it is the individuals themselves who are the agents of their own "oppression" and discipline.

How are individuals co-opted for their own oppression? According to Foucault, it is through the *epistemic* (and consequent *practical*) authority that accrues to what I'll call "judgments of normality," namely, judgments about what constitute not simply statistically normal ways of being human, but what constitute the *best* ways, that contribute to flourishing lives: how much one should eat, how one should care for the body, what kind of sex one should have, how one should raise children, what constitutes a "healthy" marriage, and on and on. Any readers of *The New York Times* will be familiar with instruction on all these topics, backed by the latest research from the human sciences. Of course, it is also true that all societies, ancient and modern, have been suffused with "judgments of normality," even if the particular norms and their particular objects have differed in various respects. Any student of Christianity, Islam, or Judaism knows, for example, that the ancient and modern communities in each religious tradition are permeated to the core with "judgments of normality" of the kinds just noted.

So what distinguishes "judgments of normality" in the putatively "modern" era of bio-power? It cannot be the emphasis on the regulation of the "body" per se, since Foucault's own work—especially in the later volumes on *The History of Sexuality*[9]—makes clear how far back these concerns go.[10] Rather, Foucault's

[7] In *The History of Sexuality, Vol. 1: An Introduction*, Foucault says he uses "bio-power" to mark "an explosion of numerous and diverse techniques for achieving the subjugation of bodies and the control of populations" which began in the seventeenth century. Michel Foucault, *The History of Sexuality, Vol. 1: An Introduction*, trans. Robert Hurley (Vintage Books, 1980), 140.

[8] Michel Foucault, "Truth and Power," in *Power/Knowledge*, ed. Colin Gordon (Pantheon, 1980), 121.

[9] See especially Michel Foucault, *The Uses of Pleasure*, trans. Robert Hurley (Vintage Books, 1990), and Michel Foucault, *The Care of the Self*, trans. Robert Hurley (Vintage Books, 1988).

[10] Foucault certainly thinks, to be sure, that the techniques for regulating and "disciplining" bodies have grown more sophisticated in the modern era. The classic study is, of course, Michel Foucault, *Discipline and Punish*, trans. Alan Sheridan (Pantheon, 1977).

work suggests that what marks judgments of normality in the modern era is that their authority derives from "the human sciences," that is, from claims about how one *ought* to be whose authority is, in the first instance, *epistemic* rather than moral or religious.[11]

Even this, however, does not yet suffice to distinguish the era of bio-power: for example, even orthodox religious traditions typically ground their moral authority in a kind of *epistemic* authority (recall: "the truth will set you free"), such as knowledge of the divine will or transcendent truths. What really distinguishes the claim of epistemic authority in the era of bio-power is that the human sciences claim a distinctively modern version of such authority: they present themselves as grounded in claims about human beings that emerge from inquiries that adhere to the epistemic strictures of the natural sciences, strictures that emerged with the scientific revolution and triumphed (more or less) with the Enlightenment. The epistemic authority of judgments of normality in the era of bio-power derives from their purportedly *scientific* status, not, for example, their religious status.

The difficulty, in Foucault's view, is that the epistemic pretense of the human sciences is just that: *pretense*. What Foucault says about "a science as 'dubious' as psychiatry" is meant to apply more generally to the human sciences with which he is concerned: "the epistemological profile of psychiatry is a low one and psychiatric practice is linked with a whole range of institutions, economic requirements, and political issues of social regulation."[12] This remark is revealing about Foucault's argumentative strategy, namely, that he does not (as some writers have done[13]), engage in a frontal attack on the epistemic standing of particular human sciences, but rather reveals their history to expose the influence of economic, political, and, importantly, moral considerations on their development. This does not, strictly speaking, show these sciences to make false claims, but it aims to raise (hopefully) debilitating doubts about the warrant for those claims.[14] For we know from epistemology that beliefs caused the wrong

[11] The best, and probably best-known, examples are Michel Foucault, *Madness and Civilization*, trans. Richard Howard (Pantheon, 1965), and Foucault, *Discipline and Punish*.

[12] Foucault, "Truth and Power," 109.

[13] See, e.g., Adolf Grünbaum, *The Foundations of Psychoanalysis: A Philosophical Critique* (University of California Press, 1984); Dominic Murphy, *Psychiatry in the Scientific Image* (MIT Press, 2006).

[14] See Brian Leiter, "The Hermeneutics of Suspicion: Recovering Marx, Nietzsche, and Freud," in *The Future for Philosophy*, ed. Brian Leiter (Clarendon Press, 2004), 103–5. Alas, Foucault is extremely unclear about the character and ultimate import of his skepticism about the human sciences. Often his position echoes Rudolf Carnap's on "external" and "internal" questions (in his famous paper Rudolf Carnap, "Empiricism, Semantics, and Ontology," in *Semantics and the Philosophy of Language*, ed. L. Linsky (University of Illinois Press, 1952)), as when Foucault says he is only interested in "seeing historically how effects of truth are produced within discourses which in themselves are neither true or false." Foucault, "Truth and Power," 118. The "external" question about whether, for example, psychiatric claims about human beings are true or false is a misguided, indeed, unintelligible question. Foucault's willingness to exclude "nondubious" sciences like physics and chemistry

way are epistemically suspect, even though they can turn out to be true. If I tell you the second law of thermodynamics, because it came to me in a dream, you don't have a good reason to believe it is true since its etiology is not a reliable one. Those thinkers whom Ricoeur called members of the "school of suspicion"—namely, Marx, Nietzsche, and Freud—all exploit this simple idea, by adducing suspect etiologies of familiar beliefs about, for example, morality and religion. And we should see Foucault as belonging to this tradition when he tries to undermine our confidence in the epistemic status of claims in the human sciences by showing how the development of those sciences was so often linked not to relevant "evidence" but to moral, political, and economic interests which are, prima facie, unreliable ways of discovering truths about human beings.

How exactly does such debunking work?

III. Origins and Epistemic Status

I assume with most epistemologists that Edmund Gettier[15] demonstrated that the status of a belief as knowledge is not settled just because it is both true and justified. On one influential understanding of the import of the Gettier critique,[16] either a "fourth" condition is required for a belief to count as knowledge or, alternatively, some additional condition is needed for justification. Reliabilists propose that a true belief is only justified if produced by a *reliable process*.[17] In the famous Gettier cases, by contrast, the belief is produced by an epistemically lucky process, not a reliable one.

If reliabilism is correct, then the *etiology of belief directly matters* to justification. In particular, if a belief arises from an epistemically *unreliable* process, then it is not justified. Recall our initial example: If the Second Law of Thermodynamics comes to me (accurately!) in a dream, I am not justified in believing it (although it turns out to be true), since dreaming is not a reliable method for discovering the physical laws of nature. If, following Marx, people in capitalist societies believe that capitalism promotes the well-being of everyone only because of propaganda by the ruling class—in whose interest it is for everyone to believe this—then the people who believe this lack justification for their belief: What serves the self-interest of a dominant economic class is not, it might seem, a reliable process for forming beliefs about what promotes everyone's well-being. If, as

from his critical analysis belies what I suspect is a rather deep affinity with the "logical positivist" view of the sciences.

[15] Edmund Gettier, "Is Justified True Belief Knowledge?" *Analysis* 23 (1963): 121–23.
[16] See, e.g., Philip Kitcher, "The Naturalists Return," *Philosophical Review* 101 (1992): 59.
[17] See Alvin Goldman, *Epistemology and Cognition* (Harvard University Press, 1986), 42–44.

Nietzsche claims in the first essay of *On the Genealogy of Morality*, the oppressed classes in the Roman empire came to embrace Christian morality because of their *ressentiment*—their festering hatred of their oppressors, whose power and riches they also envied—then those moral beliefs are not justified, since there is no account of moral epistemology on which festering hatred mixed with envy is deemed a reliable mechanism for ascertaining moral truths (assuming there are any).[18] Notice that one need not be an externalist about justification for the simple skeptical etiological argument to go through. An internalist could agree that if an unreliable mechanism produces an agent's belief *and* the agent is aware of that, then the agent's belief is not justified. All this internalist will demand is awareness of the unreliable mechanism to defeat justification.

Given the preceding, an etiological critic like Marx, Nietzsche, or Foucault has a simple argument to establish the direct epistemic relevance of an etiological account of beliefs to what I will call the "Target Beliefs" (i.e., the beliefs whose epistemic status is the target of the critique). If an unreliable process produces the target beliefs, then they are not justified (although they might be true). The internalist etiological critic will only endorse this argument if the agent is aware of the etiology; the externalist etiological critic does not require that the agent be aware of the facts about the etiology.

IV. Knowledge and Action according to Foucault

What links the epistemic pretensions of the human sciences and their "discoveries" about what "normal" humans are like to practical imperatives about *how one ought to live* is never clearly articulated by Foucault, but the structure of practical reasoning he (plausibly) supposes to be at work seems to be this: First, agents want to maximize their flourishing (call this the "principle of prudential reason"); second, the human sciences illuminate how (normal) human beings flourish; consequently, and this is the third claim, agents have prudential reasons to adjust their behavior to comport with the results of the human sciences. "Flourish" here should be understood in a suitably broad sense to encompass many different senses of "living well or happily." At the same time, the normality at issue in the second claim about what the human sciences reveal to us is not simply descriptive (e.g., *statistical* normality) but fundamentally *normative*, meaning something akin to "agents who flourish." In other words, the human sciences illuminate the "facts" about what human beings do who "live well." The structure of practical reasoning just described captures, then, the

[18] See Neil Sinhababu, "Vengeful Thinking and Moral Epistemology," in *Nietzsche and Morality*, ed. Brian Leiter and Neil Sinhababu (Oxford University Press, 2007), 262–80.

truly pernicious aspect of the modern era of "bio-power": As long as the second proposition (namely, that the human sciences reveal how normal human beings flourish) is *taken to be true*, then the third proposition—the claim that agents have reasons to adjust their behavior to comport with the results of the human sciences—necessarily follows given the plausible (and uncontested, at least by Foucault) assumption that the principle of prudential reason operates. Thus, insofar as the human sciences are accorded epistemic authority, individuals will "police" and regulate themselves to conform to their findings and edicts.

Notice that centralized state power (the "juridical" model of power noted earlier) is hardly irrelevant in this story. As Foucault himself documents in *Madness and Civilization, The Birth of the Clinic, Discipline and Punish,* and elsewhere, the state in the modern era is distinguished by its profound and intimate interest in the character of the populations it rules—their health, their reproductive patterns, their productivity, and so on. As Foucault writes in an essay on "The Politics of Health in the Eighteenth Century," this period witnessed "the emergence of the health and physical well-being of the population in general as one of the essential objectives of political power. [The question becomes] how to raise the level of health of the social body as a whole."[19] In consequence, we see the state undertaking

> demographic estimates, the calculation of the pyramid of ages, different life expectations and levels of mortality, studies of the reciprocal growth of wealth and growth of population, various measures of incitement to marriage and procreation, the development of forms of education and professional training. . . . The biological traits of a population become relevant factors for economic management, and it becomes necessary to organize around them an apparatus that will ensure not only their subjection but the constant increase of their utility.[20]

Indeed, in *Discipline and Punish,* Foucault says he is exploring "the present scientifico-legal complex from which the power to punish derives its bases, justifications, and rules,"[21] meaning that the state (as the force directly behind the "legal" part of the complex) remains a central actor in this story of oppression in the era of bio-power.

Now, while the power of the human sciences derives from a claim in the first instance to *epistemic* (not moral) authority, moral or ethical norms are implicated in three ways in Foucault's picture of how persons become agents

[19] Michel Foucault, "The Politics of Health in the Eighteenth Century," in *Power/Knowledge*, ed. Colin Gordon (Pantheon, 1980), 277.

[20] Ibid., 278–79.

[21] Foucault, *Discipline and Punish*, 23.

of their own oppression. Most importantly, the claim to epistemic authority becomes practically effective only by virtue of the scheme of practical reasoning already described, a scheme that depends, fundamentally, upon an ethical imperative to treat the truth as practically decisive in realizing the agent's good; the purported truths of the human sciences, in turn, provide the occasion for an instantiation of that imperative. This point is perhaps worth emphasizing, because Foucault is often associated—indeed, he often associated himself—with Nietzsche, yet on this important issue his posture is not at all Nietzschean. For Nietzsche argued—perhaps most famously in the third essay of *On the Genealogy of Morality*, but really throughout his corpus[22]—that the truth is often "terrible," and that the "overvaluation" of truth is an expression of asceticism (of life denial), precisely because what is true is often hostile to flourishing.[23] To be sure, Nietzsche is thinking of very particular truths: human suffering is both inescapable and utterly meaningless; there is no free will or meaningful control we exercise over the contours of our lives; and ours is a world of wills in endless struggle for dominance and mastery. But the conclusion Nietzsche draws from the nature of these terrible truths is that we should *not* treat what is true as decisive in practical reasoning precisely because it *may* be incompatible with human flourishing: Most of the time, illusions are essential for life. If Foucault had been more of a Nietzschean, he might have argued *not* that the human sciences lack epistemic authority but instead that even epistemic authorities sometimes do not deserve to play a decisive role in practical reasoning! It is very striking that this is *not* Foucault's argumentative strategy, one of many respects in which he is un-Nietzschean.

Ethical norms are implicated in two additional, but closely related, ways in Foucault's story. First, the purported truths of the human sciences (about how normal individuals "flourish") are predicated on implicit and explicit moral views about what constitutes "normal" ways of being. I take it that at least part of Foucault's aim is to raise doubts about these conceptions of "normal flourishing." Second, and relatedly, a consequence of the epistemic authority accorded human sciences is that their claims affect moral attitudes about their subject matters and, in particular, tend to implicate a conception of the self, both its nature and its (morally) proper governance.[24]

[22] See the discussion in Brian Leiter, *Nietzsche on Morality*, 2nd ed. (Routledge, 2015), 213–14.

[23] See Brian Leiter, "The Truth Is Terrible," *The Journal of Nietzsche Studies* 49 (2018): 151–58. And for a (much shorter) more popular treatment, see Brian Leiter, "The Truth Is Terrible," *Times Literary Supplement*, June 21, 2018, https://www.the-tls.co.uk/articles/public/friedrich-nietzsche-truth-terrible/.

[24] These concerns are suggested, for example, by Foucault's remarks in one of the last interviews he gave before his death. See Michel Foucault, "Polemics, Politics, and Problematizations," in *The Foucault Reader*, ed. Paul Rabinow (Penguin, 1991), 386–87.

To sum up, Foucault wants to criticize and challenge each of these practical claims: He wants to argue against granting the claims of the human sciences practical authority over our lives (though not because he rejects, as Nietzsche does, the authority of *truth*, but because he rejects the idea that the human sciences have the requisite access to the truth); he wants to challenge the implicitly and explicitly moralized views of normality and normal flourishing; and he wants to call attention to and raise questions about the moral attitudes, and the ethical conception of the self in particular, that emerges from the human sciences. The first challenge seems to me the most inchoate in Foucault, though like the other two it depends crucially on the challenge to the *epistemic* authority of the human sciences. These concerns are perhaps most vividly illustrated in *Madness and Civilization* and volume one of *The History of Sexuality*, but they permeate all Foucault's works that involve an historical analysis of institutions.[25]

V. Foucault's Critique Illustrated

Let us take *Madness and Civilization* as illustrative of Foucault's critical practice.[26] He begins by describing the medieval houses in which lepers were isolated, but his real point is that "[w]hat doubtless remained longer than leprosy, and would persist when the [leper] houses had been empty for years, were the values and images attached to the figure of the leper, as well as the meaning of his exclusion."[27] In other words, the pathological category became an ethical and social one, marking a purported *kind* of person, not just physiologically, but morally. So too with the "poor vagabonds, criminals, and 'deranged minds'"[28] to whom Foucault soon turns: They too have their own "values and images attached" to them and the "meaning" of their exclusions must be decoded as well. As he puts it later: "The asylum was substituted for the [leper] house, in the geography of haunted places as in the landscape of the moral universe."[29] So one aim of Foucault's work is to bring out the *moral* status of those condemned and excluded on grounds that were not always explicitly moral, or that blurred the line between the "moral" and "nonmoral" considerations.

[25] Foucault himself says that "the prison was linked from its beginning to a project for the transformation of individuals," but in this respect it is no different from any of the other institutions to which he has turned his attention: "The prison was meant to be an instrument, comparable with—and no less perfect than—the school, the barracks, or the hospital, acting with precision upon its individual subjects." Michel Foucault, "Prison Talk," in *Power/Knowledge*, ed. Colin Gordon (Pantheon, 1980), 39–40.

[26] In assessing the success of Foucault's critique, we will later examine Foucault, *The History of Sexuality*.

[27] Michel Foucault, *Madness and Civilization*, trans. Richard Howard (Pantheon, 1965), 6.

[28] Ibid., 7.

[29] Ibid., 57.

For example, the Parisian "Hôpital Général," which Foucault treats as representative of "the great confinement" of the 1660s (when one out of every hundred Parisians was put away!),[30] had at its official mission "preventing 'mendicancy and idleness as the source of all disorders,'"[31] so that the community, in effect, "acquired an ethical power of segregation, which permitted it to eject, as into another world, all forms of social uselessness."[32] Foucault continues:

> [T]he relation between the practice of confinement and the insistence on work is not defined by economic considerations; far from it. A moral perception sustains and animates it ... [T]he origin of poverty was [taken to be] neither scarcity nor unemployment, but "the weakening of discipline and the relaxation of morals." The edict [creating the Hôpital] was full of moral denunciations ... Hence the Hôpital does not have the appearance of a mere refuge for those whom age, infirmity, or sickness keep from working; it will have not only the aspect of a forced labor camp, but also that of a moral institution responsible for punishing, for correcting a certain moral "abeyance". .. The Hôpital Général has an ethical status....
>
> [I]t is in this context that the obligation to work assumes its meaning as both ethical exercise and moral guarantee ... The prisoner who could and who would work would be released, not so much because he was again useful to society, but because he had again subscribed to the great ethical pact of human existence ... [T]he very requirement of labor was instituted as an exercise in moral reform and constraint, which reveals, if not the ultimate meaning, at least the essential justification of the confinement.
>
> An important phenomenon, this invention of a site of constraint where morality castigates by means of administrative enforcement.... [I]n this great confinement of the classical age, the essential thing—and the new event—is that men were confined in cities of pure morality.[33]

The subtext of this historical account is that the underlying *moral* rationale for confinement is, itself, of dubious merit, but what really matters for Foucault is that this sociohistorical phenomenon was merely a prelude to the modern era of "scientific" psychiatry. In other words, this spectacle of moral policing under the guise of a hospital (or medical care) was not a peculiarity of this earlier era alone. Even purportedly great "medical" reformers of the treatment of mental illness in the late eighteenth century, like Pinel of France, were still writing: "How necessary it is, in order to forestall hypochondria, melancholia, or mania, to follow the

[30] Ibid., 38, 45.
[31] Ibid., 47.
[32] Ibid., 58.
[33] Ibid., 58–60.

immutable laws of morality!"[34] As Foucault explains, "[T]he asylum becomes, in Pinel's hands, an instrument of moral uniformity and of social denunciation," in which to "guarantee bourgeois morality a universality of fact and permit it to be imposed as a law upon all forms of insanity."[35] Foucault continues:

> [W]hile Pinel . . . strongly asserted that his moral action was not necessarily linked to any scientific competence [unlike later practitioners of psychiatry], it was thought, and by the patient first of all, that it was in the esotericism of knowledge, that the doctor had found the power to unravel insanity; and increasingly the patient . . . would alienate himself in the physician, accepting entirely and in advance all his prestige, submitting from the very first to a will he experienced as magic, and to a science he regarded as prescience and divination . . . If we wanted to analyze the profound structures of objectivity in the knowledge and practice of nineteenth-century psychiatry from Pinel to Freud, we should have to show in fact that such objectivity was from the start a reification of a magical nature, which could only be accomplished with the complicity of the patient himself, and beginning from a transparent and clear moral practice, gradually forgotten as positivism imposed its myths of scientific objectivity; a practice forgotten in its origins and its meaning, but always used and always present. What we call psychiatric practice is a certain moral tactic contemporary with the end of the eighteenth century, preserved in the rites of asylum life, and overlaid by the myths of positivism.[36]

Only here, toward the end of Foucault's brilliantly evocative history and polemic, do we now see what Foucault has exposed: namely, that moral considerations have driven practices of confinement and regulation throughout the modern era, and they have done so right into the present, but under the guise of an epistemic (more precisely, scientistic [what Foucault means, I take it, by "positivism"]) authority they have not really earned. The implicit invitation Foucault presents to the reader is to rethink and resist the conceptions of normality (of sanity and madness, of sexual normalcy and perversion, of criminality and law-abidingness, and so on) that permeate these systems of control.

I began by suggesting that Foucault's work is motivated by its own ethical or political impulse, namely, to liberate modern individuals from a kind of self-imposed subjugation. At the same time, as we have seen, Foucault wants to indict other ethical norms that he sees as playing a role in this subjugation. But the

[34] Ibid., 197.
[35] Ibid., 259.
[36] Ibid., 275–76.

idea of subjugation or oppression is itself a normative one, presupposing that we have a handle on what constitutes wrongful treatment of the individual in virtue of distorting or blocking their flourishing. The conception of *flourishing* that Foucault values, the kind of flourishing that presumably grounds his indignation at the practical authority underwritten by such dubious epistemic credentials, remains, alas, a bit vague. As Michael Walzer, in a highly critical essay, put it many years ago: Foucault aims not "for revolution but for local resistance"[37]—that is, resistance to the conception of "normalcy" put forward by human sciences. It is a characterization Foucault effectively endorses:

> The role for theory today seems to me to be just this: not to formulate the global systematic theory which holds everything in place, but to analyse the specificity of mechanisms of power, to locate the connections and extensions, to build little by little strategic knowledge.[38]

"Strategic knowledge" is, in context, clearly knowledge that facilitates "local resistance": against prisons, psychiatric establishments, the purveyors of sexual norms and stereotypes—precisely all those whom Foucault, in his actual political practice, resisted. What "global systematic theory" explains how all these hang together remains somewhat elusive. Perhaps as a kind of realist, Foucault didn't think one was necessary.

While Foucault emphasizes that individuals are complicit in their own oppression by *accepting* as practically decisive the purported truths of the human sciences, he certainly does not—despite the rhetoric noted earlier about "cutting off the King's head" in political theory—absolve centralized state power. For insofar as the judgments of normality that emerge from the human sciences are given practical authority over people through institutions—through courts and administrative bodies that deem people mentally unfit, through psychiatrists who testify in court, and the like—individuals can be oppressed by those judgments of normality whether or not they, as individuals, accept the epistemic authority of the human sciences. Despite his skepticism about juridical and centralized models of power (which he so often associates with Marxism), Foucault shares with Marxist critics the idea that the flourishing of individuals can be hostage to ideas and institutions beyond their control.

[37] Michael Walzer, "The Politics of Michel Foucault," in *Foucault: A Critical Reader*, ed. D. Hoy (Blackwell, 1986), 55.

[38] Michel Foucault, "Power and Strategies," in *Power/Knowledge*, ed. Colin Gordon (Pantheon, 1980), 145.

VI. Doubts about Foucault's Critique: Are Pedophiles Really Harmless?

How seriously should we take Foucault's critique? Foucault himself, it should be recalled, exempts from his critical gaze non-"dubious" sciences like physics and chemistry, focusing instead on those human sciences whose "epistemological profile" is "a low one."[39] But even with respect to the latter, he does not actually argue, as some have done, for the "lowness" of the epistemological profile, instead calling attention to the influence of economic, political, and moral considerations on their development. Yet it is now surely a familiar point in post-Kuhnian philosophy of science that the influence of social and historical factors might be compatible with the epistemically special standing of the sciences as long as we can show that epistemically reliable factors are still central to explaining the claims of those sciences.[40] And that possibility is potentially fatal to Foucault's critique.

For recall that central to Foucault's critique is the role that the epistemic pretensions of the sciences play in a structure of practical reasoning which leads agents concerned with their flourishing to become the agents of their own oppression. And the crucial bit of "pretense" is, as we noted earlier, that the human sciences illuminate the truth about how (normal) human beings flourish in virtue of adhering to the epistemic strictures and methodologies of the natural sciences. Recall also that Foucault, unlike Nietzsche, does not contest the practical authority of truth (i.e., that truth is the highest value and determines what *ought* to be done); he rather denies that the claims in question are true or have the epistemic warrant that we would expect true claims to have. So the entire Foucauldian project of liberation turns on the epistemic status of the claims of the human sciences. And on this central point, Foucault has, surprisingly, almost nothing to say beyond raising "suspicion." Perhaps *contemporary* medicine and *contemporary* psychiatry have identified *natural kinds* (i.e., real clusters of interconnected pathogenic properties of persons). In that case, Foucault's story is the story of the bogus science of the past enlisted on behalf of moral and political objectives, a story whose general outlines have long been familiar, even if Foucault tells striking new aspects of it. On the epistemic standing of the *current* human sciences, all Foucault leaves us with is a suspicion, rather than an argument. Suspicion is, as we have already argued, epistemically important, but it needs to be supplemented with a critique of the truth of the claims at issue.

[39] Foucault, "Truth and Power," 109.

[40] A classic articulation of this idea can be found in Philip Kitcher, *The Advancement of Science* (Oxford University Press, 1993), esp. ch. 5.

Even the suspicion is, however, unfortunately undercut by Foucault's sometimes cavalier attitude toward the phenomena in question. Consider the following remarkable passage from *The History of Sexuality* about which Foucault's devoted followers rarely comment:

> One day in 1867, a farm hand from the village of Lapcourt, who was somewhat simple-minded, employed here then there, depending on the season, living hand-to-mouth . . . was turned in to the authorities. At the border of a field, he had obtained a few caresses from a little girl, just as he had done before and seen done by the village urchins round about him . . . So he was pointed out by the girl's parents to the mayor of the village, reported by the mayor to the gendarmes, led by the gendarmes to the judge, who indicted him and turned him over first to a doctor, then to two other experts . . . What is the significant thing about this story? The pettiness of it all; the fact that this everyday occurrence in the life of village sexuality, these inconsequential bucolic pleasures, could become, from a certain time, the object not only of a collective intolerance but of a judicial action, a medical intervention, a careful clinical examination, and an entire theoretical elaboration.[41]

The same underlying events might, of course, be described rather differently: namely, that up until the time of this incident, pedophilia and child sexual abuse had been routinely tolerated—treated as an "inconsequential bucolic pleasure[]" in Foucault's startling phrase—but gradually people came to realize that "simple-minded" men being masturbated by young girls was not such a good thing (not so "inconsequential"), and thus the modern scientific study of pedophilia, and its harms, commenced. Why we should prefer Foucault's version to the alternative is utterly unclear. Why not say, instead, that in the nineteenth century a certain psychological *type* was discovered, namely, the pedophile (the kind of person who can only, or primarily, achieve sexual arousal with children), and that the harms of pedophilia were also discovered, even if the nineteenth-century versions of these discoveries have been superseded by a century of investigation? Absent answers to questions like this, Foucault's critical project is in danger.

To be sure, even if Foucault does not himself supply the arguments, the reasons for being skeptical about the epistemic claims of many of the contemporary human sciences have been well-articulated by others.[42] Those who want

[41] Foucault, *History of Sexuality I*, 31.

[42] See, e.g. the critiques of economics offered by Alex Rosenberg, *Economics—Mathematical Politics or Science of Diminishing Returns?* (University of Chicago Press, 1992), and Daniel M. Hausman, "Why Does Evidence Matter So Little to Economic Theory?," in *Structures and Norms in Science*, ed. M. L. Dalla Chiara et al. (Springer, 1997), 395–407; and the critique of psychology offered by Dominic Murphy, *Psychiatry in the Scientific Image* (MIT Press, 2006).

Foucault's critique to be taken seriously must—perhaps drawing on extant *direct* rather than genealogical critiques of the human sciences—put forward a systematic critique of the *truth* of the conceptions of "normality" at work in the contemporary human sciences, from psychiatry to criminology. Foucault's kinds of genealogies are not irrelevant to this purpose: if the understanding of the "homosexual" or the "sociopath" has been tainted with moral views that have no epistemic relevance, that is worth knowing. But epistemically irrelevant factors can sometimes produce true beliefs, and what is ultimately needed is a frontal attack on the truth of the claims in the human sciences.[43]

[43] This essay expands greatly on some rough ideas I first broached more than a decade ago in Brian Leiter, "Morality Critics," in *The Oxford Handbook of Continental Philosophy*, ed. Brian Leiter and Michael Rosen (Oxford University Press, 2008), 711–54. I am grateful to an audience at a conference on "How Do We Keep Knowing?" at the Glassock Humanities Research Center at Texas A&M University for helpful discussion of an earlier draft. Finally, I am indebted to Joshua Fox for research assistance and to an anonymous referee for helpful corrections and feedback.

Index

For the benefit of digital users, indexed terms that span two pages (e.g., 52–53) may, on occasion, appear on only one of those pages.

Prepared by Andrew Biondo